D0829529

A Chanticleer Press Edition

DESERTS

By James A. MacMahon

Birds
Miklos D. F. Udvardy, Professor of Biological Sciences,
California State University, Sacramento

Butterflies
Robert Michael Pyle, Consulting Lepidopterist, International
Union for Conservation of Nature and Natural Resources

Fishes
James D. Williams, Research Associate, National Museum of
Natural History

Insects and Spiders
Lorus Milne and Margery Milne, Lecturers, University of
New Hampshire

Mammals
John O. Whitaker, Jr., Professor of Life Sciences, Indiana
State University

Mushrooms
Peter Katsaros, Mycologist

Reptiles and Amphibians
John L. Behler, Curator of Herpetology, New York Zoological
Society; and F. Wayne King, Director, Florida State Museum

Trees
Elbert L. Little, Jr., former Chief Dendrologist, U. S. Forest
Service

Wildflowers
Richard Spellenberg, Professor of Biology, New Mexico State
University

Alfred A. Knopf, New York

This is a Borzoi Book.
Published by Alfred A. Knopf, Inc.

Copyright © 1985, 1998 by Chanticleer Press, Inc. All rights
reserved under International and Pan-American Copyright
Conventions. Published in the United States by Alfred A.
Knopf, Inc., New York, and simultaneously in Canada by
Random House of Canada Limited, Toronto. Distributed by
Random House, Inc., New York.

Prepared and produced by Chanticleer Press, Inc., New York.

Printed and bound by Toppan Printing Co., Ltd., Tokyo, Japan.
Type set in Garamond by Dix Type, Inc., Syracuse, New York.

Published March 1985
Tenth Printing, October 1998

Library of Congress Cataloging-in-Publication Data
McMahon, James, 1939–
The National Audubon Society nature guides. Deserts.
Includes index.
1. Natural history–West (U.S.)–Handbooks, manuals, etc.
2. Desert ecology–West (U.S.)–Handbooks, manuals, etc.
3. Zoology–West (U.S.)–Handbooks, manuals, etc.
4. Botany–West (U.S.)–Handbooks, manuals, etc.
5. Desert Fauna–West (U.S.)–Identification. 6. Desert flora
–West (U.S.)–Identification.
I. National Audubon Society. II. Title. III. Title: Deserts.
QH104.5.W4M33   1985   574.5'2652'0978   84–48674
ISBN 0-394-73139-5 (pbk.)

Cover photograph: A Birdcage Evening Primrose blooms in
solitary splendor in Anza-Borrego Desert State Park,
California.

CONTENTS

Part I   **Deserts**
How to Use This Guide 8
Preface 18
Introduction 22
The Great Basin Desert 33
The Colorado Plateau Semidesert 45
The Mojave Desert 47
The Sonoran Desert 62
The Chihuahuan Desert 83
Some Special Vegetation Types Common to All Deserts 102
Aspects of the Biology of Desert Organisms 110
How to Use the Color Plates 150

Part II   **Color Plates**
Deserts 1–36
Wildflowers 37–165
Mushrooms 166–168
Reptiles and Amphibians 169–291
Fishes 292–300
Trees, Shrubs, Cacti, and Grasses 301–366
Insects and Spiders 367–402
Butterflies and Moths 403–450
Mammals 451–528
Birds 529–618

Part III   **Species Descriptions**
Wildflowers and Mushrooms 354
Reptiles and Amphibians 417
Fishes 475
Trees, Shrubs, Cacti, and Grasses 480
Insects and Spiders 510
Butterflies and Moths 526
Mammals 546
Birds 576

Part IV   **Appendices**
Glossary 614
Bibliography 618
Credits 620
Index 625

THE AUTHOR

James A. MacMahon
Professor of biology and a member of the Ecology Center at
Utah State University, James MacMahon holds a B.S. degree
in zoology from Michigan State University and a Ph.D. in
biology from Notre Dame. He served as associate director of
the Institute of Desert Biology at Arizona State University,
and then moved to Utah State University to be assistant
director in charge of field research for the Desert Biome, a part
of the International Biological Program, before assuming his
present position.
Dr. MacMahon has published more than seventy technical
papers, many popular articles for magazines such as *Natural
History,* and a book on general zoology. He has received
awards from two universities for his teaching and research, and
is presently studying the recolonization of plants and animals
on Mount Saint Helens and the application of ecological
theory to management problems in arid lands.

HOW TO USE THIS GUIDE

This guide is designed for use both at home and in the field. Its clear arrangement in four parts—habitat essays, color plates, species descriptions, and appendices—puts information at your fingertips that would otherwise only be accessible through a small library of field guides.

The habitat essays enable you to discover the many kinds of desert habitats, the relationships among the plants and animals found there, and highlights not to be missed. The color plates feature desert scenes and over 600 photographs of different plant and animal species. The species descriptions cover the most important information about a plant or animal, including a description, the range, specific habitat, and comments. Finally, the appendices include a bibliography, a glossary, and a comprehensive index.

Using This Guide at Home

Before planning an outing, you will want to know what you can expect to see.

1. Begin by leafing through the color plates for a preview of deserts.

2. Read the habitat section. For quick reference, at the end of each chapter you will find a list of some of the most common plants and animals found in that habitat.

3. Look at the color plates of some of the animals and plants so that you will be able to recognize them later in the field. The table called How to Use the Color Plates provides a visual table of contents to the color section, explains the arrangement of the plates, and tells the caption information provided. The habitats where you are likely to encounter the species are listed in blue type so that you can easily refer to the correct habitat chapter. The page number for the full species description is also included in the caption.

4. Turn to the species descriptions to learn more about the plants and animals that interest you. A range map or drawing appears in the margin for birds, fishes, mammals, reptiles, and amphibians, and for many of the trees, shrubs, cacti, grasses, and wildflowers. Poisonous reptiles are indicated by the danger symbol ⊗ next to the species name.

5. Consult the appendices for definitions of technical terms and suggestions for further reading.

Using This Guide in the Field

When you are out in the field, you will want to find information quickly and easily.

1. Turn to the color plates to locate the plant or animal you have seen. At a glance the captions will help you narrow down the possibilities. First, verify the habitat by checking the blue type information to the left of the color plate. Next, look for important field marks, which are also indicated in blue type— for example, how and where a mushroom grows, an insect's food, or a caterpillar's host plants. To find out whether a bird, mammal, fish, reptile, or amphibian is in your area, check the range map next to the color plate.

2. Now turn to the species description to confirm your identification and to learn more about the species.

First frontispiece. An ancient Saguaro cactus in the Sonoran Desert; Organ Pipe Cactus National Monument, Arizona.

Second frontispiece. An Elf Owl in its nest cavity in an old Saguaro; Organ Pipe Cactus National Monument, Arizona.

Third frontispiece. Barrel, Cholla and Beavertail cacti dominate the landscape; Anza Borrego Desert State Park, California.

Fourth frontispiece. A Desert Tortoise feeding on vegetation in the Sonoran Desert.

Fifth frontispiece. Coral pink sand dunes in an upper elevation transition site in the Colorado Plateau Semidesert near Kanab, Utah.

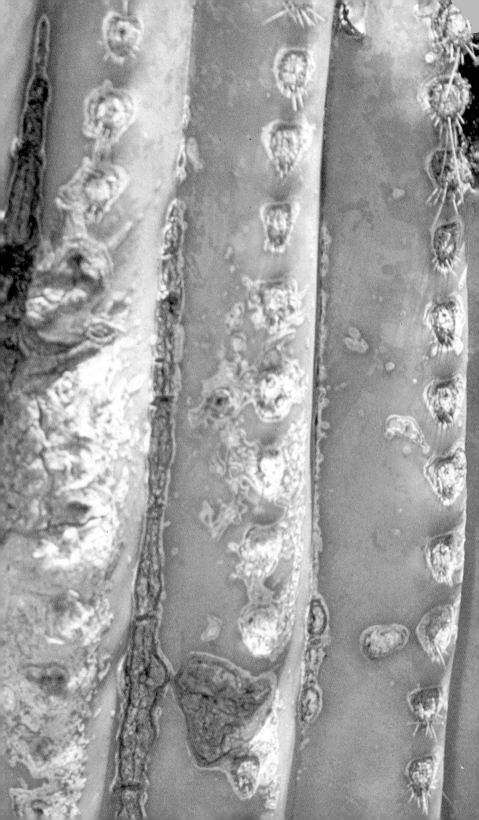

PART I   DESERTS

PREFACE

Since you have opened this book, it is clear that you are curious about deserts. But beware: If you proceed further, you may find yourself gripped by a real passion for the arid lands of North America.

Your eye will be arrested by a single photograph of a desert landscape, painted in myriad soft earth tones and highlighted by the brightest reds, the most brilliant whites, and the deepest blacks found anywhere in nature—and you may soon begin to wish that a page of this book could be your looking-glass entry into that landscape. Flipping through the dozens of photographs of birds and reptiles will reveal an enticing kaleidoscope of colors and patterns and shapes, and you will be astounded by the vast variety of organisms that survive in so apparently hostile an environment.

If you are actually in a desert at the moment you read this, you have already caught the excitement, the allure of these places. You know by just looking around you that photographs can only hint at the magnificent but subtle changes in the appearance of the landscape that are wrought by the movements of the sun. You may already be entranced by details such as the behavior of a lizard or bird trying to find a position that will minimize its heat load but still allow it to find prey. You may have learned to love the pungent fragrance of the shrubs after a rain, the feel of a dry desert wind, or the sound of silence that is so loud you cannot ignore it.

Few people are immune to the charm and splendors of the desert. Those who have experienced the desert know that it can arouse a lifelong desire to learn more—and a desire simply to be there.

It is the aim of this book to heighten your curiosity and enlarge your understanding. Together we will explore and examine the interaction of desert plants, animals, and the physical environment.

The subject matter is breathtakingly large. In this volume, we will cover the vast area of arid western North America that is wedged between the Rocky Mountains and the Sierra Nevada and that extends from southern Idaho and southeastern Oregon south into Mexico. The scope is generally limited to natural communities that occur below 5000 feet in elevation and in locales that receive less than ten inches of annual precipitation. This area contains a higher concentration of imposing landscapes than any other region of equal size in North America. The diversity of plants and animals is enormous, and their adaptations are always interesting, often remarkable, and sometimes hardly believable.

The purpose here is threefold: first, to introduce you to the differences between the four major desert zones in North America; second, to help you identify some of the plants and animals you are likely to encounter; and finally, to impart information about the biology of these organisms, particularly those aspects that are unique to deserts.

Not all of the deserts discussed receive the same degree of coverage, because some have more complex biotas than others. Similarly, not all groups of organisms are treated equally.

Most of the birds, reptiles, and mammals that you might encounter on a trip to a desert are covered here. However, we can offer you only a small sampling of the thousands of wildflowers and tens of thousands of invertebrates that you may encounter. The life of the desert is enormous, and impossible to encompass in a single book or to experience in one visit. It may even be beyond the reach of a single lifetime. Nonetheless, the sample included will, I hope, startle you, tickle you, enrapture you—but most of all excite you, as it has me.

I first set foot in a desert some thirty years ago, on a trip to the Big Bend of Texas when I was a high school student. My fascination with the desert developed rapidly, has persisted unabated, and often breaks out in the symptom of a longing to return that must be dealt with immediately. A few weeks ago, I visited the deserts in Arizona, New Mexico, and Texas. I thought about things that I had written for this book, worried a little that the real excitement of the desert would be overshadowed by my scientific writing style. Nonetheless, I know that experiencing the desert will thrill you even if I do not—while you might be immune to my words, you cannot be immune to the desert.

Tips

When you go to the desert, you can make your experience a positive one by doing two things before you go. First, be prepared to take the fullest advantage of your visit by having along the proper equipment for observing and taking notes. Second, take all of the precautions necessary to ensure your personal comfort and safety.

I recommend that everyone take copious notes whenever they are in the field. Our memories, which seem infallible and everlasting at the moment, fade with the passage of even brief periods of time. Pencils or pens with waterproof ink and pads or notebooks with waterproof paper ensure a permanent record. Write down all of your observations, your feelings, and even the manner in which each of your senses reports to you. Years from now you will be able to read such detailed notes and relive precious moments in a way that a mere photographic record cannot provide.

Good-quality binoculars will enable you to see distant geomorphic structures, to identify a bird, or to observe the uninterrupted courtship routine of a pair of flashy lizards. A hand lens (of 10 × to 20 ×) will give you access to a world of smaller—though no less interesting—desert inhabitants; through one, you can see the marvels of a plant's flower parts or the intricate sculpturing of what otherwise appears to be a plain, black beetle's back.

Since many desert animals are best seen at night, a strong, lightweight, hand-held flashlight is a must. A black light will reveal scorpions and some other animals. Although black lights are an additional expense, they are fun and a good idea for the more serious naturalist.

Desert soils are often hot and rocky, and in places are covered with spiny plants. All of these conditions dictate that you wear strong, well-made footwear. You do not need knee boots; regular hiking boots are sufficient, but be sure they give good ankle support and that their soles can grip on slippery surfaces. Loose, comfortable clothing is a big advantage. Make sure you have rain gear and a heavy shirt or sweater, because evenings can be chilly and rains are unpredictable. A hat is indispensable in the hot desert sun, and sunglasses are a wise investment. You may want to protect your exposed skin and lips with a sunscreen.

Plan your trip carefully. Detailed maps, including topographic maps, are available for most areas of the United States and are a worthwhile investment. Outdoor-equipment stores carry most maps that you might need.

If you plan an adventuresome trek on a little-traveled road, inform someone—a ranger, a sheriff, a friend—of your route. Also tell this person when you expect to return.

Take plenty of water with you, and don't spare it and cause yourself to become physiologically exhausted. Your body will let you know when water is needed; drink then, and drink a lot. Also drink any time that you eat, especially in the morning and evening. Don't tough it out, and don't skimp on water. In deserts you may need a gallon of water per person per day in order to walk.

Rest in the shade for ten minutes every hour. Don't remove your clothes to cool off, because doing so hastens dehydration. If you are dizzy, lose your appetite, and become nauseous, you may be dehydrated.

In the desert, as anywhere else, there are a few hazards. Since substrates are often loose, you are inviting trouble when you drive on little-traveled roads; even vehicles with four-wheel drive can easily become stuck. If this happens, stay with your vehicle, and don't spin your wheels further into the sand or mud. Your jack may allow you to lift the vehicle out of the trouble spot and push it to a more stable surface. Deflating your tires somewhat may offer sufficient traction to get loose. Remain calm and use your head.

Flash floods often follow heavy rains. Even when downpours occur at some distance from you, they may still flood the canyon you are in. If there are thunder clouds in your vicinity, stay out of washes and gullies. Never camp overnight in deep washes, and always try to be aware of the weather forecast for the time you expect to be in the desert.

Always carry a good first aid kit in your vehicle, and a small one in your day pack when leaving your vehicle.

Most animals and plants are innocuous, but some stab, sting, or bite. Your best plan is to avoid these organisms. Never reach with your hands or feet into places you cannot see; never sit down without looking. Pick up objects on the ground with great care.

If you are stung by an insect or a scorpion, or are bitten by a spider, try to retain the animal for positive identification. Apply ice to the bite and get to a physician, where proper help is available.

It is highly unlikely that you will be bitten by a venomous snake. If this does occur, however, kill the snake so that you can take it to the physician, or otherwise positively identify it. If you can reach medical assistance within an hour or so, it is probably wiser not to perform first aid on yourself or a friend. Be calm. Move slowly and deliberately. The "cut-and-suck" method of snakebite first aid, popularized in TV westerns, is notoriously difficult to perform properly; what is more, this treatment can have more disastrous effects than the bite. I do not recommend it, except under the direst of circumstances. In the United States, very few people are ever killed in the field by venomous snakes. Stay calm and find professional help. The use of antivenin is extremely effective, but because some people are allergic to horse serum, it can be dangerous to use without a physician in attendance. If you are going to be many hours or days away from medical help, you need to learn the details of recognizing the severity of snake bites before you leave for the desert. It is only then that you can plot a program of appropriate and effective first aid.

While in the desert, it is important to respect the plants, animals, and geologic structures there. Cacti that can be picked or kicked over in seconds may have required more than twenty years to grow, and there may be few of their seeds in the soil. Many animals are not abundant, or if they appear to be abundant do not produce offspring frequently. The capture of such species for pets can decimate local populations in a very few years.

In many areas, state and federal laws regulate the collection and possession of a variety of plants and animals. Fines can be severe, so you are well served to leave the desert with good notes and photographs rather than specimens.

Life in deserts has a hard enough time surviving the physical environment. Further pressure by man is often simply too much, and once-common species have become rare or even locally extinct. Surely none of us wants to be an agent of such destruction.

Do not let any of this dissuade you. Your desert adventure will undoubtedly be safe, and it will certainly inspire awe. In its very starkness the desert can provide thrills that will occur over and over. Sometimes you will find yourself the victim of sensory overload—and you must close your eyes to comprehend the magnitude of the wonders surrounding you. Once you have gone to the desert, you will certainly return— over and over.

INTRODUCTION

Deserts can be defined in many ways. To some people, a desert is merely a vast, hot, dry, sandy wasteland. To others it is a warm, dry area that is occupied by a myriad of interesting plants and animals. To me a desert is a fascinating, beautiful landscape where I can walk deep in contemplation and be surrounded by silence.

What is a Desert?

The one common factor in all technical definitions is that deserts are dry. Early scientists thought that low average precipitation on a given site indicated a high degree of dryness, and they considered any area receiving less than ten inches precipitation per year to be a desert. Some areas fitting this criterion, however, were clearly not deserts; they supported too many plants to look like a desert. Thus a second element was added to the definition: the amount of evaporation occurring in an area. Regardless of how much rain falls in an area, if there is more potential for the air to evaporate water than there is water, then that area will be dry. Evaporation, like rainfall, is measured in inches, and it generally refers to the amount of water that would evaporate from a completely exposed surface, such as a large pan filled with water. If a site receives less than ten inches of precipitation in a year and if the yearly evaporation exceeds ten inches, then it is likely that the place will look like a desert, whether the area is hot or cold, sandy or not. The causes of evaporation are quite complex. It is clear, however, that high radiation (for example, sunshine), high wind speed, and high temperature all contribute to high rates of evaporation. Low yearly precipitation and high evaporation help to define a dry area, but we must examine these factors in more detail to really understand the nature and causes of desert conditions. In the simplest terms, we need to explore why the organisms on a particular desert site consider their environment dry, regardless of the amount of precipitation that might fall. To do this, we must "think" like a plant. A plant needs to get sufficient water, mainly from the soil by way of its roots, to carry on all of its normal daily routines, including respiration, photosynthesis, reproduction, and growth. In dry areas, plants must get water when it is available and then conserve it for use during periods when it is not.

One inch of precipitation does not mean that a plant's roots have one inch of water available to them. Rather, the availability of water depends on the timing and type of precipitation. For example, precipitation during a cold period of the year may be of little value to a plant that is physiologically dormant in cold weather; it passes through the soil without being absorbed by the plant's roots. If low temperatures cause precipitation in the form of snow, much water can be lost to plants when the snow evaporates without ever melting; it is thus never close to the plant roots.

The intensity of rainfall also affects its availability to plants. The brief, intense thunderstorms of summer quickly wet the soil surface during the first few minutes, making the soil repellent to any additional input of water because the surface layer is saturated and there isn't sufficient time for this water to percolate into lower layers. Subsequent rainfall accumulates on the soil surface and flows along it, a sheet of water that does not penetrate deeply enough to reach a plant's roots, regardless of a plant's physiological status. This type of high-intensity, short-duration rainfall and the consequent water repellency of the soil cause the flash floods characteristic of some desert environments.

The nature of the soil has a role in determining how much of the rainfall is available to plants as well. Soil that is composed of very fine particles doesn't allow much water to penetrate through to plant roots. Conversely, coarse soil that contains various sized particles from sand to rocks and pebbles allows water to flow rapidly downward. The ideal desert soil is a mix of particle sizes: large particles to allow the infiltration of precipitation into the soil, and small particles to retain the water long enough for plants to absorb it.

Finally, one obvious attribute of the desert is that not many plants usually grow there. This sparseness of vegetation gives the desert its characteristic appearance, or physiognomy. Regardless of location, the physiognomy of the vegetation identifies a site as a desert. A place that looks desertic probably has low rainfall, high evaporation, and other conditions associated with true desert conditions.

No one environmental characteristic can define a desert, but particular combinations of characteristics—all of which cause dryness—seem to be related to the presence of certain plant types. These plants create a distinctive landscape that can occur only under dry conditions—in deserts.

Where are the Deserts of North America?

The deserts of the United States are located between two major mountain masses, the Rocky Mountains on the east and the Sierra Nevada on the west. The deserts are of two general types. The first, which occurs in more northern areas, is the cold desert, a term applied to the Great Basin Desert because more than half of the annual precipitation that falls there occurs in the form of snow, and because this desert's northern position gives it low average annual temperatures. The second type, the hot desert, receives precipitation in either winter or summer—or both—and the precipitation occurs predominantly as rainfall.

Exactly where deserts occur is a matter of some conjecture, for it is difficult to define exact boundaries for the various desert types. This difficulty is due in part to the fact that scientists disagree about which plants and animals best characterize the deserts. As we will see, some of the desert's most common and conspicuous plants and animals occur in many other habitats as well. Conversely, some species that are clearly confined to deserts—for example, the Saguaro Cactus—do not occur in every area that is considered desert. Consequently, we cannot use such species' distribution patterns to delimit desert boundaries.

The two maps presented here rely on different scientific philosophies to define the boundaries of deserts. The first one, drawn by Dr. Forrest Shreve, one of the foremost desert plant ecologists, has been used for over forty years. It is based on the distribution of plant species and on Dr. Shreve's concept of deserts. The second map takes both plant and animal distributions into account to determine its desert boundaries. Despite minor differences of interpretation, the maps clearly depict the extent of the various deserts.

The Great Basin Desert occupies approximately the southern third of Idaho, the southeastern corner of Oregon, the western half of Utah, and the northern three quarters of Nevada. This area covers over 158,000 square miles and represents the largest desert area in the United States.

The hot deserts to the south of the Great Basin Desert are subdivided into three types: the Mojave Desert, which covers southern Nevada, the extreme southwestern corner of Utah, and part of California; the Sonoran Desert, in Arizona and California; and the Chihuahuan Desert, which occupies a small area of southern New Mexico and extreme western Texas. These last two deserts are much more extensive in Mexico. If we include both the Mexican and the U.S. portions, the Chihuahuan is the largest desert in North America, occupying 175,000 square miles, or thirty-six percent of the total North American desert area; the Great Basin is the second largest (thirty-two percent); the Sonoran, the third largest (106,000 square miles and twenty-one and a half percent); and the Mojave, the smallest, with its 54,000 square miles comprising only eleven percent of the total desert area.

Physiography of Desert Landscapes

All of the deserts in the United States—both hot and cold—are essentially contained in the area that is called the Basin and Range Province. Extending across thirty degrees of latitude and encompassing between ten and twelve degrees of longitude, this area covers about 300,000 square miles and represents about eight percent of the country's land area. Surrounded by the Rockies and the Sierra Nevada, the main western U.S. mountain masses, the Province derives its name from the way it appears from the air. The entire landscape consists of rather large basins dotted with much smaller mountain ranges. Generally, more than fifty percent of the land surface is covered by these basins, although the amount of basins often exceeds seventy-five percent, especially in the Sonoran Desert. The mountain ranges number more than 200. Elevations of the basins may range from more than 250 feet below sea level (in Death Valley) to about 5000 feet above. The surrounding ranges may exceed 13,000 feet.

Despite their general aridity, these basins are dotted with lakes; nearly 5000 square miles are covered by two types of lakes. The first is a normal perennial lake, which has a free water surface the year around. A conspicuous example of the twenty-four or so lakes of this sort is Utah's Great Salt Lake. The second type of lake is much more characteristic of arid

Classical Interpretation of Desert Boundaries

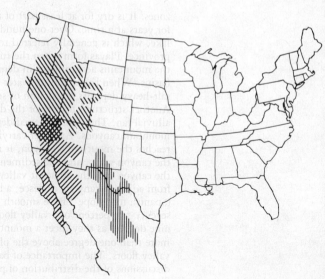

Desert Boundaries Used in This Guide

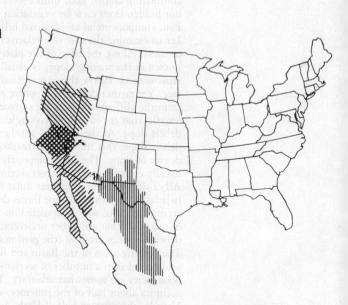

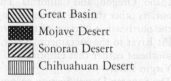

Great Basin

Mojave Desert

Sonoran Desert

Chihuahuan Desert

zones: It is dry for at least part of the year and often remains so for years at a time. Over one hundred examples of this kind of lake, which is generally referred to as a playa, occur in the province. Playas form when the runoff of precipitation from the mountains accumulates in depressions in the surrounding basins. When this standing water evaporates, it leaves behind salt-heavy deposits of calcium or sodium (plates 7 and 8). Another structural feature of the desert landscape is the alluvial fan. These cone-shaped deposits originate from mountain canyons. As water carrying sediments (alluvium) reaches the mouth of a canyon, it is suddenly unrestricted by the canyon walls, and the sediments fan out from the mouth of the canyon into the adjacent valley. Where several alluvial fans from adjacent canyons coalesce, a bajada is formed. Bajadas (Spanish for "slope") have smooth surfaces and may cover up to seventy-five percent of a valley floor. They have slopes of six to nine degrees as they meet a mountain range, but seldom rise more than one degree above the plains or the playas on the valley floors. The importance of bajadas will recur often in our discussions of the distribution of plants and animals.

Slopes in desert systems are generally very dramatic. This is because the geological portions are often composed of starkly contrasting colors, and, unlike forested areas, the structure is not hidden from view by vegetation (plate 19).

Four components of an idealized hillslope can be recognized. Let us examine the case of a relatively flat, isolated mountain or mesa. Along the edge of the plateau, the upper slope, known as the waxing slope, is usually somewhat convex in cross section. Below this is a vertical portion, a cliff or a free face. Yet farther downslope, where material has accumulated from the cliff and the waxing surface, is a slope of varying lengths that is constant in its angle and has a flat surface—the debris slope. At the bottom, another slope usually abuts the debris slope; this transition is marked by a sudden change in degree of slope. The lower slope, the piedmont, is usually concave to flat in cross section and is a waning slope. All of the hillslope structures differ from alluvial fans and bajadas in that the hillslope forms do not result from an accumulation of water-deposited materials. Rather they consist of materials that are either undergoing transportation (e.g. the debris slope) or eroding (the piedmont).

The desertic areas of the Basin and Range Province have been subdivided into a number of sections; however these boundaries are somewhat arbitrary. The Great Basin Section occupies about half of the province, including most of Nevada, the western half of Utah, and minute portions of Idaho, Oregon, and California. This section has few drainage outlets other than an area emptying into the Snake River in the northeast, a portion of the northwest that drains via the Pit River to the Sacramento River, and an area in the southeast corner that empties into the Colorado River via the Virgin River.

The Sonoran Desert Section encompasses the southwestern quarter of Arizona and the adjacent desert areas of California.

The major portion of the Mojave and Sonoran deserts is contained in this section. Common rock substrates in this section include Precambrian granites and gneisses. Lakes were common here during the Pleistocene Epoch. Since the slopes are often composed of metamorphic rocks, they may occur at rises (angles) of up to twenty percent.

The Salton Sea Trough Section is merely an extension of the trough occupied by the Gulf of California, but obviously is the part not inundated by the Gulf. In the United States, the section includes a very small area in California centered around the cities of Brawley and El Centro. It occurs just south of the mountains, which form the southern boundary of Joshua Tree National Monument. A main feature of the trough is the Salton Sea. This body of water was inundated by floods in 1904, doubling its depth. The flooding was checked in 1907.

The Mexican Highland Section occurs as a diagonal band across the middle third of Arizona, the southwestern quarter of New Mexico, and southward into Mexico. Excluding the mountainous portions, the Chihuahuan Desert and the Chihuahuan-Sonoran transition are essentially contained within this section. The area is characterized by high valleys (4500 feet); its lowest elevations are along the Rio Grande River, with the land rising both to the north and to the south. Unlike other portions of the basin and range province, this section contains well-developed drainage systems, though internal drainages and their associated playas do occur.

The Basin and Range Province is so vast and covers such a diversity of landscapes that it is impossible to generalize about any aspect of its geology or geological history. It is clear, however, that the mineral resources of the province have been and continue to be of great economic importance in the United States. American deserts are famous in contemporary mythology for the lonely miner and his faithful burro, who traversed the bleak landscape looking for that one lucky claim. Indeed some people made and lost fortunes here by discovering gold, silver, copper, mercury, zinc, antimony, or any one of several other minerals. Especially significant were the copper finds, which today provide some seventy percent of all of the metal produced in the United States.

You will have no trouble seeing the old digs—both successful and unsuccessful ones—which dot the landscape as you travel across America's deserts. You may feel a romantic twinge and the desire to stop for a few days to prospect for your fortune when you find an old mine. Frankly, my advice is to prospect for the biological beauties of the desert rather than the minerals. Biological treasures are a sure find, and they are not taxable.

Desert Climates

Deserts, by definition, are warm and dry. While true, this generalization—like many general statements—is not very revealing or interesting. In fact, deserts are complex and diverse, as the degree of warmth (i.e. the annual temperatures) and the pattern and magnitude of precipitation in North

American deserts are highly variable. To a large extent, we can classify American deserts by their precipitation patterns. As was mentioned previously, the Great Basin Desert, a cold desert, receives most of its precipitation in the form of winter snowfall, while the three hot deserts receive their precipitation in the form of rainfall. These three hot deserts, however, are quite dissimilar; the rain falls at different times of year and in different ways.

In essence, American deserts lie in a zone of the earth's surface where there are strong seasonal shifts in storm tracks, which are areas where precipitation is likely to occur. In part, this shifting is caused by the seasonal heating of the earth's surface, and in part, by global wind patterns.

In the winter, storms originating in the Pacific Ocean move eastward and inland. As the moisture-laden air moves across the mountain chains formed by the Coast Ranges, the Sierra Nevada, and the Sierra Madre Occidental, condensation and rain occur. Thus the westernmost portions of the United States receive winter precipitation.

In the spring, the storm tracks responsible for this winter precipitation move north of the United States, and the eastward flow of air from the Pacific Ocean becomes weaker. During this period, stronger storm cells move westward and northwestward from the Gulf of Mexico. Rainfall caused by this weather system occurs from spring to fall, a pattern called summer rainfall.

Each of these rainfall patterns becomes less pronounced as one moves away from either the Pacific or the Gulf, where the storms originate. The Mojave and Great Basin deserts receive winter precipitation, as rain in the south or snow in the north. The Chihuahuan Desert is too far east to receive the winter influences. It is directly in the path of the summer rainfall system, however, and thus gets summer rain. The Sonoran Desert is intermediate between the two storm systems. As a result, it gets both summer and winter rains, a biseasonal rainfall pattern whose relative proportions depend on the particular location in the Sonoran.

These two rainfall patterns differ not only in the season with which each is associated, but also in their very nature. The winter rains tend to be of low intensity and long duration (they settle in for hours to days), and they cover large areas at a time. By contrast, summer rains are convective thunderstorms of high intensity and short duration (minutes to hours), and they are limited in size.

Little rain falls in deserts, usually less than ten inches per year. In some places, such as Death Valley, California, there may be none at all for twelve-month periods. Of equal significance is the unpredictability of the precipitation. In fact, the two conditions are related. A worldwide correlation exists between total annual rainfall and the degree to which that rainfall is predictable; thus, the smaller the annual rainfall, the greater the year-to-year variation in the amount that occurs. This rule holds for both winter and summer rainfall patterns. And it is the combination of the low levels and the unpredictability of the rainfall that makes the environment difficult for many organisms—not merely the fact that rainfall is scant.

Temperatures in deserts are a function of both latitude and altitude. The Great Basin Desert, which is the farthest north and has base elevations that generally exceed 4000 feet, is the coolest American desert. In general, the Sonoran Desert is, year around, the warmest, because it is southern and has the lowest average elevation. Although the Mojave Desert has the lowest absolute elevation and the highest maximum temperatures (in Death Valley, California), it is north of the Sonoran and its average elevations are higher. As a result, its average temperatures are lower than those of the Sonoran. The Chihuahuan Desert has elevations exceeding 4000 feet, but its southern location moderates the coolness.

Since humidity varies inversely with temperature, the winters in the desert are more humid than the summers. The general paucity of water in desert air coupled with high temperatures tends to cause the air to be relatively dry. The low humidity influences our perception of the actual temperature; that is, a given temperature feels quite different in moist air (say eighty-five percent relative humidity) than it does in dry air (fifteen percent relative humidity). This partly accounts for the lure of the Southwest: The dry summer heat of Tucson is less oppressive than the moist heat of Washington, D.C., even when temperatures in the two cities are exactly the same. Let there be no mistake, however. If you are in Phoenix after a July or August rain when the air temperature exceeds 100° F, Washington might seem a paradise.

One of the reasons you feel relatively cooler in deserts at high temperatures and low humidities is that your perspiration evaporates rapidly. The evaporation cools the skin surface; in addition, your clothes aren't likely to stay uncomfortably sweat-soaked. The generally strong winds of the open deserts also aid in the evaporation process and thus add an additional measure of relief.

Although high evaporation rates are good for your personal comfort, they can be a problem for the resident plants and animals, which must replace the water lost. As noted before, evaporation potential—the amount of water that will evaporate from an exposed water surface in one year's time— can be expressed in inches of evaporation. Remarkably, evaporation in the American deserts ranges from seventy to 160 inches per year. Moreoever, most desert sites receive only four to eight inches of precipitation a year. Thus the disparity between precipitation and evaporation is enormous.

Solar radiation is extreme in the North American deserts for a number of reasons. First, except for the Great Basin, these deserts are at low latitudes, and so the sun is more directly over head. Second, because there is little moisture in the air, there are few clouds, and thus more sunshine reaches the ground. This lack of cloud cover also causes the thermal energy in the desert surface to reradiate—go back into the sky —very rapidly at night. This causes rapid cooling and

accounts for the high variation between daytime and
nighttime desert temperatures.

Freezing temperatures occur in all of the North American
deserts but the southernmost parts in Mexico. Cities like
Phoenix may have as many as fifteen days per year during
which the mean temperature is below freezing. Generally
speaking, any desert in the United States may experience
freezing temperatures, and the organisms occurring there may
not be well adapted to such extreme cold. A rare freeze of
sufficiently low temperatures and long enough duration can
severely affect desert organisms, especially plants. Sometimes
the nature of the vegetation at any given moment may have
been determined by several days of below-freezing
temperatures that occurred only once in a fifty-year span—and
not by weeks or months of drought and years of little rain and
high temperatures.

As unlikely as it may seem, fog and dew are important
phenomena. In many desert areas worldwide, they are critical
sources of moisture for plants and animals. Unfortunately, we
have very little precise data concerning the frequency and
extent of the occurrence and use of this source of water.

Soils in Desert Environments

A soil is the product of a complex process called weathering,
which is any action that works on geological materials to alter
their physical and chemical composition. Agents of weathering
may be physical, chemical, or biological in nature. In a sense,
a soil has a life history much like that of an organism, as it
undergoes change and is subject to both its nature and its
environment. Geological materials are exposed, and the forces
of water, wind, and temperature break them into smaller
pieces. At the same time, the materials may be altered by the
addition of oxygen, carbonate, or any one of several other
chemicals to their composition. The same rock type, exposed
in two different climatic environments, may end up forming
quite different soil types.

With the passage of time, which is a critical factor in soil
formation, plants and animals may establish footholds in these
changing geological materials. The actions of the organisms—
for example, the construction of burrows, the growth of roots,
or the excretion of certain chemicals—may further alter the
substrate, both chemically and physically. At some ill-defined
point in the whole process, the geological material is referred
to as soil. Soil scientists rightfully consider soil to be a
synthesized, living entity, as it both changes and contains
floral and faunal elements—it is not merely the accumulation
of degraded geological materials.

Soils that are barely developed and that have characteristics
like those of their geological precursors (parent material) are
considered to be young. Mature soils on the other hand,
possess a character that is the result of the subtle interplay of
various forces—both organic and inorganic—over long
periods of time.

Desert areas have both well-developed soils and soils that are so young that they really are not soils at all, but are instead merely slightly altered examples of the parent material. The undeveloped type may occur as broken rock overlying bedrock. These "soils," called lithosols, generally occur on slopes, ridges, and plateaus that are actively eroding. Undeveloped soils may also occur in actively shifting sand dunes, where they are called regosols. In sand dunes, there is a fine distinction between nonsoils and sandy soils. Some dunes are sufficiently stabilized so that plants may occur on them, gradually adding various organic materials and inorganic nitrogen; over time these dunes develop a veneer of soil. However, the sands of actively moving dunes do not alter their composition and structure sufficiently to be considered soils. Mature desert soils are of two types: those that develop in a way that is characteristic of the desert environment, and those that would have developed similarly under any climatic influence. The characteristic desert soils are called aridisols. Soils are defined on the basis of their layers, or horizons. The number of layers and their physical and chemical characteristics give each soil its character. Aridisols have an upper surface layer that is not very rich in organic matter, as well as lower layers that have clays, salts, and very fine sandy materials composed of gypsum or calcium deposits. Aridisols form under the strong influences of wind, low but often torrential supplies of moisture, and high temperatures.

In desert areas, a soil horizon is often virtually cemented together by such materials as calcium carbonate, silica, or even iron compounds. The layers form hardpans, which can be impervious to water movement and penetration by plant roots. Since calcium is common in many American deserts, layers of calcium hardpans, called caliche, are abundant—especially in the calcium-rich soils of the Chihuahuan Desert. These layers are usually a half inch to three feet deep, but may be as thick as 275 feet in some large valleys. Sometimes caliche appears at the surface in places where the loose surface soils have been eroded by wind or water. The distribution of caliche—in terms of both depth and extent—can influence the distribution of desert plants and animals.

Some desert soils provide environments that are quite inhospitable to plant growth. The substrate may be so loose that plants have difficulty taking hold; this is the case with certain sandy soils and sand dunes. Sand dunes are common and extensive in deserts, especially in the Californian portions of the Mojave and Sonoran deserts, and in the northern Mexican segment of the Sonoran. Dunes formed of the chemical gypsum also occur, most often in the Chihuahuan Desert (for example, at White Sands National Monument in New Mexico; see plate 6). Besides being unstable, desert soils may also be quite saline. High evaporation can result in extreme concentrations of various salts in the upper soil horizons (plates 28 and 29). These phenomena, as well as others, can create difficulties for plants trying to become established.

A very important soil property in deserts is the relative

proportion of different-size particles in the soil mixture. At the top of bajadas, soil "particles" are coarse to large—and even include boulders. As you walk down the slope of a bajada, the average size of the soil particles decreases until, at the very bottom, you find material as fine as silt. Plants and animals respond to this difference in soil properties, and thus significant changes in fauna and flora occur over very short geographic distances.

Certain other sorting phenomena result in the development of desert pavements. In these areas, which are usually low slopes or flat plains, stones have been closely packed together to form a uniform, stony surface, generally without vegetation (plate 30). Often there are no—or at least very few—stones in the soil profile beneath the pavement. These pavements have a number of possible origins. All fine material may simply have been carried away by wind or water, leaving the stones in place to act like an armor plate, preventing further erosion. Other scenarios explaining the development of these pavements have been put forth, including the suggestion that the stones moved up in the soil profile.

An interesting feature of pavements is revealed by picking up one of the stones and examining its color. Often the exposed surface will be a darker color than the buried sides and bottom. This shiny, black material is called desert varnish. It contains seventy percent or more clay, but its unusual appearance is due to oxides of iron and manganese. This material appears to be laid down in cycles. The exact manner in which the varnish develops is a topic of some scientific debate, but chemical processes that are known to occur could easily account for its presence. Recently, however, a biological origin for the varnish has been proposed. According to this theory, bacteria aid in the precipitation and deposition of iron and manganese compounds on the rock surfaces. (A similar process is responsible for the production of iron-manganese nodules on the ocean floor.) The chances are that these varnishes may be formed by either or both mechanisms, and perhaps by others as well.

Another soil-surface structure that is common to many desert areas is the crust formed by both physical processes and biotic ones involving microorganisms. These crusts can easily be observed in soils that have not been walked upon. The surface forms a layer that can be removed by hand and that doesn't crumble when it is held carefully. Close inspection reveals a spongelike, vesicular soil structure. This structure is formed by rainfall and soil-gas dynamics, often in association with the action of algae and lichens.

It is clear that soils—the medium necessary for plant growth —are worthy objects of study. Unfortunately, desert soils— other than those used for agriculture—have been little explored. This situation must be remedied if we are to use deserts to their full potential, whether it be to cultivate economically significant native plants, develop sites for recreation, or even manage deserts to maintain their natural beauty in the face ever-increasing human populations.

THE GREAT BASIN DESERT

The Great Basin Desert lies predominantly in the
Intermountain West, a region bounded on the west by the
Sierra Nevada–Cascade mountain axis and on the east by the
Rocky Mountains. The mid-nineteenth century explorer
Captain John C. Fremont perceived the landscape to be a
gigantic enclosed basin; convinced by his 1843–44
explorations that the area lacked an outlet to the sea, he
named it the Great Basin.

In fact, the name is somewhat misleading in that it suggests a
single large basin. Actually, the Intermountain West is
composed of 150 basins and approximately 160 discrete
mountain ranges. This landscape of alternating mountain
ranges and their adjacent basins is the physiographic zone
known as the Basin and Range Province.

The Province has valley floors at high elevations, often more
than 4000 feet. Protruding from the basins are mountain
ranges, which were raised through the process of faulting.
Most of the ranges have a north-south orientation, and many
have peaks higher than 10,000 feet; several exceed 12,000
feet. This means that in some areas mountain peaks rise 5000
to 6000 feet above the surrounding basins.

The wearing away of the mountains by the inexorable forces of
wind and water has filled many of the valleys with deep
sediments, often forming broad plains. The low areas of these
plains or valleys frequently contain ephemeral lakes, called
playas, which seldom contain water except during years of
unusually high precipitation.

During the late Pleistocene epoch, beginning about 75,000
years ago and ending 8000 to 12,000 years ago, many of the
valleys contained somewhat more permanent lakes. Two of
these ancient lakes are especially notable, because at one time
or another they covered vast areas, and the sediments derived
from them continue to affect the distribution of plants and
animals even today. More important, there are existing lakes
that originated from these bodies of water. One of the
Pleistocene lakes, Lake Lahontan, existed in an area that today
includes northwestern Nevada, southern Oregon, and
northeastern California. Lake Lahontan once covered 8495
square miles and was 886 feet deep. Today it persists mainly
in a few scattered remnants, including Pyramid and Walker
lakes, in Nevada. Another lake, Lake Winnemucca, existed
until 1938; however, a diversion dam built for irrigation
caused Lake Winnemucca to go dry.

Pyramid Lake remains a viable, only slightly salty, lake
covering an area approximately thirty miles long and seven
miles wide. A form of trout, the Lahontan Cutthroat, occurs
in the lake. This species is a relict from the time when it was
the only predatory fish in Lake Lahontan. The Lahontan is the
largest cutthroat known; a specimen taken in 1925 from
Pyramid Lake weighed forty-one pounds. Other fish, native
and introduced, occur in the lake and are the source of food for
a large American White Pelican colony on Anaho Island, at
the southeastern end of the lake.

The second large Pleistocene lake occupied more than 20,000

Lahontan Cutthroat
Salmo clarki henshawi

**Physiographic Sections of
the Basin and Range
Province**

 Great Basin
 Sonoran Desert
 Salton Trough
 Mexican Highland
 Sacramento

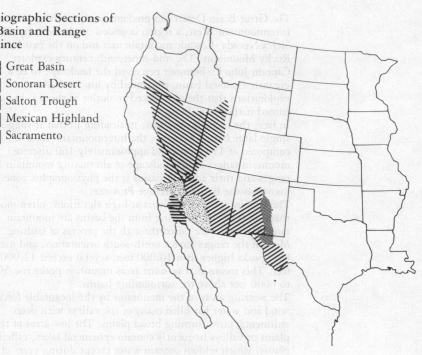

**Physiographic Provinces
of Deserts and
Surrounding Areas**

 Mountains
 Columbia Plateau
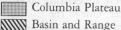 Basin and Range
 Colorado Plateau

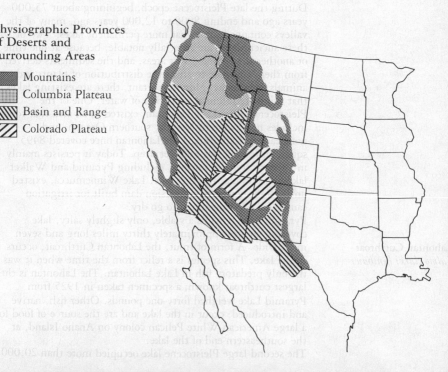

square miles in Utah, Nevada, and Idaho. This body of water, Lake Bonneville, was approximately 1083 feet deep. The remainders of the shores of Lake Bonneville form a series of terraces at roughly 5150 feet in elevation, and can easily be seen today along the Wasatch Mountains of Utah. The remnants of Lake Bonneville include the Great Salt Lake and Utah Lake in northern Utah, and Sevier Lake, a large playa in west-central Utah.

The Great Salt Lake

Since 1851, the date from which accurate records have been maintained, the Great Salt Lake has experienced dramatic changes in water level. Until recently, the lake surface had fluctuated between a high elevation of about 4211 feet (in 1873) and a low of 4191 feet (in 1963). Currently the water level, although varying, stands at 4208 feet. When the water is at an elevation of 4200 feet the lake covers an area that is about eighty miles long and thirty miles wide, and has a maximum depth of slightly over thirty feet.

Although the Great Salt Lake is too salty for fish, a variety of other organisms occur and give it its characteristic colors. Until the summer of 1984, the northern and southern portions of the lake were separated by a railroad causeway. The northern portion was much more saline (about twenty-seven percent solids by weight) than the southern portion (about thirteen percent solids by weight), and its characteristic bacteria and algae gave the water a pinkish color that varied in hue. The southern portion of the lake was dominated by blue-green algae (*Dunelilla*), which imparted blue and green tints to the lake's waters. In 1984, the causeway was breached as a flood control measure. The long-range physical and biological changes that will be caused by the breaching are not yet known. Brine shrimp exist in great abundance in some parts of the lake. These small crustaceans are harvested and sold as fish food to the home aquarist. Of more commercial significance is the extraction of various chemicals from the saline waters. The sale of magnesium, chlorine, sodium chloride, potassium sulfate, as well as by-products resulting from the extraction of these chemicals, form a multimillion-dollar industry in Utah. Until the recent floods of 1983 and 1984, and the consequent rise in the lake's level, the north end of the lake was a birder's paradise. The area was dominated by vast freshwater marshlands, which had formed behind extensive dike systems holding out the salty water of the lake. Dozens of species of waterfowl and shorebirds nested in this area and congregated in enormous numbers. Because the extent of flood damage has not been entirely assessed, the ultimate fate of the area is unclear.

Brine Shrimp
Artemia salina

Plant Life

The Great Basin Desert contains fewer plant species and life forms than do other North American deserts. The plentiful native annual plants found in our hot deserts are lacking here. Also noticeably absent are the many forms of cacti, agaves, and yuccas. Additionally, watercourses are not lined with

Big Sagebrush
Artemisia tridentata
353, 357

native "desert-wash" trees and shrubs. The plants that do exist are generally small to medium-size shrubs. While a number of species can be found in any one area, by far the vast majority of plants are either sagebrushes (*Artemisia*) or saltbushes (*Atriplex*). In the northern portions of the Great Basin Desert, grasses become conspicuous, and their dominance in the cooler, moister areas northward into Idaho, Oregon, and Washington define the boundary between the arid deserts and a moister, more steppelike vegetation zone.

The vast desert expanses of western Utah and Nevada appear to many travelers as a monotonous vista: miles of gray countryside where people are few and plants and animals are dull (plates 23 and 25). This impression is misleading. There are treasures here that, while harder to find than in the diverse Sonoran Desert, are no less interesting.

The relative proportions of the three plant types mentioned above—sagebrushes, saltbushes, and grasses—have been used to delimit three major Great Basin Desert vegetation types. In extreme northern and western Nevada and southern Idaho, there exists an area dominated by Big Sagebrush, which also includes a fair proportion of grasses. This vegetation type, Sagebrush Steppe, forms the northern portion of the Great Basin Desert (plate 27). The habitat extends well beyond the Great Basin physiographic Province northward into the Columbia Plateau Province and eastward into the Wyoming Basin Province.

Occurring in large patches across the rest of the Great Basin of Nevada and Utah is another sagebrush-dominated habitat, the Great Basin Sagebrush Zone (plate 24). These areas look very similar to the Sagebrush Steppe because Big Sagebrush is common to both zones, but the grass component, important in the Steppe, occurs less frequently in the Sagebrush Zone. Because of the dominance of Big Sagebrush, these two vegetation types are often lumped together. However, Dr. Neil West at Utah State University has argued that the more arid Great Basin Sagebrush Zone is less diverse in plant species, less productive in plant growth, and does not recover as quickly following a disturbance as does the moister Sagebrush Steppe. In line with his arguments, the two types are discussed separately here.

A third extensive vegetation type is Salt-Desert Shrub, which occurs at scattered localities throughout eight western states (plate 26). In the area under consideration in this book this type is usually, though not always, associated with saline soils. Thus, low-elevation sites where salts have accumulated and where soils composed of fine particles predominate usually contain this vegetation type.

These three main vegetation types cannot always be separated easily. Driving in a car down alluvial fans in Utah or Nevada, a careful observer can note a change from sagebrush-dominated sites on the upper slopes to virtually pure stands of various saltbushes in the valleys, even though only very short distances have been traversed. It is only at the extreme ends of this gradient that the vegetation types are absolutely different.

Similarly, along the border of Utah and Idaho or Nevada and Idaho, observers driving north or to higher elevations will see an increase in the amount of grass growing between Big Sagebrush plants, which reflects the transition from desertlike to moister, steppelike conditions.

Defining vegetation boundaries is difficult, even for ecologists. When interpreting landscapes, do not give up if a site does not exactly match the specific description of a particular community type. Many plant and animal species respond to almost imperceptible gradients of such environmental factors as rainfall, temperature, soil moisture, and salinity. The middle ranges of such gradients often contain confusing mixtures of the species that clearly dominate the extreme ends. Although two of the main Great Basin vegetation types are dominated by Big Sagebrush, other woody sagebrushes are important as well. Currently, in addition to Big Sagebrush, there are about eleven other woody sagebrush (*Artemisia*) species. More than a third of these are locally dominant in parts of the Great Basin Desert. For example, on sandy sites the beautiful Sand Sagebrush predominates, while on clay soils one finds the rather plain Black Sagebrush.

Sand Sagebrush
Artemisia filifolia

Black Sagebrush
Artemisia arbuscula

Local variations in soil chemistry and other habitat characteristics correlate to the occurrence of various sagebrush species; in addition, one species—Big Sagebrush—is so widespread and so well adapted to local conditions that botanists recognize at least four distinct forms of this species. These occur in different habitats and are as ecologically different from one another as are some of the separate species. Sagebrushes are not very tolerant of high salinity and they do not resprout after fires. Nor are they major food items for most grazing ruminant mammals, whether native or non-native. At least one bird, however, the Sage Grouse, may find over seventy percent of its diet in the form of sagebrush leaves and buds; browsing mammals such as Mule Deer and Pronghorns also eat sagebrush. In general, the presence of large grazing mammals increases the dominance of sagebrush, because the animals ignore it and feed on other species, especially grasses, thus eliminating some potential sagebrush competitors. Conversely, if an area has very saline soil or has recently been subject to fire, the importance of sagebrush will be decreased. Species that can resprout after fires, such as rabbitbrushes (*Chrysothamnus*), horsebrushes (*Tetradymia*), and snakeweeds (*Xanthocephalum*) will temporarily replace sagebrush. Therefore —as is the case with all vegetation types—the history of a particular plot of ground must be known if a proper interpretation of the relationships between plants and their environment is to be attempted.

Sage Grouse
Centrocercus urophasianus
545

Mule Deer
Odocoileus hemionus
528

Pronghorn
Antilocapra americana
527

An annual grass introduced in the 1870s, Cheatgrass Brome, also plays a role in determining the amount of sagebrush on a site. This species successfully competes with many native grasses; it also produces large quantities of stems and leaves that burn readily when dry and tend to increase the frequency and intensity of fires. This situation does not favor Big Sagebrush.

Cheatgrass Brome
Bromus tectorum

Littleleaf Horsebrush
Tetradymia glabrata
343

Mormon Tea
Ephedra spp.
364

Winter Fat
Ceratoides lanata
354

Shadscale
Atriplex confertifolia
346

Spiny Hopsage
Atriplex spinosa

Plains Pricklypear
Opuntia polyacantha
121

Bottlebrush Squirreltail
Sitanion hystrix

Indian Ricegrass
Oryzopsis hymenoides
362

Galleta
Hilaria jamesii

Bluebunch Wheatgrass
Agropyron spicatum
363

Wildrye
Elymus cinereus

Halogeton
Halogeton glomeratus

Tumble Weed
Salsola kali

Tansy Mustard
Descurainia pinnata

Clasping Pepperweed
Lepidium perfoliatum

Bur Buttercup
Ceratocephalus testiculatus

In addition to Big Sagebrush, several other shrubs occur in sagebrush-dominated areas. These include: Littleleaf Horsebrush, a species that, while attractive when covered with their yellow flowers, are toxic to cattle; Mormon teas (*Ephedra*); the highly palatable and thus prized Winter Fat; Shadscale; Spiny Hopsage; and others. The major cactus species is the very low and spreading Plains Pricklypear. Grasses vary greatly from place to place, but may include Bottlebrush Squirreltail, sacatons (*Sporobolus*), the subtly beautiful Indian Ricegrass, needle grasses (*Stipa*), Galleta, bluegrasses (*Poa*), the wheatgrasses (*Agropyron*)—especially Bluebunch Wheatgrass, as well as many wheatgrass species introduced from Eurasia—and Wildrye, a species that occurs in somewhat moist, slightly alkaline sites and may attain a height of six feet.

Forbs in the Great Basin Desert are extremely varied, but the more common include locoweeds (*Astragalus*), Sego lilies (*Calochortus,* the state flower of Utah), Indian paintbrushes (*Castilleja*), phloxes (*Phlox*), lupines (*Lupinus*), globemallows (*Sphaeralcea*), and a variety of asterlike members of the sunflower family.

There are many species of locoweeds and they are often difficult to identify. Most species are toxic, either because they accumulate selenium or because they contain a specific alkaloidlike compound (locine), or both. The Indian paintbrushes often appear to have showy red, orange, or yellow flowers. In fact these are not flowers but rather bractlike leaves.

While many of these plants may be found in either the Sagebrush Steppe or the Great Basin Sagebrush Zone, their relative proportions will differ. The Sagebrush Steppe will contain about twenty plant species in an area of approximately 1000 square feet. Shrubs range from twenty to forty inches in height and may cover from ten to eighty percent of the ground surface; forbs are about half as high as the shrubs, or even smaller. Few annual species can be found, except on disturbed sites. The Great Basin Sagebrush sites, on the other hand, rarely contain shrubs of forty inches in stature—there are also fewer individual shrub and plant species in a given area. Big Sagebrush often provides seventy percent of the plant cover and ninety percent of the biomass—the total accumulation of vegetation on the site, measured by cutting, drying, and weighing the plants.

Sites that have been disturbed often contain extensive stands of weedy annuals. Frequently these are species that are not native to North America. Among the more common "weeds" are Halogeton; Tumble Weed, a species that evokes the desolate character of the West; Tansy Mustard; Clasping Pepperweed; Bur Buttercup; and, of course, Cheatgrass Brome.

The Salt-Desert Shrub vegetation is dominated by members of the plant family Chenopodiaceae. This family contains a variety of plants, including many species tolerant of high concentrations of salt. While a number of chenopods have some economic importance, sugar beet and spinach are two

Little Greasewood
Sarcobatus baileyi

Greasewood
Sarcobatus vermiculatus
345

Iodinebush
Allenrolfea occidentalis

Rushes
Juncus balticus

Alkali Sacaton
Sporobolus airoides

Blackbrush
Coleogyne ramosissima
348

that have worldwide agricultural significance, since they are inexpensive yet nutrious dietary staples.

The various Salt-Desert Shrub species differ in their tolerance to moisture, each thriving where the water table is an optimum distance from the surface of the ground. Some species, such as greasewoods (*Sarcobatus*), can occur in lowlands where the water table is within three feet of the surface and where standing water often occurs. The areas formerly covered by Lake Lahontan harbor Little Greasewood, a species that some biologists believe to be different from the much more widely distributed Greasewood.

Other species that grow in such relatively moist areas and that can also often tolerate higher salinities than Greasewood include Iodinebush, glassworts or pickleweeds (*Salicornia*), seepweeds (*Suaeda*), and saltgrasses (*Distichlis*). On sites with deeper water tables, which seldom have surface standing water, a variety of saltbush (*Atriplex*) species predominate, as do other chenopods, such as Winter Fat and the mollies (*Kochia*).

The most characteristic shrub of the Salt-Desert area is Shadscale. This species can be found mixed in with Big Sagebrush on many sites; its greater tolerance to salinity, however, allows it to be the dominant species over vast areas of the moderately saline soils found in valley bottoms. Shadscale is an important browse plant for livestock, especially when it bears succulent young stems and leaves.

Throughout the Salt-Desert zone there exists an unusual and interesting mosaic of vegetation. Gray-green patches composed completely of Shadscale will surround white-gray patches composed entirely of Winter Fat. On some sites, several other species combine to create a striking pattern. Originally it was thought that this phenomenon was due to local soil differences; however, the situation now seems to be more complex. On the most saline sites in the Great Basin, virtually no true shrubs persist. In such areas, Iodinebush and saltgrass (*Distichlis*) predominate. Sometimes these two plants are mixed with rushes, Alkali Sacaton, and one or more species of pickleweed (*Salicornia*). This type of mixture is not confined to the desert areas of North America; plants in these genera occur together wherever highly saline soils exist.

To the north, the Great Basin Desert grades into the more grassy steppe vegetation of Oregon and Washington. Wherever elevations increase, the desert species give way to tree-dominated vegetation. Often in the Great Basin the transition is to a Pinyon Pine-Juniper community. To the south, the transition from the Great Basin Desert to the Mojave Desert is marked by a fourth vegetation type, the Blackbrush community.

A small, round, dark shrub, Blackbrush grows in a narrow band from California—along the edges of the Mojave Desert—across southern Nevada, and straddles the Utah-Arizona border. Often nearly pure stands of Blackbrush dominate mesas between 3000 and 5000 feet in elevation. In these areas, rainfall is low and the shallow soils are usually underlain

Turpentine Broom
Thamnosma montana
366

Desert Peach
Prunus fasciculata

Common Raven
Corvus corax
582

Golden Eagle
Aquila chrysaetos
540

Red-tailed Hawk
Buteo jamaicensis
536, 537

American Kestrel
Falco sparverius
542

Horned Lark
Eremophila alpestris
576

Black-tailed Jack Rabbit
Lepus californicus
509

Coyote
Canis latrans
523, 524

Pallid-winged
Grasshopper
Trimerotropis pallidipennis
369

Speckled Rangeland
Grasshopper
Arphia conspersa

Red-winged Grasshopper
Arphia pseudonietana

Sagebrush Defoliator
Moth
Aroga websteri

Western Widow
Latrodectus hesperus

by a calcium layer. Visitors to the Grand Canyon who peer into the abyss are often looking down upon stands of Blackbrush.

Although Blackbrush is usually highly dominant where it occurs, other shrubs do exist alongside it, including the extremely, almost nauseatingly pungent Turpentine Broom, Desert Peach, the ever-present Big Sagebrush, and, in some areas, other species of *Artemisia, Ephedra,* or *Atriplex.*

Animal Life

The rather stark structural nature of the Great Basin Desert is reflected in the paucity of animal species you may see when you travel there. If you are near water, there may be large numbers of birds. In the open drylands, however, there are very few species conspicuously present other than the Common Raven, Golden Eagle, Red-tailed Hawk, American Kestrel (which can be abundant), and flocks of Horned Larks. The Black-tailed Jack Rabbit, the Pronghorn, and—if you are lucky—the Coyote may also be seen.

Invertebrates

Invertebrates are not as obvious in the Great Basin as in other places. Of course there is the usual smattering of insects on shrubs, but because there are few succulent forbs, there are simply fewer insects than on more moist sites, or than on drier sites with more forbs. Grasshoppers of the band-winged group are conspicuous because of their colored wings and often noisy flight. Several species may be observed from early spring until the frosts. The most often encountered species is the Pallid-winged Grasshopper, a species that, like many other band-wings, has yellow hind wings with a prominent black band. Several red-winged species might catch your attention. In the spring and early summer, the Speckled Rangeland Grasshopper is abundant. In summer and fall it is replaced by the Red-winged Grasshopper. Ground-dwelling beetles may number more than one hundred species in some localities. Members of the families Tenebrionidae and Carabidae are especially common, but they are primarily nocturnal. Butterflies and moths are not especially abundant, but some species, such as the Sagebrush Defoliator Moth, can significantly influence the plant community. Robber flies (family Asilidae) are often easily seen as they hunt other insects. The disklike mounds of harvester ants (*Pogonomyrmex*) dot the landscape, and in some places, such as northern Utah, up to fifteen percent of the land surface may be covered by their mounds and the surrounding areas, which the ants keep stripped of plants.

Most Great Basin desert-shrub sites contain twenty to forty species of spiders. In the shrubs themselves, crab spiders, jumping spiders, and typical orb-web builders dominate, while on the ground the usual funnel-web weavers and some wolf spiders are present. The only potentially dangerous arachnid is the Western Widow, a species that is abundant in disturbed areas, even around houses in new developments. Fortunately, it is not likely to bite unless it is handled.

Mormon Cricket
Anabrus simplex
374

Great Basin Spadefoot
Scaphiopus intermontanus
277

Tiger Salamander
Ambystoma tigrinum
289, 290, 291

Western Whiptail
Cnemidorphorus tigris
206

Side-blotched Lizard
Uta stansburiana
202

Sagebrush Lizard
Sceloporus graciosus
212

Striped Whipsnake
Masticophis taeniatus
221

Western Yellowbelly
Racer
Coluber constrictor mormon
232

Great Basin Gopher
Snake
*Pituophis melanoleucus
deserticola*
263

Great Basin Rattlesnake
Crotalus viridis lutosus
258, 260

Perhaps the most famous Great Basin invertebrate is the Mormon Cricket. It is this species that is the "grasshopper" noted in Mormon diaries. At one point, a Mormon wrote, it ". . . was near turning the 'Garden of the Mountains' into a desert." From 1848 to 1850, this species reached high densities, which—according to legend—were contained by hordes of gulls. In fact, on the Mormon Temple grounds in Salt Lake City, Utah, there is a monument erected to honor the seagulls. Mormon Crickets occur in a variety of habitats, especially those with grasses, from extreme western Minnesota to the east side of the Sierra Nevada and Cascades, north to southern Canada, and south to the boundary of the Great Basin in the West and northern New Mexico farther eastward. Periodic outbreaks were common in the past. In 1938, nineteen million acres were infested in eleven western states.

Amphibians and Reptiles
Amphibians are few, but temporary bodies of water support breeding colonies of the desert-adapted Great Basin Spadefoot, a frog whose plaintive call carries for great distances in the desert night. In limited areas of the 'eastern Great Basin, you may occasionally be surprised to find the Tiger Salamander or its larvae in unlikely places, even in what appear to be stark desert landscapes.

Reptiles, while not as numerous here as in other deserts, can be locally abundant. The speedy Western Whiptail, an alert diurnal species, occurs commonly throughout the Great Basin Desert. Even more abundant, however, is the Side-blotched Lizard. The Sagebrush Lizard is frequently seen running into the cover of a Big Sagebrush shrub. In summer, a mid-morning walk in their habitat could reveal dozens of these lizards. Snakes are not often seen by the casual visitor to the Great Basin. A careful observer, however, might find the handsome Striped Whipsnake or the agile Western Yellowbelly Racer, a rather common snake that is frequently seen, especially during the warm portion of the morning. The serpent most likely to be encountered is the Great Basin Gopher Snake, which makes its presence known by hissing loudly and vibrating its tail at intruders. This distressing habit causes many Great Basin residents to call it the "Blow Snake" and to consider this harmless species—a great consumer of rodents—venomous. The only venomous snake in the area is the Great Basin Rattlesnake, a potentially dangerous species but one that has been responsible for very few bite cases, except while it was being handled. This rattlesnake occurs from the driest deserts to elevations of more than 8000 feet and usually betrays its presence by rattling.

Birds
An early morning bird walk in the Great Basin can be somewhat disappointing. While raptors are numerous in terms of both individuals and species, other types of birds are not common in the desert scrub. In part this is caused by the low-lying vegetation, but it is also partly due to the limited supply of consumable seeds. Short walks up into the Pinyon-

Sage Thrasher
Oreoscoptes montanus
591

Sage Sparrow
Amphispiza belli
611

Green-tailed Towhee
Pipilo chlorurus
605

Mountain Cottontail
Sylvilagus nuttalli

Pygmy Rabbit
Brachylagus idahoensis

Desert Cottontail
Sylvilagus audubonii
508

Least Chipmunk
Eutamias minimus
497

Townsend's Ground
Squirrel
Spermophilus townsendii
501

Ord's Kangaroo Rat
Dipodomys ordii
480

Chisel-toothed Kangaroo
Rat
Dipodomys microps
481

Deer Mouse
Peromyscus maniculatus
489

Great Basin Pocket
Mouse
Perognathus parvus
474

Kit Fox
Vulpes macrotis
521

Bobcat
Felis rufus
517, 520

Juniper area, or into higher montane sites, are usually more rewarding.

There are a few birds that tend to favor stands dominated by Big Sagebrush. These include the Sage Thrasher, Sage Sparrow, and the Sage Grouse. Unfortunately none are very easy to observe. They fly quickly to the cover of shrubs and are not very strikingly marked. Another bird of secretive habits, one not as closely associated with sagebrush, is the Green-tailed Towhee. During the breeding season in early spring, groups of Sage Grouse going through their courtship routine of athletic dances and booming sounds rival almost any sight in nature for sheer excitement. Local breeding sites are generally well known and easy for a visitor to find, although they may be off the beaten track.

Mammals

Most desert mammals are nocturnal and therefore difficult to observe. A conspicuous exception is the Badger, a species encountered when least expected, often with unnerving consequences because Badgers can be aggressive. The Black-tailed Jack Rabbit can usually be seen easily in most areas. In the northern Great Basin, however, the species experiences population cycles, and, as a result, the jack rabbits reach high densities every nine to eleven years. In different areas, the peaks may occur in different years. In response to the growth in the rabbit population, Coyotes, major predators of the rabbits, expand their populations; their peak population lags behind that of the rabbits. When the rabbit population is low, Coyotes feed instead on rodents.

The Pronghorn is locally abundant in the Great Basin Desert and can be a pest to agricultural crops. This animal forms small groups composed of a buck, several does, and young. The males are quite territorial and mark their boundaries in a number of ways, including the use of scent glands, with each individual producing a distinctive scent.

In addition to Pronghorns and jack rabbits, one of three small rabbits is usually visible: the Mountain Cottontail, a generally montane species that occurs in sagebrush stands in the northern part of the Great Basin Desert; the Pygmy Rabbit, usually seen in sagebrush clumps; and, in the southern Great Basin, the Desert Cottontail. Two rodents, the Least Chipmunk and Townsend's Ground Squirrel, are active during the day and are abundant.

A night foray with flashlight in hand, especially in sand-dune areas, may reveal a greater abundance of mammals. Various kangaroo rats, especially Ord's Kangaroo Rat or the rarer Chisel-toothed Kangaroo Rat, are easily found during such searches. Invariably, you will see the ubiquitous Deer Mouse and the Great Basin Pocket Mouse. If you are particularly lucky you may even see one of the two North American species of kangaroo mice (*Microdipodops*), both of which are confined to the Great Basin. And a fleeting glimpse of a Kit Fox or a Bobcat in the edge of your light is always possible.

THE GREAT BASIN DESERT:
PLANTS AND ANIMALS

Wildflowers
Arrowleaf Balsam Root 30
Balloon Flower 44
Birdcage Evening
Primrose 93
Clammyweed 81
Claret Cup Cactus 42
Cushion Cactus 40
Desert Candle 164
Desert Dandelion 125
Desert Four O'Clock 52
Desert Paintbrush 159
Desert Trumpet 108
Esteve's Pincushion 84
Filaree 57
Five-Needle Fetid
Marigold 134
Freckled Milkvetch 163
Golden Prince's Plume 109
Jones' Penstemon 68
Long-Leaved Phlox 58
Nuttall's Larkspur 63
Plains Pricklypear 121
Poison Milkweed 80
Puncture Vine 143
Rattlesnake Weed 102
Sego Lily 99
Simpson's Hedgehog
Cactus 38
Skyrocket 161
Spike Broomrape 76
Spreading Fleabane 89
Sulphur Flower 112
Sunray 132
Tahoka Daisy 62
Tansy-leaved Evening
Primrose 139
Threadleaf Groundsel 129
Western Peppergrass 78
Winged Dock 46
Yellow Bee Plant 111
Yellow Spiny Daisy 131

Mushrooms
Buried-Stalk Puffball 168
Desert Inky Cap 166
Desert Stalked Puffball 167

Reptiles
Black Collared Lizard 186
Coachwhip 223, 229, 230,
233
Desert Spiny Lizard 199
Gopher Snake 263

Ground Snake 225, 228,
231
Longnose Leopard
Lizard 191
Longnose Snake 238, 247
Night Snake 267
Racer 232
Sagebrush Lizard 212
Short-horned Lizard 197
Side-blotched Lizard 202
Striped Whipsnake 221
Western Blackhead
Snake 227
Western Patchnose
Snake 218
Western Rattlesnake 258,
260
Western Terrestrial Garter
Snake 215
Western Whiptail 206
Zebratail Lizard 203

Amphibians
Bullfrog 288
Great Basin Spadefoot 277
Northern Leopard Frog 286

Fishes
Golden Shiner 299
Mosquitofish 294
Speckled Dace 297
Tui Chub 298

Trees, Shrubs,
Cacti, and Grasses
Big Sagebrush 323, 327
Blackbrush 318
Bluebunch Wheatgrass 333
Four-wing Saltbush 322
Greasewood 315
Indian Ricegrass 332
Littleleaf Horsebrush 313
Mormon Tea 334
Rabbit Brush 310
Shadscale 316
Snakeweed 311
Tamarisk 304, 324
Winter Fat 324

Insects and Spiders
Arid Lands Honey Ants 384
Bee Assassin 376
Broad-necked Darkling
Beetle 381

Carolina Wolf Spider 401
Cochineal Bug 391
Green Valley
Grasshopper 367
Inconspicuous Crab
Spider 400
Jerusalem Cricket 375
Little Black Ant 386
Mormon Cricket 374
Pale Windscorpion 396
Pallid-winged
Grasshopper 369
Rough Harvester Ant 387
Spine-waisted Ants 385
Tarantula Hawk 383
Texas Carpenter Ant 388
Thistledown Velvet-ant 390

Butterflies and Moths
Anise Swallowtail 446
Becker's White 403
Behr's Hairstreak 416
Blue Copper 414, 415
Bronze Roadside
Skipper 438
California Cankerworm
Moth 449
Common Sulphur 443
Gray Marble 405
Great Basin Sootywing 437
Great Basin Wood
Nymph 431
Large California Spanworm
Moth 480
Large White Skipper 408
Monarch 419
Mormon Metalmark 428
Pahaska Skipper 434
Painted Lady 420
Pale Blue 409
Pearly Marblewing 406
Phoebus Parnassian 407
Queen 418
Sagebrush Checkerspot 423
Sandhill Skipper 433
Short-tailed Black 447
Sleepy Orange 417
Western Pygmy Blue 413
Western Tiger
Swallowtail 444
White-Lined Sphinx 448

Mammals
Badger 514

Bighorn Sheep 526
Black-tailed
Jack Rabbit 509
Bobcat 517
Botta's Pocket Gopher 469
Brazilian Free-tailed
Bat 465
California Myotis 458
Chisel-toothed Kangaroo
Rat 481
Coyote 523
Dark Kangaroo Mouse 478
Deer Mouse 489
Desert Cottontail 508
Desert Kangaroo Rat 484
Desert Woodrat 493
Gray Fox 522
Great Basin Pocket
Mouse 474
House Mouse 495
Kit Fox 521
Least Chipmunk 497
Little Pocket Mouse 473
Long-tailed Pocket
Mouse 475
Merriam's Kangaroo
Rat 485
Mountain Lion 518
Mule Deer 528
Northern Grasshopper
Mouse 491
Ord's Kangaroo Rat 480
Pale Kangaroo Mouse 479
Pallid Bat 464
Panamint Kangaroo
Rat 482
Porcupine 507
Pronghorn 527
Raccoon 512
Ringtail 511
Rock Squirrel 505
Sagebrush Vole 496
Silver-haired Bat 459
Southern Grasshopper
Mouse 488
Spotted Bat 462
Striped Skunk 515
Townsend's Big-eared
Bat 463
Townsend's Ground
Squirrel 501
Western Harvest Mouse 486
Western Pipistrelle 461
White-tailed Antelope

Squirrel 499
Yuma Myotis 456

Birds
American Kestrel 542
Ash-throated Flycatcher 573
Bewick's Wren 587
Black-billed Magpie 580
Black-chinned
Hummingbird 563
Black-throated Gray
Warbler 598
Black-throated Sparrow 610
Brewer's Sparrow 608
Brown-headed Cowbird 613
Burrowing Owl 559
Cactus Wren 584
California Quail 548
Canyon Wren 586
Chukar 544
Common Barn-owl 555
Common Nighthawk 560
Common Poorwill 562
Common Raven 582
Cooper's Hawk 532
Dark-eyed Junco 612
European Starling 597
Ferruginous Hawk 538
Golden Eagle 540
Great Horned Owl 556
Green-tailed Towhee 605
Gray Flycatcher 569
Horned Lark 576
House Finch 617
Loggerhead Shrike 596
Mourning Dove 551
Northern Flicker 568
Northern Mockingbird 590
Red-tailed Hawk 536
Rock Wren 585
Rough-legged Hawk 539
Sage Grouse 545
Sage Sparrow 611
Sage Thrasher 591
Say's Phoebe 571
Swainson's Hawk 534
Turkey Vulture 530
Vesper Sparrow 609
Violet-green Swallow 579
Western Bluebird 589
Western Kingbird 575
Western Tanager 599

THE COLORADO PLATEAU SEMIDESERT

The arid portions of the Colorado Plateau physiographic province defy easy categorization. Their enigmatic nature can be understood, in part, by examining the maps found on page 25. These maps offer two interpretations of North American deserts. On one, the Colorado Plateau is included as a part of the Great Basin Desert; on the other, it is excluded. In fact, this confusion results because the area's vegetation is a composite of mid-elevation woodland species, those found in grasslands, and some that occur in the Great Basin Desert. Since some landscapes in the Plateau superficially resemble deserts and may contain some Great Basin plants and animals —and, additionally, because some of our most spectacular National Parks and Monuments occur in this area—a brief discussion of the Plateau is included here.

The Plateau area itself includes the southeastern quarter of Utah, east of the Wasatch Mountains and south of the Uinta Mountains; the northeastern quarter of Arizona and a bit of southwestern Colorado, west of Durango; and northwestern New Mexico, north of Gallup. The region has variously been referred to as the Painted Desert, the Navahoan Desert, the Great Basin Desert, and the Colorado Plateau Semidesert. The Colorado Plateau physiographic province covers 130,000 square miles of land, most of which is higher than 5000 feet. About a quarter of the area receives less than ten inches of precipitation per year, and this occurs predominantly as snow. The geological structure consists of stacked plates of starkly beautiful layers of sedimentary rocks, which, although frequently altered by uplifting, are generally flat, dipping only slightly northward. These soft substrates have been deeply incised by streams and rivers, resulting in canyons and rock structures of awesome beauty and magnitude. In this region, this process is most often associated with the splendor of the Grand Canyon in Arizona, yet its results are also obvious in the equally beautiful, but less visited, Canyonlands, Arches, and Capitol Reef national parks in Utah. In addition to the sedimentary rocks, many areas are marked by cones and flows of dark lava. Members of the extensive Colorado River complex are located in the Province, including the spectacular Green River, which flows through Utah.

The Plateau's arid-adapted vegetation is a mixture of the salt-desert shrubland, Blackbrush, and Great Basin sagebrush floras that were discussed in the section on Great Basin Desert. In many places, the combination of trees—such as junipers (*Juniperus*) and pinyon pines (*Pinus*)—and a great variety of grasses suggests the unique character and mixed origins of the Plateau's flora. In other places, especially in saline areas, communities virtually typical of the Great Basin Desert exist. The biota of the Plateau is isolated because the area is surrounded by mountains, save in two low areas. This isolation has permitted the evolution of a large number of endemic plant species. Many of the endemics are locoweeds (*Astragalus*), cryptanthas (*Cryptantha*), or buckwheats (*Eriogonum*), but at least ten other genera are represented by endemic species in the region.

Galleta
Hilaria jamesii

Threeawn
Aristida longiseta

Ringtail
Bassariscus astutus
511

Least Chipmunk
Eutamias minimus
497

Desert Woodrat
Neotoma lepida
493

White-tailed Antelope
Squirrel
Ammospermophilus leucurus
499

Sagebrush Lizard
Sceloporus graciosus
212

Tree Lizard
Urosaurus ornatus
205

Side-blotched Lizard
Uta stansburiana
202

Gopher Snake
Pituophis melanoleucus
263

Striped Whipsnake
Masticophis taeniatus
221

White-tailed Prairie Dog
Cynomys gunnisoni

Plateau Whiptail
Cnemidophorus velox

Western Whiptail
Cnemidophorus tigris
206

Glossy Snake
Arizona elegans
268

Night Snake
Hypsiglena torquata
267

The grass component is diverse. In many places, however, certain species are so abundant that they have been accorded the rank of a separate vegetation type. The association involving Galleta and Threeawn forms one of these groups, which occurs at about 5000 feet or slightly higher, in southeastern Utah.

Animals in the arid portion of the Plateau include species that also have wide distributions in either the grasslands or the Great Basin Desert. Of the species that are discussed in the context of other deserts, those occurring here include the Ringtail, the Least Chipmunk, the Desert Woodrat, the White-tailed Antelope Squirrel, and the Black-tailed Jack Rabbit. In addition, several desert reptile species are common, among them the Sagebrush, Collared, Tree, and Side-blotched lizards and the Gopher Snake and Striped Whipsnake. Unique to the area are the White-tailed Prairie Dog; the Plateau Whiptail, a handsome striped lizard with a bluish tail; and several subspecies of lizards and snakes. These characteristic subspecies include the Northern Whiptail, a form of the Western Whiptail; the Painted Desert Glossy Snake; the Mesa Verde Night Snake; and the Midget Faded Rattlesnake, a diminutive, pinkish form of the Western Rattlesnake.

The reptile and mammal species that are characteristic of the Great Basin Desert but do not occur on the Colorado Plateau underline by their absence the unique nature of the arid areas of the Plateau. These mammals include the Sagebrush Vole, the Kit Fox, Merriam's Kangaroo Rat, several species of pocket mice, the Chisel-toothed Kangaroo Rat, and both species of kangaroo mice. Of the missing reptiles, the most prominent are the Desert Horned Lizard, the Longnose Snake, the Ground Snake, the Zebratail Lizard, and the Patchnose Snake.

The birds here are generally those that are typical in the deserts or grasslands. Most of the species common in arid areas are included in this book.

Since the Colorado Plateau contains many mountains exceeding 11,000 feet in elevation, along with their associated montane floras and faunas, a significant part of the region's biota is beyond the purview of this book.

Although the coverage of the details of the Plateau given here is scant because the region is not a true desert, this field guide will be appropriate to use in locales marked by low elevation and sparse, shrubby vegetation. This superficial coverage is not meant to demean an area that is geologically among the most spectacular in the entire world. The Colorado Plateau offers an incredible experience, one that can be a welcome break as you tour the true deserts of North America.

THE MOJAVE DESERT

Like most other North American deserts, the Mojave Desert is
contained in the Basin and Range Province. Many biologists
have claimed that there is no Mojave Desert per se, but that in
fact the area is really a transitional vegetation type wedged
between the Great Basin Desert to the north and the Sonoran
Desert to the south. This point of view has its strengths:
Physiographically the Mojave Desert is clearly intermediate
because it straddles two separate sections of the Basin and
Range Province, the Great Basin Section to the north and the
Sonoran Desert Section to the south. Since both of these
Sections are simply subdivisions of the overall Basin and
Range Province, there are obvious similarities between them;
for example, both contain mountain ranges separated by basins
that are generally drained internally and are accompanied by
playas.

The two Sections also differ in some ways. In general, the
basin floors of the Sonoran Desert are lower in elevation than
those of the Great Basin. The Great Basin has base elevations
of 4000 feet or higher, while elevations in the Sonoran section
are usually quite a bit less than 3000 feet; in the extreme,
they may be below sea level. The lowest point in the United
States occurs in the Mojave Desert at Death Valley National
Monument in California, where the elevation is 282 feet
below sea level. This is in stark contrast to the 11,049-foot
Telescope Peak in the Panamint Range just west of Badwater.
The fact that the biological boundaries of the Mojave Desert
do not coincide with the boundaries of one of the Sections
defined by landscape physiography can be confusing. As you
move to the south end of the Great Basin, there is a decrease
in elevation—and rather an abrupt one. But you must travel
even farther south at these lower elevations before you reach
the Sonoran Desert Section boundary. On the other hand, the
biologically based Great Basin Desert ends at the elevational
break and the Mojave Desert commences. Thus, the
physiographic and biological subdivisions do not coincide.
Routes along two major highways make this somewhat clearer.
Traveling from the Great Basin Desert near Tonopah, Nevada
(6030 feet), you cross the area of the Great Basin Desert/
Mojave Desert biological transition near Beatty, Nevada (3830
feet). Farther south, just past Las Vegas, Nevada (2200 feet),
you approach the Great Basin Section/Sonoran Section
physiographic boundary. A similar situation occurs traveling
south along I-15 from Cedar City (5834 feet) in the Great
Basin Desert of Utah down to St. George, Utah (2880) feet,
obviously in the Mojave Desert. Farther south of St. George,
in the Beaver Dam Wash area astride the Utah-Arizona
border, you reach the lowest point in Utah (2350 feet), but it
is still a bit farther south to the physiographic boundary.
The northern portion of the Sonoran Desert physiographic
section—that area occupied by the Mojave Desert—differs
from the rest of the Sonoran Desert Section in that its basins,
for the most part, have internal drainages. In this, they
resemble the basins of the Great Basin Province, and differ
from the southern Sonoran Desert Section, which is traversed

by rivers connecting to the Gila and Colorado rivers. Obviously, where this is the case, internally draining basins no longer exist.

The low elevations of the Mojave Desert generally foster warmer year-round temperatures than those recorded in the Great Basin. Although freezing days do occur, the number of frost-free days still greatly exceeds 200 days a year, even in the extreme northern part of the Mojave Desert. Because of this moderate environment, agriculture is quite feasible where water is available. The early pioneers soon recognized this. The Mormons attempted to produce cotton in the area around St. George, Utah, giving this area its local nickname of Dixie. Summer air temperatures, which regularly approach 120° F, can be among the highest in the United States. The all-time recorded maximum air temperature for the United States— 134° F—was recorded in Death Valley. Under Mojave Desert summer conditions, ground surface temperatures may reach 190° F.

Rainfall is scant. Total rainfall for most sites is less than six inches per year: In Las Vegas, Nevada, it is 4.13 inches; in Barstow, California, 4.25. It may be greater on the desert boundary; in St. George, Utah, for example, the average is 7.95 inches. Death Valley has an annual rainfall average of 1.7 inches, and in an average of two years out of fifty, no rainfall is recorded for twelve months. From sixty-five to ninety-eight percent of the total rainfall arrives in winter.

Warm temperatures and high winds cause high evaporation rates. Saline soils and bodies of saltwater, however, evaporate at rates lower than their freshwater counterparts. Thus, saline playas dry at a slower rate than an equivalent freshwater lake.

Plant Life

In general the vegetation of the Mojave Desert is dominated by low, widely spaced shrubs (plate 18), a growth form that develops in response to limited rainfall. In the spring, however, following winters of gentle rainfall, annual flowers make their ephemeral appearance as a kaleidoscope of colors on the landscape, a stark contrast to the Great Basin Desert. In some places, such as Lucerne Valley, California, eighty-two to eighty-eight percent of the plant species recorded on desert sites were annuals. In years of good rainfall, the density of annuals can exceed seventy plants per square yard on many sites, and may reach densities of four hundred or more per square yard in certain areas. There is no lack of diversity in this spring flora: 250 species of annuals occur in the Mojave Desert. Of that number, eighty percent are endemics, that is, their range of distribution is confined to the Mojave Desert. In comparison with typical Great Basin Desert sites, the Mojave has more species of cacti. Most grow low to the ground and are thus not as conspicuous as Sonoran Desert species. However, when the Beavertail Cactus is covered with its brilliant magenta flowers, it is quite spectacular. Species of yuccas also dominate some sites in the Mojave Desert. One of these, a treelike yucca, the Joshua-tree, is

Beavertail Cactus
Opuntia basilaris
41

Joshua-tree
Yucca brevifolia
326

Blue Yucca
Yucca baccata
336

Mojave Yucca
Yucca schidigera
329

Parry Saltbush
Atriplex parryi

Mojave Sage
Salvia mohavensis

Woolly Bur Sage
Ambrosia eriocentra

Creosote Bush
Larrea tridentata
342

Big Sagebrush
Artemisia tridentata
353, 357

Shadscale
Atriplex confertifolia
346

Blackbrush
Coleogyne ramoisissima
348

Hopsage
Atriplex spinosa

virtually synonymous with the Mojave Desert in the minds of the traveler (and the cowboy-movie enthusiast). (The "tree's" common name, it is speculated, derives from the resemblance of its upraised limbs to the arms of Joshua leading the Israelites.) In fact, the Joshua-tree generally occurs on the biological edges of the Mojave—that is, at higher elevations —where it is a sign of transition. Nevertheless, its extremes of geographic distribution essentially outline the generally accepted boundaries of the Mojave Desert. The Joshua-tree reaches great densities and large sizes in some areas; a few reach nearly fifty feet in height. Two other yuccas are characteristic of many sites here, the Blue Yucca and the Mojave Yucca. Neither usually exceeds five feet in height.

It is convenient to divide the Mojave Desert into two general vegetation types, a northern half with close affinities to the Great Basin Desert and a southern half with similarities to the Sonoran Desert. This should not, however, belittle the relative uniqueness of the Mojave Desert as a vegetation type. Nearly one quarter of all the Mojave Desert plants are endemics. In addition to the Joshua-tree, endemic perennials with broad distributions in the Mojave include Parry Saltbush, Mojave Sage, and Woolly Bur Sage. Many local areas have their own endemic species. Searching for these narrowly distributed plants—rare both ecologically and geographically—can be a source of great enjoyment.

By an accident of history, the Mojave-Great Basin desert transition has been as intensively studied as any other desert site in North America. From Mercury, Nevada, north for eighty miles there exists a bombing range and nuclear weapons test facility, the Nevada Test Site, that covers an area of 1350 square miles. The fauna and flora of this area have been scrutinized to establish the effects of radiation on natural communities. These studies have provided a vast legacy of information about the nature of the Mojave Desert.

In the area of the test site, the transition from Creosote Bush-dominated hot desert communities to those dominated by Great Basin Desert species occurs. A good indicator of the change is the amount of annual rainfall. When the annual rainfall is less than 7¼", Creosote Bush communities dominate. Above that level, Big Sagebrush and Shadscale are more abundant. When rainfall is just at or close to the 7¼" level a truly transitional community occurs, one composed of Blackbrush, squawberries, *Lycium* species, and Hopsage. Blackbrush and Hopsage occur in the Great Basin; squawberries are more characteristic of the Sonoran Desert. Often all three of these communities may be found within a few yards of one another. Thus, one can see Great Basin and Mojave Desert sites, as well as the transitional communities, in a single well-planned stop.

The more characteristic hot desert sites, those dominated by Creosote Bush, are quite variable in composition. Part of this diversity is due to the fact that bajadas are very well developed in the Mojave Desert. Differences between plant communities at the top and at the bottom of a bajada can be stark.

Desert Holly
Atriplex hymenelytra
358

Cattle Spinach
Atriplex polycarpa

At the very bottom of bajadas, where fine soils predominate, one of two saltbush species may form nearly pure stands. In areas with high percentages of carbonate rocks, Desert Holly exists in densities characteristically numbering fifty individuals per acre but sometimes reaching up to 250 plants. Where there is less carbonate, Cattle Spinach, a larger plant, predominates at about the same density.

As one moves up the bajada, Creosote Bush begins to appear, mixed in places with Cattle Spinach or Holly. Creosote Bush is found from 240 feet below sea level in Death Valley to over 4000 feet elsewhere—even to 5200 feet on southern exposures. Creosote Bush, a species that is related to the shrubs that dominate the Monte Desert of Agentina, occurs in all of the hot deserts of North America, its distribution coinciding nearly perfectly with their boundaries. In fact, Creosote Bush so dominates the hot deserts that their characteristic smell following warm rains is that of the plant's resinous leaves. Walking in a landscape steeped in this pungent odor is one of the great pleasures of my life.

The roots of Creosote Bush seem to require a relatively large amount of oxygen and to be unable to tolerate much salinity. As a result, the plant generally does not grow on fine or poorly aerated soils. Throughout the Mojave Desert, stands dominated by Creosote Bush cover more than seventy percent of the land surface. The presence of Creosote Bush is perhaps the best indication of your whereabouts in the transition zone between the Great Basin and the Mojave deserts: If Creosote Bush is present, you are in the Mojave.

It is difficult to count "individual" Creosote Bushes because the species readily reproduces vegetatively. Viewed from above, cloned individuals form a circle of shrubs, a growth pattern often called a fairy ring. This ring continues to expand over time, and its size has been used to estimate some surprising ages: Some clones have persisted for 9000 years! Because of its wide distribution, Creosote Bush is found in association with a variety of other desert shrubs. This variety is even evident in what at first appear to be similar zones on different bajadas. One of the most common associations in the Mojave, as well as the Sonoran Desert, is represented by stands covering hundreds of acres dominated essentially only by Creosote Bush and a bur sage (*Ambrosia*). This *Larrea-Ambrosia* community also occurs on the flats. In the Mojave Desert the most common species occurring with Creosote Bush is White Bur Sage, but Woolly Bur Sage may also occur in certain areas. Another species that along with Creosote Bush dominates the middle to upper portions of bajadas is Brittlebush. Its leaves are a soft gray-green, and it is often covered with bright yellow flowers. If the brittle stems are cracked, they exude a highly pungent, clear-yellowish resin. Early missionaries burned this resinous material as incense in their churches and Indians chewed it or used it as a glue. Volcanic formations are common in some sections of the Mojave Desert. At dusk, on volcanic sites where Brittlebush occurs, the shrub's gray-green leaves and bright yellow flowers

White Bur Sage
Ambrosia dumosa
355

Brittlebush
Encelia farinosa
136

Spiny Menodora
Menodora spinescens

Ratany
Krameria parvifolia

Goldenhead
Acamptopappus schockleyi

Fremont Dalea
Dalea fremontii

Spiny Senna
Cassia armata

Paperflower
Psilostrophe cooperi
137

Big Galleta
Hilaria rigida

Bush Muhly
Muhlenbergia porteri

Turpentine Broom
Thamnosma montana
366

Anderson Lycium
Lycium andersonii
351

Hopsage
Atriplex spinosa

Turpentine Bush
Haplopappus cooperi

Freckled Milkvetch
Astragalus lentigenosus
163

Shadscale
Atriplex confertifolia
346

Diamond Cholla
Opuntia ramosissima

Barrel Cactus
Ferocactus acanthodes
122

Burrobush
Hymenoclea salsola
365

Catclaw
Acacia greggii
303, 317

stand out against the black volcanic rocks—a beautiful and exciting sight.

Other locally abundant shrubs associated with Creosote Bush and characteristic of the Mojave Desert bajadas include the white-flowered Spiny Menodora, found on rocky slopes and mesas; one of three lyciums (*Lycium pallidum, L. cooperi,* or *L. andersonii*), all of which produce bitter red berries eaten by animals and occasionally man; a Mormon tea (*Ephedra*); the purple-flowered Ratany; Goldenhead; and Fremont Dalea, a species comprised of five geographically separate varieties. In addition to these, some sites are dominated by Spiny Senna, a legume species usually associated with washes, which is leafless most of the year and thus must carry on photosynthesis in its stems. Further up the slope one finds another unusual shrub, the yellow Paperflower. Paperflower looks much like any other yellow-flowered shrub, but unlike most plants, it does not lose its dead flowers.

Still farther up the bajadas, Creosote Bush is associated with Joshua-tree (plates 16 and 17). In such stands, where water is a bit more plentiful than on the lower bajada, several grasses and shrubs may also be dominant. Grasses include Big Galleta and Bush Muhly, and even certain gramas (*Bouteloua*). Blackbrush may also occur with Joshua-tree and Creosote Bush at such sites, even though Joshua-trees usually occur on more sandy or loamy soils than does Blackbrush. A species that occurs in parts of the Great Basin, Turpentine Broom, is also found in this association. Turpentine Broom is related to the orange and its fruit, though small and greenish-yellow, has the dimpled surface of an orange.

This description of a bajada is, of course, merely ideal; numerous variants occur depending on local conditions. At high elevations (3500 to 4000 feet) and in places where soils are a sandy loam, Creosote Bush is associated with Anderson Lycium and Hopsage. In some regions, particularly along the western half of the Mojave Desert, Turpentine Bush may be abundant; in good years it is joined by dense populations of a biennial locoweed, Freckled Milkvetch.

Throughout the Mojave Desert, Creosote Bush is also associated with Shadscale, particularly on sites characterized by calcareous soils. Such communities contain a greater variety of conspicuous herbs and are the main places where the Diamond Cholla occurs. A cactus of a different form that can be found in this assemblage, and in others, is the Barrel Cactus. This species, which is very noticeable in southern Utah and Nevada on rock outcrops, seems to become established only in rare years of very favorable rainfall. The result is that many individual plants in a particular area will all be of the same age.

Small drainage channels or washes have their own mixture of species. These include Burrobush, a dense, rather soft, shrub with threadlike leaves that is often covered with white flowers. Catclaw also grows here. This species forms large shrubs, or even small trees, and occurs from the Mojave, through the Sonoran, and into the Chihuahuan Desert.

Honey Mesquite
Prosopis glandulosa
308, 321

Screwbean Mesquite
Prosopis pubescens
302, 311, 320

Fremont Cottonwood
Populus fremontii

Arrow Weed
Pluchea sericea
344

Four-wing Saltbush
Atriplex canescens
352

Desert Willow
Chilopsis linearis
306

Seep Willow
Baccharis glutinosa

In the same habitat—and on sandy flats and sand dunes, and in many other places as well—one encounters a species found in all North American hot deserts, the Honey Mesquite. Mesquite is a very characteristic plant of the entire Southwest and was a significant plant to all of the region's early inhabitants. Today it has reached an unprecedented popularity as a pungent fuel for barbecuing.

In washes, or along rivers where there is even more water, native trees dominate. One desert-adapted form is Screwbean Mesquite, which has the genus's characteristic compound leaves. It is easily recognized by its tightly coiled pod, which resembles a stout spring one to two inches in length. Screwbean is a useful tree, providing browse for cattle and wildlife, and its serviceable wood is used in tool manufacture. Another tree, Fremont Cottonwood, has a wide distribution in the Southwest and may occur at elevations up to 6500 feet and in a variety of riparian habitats. Cottonwood requires water close to its roots, so early travelers used its presence to signal a good spot to dig for water in the sands of watercourses.

Associated with the native Cottonwood are the tamarisks (*Tamarix*). Three species of this Old World genus have been introduced into the southeastern United States. Their leaves make them look very much like some conifers, although they are not related. They occur in enormous densities in many places and often tend to replace native species.

Two other species associated with moist areas are Arrow Weed and Four-wing Saltbush. Both require a somewhat saline environment. The Devil's Cornfield in Death Valley, for example, is a nearly pure stand of Arrow Weed. This species, however, is not confined to saline areas, and grows in virtually impenetrable thickets along many rivers in the arid Southwest. The straight stems of Arrow Weed were used by Indians as shafts for their arrows.

Other wash species include the Desert Willow, which has large, beautiful, aromatic flowers, and the Seep Willow, which requires more moisture and is usually found near streams, ditches, or other semi-permanent waters.

In the Mojave Desert, as elsewhere, the high salinity areas, particularly those that have high water tables, contain a mixture of salt-tolerant species similar to those described for the Great Basin.

Animal Life

Scientists at the University of Nevada-Las Vegas have found the following number of species in Creosote Bush-dominated communities in the Mojave Desert of southern Nevada: thirty species of reptiles (fifteen snakes, fourteen lizards, one turtle); thirty-three species of birds, eight of them permanent residents; and forty-four species of mammals. The total number of species found in Blackbrush-dominated communities is smaller: nineteen reptiles, twenty-six birds, and thirty-three mammals. The same Creosote Bush areas contained 256 species of plants, while the Blackbrush communities contained only 185 species.

Even aquatic habitats such as desert springs and marshes were found to contain as many as twenty species of fish and seven amphibians, and they drew as many as 202 bird species. These figures show that the Mojave contrasts sharply with the Great Basin Desert, which has fewer kinds of plants and animals. The reasons for these differences are not clear; however, the shorter growing season in the North may limit the diversity of plants, which in turn may limit the diversity of animals. In addition, animals that require intense sunshine might be precluded from inhabiting the Great Basin. The paucity of reptiles in the Great Basin, especially lizards, may be related to this as well.

Invertebrates

The vast majority of visible terrestrial invertebrates in the Mojave Desert are either insects or arachnids. Other groups of invertebrates are either so tiny (like protozoans or nematode worms) that they cannot be seen with the unaided eye, or they are dormant below ground, like desert snails. One exception occurs in certain areas, where millipedes and centipedes may be common, especially following rain and at night.

Of the arachnids, scorpions and spiders are the most often seen. Another group, the solpugids, or wind scorpions, are represented by numerous species but are mainly nocturnal.

In the Mojave Desert one may encounter ten or more species of scorpions, but none of these can inflict a fatally toxic sting. In a particular area, spiders usually number from twenty to forty species, depending upon the habitat. The Western Widow is the only dangerous species. However, a relative of the notorious brown Recluse Spider of central and eastern North America does occur in the Mojave. This species is not known to be dangerous, but it must be assumed that all members of the genus can inject venom.

Two spiders frequently seen in the Mojave are the tarantulas (several species in the genus *Aphonopelma*), which despite their formidable appearance are innocuous, and a small spider of the genus *Diguetia;* the latter belongs to a family confined to the hot deserts of North America and the Monte of Argentina. All diguetid species build their webs in shrubs. The adults hide in a retreat shaped like an inverted cone and suspended in the web. Egg sacs are also hung, quite conspicuously, in the web.

Crab and jumping spiders in shrubs, wolf spiders and funnel-web weavers on the ground, along with a number of comb-footed and orb-weaving species, make up the rest of the usual spider fauna.

Of the insects, the orthopterans (crickets, grasshoppers, locusts, and others), which are well adapted to the desert, are the most obvious day-active forms. Butterflies and moths, beetles, wasps, and bees and ants are also abundant, but often they are not as noticeable. In the Mojave, the most obvious species is the Pallid-winged Grasshopper. This species occurs in a variety of habitats from Canada to South America, and is often the most abundant species in North American deserts. Three species of Mojave Desert grasshoppers are regularly

Western Widow
Loxosceles deserta

Pallid-winged
Grasshopper
Trimerotropis pallidipennis
69

Creosote Bush
Grasshopper
Bootettix argentatus
368

Desert Clicker
Grasshopper
Ligurotettix coquilletti

Furnace Heat Lubber
Tytthoytle maculata

Cream Grasshopper
Cibolacris parviceps

associated with Creosote Bush. The yellow-green and silver Creosote Bush Grasshopper lives exclusively on Creosote Bush and is camouflaged to match its leaves. The small, gray-brown Desert Clicker Grasshopper sits on stems of Creosote and other desert shrubs emitting a loud *zip-zip-zip* call. The large, fast, and elusive Furnace Heat Lubber also occurs in association with Creosote Bush from 225 feet below sea level to over 4500 feet. A widespread, common species of open Mojave Desert sites in association with various plant species is the Cream Grasshopper, which often assumes the color of the ground surface. Numerous crickets and their relatives also can be seen and heard at night in the Mojave.

As in most arid areas, the tenebrionids, or darkling beetles, are the the most abundant ground-dwelling beetle species. As many as twelve to fifteen species can be found in some Creosote Bush or *Lycium*-dominated communities. Among the more common are *Cryptoglossa verrucosa* and *Eleodes armata*. Both of these large, dark beetles are opportunistic feeders, but in deserts probably mainly feed on plant detritus.

Ants and other hymenopterous insects occur commonly in the Mojave Desert. Interestingly, many truly desert ants are harvesters, among them the harvester ants in the genus *Pogonomyrmex*. Two of these, the California Harvester Ant and the Rough Harvester Ant, occur in several Mojave Desert vegetation types. Another harvester, *Veromessor pergandei*, is very common in both the Mojave and Sonoran deserts. Termites, while not often seen, are busy decomposing the wood of desert plants, and in many areas are extremely abundant.

California Harvester Ant
Pogonomyrmex californicus

Rough Harvester Ant
Pogonomyrmex rugosus
387

Fish

The diverse aquatic habitats contained in North America's deserts often come as a surprise to visitors. In places that have permanent water, fish occur in a considerable diversity. Some sites in the Mojave Desert are especially noted for their fish. Perhaps the best-known areas are those in Death Valley. Not long ago, ten fish species inhabited this area, but recently one species has become extinct. The remaining fish include five species of pupfish (*Cyprinodon*), the easiest group of species to observe in the National Monument; one species of killifish (*Empetrichthys*); two species of minnow, each in a different genus (*Gila* and *Rhinichthys*); and a sucker (*Catostomus*). One of the pupfish, the Cottonball Marsh Pupfish, lives in Cottonball Marsh, more than two hundred feet below sea level, in water that can be five times as saline as seawater. Eight of Death Valley's existing nine species are endemic to that aquatic system and half have populations that are threatened or endangered. While changes in water supplies, caused by agricultural irrigation, are part of the problem, the introduction of fish species, both native North American forms and exotics, poses the greatest threat at present, as it has in the past.

Cottonball Marsh Pupfish
Cyprinodon milleri

Amphibians and Reptiles

The Mojave Desert supports diverse reptile and amphibian

Desert Tortoise
Gopherus agassizi
169

Gila Monster
Heloderma suspectum
180

Desert Iguana
Dipsosaurus dorsalis
188

Zebratail Lizard
Callisaurus draconoides
203

Western Whiptail
Cnemidophorus tigris
206

Western Banded Gecko
Coleonyx variegatus
176, 179

Desert Horned Lizard
Phrynosoma platyrhinos

Side-blotched Lizard
Uta stansburiana
202

Longnose Leopard Lizard
Gambelia wislizenii
191

Collared Lizard
Crotaphytus collaris
200, 201

Chuckwalla
Sauromalus obesus
189

Tree Lizard
Urosaurus ornatus
205

Brush Lizard
Urosaurus graciosus
190

Desert Spiny Lizard
Sceloporus magister
199

life. One of the most conspicuous species is the Desert Tortoise, a vegetarian that is a protected species; it can be observed throughout the Mojave. These turtles are especially conspicuous in the spring, when they can be heard snorting or banging shells as they "fight" against rivals or potential mates. During the hottest portions of the day, the tortoises retreat to burrows or to soil depressions in the shade of shrubs.

Another spectacular find in small portions of the Mojave in southern Nevada and near St. George, Utah, is the Gila Monster, one of the two venomous lizards in the world. The Gila Monster is slow and not particularly aggressive, but it has a quick bite and can inflict a painful, though rarely if ever fatal, wound. Food for this lumbering saurian includes the eggs and young of ground-nesting birds, as well as young mammals. While you may see the tracks of Gila Monsters in sandy areas, these lizards are primarily nocturnal and most often dwell in sites that have nearby boulders. Despite their ponderous appearance Gila Monsters can travel more than a mile in just a few days.

The Mojave Desert supports numerous lizards. In sandy areas dominated by Creosote Bush, the beautiful Desert Iguana is quite common, albeit wary. Primarily a herbivore, it also eats insects and even carrion, and may climb into bushes for a delicate brunch of flowers. Also in sandy areas, especially washes, you can get a glimpse of the speedy Zebratail Lizard. This lizard is especially conspicuous when it runs because it holds its tail erect. The underside of the tail is ivory-white, set off by black bands. When the lizard is at rest, however, with its tail flat, it "disappears," blending in with the ground. Nearly as quick, but proportionately more slim and less colorful, is the Western Whiptail.

Also on the ground, but in the daytime and usually hidden under debris or stones is the beautiful Western Banded Gecko. This delicate, nocturnal species can have its skin peeled off by rough handling. The Desert Horned Lizard and the Side-blotched Lizard are abundant in the Mojave, as they are in the Great Basin. While the Horned Lizard eats insects, predominantly ants, I have seen them eat the fruits of *Lycium* in Nevada, causing me to abandon my entrenched conception of their diet.

Two lizard species that often use rocks for shelter or as vantage points occur from the Great Basin through the Mojave—the Longnose Leopard Lizard and the Collared Lizard. In even more extensively rocky areas where there are crevices, a spectacular lizard, the Chuckwalla, occurs; its scientific name means "the obese, terrible lizard." Actually, Chuckwallas are neither. They are docile herbivores, and the species name derives from their ability to inflate their bodies and wedge themselves in rock crevices, a protective device.

Shrubs and trees in the Mojave Desert provide a few lizard surprises. Two related species, the Tree Lizard and the Brush Lizard, both well camouflaged to look like branches or bark, are occasionally seen. Far more conpicuous is the Desert Spiny Lizard, a five- to six-inch species covered with rough scales. To

Desert Night Lizard
Xantusia vigilis
183, 184

Great Basin Gopher
Snake
*Pituophis melanoleucus
deserticola*
263

Red Coachwhip
Masticophis flagellum
223, 229, 230, 233

Western Patchnose Snake
Salvadora hexalepis
218

Great Basin Rattlesnake
Crotalus viridis lutosus
258, 260

Sidewinder
Crotalus cerastes
252, 253

Speckled Rattlesnake
Crotalus mitchelli
251, 255

Mojave Rattlesnake
Crotalus scutulatus
259

California Kingsnake
*Lampropeltis getulus
californiae*
234

Longnose Snake
Rhinocheilus lecontei
238, 247

Spotted Leafnose Snake
Phyllorhynchus decurtatus
265, 269

Western Blind Snake
Leptotyphlops humilis
226

Great Basin Spadefoot
Scaphiopus intermontanus
277

Southwestern Toad
Bufo microscaphus
279

escape, it races up trunks and noisily crashes through leaves and vegetation. At night, try searching the arms of Joshua-trees with a flashlight to see a uniquely desert species, the Desert Night Lizard. This lizard is almost as fragile as the gecko. Its one-and-one-half inch body is covered with velvetlike skin. During the day, the Night Lizard is most often found by turning over fallen branches of Joshua-tree on the ground, or within the stick nests of pack rats (*Neotoma*), which are often built around the base of a Joshua-tree.

Unlike the Great Basin Desert species, most Mojave Desert snakes are nocturnal. Nonetheless, an early morning walk could reveal a Great Basin Gopher Snake or a Striped Whipsnake, just as in the Great Basin. More common, however, is the Red Coachwhip, a fast, slender species with variable coloration. In sandy washes and other places you may see the Western Patchnose Snake, which has a strange enlarged triangular scale covering the front of its upper lip. In the Utah portion of the Mojave, you can still find the Great Basin Rattlesnake, which does not extend into the rest of the Mojave. However, three other rattlesnake species do occur in the Mojave. The Sidewinder, which has a conspicuous horn above each eye, dwells in areas of loose sandy soil, including relatively barren sand dunes. In more rocky areas the well-camouflaged Speckled Rattlesnake is sometimes seen. Both Sidewinders and Speckled Rattlesnakes are usually colored to match their background. Thus they may be gray, brown, white, or even red in specific areas. The third species, the Mojave Rattlesnake, is a yellow-green version of a Western Diamondback, but is more aggressive, has a much more potent venom, and thus is potentially an extremely dangerous snake: Avoid it. This species occurs primarily in open desert scrubland rather than in rocky areas.

Several of the snakes occasionally seen during the day are primarily nocturnal, such as the rattlers, but there is a specifically nocturnal group as well. In this group are some of the desert's most attractive serpents. The beautiful California Kingsnake, a subspecies of the Common Kingsnake, is among these. The red, black and yellowish-white banded Longnose Snake is active at night, along with the Spotted Leafnose Snake, another species with a "patched" nose. You may also see the common Glossy Snake or the Night Snake.

After a heavy rain, if you look hard, you might even see the primitive and very diminutive Western Blind Snake, a slender animal that has no neck constriction to delimit the head. This very secretive species is primarily subterranean.

Few amphibians occur in the areas dominated by Creosote Bush in the Mojave Desert, unless there is a source of water that persists long enough for larvae to complete their life cycle. In the northern parts of the Mojave, the Great Basin Spadefoot reaches its southernmost distribution; it can be fairly common locally. A toad of spotty distribution, the Southwestern Toad, primarily nocturnal, occurs in some areas along watercourses, especially those with sufficient water to support such trees as cottonwoods. Where permanent water

Northern Leopard Frog
Rana pipiens
286

Canyon Treefrog
Hyla arenicolor
272

Black-throated Sparrow
Amphispiza bilineata
610

Le Conte's Thrasher
Toxostoma lecontei
594

Northern Mockingbird
Mimus polyglottos
590

Cactus Wren
Campylorhynchus bruneicapillus
584

Gambel's Quail
Callipepla gambelii
547

Mourning Dove
Zenaida macroura
551

Greater Roadrunner
Geococcyx californianus
554

Common Raven
Corvus corax
582

Lesser Nighthawk
Chordeiles acutipennis
560

Phainopepla
Phainopepla nitens
595

Loggerhead Shrike
Lanius ludovicianus
596

Scott's Oriole
Icterus parisorum
616

Deer Mouse
Peromyscus maniculatus
489

exists, the Northern Leopard Frog can be seen. Finally, in isolated areas with permanent moisture, such as rocky stream beds, you will find the Canyon Treefrog, a species in a family (*Hylidae*) that is not at all typical of desert sites.

Birds

The numbers of bird species that breed in the low shrub areas of the Mojave Desert can be quite limited. In wet years, five species occurred as residents of a Creosote Bush-Lycium-White Burrobush area at the Nevada Test Site. These included the Black-throated Sparrow, Sage Sparrow, Brewer's Sparrow, Le Conte's Thrasher, and the Northern Mockingbird. In dry years, only Le Conte's Thrasher and the Black-throated Sparrow persisted.

On sites with a greater diversity of vegetation forms, the bird species list jumps rapidly. For example, in Joshua Tree National Monument, California, thirty-five species have been found across the spectrum of Creosote Bush types, and fifty species in the Joshua-tree zones. In deserts the presence of trees or large cacti is the principal element in increasing the number of bird species. Nevertheless, even the presence of smaller plants—chollas (*Opuntia*), for example—adds species; the Cactus Wren is one species that often builds its domed nests in these cacti. Other conspicuous Mojave Desert birds that you are likely to see include Gambel's Quail, Mourning Doves, Greater Roadrunners, and Common Ravens. At dusk, the Lesser Nighthawk is abundant in some spots. Smaller or less obvious birds include the Ash-throated Flycatcher and Black-tailed Gnatcatcher, both of which are likely to be seen where trees like mesquites or catclaws occur. Two other quite noticeable birds are the Phainopepla and the Loggerhead Shrike. Since shrikes require open ground for foraging, deserts are ideal spots for these gray, white, and black carnivores. The Phainopepla has a diverse diet. It takes insects on the wing, but also feeds on the berries of mistletoes such as *Phoradendron californicum*. In fact, Phainopepla are major dispersing agents for these parasitic plants, since the undigested seeds in their feces are deposited on tree branches. In areas where there are stands of Joshua-tree, Scott's Oriole, with its bright lemon-yellow and black plumage, is common.

Mammals

Most hot desert sites contain ten to twelve species of mammals the size of a rabbit or smaller. The general types and the mixture of small mammals occurring in any one place are remarkably constant, though the exact species may vary from place to place, even within the same desert type. The list usually includes two kangaroo rats (*Dipodomys*), two pocket mice (*Perognathus*) of different sizes, a pack rat (*Neotoma*), a grasshopper mouse (*Onychomys*), the Deer Mouse, a diurnal ground squirrel (*Spermophilus* or *Ammospermophilus*), and a small (*Sylvilagus*) and a large (*Lepus*) rabbit.

The larger mammals usually include the same widespread species that inhabit all deserts, hot or cold: the Coyote, Badger, and Kit and Gray foxes. In the Mojave Desert, the

Bighorn Sheep
Ovis canadensis
526

Desert Cottontail
Sylvilagus audubonii
508

Black-tailed Jack Rabbit
Lepus californicus
509

White-tailed Antelope
Squirrel
Ammospermophilus leucurus
499

Round-tailed Ground
Squirrel
Spermophilus tereticaudus
504

Merriam's Kangaroo Rat
Dipodomys merriami
485

Desert Kangaroo Rat
Dipodomys deserti
484

Panamint Kangaroo Rat
Dipodomys panamintinus
482

Long-tailed Pocket Mouse
Perognathus formosus
475

Little Pocket Mouse
Perognathus longimembris
473

Southern Grasshopper
Mouse
Onychomys torridus
488

Cactus Mouse
Peromyscus eremicus
492

Canyon Mouse
Peromyscus crinitus

Botta's Pocket Gopher
Thomomys bottae
469

Desert Shrew
Notiosorex crawfordi
470

Bighorn Sheep is also conspicuous, especially in some of our national parks and monuments. They rarely stray far from water and are most often associated with mountainous slopes. Because the small mammals of the Mojave Desert are generally nocturnal, daytime walks are not likely to yield much more than the Desert Cottontail, or the abundant Black-tailed Jack Rabbit. In some places you may see isolated individuals of the White-tailed Antelope Squirrel. This species is usually solitary and has the habit of flicking its tail to display its white underside, and of emitting a long, clear trill. It is by no means restricted to the desert and occurs well up into the Pinyon Pine zone. Another somewhat less flashy diurnal animal is the Round-tailed Ground Squirrel. Antelope (*Ammospermophilus*) and ground (*Spermophilus*) squirrels can be distinguished by the former's trait of running with the tail held vertically to expose its underparts.

Nighttime forays may yield the Merriam's Kangaroo Rat, a species that occurs in a wide variety of soil and vegetation types. More confined in terms of habitat is the sand-dwelling Desert Kangaroo Rat and of more limited geographic extent is the Panamint Kangaroo Rat. The two pocket mice most likely to be observed are the Long-tailed Pocket Mouse and the Little Pocket Mouse. Both of these nocturnal species also occur in the Great Basin; the Little Pocket Mouse, in particular, has an extensive Great Basin distribution. Both species are most obvious during the summer months, for they readily go into torpor during cool periods. Several other pocket mice occur locally but are not likely to be encountered.

The final array of nocturnal forms includes the ubiquitous Deer Mouse, the Southern Grasshopper Mouse, and two other species of the genus *Peromyscus*. The Cactus Mouse is a rather large, white-footed mouse; instead of burrowing it seeks shelter under vegetation, in crevices, or in the holes of other animals. The Canyon Mouse is generally seen in rocky areas and does not occur in the Creosote Bush flats, which the Cactus Mouse may inhabit. The two species are superficially quite similar.

Two additional mammals should be mentioned. The conspicuous mounds of freshly turned, loose soil you see on a walk may have been created by Botta's Pocket Gopher. These creatures make their homes nearly anywhere that they can burrow—only rocky areas, where they cannot dig, or sand dunes, where their tunnels collapse, are outside of their range of habitats. They are often associated with the bases of shrubs. It is not likely you will see the animal itself because it usually remains below ground. The Desert Shrew is not very likely to be seen either, but can be abundant in some places. Its nests are often constructed in areas of dense vegetation. Occasionally you will scare one out by kicking the bases of yuccas.

Despite its physical rigors, the Mojave Desert is a treasure trove of biological diversity. There you can observe beautiful, even elegant, plants and curious animals, if you time your visit to avoid the hottest summer months, and if you take the time to search out the plants and animals.

THE MOJAVE DESERT: PLANTS AND ANIMALS

Wildflowers

Apache Plume 96
Barrel Cactus 122
Beavertail Cactus 41
Birdcage Evening
Primrose 93
Bladder Sage 75
Brittlebush 136
Buffalo Gourd 140
Chia 64
Chinchweed 133
Claret Cup Cactus 42
Climbing Milkweed 83
Common Ice Plant 88
Coulter's Lupine 72
Crescent Milkvetch 50
Cushion Cactus 40
Death Valley Sage 77
Desert Anemone 91
Desert Bell 70
Desert Candle 164
Desert Chicory 86
Desert Dandelion 125
Desert Five Spot 43
Desert Four O'Clock 52
Desert Globemallow 158
Desert Gold 145
Desert Marigold 128
Desert Primrose 156
Desert Rock Nettle 150
Desert Sand Verbena 53
Desert Sunflower 135
Desert Tobacco 103
Desert Velvet 118
Desert Trumpet 108
Esteve's Pincushion 84
Filaree 57
Five-needle Fetid
Marigold 134
Freckled Milkvetch 163
Ghost Flower 147
Great Desert Poppy 95
Jackass Clover 110
Mojave Aster 61
Mojave Desert Star 90
Pale Trumpets 66
Paperflower 137
Plains Pricklypear 121
Puncture Vine 143
Purple Mat 54
Ratany 56
Rattlesnake Weed 102
Scalloped Phacelia 65
Snakehead 126

Southwestern Ringstem 105
Southwestern Thorn
Apple 100
Spike Broomrape 76
Spotted Langloisia 97
Spreading Fleabane 89
Sunray 132
Sweet-scented
Heliotrope 101
Tahoka Daisy 62
Tobacco Weed 85
Trailing Four O'Clock 59
Tree Tobacco 114
Western Peppergrass 78
Whispering Bells 115
White Horsenettle 73
Wooly Daisy 127
Yellow Bee Plant 111
Yellow Head 124
Yellow Peppergrass 113
Yellow Spiny Daisy 131
Yellow Twining
Snapdragon 116

Mushrooms

Buried-stalk Puffball 168
Desert Inky Cap 166
Desert Stalked Puffball 167

Reptiles

Black Collared Lizard 186
Brush Lizard 190
Chuckwalla 189
Coachwhip 223, 229, 230,
233
Common Kingsnake 234,
246
Desert Iguana 188
Desert Night Lizard 183,
184
Desert Spiny Lizard 199
Desert Tortoise 169
Gila Monster 180
Glossy Snake 268
Gopher Snake 263
Ground Snake 228, 231,
239
Longnose Leopard
Lizard 191
Longnose Snake 238, 247
Lyre Snake 262, 270
Mojave Fringe Toed
Lizard 181
Mojave Rattlesnake 259

Night Snake 267
Rosy Boa 219
Side-blotched Lizard 202
Sidewinder 252, 253
Speckled Rattlesnake 251, 255
Spiny Softshell 174
Spotted Leafnose Snake 265, 269
Tree Lizard 205
Western Banded Gecko 176, 179
Western Blackhead Snake 227
Western Blind Snake 226
Western Patchnose Snake 218
Western Rattlesnake 258, 260
Western Shovelnose Snake 235, 237
Western Whiptail 206
Zebratail Lizard 203

Amphibians
Bullfrog 288
Canyon Treefrog 272
Great Plains Toad 283
Northern Leopard Frog 286
Red-spotted Toad 278

Fishes
Golden Shiner 299
Mosquitofish 294
Speckled Dace 297
White River Springfish 292

Trees, Shrubs, Cacti, and Grasses
Anderson Lycium 321
Arrow Weed 314
Burrobush 335
Bur Sage 330
Creosote Bush 312
Desert Buckwheat 329
Desert Holly 328
Fluffgrass 331
Four-wing Saltbush 322
Gregg Catclaw 303, 317
Honey Mesquite 308, 321
Indian Ricegrass 332
Jojoba 317
Joshua-tree 326
Mojave Yucca 329

Mormon Tea 334
Ocotillo 305
Parry's Century Plant 309
Rabbit Brush 310
Saguaro 301
Screwbean Mesquite 302, 311, 320
Smoke Tree 304
Snakeweed 311
Sotol 308
Tamarisk 304, 324
Teddybear Cholla 302
Turpentine Broom 336
White Bur Sage 325

Insects and Spiders
Arid Lands Honey Ants 384
Aztec Pygmy Grasshopper 373
Bee Assassin 376
Broad-necked Darkling Beetle 381
Carolina Wolf Spider 401
Centruroides Scorpions 394
Cochineal Bug 391
Creosote Bush Grasshopper 368
Desert Tarantula 399
Giant Vinegarone 398
Green Valley Grasshopper 367
Inconspicuous Crab Spider 400
Jerusalem Cricket 375
Little Black Ant 386
Mormon Cricket 374
Obscure Ground Mantid 377
Pale Windscorpion 396
Pallid-winged Grasshopper 369
Red Velvet-Ant 389
Rough Harvester Ant 387
Spine-waisted Ants 385
Tarantula Hawk 383
Texas Carpenter Ant 388
Thistledown Velvet-ant 390

Butterflies and Moths
Antillean Blue 411, 412
Becker's White 403
Behr's Hairstreak 416
Bordered Patch 429, 430
California Cankerworm 449

Chara Checkerspot 422
Common Sulphur 443
Desert Checkerspot 421
Desert Gray Skipper 436
Desert Green
Hairstreak 441
Desert Orange Tip 404
Desert Swallowtail 445
Great Basin Sootywing 437
Gray Metalmark 427
Large California Spanworm
Moth 450
Large White Skipper 408
Leda Hairstreak 440
Monarch 419
Pahaska Skipper 434
Painted Lady 420
Pale Blue 409
Pearly Marblewing 406
Phaon Crescentspot 426
Queen 418
Sandhill Skipper 433
Short-tailed Black 447
Sleepy Orange 417
Small Blue 410
Texan Crescentspot 425
Western Pygmy Blue 413
White-lined Sphinx 448
Yucca Giant Skipper 439

Mammals
Badger 514
Big Free-tailed Bat 467
Bighorn Sheep 526
Black-tailed
Jack Rabbit 509
Bobcat 517, 520
Botta's Pocket Gopher 469
Brazilian Free-tailed
Bat 465
Brush Mouse 490
Cactus Mouse 492
California Leaf-nosed
Bat 452
California Myotis 458
Coyote 523
Deer Mouse 489
Desert Cottontail 508
Desert Kangaroo Rat 484
Desert Pocket Mouse 477
Desert Shrew 470
Desert Woodrat 493
Gray Fox 522
House Mouse 495

Kit Fox 521
Little Pocket Mouse 473
Long-tailed Pocket
Mouse 475
Merriam's Kangaroo
Rat 485
Mountain Lion 518
Mule Deer 528
Pallid Bat 464
Panamint Kangaroo
Rat 482
Porcupine 507
Pronghorn 527
Raccoon 512
Ringtail 511
Rock Squirrel 505
Round-tailed Ground
Squirrel 504
Southern Grasshopper
Mouse 488
Spotted Bat 462
Striped Skunk 515
Townsend's Big-eared
Bat 463
Western Harvest
Mouse 486
Western Pipistrelle 461
White-tailed Antelope
Squirrel 500
Yuma Myotis 456

Birds
Abert's Towhee 606
American Kestrel 542
Ash-throated
Flycatcher 573
Bewick's Wren 587
Black-chinned
Hummingbird 563
Black Phoebe 570
Black-tailed
Gnatcatcher 588
Black-throated
Sparrow 610
Blue Grosbeak 604
Brewer's Sparrow 608
Brown-headed
Cowbird 613
Burrowing Owl 559
California Quail 548
Canyon Wren 586
Common Barn Owl 555
Common Poorwill 562
Common Raven 582

Cooper's Hawk 532
Costa's Hummingbird 564
European Starling 597
Gambel's Quail 547
Golden Eagle 540
Great Horned Owl 556
Greater Roadrunner 554
Hooded Oriole 614
Horned Lark 576
House Finch 617
Ladder-backed
Woodpecker 567
Le Conte's Thrasher 594
Lesser Nighthawk 560
Loggerhead Shrike 596
Mourning Dove 551
Northern Flicker 568
Northern
Mockingbird 590
Phainopepla 595
Red-tailed Hawk 536
Rock Wren 585
Sage Thrasher 591
Say's Phoebe 571
Scott's Oriole 616
Turkey Vulture 530
Verdin 583
Violet-green Swallow 579
Western Kingbird 575
Western Tanager 599
White-winged Dove 550

THE SONORAN DESERT

The Sonoran Desert extends over twelve degrees of latitude, from roughly 23° N, on the tip of Baja California, to 35° N, on the border between Arizona and California on the Colorado River. More than two-thirds of its total area lies within Mexico in two separate areas: One section occupies two-thirds of Baja California, and the other portion covers more than half the state of Sonora. In the United States, the Sonoran occurs in extreme southeastern California and in the southern third of Arizona, especially in the southwestern quarter. In an altered form, with fewer species, it also occurs in scattered patches virtually to the Arizona–New Mexico border.

The Sonoran is a young desert. In its current form it has probably existed for no more than 10,000 years. Despite its youth, the Sonoran is the most complex of any of our desert types—complex in the sense that a great diversity of species can be found within its boundaries and also in its general structure, both biological and geological. Surface features include sedimentary, metamorphic, and volcanic rocks that vary widely in age. The Precambrian rock outcroppings in the northern parts of the desert (between 33 and 35° latitude in Arizona) are about two billion years old. Certain lava fields, including the Pinacate region of northern Mexico along the United States border, were formed mainly 100,000 years ago, yet experienced eruptions as recently as 1300 years ago.

While the diversity of plant and animal life in the Sonoran can in part be accounted for by its unique geologic history—the working and reworking of the rocks by water and wind, and the development of soil complexes on slopes and in the basins —geological substrates are not the only explanation.

The Sonoran is a subtropical desert. Tropical and subtropical locations tend to have more plant and animal species, in areas of comparable size, than do more temperate habitats, and the Sonoran is no exception.

Further, the Sonoran's biseasonal pattern of rainfall promotes the existence of more species than in our other deserts. This is just what one might anticipate. If the Mojave Desert can have winter annuals in response to the long-duration, low-intensity winter rains, and if the Chihuahuan can have summer annuals in response to the high-intensity, short-duration summer rains, then the Sonoran should be expected to have a number of annuals of each type.

The Sonoran's diversity is more than a diversity of species. The plants come in more shapes and sizes on average Sonoran Desert sites than on average sites in other deserts. Large, tall, columnar cacti such as Saguaros tend to dominate the horizon. Their prominence sometimes masks the presence of other cactus forms. Add to this the presence of several species of very tall, single-stemmed shrubs (called subtrees—palo verde is an example) and you begin to get an idea of the structural diversity of Sonoran plant communities.

Saguaro
Cereus giganteus
331

Plant Life

A number of interpretations of Sonoran Desert biogeography have been proposed. The system presented by the eminent

Hot Desert Subdivisions

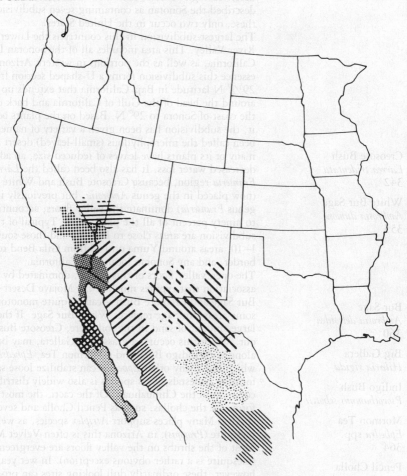

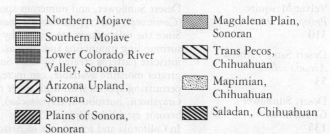

- ▭ Northern Mojave
- ▦ Southern Mojave
- ▦ Lower Colorado River Valley, Sonoran
- ◩ Arizona Upland, Sonoran
- ◪ Plains of Sonora, Sonoran
- ◆ Vizcaino, Sonoran
- ◌ Magdalena Plain, Sonoran
- ◩ Trans Pecos, Chihuahuan
- ⁙ Mapimian, Chihuahuan
- ◩ Saladan, Chihuahuan

Creosote Bush
Larrea tridentata
342

White Bur Sage
Ambrosia dumosa
355

Bur Sage
Ambrosia deltoidea
360

Big Galleta
Hilaria rigida

Indigo Bush
Psorothamnus schottii

Mormon Tea
Ephedra spp.
364

Pencil Cholla
Opuntia ramosissima

Velvet Mesquite
Prosopis velutina
310

Desert Sand Verbena
Abronia villosa
53

Desert Sunflower
Geraea canescens
135

Graythorn
Ziziphus obtusifolia

Beavertail Cactus
Opuntia basilaris
41

desert ecologist Forrest Shreve in 1951 is used here. Shreve described the Sonoran as containing seven subdivisions; of these, only two occur in the United States.

The largest subdivision in this country is the Lower Colorado River Valley. This area includes all of the Sonoran Desert in California, as well as the portions in western Arizona. In essence this subdivision forms a U-shaped section from 29½° N latitude in Baja California that extends up and around the head of the Gulf of California and back down along the coast of Sonora to 29° N. Based on the plants occupying it, the subdivision has been given a variety of names. It has been called the microphyllous (small-leaved) desert because many of its plants have leaves of reduced size, an adaptation to decreased water loss. It has also been called the *Larrea-Franseria* region, because Creosote Bush and White Bur Sage (now placed in the genus *Ambrosia,* but previously in the genus *Franseria*) dominate the valley floors, accounting for up to ninety percent of all the plant cover. Typical of this subdivision are areas close to Phoenix and those south on I–10, areas around Yuma on I–8 from Gila Bend to the border, and any Sonoran locality in California.

The open valley floors of this region, dominated by the same association that typifies much of the Mojave Desert—White Bur Sage and Creosote Bush—can be quite monotonous. In some areas Bur Sage replaces White Bur Sage. If there is a large amount of sand in the soils here, Creosote Bush drops out. When this occurs, a grass, Big Galleta, may be common, along with Indigo Bush and a Mormon Tea, *Ephedra trifurca,* which like many other *Ephedras* can stabilize loose sandy soils, forming pedestals. This species is also widely distributed and common in the Chihuahuan. Of the cacti, the most obvious forms are the chollas, such as Pencil Cholla and several larger species. Many places support *Atriplex* species, as well as mesquite (*Prosopis*); in Arizona this is often Velvet Mesquite. Most of the shrubs on the valley floors are evergreens (mesquite is a rather obvious exception). In wet years, however, these ordinarily dull looking sites can produce more than sixty species of annuals, including Desert Sand Verbena, Desert Sunflower, and numerous species of evening primroses (*Camissonia*) and cryptanthas (*Cryptantha*).

Since the valley floors are crossed by runoff from the surrounding mountains and bajadas, they are often covered by intricate patterns created by rills. Such areas, with slightly greater moisture available, can increase the plant diversity by permitting species with high water requirements, such as Graythorn, burrobush, (*Hymenoclea*), or lycium (*Lycium*), to become established (plate 15).

In California and some parts of Arizona you are likely to see the gray pads of the Beavertail Cactus, and if you are lucky, you may see its brilliant red-magenta flowers. Be careful, however! Beavertail does not have obvious spines so it is often touched by the unwary. To their surprise, the tufts of rusty, hairlike, barbed structures called glochids, which are on the pads, embed themselves painfully into the skin.

Blue Palo Verde
Cercidium floridum
301, 316

Ocotillo
Fouquieria splendens
335

Golden Cholla
Opuntia echinocarpa

Barrel Cactus
Ferocactus acanthodes
122

Desert Ironwood
Olneya tesota
319

Teddybear Cholla
Opuntia bigelovii
332

Hedgehog Cactus
Echinocereus engelmannii

Desert Agave
Agave deserti

Trixis
Trixis californica
106

Chuparosa
Beloperone californica
160

Desert Lavender
Hyptis emoryi

Sweetbush
Bebbia juncea

As you ascend the bajada, the plant diversity picks up rapidly. Blue Palo Verde, a subtree, can be locally common (plate 12), often in association with bur sages. Ocotillo, a tall multi-stemmed species, occurs on the slopes and is often mixed with one of the more evident and widespread of the chollas, Golden Cholla (plate 10). It is in these upper bajada areas that you are most likely to see the Barrel Cactus and the stately Saguaro. Even the Desert Ironwood, a subtree less common than the palo verdes, may be abundant on upper bajadas (plate 13). Two additional conspicuous species are the incredibly densely spined Teddybear Cholla and the low growing Hedgehog Cactus. In these areas, you will also see the Desert Agave. Its flower stalk may be more than eighteen feet tall.

A careful look among the rocks on the uppermost portions of the bajada will reveal a surprising diversity of smaller perennials. Desert ferns and spike mosses can be found at some localities, especially in the shade of rocks.

Many spectacular sand dune areas occur in the Lower Colorado River subdivision. Visits to places like the Algodones dunes in California (only a few miles from Yuma, Arizona) will add a great number of sand dune endemics to your life list of plants. One of the more spectacular of these may resemble a stand of mushrooms or dried feces. This plant, *Ammobroma sonorae*, is a parasite on six other plant species. Its bloom consists of dozens of tiny purple flowers covering the fleshy mound that sits on the sand surface. While the species is rare today, in the past it was commonly eaten by Indians. In fact, it was first discovered by scientists in the 1850s, when it was served to them for dinner by Sand Papago Indians.

Other specialized habitats contain some interesting and attractive plants. Washes of various types are always good bets for finding unusual plants. Rocky washes contain plants like *Trixis californica*, a shrub with yellow flowers, while sandy washes are home to two species, *Justicia* (*Beloperone*) *californica* and *Anisacanthus thurberi*, both of which have the common name Chuparosa (Spanish for hummingbird) and whose bright red, tubular flowers draw hummingbirds. Also found here are Desert Lavender and Sweetbush.

The second subdivision of the Sonoran Desert in the United States is the Arizona Upland Division, an area also called the palo verde cacti desert. This subdivision is often used for movie locations and frequently shows up in "beautiful" desert pictures in magazines around the world. Often there are shrubs of various heights: one vegetation layer is less than eighteen inches high; another is about three feet tall; and there is an upper layer of subtrees. Superimposed is a mixture of cactus types, including the dominant, majestic Saguaro—the trademark of the Sonoran Desert. This subdivision forms the eastern boundary of the Sonoran in Arizona and in Sonora, Mexico. It is a rather narrow band, less than a third the area of the Lower Colorado River Valley subdivision. The area around Tucson, Organ Pipe Cactus National Monument, and many areas of the Tonto National Forest east of Phoenix are excellent places to see this habitat. Try stopping for a few hours at the

Buckthorn Cholla
Opuntia acanthocarpa

Cane Cholla
Opuntia spinosior

Jumping Cholla
Opuntia fulgida
325

Prickly Pear Cactus
Opuntia phaeacantha

Desert Christmas Cactus
Opuntia leptocaulis
162

Night-blooming Cereus
Cereus greggii
87

Fishhook Cactus
Mammilaria microcarpa
39

Fishhook Barrel Cactus
Ferocactus wislizenii

Organ Pipe Cactus
Cereus thurberi

Senita
Cereus schottii

Purple Martin
Progne subis
577, 578

Gila Woodpecker
Melanerpes uropygialis
565

Boyce Thompson Southwestern Arboretum at Superior, Arizona. Here you may see the natural desert communities, as well as a collection of Sonoran Desert plants from the other desert subdivisions. Similarly good plant collections can be found at the Desert Botanical Garden in Phoenix. And, of course, no place can match the Arizona-Sonora Desert Museum in Tucson in its rich collection of plants, animals, geological exhibits, and other desert interests.

The diversity of cacti in the Arizona Upland cannot be overemphasized. All forms are abundant. Chollas include the abundant, highly variable Buckthorn Cholla, the Cane Cholla with its characteristic gray spines, and the Jumping Cholla, a species whose fruits may accumulate over a period of years, thus forming chains. Four or five chollas may occur in close proximity to one another, and when this happens, hybridization may occur. Another abundant cactus is the Prickly Pear, a species common in all of our hot deserts. Several low chollalike forms also occur. Desert Christmas Cactus and Pencil Cholla are two; they are often found among or near shrubs such as Creosote Bush. Another common associate of Creosote Bush is the marvelously fragrant, but seldom observed, Night-blooming Cereus. This plant has stems that look like dead sticks or the branches of Creosote Bush. Thus it is well hidden, belying the fact that it has a huge underground tuberous root that is used as a water storage organ. The minute Fishhook Cactus and its relatives are often found under a variety of shrubs. The crowns of small flowers encircling their tops are a desert delight. Barrel cacti, such as Fishhook Barrel, can be very abundant and are often mistaken for young Saguaros even though their spine patterns are very dissimilar. Two large cacti that are more common in Mexico extend into the United States in the vicinity of Organ Pipe Cactus National Monument. Organ Pipe Cactus is by far the more common of the two. The other species, Senita, is less abundant, but shares the same multiple-branched, upright structure as the Organ Pipe.

The star of all these cactus scenarios is the Saguaro (plates 10 and 11). Its commanding presence in the Sonoran Desert not only captures the eye, but is also a focus of animal activity. Woodpeckers, wood rats, Purple Martins, owls, lizards, and other animals make their homes in the Saguaro in cavities originally excavated by woodpeckers, including the Gila Woodpecker. The hole consists of an opening and a downward-positioned chamber. The cactus forms a hardened covering, a callus, over these "injured" surfaces, leaving the cavity lined with a thin, woodlike layer. When a Saguaro dies, these cavity linings sometimes resist decomposition and can be found on the desert surface, where their shoelike appearance gives them the name "Apache boots."

For some years, biologists were shocked at the apparent lack of Saguaro reproduction on some sites in the Southwest, including parts of Saguaro Cactus National Monument near Tucson. This lack of reproduction and a decline in adult populations in some areas were variously attributed to frost, disease, pathogens, animals, or a combination of these agents. A detailed series of studies was conducted by university and park service personnel at the University of Arizona, particularly by Warren F. Steenbergh and Charles H. Lowe. The research suggests that Saguaro is a semitropical species that has only within the last few thousand years moved into more northern climates. In fact, Saguaro is the most northern of the columnar cacti, ranging to 35° 6' N. The result of this incursion into a northern and less hospitable environment is that when frosts of sufficient intensity and duration occur, many individual plants die. Death can be caused either directly by frost damage, or by pathogens that attack the injured cactus tissues following frost damage. Especially vulnerable are young plants that are less than four years old, and the very old, many-branched giants. Individuals that are unbranched and between eighteen inches and sixteen feet in height suffer the lowest mortality.

The role of native animals in the death of Saguaros is much smaller than once thought. Woodpecker holes have little effect other than to weaken the plant's structure. Attacks by the larvae of a noctuid moth which burrow in the cactus tissue and by woodrats (*Neotoma*) or other mammals may increase the probability of freezing damage, but their actions do not directly kill many cacti.

Grazing by domestic animals, especially cattle, however, does have an important effect. Cattle can remove much of the plant cover on a site, cover that provides protection to young Saguaros while they become established. Without such "nurse plants," the mortality of young Saguaros increases dramatically, especially in areas without rocks, since rocky slopes make it more difficult for cattle to graze.

Once Saguaro is established, the probability of its survival greatly increases with each passing year. The age of a Saguaro can be roughly estimated by its size. A six- to seven-inch specimen is roughly fourteen years old; a six- to seven-foot individual is thirty-five to forty years old. When a Saguaro is twelve to thirteen feet high, it is about fifty years old; it is then that the cactus is ready to begin developing its first arm. An eighteen- to twenty-foot plant is about sixty-five years of age and has one arm, and a cactus that is twenty-five feet tall or taller is more than eighty-five years old—a branched adult. The stately individuals we admire the most are well over one hundred years of age. These older plants are the tallest features of the landscape and are often damaged by lightning.

Although Saguaros are threatened in certain spots, the populations in many places in the United States are very stable, and we are not in any danger of losing these desert monarchs.

In many areas cacti are protected by law, a move necessitated by the massive collecting of cacti for use as house plants. No species is exempt from this pressure: Even large Saguaros are "rustled" to use as landscape accents. For some species, this human influence is more significant than any natural process as a source of possible extinction.

Foothill "Yellow" Palo
Verde
Cercidium microphyllum
309, 318

Brittlebush
Encelia farinosa
136

Whitethorn Acacia
Acacia constricta

Fairy Duster
Calliandra eriophylla
48

Limber Bush
Jatropha cardiophylla

Jojoba
Simmondsia chinensis
347

Ratany
Krameria parvifolia
56

Desert Buckwheat
Eriogonum fasciculatum
359

Paperflower
Psilostrophe cooperi
137

Desert Willow
Chilopsis linearis
306

Desert Broom
Baccharis sarothroides

Dock
Rumex hymenosepalus

Canyon Ragweed
Ambrosia ambrosioides

Desert Hackberry
Celtis pallida

Mexican Jumping Bean
Sapium biloculare

A noncactus dominant of the Arizona Upland subdivision is the Foothill Palo Verde. The Saguaro and the Foothill Palo Verde occur on all sites but the valley floors, and reach high densities on middle to upper bajadas (plates 11 and 14). In the same location, White Bur Sage is replaced by Bur Sage, and Brittlebush can be locally dominant.

While Creosote Bush also occurs in the Arizona Upland, it is not as dominant as in the Lower Colorado River Valley subdivision. Desert Ironwood, another species that occurs in the Lower Colorado River Valley, is much more characteristic of the Arizona Uplands. It is not as widely distributed on slopes as palo verde, probably because it is not as tolerant of cold. Ironwood has many important uses. Its wood is so dense that it does not float in water. This denseness makes it ideal for the production of elegant carvings, though it easily dulls carving tools. The seeds are edible when roasted or when ground. Personally, I prefer Ironwood to mesquite for broiling fish and steaks over a desert campfire.

There are so many other shrubs that can be associated with the "big four" (Saguaro, Bur Sage, palo verde, and Ironwood) that it is difficult to do more than provide a list. Several small leguminous shrubs can attain local dominance. Whitethorn Acacia is one of the more conspicuous, but it is not nearly so attractive as the much smaller, delicately flowered Fairy Duster. The very flexible, reddish branches of Limber Bush attract notice most of the time, especially when they are covered by shiny, bright green, heart-shaped leaves. Also very noticeable is the leathery, gray-green Jojoba. Jojoba has a very large fruit, remotely reminiscent of the lower portion of an acorn. When processed, Jojoba fruits yield an oil of very high quality that can be used for purposes such as high-temperature lubrication, that previously called for the oil obtained from sperm whales. In addition, the meaty portions of the Jojoba fruit may be suitable as feed supplements for farm animals. Because of its potential economic significance, there has been great deal of research on Jojoba over the past fifteen years. It is currently being planted on an experimental basis in several states and may become an extremely important cash crop in the near future.

Mixed in with these other shrubs is Ratany, a plant with finely divided grayish stems and bright purple flowers. Desert Buckwheat also grows in local abundance. Add to this a lycium (*Lycium*), a zinnia (*Zinnia*), Paperflower, and one of several other shrubs, and the potential complexity of the area will become apparent.

Where washes dissect the land surface, a whole new complex of vegetation exists. Here burrobush (*Hymenoclea*), Desert Willow, and Desert Broom are dominants. These same species also commonly occur along the edges of roads where road surface runoff simulates wash conditions.

Sandy washes may harbor the large-leaved, but low growing, Dock or the Canyon Ragweed, another large-leaved species, but one that is more erect. Edges of washes sometimes contain Desert Hackberry and Mexican Jumping Bean, usually without an insect (the larva of the moth *Carpocapsa saltitans*) to make the fruit of this shrub, the "beans," jump. The five subdivisions of the Sonoran Desert that do not reach the United States contain an especially rich variety of species and some striking new forms. Along the coast of Sonora and the east coast of Baja California lies the Central Gulf Coast subdivision. This area is dominated by subtrees of the genus *Bursera* and by various species of *Jatropha*. The smaller layer of shrubs (up to eighteen inches tall) characteristic of many of our desert sites is generally absent, and Creosote Bush is only locally abundant. One species typical of this subdivision,

Elephant Tree
Bursera microphylla
312, 315

Elephant Tree, extends into the United States all the way to mountain slopes near Phoenix. This magnificent species, a subtree, resembles a bonsai tree. Rich golden, exfoliating bark covers the lower parts of its trunk, while its branch tips are a deep reddish brown; its compound leaves are a beautiful green. Although its flowers are inconspicuous, the odor of this magnificent plant is highly pungent.

The Central Gulf Coast subdivision also contains more species related to ocotillo (*Fouquieria*). Among these are the

Boojum Tree
Fouquieria columnaris

remarkable Boojum Tree, a gray, spiny species that is more than thirty feet tall and resembles an upside-down carrot. It is not easy to find the Boojum on the mainland portion of Sonora, though it does occur on the slopes near the ocean. It is more accessible in Baja California, where it occurs as a highly conspicuous dominant in the Vizcaino subdivision.

The Vizcaino subdivision extends from 26 to 30° N, occupying the western two-thirds of the peninsula. Here eerie landscapes, dominated by a variety of large agaves—especially

Maguey
Agave shawii

Cardon
Cereus pringelei

Ball Moss
Tillandsia recurvata

Maguey—many yuccas, Boojum, and a columnar cactus, the Cardon, form architecturally complex scenes. Probably the world's largest cactus, Cardon replaces Saguaro here; they resemble one another, but Cardon has more, and longer, arms. Interestingly, despite the aridity of this subdivision, many of the large plants are covered with a Ball Moss much as one would expect in a more tropical environment. This is due to the presence of humid Pacific Ocean air, which these plants use as a water source.

Further south on the west coast of the Baja California Peninsula is the Magdalena Plain subdivision. Gone are the Boojum, the Maguey, and many other treelike forms. Some remain, however, and a few new ones occur. These include different mesquites (*Prosopis*), more Ocotillo relatives, and yet another *Bursera*. There are many large columnar cacti and a moderate number of medium-size shrubs.

The last two subdivisions show more clearly the subtropical affinities of the Sonoran. The Plains of Sonora subdivision is a small area wedged between the Central Gulf Coast subdivision on the west and the southern extension of the Arizona Uplands subdivision on the east. Here the genera are much like those of the Arizona Uplands division and in general appearance it resembles the Arizona Uplands division as well. The ground, however, is more open and supports fewer cacti and a smaller variety of shrubs. In general, it looks like an open woodland.

Mexican Palo Verde
Parkinsonia aculeata
307, 322

Tree Ocotillo
Fouquieria macdougalii

Mexican Palo Verde, commonly planted in Arizona, is native here, as is the unusual Tree Ocotillo. Many tropical trees extend into the area, but are not as dominant as they are in the last, most southern subdivision, the Sonora Foothills. The Sonora Foothills division is dominated by a complex variety of subtrees. Indeed this vegetation form is so prevalent that some biologists consider the subdivision to belong to a tropical thornscrub series rather than to the desert. The diversity of subtropical trees in this subdivision shows the derivation of the subtree component of the vast area of the Sonoran Desert as a whole. Desert subtrees originated in the south, and their northward distribution into the United States is primarily determined by favorably warm temperatures.

The Sonoran Desert has many vegetation transitions. At its upper elevation, it meets grassland and a complex of junipers and oaks. Along its northern border in Arizona, the transition is marked by the presence of a characteristically transitional subtree, the Crucifixion Thorn. At a distance this species looks like palo verde with darker bark and it replaces palo verde as a codominant with Creosote Bush. In some places where the Mojave and Sonoran deserts meet at the Sonoran's upper elevational limits (at numerous places along US-83 between Wickenburg, Arizona, and I-40, for example), you can see plants of the grassland transition such as agaves, yuccas, and bear grass (*Nolina*) mixed in with Saguaros, Joshua-tree, junipers, Crucifixion Thorn, and a host of other species. These transitions can easily confuse the naturalist inclined toward tidiness and clarity of habitat boundaries.

The eastward plant transitions of the Sonoran Desert with the Chihuahuan are subtle. The visual dominants, such as Saguaro and palo verde, do not reach the Arizona–New Mexico border, but many plant species of lesser stature do. Given the plant distributions and the fact that the two desert faunas meet on the state boundaries, it is fair to say that the two deserts "switch over" virtually at the state borders.

Crucifixion Thorn
Canotia holacantha
314

Animal Life

The animals of the Sonoran Desert are as diverse as the plants. Unlike the plants, however, their occurrence does not coincide so neatly with subdivision boundaries or even with the more clearly defined boundaries of the four major desert vegetation types. Thus many species occur in all four desert types, including the seven subdivisions of the Sonoran.

Invertebrates

The Sonoran Desert's invertebrates are probably no more numerous than in other deserts, but they are often more conspicuous, in part because their diversity includes colorful or bizarre forms. Scorpions can be quite common, though they are not encountered often in the daytime. If you want to see them, a night trip with a black-light can be quite rewarding. The cuticle of many species of scorpions fluoresces under black-light, much like many minerals.

The scorpion's method of operation is to sit and wait for its

Giant Desert Hairy
Scorpion
Hadrurus arizonensis
395

Carolina Wolf Spider
Lycosa carolinensis
401

Desert Brown Spider
Loxosceles deserta

prey to amble by, then grab it with pincerlike front appendages called pedipalps. Thus held, the prey is stung and devoured. The pedipalps are also used during "courtship." Males grasp the pedipalps of females and "dance" around. This dance actually represents the search for a suitable substrate upon which the male can deposit a sperm package, or spermatophore. Subsequently the female is pulled over the spermatophore, picking the package up with her genital opening; thus mating is accomplished.

Scorpion stings can be quite painful. Large species like the Giant Desert Hairy Scorpion may inflict damage simply because of the size of the "stinger." Most species, however, are of little consequence. Unfortunately, one potentially dangerous genus, *Centruroides*, does occur, in the Sonoran Desert of Arizona; stings from these animals, especially *Centruroides sculpturatus*, deserve immediate medical attention. Unlike many other common desert scorpions, *Centruroides* scorpions do not burrow. They hide by moving beneath stones or between the bark and wood of dead trees. Because they cling to such surfaces, extreme caution should be exercised when picking up firewood or turning over stones. Simply looking on the ground to avoid danger is not enough: The scorpion could be on the stone or the wood in your hand. In Arizona, mortality from scorpion stings is extremely rare. This is not the case in Mexico, where there are more types of dangerous scorpions and where scorpions with more toxic venoms occur.

Solpugids also inhabit the Sonoran. Like scorpions, which they resemble, these fast-moving creatures are nocturnal, but they can be found under objects on the ground during the day. At night you will occasionally see them under the lights of restrooms in campgrounds where they are hunting insects. They have powerful "jaws" and can inflict an unpleasant, though harmless, bite.

Spiders are common in deserts. After rains, roads may be alive with tarantulas (*Aphonopelma*). The ground surface is home to other species, such as the large Carolina Wolf Spider and the Desert Brown Spider or another species in this genus. Shrubs may harbor a variety of species, including jumping spiders, whose large eyes and often bright, sometimes metallic colors make them a surprising joy to find.

Most desert visitors fear the spiders and scorpions that conventional wisdom tells us are lurking out there. In fact, few accidents occur as a result of encounters with these animals. In all my years of sleeping on the ground in desert areas, I have never encountered a scorpion among my personal items. However, caution is certainly advised.

The beasts that cause the most discomfort in deserts are ants. Desert areas usually contain numerous ant species, any one of which can provide a surprise nip. As you move from Creosote Bush flats across a wash dominated by mesquite and acacia, and then up a bajada into an area with Saguaros and subtrees, you might easily encounter twenty to thirty ant species. Like the plants, ants can have habitat preferences that are narrowly

Rough Harvester Ant
Pogonomyrmex rugosus
387

Spine-waisted Ants
Aphaenogaster spp.
385

Texas Carpenter Ant
Camponotus festinatus
388

Little Black Ant
Monomorium minimum
386

restricted or quite wide. The Rough Harvester Ant occurs on the *Larrea* flats and edges of the wash. Its range coincides with that of the Spine-waisted Ant. The Texas Carpenter Ant avoids the flats but occurs from the washes all the way up the bajada, a distribution that complements the preferred habit of the first two species. In contrast to the rather wide distributions of these other species, the Little Black Ant occurs only in the washes. Other species occur in equally defined patterns, broad or narrow.

Many of the ant species living in deserts have morphological specializations called psammophores that allow them to move sand. In the Rough Harvester Ant the task is accomplished with a ring of inward-facing hairs behind the mouth, while in honey ants (*Myrmecocystus*) some of the mouth parts are modified with a fringe to form a sand-moving basket.

Many other hymenopterous insects occur in deserts. Bees are common. Some eighty-four species in eight families occur on *Larrea* alone.

Wasps, flies, and beetles are abundant when flowers are in bloom and some groups can be observed at all times, with or without flowers. Particularly obvious at times are the blister beetles of the family Meloidae. These beetles get their common name for their habit of emitting "blood" from their knee joints and other parts of their bodies when they are alarmed. This fluid can cause painful blisters on your skin. Genera such as *Lytta* are common on flowers, but should not be handled, even though some species are strikingly attractive.

As is the case in all our deserts, grasshoppers and their relatives are abundant and conspicuous because of their calls, their often bright wing colors, and their sometimes very noisy flight. When they alight, however, many species disappear because they are so cryptically colored. A good example is the

Green Valley Grasshopper
Schistocerca shoshone
367

Green Valley Grasshopper. In flight this large green grasshopper is quite noticeable. When it lands on a palo verde, though, its green blends in well with the tree's green bark and branches, and it is difficult to find.

Generally speaking, the more plant species you find on a desert site, the more grasshopper species you will find, regardless of which desert you visit. The relationship, however, is not one-to-one: Adding one plant species to a community does not necessarily add one grasshopper. The ratio in the Sonoran Desert, for example, is closer to one additional grasshopper for each additional two plant species.

Termites are also common and important components of Sonoran Desert ecosystems. Although they are rarely obvious, the tubes of soil that they construct on or around dead wood and grass clumps signal their presence.

Fish

A list of all the freshwater fishes that live in the Sonoran Desert, including Mexico, would contain more than eighty species. Many of these are introduced or not specifically characteristic of the deserts. Several species, however, are true desert forms. The one most likely to be observed is the Desert

Desert Pupfish
Cyprinodon macularius
293

Western Spadefoot
Scaphiopus hammondi
276

Couch's Spadefoot
Scaphiopus couchi
274

Great Plains Toad
Bufo cognatus
283

Red-spotted Toad
Bufo punctatus
278

Sonoran Green Toad
Bufo retiformis
284

Colorado River Toad
Bufo alvarius
281

Canyon Treefrog
Hyla arenicolor
272

Desert Tortoise
Gopherus agassizi
169

Side-blotched Lizard
Uta stansburiana
202

Chuckwalla
Sauromalus obesus
189

Collared Lizard
Crotaphytus collaris
200, 201

Longnose Leopard Lizard
Gambelia wislizenii
191

Desert Iguana
Dipsosaurus dorsalis
188

Zebratail Lizard
Callisaurus draconoides
203

Pupfish. This species occurs in a number of sites, but one of the most pleasant places to observe it is at Quitoboquito Springs in Organ Pipe Cactus National Monument, Arizona.

Amphibians and Reptiles
Amphibians are not overly abundant in the Sonoran Desert. The six species you are most likely to see are best observed following a heavy summer rain, when a nighttime drive down a little-traveled desert road with your windows down and your eyes open can be quiet rewarding. The loud sound of a hoarse snore or a plaintive cry will usually lead you to a ditch or temporary pond where you will find spadefoot toads. The "snorer" is the Western Spadefoot, which typically calls while floating on the water surface. The crying comes from Couch's Spadefoot, a species similarly tolerant of dry conditions. A more harsh, explosive clatter may indicate the presence of the Great Plains Toad, which can occur in numbers sufficient to make you fear for your hearing. Two other very attractive toads have more musical trills. The Red-spotted Toad is particularly common in rocky areas, while the Sonoran Green Toad, with its attractive green skin marked with a network of black, is more likely to be found at the edges of a temporary body of water that is surrounded by grasses or shrubs. The giant you see on the road in southern Arizona is the magnificent Colorado River Toad. This species is usually olive drab in color and has a white wart near the angle of its jaw. These animals do not usually stray too far from permanent water, but can be found on the flats on rainy nights. Along certain streams you might see the Canyon Treefrog among the rocks.

Reptiles, especially lizards, are abundant and easy to find in the Sonoran. The Desert Tortoise can be seen travelling at an ambling pace before the sun gets too hot, or during the heat of the day it may be spotted resting in a shallow depression beneath a shrub. The ever-present Side-blotched Lizard seems to be almost everywhere, as is the Western Whiptail. The Whiptail can often be seen turning over pieces of wood with its head, then eating the insects that it uncovers.

In rocky areas, carefully search crevices for the Chuckwalla. Also among the rocks you may see either the spectacularly beautiful Collared Lizard or its near relative the Longnose Leopard Lizard. Leopard Lizards often can be found under shrubs. These lizards are somewhat plain in color; when the females are carrying eggs, however, they develop large bright orange spots on their bodies.

In more sandy areas the Desert Iguana can be found, often near Creosote Bushes, where its burrows are frequently located. Both male and female Desert Iguanas develop light pinkish areas along the sides of their bellies during the breeding season. In the same areas, the Zebratail Lizard may race by. If you should happen to catch one, you will be surprised by the beauty of its stomach, which is ivory white and, in the male, marked with ebony black bars against a brilliant blue background.

Fringe-toed Lizard
Uma notata
182

Desert Horned Lizard
Phrynosoma platyrhinos
195

Regal Horned Lizard
Phrynosoma solare
195

Flat-tail Horned Lizard
Phrynosoma m'calli
194

Desert Spiny Lizard
Sceloporus magister
199

Gila Monster
Heloderma suspectum
180

Western Banded Gecko
Coleonyx variegatus
176, 179

Gopher Snake
Pituophis melanoleucus
263

Coachwhip
Masticophis flagellum
223, 229, 230, 233

Western Patchnose Snake
Salvadora hexalepis

Sonoran Whipsnake
Masticophis bilineatus
222

Common Kingsnake
Lampropeltis getulus
234, 246

Longnose Snake
Rhinocheilus lecontei
238, 247

Glossy Snake
Arizona elegans
268

Lyre Snake
Trimorphodon biscutatus
262, 270

Ground Snake
Sonora semiannulata
228, 231, 239

On very sandy areas, such as dunes, the Fringe-toed Lizard, which is perfectly adapted to its habitat, may surprise you as it dashes down the face of a dune, then dives into the sand and squiggles out of sight. Even in places with little vegetation, this species can be locally abundant, and its stomach, often marked with orange, is as spectacular as that of the Zebratail. Three species of horned lizards might be encountered in the Sonoran Desert. In the western portions, the Desert Horned Lizard is often quite common, especially along washes. The largest of the group, the Regal Horned Lizard, with its large horns, can be found in gravelly to rocky areas in south-central Arizona. The Flat-tail Horned Lizard is limited to fine, windblown sands in extreme southeastern California, southwestern Arizona, and adjacent Mexico.

The Desert Spiny Lizard may be seen in the early morning, often as it climbs a subtree. On the bark of these plants you might also see one of several tree lizards (*Urosaurus*).

The Gila Monster occurs widely in the Arizona portions of the Sonoran Desert. Interestingly, the completely harmless Western Banded Gecko, which occurs along with several other species throughout both the Sonoran and Mojave deserts, is sometimes mistaken for a baby Gila Monster, probably because both species are salmon-colored with dark markings.

As in other deserts, only a few snakes are active during the day during the hottest parts of the year. Day-active snakes in the Sonoran include some of the same ones found in the Mojave, like the Gopher Snake, the Coachwhip, or the Western Patchnose Snake. One diurnal species that does not occur in any other desert is the Sonoran Whipsnake, a species that moves rapidly across the ground and may climb up into bushes or trees.

At night, as the whole desert comes alive, so do the snakes. The desert forms of the Common Kingsnake are active at night, especially following a rainstorm. The brightly banded Longnose Snake is likely to be found along with the Kingsnake, as are the widely distributed Glossy Snake and the Night Snake. The Night Snake is a very inoffensive species; however, it does have a mild venom, as does the larger Lyre Snake. Both species have a pair of grooved fangs at the back of their mouths; hence they are commonly called rear-fanged snakes. Neither species can harm a human, though the Lyre Snake is large enough to inflict a painful bite. Both species have elliptical pupils, a characteristic of truly nocturnal snakes. The Night Snake can occur in almost any habitat in the desert, while the Lyre Snake is usually associated with rocky areas in the higher portions of the Sonoran.

In certain areas a night drive may produce a look at one of a number of small desert specialists not usually encountered because of their secretive habits. Species such as leafnose snakes (*Phyllorhynchus*) are found in sandy to gravelly areas, often where Creosote Bush and palo verde are common. More closely tied to sandy areas or to soils where there is some moisture below the surface is the Ground Snake, a species that exhibits a bewildering array of color patterns. Also in such

Banded Sand Snake
Chilomeniscus cinctus
236

Western Shovelnose
Snake
Chionactis occipitalis
235, 237

Sonoran Shovelnose Snake
Chionactis palarostris
240

Arizona Coral Snake
Micruroides euryxanthus
241

Western Blind Snake
Leptotyphlops humilis
226

Rosy Boa
Lichanura trivirgata
219, 224

Sidewinder
Crotalus cerastes
252, 253

Western Diamondback
Rattlesnake
Crotalus atrox
256

Mojave Rattlesnake
Crotalus scutulatus
259

Speckled Rattlesnake
Crotalus mitchelli
251, 255

Blacktail Rattlesnake
Crotalus molossus
248

Tiger Rattlesnake
Crotalus tigris
249

areas, but more limited, is the Banded Sand Snake. Several small snakes with unusual noses might also be encountered. Two species of shovelnose snakes (*Chionactis*) can be found in desert areas that have scant vegetation. The Western Shovelnose is found in sandier areas than the Sonoran Shovelnose.

Following rain, you might sight the beautiful, but venomous, Arizona Coral Snake searching for its secretive prey, the Western Blind Snake. The Coral Snake can be distinguished from other snakes banded with red, yellow-white, and black because the front portion of its head is black and the red band on its body is always separated on each side from the black bands by yellow bands. This latter characteristic has been popularized by a rhyme: Red and yellow, kill a fellow; red and black, friend of Jack. While this alone is a sufficient identifier for snakes in eastern North America, the Sonoran Shovelnose Snake has a banding pattern similar to that of the coral snake, but it has a white front half to its head.

If you are very fortunate, you may happen on to the stocky Rosy Boa. This attractive, mauve-striped snake of rocky areas is one of only two species of true boas that occur in the United States.

While all of these snakes are interesting and often extraordinarily pretty, there are many venomous snakes in the Sonoran Desert that can inflict a painful or even fatal bite. Six rattlesnake species can be found in the Sonoran, and three of these are locally common. In sandy areas the small Sidewinder can be traced by following its characteristic J-shaped tracks in the sand. This species is well camouflaged and can give you quite a start when it rattles close to your feet. The Western Diamondback Rattlesnake is common in a variety of situations, from open flats to rocky hillslopes. The color of this snake often includes a very attractive mauve shade, quite different from the appearance of the same species farther to the east. Looking very much like the Diamondback, but more greenish-yellow in color is the extremely venomous Mojave Rattlesnake. Often found with the Western Diamondback, this species should surely be avoided.

Three less common rattlesnakes also occur here. The Speckled Rattlesnake prefers rocky areas, which it matches by the patterning and coloration of its skin. Also associated with rocky areas, but not to the same extent as the Speckled Rattlesnake, is the beautiful and unaggressive Blacktail Rattlesnake. Blacktails occur up into the mountains to considerable altitudes, and they can often be found on the upper portions of the bajadas with Saguaros and subtrees. Similarly associated with rocky areas is the Tiger Rattlesnake, which has a rather incongruous appearance because of its small head and large rattle. Many specimens have soft, attractive blue-gray or lavender colors between their "tiger" crossbands. Rattlesnakes are not out to attack the visitor, but they should be avoided. This is most easily done by not placing your hands or feet where you cannot see them and by watching where you sit.

Birds

Despite the fact that some desert areas, such as Organ Pipe Cactus National Monument, publish lists that include more than 250 bird species seen within their boundaries, typical Sonoran Desert sites generally have fewer than twenty-five breeding bird species.

In the most austere sites, such as a Creosote Bush flat, there may be only a single breeding species, the Black-throated Sparrow. As you move up a bajada into increasingly complex vegetation, especially where there are taller subtrees and columnar cacti, the species list increases. The density of breeding species can be quite low in deserts. On the lower parts of bajadas and on valley plains there may be no birds or just one for each three acres of land.

Black-throated Sparrow
Amphispiza bilineata
610

Gambel's Quail
Callipepla gambelii
547

You may see the Gambel's Quail running on the ground, though it is most common close to springs or in places with succulent vegetation. You might also spot the elusive Roadrunner out on a morning search for lizards. Roadrunners mate for life and have a year-round territory. In some places in Arizona they are known to have two breeding seasons. Nests are built off the ground, in tall shrubs, subtrees, or cacti.

Greater Roadrunner
Geococcyx californianus
554

Le Conte's Thrasher
Toxostoma lecontei
594

Also running on the ground are the thrashers, smaller birds with long, somewhat down-curved bills. Le Conte's prefers Creosote Bush flats with some chollas for nesting. It feeds on insects found in the litter. The Crissal Thrasher is much more at home in denser vegetation, where it hides quite effectively from the bird enthusiast. This preference of habitat usually limits the species to areas along rivers or in large washes. Both Bendire's and Curve-billed Thrashers also occur in the Sonoran. Although California and New Mexico are included in its range, Bendire's Thrasher is essentially limited to Arizona in terms of the likelihood of viewing it. Unlike other desert thrashers, it is a migratory species. The Curve-billed is by far the most commonly seen thrasher in the Sonoran Desert. It is found nesting in the most complex vegetation types where subtrees, Saguaros, and chollas abound, but can nest in other areas where there are suitable nesting sites, including cities and towns. In some areas of the Sonoran in California you may sight a Burrowing Owl. In Arizona this is not as likely except in the winter; I have seen this bird many times in the summer, however, on desert flats near Phoenix.

Crissal Thrasher
Toxostoma dorsale

Bendire's Thrasher
Toxostoma bendirei
592

Curve-billed Thrasher
Toxostoma curvirostre
593

Burrowing Owl
Athene cunicularia
559

Mourning Dove
Zenaida macroura
551

You are quite likely to see a variety of doves pecking around on the ground. The Mourning Dove occurs in a wide variety of desert sites, including the flats, while the White-winged Dove is more often seen in the portions of bajadas that have a greater diversity of vegetation. The best nesting sites for White-wings are the mesquite bosques (clumps of trees) along major streams and rivers. On the ground in such riparian situations you may see yet another dove, the Common Ground-Dove. Its bright rufous wings, seen when the bird flies, set it apart from doves other than the Inca Dove, which is much more common in desert cities than in uninhabited areas.

White-winged Dove
Zenaida asiatica
550

Common Ground-Dove
Columbina passerina
553

Inca Dove
Columbina inca
552

In the shrubs and subtrees look for the domed nest of the

Verdin
Auriparus flaviceps
583

Black-tailed Gnatcatcher
Polioptila melanura
588

Ash-throated Flycatcher
Myiarchus cinerascens
573

Say's Phoebe
Sayornis saya
571

Lucy's Warbler
Vermivora luciae

Yellow-rumped Warbler
Dendroica coronata

Northern Mockingbird
Mimus polyglottos
590

Cactus Wren
Campylorhynchus brunneicapillus
584

Ladder-backed Woodpecker
Picoides scalaris
567

Northern Flicker
Colaptes auratus
568

Elf Owl
Micrathene whitneyi
558

Common Raven
Corvus corax
582

Turkey Vulture
Cathartes aura
530

Red-tailed Hawk
Buteo jamaicensis
536, 537

American Kestrel
Falco sparverius
542

Verdin, a very small insect-eating species. Another small bird that coexists with Verdins is the Black-tailed Gnatcatcher. While both species nest in larger shrubs and subtrees, they each have been seen feeding in Creosote Bush, an unusual habit for desert birds, which seem to avoid this shrub, despite its abundance.

The most common desert flycatcher is the Ash-throated Flycatcher, a cavity nester that seeks out holes in plants or even in posts and pipes. One might also see a phoebe, especially Say's Phoebe, or very rarely the Black Phoebe.

Lucy's Warbler occurs on upper portions of bajadas, though it is more common in riparian habitats, where the Yellow Warbler is also found. The Yellow-rumped Warbler—formerly called Audubon's Warbler—a bird of conifer forests, is a very common winter visitor to the Sonoran Desert.

The conspicuous Mockingbird, with its white wing patches, is common in all but the most barren Creosote Bush flats. Its curious habit of singing on moonlit nights suprises some desert visitors. Conspicuous for its noisiness—it has a rather rasping cry—is the Cactus Wren, the state bird of Arizona. Cactus Wrens, while often nesting in chollas, also nest in mesquites and palo verdes; they frequently build dummy nests, a characteristic trait of wrens.

Associated with the Saguaros are three woodpeckers. The loudest and most common of these is the Gila Woodpecker, a species that in the deserts is chiefly confined to areas where the Saguaro abounds, but which can become a pest and inflict serious damage in areas such as orange groves. The Ladder-backed Woodpecker has a more extensive geographic and ecological distribution. Because of its small size, the Ladderback nests in a variety of plants, including yuccas and mesquites; they are true desert woodpeckers, confined to this environment. The gilded race of the Northern Flicker finishes out the trio.

At night, by watching holes in Saguaros made by Gila Woodpeckers, you may see the Elf Owl, the smallest owl in the world. This species has a wide distribution and is not limited to Saguaros, nor even to deserts.

Numerous large birds can be seen perched atop tall plants. The Common Raven and Turkey Vulture are two such birds. In the early morning they may also frequently be seen picking up carrion along desert roads. Red-tailed Hawks are common, and their nests can sometimes be seen in the crotches formed between the arms and trunk of Saguaros. In some places, especially areas wooded by mesquites, you may see the handsome chestnut, black, and white Harris' Hawk. In many desert areas, American Kestrels may be seen catching grasshoppers, often hovering to position themselves above their prey.

Many other birds might be seen in the Sonoran, especially in park areas where there is more lush plant growth to provide a source of food and nesting sites. Many of these species are temporary visitors or opportunists rather than true desert inhabitants.

Coyote
Canis latrans
523, 524

Badger
Taxidea taxus
514

Black-tailed Jack Rabbit
Lepus californicus
509

Desert Cottontail
Sylvilagus audubonii
508

Bighorn Sheep
Ovis canadensis
526

Round-tailed Ground
Squirrel
Spermophilus tereticaudus
504

Rock Squirrel
Spermophilus variegatus
505, 506

White-tailed Antelope
Squirrel
Ammospermophilus leucurus
499

Harris' Antelope Squirrel
Ammospermophilus harrisii
498

Kit Fox
Vulpes macrotis
521

Merriam's Kangaroo Rat
Dipodomys merriami
485

Desert Kangaroo Rat
Dipodomys deserti
484

Mammals

In the Sonoran, mammals, especially small species, tend to be nocturnal. Animals that might be seen during the day are rabbits, Coyotes, some ground squirrels, and, somewhat less likely, the Collared Peccary and Badger.

The Black-tailed Jack Rabbit can be found in almost any desert habitat. These animals are quite conspicuous because of their size. During the day they seek shelter beneath shrubs. Desert Cottontails require more densely shrubbed habitats than jack rabbits. They also avoid the midday sun, and may enter burrows. Cottontails are more patchy in their distribution than jack rabbits, but where they occur, they are often more numerous.

Coyotes can be seen shyly running across the desert in the day, usually in the early morning or late afternoon. You are probably more likely to encounter a Badger attempting to dig potential prey out of the ground.

Because of its size, the Bighorn Sheep is a species that you might expect to find. While this magnificent animal can be seen, it is very wary and blends in with its background. Search very quietly for Bighorn near watering places such as small springs in rocky areas.

Depending on where you are in the Sonoran Desert, you will see one or another species of diurnal ground squirrel. The Round-tailed Ground Squirrel occurs commonly throughout the Sonoran, occupying areas from the flats all the way into those dominated by subtrees. In rocky areas, and at upper elevations of the desert, look for the Rock Squirrel among boulders where it nests, though it is also a good climber in plants. Two species of antelope ground squirrel occur in the Sonoran. The White-tailed Antelope Squirrel occurs in the California and Baja California portion of the desert, while Harris' Antelope Squirrel occupies the Arizona and Sonoran portions. Both species attract attention because of their tail-flicking habits—the White-tail especially, because the tail's underside is quite white. Harris' is more tied to desert areas; the White-tail ranges well up into cool montane environments.

As night falls, the rodents and their mammalian hunter, the Kit Fox, dominate the scene. Kit Foxes are agile and are almost exclusively carnivorous, feeding mostly on kangaroo rats in many parts of their range. These foxes often den great distances from any water and are assumed to obtain sufficient moisture from their food. Their dens have multiple openings and multiple dens are constructed and used in the course of a year. Kangaroo rats (*Dipodomys*) and pocket mice (*Perognathus*) may appear in great abundance. Usually there are at least two species of each in any area. The most likely species to be encountered is Merriam's Kangaroo Rat, a resident of all North American deserts. This "K-rat" occurs in any spot where the soil can be dug and where a sufficient number of seeds can be harvested and cached. In sandy sites in the western portion of the Sonoran, Merriam's Kangaroo Rat may be associated with the Desert Kangaroo Rat; it is found with

Ord's Kangaroo Rat
Dipodomys ordii
480

Banner-tailed Kangaroo Rat
Dipodomys spectabilis
483

Desert Pocket Mouse
Perognathus penicillatus
477

Rock Pocket Mouse
Perognathus intermedius

Bailey's Pocket Mouse
Perognathus baileyi
476

Long-tailed Pocket Mouse
Perognathus formosus
475

Silky Pocket Mouse
Perognathus flavus
471

Deer Mouse
Peromyscus maniculatus
489

Cactus Mouse
Peromyscus eremicus
492

Canyon Mouse
Peromyscus crinitus

Southern Grasshopper Mouse
Onychomys torridus
488

Desert Woodrat
Neotoma lepida
493

White-throated Woodrat
Neotoma albigula
494

Botta's Pocket Gopher
Thomomys bottae
469

Mexican Long-nosed Bat
Leptonycteris nivalis
454

Ord's Kangaroo Rat in the eastern portions. In grassland/desert transition areas, the large, handsome Banner-tailed Kangaroo Rat may be an associate; its extensive communal burrow sites are very evident.

Of Sonoran pocket mice, the Desert Pocket Mouse is the most abundant. These animals prefer valley plains with loose soil, a habitat in stark contrast to the rocky areas occupied by the similarly distributed Rock Pocket Mouse. In the Arizona and Baja California portions of the Sonoran, the large, grayish Bailey's Pocket Mouse may be encountered, while in California the Long-tailed Pocket Mouse dominates on gravelly soils. The eastern portions of the Sonoran are occupied by the Silky Pocket Mouse, a small, attractive species. All of these animals are predominantly seed-eaters. Like certain other desert rodents, pocket mice can go into a state of torpor when seeds are not available.

Rounding out our nocturnal cast of characters is the ubiquitous Deer Mouse, which avoids the driest desert sites, and one of its relatives, the Cactus Mouse. The latter occurs in all of our hot deserts, nesting in burrows amid even the most open vegetation. The Canyon Mouse, by contrast, prefers rocky canyon areas in the western Sonoran Desert. Some areas, especially upper elevations, may harbor the Southern Grasshopper Mouse, an omnivore that can make a meal on such unpromising creatures as scorpions or tenebrionid beetles, overcoming the latter's chemical defenses.

Daytime strolls will reveal the presence of two other types of mammals, though you won't see the animals themselves, but signs of their activity. The Desert Woodrat often accumulates pieces of cholla to add to the sticks, yucca leaves, and even cow chips it uses to make its home. It may also be found nesting within yucca stems in chambers it has hollowed out. Somewhat restricted to the drier parts of the desert and to desert transitional sites is the White-throated Woodrat.

As in the Mojave Desert, the characteristic earthen mounds formed by Botta's Pocket Gopher may dot local landscapes. Bats, as usual, are present, numerous and diverse, but they are very difficult to observe. In the Mexican Sonoran, an exception might be a chance observation of the Mexican Long-nosed Bat, which hovers as it feeds on pollen and nectar from the flowers of an agave or Saguaro.

The Sonoran Desert is our most diverse desert habitat. Since there are a variety of national monuments, national forests, state parks, botanical gardens, and museums close to large cities, it is even among the most accessible deserts in North America, even to the least intrepid traveler. Even a one-day trip will reward you with breathtaking scenes and a unique biota.

THE SONORAN DESERT: PLANTS AND ANIMALS

Wildflowers

Angel Trumpets 104
Apache Plume 96
Arizona Blue-eyes 69
Arizona Jewel Flower 107
Barrel Cactus 122
Beavertail Cactus 41
Birdcage Evening
Primrose 93
Blackfoot Daisy 92
Bladder Sage 75
Brittlebush 136
Buffalo Gourd 140
Chia 64
Chinchweed 133
Chuparosa 160
Claret Cup Cactus 42
Climbing Milkweed 83
Common Ice Plant 88
Coulter's Globemallow 157
Coulter's Lupine 72
Crescent Milkvetch 50
Cushion Cactus 50
Desert Anemone 91
Desert Bell 70
Desert Calico 51
Desert Candle 164
Desert Chicory 86
Desert Christmas
Cactus 162
Desert Dandelion 125
Desert Five Spot 43
Desert Four O'Clock 52
Desert Globemallow 158
Desert Gold 145
Desert Lily 98
Desert Mariposa Tulip 152,
154
Desert Marigold 128
Desert Poppy 155
Desert Primrose 156
Desert Rock Nettle 150
Desert Rosemallow 151
Desert Sand Verbena 53
Desert Sunflower 135
Desert Tobacco 103
Desert Trumpet 108
Desert Velvet 118
Devil's Claw 117
Dingy Chamaesarcha 119
Esteve's Pincushion 84
Fagonia 55
Fairy Duster 48
Feather Dalea 49

Filaree 57
Fishhook Cactus 39
Five-needle Fetid
Marigold 134
Freckled Milkvetch 163
Ghost Flower 147
Great Desert Poppy 95
Indian Blanket 60
Jackass Clover 110
Little Snapdragon Vine 74
Melon Loco 141
Mexican Gold Poppy 148
Mojave Aster 61
Mojave Desert Star 90
Night-blooming Cereus 87
Pale Face 45
Pale Trumpets 66
Paperflower 137
Puncture Vine 143
Purple Groundcherry 67
Purple Mat 54
Rain Lily 153
Rainbow Cactus 123
Ratany 56
Rattlesnake Weed 102
Rough Mendora 142
Scalloped Phacelia 65
Snakehead 126
Southwestern Ringstem 105
Southwestern Thorn
Apple 100
Spectacle Pod 79
Spike Broomrape 76
Spotted Langloisia 97
Spreading Fleabane 89
Sunray 132
Sweet-scented
Heliotrope 101
Tahoka Daisy 62
Tobacco Weed 85
Trailing Four O'Clock 59
Tree Tobacco 114
Trixis 106
Twinleaf 144
Western Peppergrass 78
Whispering Bells 115
White-bracted Stick
Leaf 120
White Horsenettle 73
White Milkweed 82
Wooly Daisy 127
Yellow Bee Plant 111
Yellow Head 124
Yellow Peppergrass 113

Yellow Spiny Daisy 131
Yellow Twining
  napdragon 116

Reptiles
Arizona Coral Snake 241
Banded Sand Snake 236
Black Collared Lizard 186
Blackneck Garter Snake 220
Blacktail Rattlesnake 248
Bluntnose Leopard
  Lizard 187
Brush Lizard 190
Checkered Garter Snake 216
Chihuahuan Spotted
  Whiptail 210
Chuckwalla 189
Coachwhip 223, 229, 230,
  233
Collared Lizard 200, 201
Common Kingsnake 234,
  246
Desert Iguana 188
Desert Night Lizard 183,
  184,
Desert Spiny Lizard 199
Desert Tortoise 169
Flat-tail Horned Lizard 194
Fringe-toed Lizard 182
Gila Monster 180
Glossy Snake 268
Gopher Snake 263
Granite Night Lizard 185
Greater Earless Lizard 204
Ground Snake 225, 228,
  231
Leaf-toed Gecko 175
Lesser Earless Lizard 192
Longnose Leopard
  Lizard 191
Longnose Snake 238, 247
Lyre Snake 262, 270
Mojave Rattlesnake 259
Night Snake 267
Red Diamond
  Rattlesnake 254
Regal Horned Lizard 195
Rosy Boa 219, 224
Saddled Leafnose Snake 245
Side-blotched Lizard 202
Sidewinder 252, 253
Sonoran Mud Turtle 171
Sonoran Shovelnose
  Snake 240

Sonoran Whipsnake 222
Speckled Rattlesnake 251,
  255
Spiny Softshell 174
Spotted Leafnose Snake 265,
  269
Tiger Rattlesnake 249
Tree Lizard 205
Western Banded
  Gecko 176, 179
Western Blackhead
  Snake 227
Western Blind Snake 226
Western Diamond
  Rattlesnake 256
Western Patchnose
  Snake 218
Western Shovelnose
  Snake 235, 237
Western Whiptail 206
Zebratail Lizard 203

Amphibians
Bullfrog 288
California Treefrog 271
Canyon Treefrog 272
Colorado River Toad 281
Great Plains Toad 283
Lowland Burrowing
  Treefrog 273
Northern Leopard Frog 286
Red-spotted Toad 278
Rio Grande Leopard
  Frog 285
Sonoran Green Toad 284

Fishes
Desert Pupfish 293
Gila Topminnow 295
Golden Shiner 299
Longfin Dace 296
Mosquitofish 294
Speckled Dace 297
Spikedace 300

**Trees, Shrubs, Cacti, and
Grasses**
Anderson Lycium 321
Arrow Weed 314
Bitter Condalia 323
Blue Palo Verde 301, 316
Burrobush 335
Bur Sage 330
California Washingtonia 327

Creosote Bush 312
Crucifixion Thorn 314
Desert Buckwheat 329
Desert Holly 328
Desert Willow 306
Elephant Tree 312, 315
Fluffgrass 331
Four-wing Saltbush 322
Greasewood 315
Gregg Catclaw 303, 317
Honey Mesquite 308, 321
Indian Ricegrass 332
Jumping Cholla 325
Littleleaf Horsebrush 313
Mojave Yucca 329
Mexican Palo Verde 307,
  322
Mormon Tea 334
Screwbean Mesquite 302,
  311, 320
Shadscale 316
Smoke Tree 305, 313
Snakeweed 311
Soaptree Yucca 328
Tamarisk 304, 324
Turpentine Broom 336
White Bur Sage 325
Winter Fat 324
Yellow Palo Verde 309, 318

Insects and Spiders
Agave Billbug 380
Arid Lands Honey Ants 384
Arizona Blister Beetle 382
Aztec Pygmy
  Grasshopper 373
Bee Assassin 376
Broad-necked Darkling
  Beetle 381
Carolina Wolf Spider 401
Centruroides Scorpions 394
Cochineal Bug 391
Creosote Bush
  Grasshopper 368
Desert Tarantula 399
Dragon Lubber
  Grasshopper 372
Giant Vinegarone 398
Green Valley
  Grasshopper 367
Horse Lubber
  Grasshopper 371
Inconspicuous Crab
  Spider 400

Ironclad Beetle 379
Jerusalem Cricket 375
Little Black Ant 386
Lubber Grasshopper 370
Mormon Cricket 374
Obscure Ground
Mantid 377
Pale Windscorpion 396
Pallid-winged
Grasshopper 369
Red Velvet-ant 389
Rough Harvester Ant 387
Spine-waisted Ants 385
Tarantula Hawk 383
Texas Carpenter Ant 388
Thistledown Velvet-ant 390

Mammals
Antelope Jack Rabbit 510
Arizona Pocket Mouse 472
Badger 514
Bailey's Pocket Mouse 476
Banner-tailed Kangaroo
Rat 483
Big Free-tailed Bat 467
Bighorn Sheep 526
Black-tailed Jack
Rabbit 509
Bobcat 517, 520
Botta's Pocket Gopher 469
Brazilian Free-tailed Bat 465
Brush Mouse 490
Cactus Mouse 492
California Leaf-nosed
Bat 452
California Myotis 458
Cave Myotis 457
Coati 513
Collared Peccary 525
Coyote 523
Deer Mouse 489
Desert Cottontail 508
Desert Kangaroo Rat 484
Desert Pocket Mouse 477
Desert Shrew 470
Desert Woodrat 493
Fulvous Harvest Mouse 487
Ghost-faced Bat 451
Gray Fox 522
Harris' Antelope
Squirrel 498
Hog-nosed Skunk 516
House Mouse 495
Kit Fox 521

Little Pocket Mouse 473
Long-tailed Pocket
Mouse 475
Long-tongued Bat 453
Merriam's Kangaroo
Rat 485
Mountain Lion 518
Mule Deer 528
Ord's Kangaroo Rat 480
Pallid Bat 474
Panamint Kangaroo
Rat 482
Pocketed Free-tailed
Bat 466
Porcupine 507
Pronghorn 527
Raccoon 512
Ringtail 511
Rock Squirrel 505
Round-tailed Ground
Squirrel 504
Sanborn's Long-nosed
Bat 455
Silky Pocket Mouse 471
Southern Grasshopper
Mouse 488
Southwestern Myotis 460
Spotted Bat 462
Spotted Ground
Squirrel 503
Striped Skunk 515
Townsend's Big-eared
Bat 463
Western Harvest Mouse 486
Western Pipistrelle 461
White-tailed Antelope
Squirrel 500
White-throated
Woodrat 494
Yuma Myotis 456

Birds
Abert's Towhee 606
Aplomado Falcon 543
Ash-throated Flycatcher 573
Bendire's Thrasher 592
Bewick's Wren 587
Black-chinned
Hummingbird 563
Black Phoebe 570
Black-tailed
Gnatcatcher 588
Black-throated Gray
Warbler 598

Black-throated Sparrow 6
Black Vulture 529
Blue Grosbeak 604
Brown-crested
Flycatcher 574
Brown-headed Cowbird 6
Brown Towhee 607
Burrowing Owl 559
Cactus Wren 584
Canyon Wren 586
Caracara 541
Common Barn-owl 555
Common Poorwill 562
Common Raven 582
Cooper's Hawk 532
Costa's Hummingbird 56
Curve-billed Thrasher 59:
Elf Owl 558
European Starling 597
Ferruginous Pygmy-owl 5
Gambel's Quail 547
Gila Woodpecker 565
Golden Eagle 540
Great Horned Owl 556
Greater Roadrunner 554
Ground Dove 553
Harris' Hawk 533
Hooded Oriole 614
Horned Lark 576
House Finch 617
Inca Dove 552
Ladder-backed
Woodpecker 567
Le Conte's Thrasher 594
Lesser Nighthawk 560
Loggerhead Shrike 596
Mourning Dove 551
Northern Cardinal 600
Northern Flicker 568
Northern Mockingbird 59
Phainopepla 595
Purple Martin 577
Pyrrhuloxia 602
Red-tailed Hawk 536
Rock Wren 585
Say's Phoebe 571
Scott's Oriole 616
Turkey Vulture 530
Verdin 583
Vermillion Flycatcher 57.
Violet-green Swallow 579
Western Kingbird 575
Western Tanager 599
White-winged Dove 550

THE CHIHUAHUAN DESERT

The Chihuahuan Desert occurs in the United States as a band across west Texas (from between 102° to 103° westward), including the Big Bend area and the area between the cities of Pecos and El Paso. In New Mexico, the Chihuahuan is represented as four fingerlike projections. The smallest is the easternmost portion, which lies just west of Carlsbad and extends to slightly northwest of Artesia. The second finger includes White Sands National Monument near Alamogordo, and continues to north of Tularosa. The third area extends the farthest north, covering the valleys from Las Cruces to a point just north of Socorro. Each of these extensions runs from north to south between mountain ranges. The fourth finger, interrupted by mountains, extends in a northwest direction to Clifton, Arizona, and to areas near Benson. Several sites farther into Arizona have isolated patches of Chihuahuan Desert vegetation, especially on limestone outcrops, but because these sites are so remote from the main body of the Chihuahuan, they lack the characteristic vertebrate species found in areas closer to the Arizona-New Mexico border. Limestone outcrops in the Santa Catalina Mountains just outside of Tucson contain some of these vegetation patches. In Mexico, where the Chihuahuan Desert is much more extensive, it occupies considerable portions of the states of Chihuahua, Coahuila, Zacatecas, and San Luis Potosí. Smaller sections of Durango, Nuevo León, and Hidalgo are also a part of this desert.

The Chihuahuan Desert is an area of high elevations. The lowest portions, at about 1000 feet, are on the Rio Grande River, and the highest portions, in Mexico, may exceed 6500 feet. A more typical limit in the United States is 5000 feet, and 3500- to 4200-foot elevations represent a characteristic range. These high elevations are related to the cool winters experienced in the Chihuahuan Desert, especially in the portions that lie in the United States, where nighttime temperatures drop below freezing at least one hundred times per year. Do not let the cool winters mislead you, however: Summer temperatures are high, and the climate overall is moderate compared to those of continental nondesert areas. Rainfall varies from 7.8 inches a year to nearly twelve, particularly at high sites. Areas with more than ten inches per year are often those that, while currently supporting desert vegetation, were desert grasslands at one time until overgrazing turned them into deserts. While rainfall is characteristically a summer phenomenon, winter rains and snow do occur, although snow never remains on the ground for long. The winter precipitation is sufficient in some areas for winter annuals to occur.

The Chihuahuan lies within an area surrounded by the Rocky Mountains, the Sierra Madre Oriental, and the Sierra Madre Occidental. Like other North American deserts, it consists of alluvial plains, bajadas, and scattered mountains. Nearly eighty percent of the entire area is dominated by soils that are derived from calcareous parent materials. Such desert areas may also contain volcanic materials, generally of Eocene-

Miocene derivation (58 to 13 million years ago). Where volcanism has occurred, you may observe complex mosaics of soils and their attendant vegetations.

The combination of relatively high rainfall, high-calcium soils, and cool temperatures during parts of the year promotes the establishment of grasses, yuccas, and agaves. They give th Chihuahuan Desert a different, nontropical character compared with the Sonoran Desert. In many sites, the distinction between desert and grassland is virtually impossible to draw.

Plant Life

The most prevalent lowland vegetation type in the Chihuahuan Desert is dominated by Creosote Bush (plate 21). The genetic makeup of Creosote Bush differs in each of our hot deserts, and you can sometimes recognize the origin of a particular plant by its appearance. The Chihuahuan plants are not as densely leaved as the others and they have straighter stems. Along with Creosote Bush you may encounter Tarbush a species that is often prevalent enough to rank as a co-dominant; at some sites it may even be dominant. The distribution of Tarbush in the United States essentially outlines the Chihuahuan Desert, and it is thus often considered to be a good indicator of a true Chihuahuan habitat.

Both Tarbush and Creosote Bush prefer calcareous soils. Creosote Bush in particular requires well-drained sites and thus is associated with calcareous gravels, often underlain by a layer of caliche. Other species you are likely to see in these areas include Mariola, a very pungent-leaved shrub. On some sites you may observe Honey Mesquite, though it is usually more abundant in sandy areas along washes or fringing the edges of playas. Often, if the area has been grazed, Snakeweed may be a dominant. The presence of Snakeweed is a good indicator of land disturbance, and its dominance suggests a history of overgrazing. Similarly associated with disturbed areas is the Russian Thistle, or Tumble Weed. The globular skeletons of this species accumulate as they are caught in fences along highways, and the succulent bright green living plants line road edges in all of our deserts. Russian Thistle produces plant material with a high energy content while using very little water. Its skeletons can be pressed into fire logs.

Rounding out the rather austere set of Chihuahuan woody perennials are an occasional yucca, particularly Soaptree Yucca, a Mormon tea (*Ephedra*), and one or two species of *Opuntia*, either a prickly pear or a cholla.

As unprepossessing as these sites appear at first glance, they may contain up to thirty species of annuals and many small perennial forbs. Among the forbs, Desert Marigold is conspicuous. This yellow-flowered species with powdery-gray leaves occurs as one of the most readily apparent plants along highway edges in all our hot deserts. Because of the water available from pavement runoff, some individuals are in bloom nearly every month of the year.

Creosote Bush
Larrea tridentata
342

Tarbush
Flourensia cernua
350

Mariola
Parthenium incanum
356

Honey Mesquite
Prosopis glandulosa
308, 321

Snakeweed
Xanthocephalum sarothrae
341

Tumble Weed
Salsola kali

Soaptree Yucca
Yucca elata
328

Desert Marigold
Baileya multiradiata
128

Desert Zinnia
Zinnia acerosa

Little Golden Zinnia
Zinnia grandiflora
38

Fluffgrass
Erioneuron pulchellum
61

Desert Holly
Perezia nana

Buffalo Gourd
Cucurbita foetidissima
40

Banana Yucca
Yucca baccata
36

Lechuguilla
Agave lecheguilla
37

Goldeneye
Viguiera stenoloba

Feather Dalea
Dalea formosa
9

Rubber Plant
Jatropha dioica

False Agave
Hechtia texensis

Other forbs that recur include the white-flowered Desert Zinnia and the yellow-flowered *Zinnia grandiflora*. On some sites, and commonly along roads, the purple flowers of one of the species in the genus *Solanum* may be common and conspicuous. When the light is just right, small, dense tufts of silver or gold may bring to your notice a small, compact plant, Fluffgrass. Similar areas contain the holly-like leaves of Desert Holly. Also in low areas, particularly on sandy soil or less frequently along road edges, are one or two species of gourds, especially the Buffalo Gourd. This trailing vine has large, heart-shaped leaves and occurs in all of our hot deserts. As you proceed up a bajada, there is an increase in yuccas and agaves (plate 20). One yucca in particular, Soaptree Yucca, dominates vast areas of the Chihuahuan Desert. Also occurring in the Sonoran Desert and on some grassland sites, it can reach fifteen feet in height and its tall flowering stalks, covered with creamy flowers and set off against an azure desert sky, can be an impressive sight. The Banana Yucca is also found in this habitat. Its stout leaves and blue-gray color make it easily recognizable.

A narrow-leaved agave, Lechuguilla, is often mistaken for a yucca. This species is another good indicator of the Chihuahuan Desert, although its range does not extend very far into New Mexico.

Agaves have long been used by man. Evidence taken from sites in Mexico reveal that agave fibers were used more than 9000 years ago. Fibers from Lechuguilla can be made into nets, baskets, mats, ropes, and sandals. Its stems yield a soap substitute, and its pulp has been used as a spot remover. Certain compounds in Lechuguilla are poisonous, and the Tarahumara Indians in Mexico once used these compounds on their arrows and in water to poison fish. Livestock can die from eating the leaves during a drought when the succulent Lechuguilla leaves become the forage of last resort.

On the mainland areas of North America, not counting Baja California, there are some 136 species of agaves. Nine occur in the Chihuahuan Desert, five in the United States portions. Various species are used to produce drinks such as the fermented aguamil or pulque, or the fermented and distilled mescal or tequila. Desert species of agaves are generally not used to produce these beverages.

Remaining on the slopes, you might encounter the Goldeneye or the more showy Feather Dalea, whose range includes oak woodlands, where it provides food for deer.

The Rubber Plant also grows in such areas, although its distribution is spotty. Rubber Plants form colonies of highly flexible, reddish-brown stems, leafless for long periods. When a stem is injured, a yellowish watery substance, which may turn red in color, is exuded. The species has a variety of medicinal uses. The roots, for example, were chewed to relieve toothaches. It occurs as far North as the Guadalupe Mountains, but is a much more common species in the Big Bend area. In some sites in west Texas the hillsides may foster a mixture of Lechuguilla and its look-alike, False Agave, a

Ocotillo
Fouquieria splendens
335

Candelilla
Euphorbia antisyphilitica

Ratany
Krameria parvifolia
56

Texas Silverleaf
Leucophyllum frutescens
47

Parry's Century Plant
Agave parryi
339

Harvard Agave
Agave harvardiana

Bear Grass
Nolina microcarpa

Sacahuista
Nolina texana

Sotol
Dasylirion wheeleri
338

Prickly Pear Cactus
Opuntia phaeacantha

Texas Prickly Pear
Opuntia lindheimeri

Tree Cholla
Opuntia imbricata
333

plant with spiny, reddish leaves that belongs to the same family as the pineapple, Bromeliaceae.

Ascending further, the numbers of Ocotillo increase. The spiny branches of this species are sometimes planted as cuttings, which root to create an impenetrable living fence. Also present in such areas, but primarily from the Big Bend southward, are eye-catching clusters of the rod-like branches o Candelilla. This species is often pirated from Big Bend National Park because its juices can be used to produce candles, shoe polish, and a variety of other products. In Mexico it is alleged to be a treatment for venereal disease— hence its species name *antisyphilitica*.

Ratany is frequently found on Chihuahuan Desert slopes, but its distribution includes all our hot deserts. The purple flowers of Ratany, while quite showy, are upstaged by an even more handsome plant found in the Texas portions of the Chihuahuan Desert, Texas Silverleaf. It and its smaller cousin, *Leucophyllum minus*, have soft gray leaves. They are covered with lavender flowers following rains, a habit from which they derive their other common name, Barometer Bush.

As you further ascend the bajada, you note more grassland or a combination of desert and grassland elements (plate 19). Here there are more species of yucca and more agaves. Large-leaved agaves like Parry's Century Plant in New Mexico and Texas and the Harvard Agave in Texas become abundant, and their flowering stalks, new and old, dot the horizon.

Also in this zone are two unusual members of the lily family. The first comprises a small group of species that look like large bunch-grasses—the bear grasses, or nolinas. Bear Grass occurs in Arizona and New Mexico, but in Texas it is replaced by Sacahuista. The fact that these plants are not grasses becomes obvious when they put up their flowering stalks, tall structures somewhat like yucca stalks but more intricate and covered with numerous small flowers.

Mixed in with the nolinas are the sotols (*Dasylirion*). In New Mexico, *D. wheeleri* predominates, while in Texas, *D. leiophyllum* replaces it. These species have numerous prickles along the margins of their leaves, and their leaf bases are expanded to form a spoonlike structure. Sotols have a wide distribution and can also be found in the Sonoran Desert/ grassland transition.

Of course, this upper elevational aspect of the Chihuahuan Desert is marked by the presence of numerous grasses.

Up to this point I have not mentioned the Chihuahuan Desert cacti. It is difficult to know where to begin—there are so many interesting species that might catch your eye. By far the most conspicuous prickly pear is *Opuntia phaeacantha*. To naturalists, this is a complex species composed of numerous varieties, some of which are found in the same place and interbreed. A somewhat similar species is the Texas Prickly Pear. A horticultural variety of the prickly pear that has long narrow tonguelike pads is called the Cow's Tongue. It is often grown around houses in the towns of arid areas.

One of the largest, most noticeable chollas is the Tree Cholla,

Desert Christmas Cactus
Opuntia leptocaulis
62

Clavellina
Opuntia schottii

Turk's Head
*Echinocactus
horizonthalonius*

Horse Crippler
Echinocactus texensis

Peyote
Lophophora williamsii
7

Whitethorn
Acacia neovernicosa

Sandpaper Bush
Mortonia scabrella

Little Leaf Desert Sumac
Rhus microphylla

Apache Plume
Fallugia paradoxa
6

Crucifixion Thorn
Koeberlinia spinosa

a species whose dark green branches have a purple or reddish cast. Usually its spines are red or pink, but a variety in the Big Bend has silver spines. The smaller, but generally more common, Desert Christmas Cactus is abundant throughout the desert. A clump or mat-forming cholla, Clavellina, occurs in western Texas. These plants may form mats that are up to ten feet in diameter, but are only about four inches high.

Several species of hedgehog cacti occur in the Chihuahuan Desert. Their cylindrical stems branch near the ground; they form tight groups, with up to five hundred stems in a patch. Small barrel-like cacti of the genus *Echinocactus* are represented throughout the Chihuahuan by the Turk's Head and by the Horse Crippler.

Perhaps the most notorious of the Chihuahuan Desert cacti is the Peyote. This species has a very limited distribution in the Big Bend area, where it occurs on the limestone soils of both hills and flats. Its gray color and low profile make it very difficult to find. It has been so thoroughly collected that it is no longer common anywhere you are likely to travel.

The small, attractive cacti of the genus *Mammilaria* are relatively abundant, but there is very little agreement among specialists as to how many species exist anywhere, particularly in the Chihuahuan Desert. A recent analysis of the entire United States lists thirteen species, but some popular works list fourteen species in the Big Bend area alone. Suffice it to say, these pincushions, fishhooks, or cob cacti are abundant, especially beneath shrubs. There are many other cacti to see in the Chihuahuan. Good luck in trying to identify them. You'll need it!

Variants of the vegetation types we have discussed also occur in the Chihuahuan. In fairly extensive areas, Creosote Bush is associated with Whitethorn. This acacia, identified by its white thorns arising from reddish-brown stems, is common in many areas on limestone slopes and along washes, including the outlying Chihuahuan Desert sites in Arizona, especially near Tombstone. As a dominant vegetation, Whitethorn is most common in Texas.

Associated with Whitethorn is Sandpaper Bush. In some places this shrub, with its small, rough, yellowish-green leaves curled against the stem, can comprise all the plant cover, especially on limestone sites. Another form of Sandpaper Bush occurs in the Mojave Desert, even into the Virgin River highway gorge (I–15), on the Utah-Arizona border.

Other plants that may catch your attention include Little Leaf Desert Sumac. This species occurs throughout the Chihuahuan on sandy and gravelly soils, often along washes, where it may mix at cooler sites with Apache Plume. The purplish, feathery fruit of Apache Plume makes it an easy species to recognize.

A rather ominous looking plant found on the sandy soils of the Creosote Bush plains is the Crucifixion Thorn. Crucifixion Thorn resembles a pile of stout, dark green thorns (actually branches), which are not brightened up much by its black fruits. Its distribution rather closely follows the Chihuahuan Desert limits into Mexico.

Graythorn
Ziziphus obtusifolia

Tobosa
Hilaria mutica

Burrograss
Scleropogon brevifolius

Four-wing Saltbush
Atriplex canescens
352

Gypsum Grama
Bouteloua breviseta

Another thorny plant, but one with much less robust branches and small leaves, is Graythorn, a species most frequently found on slopes. Here its fruits are eaten by birds.

A few other local habitats should be mentioned. In swales, a different group of plants exists. The most obvious is a coarse grass, Tobosa. It is often joined by Burrograss and the familiar Four-wing Saltbush.

A common group of species that occurs on gypsum soils includes Soaptree and Little Leaf Desert Sumac. These are often joined on such sites by a matted plant spreading from a woody taproot, *Tequilia (Coldenia) hispidissima,* and by Gypsum Grama, as well as a host of lesser species.

One more striking scene in the portion of the Chihuahuan Desert that lies in the United States becomes starkly evident as the traveler motors between Las Cruces and Lordsburg, New Mexico on I–10 or east of El Paso, Texas, also along I–10. Here much of the landscape is dotted by tall mounds of sand, each capped by a low-growing shrub. You may well be surprised to find that this strange, apparently unfamiliar, species is actually our old friend the Honey Mesquite. About one hundred years ago, the loss of the original grass cover in these areas permitted the rapid entry of mesquite, which can sprout when covered by sand. Under these conditions, it assumes a prostrate form that stabilizes the areas of soil beneath its canopy. Wind erosion between the shrubs creates the mound-depression aspect of the landscape. It is theorized that the changes in vegetation that occurred in native grasslands resulted from overgrazing, perhaps in concert with a subtle change in climate and by changes in the animal populations.

The portions of the Chihuahuan Desert in Mexico contain many more species than do those in the United States. In part this is due to the greater size of the area, but the more southern distribution is important as well. Large columnar cacti reminiscent of those in the Sonoran Desert occur in great abundance. A plethora of cactus species of every form, color, and habit can be found on the hillslopes. Several treelike yuccas are common. Despite this diversity, many of the dominants are still species familiar in the United States, and even with the greater variety of species, most areas do not surpass in appeal the vistas of the Big Bend area in Texas.

Animal Life

The Chihuahuan Desert supports numerous animal species, ranging from tiny insects and arthropods to large mammals, such as the Bobcat. Even the briefest visit to this area can be rich in wildlife discoveries.

Bobcat
Felis rufus
517, 520

Invertebrates

Like other deserts, the Chihuahuan is home to thousands and thousands of invertebrates. Many of these species are conspicuous, and even the most casual visitor is likely to encounter them. Others are not so obvious, but they are no less interesting. The invertebrates of two areas of the United States portion of the Chihuahuan Desert are especially well known. In Texas, the Big Bend National Park has been surveyed by biologists investigating everything from snails to grasshoppers. Being a border area, Big Bend contains many species whose range barely reaches the United States.

Although rather exhaustive lists of invertebrate species known to inhabit the Big Bend are available in scientific journals, surprisingly few studies have been conducted on the roles these species play in nature. By contrast, areas near Las Cruces, New Mexico, have been the sites for studies of the interaction between plants and animals as they influence the dynamics of Chihuahuan Desert ecosystems. These studies, conducted by Dr. Walter Whitford and his colleagues at New Mexico State University, have especially emphasized the biological roles of the invertebrates, which may be quite significant in deserts.

As with amphibians, there is nothing like a good rain to make desert invertebrates move. Following rains in the Big Bend, you may see a conical, creamy white snail, *Rhabdotus schiedeanus*, moving on the ground or on the vegetation. This snail attaches itself to plants with a mucous secretion and goes into a resting state during dry periods. In many desert areas, you may encounter the large Desert Millipede. This species feeds on organic matter lying on the ground surface.

At night, or turning over a flat rock, you may also encounter a large centipede, *Scolopendra heros*. Beware! Unlike millipedes, these animals are active and voracious predators and can inflict a very painful bite. As in other deserts, the same pattern of searching with a black light may uncover any one of a dozen or so fairly common scorpions. None of the Chihuahuan Desert species are known to be deadly, but care is still advised because people vary in their individual responses to stings. You can also find various wind or sunscorpions, the solpugids.

Another nocturnal species you might meet—and one that would certainly command your attention—is the Giant Vinegarone. These animals are dark in color, about five inches in length, and have prominent pincers and a whiplike tail. I usually see them only at the upper elevations of the deserts, at points of transition with other vegetation types; some people, however, find them along rocky ravines well into the desert. Vinegarones are commonly seen on the roads at night; during the day, they remain hidden under debris or rocks.

Many spiders occur in the Chihuahuan Desert; nearly any site contains at least twenty or so species. The list usually includes at least one large but harmless tarantula, such as *Dugesiella echina*.

Of the insects, the grasshoppers are still among the most conspicuous: A dozen species may be found at any one place. The Pallid-winged Grasshopper is likely to be among the most abundant species anywhere you look in scattered open shrublands, as it has been in each of the other three deserts. The Creosote Bush Grasshopper is again to be found in the foliage of *Larrea*.

Two large grasshoppers may also be encountered in late summer or early fall—both in desert-grassland transitional

Desert Millipede
Orthoporus ornatus
393

Giant Vinegarone
Mastigoproctus giganteus
398

Pallid-winged Grasshopper
Trimerotropis pallidipennis
369

Creosote Bush Grasshopper
Bootettix argentatus
368

Horse Lubber
Grasshopper
Taeniopoda eques
371

Lubber Grasshopper
Brachystola magna
370

sites and in the typical Chihuahuan Desert habitat. The more beautiful of the two is the Horse Lubber, a black grasshopper with yellow markings on the head and pronotum (back). It has beautiful rose-colored wings, although you will probably not see it fly too far. When handled, the Horse Lubber produces a hissing, bubbling sound by forcing air and liquid through the breathing pores, or spiracles, on the sides of its body. This froth is foul-tasting to predators and thus acts as a deterrent. The Horse Lubber occurs in the Sonoran Desert across southern Arizona and into the Chihuahuan, across southern New Mexico and into the Big Bend of Texas.

The other large species you are likely to see occurs in all these areas, but also extends up into the Great Plains nearly to Canada. This large, brown, short-winged species, which is often splashed with greenish patches, is simply called the Lubber Grasshopper. While it is a typical grassland species, it is also found on creosote-tarbush flats, and is particularly common around mesquites.

Another group of grasshoppers to watch for are the slant-faces of the subfamily Gomphocerinae. Many of these species have curiously slanted faces and present a bizarre appearance. This group is generally more attracted to grass-dominated areas and as a result is often a common component of the Chihuahuan. Other orthopterans—including praying mantids ranging from small, ground-dwelling species of the genus *Litaneura* to large species of the genus *Stagmomantis*—may be common but are difficult to see because of their cryptic coloration. Similarly hidden are at least three species of walkingsticks, including one, *Diapheromera covilleae*, that occurs mainly in association with Creosote Bush. Often in the fall I have found *Diapheromera* or the gray walkingstick *Pseudosermyle straminea* to be abundant on shrubs where dozens can be observed in just a few hours; most often they appear in a pair—one male and one female—on a particular shrub.

Beetles are abundant, conspicuous, and often colorful, especially darkling beetles at night, and blister beetles during the day. The large, bizarre blister beetle *Megetra cancellata* grows up to three inches in length and looks like an inflated, oblong balloon of black marked with red with a head attached. It can be so abundant along roadways between El Paso and Carlsbad that cars stop to see what that strange animal is.

Butterflies can be quite common, too, especially during the months when their host plants are available for egg-laying. Even day-flying moths such as the black-blue members of the genus *Ctenucha* may catch your eye; they have metallic-colored wings that are often striped with yellow, and yellow-orange heads. These moths apparently mimic wasps as they feed sitting on flowers.

Ants, wasps—particularly tarantula hawks—and bees are numerous, and many bees are handsome indeed. One family of wasps, the mutilids, or velvet-ants, can be quite common. These insects have a scruffy or furry appearance, and are usually red or white. One of the white species often rests on

Creosote Bush, where, to my eye at least, it looks much like the fuzzy grayish fruit of this plant. Velvet-ants, while attractive, can deliver a painful sting.

Ten or so species of ants may coexist on a single Chihuahuan Desert site. Often these will include five or six seed-foragers, such as the harvesting ants of the genera *Pogonomyrmex* and *Pheidole*. Also included may be two or three arthropod feeders and an omnivore. The seed-foragers vary greatly in their habits, even within the same genus. For example, the Rough Harvester Ant forages in columns, while *Pogonomyrmex imberbiculus* is an independent forager. Some species collect only the cleaned seeds of plants, while closely related species collect the seed and its associated structures (the chaff), which they discard later. It is possible to sit and watch ants for a few hours and to see a diversity of biological strategies that are so complex that they even astonish biologists.

Not as noticeable as the ants are the large numbers of termites that inhabit the Chihuahuan Desert, as well as the Sonoran. Two species, *Gnathitermes tubiformans* and *Amitermes wheeleri*, are subterranean. Both decompose animal feces, especially cattle dung, as well as the dead leaves, branches, and roots of many plants. In a single autumn, they can consume fifty percent of the biomass of Creosote Bush leaves lying on the soil surface. This process releases important chemicals, such as nitrogen, into the soil where plant roots can obtain them for further growth.

In many areas in the Chihuahuan and Sonoran deserts, you can see the surface activities of these or other termite species as they build mudlike tubes over dead wood and on some plants. Some termites damage buildings in desert areas, and termite control is often a big business in our arid-zone cities.

Because of their influences on nutrient cycling, termites, as well as a host of other insects, nematodes, and soil microorganisms, are in part responsible for the marvelous array of plants you see as you stroll the Chihuahuan Desert. Try digging around in the soil a little, particularly where there is dead plant material, and inspect the soil with a hand lens: A remarkable world exists down there awaiting your inspection.

Fish

While more species of pupfish (*Cyprinodon*) occur in the general area of the Chihuahuan Desert than in any other desert, few of these live under truly desert conditions. The exceptions are the White Sands Pupfish, which occurs in pools and creeks associated with Malpais Spring, Otero County, New Mexico, and some populations of the Pecos River Pupfish, a much more widely distributed species traversing nearly the whole of the Pecos River of New Mexico and Texas. Many populations of this species occur in gypsum sinkholes or desert streams, in highly saline water. In the cattail marshes near Boquillas Spring in the Big Bend area of Texas, there occurs an endemic mosquito fish, the Big Bend Gambusia. While many large stream or river fish occur in the Chihuahuan, they are beyond the purview of our coverage.

Rough Harvester Ant
Pogonomyrmex rugosus
387

White Sands Pupfish
Cyprinodon tularosa

Pecos River Pupfish
Cyprinodon pecosensis

Big Bend Gambusia
Gambusia gaigei

Tiger Salamander
Ambystoma tigrinum
289, 290, 291

Couch's Spadefoot
Scaphiopus couchi
274

Western Spadefoot
Scaphiopus hammondi
276

Plains Spadefoot
Scaphiopus bombifrons
275

Woodhouse's Toad
Bufo woodhousei

Great Plains Toad
Bufo cognatus
283

Red-spotted Toad
Bufo punctatus
278

Great Plains
Narrowmouth Toad
Gastrophryne olivacea
282

Rio Grande Leopard Frog
Rana berlandieri
285

Spiny Softshell
Trionyx spiniferus
174

Slider
Pseudemys scripta
172

Yellow Mud Turtle
Kinosternon flavescens
170

Western Box Turtle
Terrapene ornata
173

Texas Banded Gecko
Coleonyx brevis
177, 178

Big Bend Gecko
Coleonyx reticulatus

Amphibians and Reptiles

If you want to see a salamander in a desert, your best chance would be in the Chihuahuan, where you could watch adult Tiger Salamanders crossing the road during a rainfall, or see their larvae in cattle tanks. On rainy nights, you might also find one of three desert spadefoots. Couch's Spadefoot is the most common and thus most likely to be seen. It may be accompanied by the Western Spadefoot in playas and in all but the most extreme desert sites. On grassland-desert transition sites, you might see the Plains Spadefoot.

In these same areas, you may also hear the trills of toads. Woodhouse's Toad can be common along streams and can even be seen in some towns under lights, where it catches insects. The Great Plains Toad is more abundant and more characteristic of desert sites, although it can be found near irrigation ditches and in riparian situations. In sandy soils, especially where there are mesquites, you might encounter a robust but nondescript species, the Texas Toad. Where there is persistent water, the Red-spotted Toad can be locally common. In moist habitats, all of these toads may be found hopping about during the day. The Green Toad is encountered only following heavy summer rains, when it can be heard calling around the edges of temporary ponds.

A call that has been likened to that of a bleating sheep signifies the presence of the small, odd-shaped Great Plains Narrowmouth Toad. This species has a pointed snout and is an ant-eater. It often hides in the burrows of other animals, including tarantulas, both in the Chihuahuan and in the extreme southern portions of the Sonoran Desert.

It should be pointed out that while none of our North American desert frogs are dangerous, several species can cause alarm if you get their skin secretions in your mouth or eyes. Spadefoots can make you sneeze and cry, and Narrowmouths can cause a sharp, alarming pain in your eyes, as can some toads. Wash your hands after handling any amphibian.

In permanent-water situations, such as riparian areas, you may see the Rio Grande Leopard Frog, a very common species in some places. Along the rivers of the Chihuahuan, you might spot a swimming Spiny Softshell, and along the Rio Grande you might see a Slider, a turtle formerly sold in pet shops (plate 3). In cattle tanks or streams you may find the lumbering Yellow Mud Turtle. There is no desert tortoise in the Chihuahuan. The only terrestrial turtle you are likely to encounter is the Western Box Turtle.

A host of lizards inhabit the Chihuahuan Desert. Many, including the Side-blotched, Longnose Leopard, Collared, Western Whiptail, Tree, and Desert Spiny, also occur in the Sonoran and Mojave, and all but the Desert Spiny Lizard occur in the Great Basin Desert.

Less widely distributed species include the nocturnal Texas Banded Gecko, which can be seen on the roads at night. The Big Bend Gecko is much rarer and, indeed, was not discovered until the mid-1950s. Two horned lizards, the Texas Horned Lizard and the Roundtail Horned Lizard, can be

Chihuahuan Spotted
Whiptail
Cnemidophorus exsanguis
210

Desert Grassland
Whiptail
Cnemidophorus uniparens
209

New Mexico Whiptail
Cnemidophorus neomexicanus
211

Colorado Checkered
Whiptail
Cnemidophorus tesselatus
207

Little Striped Whiptail
Cnemidophorus inornatus
208

Crevice Spiny Lizard
Sceloporus poinsetti
198

Eastern Fence Lizard
Sceloporus undulatus

Great Plains Skink
Eumeces obsoletus
213

Lesser Earless Lizard
Holbrookia maculata
192

Greater Earless Lizard
Cophosaurus texanus
204

Glossy Snake
Arizona elegans
268

Longnose Snake
Rhinocheilus lecontei
238, 247

Common Kingsnake
Lampropeltis getulus
234, 246

Night Snake
Hypsiglena torquata
267

Trans-Pecos Rat Snake
Elaphe subocularis
214

found abroad on warm sunny days. The Texas Horned Lizard is much more common and active than the Roundtail and is thus more often encountered, though the Roundtail is by no means rare.

In the other North American deserts, the principal whiptail lizard is the Western Whiptail. Whiptails have evolved more abundantly in disturbed grasslands and desert/grassland transition areas. As a result, the Chihuahuan is an ideal place to see a greater variety of these animals. The Chihuahuan Spotted Whiptail inhabits disturbed areas, such as overgrazed grasslands that have been invaded by shrubs, or washes subject to the disturbance of flooding. All Chihuahuan Spotted Whiptails are females and thus reproduction is by asexual means. A lizard with similar habits, but a slightly different distribution, the Desert Grassland Whiptail is also an all-female species. Of even more limited distribution, and found in disturbed areas of floodplains, is yet another all-female species, the New Mexico Whiptail. Associated with rocks, and occurring as a series of isolated populations, is our largest whiptail, the Colorado Checkered Whiptail. This lizard frequently inhabits floodplains and can be found along the Rio Grande in Big Bend National Park. In more open plains and on desert sites, the blue head and tail of the Little Striped Whiptail are a distinctive sign of this species, one that contains both genders.

Of the spiny lizards, the Crevice Spiny Lizard is often the most noticeable but the hardest to capture. This large lizard has a dark neck band and occurs in rocky areas. When frightened, it wedges itself into crevices, where it resists capture effectively. Among the yuccas and shrubs you may spot a smaller spiny lizard, one of the forms of the Eastern Fence Lizard.

Two diurnal skinks—sleek, shiny lizards—can be found in the Chihuahuan Desert, but only the large Great Plains Skink is abundant. This secretive animal is hard to find without turning over rocks, especially along riparian areas.

Two other lizards deserve mention. The Lesser Earless Lizard occurs in grassy areas and on bajadas with sandy soils. A very light, almost white, form occurs on the dunes of White Sands National Monument in New Mexico. Usually more common in desert shrub areas is the fast and elusive Greater Earless Lizard. This speedster occurs in rocky flats and along washes; it is often seen crossing the road in the daytime.

Most of the Chihuahuan snakes are similar to those encountered in other North American deserts. The common species you might see during the day include the Gopher Snake, Western Patchnose Snake, and Coachwhip. At night the Glossy Snake, Longnose Snake, Common Kingsnake, and Night Snake are common and widespread.

Nighttime wanderings may also reveal some Chihuahuan Desert specialities. Two of these are among the most beautiful snakes in North America. The Trans-Pecos Rat Snake has H-shaped black markings against a yellowish background. These snakes are partial to rocky areas on desert slopes but are

Mexican Kingsnake
Lampropeltis mexicana
242, 243

Lyre Snake
Trimorphodon biscutatus
262, 270

Texas Blind Snake
Leptotyphlops dulcis
225

Western Blind Snake
Leptotyphlops humilis
226

Western Hooknose Snake
Gyalopion canum
266

Western Hognose Snake
Heterodon nasicus
261

Western Diamondback
Rattlesnake
Crotalus atrox
256

Prairie Rattlesnake
Crotalus viridis viridis
258, 260

Blacktail Rattlesnake
Crotalus molossus
248

Mojave Rattlesnake
Crotalus scutulatus
259

Rock Rattlesnake
Crotalus lepidus
250, 257

Massasauga
Sistrurus catenatus
264

Trans-Pecos Copperhead
*Agkistrodon contortrix
pictigaster*
244

often seen on the road at night. A snake with less subtle coloration is the Mexican Kingsnake. This species is quite variable in appearance, with different combinations of gray, black, and orange crossbands in varying hues and intensities. A distinct form of the mildly poisonous Lyre Snake, a rear-fanged species, occurs in areas with limestone outcrops and rocks. Two species of blind snakes occur in the Chihuahuan Desert. The Texas Blind Snake and the Western Blind Snake both have specialized feeding habits, eating ants and termites at all stages of development, and are seldom seen except following rains or when digging.

Two snakes with conspicuously upturned noses can be encountered in grassland-desert transition areas. The small Western Hooknose Snake is usually less than a foot in length. The Western Hognose Snake is typically twice this size and is more often found in desert areas than the Hooknose. This Hognose has enlarged rear teeth with which it punctures toads that have inflated themselves to prevent being eaten.

Several venomous snakes occur in the Chihuahuan Desert. Of the rattlesnakes, the largest is the Western Diamondback, a species common throughout the desert. A form of the Western Rattlesnake, the Prairie Rattlesnake, can be found along with the Diamondback in many areas, particularly in New Mexico. The attractive Blacktail is usually found on slopes, particularly at higher elevations. The highly toxic Mojave Rattlesnake occurs on Creosote Bush flats. Occasionally, you may come upon a small, darkly banded rattlesnake whose base coloration varies from near purple, through browns and blues to whites. This is the Rock Rattlesnake, a reptile common on talus slopes in pine-oak forests, but that also occurs in arroyos on desert flats, among rocks on limestone outcrops, and among boulders on the upper portions of bajadas.

Finally, two types of venomous snake that do not occur in our other deserts can be seen in isolated areas of the Chihuahuan. In the grassland/desert transition areas all the way to the Arizona/New Mexico border, you may encounter a rather uncommon rattlesnake, the Massasauga. There is one section of Creosote Bush flat in New Mexico where, at least once a week for short periods in the summer, I would see one on the road at night, or killed the next morning. This is a spottily distributed, retiring species.

A form of Copperhead, the Trans-Pecos, is sometimes found in the desert areas of the Big Bend of Texas. More likely, however, you would see it in riparian situations, such as the cane bottoms along the Rio Grande in Big Bend National Park.

As in the other hot deserts, reptiles abound in number and diversity in the Chihuahuan. Patience, care, and a sharp eye can enable even the rank amateur to see ten or more species of these fascinating creatures in the course of a few days of desert trekking.

Birds

As is the case in the Sonoran, the avifauna of the Chihuahuan

Turkey Vulture
Cathartes aura
30

Red-tailed Hawk
Buteo jamaicensis
36, 537

Common Raven
Corvus corax
82

Chihuahuan Raven
Corvus cryptoleucus
81

Loggerhead Shrike
Lanius ludovicianus
96

Northern Mockingbird
Mimus polyglottos
90

Crissal Thrasher
Toxostoma dorsale

Gambel's Quail
Callipepla gambelii
47

Scaled Quail
Callipepla squamata
46

Green-tailed Towhee
Pipilo chlorurus
05

Ash-throated Flycatcher
Myiarchus cinerascens
73

Vermilion Flycatcher
Pyrocephalus rubinus
72

American Kestrel
Falco sparverius
42

Swainson's Hawk
Buteo swainsoni
34, 535

Harris' Hawk
Parabuteo unicinctus
33

Zone-tailed Hawk
Buteo albonotatus

Desert is limited in richness. Breeding species number roughly thirty across the United States portion of the desert, twenty to twenty-five in any one good area, but ordinarily ten to twelve species in the more extreme desert areas. Densities are not high. There may be seventy breeding pairs per one hundred acres, a figure a bit lower than averages in the Sonoran. In the more extreme sites, the species list is virtually the same as in similar areas of the Sonoran Desert.

Birds you are likely to see soaring overhead are the Turkey Vulture, the Red-tailed Hawk, and the Common Raven. In some places you actually may be confusing the Common Raven for the Chihuahuan Raven. The two are very difficult to differentiate, but the Chihuahuan is a somewhat smaller and more social bird. It is a bit more common in desert grasslands than in more extreme desert environments. The Mourning Dove is common, much more so than the White-winged Dove, which has a limited distribution in the Chihuahuan.

In scrub areas, two domed-nest builders, the Verdin and the raucous Cactus Wren, can be found nesting in tall shrubs and chollas. A bright flash of gray, black, and white might draw your eye to either the silent, voracious predator, the Loggerhead Shrike, or to the noisy Northern Mockingbird. Two small, abundant birds are the desert-specializing Black-throated Sparrow, a species found in the harshest areas of all four North American deserts, and the Black-tailed Gnatcatcher, a hot-desert specialist most often associated with washes or riparian situations.

The Crissal Thrasher, the Curve-billed Thrasher, and the Sage Thrasher may be seen, sometimes even together, during a warm winter. The Crissal Thrasher is most often sighted. In many areas, you may see or hear the very loud call of Gambel's Quail, but the most characteristic quail of the Chihuahuan Desert and the surrounding grasslands is the Scaled Quail. Its blue-gray, scaled appearance makes it easy to identify.

In shrubby areas or places where mesquites abound, you can see the Greater Roadrunner, perhaps carrying a whiptail lizard in its mouth. In such areas you might also spot one or both elusive towhees. The Green-tailed actually prefers higher elevations or more northern sites. It is common in the Great Basin, but winters in the Chihuahuan Desert area. The Brown Towhee is more common but is a rather drab, retiring bird and is easily overlooked.

In riparian areas, the Ash-throated Flycatcher can be seen, as can Say's Phoebe. In some areas, such as Big Bend National Park, you might even see the spectacular scarlet and black Vermilion Flycatcher.

Hawks and owls of the Chihuahuan include the American Kestrel, often seen sitting on power or telephone lines; Swainson's Hawk, a dark-breasted species that "cruises" the plains; and the attractive but much less common Harris' Hawk. Occasionally you can spot a Zone-tailed Hawk, a species that generally prefers canyons, flying over desert rivers. At dusk the Lesser Nighthawk takes to the sky. Later you may hear the call of the Elf Owl, although you'll probably have to

Black-chinned
Hummingbird
Archilochus alexandri
563

Sage Sparrow
Amphispiza belli
611

House Finch
Carpodacus mexicanus
617, 618

Horned Lark
Eremophila alpestris
576

Northern Cardinal
Cardinalis cardinalis
600, 601

Pyrrhuloxia
Cardinalis sinuatus
602, 603

Scott's Oriole
Icterus parisorum
616

Hooded Oriole
Icterus cucullatus
614, 615

Blue Grosbeak
Guiraca caerulea
604

Varied Bunting
Passerina versicolor

Ladder-backed
Woodpecker
Picoides scalaris
567

Black-tailed Jack Rabbit
Lepus californicus
509

Coyote
Canis latrans
523, 524

be near a tree, such as those that grow in the riparian zones. The hummingbird most likely to be seen is the Black-chinned. A short trip into the mountains in places like Big Bend National Park could yield an additional ten species.

The Sage Sparrow is locally common at upper elevations, as is the House Finch. In grassy areas, Horned Larks, moving in active flocks, can be quite numerous.

Finally, there is a group of rather striking birds, hard to miss when present. They may have limited distributions, however, or small population sizes, and you may not see them. These include the Northern Cardinal and its cousin the Pyrrhuloxia. Both birds are most apt to be seen where large trees occur, such as along streams. The same is true for the orioles that occur in desert areas. The most common of this group is Scott's Oriole, whose lemon-yellow body and black head and chest distinguish it from the more spottily distributed Hooded Oriole. Two other eye-catching birds are the Blue Grosbeak and the less common Varied Bunting.

You might also see one of several woodpeckers, also colorful birds. The most likely candidate is the Ladder-backed Woodpecker, a species typically found in areas with mesquite, and one that favors Century Plants, which it uses for nesting sites and where it feeds on the larvae of the Agave Beetle.

Winter or spring birding in the Chihuahuan Desert can be quite rewarding. Midsummer can be disappointing, but some careful searching at the right times will produce numerous species to add to your life list.

Mammals

The mammals of the Chihuahuan Desert are diverse, and to me they have always seemed more conspicuous than the mammals of the other deserts. To be sure, there is still a strong nocturnal component that is difficult to observe; nonetheless, several large mammals reach fairly high population densities and are easily seen. This probably has something to do with the relative abundance of vegetation and its annual productivity in the Chihuahuan compared with other deserts. The direct result of more available plant matter, especially grasses, is the presence of a greater number of plant-eaters (herbivores); in turn, these herbivores are available as food for more carnivores.

Daytime desert strolls reveal some of the same species encountered in other deserts. As in other deserts, Black-tailed Jack Rabbits are usually the most obvious species. This is not always the case, however. In some years you might not be able to find a single individual, because their numbers seem to vary in a somewhat cyclic fashion, as do those of their main predator, the Coyote. These population fluctuations are not as predictable as those described for the same species in the Great Basin. Coyotes and jack rabbits both range over a variety of habitats, especially the Coyote, but they are most abundant in desert and desert/grassland areas of the Chihuahuan.

Desert Cottontail
Sylvilagus audubonii
508

Spotted Ground Squirrel
Spermophilus spilosoma
503

Mexican Ground Squirrel
Spermophilus mexicanus
502

Texas Antelope Squirrel
Ammospermophilus interpres
500

Rock Squirrel
Spermophilus variegatus
505, 506

Mule Deer
Odocoileus hemionus
528

Pronghorn
Antilocapra americana
527

Collared Peccary
Dicotyles tajacu
525

Badger
Taxidea taxus
514

Kit Fox
Vulpes macrotis
521

Gray Fox
Urocyon cinereoargenteus
522

Ringtail
Bassariscus astutus
511

The Desert Cottontail may also be seen during the day, though both cottontails and jack rabbits are much more apt to be spotted at dawn or dusk, or in the lights of your car.

A number of diurnal ground squirrels might also be observed. Two of these have spotted backs. The Spotted Ground Squirrel is characterized by small, irregular spots on a reddish-brown background. This squirrel ranges widely through the Chihuahuan Desert and arid grasslands of North America. In desert areas, it can be associated with mesquites, ephedras, and yuccas, but it occurs in Creosote Bush–dominated areas as well. The Mexican Ground Squirrel, a considerably larger animal, actually has larger, more conspicuous spots that are arranged in nine rows. It does not cover the same extremes of habitat as the Spotted and it has a more restricted geographic range; however, it is common around farms, and in areas near the Rio Grande in Big Bend National Park.

The Texas Antelope Squirrel, a striped rodent, prefers rocky areas, particularly in middle elevations, but it also occurs with chollas and Creosote Bush at lower elevations. The Rock Squirrel is found in rocky areas ranging from Creosote Bush–Lechuguilla habitats up into the mountains.

Mule Deer might be seen in the cool of winter, but you have a greater prospect of seeing—usually at a considerable distance—the unusual and elegant Pronghorn. Pronghorns are most common in areas with a good cover of grasses and forbs, and thus are found regularly only in the grassland/desert transitions.

Another large animal to look for is the Collared Peccary, or Javelina. Peccaries are usually social, forming small herds of five to ten individuals. In the winter, they occur on desert bajadas, where breeding takes place from November to February. From March to June they spend more time in the cooler washes and they drop their young from May to July. Peccaries eat a great number of plants, but Lechuguilla constitutes between eleven and forty-one percent of their diets. They eat mainly the roots and center core, discarding the tough outer leaves. The pads of prickly pear are often included in their diets, but not as often as in the Sonoran Desert.

Occasionally you may also spot a Bobcat bounding up a boulder-strewn slope or in riparian areas, where they hunt for rodents and rabbits. In more open areas, you may sight a Badger in search of lizards or rodents. This is a good animal to leave alone: Badgers can be aggressive.

To see other carnivores, take a nighttime stroll armed with a flashlight. As you walk, particularly in winter, you may hear Coyotes and see the quick movements of one of two foxes. The more "deserty" fox is the Kit Fox. In moister, cooler sites you might see the Gray Fox. The two are easily distinguished by the size of their bodies and ears and by the black stripe that runs down the top of the Gray Fox's tail. (The only black on the Kit Fox's tail is at the tip.) Both species are omnivorous. Also likely to be seen at night are a series of striped, or banded, medium-size mammals. The graceful Ringtail is usually seen near areas with large rocks or boulders; it

Raccoon
Procyon lotor
512

Western Spotted Skunk
Spilogale gracilis

Hooded Skunk
Mephitis macroura

Striped Skunk
Mephitis mephitis
515

Hog-nosed Skunk
Conepatus mesoleucas
516

Merriam's Kangaroo Rat
Dipodomys merriami
485

Ord's Kangaroo Rat
Dipodomys ordii
480

Banner-tailed Kangaroo
Rat
Dipodomys spectabilis
483

Silky Pocket Mouse
Perognathus flavus
471

Desert Pocket Mouse
Perognathus penicillatus
477

Rock Pocket Mouse
Perognathus intermedius

Nelson's Pocket Mouse
Perognathus nelsoni

Plains Harvest Mouse
Reithrodontomys montanus

Hispid Cotton Rat
Sigmodon hispidus

Northern Grasshopper
Mouse
Onychomys leucogaster
491

Southern Grasshopper
Mouse
Onychomys torridus
488

generally does not occur on the flats, but can be common on rocky slopes, covered with desert vegetation, that are dissected by washes or canyons. The Raccoon can be found virtually anywhere there is permanent water.

The black-and-white pattern seen in the beam of your light signals the presence of a skunk and is always a warning to proceed cautiously. Four skunks occur in the Chihuahuan Desert and are frequently seen as road kills. All are associated with moist situations, such as ravines, riparian zones, and high elevations. The smallest and most distinctive is the Western Spotted Skunk. The Hooded Skunk, a typical striped species, is much less common and has a limited distribution. The distinctive hood of long hairs on its neck is usually white. The two more frequently encountered skunks are the Striped, a very common species that can be a pest around campgrounds, and the Hog-nosed. The Hog-nosed Skunk has a single wide white stripe extending from its head through its nearly all-white tail. This large, strong skunk has a long, broad nose and long claws that are adapted for digging.

The nocturnal mouse brigade is quite diverse. Depending on where you are, you could see one or two of four Chihuahuan kangaroo rats (*Dipodomys*), as well as perhaps five pocket mice (*Perognathus*). In most places, regardless of soil type, you will encounter Merriam's Kangaroo Rat. Like other kangaroo rats, Merriam's are seed-eaters, but supplement their diets with insects and leaves. Roughly the same size, but with five hind toes rather than four, and living predominantly in sandy areas, is Ord's Kangaroo Rat. The Banner-tailed Kangaroo Rat is much larger in size and has a striking white tuft on its tail. This animal prefers grass habitats more than the other two, but may also be found in many areas containing Creosote Bush. Like all kangaroo rats, these giants—the largest in their genus—are gentle, except to one another—the males can be quite quarrelsome.

Of the pocket mice the small, soft Silky Pocket Mouse or the medium-sized Desert Pocket Mouse are most likely to be seen. They often occur together, though the desert pocket mouse is less often found in gravel- or rock-dominated soils. The Rock Pocket Mouse can occur with these other two, especially in New Mexico and extreme western Texas, though it is more characteristically found, as its name implies, in rocky areas. To the east and south of the Rock Pocket Mouse, in areas such as the Big Bend of Texas, Nelson's Pocket Mouse dominates the rocky areas.

The grass component of Chihuahuan Desert communities permits several mammals more characteristic of grasslands to occur. Two harvest mice are occasionally found. Very rarely, you might see the Plains Harvest Mouse. You have a better chance of seeing the Western Harvest Mouse in grassy areas, such as the edges of playas on sandy soils. The Hispid Cotton Rat is also associated with grassy sites, such as tobosa swales and riparian situations. This is a large rodent, the size of a house rat, and can be seen in its runways, even during the day. Either the Northern or Southern Grasshopper Mouse

Cactus Mouse
Peromyscus eremicus
92

Deer Mouse
Peromyscus maniculatus
89

White-ankled Mouse
Peromyscus pectoralis

Botta's Pocket Gopher
Thomomys bottae
69

Desert Pocket Gopher
Geomys arenarius

Yellow-faced Pocket Gopher
Pappogeomys castanops

Southern Plains Woodrat
Neotoma micropus

White-throated Woodrat
Neotoma albigula
494

Beaver
Castor canadensis

Porcupine
Erethizon dorsatum
507

Spotted Bat
Euderma maculatum
462

Brazilian Free-tailed Bat
Tadarida brasiliensis
465

Pallid Bat
Antrozous pallidus
464

could be seen in extreme western Texas, near El Paso, and in New Mexico. The Northern is most common in sandy areas, while the Southern is more often found on gravelly sites. Only the Southern Grasshopper Mouse extends into the Big Bend area.

The Cactus Mouse and the Deer Mouse occur in habitats similar to those in which they are found in the Sonoran. The Cactus Mouse is a true desert form occurring even in quite arid sites, while the Deer Mouse is tied to much less arid areas. In the rocky upper elevations of the desert/grassland transition, you might see the White-ankled Mouse, a species not met with elsewhere.

Pocket gopher mounds dot the Chihuahuan Desert landscape. Botta's Pocket Gopher can be found throughout, while the Desert Pocket Gopher is confined to the El Paso area and to New Mexico. On dry sites with more than eight inches of soil, a third species, the Yellow-faced Pocket Gopher may abound. On your walks you may see the homes of two woodrats. In the open desert scrub areas, usually in patches of cactus or dense thorny shrubs, you may spot the home of a large steel-gray species, the Southern Plains Woodrat. Sometimes in the same type of habitat, especially in New Mexico and the northern portions of the Chihuahuan Desert in Texas, you will see the White-throated Woodrat. This is a buff-colored species that, while found in deserts in the north, is typically associated with rocky areas and higher elevations in the south, particularly in the Big Bend country.

The largest rodent in desert areas is the Beaver, a species found only in riparian habitats with permanent water; today it is much less common in desert streams and rivers than it was in presettlement times. Another large rodent you might see is the Porcupine. While some people doubt that this is a desert species, it is often seen in areas dominated by Creosote Bush, but also where other plant species are common. I have seen dozens of dead Porcupines between El Paso and Carlsbad and also south into the Big Bend. They also occur in certain areas of the Sonoran Desert, where I once watched one level a Creosote Bush.

Finally, at dusk you may see any one of a dozen bat species, especially along riparian zones. Even though bats can fly in from elsewhere and could thus be found in virtually any vegetation type, several species are desert specialists. Included is the attractive Spotted Bat, named for the three large white spots on its black back. Its very conspicuous ears can be seen even at night. Two more common species, with wider habitat distributions, are the Brazilian Free-tailed Bat, famous for its great numbers in "guano caves," and the most abundant bat of all, the large pale, Pallid Bat.

With its rich and diverse animal life, the Chihuahuan Desert offers the visitor countless opportunities to learn much about desert wildlife, both day and night.

THE CHIHUAHUAN DESERT: PLANTS AND ANIMALS

Wildflowers

Angel Trumpets 104
Apache Plume 96
Arizona Blue-Eyes 69
Arizona Jewel Flower 107
Blackfoot Daisy 92
Buffalo Gourd 140
Chia 64
Chihuahua Flax 149
Claret Cup Cactus 42
Climbing Milkweed 83
Coulter's Lupine 72
Crescent Milkvetch 50
Cushion Cactus 40
Desert Anemone 91
Desert Christmas
Cactus 162
Desert Four O'Clock 52
Desert Gold 145
Desert Marigold 128
Desert Poppy 155
Desert Rosemallow 151
Desert Tobacco 103
Devil's Claw 117
Fairy Duster 48
Feather Dalea 49
Fendler's Bladderpod 146
Filaree 57
Freckled Milkvetch 163
Golden Prince's
Plume 109
Indian Blanket 60
Jackass Clover 110
Little Golden Zinnia 138
Little Snapdragon Vine 74
Melon Loco 141
Mexican Gold Poppy 148
Night-blooming
Cereus 87
Pale Trumpets 66
Paleface 45
Peyote 37
Plains Pricklypear 121
Puncture Vine 143
Rainbow Cactus 123
Ratany 56
Rattlesnake Weed 102
Rough Menodora 142
Scalloped Phacelia 65
Speading Fleabane 89
Spectacle Pod 79
Spike Broomrape 76
Sweet-scented
Heliotrope 101

Tahoka Daisy 62
Texas Silverleaf 47
Trailing Four O'Clock 59
Tree Tobacco 114
Trixis 106
Western Peppergrass 78
White Horsenettle 73
Yellow Spiny Daisy 131

Reptiles

Blacktail Rattlesnake 248
Chihuahuan Spotted
Whiptail 210
Coachwhip 223, 229,
230, 233
Collared Lizard 200, 201
Colorado Checkered
Whiptail 207
Common Kingsnake 234,
246
Copperhead 244
Crevice Spiny Lizard 198
Desert Grassland
Whiptail 209
Desert Spiny Lizard 199
Glossy Snake 268
Gopher Snake 263
Great Plains Skink 213
Greater Earless Lizard 204
Little Striped
Whiptail 208
Longnose Leopard
Lizard 191
Longnose Snake 238, 247
Lyre Snake 262, 270
Massasauga 264
Mexican Kingsnake 242,
243
Mojave Rattlesnake 259
New Mexico Whiptail 211
Night Snake 267
Rock Rattlesnake 250, 257
Roundtail Horned
Lizard 193
Side-blotched Lizard 202
Slider 172
Spiny Softshell 174
Texas Banded Gecko 177,
178
Texas Blind Snake 231
Texas Horned Lizard 196
Trans-Pecos Rat
Snake 214
Tree Lizard 205

Western Blind Snake 226
Western Box Turtle 173
Western Diamond
Rattlesnake 256
Western Hognose
Snake 261
Western Hooknose
Snake 266
Western Rattlesnake 258,
260
Western Whiptail 206
Yellow Mud Turtle 170

Amphibians
Great Plains Toad 283
Green Toad 287
Plains Spadefoot 275
Red-spotted Toad 278
Rio Grande Leopard
Frog 285
Texas Toad 280
Western Spadefoot 276

**Trees, Shrubs,
Cacti, and Grasses**
Arrow Weed 314
Banana Yucca 306
Creosote Bush 312
Fluffgrass 331
Four-wing Saltbush 322
Gregg Catclaw 303, 317
Honey Mesquite 308, 321
Indian Ricegrass 332
Lechuguilla 307
Mariola 326
Mexican Palo Verde 307
Mormon Tea 334
Ocotillo 305
Rabbit Brush 310
Screwbean Mesquite 302
Snakeweed 311
Soaptree Yucca 328
Sotol 308
Tamarisk 304, 324
Tarbush 320
Torrey Yucca 330
Tree Cholla 303
Winter Fat 324

Insects and Spiders
Creosote Bush
Grasshopper 368
Desert Tarantula 399
Giant Vinegarone 398

Lubber Grasshopper 370
Pallid-winged
Grasshopper 369
Rough Harvester Ant 387

Mammals
Badger 514
Banner-tailed Kangaroo
Rat 483
Black-tailed
Jack Rabbit 509
Bobcat 517, 520
Botta's Pocket Gopher 469
Brazilian Free-tailed
Bat 465
Cactus Mouse 492
Collared Peccary 525
Coyote 523
Deer Mouse 489
Desert Cottontail 508
Desert Pocket Mouse 477
Fulvous Harvest
Mouse 487
Ghost-faced Bat 451
Gray Fox 522
Hog-nosed Skunk 516
Merriam's Kangaroo
Rat 485
Mexican Ground
Squirrel 502
Mule Deer 528
Northern Grasshopper
Mouse 491
Ord's Kangaroo Rat 480
Pallid Bat 464
Porcupine 507
Pronghorn 527
Raccoon 512
Ringtail 511
Rock Squirrel 505
Spotted Bat 462
Spotted Ground
Squirrel 503
Striped Skunk 515
Texas Antelope
Squirrel 500
Western Harvest
Mouse 486
White-throated
Woodrat 494

Birds
Ash-throated
Flycatcher 573

Bewick's Wren 587
Black-chinned
Hummingbird 563
Black Phoebe 570
Black-tailed
Gnatcatcher 588
Black-throated
Sparrow 610
Black Vulture 529
Brown-headed
Cowbird 613
Brown Towhee 607
Burrowing Owl 559
Cactus Wren 584
Canyon Wren 586
Common Nighthawk 560
Common Poorwill 562
Curve-billed Thrasher 593
Elf Owl 558
Gambel's Quail 547
Golden Eagle 540
Golden-fronted
Woodpecker 566
Great Horned Owl 556
Greater Roadrunner 554
Ground Dove 553
Harris' Hawk 533
Hooded Oriole 614
Horned Lark 576
House Finch 617
Inca Dove 552
Ladder-backed
Woodpecker 567
Lesser Nighthawk 560
Loggerhead Shrike 596
Mourning Dove 551
Northern Cardinal 600
Northern Flicker 568
Northern
Mockingbird 590
Pyrrhuloxia 602
Red-tailed Hawk 536
Rock Wren 585
Sage Thrasher 591
Say's Phoebe 571
Scaled Quail 546
Scott's Oriole 616
Swainson's Hawk 534
Turkey Vulture 530
Verdin 583
Vermillion Flycatcher 572
Western Kingbird 575
White-necked Raven 581
White-winged Dove 550

SOME SPECIAL VEGETATION TYPES COMMON TO ALL DESERTS

Some habitat types are highly localized within the general desert landscape, frequently because the plants that they support require specific soils. The vegetation structure and even the species composition within these specialized habitats may be virtually the same anywhere these conditions occur. Thus habitats such as playas, sand dunes, sites containing gypsum soils, and riparian situations may be quite similar anywhere they occur in the four North American deserts. Because of this similarity, these habitats are dealt with separately here.

Riparian Vegetation

The term riparian has quite different meanings to different people. The concept used here is that riparian vegetation is made up of those plants that occur along drainageways and associated floodplains that differ from the species in the surrounding desert.

This definition specifically considers as riparian habitats a wide spectrum of drainage-channels. Even small rills in desert landscapes may alter vegetation composition and form. In a particular spot, for example, a quick look might suggest that the area is dominated by Burrobush and Creosote Bush, and perhaps supports a few other species. Closer scrutiny reveals that in fact the majority of the Burrobushes are arrayed in lines that follow tiny drainages that are less than two inches deep. This situation, of course, is more subtle than are riparian systems along a major watercourse, where a stream channel and usually two well-developed terraces parallel the river (plate 3). The first terrace is the area encompassing the normal flood excursions of the river. One to eight feet above this is the second terrace, which marks the area covered only by extreme floods.

On the first terrace, trees such as willows and cottonwoods grow close to the water. Farther back on the terrace, where th soil is saturated, is a band of Arrow Weed. Even farther back is a zone containing Screwbean and Quail Bush, as well as a variety of plants from other genera.

The second terrace is the zone most often occupied by the mesquites. These trees may form veritable forests, which are generally referred to as bosques, a word of Spanish origin. Bosques were a common sight along desert rivers at the turn o the century. They stabilized banks and encouraged the accumulation of silt that was rich in organic matter. The extent of such areas varied according to the flooding pattern o each river. However, these natural patterns were altered by th appearance of dams and irrigation channels.

In addition, the introduction of Tamarisk and other members of the Old World genus *Tamarix* severely affected bosques composed of native species. Tamarisk was introduced into the United States in the early 1800s as a decorative species, and it is still planted for this purpose in many arid areas of the world. This species is a rapid spreader: A single plant may produce 600,000 seeds per year. Furthermore, its leaves secrete salt, an adaptation to reduce the tree's salt content. As

Burrobush
Hymenoclea salsola
365

Creosote Bush
Larrea tridentata
342

Arrow Weed
Pluchea sericea
344

Screwbean
Prosopis pubescens
302, 311, 320

Quail Bush
Atriplex lentiformis

Tamarisk
Tamarix chinensis
304, 324

esert Willow
hilopsis linearis
06

eep Willow
accharis glutinosa

esert Broom
accharis sarathroides

pache Plume
allugia paradoxa
6

alifornia Washingtonia
'ashingtonia filifera
27

noke Tree
alea spinosa
05, 313, 334

ermilion Flycatcher
rocephalus rubinus
72

a result, surface soils under the tree accumulate salts, which inhibit the germination and establishment of non-salt-tolerant natives. Finally, the large quantities of litter produced by Tamarisk encourage fire. Tamarisk can resprout from its roots following fire, while many native species cannot. All these factors aid the spread of Tamarisk and reduce the numbers (and influence) of such native species as mesquite.

Other second-terrace or minor-channel species include Desert Willow, a relative of the Catalpa, whose linear leaves and lavender flowers catch the eye; Seep Willows and Desert Broom, species whose brilliant green colors set them off, even during dry periods; and Apache Plume, which has beautiful white flowers, and fruits that are characterized by light pink featherlike plumes. At least two species of acacias are also abundant in this area.

The predominance of acacias and mesquites in riparian situations has been attributed to their semitropical origins. In the areas where these genera probably evolved, warm, moist conditions prevail. Their presence in a warm desert along a moist watercourse should therefore be of no great surprise.

A few quite unusual plants are bound to riparian situations. The most spectacular is probably the California Washingtonia, an attractive palm that occurs in California and in a very few scattered locations in western Arizona.

Another species, one that follows very closely the middle of drainage channels without permanent water, is Smoke Tree. At a distance, this plant resembles a puff of smoke.

Permanent water is, of course, required by many fishes and some amphibian species. However, it should be equally obvious that animals requiring vertical structure in their environment, and not necessarily a stream *per se,* can find a haven among riparian plants. It has been documented that fifty to eighty percent of all species known to occupy broad geographic ranges within American deserts are influenced by the presence of a riparian environment.

Of some 308 bird species in the Sonoran Desert, about twenty percent are confined to riparian settings; another sixty percent or so can live in, and are frequently found in, riparian environments. Certainly the hordes of White-winged Doves that nest in these areas—they are intimately related to the presence of mesquites—attest to the importance of the riparian zone for some bird species. Some, such as the Vermilion Flycatcher, are seen almost exclusively in riparian situations or near spring-fed ponds.

In deserts, bats are most often associated with free-standing water. Most species can be observed as they swoop to obtain a drink or to feed on insects hovering above the water. Large mammals find refuge in riparian bosques. Although they may occur in other habitats or throughout the desert, the population densities of medium-size and large mammals are greatest in riparian systems. Certain species—for example, Muskrats and Beavers—are virtually confined to riparian habitats.

The management of riparian areas is of considerable

importance to humans. Flood control, hunting, fishing, boating, swimming, picnicking, irrigation, and erosion control are all important uses of riparian systems. These actions are not only related to the health of the systems, but they also influence man. You need only watch the thousands of people who sit in innertubes and float down desert rivers (such as the Verde and Salt rivers in Arizona), and who follow their ride with a picnic and "a cool one" under the mesquites, to realize the recreational value of riparian systems, to say nothing of their economic importance—both direct and indirect. Historically, riparian zones were of utmost importance to native Americans, who often positioned their villages in relation to riparian habitats. Although we sometimes try to ignore their importance to the contemporary citizens of the desert, these ecological systems will not let us forget their importance. In many desert areas, including some farmlands and towns, floods would not have taken place—or at least would have been less severe—if the protective nature of riparian vegetation had been left unaltered.

Sand Dunes

Sand dunes occur in all North American deserts, where they cover approximately six percent of the land surface (plates 4 and 5). For the most part, the dunes are composed of particles ranging between 0.13 mm and 0.5 mm in diameter. These grains are generally silicon dioxide but they may also derive from gypsum, a calcium sulfate compound (plate 6).

Sand dunes are principally formed by the action of wind, specifically—because of the tiny size of sand particles—by a process termed eolian saltation (a wind-induced bouncing of the grains along the surface). Such movement results in the formation of a variety of dune types. These can be classified into three general categories based on the relative strength of the wind, the supply of sand, and the amount of vegetation cover (which is not independent of the other two factors). Longitudinal dunes are long in comparison to their width, and they are symmetrical in cross section. They form where there are strong winds and little sand. Transverse dunes are shorter and somewhat asymmetrical in cross section. They lie close to one another and are of variable length. Transverse dunes usually support little vegetation and develop under low to moderate winds in areas of moderate to enormous supplies of sand. U-shaped dunes, as their name implies, are shaped like gigantic letter U. Their arms trail behind the advancing dune. (This situation differs from another dune with a horseshoelike shape, the barchan, a type of transverse dune whose arms precede the dune in its forward movement.) U-shaped dunes develop where there is moderate wind, moderate vegetation coverage, and moderate supplies of sand.

Active, or moving, dunes of any type can create problems for plants. Established plants may be covered by moving sand, or conversely, the movement of sand away from plant roots may expose them. In addition, active dunes contain few plants to enrich the sandy "soil," and the sand grains themselves do no contain many of the nutrients essential to plant growth. These disadvantages are somewhat balanced by an advantage: the relatively high availability of water in sand dunes. With soils that are composed of particles that are finer than sand—especially clays—water is bound tightly to soil particles and may not be very available to plants' root hairs. However, because of the larger size of sand particles, all of the rainfall occurring on a dune is essentially sopped up, sponge-fashion, by the dune sands. Little runoff or erosion occurs; the water is loosely held to the sand grains and is thus available to plants. Thus, a dune—seemingly dry on the surface—is one of the more mesic sites in a desert.

Plants overcome the negative aspects of dune existence by employing a number of mechanisms. The rapid growth of stems and branches can prevent a plant from being buried, while the production of long, horizontally directed roots helps to keep part of the root anchored in the soil. In the Algodones Dunes (on the southern portion of the Arizona-California border), you can see large numbers of these exposed root systems. Follow one of them for several yards to the "shrub" portion of the plant, and you will find sand dune specialists such as Sand Dune Buckwheat and Croton. The rapid growth rates necessary for the plant to keep ahead of the sand occur in over fifteen families of North American plants. These high rates also require that the dune plants have very high rates of photosynthesis and that these high rates occur throughout the year—not just during short growing seasons—for sand may move any time there is wind, regardless of season.

The nutrient problems facing dune plants are solved by at least two mechanisms. Some dune plants survive simply by being tolerant of low nutrient conditions. Other species may form symbiotic relationships, either with vesicular-arbuscular mycorrhyzal fungi that aid in the uptake of water and phosphorus, or with nitrogen-fixing bacteria, or with both. Dunes may contain numerous plant species. One can find sixty species on the gypsum dunes of White Sands National Monument in New Mexico; ninety-seven species on the Algodones Dunes in California; and fifty-three species on the Coral Pink Sand Dunes in Utah. This plethora of plants includes species that are endemic to the particular dune systems; dune specialists with wider distributions; and, in dunes that have become more stabilized, an assortment of desert plants from nearby areas. The latter may include Creosote Bush, any one of several saltbushes or even mesquites.

Gypsic Soils

Gypsum, a form of hydrous calcium sulfate, occurs around the world in many climates. Most commonly, however, gypsum soils—which range from gypsic rock outcrops to moving dunes, ninety-six percent of which are composed of gypsum "sands"—occur in semiarid or arid areas.

Plants that occur on gypsic soils may be highly selected, depauperate (undersized) samples of the flora growing on the

[marginal notes:]
Sand Dune Buckwheat
Eriogonum deserticola

Croton
Croton wigginsii

surrounding nongypsic soils. In most cases, however, there is also a group of obligate gypsophiles (species that live only on gypsum soils).

In the United States, gypsum soils occur in both deserts and other areas, but they are especially common in the West. Perhaps the best-known of such sites is the 225-square-mile area in New Mexico that includes the White Sands National Monument, whose "white sands" are actually gypsum particles. This area contains about sixty species of plants. Of this number, roughly ten percent are obligate gypsophiles. These include a perennial grass, *Bouteloua breviseta*, which occurs in a number of gypsic areas of the Chihuahuan Desert; some perennial herbs (*Nerisyrenia linearifolia, Nama carnosum,* and *Tequila [Coldenia] hispidissima*); and some dwarf shrubs (*Frankenia jamesii* and *Pseudoclappia arenaria*). In general, this array of grasses, perennial herbs, and dwarf shrubs typifies the gypsophiles found in all gypsum soils.

Few true gypsophiles occur as tree forms. Although a number of relatively large plants—from shrub-size species to small treelike plants—occur on gypsic soil, all of them occur on

Fremont Cottonwood
Populus fremontii var.
wislezenii

Soaptree
Yucca elata
328

Squaw Berry
Rhus aromatica

other soils as well. These include a variety of Fremont Cottonwood (*Populus fremontii* var. *wislezenii*), as well as Soaptree and Squaw Berry, all of which show contorted stem and root forms on gypsic dunes.

It is not at all clear why plants find gypsum soil to be such a harsh environment. While some scientists have suggested that gypsum soils are saline as well, and that salinity is the limiting factor, this often does not seem to be the case. It may be that a high amount of calcium or sulfur is the culprit. The question of whether sulfur is a toxic component for plants in general is actively being researched, and answers concerning the possibility of sulfur acting as a plant poison in gypsum soils may be forthcoming in the near future.

Nonetheless, some genera of plants are tied to gypsum soils. Where gypsic and nongypsic soils abut one another in a clearly demarcated way, the gypsophilic and nongypsophilic plants undergo an equally abrupt transition. In places where gypsum soils are covered by as little as an inch of nongypsic materials, the flora contains no gypsophiles. The species with such sharp responses belong to a number of families and genera. Three of the more prevalent ones in the United States are *Tequilia,* a genus in the forget-me-not family, which contains seven gypsophiles within one group of nine closely related species; *Sartwellia,* a genus in the sunflower family, whose four species are all gypsophiles; and *Nerisyrenia,* an herbaceous genus in th mustard family that is composed of nine species, all but one o which are gypsophiles. This is but a small portion of the North American genera that contain gypsophiles; they occur in some fourteen plant families.

The best representation of gypsophiles occurs in the Chihuahuan Desert. This is in line with the general geographic pattern, which is that gypsum areas in the North have fewer gypsophiles than do apparently equivalent areas in the South.

The flora occurring on gypsic soils consists of an unusual, albeit geographically limited, assemblage of plants. A number of species may be rare enough to qualify as threatened or endangered. Indeed, certain species that have existed since before 1950 in White Sands National Monument have not been conspicuous in more recent times.

Animals do not seem to differentiate as readily between gypsic and nongypsic soils as do the plants. The most obvious adaptation in a place like the White Sands National Monument is that the animals that live in the white-colored gypsum areas are lighter in color than the same species in the immediately adjacent, nongypsic areas. The visitor is most likely to notice this in one of two light-colored lizards, or perhaps a light-colored weevil or tiger beetle. This concession to the environment is not intrinsically related to gypsum; the same adaptation would occur in response to any light substrate.

Playas and Saline Soils

In arid zones, standing water usually contributes to an increase in the salinity of the soils beneath it. Ordinarily this is merely a result of the accumulated water evaporating; as it does, salt is concentrated in the remaining water until all the water is evaporated, whereupon salts are left in the lowest ground areas. The salinization of the surface soil can also occur when salts move upward within the soil profile as water evaporates. Saline soils and playas, or ephemeral lakes, are closely linked. During dry periods, playas are merely expanses of saline soil. Playas are, in essence, temporary lakes that are dry for much longer periods than they are wet. Ordinarily they are formed by the runoff from entire watersheds, but some have more localized origins. Playas lose very little of their water through percolation into the soil; as a result, water flowing into a playa translates directly into variations in the lake volume.

There are nearly 50,000 playas in the deserts of the world. Most are small, seldom exceeding thirty-six square miles. Playas are not uniform in physical, chemical, or biological properties from one place to another. The lowest areas—those that are wet for the longest time—usually contain very fine soil particles, such as silts and clays. Toward the edges, coarser particles, such as sands, occur. Salinity follows a similar gradient; it is highest in the middle and decreases toward the outside edges. The depth of the water table with respect to the surface also varies from playa to playa. The combination of these three factors—the salinity, the soil characteristics, and the proximity of the water table—to a large extent determines the distribution of plants around various playas.

Many secondary features develop in playas. If springs are involved, the sediments they deposit may be cemented into mounds. In some places in the world (for example, Lake Eyre in Australia) these mounds may be over thirty feet tall. Mound structures may also develop from wind-borne sediments that are trapped by the bases of plants. The size of a mound is determined by the plants' ability to get their roots to water.

Greasewood
Sarcobatus vermiculatus
345

Iodinebush
Allenrolfea occidentalis

Sea Purslane
Sesuvium verrucosum

Pickleweed
Salicornia rubra

Saltgrass
Distichlis spicata

Thus if the water table is too deep, significant mounding does not occur. A good example of a plant-mediated mound formation can be seen on the salt flats at the northern end of Utah's Great Salt Lake, where large areas are covered with mounds that are a foot or two high; these have formed in nearly pure stands of Greasewood. In other places in the Southwest, such mounds may reach almost ten feet in height. Salt crusts of varying shapes and patterns can develop. Often the crusts are formed as polygonal plates of fine-grained soil, which are separated from each other by cracks. Together they look like the scales on a giant turtle's back. Pits, which are formed when gases from decomposing organic matter escape, are another example of secondary saline-soil structures.

Most plants have a relatively low tolerance for salinity. In crop plants, salinities above one tenth of a percent can cause physiological reactions. On the other hand, salt-tolerant desert species and plants occuring in salt marshes along the edges of oceans may tolerate up to six percent salinity.

Plants in saline areas face unique difficulties. First, they must be tolerant of the specific chemicals forming the salts on a given site. Salt types vary but usually involve compounds that have been formed from calcium, magnesium, or sodium, and that have reacted with chloride, sulfate, or carbonates.

Second, because the soil is saline, water moves toward the area of highest salt concentration, not toward the plant—a situation that can make it difficult for a plant to take up water. Some plants may take up particular salts; this gives their cells high salt concentrations while allowing them to retain water, or, in technical terms, to maintain their turgor (a plant that has not kept its turgor is wilted).

But there is a limit to how much salt can be accumulated without ill effect. Plants deal with this constraint in several ways. Some develop a tolerance to high salt concentrations. Others become succulent. A succulent plant stores water in its tissues; this gives its leaves or stems a watery, distended appearance. The stored water enables the plant to dilute the salts it takes up. Finally, some plants actively excrete salts through hairs or pores on their leaves. This is the case with certain species of saltbushes (*Atriplex*).

The variation in the capacity of different plants to manage salts and the differences in salt content in the soils around playas together cause zones of vegetation to develop.

The most highly saline areas characteristically contain the succulents Iodinebush, Sea Purslane, seepweeds (*Suaeda*), and Pickleweed, as well as a species of grass, Saltgrass. Pickleweed, one of the most salt-tolerant species in the United States, can endure up to six percent salinity. It is often the only species on open, flat salt pans. Interestingly, it is not very drought-tolerant; thus it is often excluded from certain saline areas because they are too dry, not because they are too salty. The seepweeds are very salt-tolerant; there are some fourteen species in North America, and several of these are locally common in the deserts. Certain species, such as the widespread *Suaeda depressa*, are very plastic: They can alter their form to suit the environment. In saline soils, this species adopts a dwarfed, prostrate growth form or, alternatively, exists as a single-stemmed, upright plant. In soils with lower salinities, the plant is much more robust and may have several upright stems. (Such variation in the very form of a plant is a taxonomist's nightmare.)

Iodinebush, though often occurring with Pickleweed, has a lower salt tolerance. It frequently forms low hummocks by trapping wind-borne soil particles, and such areas can dominate large areas around playas or swales (depressions). Saltgrass has shallow roots and forms rhizomes in areas that are less saline than those tolerated by the other species mentioned. In somewhat less saline areas of the playa, we begin to see a moderate number of shrubs, representing roughly two to six species. These are frequently saltbushes (*Atriplex*) or greasewoods (*Sarcobatus*). Numerous grasses or grasslike plants also occur in such areas, and they may be quite dense.

Where there is some standing water, as in saline springs or seeps, several submerged aquatic plants, all extremely salt-tolerant, may occur. Perhaps the three most common species from the Great Basin to the Chihuahuan Desert are Horned Pondweed, Widgeongrass, and Fennelleaf Pondweed. All three have virtually worldwide distributions. These species often provide food for ducks and other migratory birds.

Horned Pondweed
Zannichellia palustris

Widgeongrass
Ruppia maritima

Fennelleaf Pondweed
Potamogeton pectinatus

When playas fill with water, numerous invertebrates may occur in great numbers. These include ostracods and cladocerans (both are groups of tiny crustaceans); the larvae of a variety of insects, especially including hardy species like the brine flies of the family Ephydriadae; and certain mosquitoes. All of these species usually have broad environmental tolerances and are able to occupy fresh to saline water.

Vertebrates capable of responding to ephemeral sources of water are generally amphibians. As if from nowhere, spadefoot toads (*Scaphiopus*) come out following rains to form deafening choruses. They are often accompanied by true toads (*Bufo*) and occasionally by a few other frogs as well. When flooded, playas may harbor the Tiger Salamander or even an occasional mud turtle (*Kinosternon*), as long as the salinity is not too great.

Tiger Salamander
Ambystoma tigrinum
289, 290, 291

Human beings have more than a passing interest in saline soils and the plants that grow in them. Expansion of agricultural productivity into the desert areas of the world will require either the creation of salt-tolerant varieties of current agricultural crops or the selection of new species with the potential for human use. Four-wing Saltbush has promise as a forage crop. Eighteen to twenty percent of its content is protein, a level comparable to that in alfalfa. It is easily digested by cattle and sheep. This species and others such as Russian thistles (*Salsola*) and mollies (*Kochia*), which can be burned as fuel, may allow us to put arid "wastelands" into agricultural production. While work is going forward at a rapid rate with regard to using native, salt-tolerant plant species for agriculture, much remains to be done. We have barely tapped the potential of our desert areas to provide resources for human beings.

Four-wing Saltbush
Atriplex canescens
352

ASPECTS OF THE BIOLOGY OF DESERT ORGANISMS

The extreme nature of desert environments presents a myriad of problems to the plants and animals that inhabit them. But just as there are a variety of problems, there are also a great number of solutions to these difficulties. Desert animals and plants fascinate and amaze me with their adaptations, which in some cases, are quite complex. In others they are simple, even though they solve complex problems.

Just a few of the adaptational problems faced by desert species are listed below. In fact many species have developed adaptations to several of these problems, and some individual adaptations solve more than one problem. Remember that one of the most common adaptations to desert conditions is simply to avoid its rigors altogether.

Some of the problems are these: 1. Water is in low supply most of the time. When present, it often occurs in floodlike quantities. 2. Water occurs at unpredictable intervals and in unpredictable quantities. 3. Summer daytime temperatures may be extremely high. 4. The difference between daytime and nighttime temperatures may be extreme. 5. Loose substrates, which are easily blown about and difficult to traverse, may dominate the landscape. 6. Because vegetation is sparse and open, concealment from enemies is difficult, and there is little protection against the harsh environment.

Plants

We are used to seeing trees, shrubs, flowers, and cacti in deserts. It may be surprising, however, to realize that algae and fungi occupy deserts as well, since these plants are usually thought to inhabit moist areas. Actually, certain algae and fungi, as well as lichens—the symbiotic outcome of the association of the other two—may be significant elements in the desert landscape.

Nonflowering Plants

Algae—both green and blue-green forms—are common in the surface soils of deserts. More than one hundred species are known to inhabit the deserts of North America. Their prevalence is often inversely related to the proportion of land area covered by taller plants: Where shrubs are common, algae are not as abundant. The number of soil algae also decreases with depth. Virtually no algae are found twenty inches below the surface of the ground.

The algae in deserts survive the high temperatures and low water levels as a result of their physiological durability. Algae preserved in dry soil for over fifty years may remain viable, "greening up" when they come in contact with water. These microorganisms have certain advantages because of their small size. Because they can live in the spaces between soil particles, they can derive moisture from the dew condensed on the soil surface out of the cool night air, or from condensation within the soil pores themselves. They may even obtain the water that condenses under rocks. An interesting example of this desert adaptation can be seen by picking up a somewhat translucent rock, such as quartz, that is exposed at the surface of the desert soil. Often the sides and bottoms of such rocks are covered with algae. These plants receive sufficient light *through* the rock to carry on photosynthesis, and they use as a source of water the moisture on the underside of the rock.

In addition to occurring in the soil and under rocks, algae can also be found in rock crevices and, astonishingly, within the very fabric of the rock itself. In both of these cases, water is made available to the plants, and the rocks provide protection, to some extent, from extreme heat.

Fungi occur in desert soils, and in part are responsible for the development of crusts on the soil surface. If you wish to examine a crust, you can, with care, remove a hand-size chunk that is up to an inch thick. Microorganisms, including algae, fungi, and lichens, bind the soil particles together with their "bodies"; this helps to hold down soil erosion.

More commonly recognized, above-ground, mushroom forms of fungi also occur in deserts. Such species include the common Desert Inky Cap, which occurs practically worldwide in desert areas that are as low as sixty-five feet below sea level. A species of more northern distribution is the Desert Stalked Puffball, which ranges as far north as Alaska. Another species, the Buried-stalk Puffball, is most common in sandy areas, including sand dunes.

Some fungi form a symbiotic relationship with higher plants. The structure resulting from this association, called a mycorrhiza, resembles root hairs and occurs in the same place on plants as roots do. The association helps the plant take up water and phosphorus. Many desert shrubs, trees, and flowers have such an arrangement; indeed, virtually ninety percent of all plant species worldwide are involved in these mycorrhizal associations. Scientists are studying this relationship with great intensity. One reason for such studies involves the difficult task of reestablishing plants in arid lands that have been used for mining. In cases where the plants being used for restoration are mycorrhizal species, it is important that the fungus be locally available to form the mycorrhizae. Such plants will fare much better in the harsh environment when the proper fungus exists and the symbiosis develops.

Lichens are quite abundant in deserts, both on the soil surface and when attached to plants in areas where fog occurs. They are also found on rock surfaces on the upper portions of bajadas. The lichens and algae that form soil crusts can capture nitrogen from the air. They put the nitrogen compounds required for plant growth into the biological cycle and, as a result, improve soil fertility. During times of the year when moisture is available, it "activates" the crusts, stimulating high rates of biochemical activity.

Other nonflowering plants may be common on certain specialized desert sites. Ferns occur in rock crevices or beneath the edges of boulders, places that funnel water to the plant. Such strategic locations, which also reduce insolation, help the fern to survive the desert's rigors. Desert ferns have adapted to tolerate repeated and prolonged dehydration; in addition, they are covered with "hairs" that reflect light and may thus insulate the fronds. Both of these strategies aid survival. The

Desert Inky Cap
Podaxis pistillaris
66

Desert Stalked Puffball
Battarrea phalloides
67

Buried-stalk Puffball
Tulostoma simulans
68

Resurrection Plant
Selaginella lepidophylla

capacity to rehydrate following prolonged desiccation is a rather spectacular adaptation in a fern ally, the Resurrection Plant of the Chihuahuan desert.

Mosses occur sporadically in deserts. You may walk for miles and never see one, and then suddenly be surrounded by them. They are often concentrated in small mats beneath shrubs or under cactus clumps. While they frequently look dried and dead, simply spitting on them will revitalize many species before your eyes, revealing—as if by magic—the green, photosynthetically active tissue.

Annuals

Annuals, or ephemerals as they are often called, cannot withstand drought. When dry conditions occur, the plant shrivels and dies. It is the function of the seed to withstand dry periods and to be the source of the next generation. Thus, these plants, which are so very characteristic of the desert, evade the worst of desert conditions.

North American desert annuals fall into two broad groups that coincide with the seasons of maximum rainfall. Thus winter annuals are those that respond to precipitation occurring in late fall, winter, and early spring, while summer annuals respond to the precipitation in summer and early fall. The hot deserts vary in their seasonal rainfall characteristics, and, as a result, so do the concentrations of the various annuals. The Mojave Desert is primarily a winter-annuals area; the Chihuahuan Desert, a summer-annuals area (plate 31); and the Sonoran Desert, with its biseasonal rainfall peaks, contains both winter and summer annuals (plates 32 and 33). The Great Basin Desert exhibits a paucity of native annuals, but, as one would expect, those that do occur are of the winter type.

The adaptation of annuals involves more than their ability to germinate in response to a particular pattern of seasonal rainfall. In contrast with winter annuals, summer annuals are taller, tend to be more weedy (to occur in disturbed sites), include many grasses, and have leaves that do not exhibit typical desert adaptations.

Of particular significance is a difference in the chemical pathways by which photosynthesis occurs in these two groups. Two types of photosynthesis are recognized. Plants of one photosynthetic group are termed C_4 plants. This name derives from the number of carbon molecules (four) in the specific chemical produced by photosynthesis. The other common group includes plants whose photosynthetic product (at an early stage) is a three-carbon chemical (C_3 plants).

Most summer annuals are C_4 plants, while most winter annuals are C_3 plants. C_4 plants carry on photosynthesis more effectively at high temperatures and high intensities of light, use water more efficiently, and produce more material than C_3 plants do under the same extreme conditions. C_3 plants, on the other hand, germinate during cool periods, often forming rosettes of leaves that hug the ground. Such rosettes may heat up quite a bit, even during cold periods, because they are at the ground surface. When the air warms later in the year, the ground surface is too hot for leaves, so these species frequently change their form and "grow up" out of the soil's surface, leaving behind its microclimate.

C_3 and C_4 plants also differ morphologically (in terms of their form and structure). To dissipate heat, the leaves of C_4 species are often subdivided into leaflets, or have serrated margins. C_3 species more often have simple (single-bladed), entire (nonserrated and nondivided) leaves. There are also internal anatomical differences that are not obvious to the unaided eye, and which we will ignore here.

The amount of rainfall greatly affects the relative abundance of annuals in different years. In general, more rainfall produces more annuals. But the situation is more complex. Winter and summer annuals both have a mechanism, involving a response to temperature and day length, that limits germination to the right time of year. This can protect a plant from responding to an unusual, potentially lethal, weather situation—one that gives favorable cues that might induce premature germination. If a winter annual were fooled into germinating by a summer rain, it might succumb to the high temperatures of the summer days—a situation to which it is not adapted. The detailed interactions of all of these environmental factors, and their effects on the germination of desert annuals, constitute an area of scientific inquiry at this time. Until explanations are forthcoming, suffice it to say that when conditions are just right, the desert bursts into a spectacular bloom.

The spatial pattern formed by adjacent annuals and perennials is also different for C_3 and C_4 plants. Winter annuals occur widely across sites, while summer annuals are more often found in the spaces between shrubs. Loosely canopied perennials such as palo verde and Creosote Bush harbor more annuals than do shrubs forming tight canopies such as bur sages (*Ambrosia*).

Certain early studies suggested that some plants might produce chemicals that inhibit annuals from growing under their canopies. This chemical inhibition of one plant by another is termed allelopathy. Allelopathic chemicals are often hypothesized or inferred to have a significant influence in desert systems. However, since some shrubs often have annuals in their shade, and certain annual species are virtually always found under shrub cover, the real importance of allelopathic chemicals in nature is still a matter of scientific debate.

One final adaptation should be mentioned. It is clear that if all the seeds of a particular species germinated under favorable conditions and then a disaster occurred, the species might not have time to reproduce. As a result, the species would be lost until other seed arrived from surrounding areas. To prevent this situation, not all seeds of the same species germinate synchronously. Thus, while many seeds germinate under favorable conditions, a number of seeds are reserved in the soil for another "good" time. This certainly underlines the fact that while annuals avoid desert conditions, this "avoidance" is based on numerous highly adapted mechanisms.

The Biology of Desert Organisms

Perennials

Since perennials, by definition, must live for more than one growing season, they cannot escape the dry conditions of the desert in the same way that annuals do. It is true that the seeds of perennials give them a hedge against repeated bad years, which might ultimately kill mature plants, and that, in this way, they perform much like the seeds of annuals. However, it is the shrubs or trees themselves that must endure the desert conditions—and to which we turn our attention.

Perennials have a variety of strategies to survive drought situations. One group of species is referred to as the drought-avoiding water-savers. These species usually have one or more structural adaptations that cause them either to lose water more slowly or to store water when it is available. Among the more common adaptations are thick leaf or stem coverings (cuticles), which seal water in the plant; reduced exposure of the plant's surface area to the air, which minimizes drying; and succulent tissues with the capacity to store water. Cacti provide good examples of all of these modifications.

When you look at a cactus plant, you are actually viewing a stem—the fleshy portion of the plant—that is covered with the remnants of leaves—the spines. By being leafless, the cactus has reduced its total surface area and thus does not lose water at as high a rate as a leafy plant does. The tissues that in its extinct forbears formed leaves have been modified into spines. These may keep some animal predators away, and they also insulate the stem surface from solar radiation.

In some temperate species of cacti, leaves develop for a short period. Such leaves are small and short-lived, and thus are seldom seen by the the casual visitor.

Virtually the whole center of a cactus (the pith), as well as the outer perimeter (the cortex), are composed of water and food-storing tissues. A woody support material exists between these two layers and can be seen in the form of the intricately sculpted pieces of cholla skeletons lying on the ground in the hot deserts, or of the long, spearlike ribs of the Saguaro in the Sonoran Desert.

Saguaro
Cereus gigantea
331

The water-impervious cuticular waxes are best developed on the sunny side of a cactus. In highly exposed species, such as the tall, columnar Saguaros, the differences in the wax thickness on various portions of the plant can be very significant. If you were to purchase a large Saguaro to be transplanted to your yard, you would want to make sure that it was replanted with its sunny side—the side with the thick cuticle—facing the sun. If you were to reverse the sides, the plant could be burned. Such damaged areas might make the Saguaro vulnerable to attack by fungi, which would cause its tissue to rot. Subsequently, the plant would die or, at the very least, its body would be deformed.

Another adaptation of cacti is to keep their stomates closed during the hot day. Stomates are the pores in the surfaces of leaves or stems, which allow plants to take in or give off gases, and through which water, usually taken up from the soil by roots, is lost. Most plants open their stomates during the day.

In deserts, cacti open their stomates during the cool of the night instead and thus decrease the amount of water lost. This adaptation creates another problem. To manufacture food, plants change carbon dioxide and water into sugar. Part of the complex series of reactions necessary to do this must be performed in the presence of light. Since the cactus takes up its carbon dioxide at night, in the dark, it cannot complete photosynthesis. Instead, in contrast with the chemistry of most other plants, the cactus takes up the carbon dioxide and then produces and stores an acid compound known as malic acid. This substance is later used to complete the food-manufacturing process during the day, when light is available but the stomates are closed. This specialized chemical system is called crassulacean acid metabolism, or CAM for short. The name is derived from a plant family—the Crassulaceae, or stonecrops, which contains a host of succulent species familiar to most peoples as hen-and-chickens, bryophyllums, or sedums—all of which possess CAM. In fact eighteen families of plants and more than 110 genera have species that use CAM. Most of these are succulents. In the American deserts, in addition to the cacti, both yuccas and agaves have CAM. The shallow, broadly spreading root systems found in most species of cacti represent yet another adaptation. This feature allows cacti to take up water, even from light rain.

Some cacti use several adaptations. They avoid drought and save water by taking up water rapidly (shallow roots), storing large quantities (succulent stems), and sealing it off from the air (impervious cuticles, low surface area of stems, leaflessness, and practice of opening stomates at night).

A different desert-plant strategy, as unlikely as it may sound, is to be a water spender. Phreatophytes, the species that have this adaptation, use water at very high rates. In order to do this, these species must exist where there are quantities of water, and they must have root systems that are extensive enough to get at it. They usually occur along ravines, arroyos, streams, or rivers. Such species generally have more root material below ground than they have shoot material above. This arrangement is due to the fact that the plant's uptake of water is proportional to the amount of root material, and its loss of water is proportional to the amount of above-ground material. Many desert plants—not just water spenders—have nine times as much root material, by weight, as shoot material.

Phreatophytes have been a topic of controversy in the American Southwest. Because they take up so much water and simply "spend" it by way of transpiration into the air, some observers have believed that their presence along watercourses decreases the water available for human use. They have thus been regarded as pests that must be removed or controlled. The situation is a bit more complex, however. In general an area of land covered by phreatophytes loses less water than a site of equal size where they have been removed, because of the lower temperatures produced by the shading the plants provide. Furthermore, the organic matter produced by such plants increases the water-holding capacity of the soil, and the plants' presence helps prevent the runoff of rainfall. Such plants also provide excellent wildlife habitat in areas characteristically devoid of dense vegetation. On balance, phreatophytes would seem to be a positive presence, though they can be nuisances, as when you are trying to force your way through almost impenetrable stands.

Still other strategies of coping with the desert exist. Some species of perennials have the capacity to withstand drought by avoiding dehydration. These plants generally have small, deciduous leaves. When water is in short supply, they shed their leaves, reducing the surface area exposed to water loss. Certain of these species have green stems, branches, or trunks, and can carry on photosynthesis even without their leaves, in a manner parallel to that exhibited by the cacti. The palo verdes (*Cercidium*) are of this type. The translation of their common name, "green stick," alludes to their trunk color, which is imparted by the presence of chlorophyll. Palo verdes may produce forty percent of their annual food supply through stem photosynthesis.

Ocotillo
Fouquieria splendens
335

Other plants that can avoid dehydration are the Ocotillo and its relatives. Like cacti, the Ocotillo has shallow, spreading root systems. During the dry season, its long, spiny stems are leafless. These spines actually develop from the midribs and petioles (stems) of the leaves. During wet periods, leaves develop along the whole wandlike axis of the stem. When several periods of rainfall occur, separated by drought, Ocotillo responds to each with a flush of leaves, which it subsequently sheds. Thus, on many Sonoran Desert sites, there are regularly two crops of leaves per year, coinciding with the biseasonal rainfall.

Most of these dehydration-avoiders close their stomates when even very slight water stress occurs. This closure, while preventing water loss, also prevents the exchange of gases. Thus, since these species cannot use CAM, as the cacti do, they cannot carry on photosynthesis. As a result, the plants begin to starve: Their leaves turn yellow, probably because they are moving nutrients out of their leaves into their stems as a conservation device. The leaves then die and drop off.

The last general group of species are termed the drought- and dehydration-tolerant species. These simply dry out. They manage to survive because their tissues can withstand drying without damage. Extreme examples from this category are lichens, mosses, and the Resurrection Plant. Some of these species can produce two very different types of leaves: one suited for moist periods, and another set that is better adapted to dry periods. The Brittlebush is capable of this, as are certain salt bushes (*Atriplex*) and Big Sagebrush. When water is particularly scarce, such plants may shed their leaves, though some, such as Creosote Bush, remain evergreen. The production of these different leaf types is quite complex. Leaves may differ in a number of ways, including size; pubescence, or hairiness; and thickness. Not all of these characteristics are equally affected by all environmental

Brittlebush
Encelia farinosa
136

Big Sagebrush
Artemisia tridentata
353, 357

factors. For example, in Brittlebush at least, solar radiation primarily affects leaf thickness, while soil-water availability is a primary regulator of leaf length and growth rate.

Up to this point, I have ignored the biotic interactions of plants in deserts. Rather we have discussed the ways in which plants cope with the extremes of the desert's abiotic milieu. Here I turn to the biological interactions that represent responses to desert environments.

The spatial distribution of perennials follows various patterns. Broadly speaking there are three such general dispersion patterns. In the first one, each plant is roughly equidistant from every other plant; this is referred to as a regular dispersion pattern. Plants that follow this pattern to the extreme are spaced as equally as corn plants in a field or trees in an orchard. The second category consists of plants that follow a clumped dispersion pattern. These individuals grow close to each other in patches that are scattered across the landscape. In the third dispersion pattern, plants are distributed at random. This random dispersion pattern is not as likely to occur as the other two patterns, because organisms and their resources are not usually distributed at random in nature. An understanding of the reasons for these various patterns can reveal a great deal about the biology of the organisms involved.

The usual explanation for the regular dispersion pattern is that the organisms are competing for a resource such as water or nitrogen, and that each plant has defended its own living space. Experiments have shown that this is sometimes the case in deserts. The best example of this is probably Creosote Bush. These plants are thought to compete with one another for water. Since Creosote Bush is so long-lived, it may grow until its roots extend and interfere with the roots of another, adjacent Creosote Bush. This is in fact likely, because the roots of Creosote Bushes all eventually reach a similar depth, and horizontal spread of their roots is also similar.

In many areas of the desert, plants—including Creosote Bush —are not found in regular arrays. Instead they form clusters, arranging themselves according to the clumped dispersion pattern. It is believed that a particular resource that the plants require also has a clumped dispersion pattern, and that the plants can survive only where that resource is present. For example, they may cluster around a resource such as a localized zone of soil nitrogen, existing like a lens of nutrient material in the soil column. If the clump consists of a mixture of different species, the plants may be able to avoid competition: As long as each species has a different rooting strategy, it can obtain the resources it needs from a different soil level than the others do.

In each of North America's hot deserts, large complicated clusters of three to ten perennial species occur. These clusters have been best studied in the Mojave. In many places, annuals cluster under the cover of perennials.

Some clumped patterns are particularly interesting. Young Saguaro plants often grow under subtrees—especially beneath palo verdes. The young cactus benefits in several ways. It is shaded from intense sun and has available a good deal of organic matter derived from the litter collected under the palo verde. At the Saguaro's northern distributional limit, it may even gain some protection from freezing because of certain complex relations of radiation patterns. As the Saguaro grows, it begins to compete with the palo verde. The shallow, widely spread roots of the cactus intercept rainfall before it can percolate into the soil where the deeper palo verde roots occur. The palo verde, unable to acquire sufficient water, then dies, and the adult Saguaro survives. As palo verdes become established and grow on other sites nearby, Saguaros begin to germinate in their shade, and this long-term cycle repeats itself. The desert landscape is a rich mosaic of all the stages of this dynamic interaction.

It has been suggested that a similar cyclical situation exists in the Chihuahuan Desert. Birds and mammals feed on the fruits of the Desert Christmas Cactus and deposit its seeds beneath Creosote Bushes. The cactus grows and its superficial root system begins to take up the water that the Creosote Bush needs. The Creosote Bush dies. Exposed, the cactus eventually succumbs to the influences of rodents and wind, and dies, leaving an open space that can be colonized by Creosote Bush —and the cycle begins again.

Plants also interact with animals. On the positive side, there are a host of plant-pollinator interactions. The forty-odd species of the genus *Yucca*, for example, are all pollinated by three moth species in the genus *Tegeticula*. Of the desert yuccas, the Joshua-tree is pollinated by *T. synthetica*, while all others are pollinated by *T. yuccasella*.

The cycle begins when the female moth mates with the male moth inside a yucca flower. She gathers pollen from that flower, then speeds off to another plant and inadvertently fertilizes it. Her eggs are then laid in the ovary of the flower, and the larvae feed on the developing fruit, killing some—but not all—of the developing seeds. Ultimately the larvae leave the fruit and drop to the ground. In this complex relationship, the plant gets pollinated and the moth has a site and food for larval development.

Many other desert plants require insect pollinators, but not always in such a specific relationship. The Desert Willow can be pollinated by any of a number of bee species, whose common characteristic seems to be their large size. Although dozens of bees and beetles are known to pollinate cacti, the number of individuals of one species that you see visiting a flower doesn't attest to that species' importance as a pollinator. Some visitors are simply nectar thieves.

Vertebrates also pollinate some desert plants. Bats are known to pollinate agaves and Saguaros and hummingbirds pollinate red-flowered species such as Ocotillo.

Even though all of these examples of plant-animal pollination are interesting, deserts are prime areas for wind-based pollination as well, since they are open and windy. Many dominant desert species are wind-pollinated.

Desert Christmas Cactus
Opuntia leptocaulis
162

Joshua-tree
Yucca brevifolia
326

Desert Willow
Chilopsis linearis
306

Indian Ricegrass
Oryzopsis hymenoides
362

Buckthorn Cholla
Opuntia acanthocarpa

Pollination is not the only positive relationship existing between desert animals and plants. Seeds stored in soil caches by rodents are sometimes the ones most likely to germinate and become the next generation of plants. This has been observed in the Great Basin, where several rodent species store the seeds of Indian Ricegrass.

Animals can also protect plants from other animals. The Buckthorn Cholla produces nectar, not only in its flowers, but also within the developing tissue of new stems. This nectar attracts ants. One pugnacious ant species (*Crematogaster opuntiae*) attacks cactus-feeding insects in the Sonoran Desert and thus offers the plant a degree of biological protection.

Despite the many positive associations that exist between plants and animals, their roles are usually that of food and feeder. Many plants, however, have evolved mechanisms to prevent becoming food. Some build up chemical compounds in their leaves and stems that deter animals. In deserts a more obvious adaptation is the presence of spines, thorns, and prickles, which deflect herbivores.

If an animal removes a chunk of a plant, the plant suffers in two ways. First, the integrity of the plant's body surface is broken, and it may desiccate or become prone to disease attack. Second, since many resources, such as water, are not constantly available in deserts, a stem or a leaf cannot be replaced readily.

Interestingly, many of the browsers that may have prompted the evolution of spines—for example, the giant ground sloth of Pleistocene times—are extinct. Thus the presence of spines on desert plants today may be a result of interactions that occurred thousands of years ago, rather than one that we are likely to observe now.

There are thousands—even millions—of interactions between species that occur daily in deserts; biologists have not even begun to catalog them, to say nothing of understanding them. Any avid naturalist in the desert may happen onto one of these interesting relationships simply by sitting quietly and watching desert plants.

Animals

Desert animals face the same problems as plants and often solve them in a similar manner. For example, the hairiness of some animals and the dense spininess or hairiness of some plants may reflect solar radiation, which would otherwise increase the organisms' body temperature. Similarly, thick layers of waxes or other material seal the water of plants or insects inside their bodies.

One striking difference does exist between the two groups: Animals are more mobile than plants and can often avoid environmental problems by moving away. Such avoidance adaptations take a variety of forms. On a daily basis, an animal may adjust the time of its activity to reduce exposure to environmental stress. Active only at night, nocturnal animals feed and seek mates during the coolest, most humid part of the day. Other animals are crepuscular—active at dawn and dusk. During these periods, there is more light, but favorable temperature and humidity conditions still persist. Animals can also avoid stress by migrating out of the desert during extreme periods, then returning during more hospitable times. Despite these vagility considerations, many animals stick it out; they have evolved morphological, physiological, and behavioral traits that are astonishingly diverse.

Invertebrates Other Than Arthropods

Except for arthropods, which have impervious body coverings that resist water loss, invertebrates are not conspicuous in deserts. Some groups, such as snails, are abundant and conspicuous in some desert areas of the world, but are not nearly so obvious in the United States, though they may be observed locally. Minute forms such as protozoans undoubtedly occur as common elements of the soil fauna, but they have not been studied in detail, and thus we know little about their role in desert ecosystems or their adaptations, if any, to desert conditions. Their ability to form cysts, an encapsulated resting stage that may last for tens of years, makes them well-suited to desert environments, though this adaptation occurs wherever they exist and consequently is not really a desert-specific adaptation. Food sources such as bacteria and fungi, organisms that feed on plant residues, are periodically abundant in desert soils. We would expect then that periodically protozoans might also be common, and the few available studies suggest that they are.

Two groups of worms, the round worms (nematodes) and the segmented worms (annelids), have desert representatives. The most familiar annelids are the earthworms. Since earthworms require moist conditions, they rarely occur in the desert, except in sites such as riparian situations that are unusually high in soil moisture and organic matter.

A less familiar group of annelids, the enchytraeids, have been isolated in plant-litter samples retrieved from Chihuahuan Desert soils. They often feed on fungi, which, as we have noted above, are often abundant in desert soils.

Nematodes are as difficult to work with as enchytraeids. Luckily, however, scientists have expended considerable energy to find ways of studying them in desert soils. In general, they have found that nematodes occur in greater numbers beneath shrubs than in the open areas between shrubs. Also, their numbers decrease with depth. Thus, under a shrub in the Mojave Desert, there may be as many as 230 nematodes in a cubic inch of soil near the surface. The number drops to about sixty just ten inches below the surface, and to thirty or so in the surface soils between the plants.

Nematodes display a variety of feeding adaptations. Some species are fungus-feeding specialists, while others feed on microbes; still others are voracious predators or even parasites of plants. According to the available studies, microbe feeders predominate in desert soils.

Even though you could capture about one million nematodes

for each square yard of desert soil, not all of these individuals would be biologically active at any one instant. During unfavorable times, nematodes have the ability to go into a resting state, during which their metabolism is virtually unmeasurable. In essence the animals wrinkle up and dry out, but do not die. When water is again available, the nematodes "return to life." A great deal of variability exists in the spatial distribution of soil characteristics such as water content. This means that in one zone of a few cubic inches, there may be a veritable riot of nematode activity, while in an adjacent few cubic inches, all life may be in a resting state.

Arthropods

The vast majority of conspicuous desert invertebrates are arthropods, which include wind or sun scorpions (solpugids), true scorpions, spiders, mites, insects, millipedes, centipedes, and even forms more generally thought to be aquatic, such as crustaceans.

Desert-avoidance adaptations are numerous in arthropods. Crustaceans such as fairy shrimp, clam shrimp, and tadpole shrimp, which inhabit playa lakes during periods of water sufficiency, undergo periods of inactivity, during which their development is arrested and their metabolism is diminished. This period of arrested metabolism is termed diapause. It can occur at almost any developmental stage, and it occurs widely within the phylum Arthropoda. When the proper environmental cues recur—especially the presence of water—these species commence development at a rapid rate and complete their life cycles in a short time.

A variety of insects and arachnids spend the hottest and driest portions of the day and year in burrows. Sometimes these burrows have been constructed by other animals, such as rodents. Other times, however, the arthropod must construct the burrow itself, which it usually does at the bases of plants. Here plant roots may have loosened the soil so that digging is easier. Additionally, plant roots reinforce loose soil so that tunnels do not collapse as easily. Digging species—certain scorpions, for example—may have enlarged palps or legs to aid in soil movement, while closely related species that merely retreat below surface cover do not show this development. Some species adjust body temperature by moving deeper into the soil during the day. A good example of this behavioral thermoregulation is provided by nocturnal scorpions, which can essentially maintain low body temperature—even during the hottest portions of the day—by moving downward into their burrows. Despite this avoidance of high temperatures, scorpions can still endure very high body temperatures, even in excess of 115° F. Such temperatures are higher than those endured by most other arthropods.

On days when there is cloud cover, or cool air temperature, some predominantly nocturnal species can be seen on the surface during daylight hours. It is fascinating to explore the Sonoran Desert on a beautiful, cool, early spring day, as many animals that are nocturnal during the summer will appear.

Normally, day-active arthropods are not necessarily exposed to the high heat regimes that one might expect. Since these animals are small, their size alone offers them some advantages. First, the ratio of the animal's surface area to its volume is great, so that gained heat can be lost quickly. Of course the animals also heat up quickly. Second, and more important, these animals can fit into microenvironments that are much more favorable for them, a form of "escape" not available to a large species. An insect resting on a plant need only keep itself on the shady side of a slender stem or small leaf to reduce its heat load. Thus many day-active insects regulate their body temperature mainly by behavioral means. They expose their bodies to direct sunlight during the early morning to get their body temperatures up to optimum operating levels so that they can feed, fly, and mate. Then, as the daytime heat increases, they use shade-seeking behavior to avoid any further temperature increase. Even subtle changes in the angle of an insect's body to the rays of the sun can alter its body temperature. Thus, a grasshopper sitting on the open ground can lessen its heat load by resting with its body axis parallel to the sun's rays rather then perpendicular to them. Some species actually manufacture their own shaded microsites. Several species of web-building spiders spin conical retreats that hang in their webs. Since these are placed in bushes—above the ground surface, where the temperatures are extraordinarily high—they are in relatively cooler air. The bush prevents reflections off of the ground from heating the cone's opening from below, and the white silk reflects the sun's rays from above. Such webs are built by common orb-web weavers of the genus *Metapeira* and by members of the single genus in the family Diguetidae, whose species are confined to the deserts of North and South America.

High temperatures are not the only problem a desert invertebrate must face. A cloudless night can cause the temperature to plunge, and so animals must also adapt to freezing conditions. In some invertebrates, body tissues are adapted to prevent damage even though freezing occurs. In addition, various "antifreeze" compounds may be present in some animals' body fluids. These compounds prevent freezing even when the animal's body temperature drops well below the freezing point of water.

If an arthropod must face harsh desert conditions, it must cope with or endure the environmental excesses. Once arthropods have taken up water, they dare not lose it. Water uptake can be accomplished in a number of ways. Species that feed on wet plant materials or on other animals may meet their water requirements by eating foods with a high moisture content. Other avenues of water uptake include the direct diffusion of water through the body surfaces by contact with free water, the ingestion of water by drinking, the production of water by metabolic activities, and the intake of water from the air. The availability of free water in a desert for either ingestion or uptake by diffusion seems at first to be at variance with the very nature of deserts. Remember, however, that at night condensation can occur, and even small droplets of water that are of no use to large organisms are readily available to invertebrates.

More amazing is the fact that some species can actually extract water directly from air, even when the relative humidity is as low as fifty percent; more commonly they do so when the relative humidity ranges from eighty to ninety percent. Since water tends to move out of organisms in all but saturated air (one hundred percent relative humidity), this means that the animals are using some active chemical mechanism to harvest water from unsaturated air. This phenomenon has been especially well studied in a desert cockroach (*Arenivaga investigata*) that inhabits the Mojave and Sonoran deserts.

A final mode of obtaining water is to biochemically derive it from food. The biochemical breakdown of fat and carbohydrates produces water, and may be as important a water source for insects as it is for vertebrates.

Desert arthropods usually have mechanisms that allow them to resist desiccation rather than endure it. In contrast with plants, arthropods exhibit a quite limited range of variation in their tolerance to desiccation. An arthropod loses water in one of three ways: transpiration through its body surface; respiration; and excretory products.

Several cellular and noncellular layers help to seal the body surfaces of arthropods. Lipid compounds in the cuticle, chitin-protein complexes, and even the cell layers that produce these chemicals all help prevent water loss. Interestingly, the ability to prevent water loss may vary seasonally, and there is a concomitant seasonal change in the chemistry of body surfaces. In the winter, for example, tenebrionid beetles lose water rapidly. If, however, they are exposed to dry air, their cuticular chemistry changes and they reduce their rate of water loss. This form of physiological adjustment is termed acclimation. High temperatures can disorganize the molecular layers that prevent water loss, though usually these temperatures are so high ($150°$ F) that if they occur, the animal would have succumbed to them for other reasons.

Although there are advantages to being small, disadvantages exist as well. There is proportionately more surface area that can lose water and a lesser volume of water to be lost in a small arthropod than in a large one. Some argue that this is the reason for the presence of large scorpions, spiders, and other arthropods in deserts, though this argument is not compelling when you observe similar animals in lush rain forests.

Excretion of both nitrogenous wastes and fecal material can use a lot of water. To prevent this source of loss, desert arthropods reabsorb water from feces in their gut tracts and thus deposit very dry fecal matter. Similarly, the water-wasting production of urine is a luxury a desert arthropod cannot afford, so insects produce uric acid, a dry nitrogenous form of waste, and scorpions and spiders produce the even more water-efficient compound, guanine.

Desert arthropods usually have low respiration rates, especially since they may rest during drought periods. Both spiders and scorpions have amazingly low oxygen requirements. In France, scientists inactivated seven of eight of a scorpion's book lungs —specialized respiratory structures found in some invertebrates—and the remaining book lung was more than sufficient to meet all of the individual's respiratory needs. Finally, the ability to endure the loss of a large percentage of body water without irrevocable damage is an important desert adaptation. Desert scorpions and spiders can easily withstand the loss of thirty percent of their body weight. In fact in one study, scorpions withstood forty percent body-weight loss with no serious consequences. This stands in sharp contrast with the lower tolerance for water loss found in their nondesert relatives.

Fishes

Some desert sites in the United States contain permanent flowing or standing water. Fishes that inhabit such locales may not show much in the way of specialized adaptations to desert environments, because the physical and chemical conditions of these large water masses are stable and well within the normal limits of fish tolerances.

On the other hand, small streams or ponds may be subject to extreme daily and seasonal fluctuations of dissolved oxygen, temperature, and salinity. Under such conditions, specialized adaptations are required to ensure the survival of the fish population. Desert fishes must endure low quantities of oxygen dissolved in their water. In fact, North American desert pupfishes (*Cyprinodon*) have survived at the lowest oxygen concentrations known for any fish, that is at one fiftieth to one seventieth of the level present in normal water. In deserts in other parts of the world, certain fishes can occur in ephemeral ponds or streams. They do this by producing eggs, which, like the seeds of annual plants, survive when the adults die off as the pond or stream bottom becomes dry soil. Alternately, adults may survive in moist to dry sediments in a state of aestivation. No desert fishes in the United States can do this. The only species that comes close is the Longfin Dace, which can survive for at least a day under water-saturated mats of algae and debris in Sycamore Creek in Arizona.

In the United States, most desert fish live in essentially permanent ponds or streams. The minnow family (Cyprinidae) and the sucker family (Catostomidae) are stream forms, while the tooth carp (Cyprinodontidae) and the live bearers (Poecilidae) are spring or pond forms.

Interestingly, these desert fishes are in great peril. Of the approximately thirty-one North American fish species that are endangered, twenty-three occur in the deserts of the southwestern United States. This danger stems, in part, from the introduction of non-native species such as the Golden Shiner, the Mosquitofish, bass, and others that compete with, consume, or otherwise interfere with the native populations. The precarious status of some of these populations is also related to the fact that most species live in habitats that are

Longfin Dace
Agosia chrysogaster
296

Golden Shiner
Notemigonus chrysoleucas
299

Mosquitofish
Gambusia affinis
294

physically small, which makes these habitats much more susceptible to catastrophic disturbance due to irrigation and other human activities.

Despite their sensitivity to the altered biological milieu within their habitats, American desert fishes exemplify the extremes of physiological adaptations to deserts. For example, pupfishes can withstand temperatures that range from 34° to 112° F, even though successful reproduction can only be accomplished within the much narrower temperature range of 75° to 86° F. At higher or lower temperatures, the female is unable to produce eggs.

Like insects, desert fishes employ behavioral thermoregulation. In the morning, they leave the cooler water of spring-fed ponds or streams and spend the day feeding in water that is within three to five degrees of their upper thermal-tolerance limit. They live life at the edge of their upper limit because high temperatures permit the fish's biochemical system to work optimally while the animal feeds. The lower nighttime temperatures are adequate for the fish's normal resting requirements.

In addition to broad thermal ranges and low quantities of dissolved oxygen, the desert fishes must endure wide fluctuations in salinity. As water evaporates from streams and ponds, the salt concentration can increase to a level equal to three to five times that of seawater. Water in solutions that are separated by membranes moves across these membranes in response to the concentrations of salts on either side of the membranes, a process termed osmosis. Thus the cells of fish, which are obviously surrounded by membranes, gain or lose water in response to the concentration of the water in which they live. When their environment has a higher salt concentration than their cells, they lose water. Conversely, when their cells have a higher concentration than their environment, they take up water by osmosis. The fluids in the bodies of fish contain about fifteen parts per thousand of salt. In fresh water, because of their high salt concentrations, these fish can simply take up water through their body surfaces. In seawater, however, which is about thirty-five parts per thousand of salt, water tends to leave the fish's body. Therefore the fish must drink salt water and retain the water but excrete the salts—both via the kidneys and, especially, through the gills. In a desert spring, where the water is commonly two and a half times as salty as seawater (eighty-eight parts per thousand) and is occasionally five times as salty (175 parts per thousand), fish are under almost constant physiological stress. Efficient excretory mechanisms permit survival.

These remarkable fish deserve our protection. Anything that can survive in such a harsh natural environment should be revered, not extirpated by humans through the destruction of its limited habitats and the introduction of an alien fauna.

Amphibians and Reptiles

Amphibians require moist places for breeding, with most

species needing the water of a pond or a stream, or at the very least, moist soil. Because their skins are moist and lose water rapidly, the adults generally must also have a moist substrate to replenish their body water. In addition, the vast majority of amphibians are not very tolerant of salt. All of these requirements are in stark contrast with typical desert conditions, so it is no surprise that very few species of amphibians have adapted to these environments. Only one

Tiger Salamander
Ambystoma tigrinum
289, 290, 291

North American species of salamander, the Tiger Salamander, occurs regularly in deserts, principally in the Chihuahuan. The Tiger Salamander is opportunistic and survives under locally favorable conditions. Since such favorable sites occur sporadically over a wide geographic area, this species appears in a number of desert localities. A few other salamanders live in canyons that extend into the desert, and thus might be encountered in a desert area.

In general, frogs are the only amphibian denizens of the desert. And among frogs, only two families—the spadefoots (Pelobatidae) and the toads (Bufonidae)—make up the overwhelming majority of amphibians you are likely to see amidst true desert conditions in the United States.

Northern Leopard Frog
Rana pipiens
286

Canyon Treefrog
Hyla arenicolor
272

Southwestern Toad
Bufo microscaphus
279

Colorado River Toad
Bufo alvarius
281

True frogs, or the family Ranidae—one typical species is the Northern Leopard Frog—are often found in deserts, but they are associated with permanent water. The story is the same for "desert" treefrogs, such as the Canyon Treefrog and even for some toads. The Southwestern Toad occurs in isolated populations that are scattered around the Southwest. Many of these areas have been irrigated for thousands of years, from the times of prehistoric cultures to the present; this habitual irrigation may have permitted this toad to persist in desert situations. The Colorado River Toad is another toad with similar requirements: It is semiaquatic and must have permanent water. All of these frog species avoid the water problems of the desert by finding a consistent source of available water.

Some toads and spadefoots, on the other hand, show remarkable adaptations to desert conditions. Many species have no definite breeding season—these animals can respond instantly to the availability of water and commence the process of reproduction. This differs from the behavior of species with well-defined breeding periods, which are often regulated, in part, by such seasonal environmental factors as the length of the day. In these latter cases, when the proper day length exists, the frogs are physiologically able to breed; however, they cannot breed either before or after that time, regardless of other environmental conditions. The disadvantage of this restriction in a desert is obvious. If day length is correct, but no rain falls, the frog cannot successfully produce offspring. Similarly, if rain occurs but day length is incorrect, the frog will again fail to breed. The most limiting and unpredictable factor, water, must be the ultimate cue to begin reproduction. This allows the desert-adapted frog to use even very temporarily available water.

The presence of loud voices in male desert frogs is thought to be an adaptation to bring males and females together, quickly, at the site of temporary water. When the eggs are laid, they develop rapidly, as do the tadpoles. This permits these species to avoid desiccation as the water body shrinks. Sources of food may be scarce in a temporary pool, so a desert tadpole, instead of being an herbivore like the tadpoles of most frog species, must be omnivorous, consuming both animal and plant matter. In extreme situations, when resources are limited, tadpoles may even become cannibalistic. Since the temporary water is often exposed to direct sunlight during the day, tadpoles must have a tolerance to high temperatures. Indeed many species can endure temperatures of over 100° F.

For adults, "avoiding" desert conditions is important. During most days, and constantly during dry periods, adults must burrow to keep moist and to avoid high temperatures. To do this, the hind foot of many species has a horny, bladelike structure to loosen and dig into the soil. These spades are quite conspicuous because of their dark color in spadefoots (*Scaphiopus*)—named for this adaptation—and some toads, such as the Great Plains Toad. These frogs are active on the surface most typically at night, when drying conditions are minimal.

Nevertheless, adults, despite their best efforts to avoid drying conditions, will inevitably begin to lose body water. It is important that they be able to withstand some loss without being incapacitated—and thus becoming easy prey. In fact desert frogs can survive body-water losses of up to fifty percent of their body weight.

Couch's Spadefoot is probably the most highly adapted to deserts of any of the American frogs. Using its spade, Couch's Spadefoot constructs burrows twenty to twenty-five inches below the soil surface, usually in close proximity to a plant, especially a shrub. Here it may remain dormant for more than two years. To prevent water loss under these conditions, the Spadefoot has several adaptations. The first, a morphological adaptation, is the Spadefoot's ability to encase itself within a dry, hard covering. Careful inspection shows that this covering is composed of several layers of skin that have been shed from the body surface, but which remain to surround the frog as a protective cocoon.

Buried in this way, the animal has a tendency to lose water more slowly, but it still loses water where its wet body touches dry soil. In this circumstance, certain physiological adaptations are helpful. As the soil continues to dry, the Spadefoot accumulates urea—the compound found in urine—in its tissues. This concentrates the Spadefoot's body fluid and slows the loss of water. In addition, before they begin to burrow, Spadefoots accumulate very dilute urine in their bladders. This adaptation allows them to accumulate an amount of water equal to thirty percent of their body weight to use as needed. To endure the extreme chemical changes occurring in their body fluids, the muscles of the Spadefoot are able to tolerate a much higher urea concentration than can those in most other vertebrates. Stored fat is used to fuel the

Great Plains Toad
Bufo cognatus
283

Couch's Spadefoot
Scaphiopus couchi
274

Spadefoot's very low rate of metabolism during this phase. As water is lost, the Spadefoot's tissues endure the drying, up to the point of losing fifty percent or more of their weight. When the rains come and the toad digs its way to the surface, it quickly replenishes its body water merely by being stationary. There is a patch of thin, highly veined skin on the abdomen between the hind legs. This "sitting spot," equivalent to perhaps ten percent of the body area, may absorb up to seventy percent of the water taken up through the body surfaces.

Once on the surface, males make their way to a temporary body of water, where they utter breeding calls that can be heard literally for miles across the desert.

Breeding is accomplished rapidly. Usually the adults are out of the ponds within three to five days, with most breeding having occurred on the first two nights. The freshly laid eggs are not as tolerant of high temperatures as later embryonic stages are, but their development is so fast that within ten hours—by morning—they can withstand temperatures in excess of 100° F for two-hour periods. By the time the eggs are thirteen hours old, they have hatched into tadpoles. The same progression may take many days in other frogs. In just seven to ten days from the moment of fertilization, the cycle is complete, and small Spadefoots are ready to emerge from the ponds. In the northeastern United States the same process may require a period of months, and over a year for certain species. The upshot of its adaptations is that the Spadefoot can maintain large, viable populations in many areas that seem quite unfit for habitation, for months or even years at a time.

The evolutionary jump from amphibians to reptiles included, among other things, the development of adaptations to a terrestrial environment. A better skeletal system to support a body not buoyed up by water, a covering of scales to reduce the rate of water loss, and a shelled egg that did not have to be placed in water were three of the prominent developments. It is not surprising, then, that reptiles are better adapted to deserts, the most extreme of terrestrial environments, than are the amphibians.

For reptiles there are three major sources for the gain or loss of heat. Heat can be conducted to or from the air; it can be conducted to or from the ground or any substrate upon which the reptile lies; and, finally, of course, heat is conducted by radiation from the sun. Reptiles, like amphibians, regulate their body temperatures mainly by gaining heat from their environment in these three ways. The amount of heat produced by their own metabolic processes is a very small portion of the heat required to maintain their body temperatures. They are thus called ectotherms—a word denoting creatures that use outside thermal sources to maintain body temperature. By contrast, birds and mammals have very high metabolic rates and are very well insulated by their body coverings of feathers or fur. Their body temperatures are regulated by using metabolic heat from internal sources, and they are termed endotherms.

This difference between ectotherms and endotherms has important consequences in the desert. When animals breathe to meet their metabolic demands for oxygen, they also lose water from their lungs. A lizard of the same body mass as a rodent has one-seventh the mammal's metabolic rate at 100° F; thus it breathes less often and conserves water.

To regulate its body temperature, a lizard or a snake crawls out of its overnight refuge and exposes its body to the sun. It gains heat from the warm soil, from the air, and directly from the sun's radiation. When its internal body temperature is at an optimum level, the reptile attempts to prevent the gain or loss of additional heat. This can be accomplished in several ways. If too hot, for example, it may move to the cover of a shaded bush. There the sun is no longer heating it up, and in the cool shade, heat loss can take place as well. The heat from the soil can be avoided by lifting the body off the surface: There is less body-surface area in contact, and thus less heat is gained. Some lizards avoid contact with the ground by running only on their hind legs, keeping the front part of the body off the soil surface.

Some species, such as the Desert Iguana, employ the opposite technique: They hug the ground. In such cases, the lizard actually pushes aside the hot surface soil and puts its belly in contact with the cooler subsurface soil, thus losing heat by conduction.

Even the position of a reptile makes a difference in its body temperature. If it places its body perpendicular to the sun's rays, it will absorb the greatest amount of heat. If it turns ninety degrees, parallel to the sun's rays, it can minimize its absorption of radiant energy. Additionally, changes in color affect temperature. A dark lizard absorbs sunlight; a lighter one reflects more sunlight and thus heats up less. The skin of desert lizards may reflect thirty-five percent of the radiation falling on them, in contrast with about six percent for tropical species.

The scales of reptiles can also influence their thermal relations. Rough scales may form air spaces, which have the effect of insulating the animal to some extent. On the other hand, scales like these may prevent water loss—and also evaporative cooling—under circumstances when water loss is called for. Thus a hot lizard or snake that cannot control its temperature by its position within the environment must pant. It cannot sweat. Panting provides the cooling effects that occur when water evaporates from the lungs, and thus lowers the body temperature. A lizard that respires nineteen times per minute at 104° F may pant fifty-nine times a minute at 110°, a temperature close to its lethal upper limit.

Different species can withstand different body temperatures. For reptiles in general, active body temperatures fall in the range of 88–102° F, with a mean of about 95°. The highest body temperature at which an animal is voluntarily active seems to be that of the Desert Iguana, which is regularly active at 115°, a value quite close to its lethal temperature of about 118°.

Desert Iguana
Dipsosaurus dorsalis
88

Sidewinder
Crotalus cerastes
252, 253

Coachwhip
Masticophis flagellum
223, 224, 227, 229

Chuckwalla
Sauromalus obesus
189

Fringe-toed Lizard
Uma notata
182

The lethal temperatures of snakes are lower than those of lizards. This may in part explain why most desert snakes are nocturnal, avoiding the heat, while most lizards are diurnal. The nocturnal Sidewinder often lives in the same places as the diurnal Desert Iguana. Its lethal temperature of about 105° F is thirteen degrees lower than that of the Desert Iguana. Even the diurnal Coachwhip can withstand only about 111° F and is usually active at body temperatures of less than 95° F.

Desert reptiles cannot obtain water through their skins as easily as the amphibians can. Their protective scales prevent not only water loss, but water uptake as well. Reptiles in deserts usually do not have the opportunity to drink, though some species may use dew. The result is that food is the principal means of water uptake for most species. In fact desert reptiles generally cannot exist on food with a water content of less than sixty percent.

Most reptiles—and all amphibians—are carnivores. Thus their water-uptake problems are solved by eating moist prey. For the few herbivorous reptiles, plant material may provide water, but there is frequently an associated problem. Desert plants often contain high salt concentrations. This extra salt is lost by most reptiles in their fecal matter, but nasal passages in some lizards, including the Desert Iguana and the Chuckwalla, contain salt-secreting glands that aid in maintaining the correct concentration of salt in their body fluids.

Of the water lost by reptiles, thirty to forty percent is lost through their feces—though these are relatively dry and contain nitrogenous body wastes in the form of dry uric acid. The remaining sixty percent or so of the body water is lost equally via respiration and through the skin.

Some species can lose water until they have lost fifty percent of their body weight—a high tolerance. Certain reptiles, such as Desert Tortoises, actually store water in their bladders.

Reptiles deal with loose substrates in a variety of ways. Fringe-toed Lizards, which are confined to sandy areas, have fringed scales on their toes to permit running across the sand. The scales operate somewhat like snowshoes, dissipating the animal's weight over a larger area of the sand. To prevent sand from getting into its nose, the Fringe-toed Lizard has closing valves, and its lower jaw is overhung by the upper, which keeps its mouth sandless. Its flat body and smooth scales minimize friction, allowing it to "swim" through the sand.

A few snakes, such as the shovelnose snakes (*Chionactis*), have similar mouth, nose, and scale adaptations. In addition, when such a snake comes to rest beneath the sand, it bends its head downward, leaving a space beneath its throat. In this small space, the snake can pump the muscles of its throat, bellows-fashion, pulling air from between the sand grains. It may be that many desert snakes and lizards with pushed-up or hooked noses use these to hold their heads at an angle in order to produce the same type of space beneath their necks.

A unique form of locomotion, sidewinding, is another adaptation to loose substrates. The J-shaped tracks resulting from this serpentine movement are caused by the animal throwing a loop of its body forward rather than sliding the whole body along an undulating, continuous pathway. This strategy prevents sideslipping, and increases efficiency of movement.

It is clear that reptiles, through a myriad of adaptations, have come to terms with the desert. Their abundance as you walk the deserts, day or night, attest to their success. Careful observation will allow you to see that the repertoire of behaviors of desert animals is not a series of random happenings, but is rather a highly orchestrated program, adapting the animal to a harsh and unpredictable environment.

Birds

Bird species are not numerous in North American deserts, compared with other habitats. Those that do occur in deserts frequently do not exhibit unique morphological or physiological adaptations to desert environments. This is partly because, due to their flight ability, birds are so vagile that they can travel several miles to sources of water and fly up to high altitudes, where the air can cool them and they can escape the rigors of the desert. In sharp contrast, small mammals are, over the course of a day, essentially confined to a narrow environmental zone, which extends from the vegetation a few feet above ground to burrows a few feet below. This zone covers an area that is generally much less than a mile in diameter, and quite often less than a few hundred feet. Nonetheless birds do have some adaptations to dryness and heat that suit them to a desert existence.

Birds have higher normal body temperatures than most other vertebrates; these often exceed 104° F. Obviously, they do not have to cool their bodies in response to the air temperature until the air temperature exceeds that of their bodies. Since cooling often involves the loss of water by evaporation, birds are better off than mammals, whose normal body temperatures are closer to 99° F, and who must thus cool themselves at lower air temperatures. Additionally, birds may allow their body temperatures to rise an additional 5° or 6° F, putting off the need to cool themselves until the environmental temperature reaches 110°, a condition that seldom occurs in the shade of plants, even those that form a very loose, open canopy, such as desert subtrees. There is a limit to this, however: Few birds can endure a body temperature in excess of 115°. In part, the mechanism for heat loss from birds when they are warmer than the air involves direct radiation of body heat to areas of lower temperature. This direct radiation does not involve the water loss of evaporative cooling.

Behaviorally, birds avoid the thermal problems of the desert day by confining their activities to the cool early morning and, to a lesser extent, to the late afternoon. During the warm periods, most species rest in the shade of vegetation or rocks. Since flying may increase body temperature, some birds may not be able to fly during the desert day, because the

Lesser Nighthawk
Chordeiles acutipennis
560

Roadrunner
Geococcyx californicus
554

Black-throated Sparrow
Amphispiza bilineata
610

combination of their metabolic heat and that of the air might cause their body temperatures to exceed their thermal limits. As alluded to earlier, high-flying birds can be active during the day because they are flying in air of lower temperature than are their kin close to the ground.

The position of the feathers when the bird is at rest can contribute to cooling. Some feathers are compressed. This destroys the insulating air space between the feathers and the body surface, and allows heat loss. Extending or raising the wings exposes lightly feathered areas along the sides of the body. Such positions increase heat loss, much as does raising your arms on a hot day.

If all of these methods of heat loss prove to be insufficient, birds use evaporative cooling. Panting through the mouth is the main avenue for the evaporative water loss; however, some species, such as the Lesser Nighthawk and the Greater Roadrunner, use their throat muscles to pump air in a process called gular fluttering. Gular fluttering is metabolically less costly than panting.

Regardless of whether a bird loses its body water to general evaporation or to evaporative cooling, the water must be replenished. Three sources of water are available. As birds metabolically oxidize food that contains hydrogen, some water is produced, though this is a very minor portion of the water they require. Water that is preformed in food—that is, it exists in the food as water and does not have to be chemically manufactured—is another, more important source. Black-throated Sparrows, among the most desert-adapted American birds, can survive using only preformed water if sufficient green plant matter or insects are available. Perhaps most of the birds that feed on animals, nectar, and fruit find sufficient water in their normal food to survive, while seedeaters may generally have to augment their diet. Few birds in the world feed entirely on green matter, so succulent leaves are not a common source of water.

Finally, the most important water is free water, that which is available for drinking. Many seed-eating birds flock to water holes to drink, even though they must sometimes travel many miles to do so. Bird-flock movement can provide a stranded traveler with a clue as to the whereabouts of free water.

Birds are not well adapted to drinking salt water. Their kidneys are not as efficient as those of mammals, because they are structurally less well developed. Thus they cannot conserve the water or excrete the salts from salty water sources. Some marine species have salt-secreting glands in their nasal passages, but most desert species do not. An exception in the United States is the Roadrunner. However, the function of its salt gland seems to be unrelated to drinking salty water. Rather, because nestlings lose water by evaporation, the only way to keep their fluid concentration within the correct range is to excrete salt via the nasal glands. The bottom line is that, as far as we now know, desert birds can make only limited use of saline water as a source of drinking water.

Water-conserving adaptations occur in birds as they do in

most desert animals. The nitrogenous waste product of birds is uric acid, which does not dissolve well in water and which is excreted in a dry, semisolid form. This conserves a great deal of water, considering the amount that goes into the watery urine of mammals.

Birds do not have sweat glands. This lack is an adaptation to flight, but it also reduces evaporative loss through the body surface. Nonetheless, their small body size and the consequent high proportion of body surface area causes birds to lose water through this avenue, especially during exercise such as running or flying.

Losses from the nasal passages are reduced in some species by a unique pattern of condensation. Birds lower the temperatures of their nasal passages so that as warm, expired air passes from the lungs through this zone, condensation occurs, and this condensed water is recaptured. The Cactus Wren is known to recover up to three-quarters of the water from its expired air in this manner.

actus Wren
ampylorhynchus
unneicapillus
84

The water that would ordinarily be lost in feces is resorbed in the gut tracts of birds. There is some indication that this is done more efficiently in arid-land species than in those of humid areas.

It is not clear that desert birds can tolerate a greater degree of water loss than nondesert species. In part this is because there is so much variation among birds in general with respect to how much water loss they can withstand. Desert species range in tolerance from the House Finch, which can survive the loss of up to twenty-six percent of its body weight, to certain quails that can withstand water losses equaling fifty percent of their body weight.

Iouse Finch
arpodacus mexicanus
17, 618

There are other problems in deserts besides heat and dryness. Bouts of cold can catch year-round residents without enough food to meet their daily energy requirements. Mammals avoid these conditions by going into torpor, a resting state not possible for most birds. In American deserts, however, several birds use torpor to avoid cold conditions. Species saving their energy in this way include the Lesser Nighthawk, the Violet-green Swallow, the White-throated Swift, and the Common Poorwill. Birds adjust to the desert in a variety of other ways. Domed nests protect some species. Regulation of the breeding season to coincide with the periodic availability of food is an adaptation to desert irregularity.

iolet-green Swallow
achycineta thalassina
79

/hite-throated Swift
eronautes saxatalis

ommon Poorwill
halaenoptilus nuttallii
52

However, these and all of the physiological adaptations we have discussed occur to some degree in nondesert birds, often to nearly the same extent. Clearly, while some birds inhabit deserts, they are not the favored spots of the vast majority of species in the United States during the hottest, driest portion of the year.

Mammals

Mammals—especially rodents of the family Heteromyidae—are common and, at least at night, conspicuous components of desert ecosystems in North America. The small size, nocturnal habits, and seed-based diet of these rodents form a suite of adaptations that permit them to persist in the face of the high heat and the low, irregular availability of water. There are several other ways to cope with the same environmental conditions, however. Thus some mammals are large rather than small, some are active diurnally rather than nocturnally, and not all desert mammals specialize in eating seeds. We shall consider several of these contrasting strategies and their relative advantages as we dissect the complexities of mammalian adaptations to deserts.

Response to high temperatures usually involves sweating or panting. While large desert mammals may employ these two modes of evaporative cooling, rodent-size mammals do not. In rodents higher temperatures do not induce the increased respiratory rates characteristic of panting, and rodents do not have sweat glands, although they do lose water through the body surface and in expired respiratory "air." As a result, their main relief from thermal stress is to escape to a more favorable thermal environment. There is, however, one interesting cooling method used by a number of species when they are under thermal stress: They lick their fur. This water evaporates and cools the body surface, yet it requires a lower energy output than panting.

Burrowing and being nocturnal are the main methods by which small desert mammals avoid thermal problems. The temperature of a burrow that is as shallow as eighteen inches below the surface does not vary more than two degrees in the course of a day and, even during the hottest portion of the year, probably never exceeds 85–90° F. This constancy contrasts with the temperature of the soil surface, which may heat to 170° during a day with air temperatures of 105°.

At night the heat of the ground surface is rapidly radiated to the clear sky. This can cause the temperature of the soil surface to fall below the air temperature, and to be as much as ninety degrees cooler than the daytime soil temperature. While many mammals simply remain in burrows until nightfall, ground squirrels (*Spermophilus* and *Ammospermophilus*) are active during the day. These animals can feed until their body temperatures increase. Then, by running down their burrows and hugging the substrate, they lose the accumulated heat, by conduction, to the cooler burrow. Once they have cooled off, they return to the surface for another cycle of foraging followed by burrow entry and heat loss.

Black-tailed Jack Rabbit
Lepus californicus
509

Larger mammals, such as the Black-tailed Jack Rabbit, do not usually burrow, and so must seek the shade of rocks or vegetation to keep cool. In very hot weather, however, an individual may dig a hole that completely conceals it, but this does not comprise an elaborate tunnel system. The large surface area and high vascularity of the Jack Rabbit's ears allows the ears to act as radiators, losing heat to areas of lower temperature, especially the sky. Unlike the smaller rodents, Jack Rabbits "pant" through their noses and use this action as a form of evaporative cooling. Since they are herbivores and favor succulent vegetation, they replenish their water from preformed water in their food. In the hottest portions of the day, these rabbits may allow their body temperatures to increase very slightly.

Mammals that are even larger than the rabbits gain some thermal advantages in deserts because of their body size alone. First, large animals are generally more mobile than small species. They can travel great distances to permanent water such as isolated springs or temporary pools in watercourses. Thus they do not depend on metabolic and preformed water from their food alone, and they can afford the luxury of evaporative cooling for some part of their thermal regulation. The large body size also reduces the surfaces that are exposed to heating in proportion to the mass of the body. This resistance to heating is further augmented by the thick, insulating fur of larger mammals. Another consequence of large body size is that, because of their mass alone, their body temperatures increase more slowly than those of smaller animals. This is because tremendous heat is required to raise the temperature of an ounce of water, and large animals have many more ounces of water than their diminutive relatives. Thus they can accumulate heat during the day and lose this thermal load either at night by radiation or during the day by retiring to shade.

Problems of water conservation are solved by mammals in a number of ways, but perhaps the most significant adaptations are those related to kidney function. Small rodents such as

Merriam's Kangaroo Rat
Dipodomys merriami
85

Merriam's Kangaroo Rat can produce urine that is so concentrated that it crystalizes as soon as it is passed from the body. Such a concentration is five times that of the most concentrated urine that human beings can produce. This is accomplished through a complex series of morphological and physiological adaptations of the kidney. One of the more easily understood is that the tubules in the kidney, which are used to reabsorb water before urination takes place, are longer in desert mammals than in nondesert species and therefore recapture more of the water. Similarly, rodents can drink saline water, as their kidneys can extract the water and excrete the salts.

Dry feces are also produced by small desert mammals to aid in water retention, and even the shape of the nasal passages in many species conserves water from expired air by condensing and absorbing the water before exhalation occurs.

Many desert heteromyids have metabolic rates that are lower than those of nondesert rodents of similar size. Lower metabolic rates conserve energy and, consequently, the loss of water. A further metabolic adaptation of some heteromyids is the ability to enter a state of torpor, during which time body temperatures and energy metabolism are decreased. This state can be entered daily or for a longer term. Torpor is an energy-conserving adaptation used by any heteromyids that are less than about forty grams in weight. This weight represents the size break between the small pocket mouse (Perognathus) or kangaroo mouse (Microdipodops) species, and the larger kangaroo rats (Dipodomys). Small kangaroo rats—for example, the thirty-five-gram Merriam's Kangaroo Rat—can go into a

Round-tailed Ground
Squirrel
Spermophilus tereticaudus
504

torpor induced by cold or starvation, but it lasts for short periods and occasionally results in death. Some nonheteromyid rodents, such as the Round-tailed Ground Squirrel, exceed the forty-gram torpor boundary, but nonetheless effectively use torpor to conserve water and energy.

In some species, such as heteromyids, the combination of efficient kidneys, nocturnal habits, and highly adapted nasal passages, among other adaptations, permits them to exist on only the water found in dry seeds. Thus these species are completely independent of the need to drink. It should be noted that "dry" seeds contain a considerable amount of preformed water, perhaps up to twenty percent by weight when they are stored in the relatively high humidity of burrows.

Many small desert mammals are bipedal—that is, they run on their hind feet, which are often enlarged compared with those of other mammals of similar size. There are many possible interpretations of the adaptiveness of this condition, but the most reasonable seems to be that bipedality permits fast, erratic, balanced movement, an aid to avoiding predators in open habitats. Additionally, kangaroo rats and, to a lesser extent, pocket mice, have bulges on the back and side portions of their heads. These enlarged skull areas are related to the middle-ear chamber; through a complex series of relationships, they permit animals to detect low-frequency sounds. This detection process is effective in determining the presence of predators in the dim light that often exists at night when heteromyids are foraging.

Much has been made of the color of desert animals. Some observers have argued that coloration is more important in determining thermal balance than any other function. The presence of many black desert animals does not seem to agree that this is the most plausible explanation. Other suggestions have been advanced, but the result of all of these cerebrations is neither clear nor compelling. However, the general thesis is that most color patterns are meant either to conceal animals or, quite to the contrary, to advertise an organism's presence because it is toxic. For mammals, the cryptic-coloration hypothesis seems an adequate explanation for the North American species.

Most medium-size mammals—such as foxes, Badgers, and Coyotes—are nocturnal carnivores. As such, these species get water from their food, and they avoid the heat and drying air of the daylight hours. This combination avoids the problems of the desert just as effectively as the more complex adaptations of some of the smaller species.

Many mammals are adapted to the rigors of the desert environment. Some families are especially finely tuned—both physiologically and morphologically—to deserts. In North America, the heteromyid rodents, the most characteristic desert mammals, are a good example of animals that exhibit a plethora of such adaptations. You need only follow a kangaroo rat for an evening in the light of a flashlight to gain a sense of awe for these desert specialists.

1 Spring-fed pond   Quitobaquito, Organ Pipe Cactus National Monument, Arizona

Sonoran

'2 Desert spring   Death Valley National Monument, California

Mojave

3 Riparian vegetation   Rio Grande, Big Bend National Park, Texas

Chihuahuan

4 Sand dunes Coral Pink Sand Dunes State Park, Utah

Colorado Plateau
Semidesert

5 Sand dunes Stove Pipe Wells, Death Valley National Monument,
California

Mojave

6 Gypsum dunes White Sands National Monument, New Mexico

Chihuahuan

7 Dry playa lake   Death Valley National Monument, California

Mojave

8 Dry playa lake   Death Valley National Monument, California

Mojave

9 Wet playa lake   Owens Lake, California

Mojave

13 Middle bajada　　　Near Superstition Mountains, Arizona

Sonoran

14 Middle bajada　　　Near Ajo, Arizona

Sonoran

15 Lower bajada　　　Near Gila Bend, Arizona

Sonoran

6 Upper bajada

Joshua Tree National Monument, California

Mojave

7 Upper bajada/transition

Joshua Tree National Monument, California

Mojave

8 Lower bajada

Eureka Valley Dunes, Nevada

Mojave

19 Upper bajada — Near Big Bend National Park, Texas

Chihuahuan

20 Middle bajada — Near Terlingua, Texas

Chihuahuan

21 Lower bajada — Near Las Cruces, New Mexico

Chihuahuan

2 Desert grassland/ desert transition

Near Santa Rita Mountains, southeastern Arizona

Sonoran

3 Sagebrush Steppe

Little Jack's Creek Canyon, Idaho

Great Basin

4 Colorado Plateau semidesert

La Sal, Utah

Great Basin

25 Transition zone
Antelope Valley, Utah

Great Basin

26 Shrub zone
Eastern Nevada

Great Basin

27 Sagebrush Steppe
Owens Valley, California

Great Basin

28 Pedestals on salt flats

Death Valley National Monument, California

Mojave

29 Salt formations

Badwater salt flats, Death Valley National Monument, California

Mojave

30 Desert pavement

Owyhee Uplands, Idaho

Great Basin

31 Spring wildflowers   Lancaster, California

Mojave

32 Spring wildflowers   Southern Arizona

Sonoran

33 Spring wildflowers   Organ Pipe Cactus National Monument, Arizona

Sonoran

34 Spring wildflowers Anza-Borrego Desert State Park, California

Sonoran

35 Spring wildflowers Algodones Dunes, California

Sonoran

36 Spring wildflowers Ajo Mountains, Organ Pipe Cactus National Monument, Arizona

Sonoran

HOW TO USE THE COLOR PLATES

The color plates on the following pages include nine major groups of plants and animals: wildflowers; mushrooms; reptiles and amphibians; fishes; trees, shrubs, cacti, and grasses; insects and spiders; butterflies and moths; mammals; and birds.

Table of Contents
For easy reference, a table of contents precedes the color plates. The table is divided into two sections. On the left, we list each major group of plants or animals. On the right, the major groups are usually subdivided into smaller groups, and each small group is illustrated by a symbol. For example, the large group of wildflowers is divided into small groups based on color. Similarly, the large group of reptiles and amphibians is divided into small groups made up of distinctive animals such as turtles or snakes.

Captions for the Color Plates
The black bar above each color plate contains the following information: the plate number, the common and scientific names of the plant or animal, its dimensions, and the page number of the full species description. To the left of each color plate, the habitats where you are likely to encounter the species are always indicated in blue type. Additionally, you will find either a fact helpful in field identification, such as the food that an insect eats (also in blue type), or a range map or drawing.
The chart on the facing page lists the dimensions given and the blue-type information, map, or drawing provided for each major group of plants or animals.

CAPTION INFORMATION

Dimensions	Blue Type/Art
Wildflowers	
Plant height and flower length or width	Drawing of plant or flower
Mushrooms	
Height of mature mushroom	Specific habitat
Reptiles and Amphibians	
Maximum length of adult	Range map of species
Fishes	
Maximum length of adult	Range map
Trees, Shrubs, Cacti, and Grasses	
Leaf or leaflet length; plant height	Drawing of tree, shrub, cactus, or grass
Insects and Spiders	
Length of adult, excluding antennae and appendages	Major food
Butterflies and Moth	
Wingspan of fully spread adult	Caterpillar's host plants
Mammals	
Length of adult	Range map
Birds	
Length, usually of adult male, from tip of bill to tail	Range map showing breeding, winter, and/or permanent range

Wildflowers	Pink 37–61	
	Blue or Purple 62–77, 97	
	White 78–105	
	Yellow 106–153, 156	
	Orange 154–157	
	Red or Brown 158–164	
	Green 165	
Mushrooms	Mushrooms 166–168	
Reptiles and Amphibians	Turtles 169–174	
	Lizards 175–213	

tiles and Amphibians
tinued)

Snakes
214–270

Frogs and Toads
271–288

Salamanders
289–291

hes

Fishes
292–300

es, Shrubs, Cacti,
d Grasses

Flowers
301–306

Pods
307–311

Berrylike Fruit
312

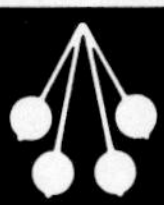

Simple Leaves
306, 313–314, 323

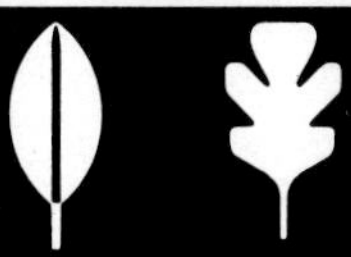

Compound Leaves
310, 315–322

Scalelike Leaves
324

Trees, Shrubs, Cacti, and Grasses (*continued*)

Cacti, Palm, Yuccas, and Other Plants
325–333, 335–339

Shrubs
334, 340–360, 364–366

Grasses
361–363

Insects and Spiders

Grasshoppers and Crickets
367–375

Bee Assassin and Tarantula Hawk
376, 383

Mantid
377

Beetles
378–382

Ants and Termites
384–390, 392

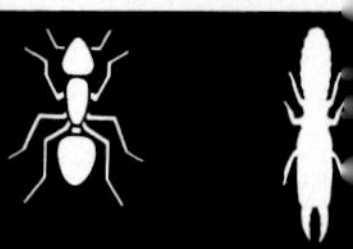

Cochineal Bug
391

Millipede
393

Insects and Spiders
(continued)

Scorpions
394–398

Spiders
399–402

Butterflies and Moths

White-patterned
403–410, 414

Blue
409–410, 412, 414, 439

Copper-colored
411, 413–417, 433

Orange-patterned
418–429

Brown- or Black-patterned
430–432, 434–438

Green
440–441

Yellow
442–443

Swallowtails
444–447

Butterflies and Moths *(continued)*

Moths
448–450

Mammals

Bats
451–468

Mouselike Mammals
469–496

Chipmunk and Squirrels
497–506

Porcupine
507

Rabbits
508–510

Raccoon, Skunks, and Others
511–516

Wild Cats
517–520

Foxes and Coyote
521–524

Deer and Other Hoofed Mammals
525–528

Birds

Hawklike Birds
529–543

Chukar, Grouse, and Quails
544–549

Doves and Roadrunner
550–554

Owls
555–559

Nightjars
560–562

Hummingbirds
563–564

Woodpeckers
565–568

Perching Birds
569–618

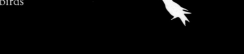

| **37 Peyote** | *Lophophora williamsii*
p. 355 | Plant height: 1–3″
Flower width: ½–1″ |

Chihuahuan

| **38 Simpson's Hedgehog Cactus** | *Pediocactus simpsonii*
p. 355 | Plant height: 2–8″
Flower width: 1–1½″ |

Great Basin

| **39 Fishhook Cactus** | *Mammilaria*
microcarpa
p. 355 | Plant height: to 6″
Flower width: ¾–1″ |

Sonoran

Great Basin
Mojave
Sonoran
Chihuahuan

1 Beavertail Cactus   *Opuntia basilaris*   Plant height: 6–12″
                           p. 357   Flower width: 2–3″

Mojave
Sonoran

42 Claret Cup Cactus   *Echinocereus*   Plant height: 2–12″
                            triglochidiatus   Flower width: 1¼–2″
                            p. 357

Great Basin
Mojave
Sonoran
Chihuahuan

43 Desert Five Spot

Malvastrum
rotundifolium
p. 358

Plant height: 4–24"
Flower width: ¾–1¼"

Mojave
Sonoran

44 Balloon Flower

Penstemon palmeri
p. 358

Plant height: 2–7'
Flower length: 1–1½"

Great Basin

45 Pale Face

Hibiscus denudatus
p. 358

Plant height: 1–3'
Flower width: 1–1½"

Sonoran
Chihuahuan

| 46 Winged Dock | *Rumex venosus*
p. 359 | Plant height: 6–20″
Flower length: ½–1½″ |

Great Basin

| 47 Texas Silverleaf | *Leucophyllum frutescens*
p. 359 | Plant height: to 8′
Flower length: ¾–1″ |

Chihuahuan

| 48 Fairy Duster | *Calliandra eriophylla*
p. 360 | Plant height: 8–20″
Flower width: 2″ |

Sonoran
Chihuahuan

49 Feather Dalea

Dalea formosa
p. 360

Plant height: 1–3"
Flower width: ½".

Sonoran
Chihuahuan

50 Crescent Milkvetch

Astragalus amphioxys
p. 361

Plant height: 2–10"
Flower length: ¾–1"

Mojave
Sonoran
Chihuahuan

51 Desert Calico

Langloisia matthewsii
p. 361

Plant height: 1–2"
Flower width: about ½"

Sonoran

52 Desert Four O'Clock   *Mirabilis multiflora*   Plant height: to 18″
p. 362   Flower width: about 1″

Great Basin
Mojave
Sonoran
Chihuahuan

53 Desert Sand Verbena   *Abronia villosa*   Creeper
p. 362   Flower head width: 2–3″

Mojave
Sonoran

54 Purple Mat   *Nama demissum*   Creeper
p. 363   Flower width: ⅜″

Mojave
Sonoran

55 Fagonia

Fagonia californica
p. 363

Plant height: 8–24"
Flower width: about ½"

Sonoran

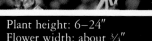

56 Ratany

Krameria parvifolia
p. 364

Plant height: 6–24"
Flower width: about ¾"

Mojave
Sonoran
Chihuahuan

57 Filaree Storksbill

Erodium cicutarium
p. 364

Creeper
Flower width: about ½"

Great Basin
Mojave
Sonoran
Chihuahuan

58 Long-leaved Phlox   *Phlox longifolia*   Plant height: 4–16″
                          p. 365   Flower width: about 1″

Great Basin

59 Trailing Four   *Allionia incarnata*   Creeper
O'Clock   *p. 365*   Flower width: ¼–1″

Mojave
Sonoran
Chihuahuan

60 Indian Blanket   *Gaillardia pulchella*   Plant height: 1–2′
                        p. 366   Flower width: 1½–2½″

Sonoran
Chihuahuan

61 Mojave Aster

Machaeranthera
tortifolia
p. 366

Plant height: 1–2½'
Flower width: about 2"

Mojave
Sonoran

62 Tahoka Daisy

Machaeranthera
tanacetifolia
p. 367

Plant height: 4–16"
Flower width: 1¼–2½"

Great Basin
Mojave
Sonoran
Chihuahuan

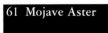

63 Nuttall's Larkspur

Delphinium
nuttallianum
p. 367

Plant height: 4–16"
Flower width: about 1"

Great Basin

64 Chia   *Salvia columbariae*   Plant height: 4–20"
                       p. 367   Flower length: about ½"

Mojave
Sonoran
Chihuahuan

65 Scalloped Phacelia   *Phacelia integrifolia*   Plant height: 6–30"
                               p. 368   Flower width: about ¼"

Mojave
Sonoran
Chihuahuan

66 Pale Trumpets   *Ipomopsis longiflora*   Plant height: to 2'
                         p. 368   Flower length: 1–1½"

Mojave
Sonoran
Chihuahuan

67 Purple Groundcherry
Physalis lobata
p. 369
Creeper
Flower width: about ¾"

Sonoran
Chihuahuan

68 Jones' Penstemon
Penstemon dolius
p. 369
Plant height: 2–8"
Flower length: ½–¾"

Great Basin

69 Arizona Blue-eyes
Evolvulus arizonicus
p. 370
Plant height: to 1'
Flower width: ½–¾"

Sonoran
Chihuahuan

Mojave
Sonoran

71 Net-cup Snapdragon
Vine

Maurandya wislizenii
p. 371

Vine
Flower length: 1″

Chihuahuan

Mojave
Sonoran
Chihuahuan

**74 Little Snapdragon
Vine** *Maurandya* Vine
antirrhiniflora Flower length: ¾–1"
p. 372

Sonoran
Chihuahuan

76 Spike Broomrape | *Orobanche multiflora* p. 373 | Plant height: 4–20″ Flower length: ½–1½″

Great Basin
Mojave
Sonoran
Chihuahuan

77 Death Valley Sage | *Salvia funerea* p. 374 | Plant height: 1½–4′ Flower length: about ½″

Mojave

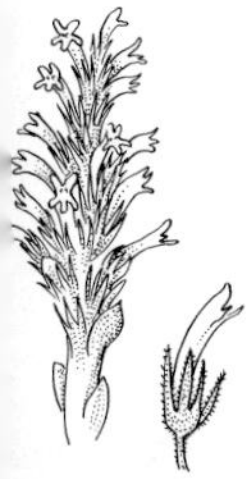

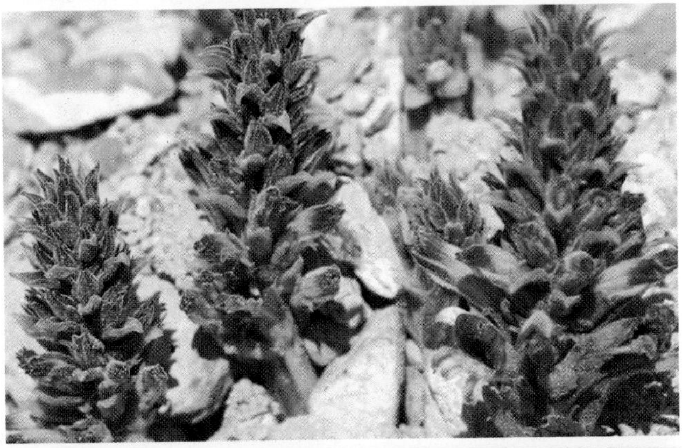

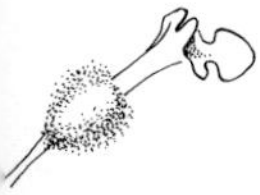

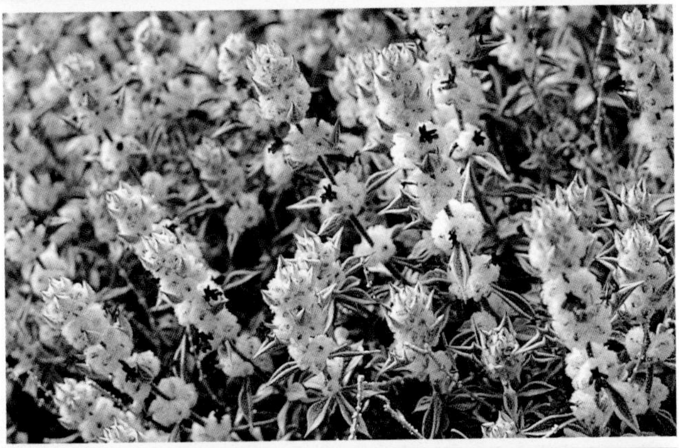

78 Western Peppergrass | *Lepidium montanum* p. 374 | Plant height: to 16″ Flower length: ⅛″

Great Basin
Mojave
Sonoran
Chihuahuan

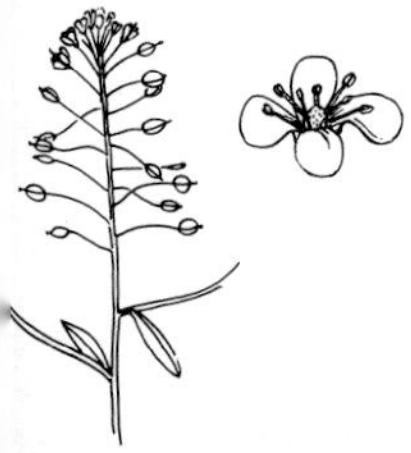

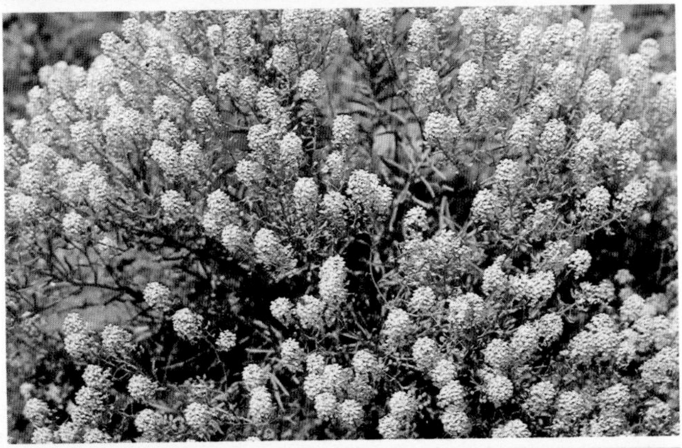

79 Spectacle Pod *Dithyrea wislizenii* Plant height: to 2'
p. 375 Flower length: about ½"

Sonoran
Chihuahuan

80 Poison Milkweed *Asclepias* Plant height: to 4'
subverticillata Flower width: ¾–1¼" .
p. 375

Great Basin

81 Clammyweed *Polanisia dodecandra* Plant height: 4–32"
p. 376 Flower length: ¼–¾"

Great Basin

32 White Milkweed · *Asclepias albicans* · p. 376 · Plant height: 3–10′ · Flower width: about ½″

Sonoran

33 Climbing Milkweed · *Sarcostemma cynanchoides* · p. 377 · Vine · Flower width: about ½″

Mojave
Sonoran
Chihuahuan

34 Esteve's Pincushion · *Chaenactis stevioides* · p. 377 · Plant height: 4–10″ · Flower width: about 1″

Great Basin
Mojave
Sonoran
Chihuahuan

85 Tobacco Weed

Atrichoseris platyphylla
p. 378

Plant height: 12–28"
Flower width: 1–2"

Mojave
Sonoran

86 Desert Chicory

*Rafinesquia
neomexicana*
p. 378

Plant height: 6–20"
Flower width: 1–1½"

Mojave
Sonoran
Chihuahuan

87 Night-blooming Cereus

Cereus greggii
p. 379

Plant height: 1–3'
Flower width: 2–3"

Sonoran
Chihuahuan

88 Common Ice Plant *Mesembryanthemum* Creeper
crystallinum Flower width: 1″
p. 379

Mojave
Sonoran

89 Spreading Fleabane *Erigeron divergens* Plant height: 4–28″
p. 380 Flower width: about 1″

Great Basin
Mojave
Sonoran
Chihuahuan

90 Mojave Desert Star *Monoptilon bellioides* Plant height: usually 1–2″
p. 380 Flower width: ¾″

Mojave
Sonoran

91 Desert Anemone

Anemone tuberosa
p. 381

Plant height: 4–16"
Flower width: 1–1½"

Mojave
Sonoran
Chihuahuan

92 Blackfoot Daisy

Melampodium
leucanthum
p. 381

Plant height: 6–20"
Flower width: about 1"

Sonoran
Chihuahuan

93 Birdcage Evening Primrose

Oenothera deltoides
p. 381

Creeper
Flower width: 1½–3"

Great Basin
Mojave
Sonoran

| 94 **Velvety Nerisyrenia** | *Nerisyrenia camporum*
p. 382 | Plant height: 8–24″
Flower width: about ¾″ |

Chihuahuan

| 95 **Great Desert Poppy** | *Arctomecon merriami*
p. 382 | Plant height: 8–20″
Flower width: 2–3″ |

Mojave
Sonoran

| 96 **Apache Plume** | *Fallugia paradoxa*
p. 383 | Plant height: to 7′
Flower width: 1–1½″ |

Mojave
Sonoran
Chihuahuan

| 97 Spotted Langloisia | *Langloisia punctata*
p. 383 | Plant height: 1½–6″
Flower width: about ½″ |

Mojave
Sonoran

| 98 Desert Lily | *Hesperocallis undulata*
p. 384 | Plant height: 1–6′
Flower length: to 2½″ |

Sonoran

| 99 Sego Lily | *Calochortus nuttallii*
p. 384 | Plant height: 6–18″
Flower width: 1–2″ |

Great Basin

| 100 Southwestern Thorn Apple | *Datura wrightii* p. 385 | Plant height: to 5′ Flower length: 6″ |

Mojave
Sonoran
Chihuahuan

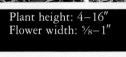

| 101 Sweet-scented Heliotrope | *Heliotropium convolvulaceum* p. 385 | Plant height: 4–16″ Flower width: ⅝–1″ |

Mojave
Sonoran
Chihuahuan

| 102 Rattlesnake Weed | *Euphorbia albomarginata* p. 386 | Creeper Flower width: less than ⅛″ |

Great Basin
Mojave
Sonoran
Chihuahuan

103 Desert Tobacco

Nicotiana trigonophylla
p. 386

Plant height: 1–3'
Flower length: ½–¾"

Mojave
Sonoran
Chihuahuan

104 Angel Trumpets

Acleisanthes longiflora
p. 387

Creeper
Flower length: 3½–6½"

Sonoran
Chihuahuan

105 Southwestern Ringstem

Anulocaulis leiosolenus
p. 387

Plant height: to 4'
Flower length: 1¼–1½"

Mojave
Sonoran
Chihuahuan

106 Trixis

Trixis californica
p. 388

Plant height: 1–3′
Flower length: ³⁄₄″

Sonoran
Chihuahuan

107 Arizona Jewel Flower

Streptanthus arizonicus
p. 388

Plant height: 1–2′
Flower length: about ¹⁄₂″

Sonoran
Chihuahuan

108 Desert Trumpet

Eriogonum inflatum
p. 389

Plant height: 8–40″
Flower width: ¹⁄₄–¹⁄₂″

Great Basin
Mojave
Sonoran

109 Golden Prince's Plume

Stanleya pinnata
p. 389

Plant height: 1½–5'
Flower length: ⅜–⅝"

Great Basin
Chihuahuan

110 Jackass Clover

Wislizenia refracta
p. 390

Plant height: 16–28"
Flower length: about ⅛"

Mojave
Sonoran
Chihuahuan

111 Yellow Bee Plant

Cleome lutea
p. 390

Plant height: 1½–5'
Flower length: about ¼"

Great Basin
Mojave
Sonoran

112 Sulphur Flower *Eriogonum umbellatum* Plant height: 4–12″
p. 391 Flower width: 2–4″

Great Basin

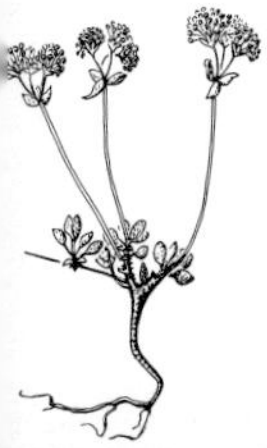

113 Yellow Peppergrass *Lepidium flavum* Creeper
p. 391 Flower length: 1/8″

Mojave
Sonoran

114 Tree Tobacco *Nicotiana glauca* Plant height: to 26′
p. 392 Flower length: 1 1/4–2″

Mojave
Sonoran
Chihuahuan

| 115 Whispering Bells | *Emmenanthe*
penduliflora
p. 392 | Plant height: 6–20″
Flower length: about ½″ |

Mojave
Sonoran

| 116 Yellow Twining
Snapdragon | *Antirrhinum filipes*
p. 393 | Vine
Flower length: about ½″ |

Mojave
Sonoran

| 117 Devil's Claw | *Proboscidea altheaefolia*
p. 393 | Creeper
Flower length: 1–1½″ |

Sonoran
Chihuahuan

Mojave
Sonoran

**19 Dingy
Chamaesaracha**

Chamaesaracha sordida
p. 394

Creeper
Flower width: about ½″

Sonoran
Chihuahuan

**20 White-bracted
Stick-leaf**

Mentzelia involucrata
p. 394

Plant height: 6–12″
Flower length: 1–1¼″

Sonoran

121 Plains Pricklypear

Opuntia polyacantha
p. 395

Plant height: 3–6"
Flower width: 2–3"

Great Basin
Mojave
Chihuahuan

122 Barrel Cactus

Ferocactus acanthodes
p. 395

Plant height: 3–10'
Flower width: 1½–2½"

Mojave
Sonoran

123 Rainbow Cactus

Echinocereus pectinatus
p. 396

Plant height: 4–12"
Flower width: 2½–5½"

Sonoran
Chihuahuan

Mojave
Sonoran

Great Basin
Mojave
Sonoran

Mojave
Sonoran

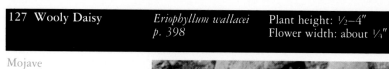

| 127 Wooly Daisy | *Eriophyllum wallacei* p. 398 | Plant height: ½–4″ Flower width: about ¼″ |

Mojave
Sonoran

| 128 Desert Marigold | *Baileya multiradiata* p. 398 | Plant height: 12–20″ Flower width: 1½–2″ |

Mojave
Sonoran
Chihuahuan

| 129 Threadleaf Groundsel | *Senecio douglasii* p. 399 | Plant height: 1–3′ Flower width: about 1¼″ |

Great Basin

30 Arrowleaf Balsam Root *Balsamorhiza sagittata* Plant height: 8–32″
  p. 399 Flower width: 4–5″

Great Basin

31 Yellow Spiny Daisy *Haplopappus spinulosus* Plant height: 6–14″
  p. 400 Flower width: about 1″

Great Basin
Mojave
Sonoran
Chihuahuan

32 Sunray *Enceliopsis nudicaulis* Plant height: 6–18″
  p. 400 Flower width: 3–4″

Great Basin
Mojave

| **133 Chinchweed** | *Pectis papposa*
p. 400 | Plant height: 2–8″
Flower width: about ½″ |

Mojave
Sonoran
Chihuahuan

| **134 Five-needle Fetid Marigold** | *Dyssodia pentachaeta*
p. 401 | Plant height: 4–8″
Flower width: ¼–½″ |

Great Basin
Mojave
Sonoran
Chihuahuan

| **135 Desert Sunflower** | *Gerea canescens*
p. 401 | Plant height: 1–3′
Flower width: about 2″ |

Mojave
Sonoran

36 Brittlebush

Encelia farinosa
p. 402

Plant height: 3–5'
Flower width: 2–3"

Mojave
Sonoran

37 Paperflower

Psilostrophe cooperi
p. 403

Plant height: 4–20"
Flower width: ½–1"

Mojave
Sonoran

38 Little Golden Zinnia

Zinnia grandiflora
p. 403

Plant height: 3–9"
Flower width: 1–1½"

Chihuahuan

| 139 Tansy-leaved Evening Primrose | *Oenothera tanacetifolia* p. 403 | Plant height: 1–4″ Flower width: about 1″ |

Great Basin

| 140 Buffalo Gourd | *Cucurbita foetidissima* p. 404 | Creeper Flower width: 2–3″ |

Mojave
Sonoran
Chihuahuan

| 141 Melon Loco | *Apodanthera undulata* p. 404 | Creeper Flower width: 1½″ |

Sonoran
Chihuahuan

42 Rough Menodora

Menodora scabra
p. 405

Plant height: 14″
Flower width: ½–¾″

Sonoran
Chihuahuan

143 Puncture Vine

Tribulus terrestris
p. 405

Creeper
Flower width: ¼–½″

Great Basin
Mojave
Sonoran
Chihuahuan

44 Twinleaf

Cassia bauhinioides
p. 406

Plant height: 4–16″
Flower width: ½″

Sonoran
Chihuahuan

| 145 Desert Gold | *Linanthus aureus* | Plant height: 2–4" |
| | *p. 406* | Flower width: ¼–½" |

Mojave
Sonoran
Chihuahuan

| 146 Fendler's | *Lesquerella fendleri* | Plant height: 1–16" |
| Bladderpod | *p. 407* | Flower width: about ½" |

Chihuahuan

| 147 Ghost Flower | *Mohavea confertiflora* | Plant height: 4–20" |
| | *p. 407* | Flower length: about 1¼" |

Mojave
Sonoran

| 148 Mexican Gold Poppy | *Eschscholtzia mexicana* p. 408 | Plant height: to 16″ Flower width: ¾–1½″ |

Sonoran
Chihuahuan

| 149 Chihuahua Flax | *Linum vernale* p. 408 | Plant height: 4–20″ Flower width: about ¾″ |

Chihuahuan

| 150 Desert Rock Nettle | *Eucnide urens* p. 408 | Plant height: 1–2′ Flower width: 1–2″ |

Mojave
Sonoran

151 **Desert Rosemallow**	*Hibiscus coulteri* p. 409	Plant height: to 4′ Flower width: 1–2″

Sonoran
Chihuahuan

152 **Desert Mariposa Lily**	*Calochortus kennedyi* p. 409	Plant height: 4–20″ Flower width: 1–2″

Sonoran

153 **Rain Lily**	*Zephyranthes longifolia* p. 410	Plant height: to 9″ Flower length: ¾–1″

Sonoran
Chihuahuan

154 Desert Mariposa Lily	*Calochortus kennedyi* p. 409	Plant height: 4–20″ Flower width: 1–2″

Sonoran

155 Desert Poppy	*Kallstroemia grandiflora* p. 410	Creeper Flower width: 2″

Sonoran
Chihuahuan

156 Desert Primrose	*Oenothera brevipes* p. 411	Plant height: 1–30″ Flower width: ¼–1½″

Mojave
Sonoran

| 157 Coulter's Globemallow | *Sphaeralcea coulteri* p. 411 | Plant height: 8–60″ Flower width: ¾–1″ |

Sonoran

| 158 Desert Globemallow | *Sphaeralcea ambigua* p. 412 | Plant height: 20–40″ Flower width: ½–1½″ |

Mojave
Sonoran

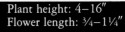

| 159 Desert Paintbrush | *Castilleja chromosa* p. 412 | Plant height: 4–16″ Flower length: ¾–1¼″ |

Great Basin

160 Chuparosa

Beloperone californica
p. 413

Plant height: to 5'
Flower length: 1–1½"

Sonoran

161 Skyrocket

Ipomopsis aggregata
p. 413

Plant height: 6–84"
Flower length: ¾–1¼"

Great Basin

162 Desert Christmas Cactus

Opuntia leptocaulis
p. 414

Plant height: to 3'
Flower width: ½–1"

Sonoran
Chihuahuan

163 Freckled Milkvetch

Astragalus lentigenosus
p. 414

Plant height: 4–16"
Flower length: ⅜–¾"

Great Basin
Mojave
Sonoran
Chihuahuan

164 Desert Candle

Caulanthus inflatus
p. 415

Plant height: 1–2'
Flower length: about ½"

Great Basin
Mojave
Sonoran

165 Devil's Claw

Proboscidea altheaefolia
p. 393

Creeper
Flower length: 1–1½"

Sonoran
Chihuahuan

Great Basin
Mojave
Sonoran

Habitat
Desert areas

Great Basin
Mojave
Sonoran
Chihuahuan

Habitat
Desert areas and sandy
coastal soils

Genus in
Great Basin
Mojave
Sonoran
Chihuahuan

Habitat
Sand and very sandy soil

169 Desert Tortoise
Gopherus agassizii
p. 418
Length: 9¼–14½"

Mojave
Sonoran

170 Yellow Mud Turtle
Kinosternon flavescens
p. 418
Length: 3½–6⅜"

Chihuahuan

171 Sonoran Mud Turtle
Kinosternon sonoriense
p. 419
Length: 3⅛–6½"

Sonoran

172 Slider *Pseudemys scripta* Length: 5–11⅜"
p. 419

Chihuahuan

173 Western Box Turtle *Terrapene ornata* Length: 4–5¾"
p. 420

Chihuahuan

174 Spiny Softshell *Trionyx spiniferus* Length: 5–9¼" (males);
p. 420 6½–18" (females)

Mojave
Sonoran
Chihuahuan

175 Leaf-toed Gecko
Phyllodactylus xanti
p. 421
Length: 4–5"

Sonoran

176 Western Banded Gecko
Coleonyx variegatus
p. 422
Length: 4½–6"

Mojave
Sonoran

177 Texas Banded Gecko
Coleonyx brevis
p. 422
Length: 4–4¾"

Chihuahuan

178 Texas Banded Gecko *Coleonyx brevis* *p. 422* Length: 4–4¾″

Chihuahuan

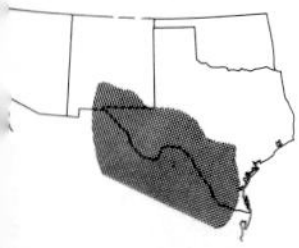

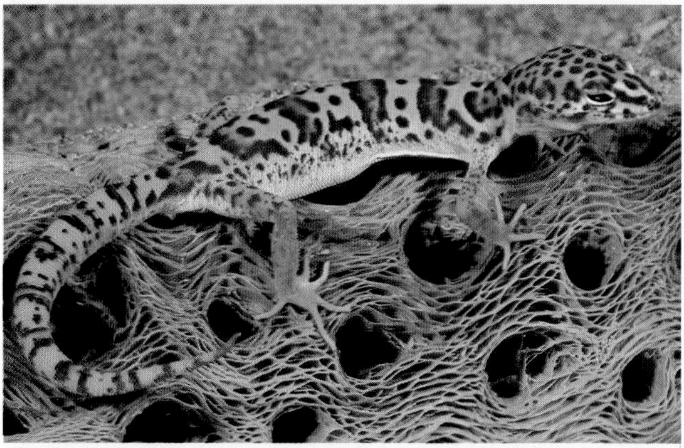

179 Western Banded Gecko *Coleonyx variegatus* *p. 422* Length: 4½–6″

Mojave
Sonoran

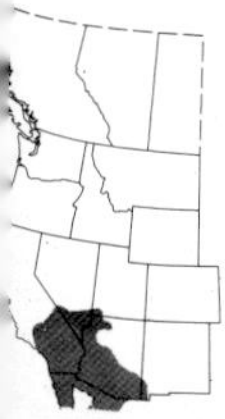

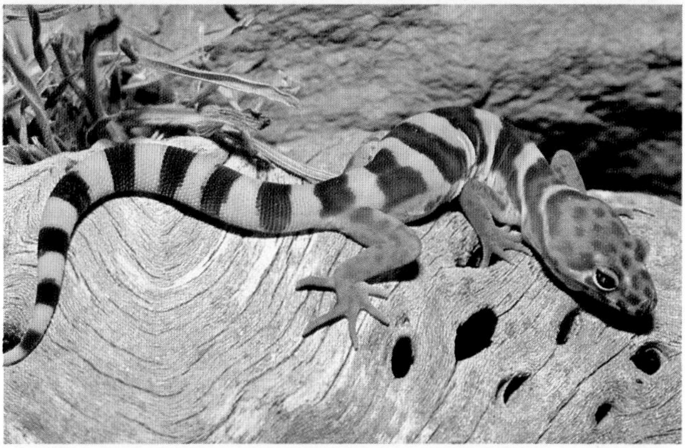

180 Gila Monster *Heloderma suspectum* *p. 423* Length: 18–24″ ⊗

Mojave
Sonoran

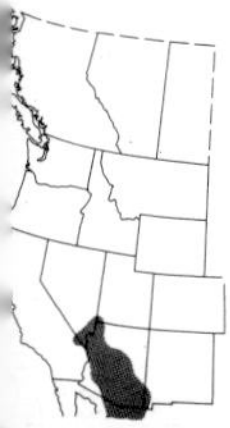

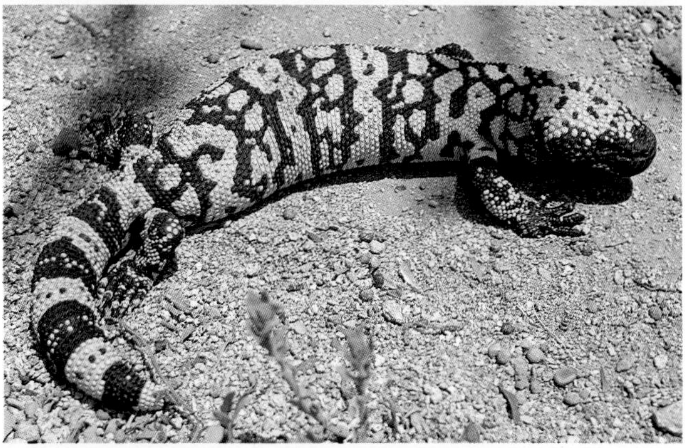

181 Mojave Fringe-toed Lizard
Uma scoparia
p. 423
Length: 5–7"

Mojave

182 Fringe-toed Lizard
Uma notata
p. 424
Length: 5–7"

Sonoran

183 Desert Night Lizard
Xantusia vigilis
p. 424
Length: 3¾–5¹⁄₁₆"

Mojave
Sonoran

84 Desert Night Lizard *Xantusia vigilis* Length: 3¾–5¹⁄₁₆"
p. 424

Mojave
Sonoran

85 Granite Night Lizard *Xantusia henshawi* Length: 4–5⅝"
p. 425

Sonoran

86 Black-collared Lizard *Crotaphytus insularis* Length: 6–13"
p. 425

Great Basin
Mojave
Sonoran

187 Bluntnose Leopard Lizard

Gambelia silus
p. 426

Length: 8–9¼"

Sonoran

188 Desert Iguana

Dipsosaurus dorsalis
p. 426

Length: 10–16"

Mojave
Sonoran

189 Chuckwalla

Sauromalus obesus
p. 427

Length: 11–16½"

Mojave
Sonoran

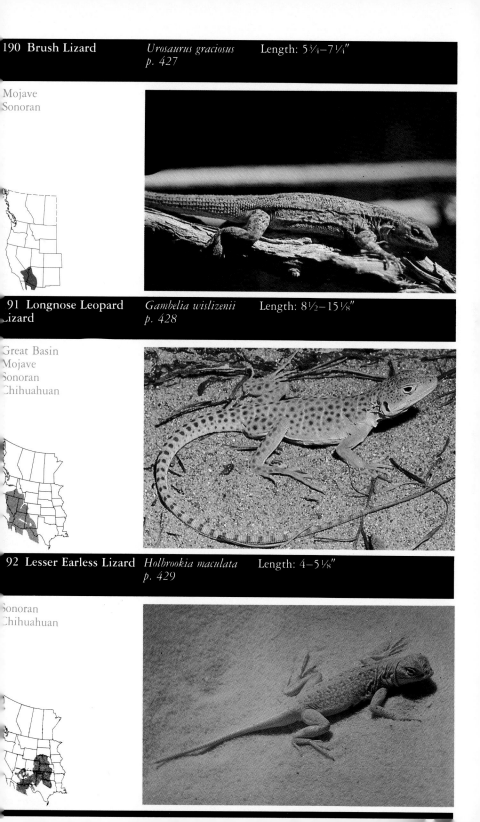

190 Brush Lizard *Urosaurus graciosus* Length: 5¾–7¼"
p. 427

Mojave
Sonoran

91 Longnose Leopard Lizard *Gambelia wislizenii* Length: 8½–15⅛"
p. 428

Great Basin
Mojave
Sonoran
Chihuahuan

92 Lesser Earless Lizard *Holbrookia maculata* Length: 4–5⅛"
p. 429

Sonoran
Chihuahuan

193 Roundtail Horned Lizard	*Phrynosoma modestum* *p. 429*	Length: 3–4⅛″

Chihuahuan

194 Flat-tail Horned Lizard	*Phrynosoma m'calli* *p. 430*	Length: 3–4¾″

Sonoran

195 Regal Horned Lizard	*Phrynosoma solare* *p. 430*	Length: 3½–6½″

Sonoran

96 Texas Horned Lizard   *Phrynosoma cornutum*   Length: 2½–7⅛"
p. 430

Chihuahuan

97 Short-horned Lizard   *Phrynosoma douglassi*   Length: 2½–5⅞"
p. 431

Great Basin

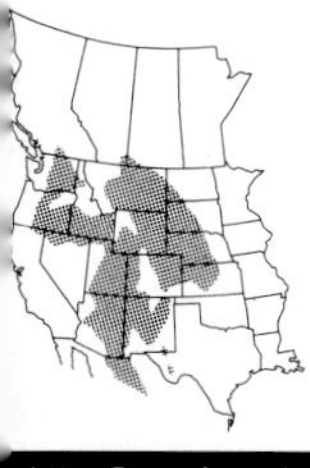

98 Crevice Spiny Lizard   *Sceloporus poinsetti*   Length: 8½–11¼"
p. 431

Chihuahuan

199 Desert Spiny Lizard
Sceloporus magister
p. 432
Length: 7–12"

Great Basin
Mojave
Sonoran
Chihuahuan

200 Collared Lizard
Crotaphytus collaris
p. 433
Length: 8–14"

Sonoran
Chihuahuan

201 Collared Lizard
Crotaphytus collaris
p. 433
Length: 8–14"
Female

Sonoran
Chihuahuan

202 Side-blotched Lizard

Uta stansburiana
p. 433

Length: 4–6⅜"

Great Basin
Mojave
Sonoran
Chihuahuan

203 Zebratail Lizard

Callisaurus draconoides
p. 434

Length: 6–9⅛"

Great Basin
Mojave
Sonoran

204 Greater Earless Lizard

Cophosaurus texanus
p. 435

Length: 3¼–7¼"

Sonoran
Chihuahuan

205 Tree Lizard

Urosaurus ornatus
p. 435

Length: 4½–6¼"

Mojave
Sonoran
Chihuahuan

206 Western Whiptail

Cnemidophorus tigris
p. 436

Length: 8–12"

Great Basin
Mojave
Sonoran
Chihuahuan

207 Colorado Checkered Whiptail

Cnemidophorus tesselatus
p. 437

Length: 11–15½"

Chihuahuan

208 Little Striped Whiptail

Cnemidophorus inornatus
p. 437

Length: 6½–9⅜"

Chihuahuan

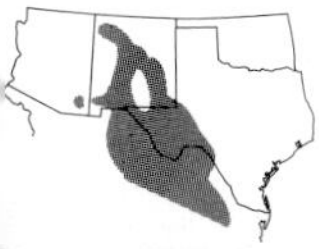

209 Desert Grassland Whiptail

Cnemidophorus uniparens
p. 438

Length: 6½–9⅜"

Chihuahuan

210 Chihuahuan Spotted Whiptail

Cnemidophorus exsanguis
p. 438

Length: 9½–12⅜"
Female

Sonoran
Chihuahuan

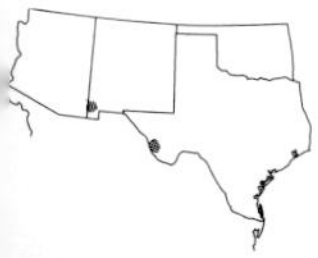

Chihuahuan

Great Basin

Chihuahuan

214 Trans-Pecos Rat Snake   *Elaphe subocularis*   Length: 34–66"
   p. 440

Chihuahuan

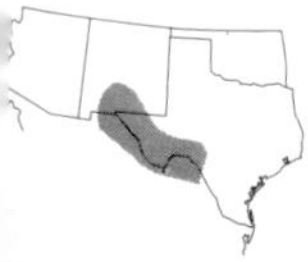

215 Western Terrestrial Garter Snake   *Thamnophis elegans*   Length: 18–42"
   p. 441

Great Basin

216 Checkered Garter Snake   *Thamnophis marcianus*   Length: 18–42½"
   p. 441

Sonoran
Chihuahuan

217 Big Bend Patchnose Snake
Salvadora deserticola
p. 442
Length: 22–40"

Chihuahuan

218 Western Patchnose Snake
Salvadora hexalepis
p. 442
Length: 22–45"

Great Basin
Mojave
Sonoran

219 Rosy Boa
Lichanura trivirgata
p. 443
Length: 24–42"

Mojave
Sonoran

Thamnophis cyrtopsis p. 444   Length: 16–43"

Sonoran
Chihuahuan

221 Striped Whipsnake   *Masticophis taeniatus* p. 444   Length: 40–72"

Great Basin
Chihuahuan

222 Sonoran Whipsnake   *Masticophis bilineatus* p. 445   Length: 30–67"

Sonoran

223 Coachwhip
Masticophis flagellum
p. 445
Length: 36–102"

Great Basin
Mojave
Sonoran
Chihuahuan

224 Rosy Boa
Lichanura trivirgata
p. 443
Length: 24–42"

Mojave
Sonoran

225 Texas Blind Snake
Leptotyphlops dulcis
p. 447
Length: 5–10¾"

Chihuahuan

Mojave
Sonoran
Chihuahuan

Great Basin
Mojave
Sonoran
Chihuahuan

Great Basin
Mojave
Sonoran
Chihuahuan

| 229 Coachwhip | *Masticophis flagellum*
p. 445 | Length: 36–102" |

Great Basin
Mojave
Sonoran
Chihuahuan

| 230 Coachwhip | *Masticophis flagellum*
p. 445 | Length: 36–102" |

Great Basin
Mojave
Sonoran
Chihuahuan

| 231 Ground Snake | *Sonora semiannulata*
p. 448 | Length: 8–19" |

Great Basin
Mojave
Sonoran
Chihuahuan

32 Racer
Coluber constrictor
p. 449
• Length: 33–77"

Great Basin

233 Coachwhip
Masticophis flagellum
p. 445
Length: 36–102"

Great Basin
Mojave
Sonoran
Chihuahuan

34 Common Kingsnake
Lampropeltis getulus
p. 450
Length: 36–82"

Mojave
Sonoran
Chihuahuan

235 Western Shovelnose Snake

Chionactis occipitalis
p. 450

Length: 10–17"

Mojave
Sonoran

236 Banded Sand Snake

Chilomeniscus cinctus
p. 451

Length: 7–10"

Sonoran

237 Western Shovelnose Snake

Chionactis occipitalis
p. 450

Length: 10–17"

Mojave
Sonoran

238 Longnose Snake   *Rhinocheilus lecontei*   Length: 22–41"
                            p. 451

Great Basin
Mojave
Sonoran
Chihuahuan

239 Ground Snake   *Sonora semiannulata*   Length: 8–19"
                         p. 448

Great Basin
Mojave
Sonoran
Chihuahuan

**240 Sonoran Shovelnose   *Chionactis palarostris*   Length: 10–15½"
Snake**   *p. 452*

Sonoran

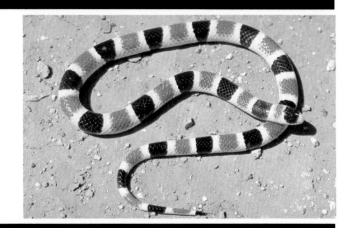

Sonoran

Chihuahuan

Chihuahuan

244 Copperhead

Agkistrodon contortrix
p. 454

Length: 22–53″

Chihuahuan

245 Saddled Leafnose Snake

Phyllorhynchus browni
p. 454

Length: 12–20″

Sonoran

246 Common Kingsnake

Lampropeltis getulus
p. 450

Length: 36–82″

Mojave
Sonoran
Chihuahuan

247 Longnose Snake	*Rhinocheilus lecontei* *p. 451*	Length: 22–41"

Great Basin
Mojave
Sonoran
Chihuahuan

248 Blacktail Rattlesnake	*Crotalus molossus* *p. 455*	Length: 28–49½"	⊗

Sonoran
Chihuahuan

249 Tiger Rattlesnake	*Crotalus tigris* *p. 455*	Length: 20–36"	⊗

Sonoran

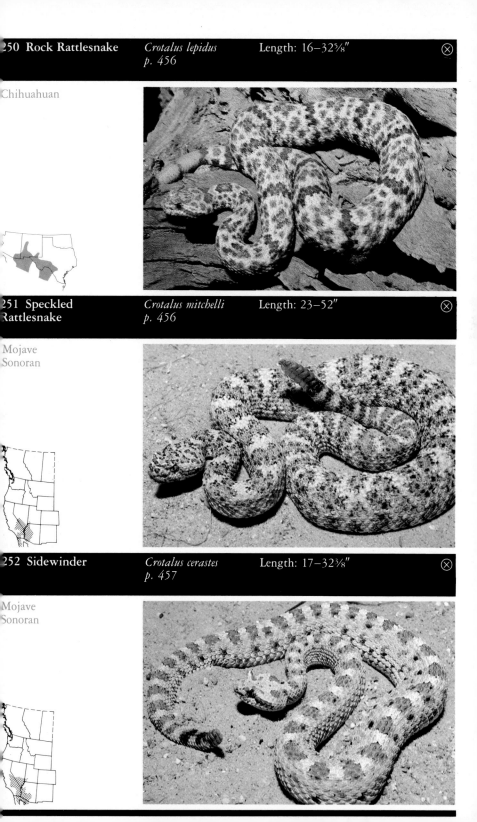

250 Rock Rattlesnake *Crotalus lepidus* Length: 16–32⅝"
p. 456

Chihuahuan

**251 Speckled
Rattlesnake** *Crotalus mitchelli* Length: 23–52"
p. 456

Mojave
Sonoran

252 Sidewinder *Crotalus cerastes* Length: 17–32⅜"
p. 457

Mojave
Sonoran

Mojave
Sonoran

Sonoran

Mojave
Sonoran

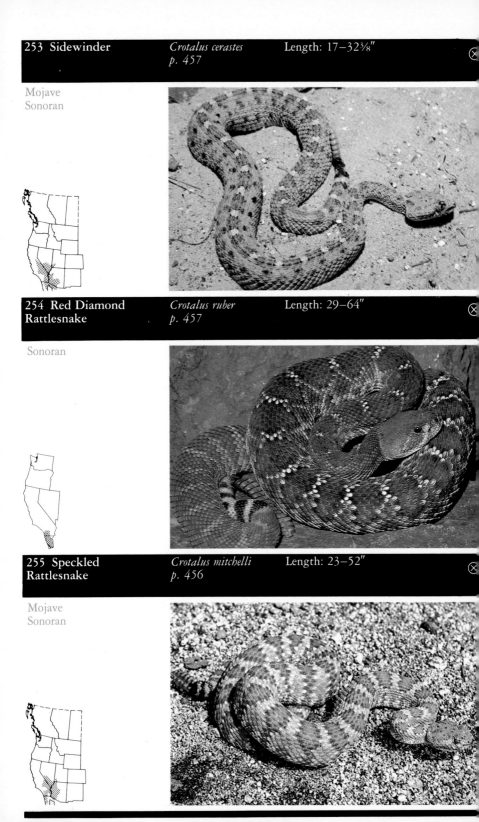

256 Western Diamondback Rattlesnake

Crotalus atrox
p. 458

Length: 34–83⅞"

⊗

Sonoran
Chihuahuan

257 Rock Rattlesnake

Crotalus lepidus
p. 456

Length: 16–32⅝"

⊗

Chihuahuan

258 Western Rattlesnake

Crotalus viridis
p. 458

Length: 16–64"

⊗

Great Basin
Small portions of Mojave
and Chihuahuan

259 Mojave Rattlesnake *Crotalus scutulatus*   Length: 24–51″   ⊗
p. 459

Mojave
Sonoran
Chihuahuan

260 Western Rattlesnake *Crotalus viridis*   Length: 16–64″   ⊗
p. 458

Great Basin
Small portions of Mojave
and Chihuahuan

**261 Western Hognose
Snake**   *Heterodon nasicus*   Length: 16–35¼″
p. 459

Chihuahuan

| **62 Lyre Snake** | *Trimorphodon biscutatus* p. 460 | Length: 24–47¾" |

Mojave
Sonoran
Chihuahuan

| **263 Gopher Snake** | *Pituophis melanoleucus* p. 461 | Length: 48–100" |

Great Basin
Mojave
Sonoran
Chihuahuan

| **264 Massasauga** | *Sistrurus catenatus* p. 462 | Length: 18–39½" | ⊗ |

Chihuahuan

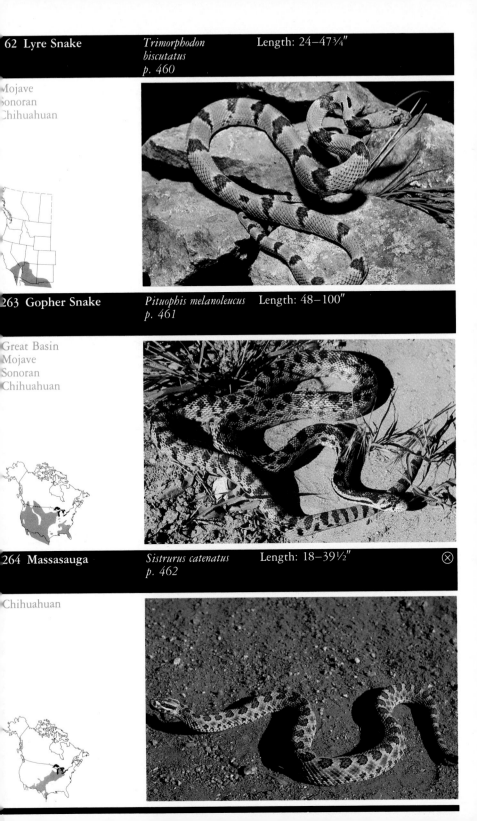

Mojave
Sonoran

Chihuahuan

Great Basin
Mojave
Sonoran
Chihuahuan

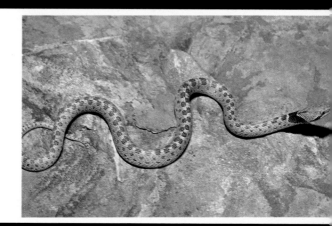

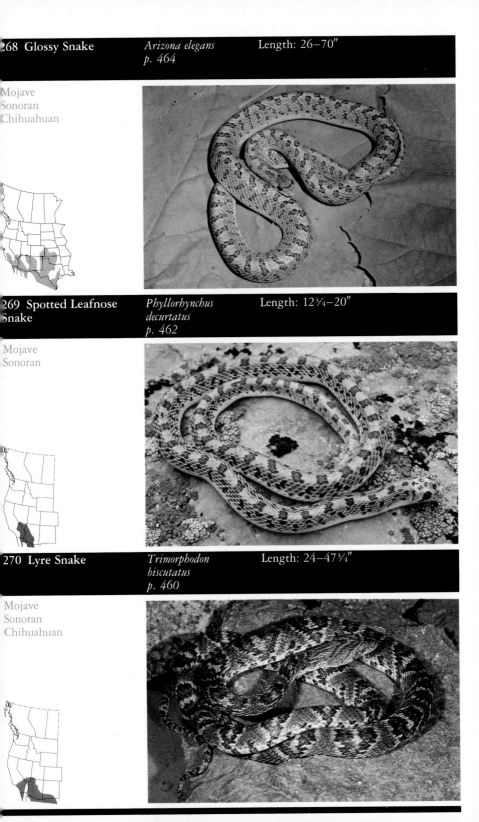

268 Glossy Snake *Arizona elegans* Length: 26–70"
p. 464

Mojave
Sonoran
Chihuahuan

269 Spotted Leafnose *Phyllorhynchus* Length: 12¾–20"
Snake *decurtatus*
p. 462

Mojave
Sonoran

270 Lyre Snake *Trimorphodon* Length: 24–47¾"
biscutatus
p. 460

Mojave
Sonoran
Chihuahuan

271 California Treefrog   *Hyla cadaverina*   Length: 1–2″
p. 465

Sonoran

272 Canyon Treefrog   *Hyla arenicolor*   Length: 1¼–2¼″
p. 465

Mojave
Sonoran
Chihuahuan

273 Lowland Burrowing Treefrog   *Pternohyla fodiens*   Length: 1–2″
p. 466

Sonoran

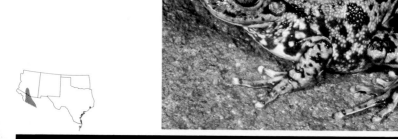

74 Couch's Spadefoot *Scaphiopus couchi* Length: 2¼–3½"
p. 466

Sonoran
Chihuahuan

275 Plains Spadefoot *Scaphiopus bombifrons* Length: 1½–2½"
p. 467

Chihuahuan

276 Western Spadefoot *Scaphiopus hammondi* Length: 1½–2½"
p. 467

Chihuahuan

| 277 Great Basin Spadefoot | *Scaphiopus intermontanus* p. 468 | Length: 1½–2" |

Great Basin

| 278 Red-spotted Toad | *Bufo punctatus* p. 468 | Length: 1½–3" |

Mojave
Sonoran
Chihuahuan

| 279 Southwestern Toad | *Bufo microscaphus* p. 469 | Length: 2–3" |

Mojave
Sonoran

80 Texas Toad

Bufo speciosus
p. 469

Length: 2–3⅝"

Chihuahuan

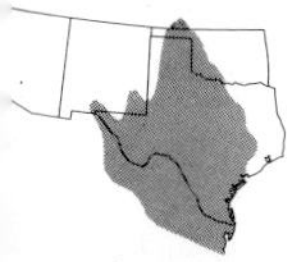

81 Colorado River Toad

Bufo alvarius
p. 470

Length: 3–7"

Sonoran

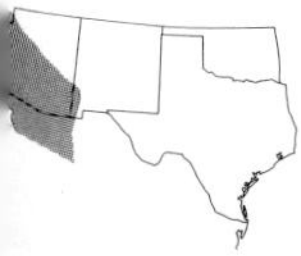

82 Great Plains Narrowmouth Toad

Gastrophryne olivacea
p. 470

Length: ⅞–1⅝"

Sonoran
Chihuahuan

283 Great Plains Toad

Bufo cognatus
p. 471

Length: 2–4½"

Mojave
Sonoran
Chihuahuan

284 Sonoran Green Toad

Bufo retiformis
p. 471

Length: 1½–2¼"

Sonoran

285 Rio Grande Leopard Frog

Rana berlandieri
p. 472

Length: 2¼–4½"

Sonoran
Chihuahuan

286 Northern Leopard Frog　*Rana pipiens*　Length: 2–5"
p. 472

Great Basin
Mojave

287 Green Toad　*Bufo debilis*　Length: 1¼–2⅛"
p. 473

Chihuahuan

288 Bullfrog　*Rana catesbeiana*　Length: 3½–8"
p. 473

Great Basin
Mojave
Sonoran
Chihuahuan

289 Tiger Salamander   *Ambystoma tigrinum*   Length: 6–13⅜″
p. 474

Great Basin
Chihuahuan

290 Tiger Salamander   *Ambystoma tigrinum*   Length: 6–13⅜″
p. 474

Great Basin
Chihuahuan

291 Tiger Salamander   *Ambystoma tigrinum*   Length: 6–13⅜″
p. 474   Larva

Great Basin
Chihuahuan

292 White River Springfish

Crenichthys baileyi
p. 476

Length: to 3"

Great Basin
Mojave

Habitat
Warm desert spring pools
and runs

293 Desert Pupfish

Cyprinodon macularius
p. 476

Length: to 2½"

Sonoran

Habitat
Marshy backwaters of
desert streams and springs

294 Mosquitofish

Gambusia affinis
p. 476

Length: to 2½"

Great Basin
Mojave
Sonoran
Chihuahuan

Habitat
Introduced into many
desert springs and ponds

295 Gila Topminnow

Poeciliopsis occidentalis
p. 477

Length: to 2"

Sonoran

Habitat
Springs, pools, edges and
backwaters of streams,
usually with debris and
aquatic vegetation

296 Longfin Dace

Agosia chrysogaster
p. 477

Length: to 3½"

Sonoran

Habitat
Warm desert streams to
cooler mountain brooks

297 Speckled Dace

Rhinichthys osculus
p. 477

Length: to 4"

Great Basin
Mojave
Sonoran

Habitat
Desert springs and their
outflow

298 Tui Chub

Gila bicolor
p. 478

Length: to 16"

Great Basin

Habitat
Quiet, shallow waters of
large, slow streams, lakes,
and ponds

299 Golden Shiner

Notemigonus crysoleucas
p. 478

Length: to 12"

Great Basin
Mojave
Sonoran
Chihuahuan

Habitat
Clear, quiet streams, lakes,
ponds, and swamps over
mud, sand, or rocks,
usually near aquatic
vegetation

300 Spikedace

Meda fulgida
p. 479

Length: to 3"

Sonoran

Habitat
Over sand or gravel in
pools of larger streams with
moderate to swift current

| 301 Blue Palo Verde | *Cercidium floridum*
p. 481 | Leaf length: 1″
Leaflet length: ¼–⅜″ |

Sonoran

| 302 Screwbean Mesquite | *Prosopis pubescens*
p. 481 | Leaf length: 2–3″
Leaflet length: ¼–⅜″ |

Mojave
Sonoran
Chihuahuan

| 303 Catclaw | *Acacia greggii*
p. 482 | Leaf length: 1–3″
Leaflet length: ⅛–⅜″ |

Mojave
Sonoran
Chihuahuan

Locally in all North
American deserts

Sonoran

Mojave
Sonoran

| 307 Mexican Palo Verde | *Parkinsonia aculeata* p. 484 | Leaf length: 8–20″ Leaflet length: ¼–⅜″ |

Sonoran
Chihuahuan

| 308 Honey Mesquite | *Prosopis glandulosa* p. 485 | Leaf length: 3–8″ Leaflet length: ⅜–1¼″ |

Mojave
Sonoran
Chihuahuan

| 309 Foothill "Yellow" Palo Verde | *Cercidium microphyllum* p. 486 | Leaf length: ¾–1″ Leaflet length: about ¼″ |

Sonoran

310 Velvet Mesquite *Prosopis velutina* p. 486

Leaf length: 5–6″
Leaflet length: ¼–½″

Sonoran

311 Screwbean Mesquite *Prosopis pubescens* p. 481

Leaf length: 2–3″
Leaflet length: ¼–⅜″

Mojave
Sonoran
Chihuahuan

312 Elephant Tree *Bursera microphylla* p. 487

Leaf length: 1–1¼″
Leaflet length: ⅕–⅖″

Sonoran

Sonoran

314 Crucifixion Thorn   *Canotia holacantha*   Usually leafless
p. 488

Sonoran

315 Elephant Tree   *Bursera microphylla*   Leaf length: 1–1¼″
p. 487   Leaflet length: ⅕–²⁄₅″

Sonoran

Cercidium floridum
p. 481

Leaf length: 1″
Leaflet length: ¼–⅜″

Sonoran

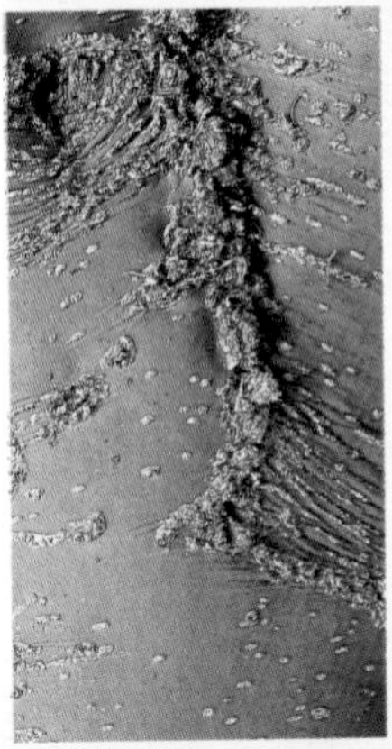

317 Catclaw

Acacia greggii
p. 482

Leaf length: 1–3″
Leaflet length: ⅛–⅜″

Mojave
Sonoran
Chihuahuan

318 Foothill "Yellow"
Palo Verde

*Cercidium
microphyllum
p. 486*

Leaf length: ¾–1″
Leaflet length: about ¼″

Sonoran

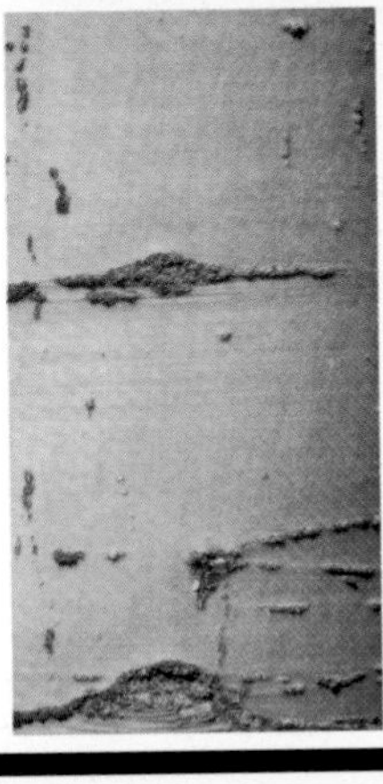

319 Desert Ironwood
Olneya tesota
p. 488

Leaf length: 1–2¼"
Leaflet length: ¼–¾"

Sonoran

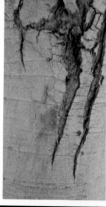

320 Screwbean Mesquite
Prosopis pubescens
p. 481

Leaf length: 2–3"
Leaflet length: ¼–⅜"

Mojave
Sonoran
Chihuahuan

321 Honey Mesquite
Prosopis glandulosa
p. 485

Leaf length: 3–8"
Leaflet length: ⅜–1¼"

Mojave
Sonoran
Chihuahuan

22 Mexican Palo Verde   *Parkinsonia aculeata*   Leaf length: 8–20"
p. 484   Leaflet length: ¼–⅜"

Sonoran
Chihuahuan

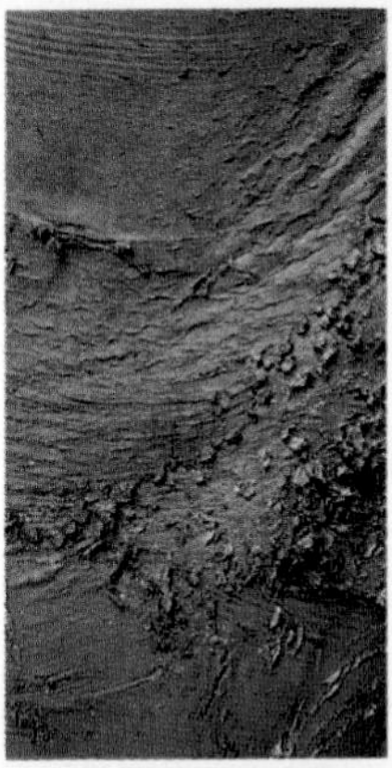

23 Bitter Condalia   *Condalia globosa*   Leaf length: ⅛–½"
p. 489

Sonoran

24 Tamarisk   *Tamarix chinensis*   Leaf length: about ¹⁄₁₆"
p. 482

Locally in all North
American deserts

325 Jumping Cholla

Opuntia fulgida
p. 490

Spine length: ¾–1¼"

Sonoran

326 Joshua-tree

Yucca brevifolia
p. 490

Leaf length: 8–14"

Mojave

327 California Washingtonia

Washingtonia filifera
p. 491

Leaf length: 3–5'

Sonoran

28 Soaptree Yucca *Yucca elata* Leaf length: 1–2½'
p. 492

Sonoran
Chihuahuan

329 Mojave Yucca *Yucca schidigera* Leaf length 18–24"
p. 492

Mojave
Sonoran

330 Torrey Yucca *Yucca torreyi* Leaf length: 2–3½'
p. 493

Chihuahuan

331 Saguaro

Cereus giganteus
p. 493

Plant height: to 50'

Sonoran

332 Teddybear Cholla

Opuntia bigelovii
p. 494

Plant height: 3–9'

Sonoran

333 Tree Cholla

Opuntia imbricata
p. 495

Plant height: 3–7'

Chihuahuan

334 Smoke Tree *Dalea spinosa* Plant height: 20'
p. 483

Sonoran

335 Ocotillo *Fouquieria splendens* Plant height: to 30'
p. 495

Sonoran
Chihuahuan

336 Banana Yucca *Yucca baccata* Plant height: to 5'
p. 495

Mojave
Sonoran
Chihuahuan

337 Lechuguilla   *Agave lecheguilla*   Plant height: 7–10'
p. 496

Chihuahuan

338 Sotol   *Dasylirion wheeleri*   Plant height: trunk to 3'
p. 496

Sonoran
Chihuahuan

339 Parry's Century Plant   *Agave parryi*   Plant height: 10–14'
p. 497

Higher elevations of
Sonoran and Chihuahuan

340 Rabbit Brush   *Chrysothamnus nauseosus*   Plant height: to 7′
p. 497

Great Basin
Mojave
Sonoran
Chihuahuan

341 Snakeweed   *Xanthocephalum sarothrae*   Plant height: 6–36″
p. 498

Great Basin
Mojave
Sonoran
Chihuahuan

342 Creosote Bush   *Larrea tridentata*   Plant height: usually less than 4′
p. 498

Mojave
Sonoran
Chihuahuan

| **343 Littleleaf Horsebrush** | *Tetradymia glabrata* p. 499 | Plant height: usually 10–20″ |

Great Basin
Mojave

| **344 Arrow Weed** | *Pluchea sericea* p. 499 | Plant height: to 10′ |

Mojave
Sonoran
Chihuahuan

| **345 Greasewood** | *Sarcobatus vermiculatus* p. 500 | Plant height: to 8′ |

Great Basin
Mojave

Great Basin
Mojave

Sonoran

Great Basin
Mojave

| 349 Desert Sage | *Salvia dorrii*
p. 502 | Plant height: 8–32″ |

Great Basin
Mojave

| 350 Tarbush | *Flourensia cernua*
p. 502 | Plant height: usually under 3′ |

Chihuahuan

| 351 Anderson Lycium | *Lycium andersonii*
p. 503 | Plant height: 3–9′ |

Mojave
Sonoran

352 Four-wing Saltbush *Atriplex canescens* Plant height: 3–6'
p. 503

Great Basin
Mojave
Sonoran
Chihuahuan

353 Big Sagebrush *Artemisia tridentata* Plant height: usually to 6'
p. 504

Great Basin

354 Winter Fat *Ceratoides lanata* Plant height: 1–3'
p. 505

Great Basin
Mojave
Chihuahuan

355 White Bur Sage *Ambrosia dumosa* Plant height: 1–2′
p. 505

Mojave
Sonoran

356 Mariola *Parthenium incanum* Plant height: usually under 3′
p. 505

Chihuahuan

357 Big Sagebrush *Artemisia tridentata* Plant height: usually to 6′
p. 504

Great Basin

358 Desert Holly   *Atriplex hymenelytra*   Plant height: 1–3′
                            p. 506

Mojave
Sonoran

359 Desert Buckwheat   *Eriogonum fasciculatum*   Plant height: to 3′
                            p. 506

Mojave
Sonoran

360 Bur Sage   *Ambrosia deltoidea*   Plant height: usually under 2′
                            p. 507

Sonoran

361 Fluffgrass

Erioneuron pulchellum
p. 507

Plant height: 3–6″

Mojave
Sonoran
Chihuahuan

362 Indian Ricegrass

Oryzopsis hymenoides
p. 508

Plant height: 7–18″

Great Basin
Mojave
Sonoran
Chihuahuan

363 Bluebunch Wheatgrass

Agropyron spicatum
p. 508

Plant height: 20–40″

Great Basin

364 Mormon Tea   *Ephedra* spp.   Plant height: over 4'
p. 508

Great Basin
Mojave
Sonoran
Chihuahuan

365 Burrobush   *Hymenoclea salsola*   Plant height: 3–6'
p. 509

Mojave
Sonoran

366 Turpentine Broom   *Thamnosma montana*   Plant height: 1–2'
p. 509

Mojave
Sonoran

367 Green Valley Grasshopper

Schistocerca shoshone
p. 511

Length: 1½–2¾"

Great Basin
Mojave
Sonoran
Chihuahuan

Food
Grasses (Poaceae)

368 Creosote Bush Grasshopper

Bootettix argentatus
p. 511

Length: ¾–1"

Mojave
Sonoran
Chihuahuan

Food
Foliage of creosote bush
(*Larrea tridentata*)

369 Pallid-winged Grasshopper

Trimerotropis
pallidipennis
p. 511

Length: 1¼–1⅝"

Great Basin
Mojave
Sonoran
Chihuahuan

Food
Herbaceous plants on range
and arid land

70 Lubber Grasshopper *Brachystola magna* Length: 1½–3⅛″
p. 512

Sonoran
Chihuahuan

Food
Vegetation and dead
insects on roads

**71 Horse Lubber
Grasshopper** *Taeniopoda eques* Length: 1½–2½″
p. 512

Sonoran
Chihuahuan

Food
Desert annuals and foliage
of perennial shrubs

**72 Dragon Lubber
Grasshopper** *Dracotettix monstrosus* Length: ¾–1¾″
p. 512

Sonoran

Food
Desert plants and dead
insects

373 Aztec Pygmy Grasshopper

Paratettix aztecus
p. 513

Length: ¼–½"

Mojave
Sonoran
Chihuahuan

Food
Algae and decaying plant material

374 Mormon Cricket

Anabrus simplex
p. 513

Length: 1–2⅜"

Great Basin
Mojave
Sonoran
Chihuahuan

Food
Lupine (*Lupinus*), sagebrush, and many plants, including grains and vegetables

375 Jerusalem Cricket

Stenopelmatus fuscus
p. 514

Length: 1⅛–2"

Great Basin
Mojave
Sonoran
Chihuahuan

Food
Other insects, plant roots, decaying vegetation, and potato tubers

reat Basin
Iojave
onoran
hihuahuan

ood
Ither insects, especially
ees

Iojave
onoran
hihuahuan

ood
nts and other insects
loving on the ground and
l low vegetation

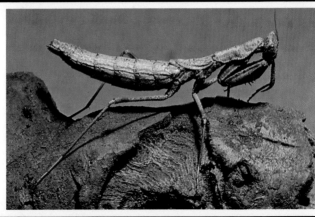

Great Basin
Mojave
onoran
Chihuahuan

ood
A wide variety of insects,
piders, and other
nvertebrates

379 Ironclad Beetle

Zopherus haldemani
p. 516

Length: ¾–1″

Sonoran
Chihuahuan

Food
Fungi

380 Agave Billbug

Scyphophorus acupunctatus
p. 516

Length: ⅜–¾″

Sonoran
Chihuahuan

Food
Adults eats the sap of agave
plants; larva feeds on their
flower stalks

381 Broad-necked Darkling Beetle

Coelocnemis californicus
p. 516

Length: ⅞–1″

Great Basin
Mojave
Sonoran
Chihuahuan

Food
Fungus and windblown
organic matter

382 Arizona Blister Beetle *Lytta magister* p. 517 Length: ⅝–1⅛″

Sonoran

Food
Plant tissues of desert shrubs; larva attacks grasshopper eggs in soil

383 Tarantula Hawk *Hemipepsis* spp. p. 517 Length: ½–¾″

Great Basin
Mojave
Sonoran
Chihuahuan

Food
Nectar; larva feeds on tarantulas (Theraphosidae) and trapdoor spiders (Ctenizidae)

384 Arid Lands Honey Ants *Myrmecocystus* spp. p. 517 Length: ⅜″ (worker); ⅜–½″ (replete worker); ¼–⅝″ (reproductives)

Great Basin
Mojave
Sonoran
Chihuahuan

Food
Honeydew from sucking bugs, nectar from flowers, and some other plant juices

385 Spine-waisted Ants
Aphaenogaster spp.
p. 518

Length: ⅜"
Workers

Great Basin
Mojave
Sonoran
Chihuahuan

Food
Small insects

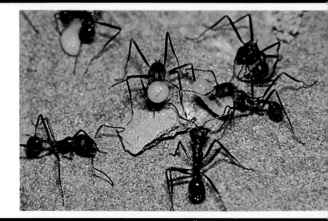

386 Little Black Ant
Monomorium minimum
p. 518

Length: ¹⁄₁₆" (worker)

Great Basin
Mojave
Sonoran
Chihuahuan

Food
Sweet substances, meat
fragments, cooked
vegetables, other human
food

387 Rough Harvester Ant
Pogonomyrmex rugosus
p. 519

Length: ¼–½"

Great Basin
Mojave
Sonoran
Chihuahuan

Food
Seeds and grains

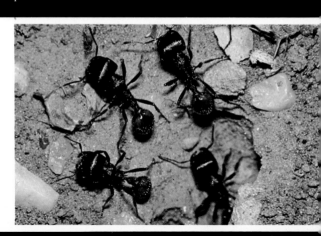

388 Texas Carpenter Ant

Camponotus festinatus
p. 519

Length: ¾–1"

Great Basin
Mojave
Sonoran
Chihuahuan

Food
Other insects, honeydew, juice from rotting fruit, and sweets

389 Red Velvet-ant

Dasymutilla magnifica
p. 519

Length: ¾" (male); ⅞" (female)

Mojave
Sonoran
Chihuahuan

Food
Adult drinks nectar; larval food unknown

390 Thistledown Velvet-ant

Dasymutilla gloriosa
p. 520

Length: ½–⅝"

Great Basin
Mojave
Sonoran
Chihuahuan

Food
Nectar; larva is external parasite of sand wasp larvae

391 Cochineal Bug

Dactylopius confusus
p. 520

Length: 1/16–1/8″ (female); 1/32–1/16″ (male)

Great Basin
Mojave
Sonoran
Chihuahuan

Food
Juices of cacti, especially
prickly pear (*Opuntia*)

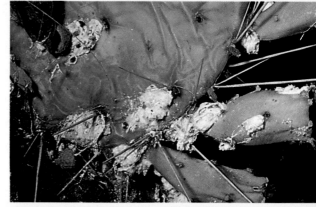

392 Termites

Order Isoptera
p. 521

Length: 1/4–5/8″

Great Basin
Mojave
Sonoran
Chihuahuan

Food
A variety of wood, other
plant parts, and cow dung

393 Desert Millipede

Orthoporus ornatus
p. 521

Length: to 7″

Sonoran
Chihuahuan

Food
Living and decomposing
vegetation; mainly dead
leaves and bark of shrubs
and cacti

394 Centruroides Scorpion

Centruroides spp.
p. 522

Length: 2–2¾"

Mojave
Sonoran

Food
Small insects

395 Giant Desert Hairy Scorpion

Hadrurus arizonensis
p. 522

Length: 5½"

Genus occurs in
Great Basin
Mojave
Sonoran
Chihuahuan

Food
Insects; occasionally small
lizards and snakes

396 Pale Windscorpion

Eremobates pallipes
p. 522

Length: ⅝–1" (male); ⅞–1¼" (female)

Great Basin
Mojave
Sonoran
Chihuahuan

Food
Insects and small vertebrate
animals, such as lizards

397 Chernetid

Family Chernetidae
p. 523

Length: 1/16–1/8"

Great Basin
Mojave
Sonoran
Chihuahuan

Food
Small flies, bark lice,
butterflies and their
caterpillars, ants, mites,
and small earthworms

398 Giant Vinegarone

*Mastigoproctus
giganteus*
p. 523

Length: 3–3 1/8"

Sonoran
Chihuahuan

Food
Small insects

399 Desert Tarantula

Aphonopelma chalcodes
p. 524

Length: 2–2 1/2" (male); 2–2 3/4"
(female)

Mojave
Sonoran
Chihuahuan

Food
Insects, lizards, and other
small animals

400 Inconspicuous Crab Spiders *Philodromus* spp. Length: ⅛–⅜″ (female); male slightly
p. 524 smaller

Great Basin
Mojave
Sonoran
Chihuahuan

Food
Small insects

401 Carolina Wolf Spider *Lycosa carolinensis* Length: ¾″ (male); ⅞–1⅜″ (female)
p. 524

Great Basin
Mojave
Sonoran
Chihuahuan

Food
Insects

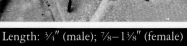

402 Apache Jumping Spider *Phidippus apacheanus* Length: ⅜–½″
p. 525

Genus occurs in
Great Basin
Mojave
Sonoran
Chihuahuan

Food
Insects and other small
arthropods

403 Becker's White
Pontia beckerii
p. 527
Wingspan: 1⅜–1⅞"

Great Basin
Mojave
W. Sonoran

Host Plants
Bladderpod (*Isomeris arborea*), golden prince's plume (*Stanleya pinnata*), black mustard (*Brassica nigra*), and probably other crucifers

404 Desert Orangetip
Anthocharis cethura
p. 527
Wingspan: 1⅛–1½"

Mojave
Sonoran

Host Plants
Include long-beaked twist flower (*Streptanthella longirostris*) and tansy mustards (*Descurainia*)

405 Gray Marble
Anthocharis lanceolata
p. 527
Wingspan: 1⅝–1¾"

Great Basin

Host Plants
Rock cresses (*Arabis*) and some other cresses

06 Pearly Marblewing *Euchloe hyantis* Wingspan: 1¼–1⅜″
p. 528

Great Basin
Mojave
W. Sonoran

Host Plants
Western tansy mustard
(*Descurainia pinnata*), desert
candle and wild cabbage
(*Caulanthus*), Arizona jewel
flower, mountain jewel
flower, other *Streptanthus*
species

407 Phoebus Parnassian *Parnassius phoebus* Wingspan: 2⅛–3″
p. 528

Great Basin visitor from
surrounding mountains

Host Plants
stonecrops (*Sedum
lanceolatum*, *S. obtusatum*,
and perhaps other species
of *Sedum*)

**408 Large White
Skipper** *Heliopetes ericetorum* Wingspan: 1⅛–1⅝″
p. 529

Great Basin
Mojave
Sonoran
Chihuahuan

Host Plants
Globemallow (*Sphaeralcea*)
and other mallows
(Malvaceae), and hollyhock
(*Althaea*)

409 Pale Blue

Euphilotes pallescens
p. 529

Wingspan: ¾–⅞"

Great Basin
Mojave

Host Plants
Wild buckwheat
(*Eriogonum kearneyi.*
E. microthecum, and
E. plumatella)

410 Small Blue

Philotiella speciosa
p. 529

Wingspan: ½–⅝"

Mojave
W. Sonoran

Host Plants
Punctured bract (*Oxytheca*
perfoliata); also trilobia (*O.*
trilobata) and kidney-leaved
buckwheat (*Eriogonum*
reniforme)

411 Antillean Blue

Hemiargus ceraunus
p. 530

Wingspan: ¾–1"

Mojave
Sonoran
Chihuahuan

Host Plants
Buds and young leaves of
legumes, including
locoweed (*Astragalus*),
mesquite (*Prosopis*), beans
(*Phaseolus*), and partridge
pea (*Chaemaecrista*)

412 Antillean Blue

Hemiargus ceraunus
p. 530

Wingspan: ¾–1″

Mojave
Sonoran
Chihuahuan

Host Plants
Buds and young leaves of
legumes, including
locoweed (*Astragalus*),
mesquite (*Prosopis*), beans
(*Phaseolus*), and partridge
pea (*Chaemaecrista*)

413 Western Pygmy Blue

Brephidium exilis
p. 530

Wingspan: ⅜–¾″

Great Basin
Mojave
Sonoran
Chihuahuan

Host Plants
Plants of goosefoot family,
including pickleweed
(*Salicornia ambigua*),
saltbush (*Atriplex*), and
pigweed (*Chenopodium*)

414 Blue Copper

Chalceria heteronea
p. 531

Wingspan: 1⅛–1¼″

Great Basin

Host Plants
Prefers thistle (*Cirsium*),
also feeds on other
composites (Asteraceae) and
mallows (Malvaceae)

415 Blue Copper

Chalceria heteronea
p. 531

Wingspan: 1⅛–1¼"

Great Basin

Host Plants
Various species of wild buckwheat (*Eriogonum fasciculatum, E. latifolium, E. umbellatum, E. nudum complex, E. microthecum*)

416 Behr's Hairstreak

Satyrium behrii
p. 531

Wingspan: ⅞–1⅛"

Great Basin
Mojave

Host Plants
Bitter brush (*Purshia tridentata* and *P. glandulosa*)

417 Sleepy Orange

Eurema nicippe
p. 531

Wingspan: 1⅜–1⅞"

Mojave
Sonoran
Chihuahuan
Very occasionally seen in Great Basin

Host Plants
Include senna (*Cassia*), clovers (*Trifolium*), and other legumes

18 Queen

Danaus gilippus
p. 532

Wingspan: 3–3⅜"

Mojave
Sonoran
Chihuahuan
Occasionally seen in
Great Basin

Host Plants
Blunt-leaved milkweed
(*Asclepias amplexicaulis*) and
climbing milkweed
(*Sarcostemma hirtellum*)

19 Monarch

Danaus plexippus
p. 532

Wingspan: 3½–4"

Great Basin
Mojave
Sonoran
Chihuahuan

Host Plants
Milkweeds (*Asclepias*) and
dogbane (*Apocynum*)

20 Painted Lady

Vanessa cardui
p. 533

Wingspan: 2–2¼"

Great Basin
Mojave
Sonoran
Chihuahuan

Host Plants
Prefers thistle (*Cirsium*),
also feeds on other
composites (*Asteraceae*) and
mallows (*Malvaceae*)

421 Desert Checkerspot

Charidryas neumoegeni
p. 534

Wingspan: 1¼–1¾"

Mojave
Sonoran

Host Plants
Goldenhead (*Acamptopappus sphaerocephalus*) and Mojave aster (*Machaeranthera tortifolia*)

422 Chara Checkerspot

Dymasia chara
p. 534

Wingspan: ¾–1⅛"

Mojave
Sonoran
Chihuahuan

Host Plants
Chuparosa (*Justicia californica*)

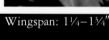

423 Sagebrush Checkerspot

Charidryas acastus
p. 534

Wingspan: 1¼–1¾"

Great Basin

Host Plants
Rabbit brush (*Chrysothamnus viscidiflorus*); asters (*Machaeranthera canescens, M. viscosa*) suspected

424 Elada Checkerspot   *Texola elada*   Wingspan: 7/8–1 1/8"
                         p. 535

Sonoran
Chihuahuan

Host Plants
Composites (Asteraceae)
and acanthus (Acanthaceae)

425 Texan Crescentspot   *Anthanassa texana*   Wingspan: 1–1 1/2"
                         p. 535

Mojave
Sonoran
Chihuahuan

Host Plants
Plants of the acanthus
family (*Dicliptera brochiata,
Jacobina carnea, Ruellia*)

426 Phaon Crescentspot   *Phyciodes phaon*   Wingspan: 7/8–1 1/4"
                         p. 536

Mojave
Sonoran
Chihuahuan

Host Plants
Fog fruit (*Lippia nodiflora,
L. lanceolata*)

427 Gray Metalmark

Apodemia palmerii
p. 536

Wingspan: ¾–⅞"

Mojave
Sonoran
Chihuahuan

Host Plant
Honey Mesquite (*Prosopis juliflora*)

428 Mormon Metalmark

Apodemia mormo
p. 536

Wingspan: ¾–1¼"

Great Basin
Scattered in Chihuahuan

Host Plants
A wide variety of
buckwheats (*Eriogonum*)

429 Bordered Patch

Chlosyne lacinia
p. 537

Wingspan: 1⅝–1⅞"

Mojave
Sonoran
Chihuahuan

Host Plants
Plants of the composite
family, especially sunflower
(*Helianthus annuus*), giant
ragweed (*Ambrosia trifida*),
and cowpen daisy (*Verbesina encelioides*)

430 Bordered Patch

Chlosyne lacinia
p. 537

Wingspan: 1⅝–1⅞"

Mojave
Sonoran
Chihuahuan

Host Plants
Plants of the composite family, especially sunflower (*Helianthus annuus*), giant ragweed (*Ambrosia trifida*), and cowpen daisy (*Verbesina encelioides*)

431 Great Basin Wood Nymph

Cercyonis sthenele
p. 537

Wingspan: 1⅜–2"

Great Basin

Host Plants
Grasses (Poaceae)

432 Desert Checkered Skipper

Pyrgus philetas
p. 538

Wingspan: ⅞–1⅛"

Sonoran
Chihuahuan

Host Plants
Probably members of the Rosaceae and Malvaceae

433 Sandhill Skipper

Polites sabuleti
p. 538

Wingspan: ¾–1⅛"

Great Basin
Mojave
Sonoran

Host Plants
Grasses (Poaceae)

434 Pahaska Skipper

Hesperia pahaska
p. 539

Wingspan: 1⅛–1½"

Great Basin
Mojave

Host Plants
Grasses (Poaceae),
including blue grama grass
(*Bouteloua gracilis*) and
desert bunchgrass (*Tridens
pulchella*)

435 Coyote Skipper

Achalarus toxeus
p. 539

Wingspan: 1⅝–2"

Chihuahuan

Host Plants
Texas ebony (*Pithecellobium
flexicaule*) and probably
other species

436 Desert Gray Skipper

Yvretta carus
p. 539

Wingspan: ⅞–1¼"

Mojave
Sonoran
Chihuahuan

Host Plants
Unknown

437 Great Basin Sootywing

Pholisora libya
p. 540

Wingspan: 1–1⅜"

Great Basin
Mojave
Sonoran

Host Plants
Common saltbush (*Atriplex canescens*) and perhaps other species of saltbush

438 Bronze Roadside Skipper

Amblyscirtes aenus
p. 540

Wingspan: ⅞–1⅛"

Barely in Great Basin
Chihuahuan

Host Plants
Grasses (Poaceae)

| **439 Yucca Giant Skipper** | *Megathymus yuccae* p. 540 | Wingspan: 2–2⅞" |

Mojave
Sonoran
Chihuahuan

Host Plants
All U.S. yuccas except
Whipple's yucca (*Yucca whipplei*)

| **440 Leda Hairstreak** | *Ministrymon leda* p. 541 | Wingspan: ¾–⅞" |

Mojave
Sonoran

Host Plant
Mesquite (*Prosopis juliflora*)

| **441 Desert Green Hairstreak** | *Callophrys comstocki* p. 541 | Wingspan: ¾–1" |

Mojave
W. Sonoran

Host Plants
Probably sulphur flower
(*Eriogonum umbellatum subaridum*) and other
buckwheats (*Eriogonum*)

442 Boisduval's Yellow
Eurema boisduvaliana
p. 542
Wingspan: 1⅛–1⅝"

Rare in Sonoran
Chihuahuan

Host Plants
Unknown

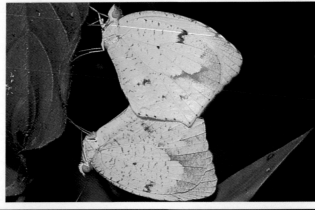

443 Common Sulphur
Colias philodice
p. 542
Wingspan: 1⅜–2"

Great Basin
Mojave
Sonoran
Chihuahuan

Host Plants
Clover, alfalfa, vetches,
and other pervasive
legumes (Fabaceae)

444 Western Tiger Swallowtail
Pterourus rutulus
p. 542
Wingspan: 2¾–3⅞"

Visitor to some Great
Basin sites

Host Plants
Include willows, poplars,
aspens (Salicaceae), several
alders (*Alnus*) and
sycamores (Platanaceae)

445 Desert Swallowtail
Papilio rudkini
p. 543
Wingspan: 2⅝–2¾"

Mojave
Sonoran

Host Plants
Turpentine broom
(*Thamnosma montana*),
Queen Anne's lace (*Daucus carota*), other members of
carrot family (Apiaceae)

446 Anise Swallowtail
Papilio zelicaon
p. 543
Wingspan: 2⅝–3"

Great Basin

Host Plants
Many species, including
fennel (*Foeniculum vulgare*),
seaside angelica (*Angelica lucida*), cow parsnip
(*Heracleum lanatum*), carrots
and parsley (Apiaceae),
citrus trees (Rutaceae)

447 Short-tailed Black Swallowtail
Papilio indra
p. 544
Wingspan: 2⅛–3⅜"

Great Basin
Mojave
W. Sonoran

Host Plants
Members of carrot or
parsley family (Apiaceae)

448 White-lined Sphinx

Hyles lineata
p. 544

Wingspan: 2½–3½"

Great Basin
Mojave
Sonoran
Chihuahuan

Host Plants
Foliage of purslane
(*Portulaca oleracea*) and
common weeds such as
chickweed (*Cerastium
arvense*); forage plants,
especially buckwheat
(*Eriogonum*); apple (*Malus*)
and grape (*Vitis*); and
foliage of truck crops

449 California Cankerworm Moth

Paleacrita longiciliata
p. 545

Wingspan: 1–1⅜"

Great Basin
Mojave
Sonoran
Chihuahuan

Host Plants
Foliage of shrubs in the
rose family (Rosaceae)

450 Large California Spanworm Moth

Procherodes truxaliata
p. 545

Wingspan: 1⅜–1¾"

All habitats in part

Host Plants
Great variety of trees and
shrubs

451 Ghost-faced Bat — *Mormoops megalophylla* — Length: 2⅜–2⅝"
p. 547

Sonoran
Chihuahuan

452 California Leaf-nosed Bat — *Macrotus californicus* — Length: 3⅜–3⅝"
p. 547

Mojave
Sonoran

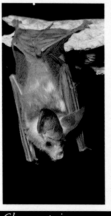

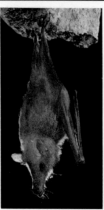

453 Long-tongued Bat — *Choeronycteris mexicana* — Length: 2¼–3⅜"
p. 547

Sonoran

Chihuahuan

Sonoran

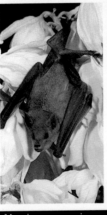 

Great Basin
Mojave
Sonoran
Chihuahuan

457 Cave Myotis

Myotis velifer
p. 548

Length: 3½–4½"

Sonoran
Chihuahuan

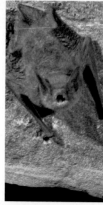

458 California Myotis

Myotis californicus
p. 549

Length: 2⅞–3⅜"

Great Basin
Mojave
Sonoran
Chihuahuan

459 Silver-haired Bat

Lasionycteris noctivagans
p. 549

Length: 3⅝–4¼"

Great Basin

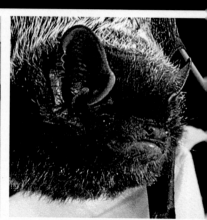

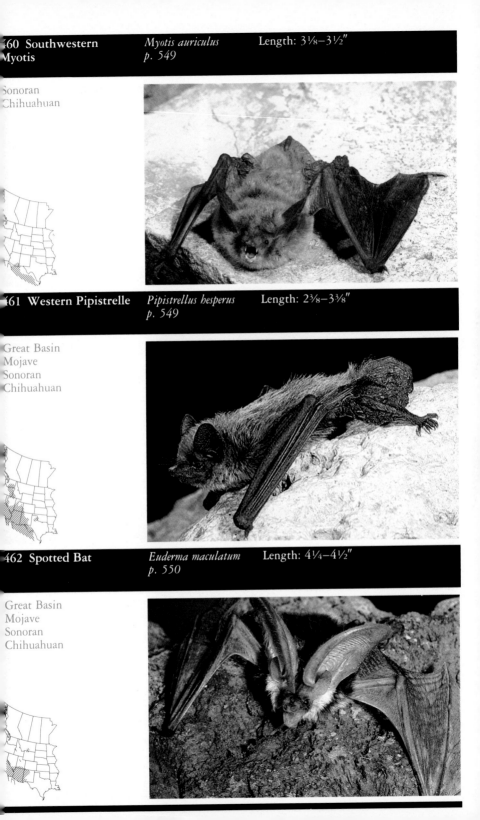

60 Southwestern Myotis *Myotis auriculus* p. 549 Length: 3⅛–3½"

Sonoran
Chihuahuan

61 Western Pipistrelle *Pipistrellus hesperus* p. 549 Length: 2⅜–3⅜"

Great Basin
Mojave
Sonoran
Chihuahuan

462 Spotted Bat *Euderma maculatum* p. 550 Length: 4¼–4½"

Great Basin
Mojave
Sonoran
Chihuahuan

463 Townsend's Big-eared Bat

Plecotus townsendii
p. 550

Length: 3½–4⅜"

Great Basin
Mojave
Sonoran
Chihuahuan

464 Pallid Bat

Antrozous pallidus
p. 550

Length: 4¼–5⅛"

Great Basin
Mojave
Sonoran
Chihuahuan

465 Brazilian Free-tailed Bat

Tadarida brasiliensis
p. 551

Length: 3½–4⅜"

Great Basin
Mojave
Sonoran
Chihuahuan

66 Pocketed Free-tailed Bat   *Tadarida femorosacca*   Length: 3⅞–4⅝"
p. 551

Sonoran
Chihuahuan

67 Big Free-tailed Bat   *Tadarida macrotis*   Length: 5⅛–5¾"
p. 552

Great Basin
Sonoran
Mojave
Chihuahuan

68 Western Mastiff Bat   *Eumops perotis*   Length: 5½–7½"
p. 552

Sonoran
Chihuahuan

469 Botta's Pocket Gopher

Thomomys bottae
p. 552

Length: 6⅝–10¾″

Great Basin
Mojave
Sonoran
Chihuahuan

470 Desert Shrew

Notiosorex crawfordi
p. 553

Length: 3–3¾″

Mojave
Sonoran
Chihuahuan

471 Silky Pocket Mouse

Perognathus flavus
p. 553

Length: 3⅞–4⅜″

Sonoran
Chihuahuan

72 Arizona Pocket Mouse

Perognathus amplus
p. 553

Length: 4⅘–6⅔"

onoran

73 Little Pocket Mouse

Perognathus longimembris
p. 554

Length: 4¼–5⅞"

Great Basin
Mojave
onoran

74 Great Basin Pocket Mouse

Perognathus parvus
p. 554

Length: 5¾–7¾"

Great Basin

475 Long-tailed Pocket Mouse	*Perognathus formosus* p. 554	Length: 6¾–8¼″

Great Basin
Mojave
Sonoran

476 Bailey's Pocket Mouse	*Perognathus baileyi* p. 555	Length: 7⅞–9⅛″

Sonoran

477 Desert Pocket Mouse	*Perognathus penicillatus* p. 555	Length: 6⅜–8½″

Mojave
Sonoran
Chihuahuan

| 478 Dark Kangaroo Mouse | *Microdipodops megacephalus* p. 555 | Length: 5¾–7" |

Great Basin

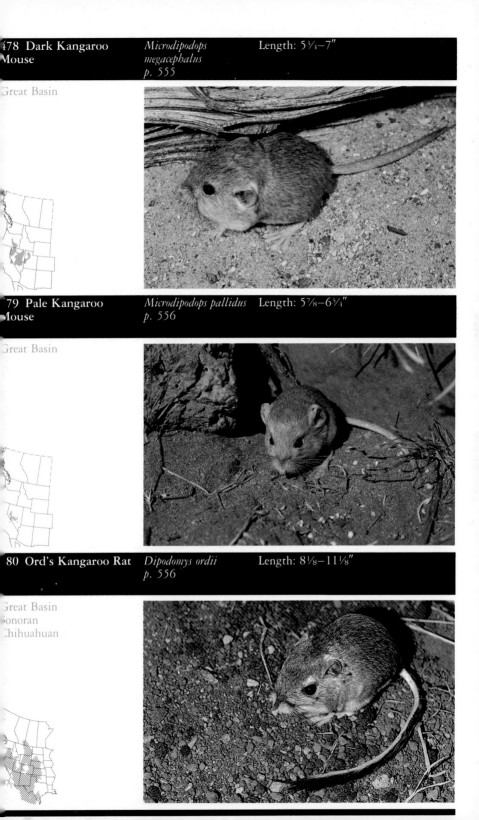

| 479 Pale Kangaroo Mouse | *Microdipodops pallidus* p. 556 | Length: 5⅞–6¾" |

Great Basin

| 480 Ord's Kangaroo Rat | *Dipodomys ordii* p. 556 | Length: 8⅛–11⅛" |

Great Basin
Sonoran
Chihuahuan

| 481 Chisel-toothed Kangaroo Rat | *Dipodomys microps* p. 556 | Length: 9⅝–11¾" |

Great Basin

| 482 Panamint Kangaroo Rat | *Dipodomys panamintinus* p. 557 | Length: 11¼–13⅛" |

Great Basin
Mojave
Sonoran

| 483 Banner-tailed Kangaroo Rat | *Dipodomys spectabilis* p. 557 | Length: 12¼–14⅜" |

Sonoran
Chihuahuan

484 Desert Kangaroo Rat

Dipodomys deserti
p. 557

Length: 12–14¾"

Great Basin
Mojave
Sonoran

485 Merriam's Kangaroo Rat

Dipodomys merriami
p. 558

Length: 8¾–10¼"

Great Basin
Mojave
Sonoran
Chihuahuan

486 Western Harvest Mouse

Reithrodontomys megalotis
p. 558

Length: 4½–6¾"

Great Basin
Mojave
Sonoran
Chihuahuan

487 Fulvous Harvest Mouse

Reithrodontomys fulvescens
p. 558

Length: 5¼–7⅞"

Sonoran
Chihuahuan

488 Southern Grasshopper Mouse

Onychomys torridus
p. 558

Length: 4¾–6½"

Great Basin
Mojave
Sonoran
Chihuahuan

489 Deer Mouse

Peromyscus maniculatus
p. 559

Length: 4¾–8¾"

Great Basin
Mojave
Sonoran
Chihuahuan

490 Brush Mouse

Peromyscus boylii
p. 559

Length: 7⅛–9⅜″

Mojave
Sonoran
Chihuahuan

491 Northern Grasshopper Mouse

Onychomys leucogaster
p. 560

Length: 5⅛–7½″

Great Basin
Chihuahuan

492 Cactus Mouse

Peromyscus eremicus
p. 560

Length: 6¾–8⅝″

Mojave
Sonoran
Chihuahuan

Great Basin
Mojave
Sonoran

Sonoran
Chihuahuan

Great Basin
Mojave
Sonoran
Chihuahuan

Great Basin

Great Basin

Sonoran

499 White-tailed Antelope Squirrel
Ammospermophilus leucurus
p. 563
Length: 7⅝–9⅜"

Great Basin
Mojave
Sonoran
Chihuahuan

500 Texas Antelope Squirrel
Ammospermophilus interpres
p. 563
Length: 8⅔–9¼"

Chihuahuan

501 Townsend's Ground Squirrel
Spermophilus townsendii
p. 563
Length: 6⅝–10¾"

Great Basin

502 Mexican Ground Squirrel

Spermophilus mexicanus Length: 11–15"
p. 564

Chihuahuan

503 Spotted Ground Squirrel

Spermophilus spilosoma Length: 7¼–10"
p. 564

Sonoran
Chihuahuan

504 Round-tailed Ground Squirrel

Spermophilus tereticaudus
p. 564
Length: 8–10½"

Mojave
Sonoran

505 Rock Squirrel

Spermophilus variegatus Length: 16⅞–20¾"
p. 565

Great Basin
Mojave
Sonoran
Chihuahuan

506 Rock Squirrel

Spermophilus variegatus Length: 16⅞–20¾"
p. 565

Great Basin
Mojave
Sonoran
Chihuahuan

507 Porcupine

Erethizon dorsatum Length: 25½–36½"
p. 565

Great Basin
Mojave
Sonoran
Chihuahuan

08 Desert Cottontail　　*Sylvilagus audubonii*　　Length: 13¾–16½"
p. 566

Great Basin
Mojave
Sonoran
Chihuahuan

09 Black-tailed Jack Rabbit　　*Lepus californicus*　　Length: 18–25"
p. 566

Great Basin
Mojave
Sonoran
Chihuahuan

510 Antelope Jack Rabbit　　*Lepus alleni*　　Length: 21⅝–26⅛"
p. 566

Sonoran
Chihuahuan

511 Ringtail

Bassariscus astutus
p. 567

Length: 24½–31⅞"

Great Basin
Mojave
Sonoran
Chihuahuan

512 Raccoon

Procyon lotor
p. 567

Length: 23¾–37⅜"

Great Basin
Mojave
Sonoran
Chihuahuan

513 Coati

Nasua nasua
p. 568

Length: 33⅜–52¾"

Sonoran
Chihuahuan

14 Badger
Taxidea taxus
p. 568
Length: 20½–34¼"

Great Basin
Mojave
Sonoran
Chihuahuan

15 Striped Skunk
Mephitis mephitis
p. 569
Length: 20½–31½"

Great Basin
Mojave
Sonoran
Chihuahuan

16 Hog-nosed Skunk
Conepatus mesoleucus
p. 569
Length: 20¼–35¾"

Sonoran
Chihuahuan

517 Bobcat

Felis rufus
p. 570

Length: 28–49⅜"

Great Basin
Mojave
Sonoran
Chihuahuan

518 Mountain Lion

Felis concolor
p. 570

Length: 59⅛–108"

Great Basin
Mojave
Sonoran
Chihuahuan

519 Mountain Lion

Felis concolor
p. 570

Length: 59⅛–108"

Great Basin
Mojave
Sonoran
Chihuahuan

20 Bobcat

Felis rufus
p. 570

Length: 28–49⅜″

Great Basin
Mojave
Sonoran
Chihuahuan

21 Kit Fox

Vulpes macrotis
p. 571

Length: 15–20″

Great Basin
Mojave
Sonoran
Chihuahuan

522 Gray Fox

*Urocyon
cinereoargenteus*
p. 571

Length: 31½–44¼″

Great Basin
Mojave
Sonoran
Chihuahuan

| 523 Coyote | *Canis latrans* p. 572 | Length: 41⅜–52" |

Great Basin
Mojave
Sonoran
Chihuahuan

| 524 Coyote | *Canis latrans* p. 572 | Length: 41⅜–52" |

Great Basin
Mojave
Sonoran
Chihuahuan

| 525 Collared Peccary | *Dicotyles tajacu* p. 573 | Length: 34¼–40" |

Sonoran
Chihuahuan

326 Bighorn Sheep

Ovis canadensis
p. 573

Length:
5¼–6' (rams);
4¼–5¼' (ewes)

Great Basin
Mojave
Sonoran
Chihuahuan

327 Pronghorn

Antilocapra americana
p. 574

Length: 49¼–57⅛"

Great Basin
Mojave
Sonoran
Chihuahuan

328 Mule Deer (includes Black-tailed Deer)

Odocoileus hemionus
p. 575

Length: 3¾–6½'

Great Basin
Mojave
Sonoran
Chihuahuan

529 Black Vulture
Coragyps atratus
p. 577
Length: 23–27"

Sonoran
Chihuahuan

530 Turkey Vulture
Cathartes aura
p. 577
Length: 26–32"

Great Basin
Mojave
Sonoran
Chihuahuan

531 Northern Harrier
Circus cyaneus
p. 577
Length: 17½–24"

Great Basin

532 Cooper's Hawk

Accipiter cooperii
p. 578

Length: 14–20"

Great Basin
Mojave
Sonoran
Chihuahuan

533 Harris' Hawk

Parabuteo unicinctus
p. 578

Length: 17½–24"

Sonoran
Chihuahuan

534 Swainson's Hawk

Buteo swainsoni
p. 579

Length: 19–22"

Great Basin
Chihuahuan

535 Swainson's Hawk
Buteo swainsoni
p. 579
Length: 19–22"

Great Basin
Chihuahuan

536 Red-tailed Hawk
Buteo jamaicensis
p. 579
Length: 19–25"

Great Basin
Mojave
Sonoran
Chihuahuan

537 Red-tailed Hawk
Buteo jamaicensis
p. 579
Length: 19–25"

Great Basin
Mojave
Sonoran
Chihuahuan

538 Ferruginous Hawk
Buteo regalis
p. 580

Length: 22½–25″

Great Basin

539 Rough-legged Hawk
Buteo lagopus
p. 580

Length: 19–24″

Great Basin

540 Golden Eagle
Aquila chrysaetos
p. 580

Length: 30–41″

Great Basin
Mojave
Sonoran
Chihuahuan

541 Crested Caracara
Polyborus plancus
p. 581
Length: 20–25"

Sonoran

542 American Kestrel
Falco sparverius
p. 581
Length: 9–12"

Great Basin
Mojave

543 Aplomado Falcon
Falco femoralis
p. 582
Length: 15–18"

Sonoran

544 Chukar

Alectoris chukar
p. 582

Length: 13–15½″

Great Basin

545 Sage Grouse

Centrocercus
urophasianus
p. 583

Length: 26–30″ (male); 22–23″
(female)

Great Basin

546 Scaled Quail

Callipepla squamata
p. 583

Length: 10–12″

Chihuahuan

547 Gambel's Quail *Callipepla gambelii* Length: 10–11½"
p. 584

Mojave
Sonoran
Chihuahuan

548 California Quail *Callipepla californica* Length: 9–11"
p. 584 Female

Great Basin
Mojave

549 California Quail *Callipepla californica* Length: 9–11"
p. 584

Great Basin
Mojave

Mojave
Sonoran
Chihuahuan

Great Basin
Mojave
Sonoran
Chihuahuan

Sonoran
Chihuahuan

553 Common Ground-Dove *Columbina passerina* Length: 6–6¾"
p. 586

Sonoran
Chihuahuan

554 Greater Roadrunner *Geococcyx californianus* Length: 20–24"
p. 586

Mojave
Sonoran
Chihuahuan

555 Common Barn-Owl *Tyto alba* Length: 14–20"
p. 586

Great Basin
Mojave
Sonoran
Chihuahuan

56 Great Horned Owl
Bubo virginianus
p. 587
Length: 18–25"

Great Basin
Mojave
Sonoran
Chihuahuan

57 Ferruginous Pygmy-Owl
Glaucidium brasilianum
p. 587
Length: 6½–7"

Sonoran

58 Elf Owl
Micrathene whitneyi
p. 588
Length: 5–6"

Sonoran
Chihuahuan

559 Burrowing Owl
Athene cunicularia
p. 588
Length: 9–11"

Great Basin
Mojave
Sonoran
Chihuahuan

560 Lesser Nighthawk
Chordeiles acutipennis
p. 588
Length: 8–9"

Mojave
Sonoran
Chihuahuan

561 Common Nighthawk
Chordeiles minor
p. 589
Length: 8½–10"

Great Basin
Chihuahuan

62 Common Poorwill

Phalaenoptilus nuttallii
p. 589

Length: 7–8½″

Great Basin
Mojave
Sonoran
Chihuahuan

63 Black-chinned Hummingbird

Archilochus alexandri
p. 590

Length: 3¼–3¾″

Great Basin
Mojave
Sonoran
Chihuahuan

64 Costa's Hummingbird

Calypte costae
p. 590

Length: 3–3½″

Mojave
Sonoran

565 Gila Woodpecker
Melanerpes uropygialis Length: 8–10"
p. 590

Sonoran

566 Golden-fronted Woodpecker
Melanerpes aurifrons Length: 8½–10½"
p. 591

Chihuahuan

567 Ladder-backed Woodpecker
Picoides scalaris Length: 6–7½"
p. 591

Mojave
Sonoran
Chihuahuan

68 Northern Flicker   *Colaptes auratus*   Length: 12½–14″
p. 592

Great Basin
Mojave
Sonoran
Chihuahuan

69 Gray Flycatcher   *Empidonax wrightii*   Length: 5½″
p. 592

Great Basin

70 Black Phoebe   *Sayornis nigricans*   Length: 6–7″
p. 593

Mojave
Sonoran
Chihuahuan

571 Say's Phoebe
Sayornis saya
p. 593
Length: 7–8"

Great Basin
Mojave
Sonoran
Chihuahuan

572 Vermilion Flycatcher
Pyrocephalus rubinus
p. 594
Length: 5½–6½"

Sonoran
Chihuahuan

573 Ash-throated Flycatcher
Myiarchus cinerascens
p. 594
Length: 7½–8½"

Great Basin
Mojave
Sonoran
Chihuahuan

74 Brown-crested Flycatcher *Myiarchus tyrannulus* Length: 8½–9½″
p. 594

Sonoran

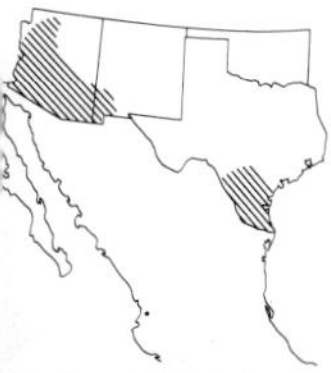

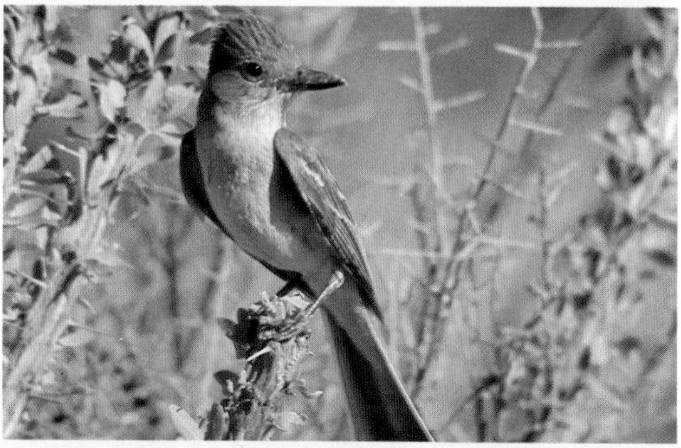

75 Western Kingbird *Tyrannus verticalis* Length: 8–9″
p. 595

Great Basin
Mojave
Sonoran
Chihuahuan

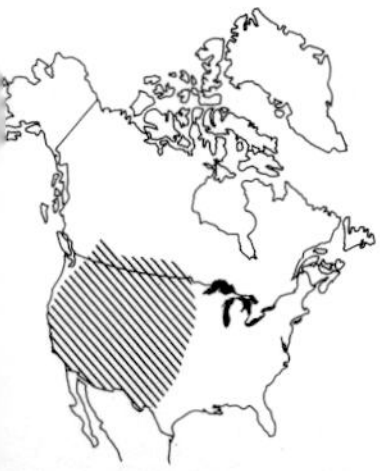

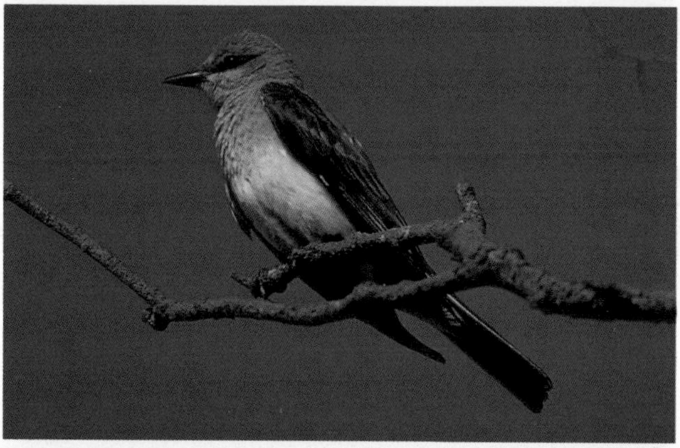

76 Horned Lark *Eremophila alpestris* Length: 7–8″
p. 595

Great Basin
Mojave
Sonoran
Chihuahuan

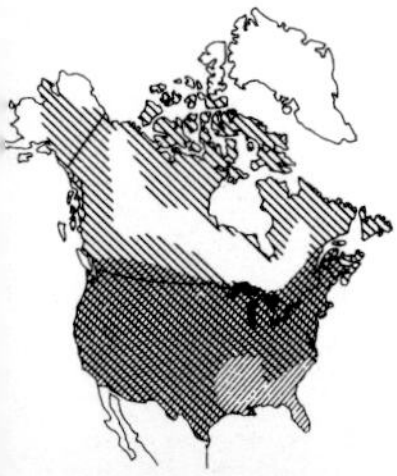

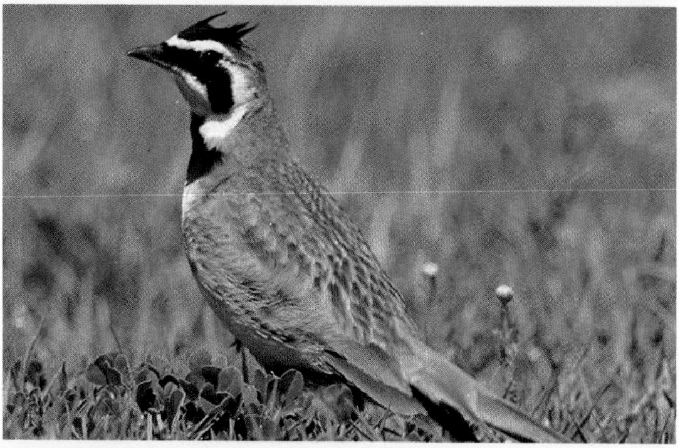

577 Purple Martin   *Progne subis*   Length: 7¼–8½"
       p. 596

Sonoran

578 Purple Martin   *Progne subis*   Length: 7¼–8½"
       p. 596   Female

Sonoran

579 Violet-green Swallow   *Tachycineta thalassina*   Length: 5–5½"
       p. 596

Great Basin
Mojave
Sonoran

580 Black-billed Magpie *Pica pica* Length: 17½–22″
p. 597

Great Basin

581 Chihuahuan Raven *Corvus cryptoleucus* Length: 19–21″
p. 597

Chihuahuan

582 Common Raven *Corvus corax* Length: 21½–27″
p. 597

Great Basin
Mojave
Sonoran
Chihuahuan

583 Verdin
Auriparus flaviceps
p. 598
Length: 4–4½"

Mojave
Sonoran
Chihuahuan

584 Cactus Wren
Campylorhynchus brunneicapillus
p. 598
Length: 7–8¾"

Mojave
Sonoran
Chihuahuan

585 Rock Wren
Salpinctes obsoletus
p. 599
Length: 5–6"

Great Basin
Mojave
Sonoran
Chihuahuan

586 Canyon Wren   *Catherpes mexicanus*   Length: 5½–5¾"
p. 599

Great Basin
Mojave
Sonoran
Chihuahuan

587 Bewick's Wren   *Thryomanes bewickii*   Length: 5–5½"
p. 599

Great Basin
Mojave
Sonoran
Chihuahuan

**588 Black-tailed
Gnatcatcher**   *Polioptila melanura*   Length: 4½–5"
p. 600

Mojave
Sonoran
Chihuahuan

Great Basin

590 Northern Mockingbird   *Mimus polyglottos*   Length: 9–11"
p. 601

Great Basin
Mojave
Sonoran
Chihuahuan

591 Sage Thrasher   *Oreoscoptes montanus*   Length: 8–9"
p. 601

Great Basin

592 Bendire's Thrasher   *Toxostoma bendirei*   Length: 9–11″
p. 602

Sonoran

593 Curve-billed Thrasher   *Toxostoma curvirostre*   Length; 9½–11½″
p. 602

Sonoran
Chihuahuan

594 Le Conte's Thrasher   *Toxostoma lecontei*   Length: 10–11″
p. 602

Mojave
Sonoran

595 Phainopepla　　*Phainopepla nitens*　　Length: 7–7¾"
p. 603

Mojave
Sonoran
Chihuahuan

596 Loggerhead Shrike　　*Lanius ludovicianus*　　Length: 8–10"
p. 603

Great Basin
Mojave
Sonoran
Chihuahuan

597 European Starling　　*Sturnus vulgaris*　　Length: 7½–8½"
p. 604

Great Basin
Mojave
Sonoran
Chihuahuan

398 Black-throated Gray Warbler

Dendroica nigrescens
p. 604

Length: 4½–5"

Great Basin
Sonoran

399 Western Tanager

Piranga ludoviciana
p. 605

Length: 6–7½"

Great Basin
Mojave
Sonoran
Chihuahuan

400 Northern Cardinal

Cardinalis cardinalis
p. 605

Length: 7½–9"

Sonoran
Chihuahuan

601 Northern Cardinal
Cardinalis cardinalis
p. 605
Length: 7½–9″
Adult female

Sonoran
Chihuahuan

602 Pyrrhuloxia
Cardinalis sinuatus
p. 605
Length: 7½–8″
Adult female

Sonoran
Chihuahuan

603 Pyrrhuloxia
Cardinalis sinuatus
p. 605
Length: 7½–8″

Sonoran
Chihuahuan

504 Blue Grosbeak *Guiraca caerulea* Length: 6–7½″
p. 606

Mojave
Sonoran
Chihuahuan

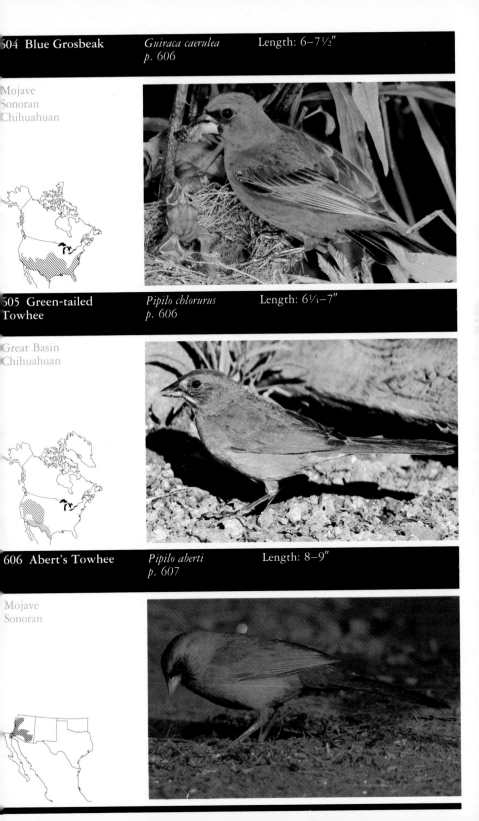

505 Green-tailed Towhee *Pipilo chlorurus* Length: 6¼–7″
p. 606

Great Basin
Chihuahuan

606 Abert's Towhee *Pipilo aberti* Length: 8–9″
p. 607

Mojave
Sonoran

607 Brown Towhee

Pipilo fuscus
p. 607

Length: 8–10"

Sonoran
Chihuahuan

608 Brewer's Sparrow

Spizella breweri
p. 608

Length: 5"

Great Basin
Mojave

609 Vesper Sparrow

Pooecetes gramineus
p. 608

Length: 5–6½"

Great Basin

reat Basin
Iojave
onoran
:hihuahuan

reat Basin

reat Basin

613 Brown-headed Cowbird

Molothrus ater
p. 610

Length: 6–8"

Great Basin
Mojave
Sonoran
Chihuahuan

614 Hooded Oriole

Icterus cucullatus
p. 611

Length: 7–7¾"

Mojave
Sonoran
Chihuahuan

615 Hooded Oriole

Icterus cucullatus
p. 611

Length: 7–7¾"
Female

Mojave
Sonoran
Chihuahuan

516 Scott's Oriole

Icterus parisorum
p. 611

Length: 7½–8¼"

Mojave
Sonoran
Chihuahuan

517 House Finch

Carpodacus mexicanus
p. 612

Length: 5–5¾"

Great Basin
Mojave
Sonoran
Chihuahuan

518 House Finch

Carpodacus mexicanus
p. 612

Length: 5–5¾"
Female

Great Basin
Mojave
Sonoran
Chihuahuan

WILDFLOWERS AND MUSHROOMS

Following rainy periods, which vary from desert to desert, the landscape is marked by brilliant flourishes of color as the desert wildflowers burst into bloom. Showy flowers in dozens of colors upstage the earth tones of the landscape that delight the visitor. In this section are included descriptions of some of the most common and beautiful wildflowers of our deserts. Also included here are several species of mushrooms that are found in deserts, especially after a prolonged rainfall.

Peyote
Lophophora williamsii
37

Low, gray, spineless, nearly hemispherical stems grow singly or in broad, dense clumps, with several pink flowers at the top.
Flowers: ½–1″ (1.3–2.5 cm) wide; petals many, pink.
Stems: 2–3″ (5–7.5 cm) wide; about 8 low ribs.
Spines: none; in their place are tufts of hair on the ribs.
Fruit: ½–¾″ (1.3–2 cm) long, fleshy, red.
Height: 1–3″ (2.5–7.5 cm).

Flowering
May–September.

Habitat
Limestone soil in desert.

Range
S. Texas to northern Mexico.

Comments
Cut, dried "buttons" of Peyote, when chewed, produce color hallucinations and are important in certain Indian religious ceremonies. A federal permit is required to possess any part of the plant. In Texas the cactus has almost been eliminated.

Simpson's Hedgehog Cactus
Pediocactus simpsonii
38

1 or a few spiny, nearly spherical stems have several white, rose, or yellow flowers at top.
Flowers: 1–1½″ (2.5–3.8 cm) wide.
Stems: 2–3″ (5–7.5 cm) wide.
Spines: ⅜–¾″ (9–20 mm) long, straight, brownish; in clusters of 5–11 on low tubercles, spreading in all directions from center, and surrounded by 15–30 white or cream ones, each about ¼″ (6 mm) long.
Fruit: about ¼″ (6 mm) long, tan and dry when mature.
Height: 2–8″ (5–20 cm).

Flowering
May–July.

Habitat
Powdery soils among sagebrush, pinyon, and juniper.

Range
E. Washington to west-central Nevada and N. Arizona; east to N. New Mexico, W. Colorado, W. South Dakota, and W. Montana.

Comments
This cactus is fairly popular with collectors. Other species of the genus are rare. Mass collecting of cacti is inexcusable, but even the person who digs only one has a detrimental effect, for eventually entire plant populations are depleted.

Fishhook Cactus
Mammilaria microcarpa
39

A low, cylindrical cactus with 1 or several stems and many hooked spines; flowers pink or lavender.
Flowers: ¾–1″ (2–2.5 cm) wide near top of stem; petals many, each about ½″ (12–15 mm) long.

Stems: 1½–3″ (3.8–7.5 cm) wide.
Spines: about ¼–½″ (6–13 cm) long, in clusters; central one ½″ (1.3 cm) long, hooked, surrounded by 18–28 shorter, straight, light tan or brownish-pink ones.
Fruit: ½–1″ (1.3–2.5 cm) long, smooth, red.
Height: to 6″ (15 cm).

Flowering
April–May.

Habitat
Dry gravelly places in deserts or arid grassland.

Range
SE. California to W. Texas and northern Mexico.

Comments
The genus name *Mammilaria* refers to the nipplelike projections on the stems. Similar species of *Mammilaria* and *Coryphantha* are distinguished by the position of the flower relative to the cluster of spines. In *Coryphantha* older nipples have a groove on the upper side. Both genera have some species with hooked spines.

Cushion Cactus
Coryphantha vivipara
40

Small, nearly spherical to barrel-shaped stems, sometimes single, but often many in a mound, have pink, red, lavender, or yellow-green flowers near top.
Flowers: 1–2″ (2.5–5 cm) wide, with many petals, each ¼–½″ (6–13 mm) long.
Stems: to 3″ (7.5 cm) wide; nipples 1–1½″ (2.5–3.8 cm) long, grooved on upper side.
Spines: in clusters; central ones 3–10, straight, tipped with pink, red, or black, each ½–¾″ (1.3–2 cm) long, surrounded by 12–40 white ones, slightly shorter.
Fruit: plump, green, smooth, ½–1″ (1.3–2.5 cm) long, with brown seeds.
Height: 1½–6″ (3.8–15 cm).

Flowering
May–June.

Habitat
Rocky desert slopes and rocky or sandy soil among pinyon, juniper, and ponderosa pine.

Range
Central Canada to Minnesota and SE. Oregon; south to SE. California, W. Texas, and northern Mexico.

Comments
The genus name comes from the Greek *koryphe* ("cluster") and *anthos* ("flower"). Nipple Cactus (*C. missouriensis*), is very similar, but has only 1 central spine in each cluster, greenish-white flowers, and reddish fruit with black seeds; it occurs mostly east of the Rocky Mountains but grows westward to central Idaho, western Colorado, southern Utah, and northern Arizona.

Beavertail Cactus
Opuntia basilaris
41

Flat, grayish-green, leafless, jointed stems in a clump lack
large spines and have vivid rose or reddish-lavender flowers on
upper edge of joint.
Flowers: 2–3" (5–7.5 cm) wide, with many petals.
Stems: joints oval, widest above middle, 2–13" (5–32.5 cm)
long, 1–6" (2.5–12.5 cm) wide, ½" (1.3 cm) thick.
Spines: ⅛–¼" (3–6 mm) long, red-brown, in many small
clusters.
Fruit: 1¼" (3.1 cm) long, egg-shaped, grayish brown, dry,
with many seeds.
Height: 6–12" (15–30 cm), with the clump of stems 6'
(1.8 m) wide.

Flowering
March–June.

Habitat
Dry, rocky, desert flats or slopes.

Range
SE. California to SW. Utah and W. Arizona; south to Sonoran
Desert.

Comments
The gray-green stems, low growth, and brilliant flowers,
which often nearly cover the plant, make this a popular
ornamental in hot, dry climates. The bristles can irritate the
skin but do not pose the danger of species with long, rigid
spines, such as the Plains Pricklypear (*Opuntia polyacantha*). It
need not be dug up; a joint broken from a plant will quickly
root in dry sand. *Opuntia* with flat joints are called Pricklypear;
in the Southwest, if the fruits are juicy and edible, they are
called *tuna* by Spanish-Americans.

Claret Cup Cactus
Echinocereus triglochidiatus
42

Brilliant scarlet flowers bloom atop spiny cylindrical stems, in
old plants many stems in a hemispherical clump.
Flowers: 1¼–2" (3.1–5 cm) wide, with many petals.
Stems: 3–4" (7.5–10 cm) thick; 5–12 ribs.
Spines: in clusters of 2–16; on ribs.
Fruit: ½–1" (1.3–2.5 cm) long, plump, red, with a few
clusters of spines that eventually drop.
Height: 2–12" (5–30 cm).

Flowering
April–May.

Habitat
Rocky desert slopes, or dry woodland in mountains.

Range
SE. California; east to S. Utah, central Colorado, and W.
Texas; south into northern Mexico.

Comments
Large plants with many stems in full flower make breathtaking
mounds of scarlet. Stems are highly variable, often with two
strikingly different forms growing in the same area.

Desert Five Spot
Malvastrum rotundifolium
43

Flowers form purplish-pink or lilac globes, each open at top and with a deep reddish center, on short branches near the top of this erect, sparsely-leaved plant.
Flowers: ¾–1¼" (2–3.1 cm) wide; petals 5; stamens many, joined at base, forming a tube around style.
Leaves: ¾–2" (2–5 cm) wide, few, round, toothed.
Height: 4–24" (10–60 cm).

Flowering
March–May.

Habitat
Desert washes and flats.

Range
SE. California, S. Nevada, and W. Arizona.

Comments
The pinkish, spherical corollas are distinctive and, when light passes through them, they resemble glowing lanterns.

Balloon Flower
Penstemon palmeri
44

A few sparsely-leaved, erect, stout stems have swollen white to reddish-pink, bilaterally symmetrical flowers mostly turned to one side in a long, narrow cluster.
Flowers: corolla 1–1½" (2.5–3.8 cm) long, the short tube at base abruptly expanded into a large swollen chamber with reddish lines on the lower inside, the opening with the 2 upper lobes bent sharply upward, the 3 lower bent downward; 4 stamens with anthers, the fifth without an anther, densely golden-bearded at tip.
Leaves: largest to 10" (25 cm) long, lanceolate, opposite, the bases of the paired upper leaves often joined, the stem appearing to go through them.
Height: 2–7' (60–210 cm).

Flowering
May–July.

Habitat
Open rocky areas among sagebrush, pinyon and juniper, or pine woods.

Range
SE. Arizona to central Arizona, S. Utah, and central New Mexico.

Comments
This is one of the most delightful species of penstemon, its cheery puffed-up flowers exquisitely fragrant.

Pale Face
Hibiscus denudatus
45

A scraggly, pale plant covered with whitish hairs. Bowl-shaped, white to pinkish-lavender flowers, more deeply colored in the center, bloom in upper leaf axils and along the ends of leafless, erect branches.
Flowers: 1–1½" (2–3.8 cm) wide; petals 5; stamens many, joined at bases, forming a tube around style.

Leaves: ½–1″ (1.3–2.5 cm) long, very few, ovate.
Height: 1–3′ (30–90 cm).

Flowering
February–October.

Habitat
Rocky slopes in deserts.

Range
S. California to W. Texas and northern Mexico.

Comments
These plants seem to have too few leaves. The delicate flowers are small for the genus and lack the flamboyance of ornamental species.

Winged Dock
Rumex venosus
46

Stout, erect, leafy, reddish stems, with conspicuous white sheaths where leaves join, have reddish-orange flowers in thick clusters.
Flowers: at first inconspicuous, with 6 sepal-like segments, the inner 3 greatly enlarging to broadly heart-shaped bracts, each ½–1½″ (1.3–3.8 cm) long, which surround a tiny fruit.
Leaves: up to 6″ (15 cm) long, numerous, ovate or lanceolate.
Height: 6–20″ (15–50 cm).

Flowering
April–June.

Habitat
Open banks, ravines, grassland or sagebrush desert, often where sandy.

Range
S. British Columbia to NE. California; east to central Canada, and throughout the Great Plains.

Comments
The reddish-orange flower clusters are conspicuous in the late spring; later the broad sepals catch the wind and tumble the seed to new places. The similar Canaigre (pronounced *can-i-gray*) or Desert Rhubarb (*R. hymenosepalus*) grows in sandy areas from Wyoming to southern California and western Texas. Its sepals are rarely more than ¾″ (2 cm) wide and its stout stems grow from a cluster of thick roots. Tannin extracted from the roots was used by early Spanish settlers to tan hides. Roots were also used medicinally. An English name for many of the more weedy *Rumex* species is Sour Dock. The sour flavor comes from oxalic acid.

Texas Silverleaf
Leucophyllum frutescens
47

A gray shrub with leaves covered with silvery hairs, and bright pink-lavender bilaterally symmetrical flowers blooming singly in crowded leaf axils.
Flowers: corolla ¾–1″ (2–2.5 cm) long, about as wide, funnel-shaped with 5 round lobes, the lower lobes hairy inside; stamens 4.

Leaves: generally about 1″ (2.5 cm) long, nearly oval, the base long and tapered.
Height: to 8′ (2.5 m).

Flowering
June–November.

Habitat
Rocky limestone plains, brushland, and deserts.

Range
S. Texas and northern Mexico.

Comments
As one travels from west to east in the Southwest, near the Mexican border, the olive-green creosote bush gives way to the gray of Texas Silverleaf, with its display of bright lavender flowers. These burst into bloom for only a few days at a time, in the summer and fall, depending on the rainfall and are responsible for its alternate name, Purple Sage.

Fairy Duster
Calliandra eriophylla
48

Pinkish puffs made by many showy, deep pink stamens decorate this low, densely branched shrub.
Flowers: in dense heads nearly 2″ (5 cm) wide, on short stems; tiny reddish calyx with 5 teeth; petals 5, reddish, only about ¼″ (6 mm) long; stamens about ¾″ (2 cm) long, projecting outward; style red, slightly longer than stamens.
Leaves: twice pinnately compound; 2–4 pairs of main divisions each bearing 5–10 pairs of oblong leaflets, each ³⁄₁₆″ (5 mm) long.
Height: 8–20″ (20–50 cm).

Flowering
February–May.

Habitat
Sandy washes and slopes in deserts or arid grassland.

Range
S. California to SW. New Mexico; south into northwestern Mexico.

Comments
This little shrub is an inconspicuous part of the arid landscape most of the year, but in spring the exquisite clusters of flowers with their many long stamens form delicate, pink balls, giving the plant a fluffy pink appearance in full bloom. It belongs to a group of mostly tropical woody plants that includes acacias and mimosas.

Feather Dalea
Dalea formosa
49

A low, scraggly shrub with tiny pinnately compound leaves, and flowers in short, headlike racemes, the petals yellow and vivid reddish lavender.
Flowers: about ½″ (1.3 cm) wide; 1 broad upper petal and 2 lateral petals nearly enclosing 2 bottom petals that are joined and shaped like prow of a boat; upper petal yellow, the

remaining 4 bright purple; long, slender teeth of calyx have silky hairs and resemble little feathers.
Leaves: less than ½" (1.3 cm) long, divided into 7 or 9 plump, folded little leaflets.
Height: 1–3' (30–90 cm).

Flowering
March—May, often again in September.

Habitat
Scrubby vegetation on high plains and in deserts.

Range
W. Oklahoma to central Arizona; south to northern Mexico.

Comments
One of many shrubby species of *Dalea,* its dark bark, contorted branches, and small leaves make it an excellent candidate for bonsai. This and other shrubby *Dalea* species are hosts of a very strange flowering parasite, Thurber's Pilostyles (*Pilostyles thurberi*), which remains under the bark most of the year, then produces tiny, inconspicuous, yellowish-brown flowers that burst through and bloom early in the summer.

Crescent Milkvetch
Astragalus amphioxys
~~5~~0

A tufted, grayish, hairy plant with pinnately compound leaves and lavender or red-violet flowers in short racemes.
Flowers: ¾–1" (2–2.5 cm) long; 1 broad upper petal and 2 lateral petals nearly enclosing 2 bottom petals that are joined and shaped like prow of a boat.
Leaves: 7–21 ovate leaflets, each ⅛–¾" (3–20 mm) long.
Fruit: pod ¾–2" (2–5 cm) long, crescent-shaped or straight, tapered at both ends, sharply pointed at the tip.
Height: 2–10" (5–25 cm).

Flowering
March–June.

Habitat
Sandy or gravelly soil in deserts, arid grassland, or among pinyon and juniper.

Range
S. Nevada to W. Colorado, central New Mexico, and extreme W. Texas.

Comments
Crescent Milkvetch can be distinguished from many similar species by its pod, which has only one chamber and has a lower seam that lies in a groove rather than forming a prominent ridge.

Desert Calico
Langloisia matthewsii
~~5~~1

Small bristly tufts or mats and colorful white to pink or lavender, bilaterally symmetrical flowers nestled among the leaves.
Flowers: corolla about ½" (1.3 cm) wide, the 3 upper lobes marked with red and white, the lower 2 generally unmarked.

Leaves: ½–1½" (1.3–3.8 cm) long, with bristles at tips of sharp teeth.
Height: 1–2" (2.5–5 cm); 1–12" (2.5–30 cm) wide.

Flowering
March–June.

Habitat
Open gravelly or sandy desert.

Range
S. California to NW. Arizona and Sonoran Desert.

Comments
All species are tufted and rather bristly. Schott's Calico
(*L. schottii*), also bilaterally symmetrical, has a pale lavender
corolla with purple spots, or a purple, arch-shaped patch.

Desert Four O'Clock
Mirabilis multiflora
52

Vibrant deep pink, broadly tubular flowers bloom in 5-lobed
cups growing in leaf axils of this bushy plant.
Flowers: about 1" (2.5 cm) wide; petal-like calyx has 5 lobes;
stamens 5.
Leaves: 1–4" (2.5–10 cm) long, opposite, broadly ovate or
heart-shaped, with short stalks.
Fruit: seedlike, ½" (1.3 cm) long, roundish, brown or black.
Height: to 18" (45 cm).

Flowering
April–September.

Habitat
Common in open sandy areas among juniper and pinyon,
extending into deserts and grassland.

Range
S. California to S. Colorado; south into northern Mexico.

Comments
Flowers open in the evening. The large root was chewed or
powdered by Indians and applied as a poultice for various
ailments. An infusion in water was used to appease the
appetite. Two similar species occur in totally separate areas.
They are Green's Four O'Clock (*M. greenei*), on dry slopes in
northern California, and MacFarlane's Four O'Clock
(*M. macfarlanei*), in canyons in northeastern Oregon and
adjacent Idaho.

Desert Sand Verbena
Abronia villosa
53

A soft-haired, sticky plant with bright pink, trumpet-shaped
flowers in heads that bloom on stalks growing from leaf axils.
Flowers: head 2–3" (5–7.5 cm) wide, with 5 lobes on end of
"trumpet."
Leaves: ½–1½" (1.3–3.8 cm) long, opposite, ovate, with
slightly wavy, scalloped edges.
Fruit: with 3–5 wings.
Height: creeper, with flower stalks to about 10" (25 cm) high
but stems trailing on the sand, up to 3' (90 cm) long.

Flowering
March–October.

Habitat
Sandy desert soil.

Range
SE. California, S. Nevada, and W. Arizona; south into
northwestern Mexico.

Comments
Following ample winter rains, Desert Sand Verbena may
carpet miles of desert with pink.

Purple Mat
Nama demissum
4

Mats of slender, hairy stems that lie on the ground, and are
leafy toward the ends, with several bell-shaped, deep reddish-
lavender flowers growing from leaf axils.
Flowers: ⅜″ (9 mm) wide; corolla with 5 round lobes at end;
stamens 5, hidden within.
Leaves: 1½″ (3.8 cm) long, sticky, spatula-shaped or ovate.
Height: creeper, flower clusters 1–3″ (2.5–7.5 cm) high,
stems to 8″ (20 cm) long.

Flowering
March–May.

Habitat
Desert flats and washes.

Range
SE. California to SW. Utah, central Arizona, and
northwestern Mexico.

Comments
Nama in Greek means "spring." There are many species, both
perennials and showy annuals, that carpet the desert floor with
purple after adequate rainfall. Hispid Nama (*N. hispidum*),
with erect, bush-branched stems and very narrow leaves, is
another low species common in deserts from southern
California to western Texas and northern Mexico.

Pagonia
Pagonia californica
5

These are low, round, open plants with green, forking,
angular stems, and flowers like pale lavender stars scattered all
over plant on ends of branches.
Flowers: about ½″ (1.3 cm) wide; petals 5, narrow; ovary has
5 lobes.
Leaves: opposite, each leaf divided into 3 lanceolate leaflets,
each ⅛–½″ (3–13 mm) long.
Height: 8–24″ (20–60 cm).

Flowering
March–May, and depending upon rains, again in November–
January.

Habitat
Rocky slopes and washes in desert.

Range
SE. California and S. Utah to northwestern Mexico.

Comments
Fagonias are so open that they cast little shadow. The stems and small leaves present little surface area to the sun and hot dry air, an adaptation to desert conditions that conserves precious water.

Ratany
Krameria parvifolia
56

A low, grayish, intricately branched, very twiggy shrub with bilaterally symmetrical reddish-lavender flowers.
Flowers: about ¾" (2 cm) wide, each on a slender stalk bearing many gland-tipped hairs; sepals 5, reddish lavender inside; upper 3 petals much smaller than sepals, reddish lavender, joined at base; lower 2 petals resembling small, greenish pads.
Leaves: ¼–½" (6–13 mm) long, very narrow, grayish, hairy.
Fruit: pod about ¼" (6 mm) wide, roundish, with long reddish prickles, each with scattered barbs near tip.
Height: 6–24" (15–60 cm).

Flowering
March–October.

Habitat
Desert slopes, flats, and dry plains.

Range
SE. California to W. Texas; northern Mexico.

Comments
This species is commonly found among creosote bush. Similar species lack glands beneath flowers and have different barb arrangements on prickles of fruit.

Filaree Storksbill
Erodium cicutarium
57

Usually reddish stems leaning or lying on the ground, small fernlike leaves, 2–10 small, deep reddish-lavender flowers in a loose cluster, and long, slender, pinlike fruits that stick straight up.
Flowers: about ½" (1.3 cm) wide; petals 5.
Leaves: 1¼–4" (3.1–10 cm) long, pinnately divided, with each segment further divided; stalk less than one quarter the length of blade.
Fruit: ¾–2" (2–5 cm) long, including slender center, with 5 lobes at base.
Height: creeper, some branches to 1' (30 cm) high, others 20" (50 cm) long.

Flowering
February–June.

Habitat
Open areas, often where the soil is disturbed.

Range
Throughout the West.

Comments

This is one of the earliest flowers to bloom in the spring.
Texas Storksbill (*E. texanum*), has flowers nearly 1″ (2.5 cm)
wide; and ovate, deeply lobed leaves. It is found on prairies
and desert from southeastern California to central Texas and
southwestern Oklahoma; also in northern Mexico.

Long-leaved Phlox
Phlox longifolia
8

Slender stems often grow in dense clumps and have bright
pink, pale lilac, or chalky white flowers in loose clusters.
Flowers: corolla about 1″ (2.5 cm) wide, with 5 round lobes
and a slender tube about ½–¾″ (1.3–2 cm) long; membranes
between pointed calyx lobes folded outward; style several
times as long as the 3 branches at its tip.
Leaves: to 3″ (7.5 cm) long, very narrow, opposite.
Height: 4–16″ (10–40 cm).

Flowering
April–July.

Habitat
Dry, open rocky places from low to moderate elevations.

Range
S. British Columbia to S. California; east to the Rocky
Mountain region from New Mexico to W. Montana.

Comments
The most spectacular phloxes have densely clumped stems
which, when in bloom, are completely hidden under a
hemisphere of pink, white, or pale lilac.

Trailing Four O'Clock
Allionia incarnata
9

Brilliant deep pink flowers bloom near the ground on this
trailing plant, 3 crowded together and resembling a single
radially symmetrical flower.
Flowers: cluster ¼–1″ (6–25 mm) wide; on a short stalk, in a
leaf axil; beneath the cluster is a calyxlike involucre of 3
bracts, each partly enclosing a fruit. Individual flowers
bilaterally symmetrical.
Leaves: ½–1½″ (1.3–3.8 cm) long, opposite, ovate.
Fruit: less than ¼″ (6 mm) wide, convex on one side, with 2
rows of 3 or 5 curved teeth on the other.
Height: creeper, with flower stalks to 4″ (10 cm) tall, stems to
3′ (90 cm) long.

Flowering
April–September.

Habitat
Dry gravelly or sandy soils in sun.

Range
SE. California to S. Utah and Colorado; south to Texas and
Mexico.

Comments
The flowers remain open most of the day, not just in the

evening as suggested by the name. The other species, Smooth Trailing Four O'Clock (*A. choisyi*), from Arizona to Texas and southward, has a perianth ³⁄₁₆″ (5 mm) long or less, and the curved edges of the fruit each bear 5–8 slender, gland-tipped teeth.

Indian Blanket
Gaillardia pulchella
60

Branched stems, mostly leafy near the base, have showy flower heads with rays red at base, tipped with yellow, each with 3 teeth at broad end.
Flowers: head 1½–2½″ (3.8–6.3 cm) wide; disk reddish maroon, domelike, with bristly scales among the flowers; rays ½–¾″ (1.3–2 cm) long.
Leaves: to 3″ (7.5 cm) long, oblong, toothed or plain on edges.
Fruit: seedlike, with tapered, white, translucent scales at tip.
Height: 1–2′ (30–60 cm).

Flowering
May–July.

Habitat
Sandy plains and desert, common along roadsides.

Range
Arizona to Texas; north to SE. Colorado and Nebraska; south into Mexico.

Comments
Frequent along roadsides in the Southwest, these wildflowers stand like hundreds of showy Fourth of July pinwheels at the top of slender stalks.

Mojave Aster
Machaeranthera tortifolia
61

Several grayish, leafy stems grow from a woody base, and have at their long, leafless ends flower heads with many narrow pale lavender or pale violet rays surrounding a yellow disk.
Flowers: heads about 2″ (5 cm) wide.
Leaves: 1–2½″ (2.5–6.3 cm) long, lanceolate or narrower, usually covered with gray hairs, bearing spiny teeth along edges and a spine at tip.
Height: 1–2½′ (30–75 cm).

Flowering
March–May, and again in October, depending on rains.

Habitat
Dry rocky desert slopes and washes.

Range
SE. California to SW. Utah and W. Arizona.

Comments
The rays' pastel hue seems unexpectedly delicate in this harsh environment. Plants occasionally line roadsides, but usually occur on rocky outwash fans. A similar species, Big Bend Aster (*M. wrightii*), grows in western Texas and nearby Mexico.

Tahoka Daisy
Machaeranthera tanacetifolia
2

Branched stems with fernlike leaves end in heads with many bright purple, very narrow rays surrounding a yellow disk.
Flowers: heads 1¼–2½″ (3.1–6.3 cm) wide.
Leaves: 2–5″ (5–12.5 cm) long, pinnately divided, the main segments also pinnately divided.
Fruit: seedlike, covered with short hairs lying flat on the surface, the top with many slender bristles.
Height: 4–16″ (10–40 cm).

Flowering
May–September.

Habitat
Sandy open ground on plains or deserts.

Range
Alberta to Texas, Arizona, and Mexico.

Comments
The fernlike leaves of this beautiful species make it one of the easiest to identify in a complex group. False Tahoka Daisy (*M. parviflora*), similar but with smaller heads and less elaborately divided leaves, grows from Utah to Arizona, Texas, and Mexico.

Nuttall's Larkspur
Delphinium nuttallianum
3

Generally only 1 stem with a few leaves, mostly at base, and blue or blue-violet bilateral flowers in one or more racemes.
Flowers: about 1″ (2.5 cm) wide; sepals 5, blue, with ovate blades, the uppermost also bearing a backward-projecting spur ½–1″ (1.3–2.5 cm) long; petals 4, blue or white with blue marks, about 3⁄16″ (5 mm) long, deeply notched on lower edge, upper petals white or bluish, angling upward from center of flower.
Leaves: to 3″ (7.5 cm) wide, nearly round, palmately divided into narrow, forked lobes.
Height: 4–16″ (10–40 cm).

Flowering
March–July.

Habitat
Well-drained soil in sagebrush deserts and open pine forests.

Range
British Columbia to N. California; east to Colorado, Nebraska, Wyoming, and Montana.

Comments
Low larkspur species are difficult to distinguish, and in the West are second only to locoweeds (*Astragalus* and *Oxytropis*) as a livestock poison, especially among cattle.

hia
alvia columbariae
4

At intervals near the top of a 4-sided stem bloom small, very deep blue bilaterally symmetrical flowers in a few dense, round clusters, beneath which are purplish bracts, each tipped with a spine.

Flowers: corolla about ½" (1.3 cm) long, with prominent upper and lower lips; stamens 2.
Leaves: to 4" (10 cm) long, mostly at base, oblong, irregularly divided.
Height: 4–20" (10–50 cm).

Flowering
March–June.

Habitat
Open places in chaparral and in deserts.

Range
Southern half of California to Baja California; east to SW. Utah, Arizona, and SW. New Mexico.

Comments
Chia (pronounced *chee-ah*) is the common name for several *Salvia* species from which Indians made pinole, a meal ground from parched seeds. When steeped in water the seeds also produced a thick, mucilaginous drink.

Scalloped Phacelia
Phacelia integrifolia
65

Glandular, bad-scented, sticky, commonly stout, leafy stems with purplish-lavender or bluish-purple flowers in coils at end of upper branches.
Flowers: corolla about ¼" (6 mm) wide, funnel-shaped, with round lobes at end; stamens 5, protruding.
Leaves: to 3" (7.5 cm) long, narrowly ovate, scalloped or shallowly lobed.
Fruit: capsule, with only 4 dark seeds, each with 2 grooves on inner side, no wrinkles in grooves as in similar species.
Height: 6–30" (15–75 cm).

Flowering
March–September.

Habitat
Rocky or sandy places in deserts and among pinyon and juniper.

Range
S. Utah to W. Oklahoma; south to W. Texas, New Mexico, Arizona, and northern Mexico.

Comments
A large, mostly western American genus that is distinguished by bluish or purplish corollas in coils and protruding stamens. Identification of individual species is determined by technical features such as seed details.

Pale Trumpets
Ipomopsis longiflora
66

Slender, pale blue-violet, pale blue, or white, trumpet-shaped flowers bloom singly or in pairs, spreading from axils of upper bracts on this spindly, openly branched, sparsely-leaved plant.
Flowers: corolla 1–1½" (2.5–3.8 cm) long, with a very narrow tube and a flared end resembling a 5-pointed star.
Leaves: near base to 1½" (3.8 cm) long, pinnately

divided into a few narrow lobes; those above, shorter and less divided.
Height: to 2' (60 cm).

Flowering
March–October.

Habitat
Sandy deserts and arid grassland.

Range
S. Utah to W. Nebraska; south to W. Texas, Arizona, and northern Mexico.

Comments
The slender, pale flowers look almost too delicate for the intense heat of the desert and plains, but these rather ungainly plants are vigorous and often grow in profusion. At night, moths attracted to the pale flowers feed on the nectar.

urple Groundcherry
hysalis lobata
7

Blue-violet or violet, nearly round, saucer-shaped flowers bloom on slender stalks in leaf axils of short, erect stems that grow from a rosette of leaves, or on longer, leafy stems that lie on the ground, their ends turning upward.
Flowers: corolla about ¾" (2 cm) wide; hairy pads alternate with bases of 5 slender stamens near center of flower, the anthers like small yellow knobs; calyx enlarges as fruit matures and forms a 5-sided bladder ¾" (2 cm) long.
Leaves: to 4" (10 cm) long, lanceolate, pinnately lobed or divided.
Fruit: berry about ¼" (6 mm) in diameter enclosed in calyx.
Height: creeper, with some branches to about 6" (15 cm).

Flowering
March–September.

Habitat
Open areas in desert plains, frequent in agricultural areas.

Range
Arizona to Kansas, south to Mexico.

Comments
The berry is edible, but caution is advised, for the flower resembles some of those of *Solanum,* a genus with both edible and deadly berries, and unripe berries of some species of *Physalis* are also poisonous. The large tomatillo, meaning "little tomato," common in Mexican and Southwestern markets, adds a pleasant tang to salads. Purple Groundcherry is sometimes put in the genus *Quincula.*

ones' Penstemon
enstemon dolius
8

A low plant with stems prostrate to erect, and with light blue or violet bilaterally symmetrical flowers in short clusters near the tips.
Flowers: corolla ½–¾" (1.3–2 cm) long, the 2 lobes of upper lip arched forward, the lower 3 spreading downward, light

blue, the tubular base violet and glandular-hairy on the outside; 4 stamens with anthers, fifth without an anther, bearded at tip.
Leaves: ½–2″ (1.3–5 cm) long, narrowly lanceolate, opposite.
Height: 2–8″ (5–20 cm).

Flowering
May–June.

Habitat
Dry gravelly or clay slopes on sagebrush or among pinyon and juniper.

Range
E. Nevada to NE. Utah.

Comments
This little penstemon with its short flower clusters and bright, short flowers is a common sight among the arid bushy lands of the Great Basin region.

Arizona Blue-eyes
Evolvulus arizonicus
69

This plant has grayish hairs, slender, erect stems, and a shallow, bowl-shaped blue flower on a slender stalk in each upper leaf axil.
Flowers: corolla ½–¾″ (1.3–2 cm) wide, with 5 round lobes; stamens 5.
Leaves: ¾–1″ (2–2.5 cm) long, lanceolate.
Height: to 1′ (30 cm).

Flowering
April–October.

Habitat
Open areas in deserts, grassland, and among pinyon and juniper.

Range
S. Arizona, SW. New Mexico, and northern Mexico.

Comments
This has the largest, prettiest flowers of several southwestern species of *Evolvulus*.

Desert Bell
Phacelia campanularia
70

Stiff, erect, leafy, glandular-hairy plant with dark blue, bell-like flowers in loose coils at the end of an open flower cluster.
Flowers: ¾–1½″ (2–3.8 cm) long, with 5 round lobes, the tubular part not constricted at base of lobes; expanded stamen bases hairless.
Leaves: ¾–3″ (2–7.5 cm) long, ovate, the edges shallowly lobed and sharply toothed.
Height: 8–30″ (20–75 cm).

Flowering
February–April.

Habitat
Dry sandy or gravelly places in deserts.

Range
S. California.

Comments
In a spring following a wet winter, thousands of these plants
will bloom, forming masses of deep, rich blue. The similar
California Bell (*P. minor*), from southern California and
northern Baja California, has a violet corolla with a cream spot
on each lobe, the opening slightly constricted, and hair on the
expanded stamen bases.

**Net-cup Snapdragon
Vine**
Maurandya wislizenii
71

Vine with rather arrow-shaped leaves and pale blue-violet
snapdragon flowers in axils of bractlike leaves.
Flowers: bilaterally symmetrical corolla 1″ (2.5 cm) long;
sepals enlarging as fruit matures, with a rigid, netlike pattern
throughout, the base of each becoming swollen and pouchlike.
Leaves: to 2″ (5 cm) long, on stalks about as long.
Fruit: capsule.
Height: vine, to 10′ (3 m) long.

Flowering
April–July.

Habitat
Among shrubs and on dunes.

Range
SE. Arizona to W. Texas and northern Mexico.

Comments
This species is much coarser-looking than its close relative,
Little Snapdragon Vine (*M. antirrhiniflora*).

Coulter's Lupine
Lupinus sparsiflorus
72

Slender, erect, branched stems have pale blue or blue-lilac
flowers in open racemes.
Flowers: ½″ (1.3 cm) long; top petal (banner) usually with
white or pale yellow center; 2 bottom petals (keel) usually
hairy on lower edge near base, and with a slender point at tip.
Leaves: palmately compound, with 5–9 leaflets, each ½–1½″
(1.3–3.8 cm) long, usually only about ⅛″ (3 mm) wide,
arranged like wheel spokes.
Height: 8–16″ (20–40 cm).

Flowering
January–May.

Habitat
Open fields, slopes, and deserts.

Range
S. California and N. Baja California, S. Nevada and SW. New
Mexico.

Comments
In a "good year" with ample fall and winter rains, Coulter's
Lupine carpets the floor of the southern Arizona desert,

competing for attention with Globemallows (*Sphaeralcea* spp.) and Desert Marigold (*Baileya multiradiata*), providing mile after mile of blue-violet, brick-red, and brilliant yellow. Found only in the Big Bend region of Texas is the similar Chisos Bluebonnet (*L. havardii*), with dark blue-violet petals.

White Horsenettle
Solanum elaeagnifolium
73

Stems grow in patches and bear fine prickles, bluish-gray lanceolate leaves, and bluish-violet, violet, or lavender, starlike flowers.
Flowers: ¾–1¼" (2–3.1 cm) wide, with 5 points on corolla; long anthers form a slender yellow cone in center of flower, especially when young.
Leaves: 1–4" (2.5–10 cm) long, usually with wavy edges.
Fruit: berry ½" (1.3 cm) wide, shiny, yellow.
Height: to 3' (90 cm).

Flowering
May–September.

Habitat
Dry open areas, now common along roads, in old lots, and in agricultural regions.

Range
Across the Southwest to central California; south into Mexico.

Comments
The lavender stars with yellow centers are beautifully set off by the silvery foliage, and large patches of the plant in full bloom are striking. However, the plants are aggressive, poisonous weeds, spreading steadily from deep rootstocks. The genus name, from the Latin *solamen* ("quieting"), alludes to the narcotic properties of many species. Southwestern Indians used the crushed berries to curdle milk in making cheese, and they have also been used in various preparations for sore throat and toothache. Many economically important plants also are in this family, including potato, tomato, chili, tobacco, eggplant, and petunia.

Little Snapdragon Vine
Maurandya antirrhiniflora
74

Stems twine through other vegetation; flowers pale blue-violet or reddish lavender, their stalks and those of leaves curved and twisted.
Flowers: corolla bilaterally symmetrical, ¾–1" (2–2.5 cm) long, with a hairy cream patch at base of lower lip near opening, 2 lobes of upper lip bent upward, the 3 lobes of lower lip bent downward.
Leaves: about 1" (2.5 cm) long, shaped like arrowheads.
Height: vine, with stems to 7' (2.1 m) long.

Flowering
June–September.

Habitat
Sandy or gravelly soil, in deserts, sometimes on rock walls, and among pinyon and juniper.

Range
SE. California to W. Texas; south into Mexico.

Comments
These little snapdragons, attractive and well worth
cultivating, can be grown from seed. They will produce small,
scrambling vines that die back to the ground each winter.

Bladder Sage
Salazaria mexicana
75

On this grayish-green shrub with spine-tipped twigs, it is
usually the papery bladders scattered over the surface that
attract attention.
Flowers: ¾" (2 cm) long, in loose racemes; calyx bladderlike,
pale orange or greenish, swelling to ¾" (2 cm) wide, corolla
bilaterally symmetrical, with a deep blue-violet upper lip and
a pale tube and lower lip.
Leaves: about ½" (1.3 cm) long, opposite, broadly lanceolate.
Height: 2–3' (60–90 cm).

Flowering
March–June.

Habitat
In deserts, commonly in washes.

Range
S. California to S. Utah, W. Arizona, SW. Texas, and
northern Mexico.

Comments
The bladderlike calyx may be blown by the wind, thus
dispersing seeds to new areas.

Spike Broomrape
Orobanche multiflora
76

The thick, purple conelike stems of this plant grow singly or
clustered, have purple or yellowish bilaterally symmetrical
flowers in axils of bracts; corolla tube lighter than lobes.
Flowers: corolla ½–1½" (1.3–3.8 cm) long, upper lip bent
back and erect, 2-lobed, lower lip 3-lobed, lobes roundish at
tips or bluntly pointed; style remains on developing capsule.
Leaves: reduced to bracts on stems.
Height: 4–20" (10–50 cm).

Flowering
March–September.

Habitat
Prairies, rangeland, and deserts.

Range
E. Washington to Mexico; east to Texas, Oklahoma, and
Wyoming.

Comments
A parasite on roots of certain Asteraceae species. The name
Broomrape refers to any species parasitic on the shrub Broom
(*Cytisus*).

Death Valley Sage
Salvia funerea
77

A compact, densely branched, ghostly white-woolly shrub with deep bluish-violet to violet bilaterally symmetrical flowers.
Flowers: about ½" (1.3 cm) long with corolla protruding from each densely woolly calyx.
Leaves: ½–¾" (1.3–2 cm) long, ovate, thick and leathery, spine-tipped, covered with white wool.
Height: 1½–4' (45–120 cm).

Flowering
March–May.

Habitat
Hot rocky washes and canyon walls.

Range
Mountains around Death Valley, California, and adjacent Nevada.

Comments
This plant's conspicuous white wool probably serves to reflect heat and reduce the effect of the strong, drying winds that sweep through the hot canyons much of the year. It is protected by law and should not be picked.

Western Peppergrass
Lepidium montanum
78

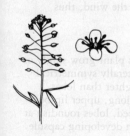

Many slender branches form a round plant, each branch ending in a short, dense raceme of minute white flowers.
Flowers: petals 4, each ⅛" (3 mm) long.
Leaves: at base about 1½–3" (3.8–7.5 cm) long, deeply and sharply pinnately lobed; ones on stem smaller and often not lobed.
Fruit: pods ⅛" (3 mm) long, ovate, flat, style at tip longer than tiny notch in which it grows.
Height: to 16" (40 cm).

Flowering
March–June and sometimes again after summer rains.

Habitat
Dry open areas in deserts and rangeland, occurring with creosote bush, sagebrush, pinyon and juniper.

Range
SE. Oregon to S. California; east to W. Texas, central Wyoming, and central Colorado.

Comments
There are at least 15 races of this species, but any perennial rather bushy mustard with small white flowers is likely to be Western Peppergrass. The showiest species is Fremont's Peppergrass (*L. fremontii*), from southeastern California to southwestern Utah, western Arizona, and northwestern Mexico. It has white flowers with petals ³⁄₁₆" (5 mm) long and pods resembling broad hearts about ¼" (6 mm) wide.

Spectacle Pod
Dithyrea wislizenii
79

A grayish, hairy plant, either branched or unbranched, with pinnately lobed leaves and white flowers in dense, thick racemes.
Flowers: petals 4, about ½" (1.3 cm) long.
Leaves: at base up to 6" (15 cm) long, edges deeply pinnately lobed; those on stem shorter and generally less deeply indented.
Fruit: pod nearly ½" (1.3 cm) wide, flat, with 2 rounded lobes.
Height: to 2' (60 cm).

Flowering
February–May and often again after summer rains.

Habitat
Open sandy soil in dry grassland and deserts.

Range
W. Oklahoma and W. Texas to S. Utah, W. Arizona, and northern Mexico.

Comments
The genus name means "two shields" in Greek and refers to the pod, which resembles a pair of spectacles. A second species, California Spectacle Pod (*D. californica*), which grows in western Arizona, southern Nevada, southern California, and northwestern Mexico, has shallowly lobed, yellowish-green leaves.

Poison Milkweed
Asclepias subverticillata
80

White starlike flowers in round umbels; 3–5 very narrow leaves in whorls at nodes form feathery clumps or patches. Sap milky.
Flowers: umbels ¾–1¼" (2–3.1 cm) wide; each flower, almost ½" (1.3 cm) wide, has 5 tiny sepals, 5 petals, bent back, and 5 roundish hoods with long horns arched toward center.
Leaves: ¾–5" (2–12.5 cm) long, with dwarf branches and very small leaves in axils.
Fruit: broad, smooth pod 2–4" (5–10 cm) long, contains many seeds with long silky hairs.
Height: to 4' (1.2 m).

Flowering
May–September.

Habitat
Sandy or rocky plains and desert flats and slopes, common along roadsides.

Range
Central Arizona, much of Utah, and W. Colorado; east to Kansas; south to Mexico.

Comments
This unpalatable species is very poisonous to livestock, which ordinarily avoid it. When better forage is unavailable, the animals may eat it, but with fatal results.

Clammyweed
Polanisia dodecandra
81

Sticky short hairs cover this strong-smelling, branched plant which has palmately compound leaves and racemes of white or cream flowers.
Flowers: petals 4, ¼–¾" (6–20 mm) long, notched at tip and tapered at base to slender stalk; 6–20 long, pink or purple stamens of unequal length.
Leaves: 3 broadly lanceolate leaflets, each ½–1½" (1.3–3.8 cm) long.
Fruit: pod ¾–3" (2–7.5 cm) long, plump, cylindrical, held erect.
Height: 4–32" (10–80 cm).

Flowering
May–October.

Habitat
Sandy slopes and flats, common along washes, in deserts, on plains, and among pinyon and juniper.

Range
SE. Oregon; east across northern states to Minnesota; south to NE. California, S. Arizona, northern Mexico, and most of Texas.

Comments
The common name, Clammyweed, refers to the sticky, moist glands on the surface of this plant.

White Milkweed
Asclepias albicans
82

Tall, leafless, waxy-white stems have woolly umbels of whitish starlike flowers on branches near the top. Sap milky.
Flowers: umbels about 2" (5 cm) wide, with flowers about ½" (1.3 cm) wide; sepals 5, small, greenish; petals 5, greenish white tinged brown or pink, bent back; 5 rounded yellowish hoods with short horns curved toward center of flower.
Leaves: ½–¾" (1.3–2 cm) long, hairlike, 3 at each node, dropping soon after development.
Fruit: Pods smooth, plump, about 4" (10 cm) long, containing many seeds with silky hairs.
Height: 3–10' (90–300 cm).

Flowering
March–May.

Habitat
Dry rocky places in desert.

Range
SE. California and SW. Arizona to northwestern Mexico.

Comments
Asklepios was the Greek god of medicine, and some species of this genus have had medicinal uses. A similar species, Rush Milkweed (*A. subulata*), grows in the same region in desert washes and on sandy flats; it is distinguished by its narrow erect hoods about as long as the petals.

Climbing Milkweed
Sarcostemma cynanchoides
33

A smooth vine with milky sap and pale white starlike flowers in umbels, the long twining stems often clambering over tops of bushes.
Flowers: umbels up to 4″ (10 cm) wide; each flower about ½″ (1.3 cm) wide, with 5 sepals, 5 spreading white, purplish, or pink pointed petals, and 5 white spherical hoods near the center.
Leaves: to 2½″ (6.3 cm) long, opposite, blades narrow, lanceolate, or narrowly triangular with one or more glands on the midrib near the base.
Fruit: pods to 3″ (7.5 cm) long, plump, downy, containing many seeds with silky hairs.
Height: vine, stems to 10′ (3 m) long.

Flowering
April–August.

Habitat
In sandy or rocky soils, mostly in deserts, but also on dry plains and in brush near the coast.

Range
S. California to S. Utah, Oklahoma, and Texas; south into Mexico.

Comments
Sarcostemma, coming from the Greek words *sarx* ("flesh") and *stemma* ("crown"), refers to the fleshy inner portion of the corona. There are several similar species in the Southwest, all hairy or downy.

Steve's Pincushion
Chaenactis stevioides
34

A small, openly branched plant with heads of white disk flowers, those around the edge larger and somewhat raylike.
Flowers: heads about 1″ (2.5 cm) wide, sometimes tinged with pink.
Leaves: ½–1½″ (1.3–3.8 cm) long, lightly woolly, pinnately divided, segments again pinnately divided into short narrow lobes.
Fruit: seedlike, club-shaped, hairy, with 4 lanceolate scales at top.
Height: 4–10″ (10–25 cm).

Flowering
March–June.

Habitat
Rocky or sandy deserts.

Range
SE. Oregon and S. Idaho to W. Wyoming and Colorado; south to New Mexico and northwestern Mexico.

Comments
Other common names sometimes used are False Yarrow and Broad-leaved Chaenactis. There are several species with white flowers.

Tobacco Weed
Atrichoseris platyphylla
85

A smooth, gray-green plant with a flat rosette of basal leaves, tall spindly stem, openly branched in the upper half, and white or pale pink flower heads at the ends of branches.
Flowers: heads 1–2″ (2.5–5 cm) wide; flowers all of ray type, those in center of head smaller.
Leaves: 1¼–4″ (3.1–10 cm) long, ovate, often purple-spotted, edges with uneven, tiny, spine-tipped teeth.
Fruit: seedlike, shaped like a 5-sided club, without hairs.
Height: 12–28″ (30–70 cm).

Flowering
February–May.

Habitat
Sandy washes in deserts.

Range
SE. California to SW. Utah and NW. Arizona.

Comments
The scientific name means the "flat-leaved" (*platyphylla*) "chicory plant without hairs" (*Atrichoseris*), referring to the absence of hairs on the fruit.

Desert Chicory
Rafinesquia neomexicana
86

A smooth, sparsely-leaved, grayish-green plant with white flower heads at the ends of the few branches. Sap milky.
Flowers: heads 1–1½″ (2.5–3.8 cm) wide, with flowers all of ray type, often purplish on back side, the longest ones ⅝″ (15 mm) long, and short outer bracts with slender tips curling back.
Leaves: those at base 2–8″ (5–20 cm) long, pinnately divided into narrow lobes; upper leaves much smaller.
Fruit: seedlike, with a slender, rigid stalk bearing feathery hairs at top, the stalk not quite as long as the narrow fruit.
Height: 6–20″ (15–50 cm).

Flowering
March–May.

Habitat
Sandy or gravelly flats or slopes in deserts, often supported by shrubs.

Range
SE. California and S. Utah to the tip of W. Texas; south to Mexico.

Comments
The genus name honors C. S. Rafinesque, a controversial early naturalist. Two similar species in the same region are California Plumeseed (*R. californica*), with smaller heads and the stalk on the fruit longer than the body, and Tackstem (*Calycoseris wrightii*), with tack-shaped glands beneath the head.

ight-blooming Cereus
reus greggii

With its few angular, gray, thin, barely spiny, twiggy stems, this white-flowered plant resembles a small dead bush.
Flowers: 2–3" (5–7.5 cm) wide, 4–6" (10–15 cm) long, very sweet-scented, with many petals.
Stems: about 1" (2.5 cm) wide; 4–6 ribs.
Spines: 11–13 in a cluster, about ⅛" (3 mm) long, mostly lying flat.
Fruit: plump, bright red, with many seeds.
Height: 1–3' (30–90 cm).

Flowering
Usually June.

Habitat
Desert flats and washes.

Range
S. Arizona to W. Texas and northern Mexico.

Comments
This cactus is inconspicuous most of the year. When in bloom, it is easily spotted only in the evening and early morning when its spectacular night-blooming flowers are open. It is very popular in desert rock gardens and in the cactus trade; when a population is found, the large, turnip-like roots are quickly dug out. It can be grown from stem cuttings, the cut end allowed to heal in shade for several weeks before it is planted in dry sand. May also be classified *Peniocereus greggi*. These and all cacti are protected in some areas. You may need a permit to collect them.

ommon Ice Plant
esembryanthemum
stallinum

A succulent plant with branched, reclining stems, covered with tiny glistening beads; white or reddish flowers in the upper axils.
Flowers: 1" (2.5 cm) wide, with many narrow petals ¼–⅜" (6–9 mm) long, and many stamens.
Leaves: ¾–4" (2–10 cm) long, wavy, ovate or spatula-shaped.
Height: creeper, about 3" (7.5 cm) high, with stems 8–24" (20–60 cm) long.

Flowering
March–October.

Habitat
On sandy flats and slopes in open areas near the coast; also in deserts.

Range
Southern half of California to Baja California.

Comments
Found also in southern Europe and Africa, this plant was probably introduced to North America from the Old World. The beads on the stems are actually swollen with water; they are easily crushed, exude their contents, and give the plant a moist feel. The species name refers to the crystalline look of the water cells.

Spreading Fleabane
Erigeron divergens
89

A well-branched plant covered with short, grayish hairs, those on stems standing straight out; at the tip of each of the many branches blooms a flower head with many narrow white, pink or lavender rays surrounding a yellow disk.
Flowers: heads about 1″ (2.5 cm) wide, with very narrow bracts, mostly lined up side by side, and not overlapping like shingles; rays each ¼–½″ (6–10 mm) long.
Leaves: largest in tufts at base, ½–1″ (1.3–2.5 cm) long, the lanceolate blade evenly tapered to the stalklike base; those on stem numerous, but slightly smaller.
Fruit: seedlike, with numerous fragile, fine bristles at top.
Height: 4–28″ (10–70 cm).

Flowering
April–September.

Habitat
Open sandy areas in deserts, plains, valleys, and foothills.

Range
S. British Columbia to California; east to W. Texas, Colorado and Montana; also Mexico.

Comments
This is one of a large number of similar species. Most usually can be recognized as *Erigeron* by their low form, many white, pink, or lavender rays, and bracts around the head all of about the same length.

Mojave Desert Star
Monoptilon bellioides
90

A small, low plant with flower heads composed of white rays often tinged with rose and a yellow disk, the longer branches tending to lie on the ground.
Flowers: heads ¾″ (2 cm) wide, with nearly 20 rays.
Leaves: to ½″ (1.3 cm) long, few, narrow, stiffly hairy.
Fruit: seedlike, plump, hairy, topped with several short scales and longer bristles.
Height: usually only 1–2″ (2.5–5 cm), but up to 1–10″ (2.5–25 cm) wide.

Flowering
January–May and again in September, depending on rains.

Habitat
Sandy or gravelly desert flats.

Range
S. California to W. Arizona and northwestern Mexico.

Comments
As is often characteristic of desert annuals, Mojave Desert Star's growth depends upon the amount of rainfall. If winter rains are ample, it and other spring wildflowers grow in profusion, even obscuring the surface of the ground; but if rainfall is scanty, the plant will be only a fraction of an inch tall, if it grows at all, with one head disproportionately large in comparison to the rest of the plant.

esert Anemone
nemone tuberosa

This plant has several stems in a cluster, and 1 pinkish-purple or white flower at end of each erect branch.
Flowers: 1–1½" (2.5–3.8 cm) wide; sepals 5–8, generally darker and hairy on back, resembling petals; petals absent; stamens many.
Leaves: at base and in a whorl of 3 about midway on stem, 1¼–2" (3.1–5 cm) wide, repeatedly divided into narrow short sections.
Fruit: many individual pistils, each woolly, all maturing into a round head.
Height: 4–16" (10–40 cm).

Flowering
March–April.

Habitat
Among rocks on desert slopes.

Range
SE. California to S. Utah and S. New Mexico.

Comments
These Anemones differ from pasque flowers by the absence of hairs on the style. There are several similar species in the western mountains.

lackfoot Daisy
elampodium leucanthum

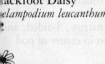

A low, round, bushy plant with flower heads of 8–10 broad white rays surrounding a small yellow disk.
Flowers: heads about 1" (2.5 cm) wide, with 5 broad outer bracts joined to one another for half or two thirds their length.
Leaves: ¾–2" (2–5 cm) long, opposite, narrow.
Fruit: seedlike, with several narrow scales at tip.
Height: 6–20" (15–50 cm).

Flowering
March–November.

Habitat
Rocky soil on dry plains and in deserts.

Range
Arizona to Kansas; south to Mexico.

Comments
At first glance Blackfoot Daisy appears the twin of White Zinnia (*Zinnia acerosa*), but heads of that species have 4–6 broad white rays and a narrow base of several overlapping scales. Both may be found in the same habitat, the range of White Zinnia ending south of Oklahoma.

rdcage Evening
rimrose
nothera deltoides

A grayish plant with large, white, tissuelike flowers blooming on a short central stalk or at the leafy ends of otherwise nearly leafless reclining stems that grow from a dense basal rosette. Buds at the stem tips droop.
Flowers: 1½–3" (3.8–7.5 cm) wide; petals 4, broad; tube between sepals and top of ovary ¾–1½" (2–3.8 cm) long.

Leaves: ¾–3" (2–7.5 cm) long, broadly ovate or diamond-shaped.
Height: creeper, with branches to 2–12" (5–30 cm) high, and reclining stems 4–40" (10–100 cm) long.

Flowering
March–May.

Habitat
Sandy deserts.

Range
E. Oregon to S. California, Arizona, and Utah.

Comments
In some years, when desert rains have been ample, these plants grow in profusion. Each evening hundreds or thousands of flowers quickly pop open. In the early morning light, before the large flowers close, the desert may appear as if strewn with tissue paper. When plants die, their stems curve upward, forming a "birdcage."

Velvety Nerisyrenia
Nerisyrenia camporum
94

This grayish, hairy plant has clumps of leafy, branched stems and at the ends of branches bears racemes of white or lavender flowers.
Flowers: about ¾" (2 cm) wide; petals 4.
Leaves: ½–2½" (1.3–6.3 cm) long, lanceolate, toothed, with short stalks.
Fruit: pods ½–1½" (1.3–3.8 cm) long, narrow, 4-sided, and slightly flattened, held erect, the partition in center of pod perpendicular to broad sides.
Height: 8–24" (20–60 cm).

Flowering
February–October.

Habitat
Gravelly or rocky soils derived from limestone, or on limestone in deserts and arid grassland.

Range
W. Texas and SW. New Mexico, and continuing south to northern Mexico.

Comments
This is the most common species of mustard with large white flowers in the region.

Great Desert Poppy
Arctomecon merriami
95

1 large, white flower blooms atop each of several stalks that have hairy leaves, most near base.
Flowers: 2–3" (5–7.5 cm) wide; sepals 3, hairy, drop when flower opens; petals 6, widest near tip; stamens many, yellow.
Leaves: 1–3" (2.5–7.5 cm) long, pale blue-green, narrowly fan-shaped, toothed across blunt end, covered with long, straight hairs.
Height: 8–20" (20–50 cm).

Flowering
April–May.

Habitat
Loose rocky slopes and deserts.

Range
SE. California and S. Nevada.

Comments
Little Desert Poppy (*A. humilis*), in southwestern Utah and
northwestern Arizona, generally less than 10″ (25 cm) tall, has
4 white petals. Yellow Desert Poppy (*A. californica*), in
southern Nevada and northwestern Arizona, has 6 yellow
petals.

Apache Plume
Fallugia paradoxa
6

A shrub with white flowers and silvery puffs of fruit heads
borne at the tips of dense, intertangled, slender branches.
Flowers: 1–1½″ (2.5–3.8 cm) wide; petals 5, round, growing
from rim of a small cup; stamens many.
Leaves: ½–1″ (1.3–2.5 cm) long, thick, divided into 5 or 7
narrow lobes, edges strongly curled downward.
Fruit: styles form a feathery plume ¾–2″ (2–5 cm) long,
above a seedlike base; many in a head.
Height: to 7′ (2.1 m).

Flowering
May–October.

Habitat
Gravelly or rocky slopes and in washes, from deserts to open
pine forests.

Range
SE. California and S. Nevada to S. Colorado, W. Texas, and
northern Mexico.

Comments
These rather thick shrubs appear unkempt, but in full flower
their white petals are attractive against the dark foliage.

Spotted Langloisia
Langloisia punctata
7

Low bristly tufts with pale violet or lilac, purple-dotted
flowers peering from among the leaves.
Flowers: corolla about ½″ (1.3 cm) wide, the 5 lobes with
many fine purple spots and, near base of each, 2 yellow dots.
Leaves: ¾–1¼″ (2–3.1 cm) long, broadest near the top, with
3–5 bristle-tipped teeth, the bristles on the stalklike base
often with 2 or 3 branches.
Height: 1½–6″ (3.8–15 cm), and in a tuft to 10″ (25 cm) wide.

Flowering
April–June.

Habitat
In dry gravelly places in deserts among creosote bush, and
among pinyon and juniper.

Range
SE. California, S. Nevada, and W. Arizona.

Comments
A relative, Bristly Langloisia (*L. punctata*), the most
widespread and northern of the few species, has bluish-
lavender flowers commonly with a few dark lines. It grows
from eastern Oregon and southern Idaho to northern Sonora.

Desert Lily
Hesperocallis undulata
98

Large, white, funnel-shaped flowers bloom in a stout raceme
above long, narrow, basal leaves with wavy edges.
Flowers: to 2½" (6.3 cm) long; 6 petal-like segments, each
with a bluish-green band on back.
Leaves: 8–20" (20–50 cm) long.
Height: 1–6' (30–180 cm).

Flowering
March–May.

Habitat
Sandy desert flats and gentle slopes.

Range
SE. California, W. Arizona, and northwestern Mexico.

Comments
Conspicuous and easily seen as one drives desert roads, it
seems at first glance an Easter Lily out of place. The bulbs of
this species, the only one in its genus, were once used by
Indians for food.

Sego Lily
Calochortus nuttallii
99

Erect, unbranched stems with a few leaves are topped by 1–4
showy, white, bell-shaped flowers in an umbel-like cluster.
Flowers: 1–2" (2.5–5 cm) wide; sepals 3, lanceolate, slightly
shorter than petals; petals 3, broad, fan-shaped; yellow around
the gland at base, marked with reddish brown or purple above
the gland; gland circular, surrounded by a fringed membrane.
Leaves: 2–4" (5–10 cm) long, narrow, the edges rolled
upward.
Height: 6–18" (15–45 cm).

Flowering
May–July.

Habitat
Dry soil on plains, among sagebrush, and in open pine forests.

Range
E. Montana and W. North Dakota; south to E. Idaho and
NW. Nebraska; across Utah and W. Colorado to N. Arizona
and NW. New Mexico.

Comments
Occasionally petals are magenta or tinged with lilac. This is
Utah's state flower; the Ute Indians called it "sago," and
taught Mormon settlers to eat the bulbs in times of scarcity.

Southwestern Thorn Apple
Datura wrightii
100

Large, trumpet-shaped, white corollas, generally withered by early morning, protrude from the coarse foliage of this stout, branched, rank-smelling plant.
Flowers: corolla 6" (15 cm) long, flared portion with 5 slender teeth on rim.
Leaves: to 6" (15 cm) long, ovate, covered with minute, low hairs.
Fruit: 1½" (3.8 cm) in diameter, spherical, hangs down, its surface prickly with many slender spines less than ½" (1.3 cm) long.
Height: to 5' (1.5 m).

Flowering
May–November.

Habitat
Loose sand, in arroyos, on plains.

Range
Central California to northern Mexico; east across the Southwest to Texas.

Comments
Extracts from this plant and its relatives are narcotic and, when improperly prepared, lethal. The narcotic properties of species have been known since before recorded history. They once figured importantly in religious ceremonies of southwestern Indians. Among several species, all with round, thorny fruits, is Jimsonweed (*D. stramonium*); the fruit has many small spines and does not hang; the corolla is only about 3" (7.5 cm) long. The common name is a corruption of Jamestown Weed, so named because of the poisoning of many soldiers sent there to stop Bacon's Rebellion in 1676. In early days the plant may have been imported for medicinal use. In all species corollas may be tinged to varying degrees with violet.

Sweet-scented Heliotrope
Heliotropium convolvulaceum
101

A hairy, sparsely-leaved plant with 1 erect, branched stem or many long, sprawling branches, the fragrant, white, broadly funnel-shaped flowers blooming in small coils along upper parts of stems.
Flowers: corolla ⅝–1" (1.5–2.5 cm) wide, with 5 low lobes and, in the center, a yellow "eye" around the tiny opening of the narrow tube.
Leaves: up to 1½" (3.8 cm) long, lanceolate or ovate, with short stalks.
Fruit: divided into 4 silky-hairy segments about ⅛" (3 mm) long.
Height: 4–16" (10–40 cm).

Flowering
March–October.

Habitat
Dunes and other sandy places in both deserts and arid grasslands.

Range
SE. California to S. Utah, Wyoming, Nebraska, and W.
Texas; south to northern Mexico.

Comments
The fragrant flowers, largest of all heliotropes in the West,
open in the cool hours of the evening. The ornamental
Common Heliotrope (*H. arborescens*), comes from Peru.

Rattlesnake Weed
Euphorbia albomarginata
102

Dense, thin mats of small, roundish opposite leaves and
slender stems have milky sap, and have many tiny white
flowerlike cups.
Flowers: attached to a cup less than ⅛" (3 mm) wide, 1 at
each node; 4 or 5 small white appendages resembling petals,
with a maroon pad at the base of each; nearly spherical,
smooth ovary on stalk in center, with 3 lobes.
Leaves: ⅛–⅜" (3–9 mm) long, round or oblong, the stalks of
the 2 leaves on opposite sides of stem connected by a single
white scale on either side.
Fruit: tiny, plump, triangular capsule that splits into 3
sections, each section containing one pale brown seed with a
white coat.
Height: creeper, with branches barely ½" (1.3 cm) high, and
stems 2–10" (5–25 cm) long.

Flowering
April–November.

Habitat
Open areas in deserts, arid grassland, and pinyon and juniper
woodland.

Range
SE. California and S. Utah to Oklahoma; south to Mexico.

Comments
One of the showiest of the low spurges, Rattlesnake Weed was
once thought useful for treatment of snakebite; hence its
common name. The cuplike structure has many simple
flowers; those producing pollen have only 1 stamen; those
producing seeds consist of just an ovary. Around the edge of
the cup are several glands which may or may not have petal-
like appendages. The entire structure mimics a single flower,
whose structure is typical of many species of *Euphorbia*. Most
are poisonous, some dangerously so.

Desert Tobacco
Nicotiana trigonophylla
103

Sticky-glandular stems and leaves, with trumpet-shaped,
white flowers in a loosely branched cluster at the top.
Flowers: corolla ½–¾" (1.3–2 cm) long, the flared ends with
5 low, bluntly pointed lobes; stamens 5.
Leaves: 2–6" (5–15 cm) long, broadly lanceolate, lower ones
on broad, flat stalks, upper ones without stalks, the bases with
earlike lobes on either side of stem.
Height: 1–3' (30–90 cm).

Flowering
November–June in the western part of the range. March–November in the eastern part.

Habitat
Sandy areas and washes.

Range
SE. California and S. Nevada to W. Texas and NW. New Mexico.

Comments
The Spanish name, pronounced *tah-bah-kee-oh,* means "little tobacco." Also once called Punche ("a punch") by Spanish Americans, who carefully tended it for tobacco and medicinal use, it is still smoked by Indians in traditional ceremonies. Coyote Tobacco (*N. attenuata*), from British Columbia to Baja California, east to New Mexico, Colorado, and northern Idaho, has fewer glands, short triangular calyx lobes, and dingy white, trumpet-shaped corollas 1–1½" (2.5–3.8 cm) long. All wild Tobaccos are poisonous, but strong-smelling and distasteful, and usually are not eaten by livestock.

Angel Trumpets
Acleisanthes longiflora
304

The highly branched stems spread on the ground or sprawl over shrubs; erect, white flowers stand like miniature trumpets in leaf axils.
Flowers: 3½–6½" (8.8–16.3 cm) long ½–¾" (1.3–2 cm) wide.
Leaves: about 1" (2.5 cm) long, opposite, triangular.
Fruit: about ¼" (6 mm) long, with 5 roundish angles.
Height: creeper, with branches to 8" (20 cm) high, and reclining stems to 3' (90 cm) long.

Flowering
May–September.

Habitat
Rocky slopes in deserts or on plains.

Range
SE. California to central New Mexico and W. Texas; south into Mexico.

Comments
During the day, flowers that bloomed the night before are bent like melted candles, and those yet to bloom are held rigidly erect as brownish-green tubes that blend with the foliage. In the cool of evening new flowers open, flaring their white funnel tops, which attract night-flying moths that drink the nectar and, more importantly, pollinate the flowers.

Southwestern Ringstem
Anulocaulis leiosolenus
305

An ungainly, spindly plant with large, fleshy leaves near the base, and pale pink or pink and white, trumpet-shaped flowers scattered about the widely branched top.
Flowers: 1¼–1½" (3.1–3.8 cm) long; slightly bilateral; 3

stamens project about 1½" (3.8 cm) beyond perianth, the
slender style even farther.
Leaves: to 10" (25 cm) wide, opposite, nearly round, rough
with small, wartlike hairs.
Fruit: resembles a wrinkled little pot with conical lid.
Height: to 4' (1.2 m).

Flowering
June–November.

Habitat
On rocky soil containing gypsum.

Range
S. Nevada, central Arizona, and W. Texas.

Comments
In the heat of the day, the tubes of spent flowers hang
bedraggled. At sundown, new flowers open, the long stamens
and style unraveling and aligning in a graceful sweep from the
narrow opening. The name Ringstem derives from the sticky
glandular rings encircling the stem.

Trixis
Trixis californica
106

A very leafy, branched shrub, often much broader than tall,
with small, yellow, rayless flower heads among lanceolate
leaves.
Flowers: heads ¾" (2 cm) long, each corolla with 3 lobes, 2
lobes toward the outside of the head narrow and curled, 1
toward the inside is broader, often with 3 teeth at the tip;
flowers surrounded by leaflike bracts, those innermost long
and narrow.
Leaves: ¾–2" (2–5 cm) long, with smooth edges or tiny
teeth.
Fruit: seedlike, topped with straw-colored bristles.
Height: 1–3' (30–90 cm).

Flowering
February–October.

Habitat
Rocky slopes in deserts.

Range
S. California to W. Texas; south to northern Mexico.

Comments
Trixis, from the Greek meaning "threefold," refers to the
3-cleft corolla.

Arizona Jewel Flower
Streptanthus arizonicus
107

A smooth, bluish-green plant with small, flask-shaped, pale
yellow or cream flowers (sometimes purplish-tinged) in open
racemes at the ends of the few erect branches.
Flowers: about ½" (1.3 cm) long; sepals 4; petals 4, narrow,
crinkled.
Leaves: about 4" (10 cm) long, pinnately lobed or undivided,
with backward-projecting lobes at base on each side of stem.

Fruit: pods, each 1¼–2½" (3.1–6.3 cm) long, slender, flat, held nearly erect.
Height: 1–2' (30–60 cm).

Flowering
January–April.

Habitat
Open gravelly or sandy areas from deserts to open pinyon and juniper woodland.

Range
Central and S. Arizona to south-central New Mexico and northern Mexico.

Comments
A very similar species, Pecos Twist Flower (*S. carinatus*), with narrow petals but violet flowers, grows mostly on limestone from western Texas to southern Arizona.

Desert Trumpet
Eriogonum inflatum
108

A spindly plant with 1 or a few leafless, erect stems swollen just below the branches.
Flowers: tiny, yellow, on very slender stalks; grow from woolly cups at ends of branches; cups with 6 teeth.
Leaves: ½–2" (1.3–5 cm) long, oval, on long stalks in a basal rosette.
Height: 8–40" (10–100 cm).

Flowering
March–July.

Habitat
Sandy or rocky ground in deserts.

Range
S. California to S. Utah, much of Arizona, and Baja California.

Comments
A common desert plant, conspicuous because of the stark swollen, gray-green stems, which have a pleasant sour taste. Dried stems were used by Indians as tobacco pipes.

Golden Prince's Plume
Stanleya pinnata
109

Slender wands of yellow flowers top tall, stout, smooth, bluish-green, leafy stems.
Flowers: petals 4, yellow, ⅜–⅝" (9–15 mm) long, densely hairy on inner side of brownish base; sepals 4, yellow.
Leaves: at base 2–6" (5–15 cm) long, pinnately divided, broadly lanceolate; those on stem smaller, often also pinnately divided.
Fruit: pod 1¼–2½" (3.1–6.3 cm) long, very slender, each on slender stalk ½–¾" (1.3–2 cm) long joined to thicker stalk.
Height: 1½–5' (45–150 cm).

Flowering
May–July.

Habitat
Plains and deserts to lower mountains, often with sagebrush.

Range
SE. Oregon to SE. California; east to W. Texas; north to W. North Dakota.

Comments
This is a conspicuous wildflower in the arid West, its flowers generally standing above any nearby shrubs. All other species have yellow flowers without hairs except White Desert Plume (*S. albescens*), which has hairs on the inside of its white petals. It occurs from northeastern Arizona to west-central Colorado and northwestern New Mexico.

Jackass Clover
Wislizenia refracta
110

An often densely branched plant with palmately compound leaves and many tiny yellow flowers in dense racemes.
Flowers: petals 4, about ⅛″ (3 mm) long; stamens 6.
Leaves: 3 elliptic leaflets, each ½–1¼″ (1.3–3.1 cm) long.
Fruit: pod about ⅛″ (3 mm) long, with 2 rounded lobes side by side, a pointed style between, the stalk of pod sharply bent in middle at joint.
Height: 16–28″ (40–70 cm).

Flowering
April–September.

Habitat
Low sandy or alkaline soil in deserts and in arid grassland, especially frequent along roads and washes.

Range
Central Valley of California to S. Nevada and W. Texas; south into Mexico.

Comments
Malodorous and poisonous to livestock, Jackass Clover is probably distasteful and rarely eaten. The 3 leaflets give it a resemblance to Clover, but there is no relationship. The origin of the name "jackass" is unknown.

Yellow Bee Plant
Cleome lutea
111

A branched plant with palmately compound leaves and racemes of small yellow flowers at the tops.
Flowers: petals 4, about ¼″ (6 mm) long; stamens 6, long.
Leaves: palmately compound, 3–7 leaflets, each ¾–2½″ (2–6.3 cm) long, lanceolate.
Fruit: pod ½–1½″ (1.3–3.8 cm) long, slender, on long arched stalks, jointed at middle.
Height: 1½–5′ (45–150 cm).

Flowering
May–September.

Habitat
Desert plains and lower valleys in mountains, commonly near water or areas formerly filled with water.

Range
E. Washington to E. California; east to S. Arizona, N. New
Mexico, W. Nebraska, and Montana.

Comments
The genus name was used by the Greek philosopher
Theophrastus for a plant resembling mustard, and while the
flowers resemble those of mustards, the ovary on a jointed
stalk and palmately compound leaves distinguish this as
Capparaceae. The similar Golden Spider Flower (*C.
platycarpa*), from eastern Oregon, southwestern Idaho, and
adjacent portions of California and Nevada, has hairs on stems
and leaves tipped with glands.

Sulphur Flower
Eriogonum umbellatum
112

Leaves at base of plant; on long, erect stalks bloom tiny,
yellow or cream flowers in balls at ends of branches of cluster.
Flowers: each individual, ball-like cluster 2–4" (5–10 cm)
wide, composed of numerous little cups, from which grow
several flowers on very slender stalks; flowers about ¼" (6 mm)
long, the 6 petal-like lobes hairy on outside; circle of bractlike
leaves immediately beneath umbel.
Leaves: ½–1½" (1.3–3.8 cm) long, clustered at ends of short
woody branches, on slender stalks, ovate, 2–3 times as long as
wide, very hairy on lower side.
Height: 4–12" (10–30 cm).

Flowering
June–August.

Habitat
Dry areas from sagebrush deserts to foothills and alpine ridges.

Range
British Columbia to S. California; east to the eastern flank of
the Rocky Mountains from Colorado to Montana.

Comments
Sulphur Flower, highly variable, adds to the difficulties of
identification in a complex group of similar western species.

Yellow Peppergrass
Lepidium flavum
113

Several stems, brittle at the joints, lie on the ground; only the
dense, short racemes of yellow flowers are turned upward.
Flowers: petals 4, about ⅛" (3 mm) long.
Leaves: ¾–2" (2–5 cm) long, the larger ones pinnately lobed.
Fruit: pod, ⅛" (3 mm) long, flat, oval.
Height: creeper, the flower clusters about 2" (5 cm) high,
stems 4–16" (10–40 cm) long.

Flowering
March–June.

Habitat
Low flats in deserts.

Range
SE. California and S. Nevada to Baja California.

Comments
Yellow Peppergrass, often so common it colors broad expanses of the desert yellow, has seeds with a peppery flavor.

Tree Tobacco
Nicotiana glauca
114

An open shrub or small tree with few branches, the yellow, trumpet-shaped flowers tending to spread or hang on slender branches.
Flowers: corolla 1¼–2″ (3.1–5 cm) long; stamens 5.
Leaves: 2–7″ (5–17.5 cm) long, smooth, ovate, gray-green.
Height: to 26′ (8 m).

Flowering
April–November.

Habitat
Roadsides, slopes, and washes.

Range
Central California, S. Arizona, and W. Texas, south into Mexico.

Comments
A common and conspicuous plant along roadsides in southern California. All species of *Nicotiana* contain the highly toxic alkaloid nicotine. An effective insecticide against aphids can be prepared by steeping tobacco in water and spraying the solution on affected parts of the plant. Tree Tobacco contains a more potent poison for aphids, anabasine.

Whispering Bells
Emmenanthe penduliflora
115

Pale yellow, bell-shaped flowers hang from very slender stalks in a branched cluster; the delicate, erect, branched stems are covered with sticky hairs that exude a pleasant, somewhat medicinal odor.
Flowers: about ½″ (1.3 cm) long; corolla has 5 round lobes; stamens 5, hidden within.
Leaves: 1–4″ (2.5–10 cm) long, narrowly oblong, pinnately lobed.
Fruit: capsule with many seeds.
Height: 6–20″ (15–50 cm).

Flowering
March–July.

Habitat
Brushy hills and desert washes.

Range
Central California south to Baja California.

Comments
The corolla remains on the plant long after it dries, a tissue-paper-like bell that rustles in gentle breezes. In the hills of southern California there is a form with a pink corolla.

**Yellow Twining
Snapdragon**
Antirrhinum filipes
16

Many slender stems twist and twine through other vegetation, and yellow bilaterally symmetrical flowers bloom on threadlike stalks growing from leaf axils.
Flowers: corolla about ½" (1.3 cm) long; the 2 upper lobes bent upward, the 3 lower bent downward and dotted with black on the hump that closes opening to the tube; stamens 4.
Leaves: to 2" (5 cm) long, lanceolate.
Height: vine, with stems to about 3' (90 cm) long.

Flowering
February–May.

Habitat
Sandy deserts.

Range
SE. Oregon to S. California and SW. Utah.

Comments
The flowers are brilliant yellow, but the plant, hidden and tangled in low bushes, is hard to find, its twining stems ordinarily obscured by leaves and twigs.

Devil's Claw
Proboscidea altheaefolia
17, 165

A coarse plant with stems lying on the ground and a few yellowish-green bilaterally symmetrical flowers blooming in racemes.
Flowers: corolla 1–1½" (2.5–3.8 cm) long, commonly flecked with maroon or rust-brown, the 5 lobes spreading from a broad opening.
Leaves: blades ¾–3" (2–7.5 cm) long, fleshy, roundish, edges plain, scalloped, or deeply lobed.
Fruit: pod about 2½" (6.3 cm) long, with curved horn nearly 5" (12.5 cm) long.
Height: creeper, with flower stalks to about 1' (30 cm) high, and stems spreading to nearly 3' (90 cm) wide.

Flowering
June–September.

Habitat
Sandy soil in arid grassland and deserts.

Range
S. California to W. Texas.

Comments
As the plump fruit matures, it divides into halves, the single "horn" forming two curved "devil's claws." Also known as the Unicorn Plant.

Desert Velvet
Psathyrotes ramosissima
8

A low compact, round, flat, gray, velvety plant with a strong turpentine odor.
Flowers: rayless yellow heads about ¼" (6 mm) wide, held erect just above the leaves.
Leaves: to ¾" (2 cm) long, thick, roundish, with prominent veins and coarsely toothed edges.

Fruit: seedlike, densely silky-hairy, with yellow-brown bristle at top.
Height: 2–5″ (5–12.5 cm).

Flowering
March–June.

Habitat
Desert flats and ledges.

Range
SE. California to SW. Utah, W. Arizona, and northwestern Mexico.

Comments
The plants form mounds resembling the shape of a turtle's shell, with the intermeshed leaves representing its scales.

Dingy Chamaesaracha
Chamaesaracha sordida
119

A low, dull green plant covered with fine glandular hairs, with a flat, round, dingy whitish-green flower blooming in each upper axil.
Flowers: corolla about ½″ (1.3 cm) wide, with 5 pale bands radiating from center to the tips of the 5 low lobes; near the center, hairy, greenish-yellow pads between bases of 5 slender stamens.
Leaves: to 1½″ (3.8 cm) long, pointed at tip, tapering to base; edges usually wavy and sometimes with low lobes.
Fruit: berry tightly enveloped by calyx.
Height: creeper, stems to 1′ (30 cm) long, mostly hugging ground.

Flowering
May–September.

Habitat
Plains and deserts.

Range
S. Arizona to W. Texas and northern Mexico.

Comments
This and other *Chamaesaracha* species are frequent but rarely very conspicuous. The corollas are dull and the foliage often has an earthen hue.

White-bracted Stick-leaf
Mentzelia involucrata
120

A low, leafy plant with satiny, white stems and narrow, translucent, pale yellow flowers at ends of branches.
Flowers: 1–1¼″ (2.5–3.1 cm) long; petals 5, erect; stamens many; 3 lobes on style; white bracts, with green, toothed margins beneath flowers.
Leaves: 1–3″ (2.5–7.5 cm) long, lanceolate, sharply and irregularly toothed, rough to the touch.
Height: 6–12″ (15–30 cm).

Flowering
March–May.

Habitat
Dry desert hillsides, flats, and washes.

Range
SE. California and W. Arizona to northwestern Mexico.

Comments
This spring wildflower has showy whitish bracts that are distinctive.

Plains Pricklypear
Opuntia polyacantha
21

Low mound of spiny, flat, nearly oval joints has bright yellow or sometimes bright magenta flowers.
Flowers: 2–3″ (5–7.5 cm) wide, with many petals on upper edge of joints.
Stems: joints bluish green, 2–4″ (5–10 cm) long.
Spines: 2–3″ (5–7.5 cm) long, 6–10 per cluster.
Fruit: ¾–1½″ (2–3.8 cm) long, egg-shaped, tan when ripe.
Height: 3–6″ (7.5–15 cm), with clumps of stems 1–10′ (30–300 cm) wide.

Flowering
May–July.

Habitat
Open areas on plains, in deserts, and among pinyon and juniper.

Range
S. British Columbia to E. Oregon and N. Arizona; east to W. Texas, Missouri, and central Canada.

Comments
This cactus is a nuisance to animals on rangeland, becoming more frequent as grass is grazed away. The spiny pads often break off and stick in the noses and throats of livestock.

Barrel Cactus
Ferocactus acanthodes
22

1 large columnar or barrel-shaped stem; flowers yellow or reddish near base of petals.
Flowers: 1½–2½″ (3.8–6.3 cm) wide, in a crown near top of stem.
Stems: 1–1½′ (30–45 cm) in diameter; 18–27 stout ribs.
Spines: stout, reddish or yellowish in dense clusters along ribs, almost hiding stem's surface, 4 in center of cluster in the form of a cross, curved, surrounded by 12–20 similarly stout ones.
Fruit: fleshy, yellow, scaly.
Height: 3–10′ (90–300 cm).

Flowering
April–May.

Habitat
Along washes, on gravelly slopes, and on canyon walls in deserts.

Range
S. California to south-central Arizona.

Comments
The genus name comes from the Latin *ferox* ("fierce"),
commonly applied to very spiny plants. Candy Barrel Cactus
or Fishhook Barrel Cactus (*F. wislizenii*), which grows from
southern Arizona to western Texas and northern Mexico, is
used for making cactus candy. It has in each cluster a large
spine oriented upward, then sharply curved downward at the
tip, and other central spines much stouter than the slender
surrounding spines.

Rainbow Cactus
Echinocereus pectinatus
123

From the top to the bottom, this low, cylindrical cactus is
girdled by bands of colorful spines of pink, gray, pale yellow,
brown, or white. Flowers pink, rose, lavender, or yellow.
Flowers: 1 or a few, 2½–5½″ (6.3–13.8 cm) wide; many
petals.
Stems: to 4″ (10 cm) wide; 15–22 ribs.
Spines: up to ½″ (1.3 cm) long, slender, in close clusters;
point at which they attach is a vertical oval.
Fruit: plump, greenish, with spines that eventually drop.
Height: 4–12″ (10–30 cm).

Flowering
June–August.

Habitat
Rocky slopes and flats, commonly on limestone.

Range
Central and S. Arizona to W. Texas; northern Mexico.

Comments
The banded colors of spines explain the name "rainbow." The
strikingly beautiful flowers seem far too large for the plant.

Yellow Head
Trichoptilium incisum
124

A low, fragrant, lightly woolly plant with small, rayless
yellow flower heads on stalks much taller than the leaves.
Flowers: heads about ½″ (1.3 cm) wide, with a few jagged,
forward-pointing teeth on edges.
Leaves: mostly near base, ¾–2″ (2–5 cm) long, lanceolate,
tapered to a long stalk.
Fruit: seedlike, tipped with 5 white or pale tan scales with
fringed edges.
Height: 2–8″ (5–20 cm).

Flowering
February–May, and October–November.

Habitat
Sandy or gravelly areas in deserts.

Range
SE. Arizona, S. Nevada, W. Arizona, and NW. Mexico.

Comments
Trichoptilium comes from Greek words meaning "hair" and
"feather," referring to the fruit tip's dissected scales.

Desert Dandelion
Malacothrix glabrata
25

A smooth plant with a few pinnately divided leaves and bright pale yellow flower heads on branched stems.
Flowers: heads 1–1½" (2.5–3.8 cm) wide; flowers all ray type.
Leaves: 2½–5" (6.3–12.5 cm) long, divided into a few threadlike lobes.
Fruit: seedlike, topped by several soft bristles, but only two of them not falling off.
Height: 6–14" (15–35 cm).

Flowering
March–June.

Habitat
Sandy desert, plains, and washes.

Range
SW. Idaho and E. Oregon to S. California, much of Arizona, and northwestern Mexico.

Comments
In wet years this showy wildflower will form masses of yellow in sandy deserts.

Snakehead
Malacothrix coulteri
26

Pale, smooth, branched stems with most leaves near the base, and at the tips pale yellow flower heads. Sap milky.
Flowers: heads 1–1½" (2.5–3.8 cm) wide, with only flowers of ray type, those in center smaller.
Leaves: those near base 2–4" (5–10 cm) long, lanceolate, the edges coarsely toothed; those on stem ovate, the bases "clasping" the stem.
Fruit: seedlike, narrow, pale greenish brown, with 4 or 5 sharp angles and 2 fine lines between the angles, and topped with slender bristles, most of which break off easily.
Height: 4–20" (10–50 cm).

Flowering
March–May.

Habitat
Open flats and hills in grassland or desert.

Range
Central California to Baja California; east to SW. Utah and S. Arizona.

Comments
The flower head's broad, round bracts have parchmentlike edges and a purplish or greenish central band that resembles a serpent's scales, and the bud resembles a fanciful snake head, thus the common name. Among similar species, Tackstem (*Calycoseris parryi*), has small tack-shaped glands on the bracts and upper stem; Scalebud (*Anisocoma acaulis*) has seedlike fruits with feathery bristles at the tip, the outer bristles half the length of the inner.

Woolly Daisy
Eriophyllum wallacei
127

A tiny, gray, woolly tufted plant with small golden-yellow flower heads.
Flowers: heads about ¼" (6 mm) wide, with 5–10 oval rays, each about ⅛" (3 mm) long, around a few disk flowers.
Leaves: to ¾" (2 cm) long, ovate, tapering to short stalks.
Fruit: seedlike, narrow, black, topped by a few short scales.
Height: ½–4" (1.3–10 cm).

Flowering
March–June.

Habitat
Sandy desert soil.

Range
SE. California to SW. Utah and NW. Arizona.

Comments
In desert annuals, such as Woolly Daisy, seed production is vital for yearly survival. During drought plants often grow only about ¼" (6 mm) before producing one head, ensuring at least some seeds. Under moister conditions plants repeatedly branch near the base, producing taller stems, many heads, and abundant seed.

Desert Marigold
Baileya multiradiata
128

A grayish, woolly plant, branched and leafy mostly in the lower half, with brilliant yellow flowers in heads, one borne at the end of each of many nearly leafless flower stalks.
Flowers: heads 1½–2" (3.8–5 cm) wide, with 25–50 oblong rays that after seed-set become papery and remain on head. No scales among the disk flowers.
Leaves: broadly ovate, blades 1½–3" (3.8–8 cm) long, pinnately divided into broad lobes, which are again divided or have roundish teeth.
Fruit: seedlike, pale tan or chalky white, lacking bristles or scales at top.
Height: 12–20" (30–50 cm).

Flowering
April–October.

Habitat
Sandy or gravelly places in deserts, common along roadsides.

Range
SE. California to S. Utah and W. Texas; south to northern Mexico.

Comments
Dense patches often form solid strips of yellow along miles of desert roadsides. In gardens a single plant grows into a perfect hemisphere of yellow, blooming throughout the hot summer and into fall. The name Marigold, given to several species of Asteraceae with sunny yellow or orange flowers, comes from "Mary's Gold," in honor of the Virgin.

Threadleaf Groundsel
Senecio douglasii
29

A bluish-green, bushy, leafy plant covered with close white wool, bearing yellow flower heads in branched clusters.
Flowers: heads about 1¼" (3.1 cm) wide, with rays about ½" (1.3 cm) long surrounding a narrow disk; most bracts about same length, lined up side by side and not overlapping.
Leaves: 1–5" (2.5–12.5 cm) long, divided into few very narrow lobes; upper leaves often simply very narrow.
Fruit: seedlike, with a tuft of slender white hairs at top.
Height: 1–3' (30–90 cm).

Flowering
April–September.

Habitat
Dry rocky plains, deserts, and pinyon-juniper rangeland.

Range
S. Colorado and Utah to Arizona, Texas, and Mexico.

Comments
One of the most toxic range plants to livestock, especially the tender new growth; because it is generally avoided, it tends to increase on overstocked ranges. Once used medicinally by southwestern Indians.

Arrowleaf Balsam Root
Balsamorhiza sagittata
30

An almost leafless stalk with 1 large bright yellow flower head at tip grows from a basal cluster of large silvery-gray leaves covered with feltlike hairs; several stalks per plant.
Flowers: heads 4–5" (10–12.5 cm) wide, with densely woolly bracts, 8–25 rays, each 1–1½" (2.5–3.8 cm) long, and many disk flowers, each enfolded by a parchmentlike scale.
Leaves: blades to 1' (30 cm) long, on petioles about the same length.
Fruit: seedlike, no hairs or scales at tip.
Height: 8–32" (20–80 cm).

Flowering
May–July.

Habitat
Open hillsides and flats in grasslands, sagebrush, or open pine forest.

Range
British Columbia south through the Sierra Nevada of California; east to W. Montana, W. South Dakota, and Colorado.

Comments
Indians prepared medicine from the roots. The very similar Deltoid Balsam Root (*B. deltoidea*), found in open places in California, western Oregon, and Washington, is only sparsely hairy, is much greener, and drops its rays soon after flowering. Several species of *Balsamorhiza* have pinnately divided leaves.

Yellow Spiny Daisy
Haplopappus spinulosus
131

A slender plant with small, weakly bristly leaves and yellow flower heads, each at the tip of one of the many upper branches.
Flowers: heads about 1″ (2.5 cm) wide, with rays about ⅜″ (9 mm) long surrounding the disk.
Leaves: ⅛–¾″ (3–20 mm) long, narrow, the lowest sometimes with a few lobes, angled upward or pressed against the stem, the edges with a spiny bristle at tip of each tooth.
Fruit: seedlike, densely covered with short hairs, bearing at top numerous, slender, pale tan bristles.
Height: 6–14″ (15–35 cm).

Flowering
August–October.

Habitat
Open places in arid grassland, in desert, and among pinyon and juniper.

Range
S. California and Arizona to New Mexico; north through the Rocky Mountain states to Alberta; on much of the Plains; also northern Mexico.

Comments
This species has the fewest number of chromosomes per cell known in any plant, 4 instead of the more usual 20 or so.

Sunray
Enceliopsis nudicaulis
132

1 or several leafless stalks, each with a broad yellow flower head at the top, grow from a basal cluster of gray-green leaves.
Flowers: heads 3–4″ (7.5–10 cm) wide, with about 20 rays and a broad central disk, each of the small disk flowers enfolded in a stiff bract.
Leaves: ovate blades ½–2½″ (1.3–6.3 cm) long, tapered to flat, long stalks.
Fruit: seedlike, flat, with hairs on sides nearly hiding 2 stiff bristles at top.
Height: 6–18″ (15–45 cm).

Flowering
May–August.

Habitat
Among the desert brush.

Range
Central Idaho to Nevada, Utah, and N. Arizona.

Comments
Its beauty—golden heads held high above a tuft of gray foliage—makes it a worthwhile ornamental in dry regions.

Chinchweed
Pectis papposa
133

Slender stems branch many times in a forked manner producing a low, small, leafy plant with small yellow flower heads in bundles at the ends of branches.
Flowers: heads about ½″ (1.3 cm) wide, with 7–9 rays

surrounding a small disk, and narrow bracts less than ¼″ (6 mm) long, lined up side by side and not overlapping, each with 3–7 conspicuous glands.
Leaves: up to 1½″ (3.8 cm) long, less than ⅛″ (3 mm) wide, dotted with glands, the leaf base broad, translucent, edges have a few lobes tipped by bristles.
Fruit: seedlike, narrow, topped with a low crown of a few scales, 1 or 2 sometimes much longer than the others.
Height: 2–8″ (5–20 cm).

Flowering
July–October.

Habitat
Open areas on arid plains or in deserts, especially on sandy soil, frequent along roadsides.

Range
S. California to W. Texas; south into Mexico.

Comments
On a hot summer afternoon where these plants are numerous, the air is saturated with a heavy, lemon odor. A look-alike, Lemonweed (*P. angustifolia*), often grows with Chinchweed but is denser and has only one gland at the tip of each bract.

Five-needle Fetid Marigold
Dyssodia pentachaeta
34

A low, tufted, dark green prickly plant with a small, deep yellow flower head on each of several leafless stalks above the foliage.
Flowers: heads ¼–½″ (6–13 mm) wide, surrounded by bracts, upper parts of which are dotted with conspicuous glands; 8–13 rays, each ⅛–¼″ (3–6 mm) long, surround a few disk flowers.
Leaves: about ½″ (1.3 cm) long, opposite, pinnately divided into a few needlelike lobes.
Fruit: seedlike, slender, with pointed scales at top.
Height: 4–8″ (10–20 cm).

Flowering
April–October.

Habitat
Open desert and arid, rocky plains.

Range
S. Utah to Arizona, New Mexico, Texas, and Mexico.

Comments
This common low plant frequently grows near creosote bush and Snakeweed or among pinyon and juniper. Its close relative, Prickly Fetid Marigold (*D. acerosa*), is more woody and prickly, with heads that sit among undivided leaves.

Desert Sunflower
Geraea canescens
35

A slender, hairy plant with a few leaves and, at the ends of the several branches, golden-yellow flower heads.
Flowers: heads about 2″ (5 cm) wide; 10–20 oblong rays, each

¾" (2 cm) long, surround the disk; bracts have long, stiff white hairs on edges.
Leaves: to 3" (7.5 cm) long, lanceolate or ovate, often with a few teeth.
Fruit: seedlike, flat, each tightly enfolded by a parchmentlike bract, the surface of the fruit hairy, the top with 2 pointed scales, the edges with a strong white margin.
Height: 1–3' (30–90 cm).

Flowering
February–May and, depending upon rains, October–November.

Habitat
Sandy, barren, flat desert.

Range
SE. California to SW. Utah; south to W. Arizona and northwestern Mexico.

Comments
Gerea comes from the Greek *geraios* ("old man"), referring to the white hairs on the fruits. After adequate rain, these plants may line mile after mile along hot, dry, desolate roadsides.

Brittlebush
Encelia farinosa
136

A round, silvery-gray, leafy bush with bright yellow flower heads that bloom in loosely branched clusters on branched stalks well above the foliage.
Flowers: heads 2–3" (5–7.5 cm) wide, with 8–18 yellow rays each ¼–⅝" (6–15 mm) long, surround a yellow disk (or brown disk in southern part of range) with scales that enfold the flowers.
Leaves: 1¼–4" (3.1–10 cm) long, ovate, hairy, with petioles.
Fruit: seedlike, without hairs or scales at top.
Height: 3–5' (90–150 cm).

Flowering
March–June.

Habitat
Dry slopes and washes in the desert.

Range
SE. California across S. Nevada to SW. Utah, W. Arizona, and northwestern Mexico.

Comments
In full flower, Brittlebush seems a solid hemisphere of brilliant yellow. The stems exude a fragrant resin that was chewed by Indians and used as incense in the churches of Baja California. A similar species, California Encelia (*E. californica*) which grows near the coast in southern California, has only one head on each stalk.

Paperflower
Psilostrophe cooperi
137

Many well-branched leafy stems, woolly at the base, form a nearly round plant covered with loose wool, usually bearing only 1 yellow flower head at the end of each branch.
Flowers: heads ½–1″ (1.3–2.5 cm) wide, with 3–5 very broad rays, each with 3 shallow teeth at end, surrounding a few small disk flowers.
Leaves: 1–2½″ (2.5–6.3 cm) long, very narrow.
Fruit: seedlike, with several pointed scales at top.
Height: 4–20″ (10–50 cm).

Flowering
April–October.

Habitat
Deserts or plains.

Range
SE. California to SW. Utah and SW. New Mexico; south to Mexico.

Comments
Paperflower forms brilliant yellow globes. Its rays become dry and papery, remaining on the plant long after flowering. There are several closely related species, all poisonous to livestock and usually avoided.

Little Golden Zinnia
Zinnia grandiflora
138

Several short, leafy, slightly woody stems in a low, round clump have numerous small flower heads with 3–6 nearly round yellow-orange rays.
Flowers: heads 1–1½″ (2.5–3.8 cm) wide; disk flowers reddish or greenish; bracts overlap, with round, translucent tips.
Leaves: 1″ (2.5 cm) long, narrow, opposite; 3 veins at base.
Fruit: seedlike, usually with 1 or 2 spines at tip.
Height: 3–9″ (7.5–22.5 cm).

Flowering
June–October.

Habitat
Dry areas on plains and in desert.

Range
E. Arizona to SE. Colorado and SW. Kansas; south to Mexico.

Comments
The genus is named for Johann Zinn, an 18th century German professor, who collected seeds of *Z. elegans* (from which the garden *Zinnia* descends) in Mexico. There he was accosted by bandits who, after searching his bag, left him alone, believing him crazy and therefore unlucky.

Tansy-leaved Evening Primrose
Oenothera tanacetifolia
139

Resembles a Dandelion, but the bright yellow flowers have 4 broad petals.
Flowers: about 1″ (2.5 cm) wide; stamens 8; tube between petals and ovary 1–3½″ (2.5–8.8 cm) long.

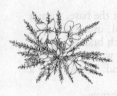

Leaves: 2–8″ (5–20 cm) long, in a rosette, lanceolate, the edges deeply cut and lobed.
Fruit: hard pod about ¾″ (2 cm) long, 4-sided, the angles narrow and wing like, sitting in the center of the rosette.
Height: 1–4″ (2.5–10 cm).

Flowering
June–August.

Habitat
In soil moist in spring but drying by summer, from sagebrush plains to pine forests.

Range
E. Washington to the Sierra Nevada of California; east to Idaho and Montana.

Comments
This is representative of several low, yellow-flowered evening primroses with no stems. The rootstock of this plant branches beneath the ground, the plants forming patches on the surface. It is also known as *Camissonia tanacetifolia*.

Buffalo Gourd
Cucurbita foetidissima
140

A malodorous plant with large, gray-green, triangular leaves growing along long, prostrate stems. Mostly hidden under leaves are funnel-shaped orange to yellow flowers.
Flowers: 2–3″ (5–7.5 cm) wide; some with stamens, others only with an ovary; corolla with 5 lobes.
Leaves: to 1′ (30 cm) long, rough.
Fruit: 3″ (7.5 cm) in diameter, spherical, hard, striped, pale and dark green when immature, lemon-yellow when ripe.
Height: creeper, with leaves reaching about 1′ (30 cm) high, on trailing stems to 20′ (6 m).

Flowering
April–July.

Habitat
Open areas on plains and deserts.

Range
S. California to E. Colorado; east to Missouri; south into Mexico.

Comments
The fruits are easily dried and often brightly painted for decorative use. They are foul-tasting, inedible, and when mature somewhat poisonous. Massive roots of large specimens may weigh several hundred pounds.

Melon Loco
Apodanthera undulata
141

A bad-smelling, grayish, hairy plant with long, coarse, prostrate stems that have tendrils, kidney-shaped leaf blades, and yellow, funnel-shaped flowers.
Flowers: 1½″ (3.8 cm) wide; petals 5, joined at base; some with 3 stamens and no functional ovary, others with an ovary and no stamens.

Leaves: 2–6″ (5–15 cm) wide, attached to stalk at indented side, edges shallowly toothed, lobed, or wavy.
Fruit: 2½–4″ (6.3–10 cm) long, oval, ribbed.
Height: creeper, the leaves up to 8″ (20 cm) high, the stems to 10′ (3 m).

Flowering
May–September.

Habitat
Sand dunes, gravelly flats and slopes.

Range
S. Arizona to W. Texas; south to Mexico.

Comments
Plants with the name "loco" are usually poisonous to some degree; several have toxins that produce madness.

Rough Menodora
Menodora scabra
142

Numerous erect, rough, leafy stems have pale yellow flowers in loose clusters.
Flowers: ½–¾″ (1.3–2 cm) wide; corolla with a short, narrow tube and 5 spreading lobes; hidden within are 2 stamens.
Leaves: ½–1½″ (1.3–3.8 cm) long, broadly lanceolate, usually erect.
Fruit: capsule of 2 translucent spheres side by side, each nearly ¼″ (6 mm) wide.
Height: 14″ (35 cm).

Flowering
March–September.

Habitat
Grassy slopes and brushy deserts.

Range
SE. California and S. Utah to W. Texas and northern Mexico.

Comments
A small genus with species only in southern North America, southern South America, and southern Africa.

Puncture Vine
Tribulus terrestris
143

This plant has sprawling stems and small yellow flowers on short stalks in the leaf axils.
Flowers: ¼–½″ (6–13 mm) wide; 5 broad petals; 10 stamens.
Leaves: 1–2″ (2.5–5 cm) long, opposite, pinnately compound, with 4–8 pairs of leaflets, each ¼–½″ (6–13 mm) long.
Fruit: a hard star-shaped capsule that divides into 5 sharply 2-horned segments.
Height: creeper, flowers and leaves rarely more than 2″ (5 cm) high, but forming mats to 3′ (90 cm) wide.

Flowering
April–November.

Habitat
Weedy open areas.

Range
Much of the arid West.

Comments
A native of the Mediterranean region, this is one of the West's most unloved weeds. The sharp spines on the fruit segments (the "goat's head") cause painful injury to bare feet and to livestock. The spines easily pierce bicycle tires, hence the common name Puncture Vine.

Twinleaf
Cassia bauhinioides
144

A low plant with few stems and 1–3 slightly bilateral yellow flowers on short stalks in axils of grayish leaves with only 2 leaflets.
Flowers: ½" (1.3 cm) wide; sepals 5, narrow; petals 5, round, with upper petal forward of others, stamens 10, brown, the 3 upper ones very small.
Leaves: leaflets ¾–2" (2–5 cm) long.
Fruit: pod ¾–1½" (2–3.8 cm) long, hairy.
Height: 4–16" (10–40 cm).

Flowering
April–August.

Habitat
Hills and flats in arid grassland and deserts.

Range
Central Arizona to W. Texas; south to northern Mexico.

Comments
This large genus, many species of which are trees or shrubs, is found primarily throughout the world's tropics.

Desert Gold
Linanthus aureus
145

A tiny, spindly plant, usually with 3 branches at a fork, and pale to deep yellow, funnel-shaped flowers on slender stalks.
Flowers: corolla ¼–½" (6–13 mm) wide, with 5 lobes, often purple spots in center, and a narrow tube.
Leaves: opposite, divided into 3 narrow, pointed lobes about ¼" (6 mm) long which form a ring of needles around stem.
Height: 2–4" (5–10 cm).

Flowering
April–June.

Habitat
Desert floor and sandy slopes.

Range
S. California to S. Nevada and SW. New Mexico; south to northern Mexico.

Comments
Northern Linanthus (*L. septentrionalis*), from Colorado to Alberta, west to the Sierra Nevada and Cascade Mountains, has a similar manner of branching but grows up to 10" (25 cm) tall and has small white, pale blue, or lavender corollas.

Fendler's Bladderpod
Lesquerella fendleri
146

Yellow flowers bloom in loose, short racemes at the ends of the stems of this low, rather tightly tufted, silvery-gray perennial whose surfaces are covered with tiny starlike scales.
Flowers: petals 4, about ½" (1.3 cm) wide.
Leaves: up to 4" (10 cm) long, lanceolate or strap-shaped, those at base sometimes with a few teeth on edges.
Fruit: nearly spherical pod, ¼–⅜" (6–9 mm) long, smooth.
Height: 1–16" (2.5–40 cm).

Flowering
March–June and often again after summer rains.

Habitat
Rocky or sandy soil, especially that derived from limestone, in arid grassland or deserts.

Range
W. Kansas to S. Utah; south through E. Arizona, New Mexico, and W. Texas to northern Mexico.

Comments
One of the earliest plants to flower in its range, its bright yellow is conspicuous against the drab ground of early spring. In the same region is the similar Gordon's Bladderpod (*L. gordonii*), which has several slender stems that lie on the ground, turning up at the tips. Unlike Fendler's Bladderpod, it is an annual, not tufted, and also has a more open appearance.

Ghost Flower
Mohavea confertiflora
147

In the upper leaf axils of this erect plant are large, bilaterally symmetrical, translucent, yellow flowers, tipped upward or even vertical.
Flowers: corolla about 1¼" (3.1 cm) long, with 5 ragged-edged lobes, lower ones with maroon speckles inside and a maroon blotch at base; opening to base closed by a hairy bump on lower side; only 2 stamens.
Leaves: 2–4" (5–10 cm) long, hairy, narrowly lanceolate.
Height: 4–20" (10–50 cm).

Flowering
March–April.

Habitat
Desert washes and rocky slopes.

Range
SE. California to S. Nevada, W. Arizona, and the northwestern Sonoran Desert.

Comments
The translucent, pale corolla gives the name Ghost Flower. There is only 1 other species, Lesser Mohavea or Golden Desert Snapdragon (*M. breviflora*), which grows in the same region and has bilaterally symmetrical yellow corollas only about ½" (1.3 cm) long.

Mexican Gold Poppy
Eschscholtzia mexicana
148

A low, smooth, pale bluish-green plant with fernlike leaves, mostly near base, and orange-yellow cup-shaped flowers borne singly on stalks.
Flowers: ¾–1½" (2–3.8 cm) wide; petals 4, yellow, orange, or yellow near tips and orange at base, occasionally cream; stamens many; sepals joined into a cone which is pushed off as flower opens; a conspicuous, flat, pinkish rim at ovary base.
Leaves: about 2" (5 cm) wide, about as long, divided into narrow segments, on a stalk as long or longer.
Height: to 16" (40 cm).

Flowering
March–May.

Habitat
Open gravelly desert slopes.

Range
SE. California to the western tip of Texas and northern Mexico.

Comments
The Spanish name, *Amapola del Campo,* means "poppy of the countryside."

Chihuahua Flax
Linum vernale
149

Very slender, erect plants with yellow-orange, bowl-shaped flowers, each with a maroon center.
Flowers: about ¾" (2 cm) wide; petals 5, fan-shaped; style with 5 branches at tip; sepals lanceolate, with gland-tipped teeth on edges.
Leaves: about ½" (1.3 cm) long, very narrow.
Fruit: 5-chambered capsule, walls between chambers open at top, fringed at opening.
Height: 4–20" (10–50 cm).

Flowering
March–October.

Habitat
Rocky, limestone soil in deserts.

Range
S. New Mexico, W. Texas, and northern Mexico.

Comments
A common species in parts of the Chihuahua Desert. Only the very bases of the petals are joined, and when the corolla falls from the flower, breezes may blow it across the ground like a fragile saucer. It is representative of a number of western yellow-flowered species, most slender and wiry, many without maroon centers in flowers.

Desert Rock Nettle
Eucnide urens
150

A rounded, bushy plant, generally much broader than tall, with stinging bristly hairs and large cream or pale yellow flowers in branched clusters that nearly obscure foliage.
Flowers: 1–2" (2.5–5 cm) wide; petals 5, broad, translucent;

5 clusters of many stamens joined to base of petals.
Leaves: ¾–2½" (2–6.3 cm) long, ovate, coarsely toothed,
covered with harsh hairs.
Height: 1–2' (30–60 cm).

Flowering
April–June.

Habitat
Dry rocky places in deserts, often on cliffs.

Range
SE. California to SW. Utah and W. Arizona; south into Baja
California.

Comments
The lovely flowers invite picking, but the hairs sting
viciously.

Desert Rosemallow
Hibiscus coulteri
151

A shrubby plant with rough hairs, undivided lower leaves,
divided upper leaves, and large, cup-shaped, whitish to yellow
flowers, often tinged with red.
Flowers: 1–2" (2.5–5 cm) wide; petals 5, broad; many
stamens joined at bases, forming a tube around style.
Leaves: lower ovate, about 1" (2.5 cm) wide; upper divided
into 3 narrow, coarsely toothed lobes.
Height: to 4' (1.2 m).

Flowering
April–August, or throughout the year in warm areas.

Habitat
Brushy desert hills and canyons.

Range
S. Arizona to W. Texas and northern Mexico.

Comments
A humble relative of the brilliant tropical Hibiscus plants,
members of a genus that contains almost 300 species.

Desert Mariposa Lily
Calochortus kennedyi
152, 154

In an umbel-like cluster on top of short stems bloom 1–6
handsome bell-shaped, vermilion, orange, or yellow flowers.
Flowers: 1–2" (2.5–3.8 cm) wide; sepals 3, lanceolate; petals
3, broad, fan-shaped, each with a dark maroon blotch near
base and a round, depressed gland surrounded by a fringed
membrane; near the gland there are a few hairs with enlarged
tips.
Leaves: 4–8" (10–20 cm) long, few, narrowly lanceolate.
Height: 4–20" (10–50 cm).

Flowering
March–June.

Habitat
Heavy soil in open or brushy areas from creosote-bush deserts
to pinyon and juniper rangeland.

Range
S. California to central Arizona; south into northwestern Mexico.

Comments
One of the most brilliant of the Mariposa lillies. In California, vermilion flowers are most frequent; orange flowers are more common eastward. The yellow phase is found throughout the range, especially at higher elevations.

Rain Lily
Zephyranthes longifolia
153

Resembling a daffodil, but much smaller and more delicate, the single yellow, funnel-shaped flower is held erect on a slender stem.
Flowers: ¾–1″ (2–2.5 cm) long, the 6 petal-like parts, yellow inside, copper-tinged outside, join above ovary.
Leaves: to 9″ (22.5 cm) long, few, basal, very narrow, often not present at flowering.
Fruit: nearly spherical 3-chambered capsule about ¾″ (2 cm) wide, filled with flat, black, D-shaped seeds.
Height: to 9″ (22.5 cm).

Flowering
April–July.

Habitat
Sandy grasslands and deserts.

Range
S. Arizona to W. Texas and northern Mexico.

Comments
Zephyranthes means "flower of the west wind." Flowers of this species appear very soon after substantial rains; hence its common name.

Desert Poppy
Kallstroemia grandiflora
155

Brilliant orange, bowl-shaped corollas, crimson in center, face upward on stalks above sprawling, forked, hairy stems.
Flowers: 2″ (6 cm) across; 5 broad petals; 10 stamens, ovary with 5 lobes.
Leaves: ¾–2½″ (2–6.3 cm) long, opposite, pinnately compound.
Height: creeper, flowering branches to 1′ (30 cm) high, stems to 3′ (1 m) long.

Flowering
May–November.

Habitat
Open sandy areas in desert.

Range
S. Arizona to W. Texas, southward through much of Mexico.

Comments
These are not poppies, and they are not closely related, but the resemblance is there and large patches provide a display as

brilliant and spectacular as those of California Poppies (*Eschscholtzia californica*). This is one of the most handsome wildflowers in the Southwest, frequent along roadsides. There are several other *Kallstroemia* species that can be recognized by the opposite, pinnately compound leaves on trailing stems. They have corollas only about ½" (1.3 cm) wide. All species are Southwestern. One, Small-flowered Carpetweed (*K. parviflora*), has orange flowers, and a beak on the fruit that is longer than the round body. Two have yellow flowers and short beaks. On Hairy Carpetweed (*K. hirsutissima*) sepals do not drop off, and the base of the fruit's beak is bristly-hairy. California Carpetweed (*K. californica*) has sepals that usually drop off after the flower opens. This wild flower has no hairs, or only small ones that grow at the base of the beak.

Desert Primrose
Oenothera brevipes
56

From a basal rosette of leaves grows a nearly leafless, reddish stem with a broad raceme of bright yellow flowers just below its drooping top.
Flowers: ¼–1½" (6–38 mm) wide; petals 4, nearly round; stamens 8, with stalks about ¼" (6 mm) long; style at least ½" (1.3 cm) long with a large round knob at tip.
Leaves: 1–5" (2.5–12.5 cm) long, pinnately lobed, the end lobe largest.
Fruit: slender pod ¾–3½" (2–8.8 cm) long.
Height: 1–30" (2.5–75 cm).

Flowering
March–May.

Habitat
Desert slopes and washes.

Range
SE. California to SW. Utah and W. Arizona.

Comments
This species, distinguished by the knob on the style, blooms at sunrise rather than sunset. It is also known as *Camissonia brevipes*.

Coulter's Globemallow
Sphaeralcea coulteri
57

Erect, slender stems with thin, grayish-velvety leaves have orange or red-orange flowers in long, wandlike clusters.
Flowers: ¾–1" (2–2.5 cm) wide; petals 5; stamens many, joined into a tube.
Leaves: ½–1¼" (1.3–3.1 cm) long, ovate or nearly round, not lobed, or with 3 or 5 deep or shallow lobes, edges scalloped.
Height: 8–60" (20–150 cm).

Flowering
January–May.

Habitat
Sandy desert flats.

Range
SE. California, S. Arizona, and northwestern Mexico.

Comment
In years of ample winter rain this species will carpet the desert
floor with red-orange.

Desert Globemallow
Sphaeralcea ambigua
158

A grayish plant often with many stems, and bright orange-red
flowers in clusters with erect branches.
Flowers: ½–1½" (1.3–3.8 cm) wide; petals 5; stamens many,
joined into a tube.
Leaves: ¾–2½" (2–6.3 cm) long, about as wide, ovate,
shallowly 3-lobed, the edges scalloped.
Height: 20–40" (50–100 cm).

Flowering
March–June.

Habitat
Desert slopes and flats, and among pinyon and juniper.

Range
S. California to SW. Utah, central Arizona and northwestern
Mexico.

Comments
One of the largest-flowered, most drought-tolerant species of
globemallow. Also known as the Desert Hollyhock. In wet
years it forms spectacular displays in the low, hot
southwestern deserts. In some forms petals are pale purplish
pink.

Desert Paintbrush
Castilleja chromosa
159

Several erect stems with bright orange to red, flowerlike tips,
the bracts brightly colored.
Flowers: corolla bilaterally symmetrical, beaklike, very
slender, ¾–1¼" (2–3.1 cm) long, lower lip a green bump at
about midlength, upper lip projecting as a beak, lightly hairy
on top, usually pale with orange to red edges; calyx bright
reddish orange, as deeply cleft on upper side as lower,
shallowly cleft on sides, the resulting 4 lobes are bluntly
pointed.
Leaves: about 1–2" (2.5–5 cm) long, lower ones very narrow,
undivided, upper ones divided into 3 or 5 very narrow lobes;
bracts in flower cluster similarly divided, but bright reddish
orange.
Height: 4–16" (10–40 cm).

Flowering
April–August.

Habitat
Dry open soil, often with sagebrush.

Range
S. Idaho to E. Oregon and E. California; east to N. Arizona,
NW. New Mexico, W. Colorado, and central Wyoming.

Comments
This is one of the West's most common dry-land paintbrushes. The genus is easily recognized but many species are notoriously difficult to identify. The genus name, which honors the Spanish botanist Domingo Castillejo, is usually pronounced *cas-til-lay-yah.*

Chuparosa
Beloperone californica
60

Numerous tubular dull-red flowers bloom on this mostly leafless, densely branched, grayish-green shrub.
Flowers: corolla 1–1½" (2.5–3.8 cm) long, deeply cleft into a 2-lobed upper lip and a 3-lobed lower lip.
Leaves: about ½" (1.3 cm) long, opposite, ovate, finely hairy, deciduous.
Height: to 5' (1.5 m), nearly as wide.

Flowering
February–June.

Habitat
Along desert watercourses, mostly below 2500' (750 m) elevation.

Range
SE. California, S. Arizona, and northwestern Mexico.

Comments
Only one of the 60 species of this New World genus extends north into the United States. The common name is Spanish for "hummingbird"; these birds frequently visit the nectar-rich plants, pollinating flower after flower as they feed. Linnets and sparrows bite off the flowers and eat the nectar-filled bases. Sometimes known locally as Honeysuckle, Chuparosa is said to have been eaten by Papago Indians. Also classified as *Justicia californica.*

Skyrocket
Ipomopsis aggregata
61

In upper leaf axils and at tops of sparsely-leaved stems are clusters of showy, red or pink, trumpet-shaped flowers.
Flowers: corollas ¾–1¼" (2–3.1 cm) long, with 5 pointed lobes.
Leaves: mostly 1–2" (2.5–5 cm) long, densest near base, pinnately divided into narrow segments.
Height: 6–84" (15–210 cm).

Flowering
May–September.

Habitat
Dry slopes from sagebrush to forest.

Range
E. Oregon to S. California; east to W. Texas; north through the Rocky Mountains and the western edge of the plains to W. North Dakota; also northern Mexico.

Comments
Skyrocket, one of the most common western wildflowers,

grows readily from seed. Its brilliant red flowers, to which the name Desert Trumpets refers, are handsome in the native garden. Its beauty compensates for the faint skunky smell of its glandular foliage, responsible for the less complimentary name Skunk Flower. This plant is also known as Scarlet Gilia.

Desert Christmas Cactus
Opuntia leptocaulis
162

Many spiny, intertangled, slender branches form a small bush. Flowers greenish, yellow, or bronze.
Flowers: ½–1″ (1.3–2.5 cm) wide, along stem.
Stems: branched, about ¼″ (6 mm) thick.
Spines: 1–2½″ (2.5–6.3 cm) long, tan or gray, 1 from each raised cluster of tiny reddish bristles.
Fruit: about ½″ (1.3 cm) long, fleshy, bright red, on stem through most of winter.
Height: to 3′ (90 cm).

Flowering
May–June.

Habitat
Flats, slopes, and along washes in deserts and grassland.

Range
W. Arizona to S. Oklahoma; south to northern Mexico.

Comments
This plant has the most slender stems of all southwestern chollas. During winter its bright red fruits add attractive color to the brown desert.

Freckled Milkvetch
Astragalus lentigenosus
163

A more or less succulent plant with stems that vary from erect to prostrate and whitish, pinkish, or purplish flowers in racemes.
Flowers: ⅜–¾″ (9–20 mm) long; 1 broad upper petal and 2 lateral petals nearly enclosing 2 bottom petals that are joined and shaped like prow of a boat; spreading or erect.
Leaves: 11–19 broadly ovate or roundish leaflets ⅜–⅝″ (9–15 mm) long, smooth or lightly hairy on upper surface.
Fruit: pod ½–1½″ (1.3–3.8 cm) long, swollen and leathery-walled or bladdery and thin-walled, 2-chambered, the end flattened sideways into a prominent upcurved beak.
Height: 4–16″ (10–40 cm) long.

Flowering
May–July.

Habitat
From deserts and salt flats to open slopes in mountains.

Range
Western Canada; south through most of the West to northwestern Mexico.

Comments
One of the most variable of western plants, with numerous

types differing in height, flowers, and pods. The common
name refers to the red-mottled pod of many races.

Desert Candle
Caulanthus inflatus
164

A stout, swollen, hollow, yellow-green stem with a few leaves,
mostly near the base, and many narrow flowers in a raceme.
Flowers: about ½" (1.3 cm) long; petals 4, narrow, white,
crinkled near tip; sepals 4, whitish or purplish brown.
Leaves: 1¼–3" (3.1–7.5 cm) long, pointed, with 2 backward-
projecting lobes at base on each side of stem.
Fruit: pods 2½–4" (6.3–10 cm) long, narrow, erect.
Height: 1–2' (30–60 cm).

Flowering
March–May.

Habitat
Sandy or gravelly soils on dry open slopes in brush or deserts.

Range
S. California and SW. Nevada.

Comments
These weird-looking plants resemble candles. Wild Cabbage
(*C. crassicaulis*), is similar but lacks backward-projecting lobes
on leaves and its sepals and petals are purplish or brownish; it
generally grows among sagebrush from western Nevada to
southern Idaho, western Wyoming, and northwestern
Colorado.

Desert Inky Cap
Podaxis pistillaris
166

Cap ⅜–1⅝" (1–4 cm) wide, ¾–4" (2–10 cm) high; stalk 2⅜–
8" tall. Cap oval to almost cylindrical, occasionally slightly
opened at base; whitish, scaly, dry. Stalk scaly or smooth,
sometimes twisted, whitish, extending to tip of cap.
Internally pale at first, darkening to almost black at maturity.

Season
Spring, summer, and fall following rain.

Habitat
Desert areas.

Range
Southwest deserts, Idaho.

Comments
The common name of this mushroom derives from the
resemblance of this species to a popular edible Inky Cap
mushroom (*Coprinus comatus*). The latter mushroom has gills.

Desert Stalked Puffball
Battarrea phalloides
167

Cap (a spore sac) 1–2" (2.5–5 cm) wide, 1–1⅝" (2.5–4 cm)
high; stalk 6–16" tall. Spore sac a flattened oval, brown,
splitting open around the middle at maturity. Internal spore
mass brown and sticky. Stalk woody and brownish, with a
volva (a small cup) at base and shaggy scales throughout
length.

Season
All year following rainfall.

Habitat
Desert areas and sandy coastal soils.

Range
Pacific Coast states (as far north as Alaska), and Rocky Mountains.

Comments
Although it is called a puffball, this species is not edible. Mushrooms of this type are interesting because of their ability to survive in harsh desert environments.

Buried-stalk Puffball
Tulostoma simulans
168

Cap (a spore sac) $3/8$–$5/8''$ (1–1.5 cm) wide; stalk $5/8$–$1\frac{1}{4}''$ tall. Spore sac rounded, with a small tubelike pore at the top, reddish-brown, but usually obscured by sand that adheres to it. At maturity, spore sac falls apart near stalk revealing brown spore mass. Stalk scaly, dry, brownish; frequently entirely buried in sand.

Season
April to December.

Habitat
Sand and very sandy soil.

Range
Widespread in North America.

Comments
This species is often overlooked because the spore sac is usually sand-covered and the stalk may be entirely obscured.

REPTILES AND AMPHIBIANS

Warm, sunny mornings in the desert are ideal for basking—one of the favorite pastimes of many reptiles and amphibians. Early in the morning, slow-moving turtles and stealthy snakes may venture out in search of a meal, retreating to a rock to bask or to a shady burrow as the day grows hotter. Some desert reptiles and most amphibians avoid the heat of the day entirely, never stirring from their homes until nightfall. In this section are included descriptions of many of the most common desert reptiles and amphibians, from the colorful, venomous Gila Monster and rattlesnakes to often drab, but noisy, toads and frogs.

Desert Tortoise
Gopherus agassizi
169

9¼–14½" (23.5–36.8 cm). Terrestrial, with domed shell and round, stumpy, elephantine hind legs. Front limbs flattened for digging and heavily scaled; all toes webless. Carapace oblong, horn-brown; plate centers often yellowish. Part of shell connecting carapace and plastron (bridge) well developed, single plate on front of bridge. Plastron yellowish, with brown along margins; adult throat plates project beyond carapace. Head small, rounded in front, reddish tan; iris greenish yellow. Front and hind feet about equal in size. Male plastron concave.

Breeding
Mates chiefly in spring; nests May–July. Lays 2–3 clutches of 2–14 hard, chalky, elliptical or spherical eggs in funnel-shaped nest, sometimes located at mouth of burrow. Hatching occurs mid-August to October. Mature in 15–20 years.

Habitat
Arid sandy or gravelly locales with creosote, thorn scrub, and cacti; also washes, canyon bottoms, and oases.

Range
SE. California and S. Nevada southeast into Mexico.

Comments
Desert Tortoises feed on grasses and forbs in early morning and late afternoon. During the heat of the day they retreat to shallow burrow dug in the base of an arroyo wall. They have been known to dig horizontal tunnels up to 30' (9.1 m) in length. This species is endangered. It has recently been suggested that the Desert Tortoise be placed in its own genus.

Yellow Mud Turtle
Kinosternon flavescens
170

3½–6⅜" (9–16.2 cm). Carapace olive to brown, smooth, keelless, and usually flattened; horny plates covering shell dark-bordered. Elevated 9th and 10th marginal plates (lacking in young). Plastron yellow to brown, with dark pigment along seams; double-hinged, with 11 plates. Jaw and throat white or yellow, often spotted. Male has concave plastron; long, thick, spine-tipped tail; and rough scale patches on insides of hind legs. Juveniles have a dark spot at edge of each carapace plate.

Breeding
Nests in June in New Mexico. 1 clutch of 1–6 hard-shelled elliptical eggs. Sexual maturity is reached in 6–7 years.

Habitat
Prefers quiet or slow-moving bodies of fresh water with mud or sandy bottoms. Often collected in cattle tanks.

Range
N. Nebraska south to Texas, E. and S. New Mexico, and SE. Arizona into Mexico. Separate populations in NW. Illinois and on Illinois-Iowa border.

Subspecies
Yellow (*K. f. flavescens*), yellow jaw, throat, and carapace;

N. Nebraska to Texas, New Mexico, and SE. Arizona.
Southwestern (*K. f. arizonense*), lower chin and throat yellow,
carapace olive; S. Arizona.

Comments
At dawn or twilight the Yellow Mud Turtle may be
encountered foraging on land. It feeds on worms and
arthropods, as well as snails and tadpoles.

Sonoran Mud Turtle
Kinosternon sonoriense
171

3⅛–6½" (8–16.5 cm). Smooth elongated carapace,
sometimes with 1 or 3 low keels. Tenth marginal plate
extends higher than other marginals. Underside of marginals
and part of shell connecting carapace and plastron yellowish
brown.

Breeding
Nests May–September and lays 2–9 elliptical eggs.

Habitat
Springs, water holes, ponds, and creeks. Desert, foothills, or
in oak and pinyon woodland and Ponderosa Pine and Douglas-
fir forests at elevations up to 6700′ (2042 m).

Range
SW. New Mexico, Arizona, and adjacent extreme SE.
California south into Mexico.

Comments
During dry periods, Sonoran Mud Turtles sometimes
congregate in water holes. They feed on snails.

Slider
Pseudemys scripta
172

5–11⅜" (12.7–28.9 cm). The "dime store" turtle. Prominent
yellow, orange, or red blotch or stripe behind eyes. Carapace
oval, weakly keeled, olive to brown, with pattern ranging
from yellow bars and stripes to networks of lines and eyelike
spots. Plastron yellow, plain to intricately patterned.
Undersurface of chin rounded. V-shaped notch at front of
upper jaw. With age, pattern and head blotch may become
masked by black pigment, making identification difficult.

Breeding
Mates March–June. Nests June–July. Lays 1–3 clutches of 4–
23 oval eggs in nest cavity, which may be located some
distance from water. Hatchlings emerge in 2–2½ months,
but often overwinter in nest. Males mature in 2–5 years.

Habitat
Sluggish rivers, shallow streams, swamps, ponds, and lakes
with soft bottoms and dense vegetation.

Range
SE. Virginia to N. Florida west to New Mexico, south to
Brazil.

Subspecies
Red-eared (*P. s. elegans*), with wide red stripe behind eye, dark

smudge on each plastron plate; Mississippi Valley from N. Illinois to Gulf. Occurs in the Pecos River of New Mexico and Texas.

Big Bend (*P. s. gaigeae*), with large black-bordered orange spot on side of head, small orange spot behind eye, carapace with netlike pattern; Big Bend region of Texas and adjacent Mexico, also Rio Grande Valley in south-central New Mexico.

Comments
Fond of basking, Sliders are often seen stacked one upon another on a favorite log. The young eat water insects, crustaceans, mollusks, and tadpoles, then turn to a plant diet as they mature.

Western Box Turtle
Terrapene ornata
173

4–5¾" (10.2–14.6 cm). Carapace high-domed, keelless, with distinctive pattern of radiating yellowish lines on a brown or black background. Plastron has distinct movable hinge; is often as long as carapace; plates continuously patterned, with radiating yellow lines. Male has red eyes, and hind portion of plastron is slightly concave; female's eyes are yellowish brown.

Breeding
Nesting May to mid–July. Early nesters may lay a second clutch in July. Lays 2–8 somewhat brittle-shelled, ellipsoidal eggs in shallow flask-shaped cavity dug in well-drained soil. Incubation takes 9–10 weeks. Maturity 8–10 years.

Habitat
Primarily open prairies; also grazed pasturelands, open woodlands, and waterways in arid, sandy-soiled terrain. Occasionally in desert flats.

Range
S. South Dakota, Iowa, and E. Illinois south to Louisiana and Texas, west to SW. Arizona. Separate population in NW. Indiana and adjacent Illinois.

Subspecies
Ornate (*T. o. ornata*), with radiating lines that sharply contrast with dark carapace; SE. Wyoming and Indiana south to Louisiana and New Mexico.
Desert (*T. o. luteola*), radiating lines less prominent; S. Arizona to Trans-Pecos region of Texas south into Mexico.

Comments
In the morning the Western Box Turtle basks briefly, then searches for food. By midday it seeks shady shelter. Where cattle share its habitat, it methodically searches dung piles for beetles. It also relishes grasshoppers, caterpillars, cicadas, mulberries, and carrion.

Spiny Softshell
Trionyx spiniferus
174

Males, 5–9¼" (12.7–23.5 cm); females, 6½–18" (16.5–45.7 cm). Shell covered with soft leathery skin, not horny plates. Carapace olive to tan, with black-bordered "eyespots" or dark blotches and dark line around shell's rim; spiny tubercles on leading edge; 2 dark-bordered light stripes on each side of head. Nostrils have a lateral ridge.

Breeding
Nests May–August. Digs flask-shaped cavity in bank of sand or gravel exposed to full sunlight and lays 4–32 spherical eggs. May nest more than once a season. Hatchlings emerge late August–October or following spring.

Habitat
Likes small marshy creeks and farm ponds as well as large, fast-flowing rivers and lakes. Occurs in several desert rivers.

Range
Throughout central United States as far west as the Continental Divide. Separate populations in Montana, S. Quebec, Delaware, and the Gila–Colorado River system of New Mexico and Utah.

Subspecies
Texas (*T. s. emoryi*), white tubercles on back third of carapace, pale marginal rim becomes conspicuously widened along rear edge; Rio Grande drainage in Texas and New Mexico, and the Gila-Colorado River system in Arizona, New Mexico, and extreme SW. Utah. Characteristics intergrade where ranges of this and other subspecies overlap.

Comments
In desert areas, softshells can be observed in shallow water along edges of sandbars by looking down on a river from a cliff.

Leaf-toed Gecko
Phyllodactylus xanti
175

4–5″ (10–12.7 cm). No eyelids, 2 expanded leaf-shaped pads on toe tips. Translucent pink to gray, occasionally with dark brown blotches. Back scales small and granular, with lengthwise rows of wartlike tubercles.

Voice
Squeaks when alarmed.

Breeding
1 or 2 eggs are laid May–July; hatchlings appear June–August.

Habitat
Cracks and crevices in granite outcrops in desert. Occasionally found beneath tree bark or dead prickly-pear pads.

Range
S. California to tip of Baja California and islands in Gulf of California.

Subspecies
Nine; 1 in our range (*P. x. nocticolus*).

Comments
Nocturnal. Emerges shortly after dark to search for insects and spiders, which are captured after a short stalk.

Western Banded Gecko
Coleonyx variegatus
176, 179

4½–6" (11.4–15 cm). Medium-size lizard with protruding eyelids. Light tan with dark brown to black crossbands, most evident in juveniles, breaking up with age into blotches, spots, and variegations. Skin supple; back scales uniformly granular. Toes slender; no pads.

Voice
Chirps when caught.

Breeding
Lays 1–3 clutches of 2 eggs, May–September. Hatchlings appear in 45 days, July–November.

Habitat
Rocky tracts, canyon walls, and sand dunes in deserts and semiarid areas. Avoids the heat of day by hiding in rock crevices or under logs, fallen limbs, or rubbish.

Range
S. California, Nevada, Utah, and Arizona, south into Baja California and Mexico.

Subspecies
Eight; 4 in our range.
Desert (*C. v. variegatus*), S. California (except coast), SW. Nevada, and W. Arizona to Gulf of California.
San Diego (*C. v. abbotti*), Pacific slopes of S. California into northern half of Baja peninsula.
Utah (*C. v. utahensis*), SW. Utah and adjacent corners of Nevada and Arizona.
Tucson (*C. v. bogerti*), SE. Arizona and SW. New Mexico.

Comments
Nocturnal. Often encountered at night, silhouetted by auto headlights against the black asphalt of desert roads.

Texas Banded Gecko
Coleonyx brevis
177, 178

4–4¾" (10–12 cm). Sleepy-looking lizard with protruding, white-rimmed eyelids. Skin supple; back scales uniformly granular. Pinkish with dark brown crossbands, most evident in juveniles, breaking up with age into nearly uniform mottling. Toes slender, no pads. Females larger.

Voice
Squeaks when alarmed.

Breeding
Clutches of 2 eggs, laid April–June.

Habitat
Rock outcrops and canyon beds in desert areas. Found beneath shelving rocks, vegetative debris, and discarded boards.

Range
S. New Mexico through S. Texas (almost to coast) and Northeastern Mexico.

Comments
Nocturnal. Most easily encountered crossing highways during

nightly movements. This gecko feeds on insects and small spiders, which it stalks with a feline twitching of the tail.

Gila Monster ⊗
Heloderma suspectum
180

18–24″ (45.7–61.0 cm). Large and heavy-bodied. Small beadlike scales on back. Broken blotches, bars, spots of black and yellow, orange, or pink, with bands extending onto blunt tail. Face black.

Breeding
Mates throughout summer. 3–5 eggs laid fall to winter.

Habitat
Arid and semiarid regions of gravelly and sandy soils, especially areas with shrubs and some moisture. Found under rocks, in burrows of other animals, in holes it digs itself.

Range
Extreme SW. Utah, S. Nevada and adjacent California, south through S. Arizona and SW. New Mexico to Mexico.

Subspecies
Reticulate (*H. s. suspectum*), adults mottled and blotched; central and S. Arizona and adjoining New Mexico.
Banded (*H. s. cinctum*), adults have broad double crossband;. SW. Utah through S. Nevada and adjoining California and W. Arizona.

Comments
Primarily nocturnal, although also active on warm winter or spring days. Gila Monsters and the related Mexican Beaded Lizards are the only venomous lizards. Their bite, although rarely fatal to humans, serves to overpower animal predators and prey. The poison is not injected like that of a snake but flows into the open wound as the lizard chews on its victim.

Mojave Fringe-toed Lizard
Uma scoparia
181

5–7″ (12.7–17.9 cm). Comblike fringe of pointed scales on trailing edge of toes. Flattened body covered with velvety granular scales. Dark bands under tail. Gray to white, with dark eyelike spots. Dark crescents across center of throat. Black blotch on each side of belly. Breeding adults have pink on sides and yellow-green on belly.

Breeding
Clutches of 1–4 eggs are laid in midsummer, probably more than 1 clutch per season. Following dry winters, little food is available, so reproduction may not occur.

Habitat
Windblown sand dunes with low-growing vegetation.

Range
Mojave Desert in California; extreme W. Yuma County, Arizona.

Comments
Diurnal. This species can move extremely fast across the loose

sand of its habitat. One specimen was clocked at a speed of 23 miles (37 km) an hour. Some consider this form to be a subspecies of *U. notata*.

Fringe-toed Lizard
Uma notata
182

5–7" (12.7–17.9 cm). Comblike fringe of pointed scales on trailing edge of toes. Flattened body covered with velvety granular scales. Dark bands under tail. Gray to white with dark eyelike spots, rough lines over shoulder, diagonal lines on throat. Black blotch on each side of belly. Orange or pink on sides.

Breeding
Clutch of 1–5 eggs laid every 4–6 weeks during summer.

Habitat
Arid stretches of windblown dunes.

Range
SE. California, SW. Arizona and adjacent Mexico.

Subspecies
Desert (*U. n. notata*), orange patch on side of belly; extreme S. California and adjacent N. Baja.
Sonoran (*U. n. rufopunctata*), no orange belly patch; extreme SW. Arizona and adjacent Mexico.

Comments
Diurnal. This species is well adapted to living in sand. The toe fringes act like snowshoes to stop the feet from sinking. Fringe-toed Lizards "swim" into the sand to avoid capture, also to avoid extreme heat or cold. The set back jaw, scaly flaps over the ear, overlapping eyelids, and valves in the nostrils all keep out sand while the lizard is burrowing.

Desert Night Lizard
Xantusia vigilis
183, 184

3¾–5⁵⁄₁₆" (9.5–12.8 cm). No eyelids; pupils vertical. Olive, yellow, brown, or orange; usually many small dark spots tending to form rows. Skin soft. Head scales large, symmetrical; back scales large, square, and smooth; 12 scales across midbelly.

Breeding
Mates May–June. 1–3 young born alive, tail first and upside down, September–October.

Habitat
Arid and semiarid granite outcroppings and rocky areas, among fallen leaves and trunks of yuccas, agaves, and Joshua-trees.

Range
S. Nevada, S. Utah, and W. and central Arizona through S. California into Mexico.

Subspecies
Six; 4 in the United States.
Desert (*X. v. vigilis*), olive-brown above, spots tend to fuse,

smallest subspecies; S. Nevada and extreme SW. Utah and NW. Arizona into S. California and N. Baja California; disjunct population in SW. Arizona (Kofa Mountains). Arizona (*X. v. arizonae*), yellow or gray above, largest subspecies; central Arizona along southern edge of Colorado Plateau (Mohave, Pinal, and Yavapai counties). Sierra (*X. v. sierrae*), spots fused into netlike pattern, broad light stripe behind eye; S. California (Kern County) in southwestern foothills of Sierra Nevada Mountains. Utah (*X. v. utahensis*), yellow-orange above; south-central Utah (Garfield County).

Comments
Diurnal. Activity may continue after dusk, hence the name. This species feeds on termites, ants, beetles, and flies.

Granite Night Lizard
Xantusia henshawi
85

4–5⅝" (10.0–14.3 cm). Flat-bodied. No eyelids; pupils vertical. Light-colored with large dark brown to black spots that expand by day, contract at night. Skin is soft. Head scales large, symmetrical; back scales small and granular; belly scales large, square, and smooth, with 14 scales across midbelly.

Breeding
Mates in late spring; 1–2 young are born alive in September.

Habitat
Arid and semiarid territory, especially in cooler areas among large peeling or flaking rocks and outcroppings.

Range
S. California into Baja California.

Comments
Nocturnal. This extremely wary and secretive lizard can be encountered only at dusk or after dark. Sometimes it can be found by prying loose the rocky flakes under which it hides. The collector should take care to restore the habitat.

Black-collared Lizard
Crotaphytus insularis
86

6–13" (15.2–33.0 cm). Large head; conspicuous black-and-white collar across back of neck. Inside of mouth light-colored. Tail flattened from side to side. Tan to olive, with pale yellow crossbands. Mature males have blue-gray throats with a black center; also large dark blotches in the groin. Gravid females show red-orange spots on sides. Young usually have vivid crossbanding, lack throat coloring, groin blotches.

Breeding
Mates May–June; lays 3–8 eggs in midsummer.

Habitat
Rocky terrain; canyons, gullies, similar protected areas where vegetation is sparse.

Range
SE. Oregon, adjacent Idaho, and W. Utah, south into Arizona and SE. California.

Subspecies
Three; 2 in our range.
Mojave (*C. i. bicinctores*), California, Oregon, Idaho, Nevada, and W. Utah and Arizona. Some consider this form a distinct species.
Baja (*C. i. vestigium*), Riverside County, California, south through Baja peninsula.

Comments
Diurnal. These lizards are frequently found basking on large boulders. They are wary and hard to catch during midday when temperatures are warm.

Bluntnose Leopard Lizard
Gambelia silus
187

8–9¼″ (20.3–23.5 cm). Head short, nose blunt. Tail round, not flattened. Narrow white to yellow crossbars separated by wide gray or brown crossbars containing numerous dark-edged brown spots. Throat blotched with gray.

Breeding
Mates April–June. 2–5 eggs are laid in June or July, hatch in August or September.

Habitat
Sandy areas, alkali flats, canyon floors, foothills, with sparse, open vegetation.

Range
San Joaquin Valley and surrounding foothills, California.

Comments
Diurnal. This lizard usually "freezes" when danger threatens, only to dash for cover if closely approached. Because much of its habitat has been converted to farms and communities, the Bluntnose Leopard Lizard is threatened with extinction.

Desert Iguana
Dipsosaurus dorsalis
188

10–16″ (25.4–40.6 cm). Large round-bodied lizard with long tail and low crest of slightly enlarged keeled scales down back. Brown around head, giving way to reddish-brown netlike pattern and gray or white spotting on neck and trunk. Netlike pattern may break into dark lengthwise lines on sides. Tail gray or white with encircling rows of dark spots. Breeding adults show pink on sides of belly.

Breeding
Mates April–May. Clutch of 3–8 eggs is laid June–August. Hatchlings appear August–September.

Habitat
Arid and semiarid regions of sand, scattered rocks, and creosote bush.

Range
S. California, Nevada, and W. Arizona south into Mexico.

Subspecies
Three; 1 in our range, *D. d. dorsalis*.

Comments

Diurnal. These are wary lizards that flee to the nearest rodent burrow or bush at the slightest hint of danger. They are tolerant of high temperatures and are active even at 115°F (46°C). When surface temperatures do get too hot for them, Desert Iguanas climb into bushes to reach cooler air layers.

Chuckwalla
Sauromalus obesus
89

11–16½" (27.9–41.9 cm). A large, potbellied lizard with loose folds of skin around neck and shoulders. Tail thick at the base and blunt at the tip. Male black on head, forelegs, and forward portion of trunk; red, gray, or yellow toward tail. Female and young tend to be banded with gray and yellow.

Breeding

Mating is believed to occur May–June. Clutches of 5–10 eggs are laid June–August; females may lay only every second year.

Habitat

Open flats and rocky areas, especially near large boulders.

Range

SE. California, S. Nevada, Utah, W. Arizona, and adjacent Mexico.

Subspecies

Four; 3 in our range.
Western (*S. o. obesus*), more than 50 scales around mid-foreleg, single row of pores on underside of thighs; California, Nevada, Utah, and W. Arizona.
Glen Canyon (*S. o. multiforaminatus*), more than 50 scales around mid-foreleg, 2 rows of pores on underside of thighs; Colorado River gorge between Garfield County, Utah, and Page County, Arizona.
Arizona (*S. o. tumidus*), fewer than 50 scales around mid-foreleg, male red toward tail; S. Arizona and into Mexico.

Comments

Diurnal. On emerging in the morning, this lizard basks until its preferred body temperature of 100°F (38°C) is reached, whereupon it begins searching for food. Strictly herbivorous, it browses on leaves, buds, flowers, and fruit. A frightened Chuckwalla retreats into a rocky crevice and wedges itself in sideways by inflating its body. It can sometimes be coaxed out of the crack by repeatedly tapping its snout with a stick.

Brush Lizard
Urosaurus graciosus
90

5¾–7¼" (14.6–18.4 cm). Medium-size lizard with fold across throat; single band of abruptly larger scales down back. Scale between eyes divided. Tail frequently twice head and body length. Gray with dark crossbars; occasionally a light stripe along side. Throat yellow or orange. Male has bluish patches on side of belly.

Breeding

Mates throughout spring. Clutch of 4 eggs is laid in May–July, hatches July–October.

Habitat
Loose sandy desert where scrub growth is plentiful, especially creosote bush.

Range
S. Nevada, W. Arizona, SE. California and adjacent Mexico.

Subspecies
Western (*U. g. graciosus*), back pattern inconspicuous; SE. California, S. Nevada and W. Arizona and Mexico.
Arizona (*U. g. shannoni*), dark markings prominent on back; south-central Arizona.

Comments
Diurnal. Although active during all the daylight hours, this lizard frequently rests head down on small branches.

Longnose Leopard Lizard
Gambelia wislizenii
191

8½–15⅛" (22–38.4 cm). Large and slender. Gray or brown with many dark spots on body and tail. Color darkens in cool temperatures. White crossbars usually evident on back, sides, and tail. Longitudinal gray streak down throat. Gravid female have red-orange spots and bars on sides. Tail round.

Breeding
In spring; 4–7 eggs are laid May–July. Occasionally second clutches are laid in August.

Habitat
Semiarid regions where soil is sandy or gravelly, and vegetation sparse or in clumps.

Range
S. Oregon and Idaho to SW. Wyoming, south to W. Texas and into Mexico, west through S. California and Baja California.

Subspecies
Five; 4 in our range.
Longnose (*G. w. wislizenii*), large dark spots encircled by white dots; extreme S. Nevada and SW. California through Arizona and New Mexico to Big Bend region of Texas and adjacent Mexico.
Cope's (*G. w. copei*), dark spots fragmented, each part with encircling white dots; extreme S. California and Baja peninsula.
Lahontan Basin (*G. w. maculosus*), large squarish dark spots without encircling white dots; SE. Oregon and S. Idaho, W. Nevada, and NE. California.
Pale (*G. w. punctatus*), small dark spots without encircling white dots; upper Colorado River basin of SE. Utah and W. Colorado, south into N. Arizona and extreme NW. New Mexico.

Comments
Diurnal. This agile lizard darts from bush to bush in search o insects or lies hidden in the shade awaiting unwary prey. It frequently eats smaller lizards.

Lesser Earless Lizard
Holbrookia maculata
92

4–5⅛" (10–13 cm). Small; with smooth granular back scales, 2 folds across throat, no external ears. Gray to brownish, depending on earth color. Usually has lengthwise rows of dark blotches separated by pale stripe down center of back and light stripe at juncture of back and sides. Male has pair of blue-bordered black marks on each side of belly behind foreleg. Female has orange throat during breeding season.

Breeding
Mates during spring and summer. Lays an average of 5–7 eggs, April–September; hatchlings appear May–October.

Habitat
Sandy soil areas in grassy prairie, cultivated fields, dry streambeds, desert grasslands.

Range
S. South Dakota through the Great Plains to central Texas, west through most of New Mexico and Arizona into Mexico.

Subspecies
Speckled (*H. m. approximans*), central Arizona through New Mexico to extreme W. Texas, south into Mexico.
Western (*H. m. thermophila*), S. Arizona below 5000′ (1500 m) and south into Mexico.
Bleached (*H. m. ruthveni*), restricted to White Sands region (Otero County), New Mexico.

Comments
Diurnal. Loss of the external ear may be an adaptation to this lizard's habit of burrowing headfirst into sand.

Roundtail Horned Lizard
Phrynosoma modestum
93

3–4⅛" (8.0–10.5 cm). Flat-bodied; short crown of spines on head. No pointed scales fringing sides. Light brown to gray, depending on surrounding soil; usually a dark blotch on neck, another in groin. Tail broad at base, becoming round and slender. Belly scales smooth.

Breeding
Mates in May; clutch of 9 eggs laid June–July, hatches July–August.

Habitat
Sandy, gravelly washes and other semiarid regions of scrub vegetation.

Range
SE. Arizona through S. New Mexico to W. Texas, and south into Mexico.

Comments
Diurnal. Camouflage coloration is the chief protection of the Roundtail. When danger threatens, it flattens itself against the sand and remains motionless, practically disappearing from sight. Like many other horned lizards, it feeds primarily on ants.

Flat-tail Horned Lizard
Phrynosoma m'calli
194

3–4¾" (7.6–12.0 cm). Flat-bodied; long slender spines crown head, 2 rows of pointed scales fringe trunk. Midbelly scales smooth. Rusty brown to gray; dark stripe down spine. Tail long, flat.

Breeding
Mates April–May. Clutches of 7–10 eggs are laid May–June.

Habitat
Dunes and other regions of fine, windblown sand with little vegetation.

Range
SE. California and adjacent Arizona and Mexico.

Comments
Diurnal. In midday this lizard will burrow into sand to avoid the heat. Burrowing is usually accomplished by quick side-to-side shuffling. It also burrows to escape the cool of night.

Regal Horned Lizard
Phrynosoma solare
195

3½–6½" (8.8–16.7 cm). Flat-bodied; head crowned by large close-set spines. Single row of pointed scales fringes trunk. Scales smooth at midbelly, weakly keeled on chest.

Breeding
Mates in summer. Clutches of 17–28 eggs are laid July–August, hatch September–October.

Habitat
Rocky and gravelly areas supporting scrub vegetation or succulents; sometimes sandy regions.

Range
S. Arizona into Mexico.

Comments
Diurnal. This species is most active during early morning, with a second, smaller show of activity just before sunset. When caught, it may become rigid, with lungs deflated and legs extended. If set down in this condition, it will flop onto its back. Some will squirt blood from the corner of the eye.

Texas Horned Lizard
Phrynosoma cornutum
196

2½–7⅛" (6.3–18.1 cm). Flat-bodied lizard with large crown of spines on head; 2 center spines longest. 2 rows of pointed scales fringe each side. Belly scales keeled. Red to yellow to gray; dark spots have light rear margins. Dark lines radiate from eye.

Breeding
Mates April–May. Clutch of 14–37 eggs is laid in burrow dug by female May–July. Young hatch in about 6 weeks, measure about 1¼" (3.1 cm).

Habitat
From sea level to 6000' (1800 m) in dry areas, mostly open country with loose soil supporting grass, mesquite, and cactus.

Range
Kansas to Texas and west to SE. Arizona. Isolated population in Louisiana; introduced in N. Florida.

Comments
Diurnal. This lizard is the common "horned toad" of the pet trade. But since it feeds almost exclusively on live large ants —generally unavailable to the pet owner—most pet horned lizards slowly starve to death over a period of months.

Short-horned Lizard
Phrynosoma douglassi
197

2½–5⅞" (6.3–14.9 cm). Flat-bodied; head crowned by stubby spines interrupted at rear by deep notch in skull. 1 row of pointed scales fringes trunk. Belly scales smooth. Gray, yellowish, or reddish brown; 2 rows of dark spots down back.

Breeding
Litters of 6–31 are born alive, July–August.

Habitat
Varies, from open rocky or sandy plains to forested areas; from sea level to above 9000′ (2700 m).

Range
S. British Columbia to N. California, S. Idaho, and most of Utah; S. Saskatchewan, southeast to Kansas, and south into Mexico. Separate populations in W. Texas.

Subspecies
Numerous; 3 in deserts of our range.
Pygmy (*P. d. douglassi*), brownish to bluish gray, with very small head spines pointed vertically; S. British Columbia through Washington, E. Oregon, and S. Idaho to N. California and N. Nevada.
Desert (*P. d. ornatissimum*), dark spots partly light-bordered, spines horizontal; extreme south-central Wyoming through W. Colorado to New Mexico and E. Arizona, with disjunct populations in SE. New Mexico and W. Texas.
Salt Lake (*P. d. ornatum*), nearly uniform gray, spines horizontal; central and N. Utah, NE. Nevada, and extreme SE. Idaho.

Comments
Diurnal. This species is most active during the midday warmth. At night it burrows into the soil. Short-horned Lizards feed primarily on ants.

Crevice Spiny Lizard
Sceloporus poinsetti
198

8½–11¼" (21.6–28.6 cm). Large rough-scaled lizard with prominent white-edged black collar and clearly marked dark crossbands on tail. Drab olive to reddish. Blue patches on throat and belly are absent in female. Young and females show more distinct crossbanding.

Breeding
7–11 young are born alive, June–July.

Habitat
Limestone and other exposed rocky outcrops in arid and semiarid areas.

Range
S. New Mexico to central Texas and south into Mexico.

Subspecies
Three; 1 in our range, *S. p. poinsetti*.

Comments
Diurnal. These are elusive lizards, quick to hide among stones and in crevices. They eat insects and occasionally consume blossoms or leaves that blow by.

Desert Spiny Lizard
Sceloporus magister
199

7–12″ (17.8–30.5 cm). A large, rough-scaled lizard. Yellow to brown, with some crossbanding and a black triangular mark with light rear edge on each shoulder. Blue throat and blue patches on sides of belly; absent in females and young, which show more prominent crossbanding.

Breeding
Mates in spring and early summer; 7–19 eggs are laid May–July, incubation lasts 8–11 weeks. More than 1 clutch may be laid in a season.

Habitat
Arid and semiarid areas at low elevation.

Range
S. Nevada south into Baja California and southeast through Arizona, New Mexico, and W. Texas. Isolated population in central California.

Subspecies
Nine; 5 in our range.
Desert (*S. m. magister*), male has dark purple to black band down center of back, bordered by narrow light stripes; SW. Arizona into Mexico.
Twin-spotted (*S. m. bimaculosus*), male has 2 rows of prominent dark spots down back and usually a dark stripe behind eye; SE. Arizona through central New Mexico to SW. Texas, south into Mexico.
Barred (*S. m. transversus*), male usually has several distinct crossbands on back and dark patches near forelegs; small area of east-central California and adjoining west-central Nevada.
Yellowback (*S. m. uniformis*), male uniform yellowish tan, sometimes with vague darker blotches; central and S. Nevada, extreme SW. Utah to central Arizona, SE. California and NE. Baja California, isolated population west of San Joaquin Valley, California.
Orangehead (*S. m. cephaloflavus*), hard yellowish orange, male has several chevron-shaped bars along back; SE. Utah, extreme SW. Colorado, NW. New Mexico, and NE. Arizona.

Comments
Diurnal. These are wary lizards that dart into rocky crevices,

rodent holes, or vegetative cover when startled. They readily climb trees or walls in search of insect prey.

Collared Lizard
Crotaphytus collaris
200, 201

8–14" (20–35.6 cm). Large head; conspicuous black-and-white collar across back of neck. Inside of mouth dark. Tail not flattened side to side. Yellow-brown to green with bluish highlights and usually light spots and dark bands. Mature male has blue-green or orange throat without black center seen in Black-collared Lizard. Gravid female has red-orange spots and bars on sides. Young show dark and light crossbanding.

Breeding
Mates April–June; lays 1–12 eggs in midsummer. Hatchlings are about 3½" (8.9 cm) long.

Habitat
Hardwood forests to arid areas with large rocks for basking. More frequent in hilly regions, especially among limestone ledges that provide crevices for good cover.

Range
E. Utah and Colorado to extreme SW. Illinois, south through central Texas, into Mexico and west into central Arizona.

Subspecies
Six; 5 in our range.
Eastern (*C. c. collaris*), S. Missouri through N. Arkansas, west to N. and central Texas.
Western (*C. c. baileyi*), central Arizona and west-central New Mexico.
Yellowhead (*C. c. auriceps*), upper Colorado and Green River basins of E. Utah, W. Colorado, and N. New Mexico and Arizona east of Colorado River.
Chihuahuan (*C. c. fuscus*), SE. Arizona, SW. New Mexico and extreme W. Texas, and south into Mexico.
Sonoran (*C. c. nebrius*), S. Arizona into Mexico.

Comments
Diurnal. A wary, feisty lizard that will bite readily and hard, given the chance. It feeds on insects and other lizards. When fleeing would-be captors, it lifts body and tail and dashes along on its hind legs, giving it the appearance of a fierce little dinosaur.

Side-blotched Lizard
Uta stansburiana
202

4–6⅜" (10.0–16.2 cm). A small lizard with small back scales, some larger scales on head; a fold with granular scales across throat. Brown; back pattern may consist of blotches, spots, speckles, stripes. Single dark blue to black spot on side behind foreleg. External ear openings.

Breeding
Mates throughout year in southernmost range, in summer elsewhere. 3 clutches of 2–6 eggs are laid. Sperm may be stored in female's oviduct for up to 3 months, so at least 2 fertile clutches can result from each mating.

Habitat
Arid and semiarid regions with coarse, gravelly soil and low-growing vegetation.

Range
Central Washington southeast to W. Texas and Mexico; west to Pacific Coast and Baja California, north through central and E. California to central Oregon.

Subspecies
Six; 5 in our range.
Northern (*U. s. stansburiana*), male has light spots and blue specks, back scales weakly keeled; central Nevada, W. Utah, NW. Arizona, and E. California.
California (*U. s. elegans*), conspicuous stripes at juncture of back and sides; S. California, W. Arizona, and into Mexico.
Nevada (*U. s. nevadensis*), back pattern weak, breeding male has orange sides; N. Nevada, Oregon, Washington, and Idaho.
Desert (*U. s. stejnegeri*), stripes at juncture of back and sides evident toward front; central New Mexico, W. Texas, south to Mexico.
Colorado (*U. s. uniformis*), back pattern weak or absent; E. Utah, W. Colorado, NE. Arizona, and NW. New Mexico.

Comments
Diurnal. These lizards live on or near the ground and are voracious consumers of insects. In the northern parts of their range they become inactive in the winter; they are active on any warm day throughout the year in the southern regions.

Zebratail Lizard
Callisaurus draconoides
203

6–9⅛″ (15.2–23.2 cm). A large lizard with granular scales, 2 folds across throat, external ears. Gray, usually with paired dusky spots running down back, becoming crossbands on tail. Black crossbars on white underside of flattened tail. Male has pair of black bars on side, extending into large blue blotches on belly. Female lacks blue blotches; bars faint to absent.

Breeding
Clutch size 2–8 eggs, average 4, laid June–August. Multiple clutches common in southern part of range. Hatchings appear July–November.

Habitat
Areas of hard-packed soil with little vegetation; occasionally among small rocks.

Range
Central Nevada and extreme SW. Utah, south through Arizona and SE. California into Mexico.

Subspecies
About 12; 3 in our range.
Nevada (*C. d. myurus*), north-central Nevada.
Mojave (*C. d. rhodostictus*), S. Nevada and extreme SW. Utah to SE. California and W. Arizona.

Arizona (*C. d. ventralis*), south-central Arizona and northern Mexico.

Comments
Diurnal. These lizards are swift runners, curling their tails over their backs to expose the "zebra" stripes. When disturbed, they curl the tail and wag it. They eat anything they can catch: insects, spiders, smaller lizards. Diet also occasionally includes flowers.

Greater Earless Lizard
Cophosaurus texanus
204

3¼–7¼" (8–18.4 cm). Relatively large, with smooth granular back scales. 2 folds across throat. Light flecks of gray to brown, depending on color of habitat. Wide black crossbands under flattened tail. Male has a pair of curved black bars within blue blotch on side just in front of hind leg. Female lacks blue blotch, usually has no black bars; has orange throat and pinkish sides when gravid.

Breeding
Some 5 eggs are laid monthly from March–August, for season total of 25.

Habitat
Stretches of broken rock, limestone cliffs, dry sandy streambeds, rocky washes.

Range
Central Arizona through central and S. Texas and into Mexico.

Subspecies
Three; 2 in our range.
Texas (*C. t. texanus*), E. New Mexico and north-central Texas into Mexico.
Southwestern (*C. t. scitulus*), SE. Arizona to south-central New Mexico and extreme W. Texas into Mexico.

Comments
Diurnal. An exceptionally active lizard, constantly dashing from rock to rock as it surveys its territory and hunts insect prey. It runs with its tail curved over its back, displaying the characteristic black bands.

Tree Lizard
Urosaurus ornatus
205

4½–6¼" (11.4–15.9 cm). Has fold across throat; band of small scales separates 2 bands of abruptly larger scales down middle of back. Scale between eyes divided. Tail less than twice head and body length. Brown to gray, with dark crossbands and blotches. Male has bright blue belly patches and blue to yellow-orange throat patches.

Breeding
Up to 6 clutches of 3–13 eggs are laid April–September. Hatchlings appear July–late October, according to range.

Habitat
Trees, rocks, fence posts, and buildings in arid regions; often near streams and dry washes.

Range
Extreme SW. Wyoming, southeast to south-central Texas and west to extreme SE. California.

Subspecies
Eight; 6 in our range.
Canyon (*U. o. levis*), 3–4 rows of enlarged back scales, belly patches not connected; north-central New Mexico.
Lined (*U. o. linearis*), bands of enlarged back scales separated by less than width of enlarged band; central and SE. Arizona to central New Mexico and into Mexico.
Big Bend (*U. o. schmidti*), irregular rows of enlarged back scales, inner series less than twice width of outer series, belly patches separate; Big Bend region of Texas (west of Pecos River) to extreme SE. New Mexico.
Colorado River (*U. o. symmetricus*), bands of enlarged back scales separated by more than width of enlarged band, belly patches separate; extreme SE. Nevada and California to W. Arizona and northern Mexico.
Northern (*U. o. wrighti*), enlarged back scales in 3–4 rows, belly patches connected; extreme SW. Wyoming to N. New Mexico and Arizona.

Comments
Diurnal. This lizard is often found in pairs or groups. Shy and wary, it is adept at hiding by agilely keeping a tree trunk or branch between itself and a pursuer. It is most commonly encountered in the morning and late afternoon.

Western Whiptail
Cnemidophorus tigris
206

8–12″ (20.3–30.5 cm). Slender; 4–8 light stripes, often with many dark spots and lines on light gray or tan. Stripes and spotting sometimes faded or absent. Throat and belly usually white or yellow (rarely all black), with black spotting on chest. 8 longitudinal rows of large, smooth, rectangular belly scales. Tail gray or gray-green, usually with black speckling on sides; bright blue in juveniles.

Breeding
Mates April–May. Clutch of 1–4 eggs is laid in June in northern range. In south first clutch is laid in May, second in July. Eggs hatch July–August.

Habitat
Arid and semiarid desert to open woodlands; where vegetation is sparse enough to make running easy.

Range
Baja California and California to E. Oregon and S. Idaho, south to W. Texas and Mexico.

Subspecies
About 15; 6 in United States.
Great Basin (*C. t. tigris*), usually 4 light stripes, vertical dark bars on sides; E. Oregon and SW. Idaho, south through central Utah and W. Arizona into extreme NW. Sonora, E. Baja peninsula, north through E. California.

Southern (*C. t. gracilis*), 4–6 distinct brown stripes with many light spots in interposed dark bands, throat and chest black; S. Arizona to extreme SW. New Mexico and N. Sonora.
Marbled (*C. t. marmoratus*), faded light gray-brown stripes and spots, vertical dark bars, chest salmon, S. New Mexico through W. Texas into Mexico.
Coastal (*C. t. multiscutatus*), 8 ill-defined light stripes, large black spots on throat; coast of S. California and W. Baja California.
California (*C. t. mundus*), 8 light stripes, distinct large dark spots and black spots on throat; north-central California south to central California coast, isolated population in north-central Oregon.
Northern (*C. t. septentrionalis*), 6 fairly distinct yellow stripes, small black spots on throat; W. Colorado to NW. New Mexico, west through S. Utah and N. Arizona.

Comments

Diurnal. This species digs burrows both for safe retreats and to find underground prey. Like most whiptails, it stalks any small moving object, even fluttering leaves. Insects, scorpions, spiders, and daddy-long-legs are eaten.

Colorado Checkered Whiptail
Cnemidophorus tesselatus
207

11–15½" (27.9–39.4 cm). Long and slender, with 6 faint light stripes separated by bold black checks, bars, or spots. Spotting faded in some populations. Back scales small and granular. Throat and belly white; small scattered black spots most prominent on chin and chest; 8 lengthwise rows of large, smooth rectangular belly scales. Tail yellow or brown, dark spots on sides. Juveniles have dark bands with a few light spots.

Breeding

Primarily unisexual; only a few males have been found. Unmated female lays clutch of 2–8 eggs in June–July, which hatches in August.

Habitat

Rocky locations on sand or gravel supporting grass or sparse brush.

Range

S. Colorado and New Mexico, W. Texas into adjacent Mexico.

Comments

Diurnal. This whiptail is a more agile rock climber than others. Food includes scorpions as well as the usual insects and spiders.

Little Striped Whiptail
Cnemidophorus inornatus
208

6½–9⅜" (16.5–23.8 cm). Slender, with 6–8 light stripes separated by dark reddish-brown to black bands without spots. Small granular scales on back. Throat and belly blue, intense in males, pale in females; 8 lengthwise rows of large smooth rectangular belly scales. Tail blue with brown base.

Breeding
Mates in spring. Clutch of 2–4 eggs, laid May–July.

Habitat
Arid and semiarid grasslands with some low brush; flatlands, gentle slopes.

Range
New Mexico, extreme SE. Arizona, W. Texas into Mexico.

Subspecies
Four; 2 in our range.
Arizona (*C. i. arizonae*), interposed dark bands blue-gray, belly light blue; SE. Arizona and W. New Mexico.
Trans-Pecos (*C. i. heptagrammus*), dark bands black, belly dark blue; W. Texas, SE. New Mexico, and northern Mexico.

Comments
Diurnal. Beetles, grasshoppers, and spiders are the chief food of this whiptail. When frightened, it tends to seek cover under shrubs, then abandon them in favor of burrows if the threat persists.

Desert Grassland Whiptail
Cnemidophorus uniparens
209

6½–9⅜″ (16.5–23.8 cm). Slender; 6 or 7 light stripes separated by dark reddish-brown or black bands without spots. Back scales small, granular. Throat white or blue-white; chin blue. Belly uniform white; 8 lengthwise rows of large, smooth rectangular belly scales. Tail olive-green; blue in juveniles.

Breeding
Unisexual; no mating. Clutch of 1–4 eggs, laid in summer, hatches in 50–55 days.

Habitat
Arid and semiarid grassland, desert scrub.

Range
Central Arizona to extreme W. Texas, and south into Mexico.

Comments
Diurnal. The range of this species seems to be expanding as more and more grassland is degraded to desert scrub. But this expansion means that the grassland range of the Little Striped Whiptail is shrinking.

Chihuahuan Spotted Whiptail
Cnemidophorus exsanguis
210

9½–12⅜″ (24.1–31.4 cm). Slender, with 6 light stripes separated by dark brown bands; light spots in both stripes and bands. Small granular back scales, 5–8 scales between light stripes down middle of back. Belly uniform light gray to white; 8 lengthwise rows of large, smooth, rectangular belly scales. Tail blue-gray to green. Juveniles have orange tail and light spots in interposed dark bands.

Breeding
Unisexual; no mating. Clutches of 1–6 eggs are laid June–August and hatch about a month and a half later.

Habitat
Desert, desert grasslands, and mountain woodlands, especially pine-oak.

Range
SE. Arizona and central New Mexico south into W. Texas and Mexico.

Comments
Diurnal. This whiptail can often be seen foraging around the edges of shrubs and vegetative litter for insects.

New Mexico Whiptail
Cnemidophorus neomexicanus
211

8–11⅞″ (20.3–30.2 cm). Slender; 7 light stripes on sides separated by light-spotted dark bands. Wavy or zigzag light stripe down middle of back, forked on head. Small granular scales on back. Throat pale blue or blue-green. Belly uniform white or pale blue; 8 lengthwise rows of large, smooth rectangular scales. Tail gray at base, gray-green toward tip; bright blue in juveniles.

Breeding
Unisexual; no mating. Clutch of 2–4 eggs, laid in summer, hatches in 50–60 days.

Habitat
Grassy areas where periodic flooding occurs; sandy arroyos, washes, playas, sandy river bottoms.

Range
Rio Grande valley of New Mexico and extreme W. Texas into Mexico.

Comments
Diurnal. This species seems to prefer disturbed areas where vegetation is sparse and ditches, fences, and trash piles abound. When frightened it flees to shelter.

Sagebrush Lizard
Sceloporus graciosus
212

5–6³⁄₁₆″ (12.7–15.75 cm). A spiny lizard. Granular scales do not overlap on rear of thigh. Grayish green to brown; some darker spots and crossbars. Faint light stripes at juncture of back and sides. Sides reddish orange behind forelegs. Males usually have light blue mottling (not patches) on throat and darker blue belly patches. Females have pinkish orange on sides and neck.

Breeding
Clutch of 2–7 eggs is laid June–July, hatches July–August.

Habitat
Primarily areas of sagebrush and gravelly soils or fine-sand dunes. Never far from shelter such as stony piles, crevices, animal burrows.

Range
S. Montana to NW. New Mexico and west to Washington, Oregon, California, and Baja California.

Subspecies
Northern (*S. g. graciosus*), with blue patches that do not meet across belly and do not meet blue of throat; Washington to Montana, south to New Mexico, west to E. California, north to coast in N. California and Oregon.
Dunes (*S. g. arenicolus*), with blue patches that do not meet across belly, throat without blue; found in sand dunes of W. Texas and SE. New Mexico.
Southern (*S. g. vandenburghianus*), with blue patches that usually meet across belly and touch blue of throat; S. California into N. Baja peninsula.

Comments
Diurnal. Primarily terrestrial, these lizards occasionally climb trees or bushes in pursuit of insect prey.

Great Plains Skink
Eumeces obsoletus
213

6½–13¾" (16.5–34.9 cm). The largest skink. Scale rows on sides oblique to rows on back. Dark edges of brown scales may align to form indistinct lengthwise stripes. Sides yellow. Juveniles black with white spots on lips, bright blue tail.

Breeding
Mates April–May. Clutch of 7–21 eggs, laid in nest excavations under rocks, May–June, hatches July–August. Female tends eggs.

Habitat
Open rocky grasslands of the Great Plains; near permanent or semipermanent water in otherwise drier areas.

Range
SE. Wyoming, S. Nebraska, and extreme SW. Iowa through the Great Plains to central Arizona, Mexico, and west-central Texas.

Comments
Diurnal. This husky skink feeds on insects, spiders, and small lizards. It will bite if handled.

Trans-Pecos Rat Snake
Elaphe subocularis
214

34–66" (86–167.6 cm). A handsome, "bug-eyed" rat snake; yellowish tan or olive-yellow, marked with a series of dark brown H-shaped blotches. Arms of H's may be partly connected, thus forming fragmented stripes at juncture of back and sides. Head unpatterned, with large eyes separated from upper lip scales by row of small scales. Scales weakly keeled. Scale in front of anus divided.

Breeding
Mates in late spring. About 3–7 soft, leathery eggs are laid in summer. Young hatch in 10½–15 weeks.

Habitat
Chihuahuan Desert. Agave–creosote bush–ocotillo-dominated slopes to rocky areas characterized by persimmon-shin oak or cedar; about 1500–4500' (450–1350 m).

Range
Big Bend and Trans-Pecos regions of Texas and S. New Mexico southward to north-central Mexico.

Comments
Most active during early evening hours on warm, dry nights. Spends day in rock crevices or abandoned burrows. This constrictor feeds on small mammals, birds, and lizards. Record longevity is 13¾ years.

Western Terrestrial Garter Snake
Thamnophis elegans
215

18–42″ (45.7–106.7 cm). Variable color and markings. Side stripe narrow, but back stripe is usually well defined. Space between stripes marked with dark spots or with scattered light specks. 8 upper lip scales; sixth and seventh enlarged. Scales keeled. Scale in front of anus undivided.

Breeding
Live-bearing. Mates in spring; 4–19 young, 6½–9″ (16.5–23 cm) long, are born July–September.

Habitat
Moist situations near water; margins of streams, ponds, lakes, damp meadows; open grassland to forest; sea level to 10,500′ (3200 m).

Range
SW. Manitoba and S. British Columbia southward into Mexico, extreme SW. South Dakota and extreme W. Oklahoma west to Pacific Coast.

Subspecies
Six; 1 in deserts of our range.
Wandering (*T. e. vagrans*), narrow back stripe dull yellow or brown, fades on tail; light areas between stripes marked with small dark spots, sometimes absent or enlarged, fused and filling space between stripes; SW. Manitoba, SW. South Dakota, and extreme W. Oklahoma west to coastal British Columbia, W. Washington, central Oregon, and east-central California.

Comments
Diurnal. Occasionally seen basking during morning hours in the open. When disturbed, it often takes to water.

Checkered Garter Snake
Thamnophis marcianus
216

18–42½″ (45.7–108 cm). Brown, olive, or tan, with bold checkered pattern of large squarish black blotches on sides. Uppermost blotches intrude into yellow back stripe. Light side stripe on neck and farther back on body. Large paired black blotches at back of head separated from corners of mouth by light crescent; 8 upper lip scales. Scales keeled. Scale in front of anus undivided.

Breeding
6–18 young, 8–9¼″ (20.3–23.5 cm) long, are born June–August.

Habitat
Arid and semiarid grassland near streams, springs, ponds, and irrigation sites; sea level to about 5000' (1500 m).

Range
Extreme SE. California, S. Arizona, E. and SW. New Mexico to E. Texas, north to SW. Kansas, south to Costa Rica.

Subspecies
Two; 1 in our range, *T. m. marcianus*.

Comments
Active during the day in the more northerly portions of its range. On warm summer nights it can be found foraging for frogs, fishes, and crayfish.

Big Bend Patchnose Snake
Salvadora deserticola
217

22–40" (56–101.6 cm). Slender snake with tan or brownish-orange back stripe, bordered by narrow black or dark brown stripes at juncture of back and sides. Narrow dark line on fourth scale row. Belly peach. Enlarged, triangular scale curves back over snout. Scales smooth. Scale in front of anus divided.

Breeding
Little is known. Mates in spring. About 5–10 eggs are laid in summer. Hatchlings are about 9" (23 cm) long.

Habitat
From flatlands, creosote bush desert and mesquite-dominated washes into foothills and mesas, 2000–5000' (600–1500 m).

Range
Big Bend region of Texas to SE. Arizona, south into northwestern Mexico.

Comments
Like the Western Patchnose Snake, this species can tolerate higher temperatures than most other snakes. Thus it is able to search out lizards active during parts of the day when other snakes are in retreats.

Western Patchnose Snake
Salvadora hexalepis
218

22–45" (56–114.3 cm). Slender gray or grayish-tan snake with wide triangular-shaped scale curved back over snout. Broad beige or yellow back stripe bordered by dark side stripes. Scales smooth. Scale in front of anus divided.

Breeding
Not well known. Presumed to mate April–June; lays 4–10 eggs in summer. Young hatch in 2–3 months.

Habitat
Barren creosote bush desert flats, sagebrush semidesert, and chaparral; sea level to 7000' (2150 m).

Range
S. California, W. and S. Nevada, and extreme SW. Utah, south into Mexico.

Subspecies
Four; 3 in our range.
Desert (*S. h. hexalepis*), top of head gray, back stripe 3 scale rows wide, 1 lip scale reaches eye; central and SW. Arizona west to SE. California, south into NE. Baja California and northwestern Mexico.
Mojave (*S. h. mojavensis*), top of head brown, black stripe obscure, often broken by narrow crossbars, lip scales do not reach eye; NW. Arizona and SW. Utah west into northern Mojave Desert in California, north into Nevada.
Coast (*S. h. virgultea*), top of head brown; back stripe narrow; 1 lip scale reaches eye; coastal California, San Luis Obispo south into NW. Baja California.

Comments
This fast-moving, agile species is active much of the day. After warming in the morning sun, it searches for lizards, young snakes, pocket mice, and reptile eggs.

Rosy Boa
Lichanura trivirgata
219, 224

24–42″ (61–106.7 cm). Stout, smooth, and shiny. Gray, tan, brown, or rosy red with 3 brown stripes down body; occasionally blotched. Head and tail somewhat short and blunt. No large symmetrical scales on top of head or under chin. Neck nearly as wide as head. Males have clawlike spur—a vestigial limb—on each side of scale in front of anus. Scales smooth. Scale in front of anus undivided.

Breeding
Habits poorly known. Mates May–June; 6–10 young are born October–November. Gestation takes approximately 130 days; newborn are about 12″ (31 cm) long.

Habitat
Desert, arid scrub, brushland, rocky chaparral-covered foothills—particularly where moisture is available, as around springs, streams, canyon floors; sea level to 4000′ (1200 m).

Range
S. California into N. Baja California, SW. Arizona, and adjacent Mexico.

Subspecies
Mexican (*L. t. trivirgata*), distinct dark brown stripes, black speckles on belly; SW. Arizona (Organ Pipe Cactus National Monument) into Mexico.
Desert (*L. t. gracia*), distinct rose, reddish-brown, or light brown stripes, brown speckles on belly; SE. California and SW. Arizona.
Coastal (*L. t. roseofusca*), ill-defined pink, rose, reddish-brown, or brown stripes; extreme SW. California into Baja.

Comments
Nocturnal. Primarily terrestrial, but occasionally climbs shrubs. A powerful constrictor, it preys on small mammals and birds. It seldom bites when handled, but when frightened may coil into a tight ball with head hidden within the coils.

Vestigial limbs, or spurs, near the vent are used by the male to stroke the female during courtship.

Blackneck Garter Snake
Thamnophis cyrtopsis
220

16–43″ (40.6–109.2 cm). Olive-gray or olive-brown, with 2 large black blotches on neck separated by back stripe. Back stripe may be wavy; orange and expanded in neck region, yellow or cream toward rear. Pale side stripes; often wavy in appearance because of intrusion of bordering black spots. 2 alternating rows of black spots between back and side stripes. Top of head gray. Scales keeled. Scale in front of anus undivided.

Breeding
Live-bearing. About 7–25 young, 8–10″ (20–25 cm) long, are born late June–August.

Habitat
Mesquite-dominated desert flats to pine-fir forests; prefers canyon and mountain streams and spring seepages; sea level to 8750′ (2700 m).

Range
S. Utah, and S. Colorado south through E. Arizona, New Mexico, and Trans-Pecos, Big Bend, and Edwards Plateau regions of Texas.

Subspecies
Three recognized; 2 in our area.
Western (*T. c. cyrtopsis*), small alternating black spots begin in neck region; SE. Utah and S. Colorado south to central Mexico.
Eastern (*T. c. ocellatus*), single large black spots in neck region; Texas, Edwards Plateau west to Big Bend.

Comments
Active during the day; may be observed basking along rocky or heavily vegetated streams in the morning. During summer rainy period, it may travel away from water. Swims on the surface of the water rather than below it.

Striped Whipsnake
Masticophis taeniatus
221

40–72″ (101.6–182.9 cm). Long, slender, and fast-moving. Gray, bluish-greenish gray, olive, reddish brown, or black; typically with 2 or more continuous or broken light lengthwise stripes on each side. Large head scales edged in white (except in S. Texas). Scales smooth. Scale in front of anus divided.

Breeding
Courts in early spring. May nest in abandoned rodent burrows. Lays 3–12 eggs, June–July. Young, 14–17″ (36–4 cm) long, hatch in August. Males mature in 1–2 years; females in 3.

Habitat
From grassland and brushy flatland to rugged mountainous

terrain dominated by pinyon-juniper and open pine-oak woodlands; sea level to 9400′ (2850 m).

Range
South-central Washington southeast in Great Basin to S. New Mexico and W. and central Texas, south to west-central Mexico.

Subspecies
Five; 2 in deserts of our range.
Desert (*M. t. taeniatus*), dark brown or blackish, white side stripes divided by thin black line; south-central Washington southeastward in Great Basin to S. New Mexico and adjacent extreme W. Texas and Mexico.
Central Texas (*M. t. girardi*), black with well-spaced lengthwise white patches on sides; central and W. Texas to central Mexico. Isolated populations in north-central Texas.

Comments
When surprised, this speedster quickly vanishes into brush, rocks, or mammal burrows. During the day, it hunts with head held high, watching for scurrying lizards or mammals.

onoran Whipsnake
Masticophis bilineatus
:22

30–67″ (76.2–170.2 cm). Long and slender; grayish brown, olive, or blue-gray, becoming lighter toward tail. 2 or 3 dark-edged light stripes on each side fade before reaching tail. Black line under eye from snout to neck. Belly cream, yellow under tail. Scales smooth. Scale in front of anus divided.

Breeding
Clutch of 6–13 rough, leathery eggs laid June–July.

Habitat
Thorny desert brushland to mountain pine-oak forest, generally in more open areas or near a stream, about 2000–6100′ (600–1850 m).

Range
Central and S. Arizona; SW. New Mexico into Mexico.

Subspecies
Three; 2 in our range.
Sonoran (*M. b. bilineatus*), chin usually unmarked; central and S. Arizona, SW. New Mexico south into Mexico.
Ajo Mountain (*M. b. lineolatus*), chin spotted; Ajo Mountains, Pima County, Arizona.

Comments
Diurnal. Readily climbs into shrubs and trees in search of lizards and birds (particularly nestlings). An alert snake, it will flee at the approach of danger.

oachwhip
Masticophis flagellum
23, 229, 230, 233

36–102″ (91.4–259 cm). Large, lithe, long-tailed and fast-moving. Western races generally yellow, tan, brown, gray, or pinkish; essentially patternless or with dark crossbars on neck. Eastern form: head and neck region dark brown to almost

black, gradually fading to light brown toward rear.
Occasionally all black. No pale side stripes. Scales smooth.
Scale in front of anus divided.

Breeding
Mates in spring. Clutches of 4–16 granular-surfaced eggs are
deposited June–July, hatch in 6–11 weeks. Young 12–16"
(30–41 cm) long.

Habitat
Dry, relatively open situations; rocky hillsides, grassland
prairies, desert scrub, thorn forest, and chaparral; sea level to
about 7000' (2150 m).

Range
SE. North Carolina, SW. Tennessee, extreme SW. Illinois,
extreme SW. Nebraska, E. Colorado, north-central New
Mexico, SW. Utah, west-central and S. Nevada, and central
California, south through Florida, Texas, and California to
central Mexico.

Subspecies
Sonoran (*M. f. cingulum*), long, dark reddish-brown bands
separated by shorter, paired, pale pink bands, or uniformly
reddish brown or black; south-central Arizona into Mexico.
Baja California (*M. f. fuliginosus*), 2 phases: yellow or light
gray with zigzag pattern of black bands along body, or dark
gray-brown above with lined pattern on sides; extreme S.
California through Baja California.
Lined (*M. f. lineatulus*), light gray or tan, each back scale on
forepart of body has a dark streak down center, underside of
tail salmon-pink; SW. New Mexico into Mexico.
Red (*M. f. piceus*), 2 phases: pink to red above with dark
crossbands on neck and forepart of body, or black above and
reddish near vent and under tail; west-central and S. Nevada
and SW. Utah, south through California and W. and SE.
Arizona and NE. Baja California and NW. Mexico.
San Joaquin (*M. f. ruddocki*), light yellow to olive-yellow
above, without dark head and dark neck bands; E. and S.
California.
Western (*M. f. testaceus*), light brown, olive, yellowish, or
pinkish red above, some with short dark crossbands on neck
and wide crossbands on forepart of body, double row of dark
spots on belly; extreme SW. Nebraska, E. Colorado, W.
Kansas, W. Oklahoma, E. New Mexico through W. and
central Texas into Mexico.

Comments
Perhaps our fastest snake. Prowls about during the day in
search of grasshoppers, cicadas, lizards, snakes, and small
rodents. When pursued, may take to a tree or disappear into a
mammal burrow. If cornered, it coils, vibrates its tail, and
strikes repeatedly—often at an enemy's face. Contrary to
popular belief, it does not chase down an adversary and whip
it to death. Record longevity is 16 years, 7 months.

Texas Blind Snake
Leptotyphlops dulcis
225

5–10¾″ (12.7–27.3 cm). Smooth, shiny, cylindrical snake; reddish brown, pink, or silvery tan, with blunt head and tail. Small spine on tip of tail. Eyes mere black spots beneath scales; more than 1 scale on top of head between large scale covering each eye.

Breeding
Clutch of 2–7 elongate, thin-shelled eggs is laid late June–July. Females tend incubating eggs and may share communal nesting sites in rocky fissures or earthen burrows. Hatchlings are about 2¾″ (7 cm) long.

Habitat
Semiarid deserts, prairies, hillsides, mountain slopes with sandy or loamy soil; sea level to 5000′ (1500 m).

Range
South-central Kansas through Oklahoma and Texas to Mexico, west to S. New Mexico and SE. Arizona.

Subspecies
Plains (*L. d. dulcis*), 1 upper lip scale between large scale containing eye and scale surrounding nostril; S. Oklahoma, central Texas into Mexico.
New Mexico (*L. d. dissectus*), 2 upper lip scales between eye scale and lower nasal scale; S. Kansas, W. Texas, S. New Mexico, SE. Arizona, and adjacent Mexico.

Comments
Nocturnal. This burrowing snake is seldom seen on the surface except in the evening following heavy summer rains. It is most frequently found in damp soil under slabs of rock, logs, or other surface debris.

Western Blind Snake
Leptotyphlops humilis
226

7–16″ (17.8–40.6 cm). Smooth, shiny cylindrical snake; brown, purplish, or silvery pink with blunt head and tail. Small spine on tip of tail. Black eyespots beneath scales; only 1 scale on top of head between large scale covering each eye.

Breeding
Mates in spring. Clutch of 2–6 slender eggs is laid July–August. Females tend eggs, and may use communal nests. Hatchlings are about 3½″ (9 cm) long.

Habitat
Deserts, grassland, scrub, canyons, and rocky foothills with moist sandy or gravelly soils; sea level to 5000′ (1500 m).

Range
Extreme SW. Utah, S. Nevada and California into Baja California, S. Arizona, SW. New Mexico, W. Texas, and Mexico.

Subspecies
Southwestern (*L. h. humilis*), 7–9 darkly colored scale rows on midback; S. California (except SE. corner) and S. Nevada, southeast to south-central Arizona.

Desert (*L. h. cahuilae*), 5 deeply colored scale rows on midback; SW. Arizona and SE. California into Mexico.
Trans-Pecos (*L. h. segregus*), 7 deeply colored scale rows on midback; SE. Arizona, SW. New Mexico, W. Texas into Mexico.
Utah (*L. h. utahensis*), 7 deeply pigmented scale rows on midback; SE. Nevada and extreme SW. Utah.

Comments
Subterranean in habit, and capable of burrowing quickly into loose soil or sand. On warm evenings it emerges at sunset from beneath moist rocks or among roots of bushes and forages for termites and ants, following their trails by smell.

Western Blackhead Snake
Tantilla planiceps
227

7–15″ (17.8–38.1 cm). Back uniformly tan, brown, or olive-gray; occasionally with faint dark stripe down midback. Belly white, becoming orange toward tail. Distinct black headcap extends downward to or below corner of mouth, ends abruptly on neck. Light collar usually borders headcap, followed by a few dark spots. Scales smooth. Scale in front of anus divided.

Breeding
Lays 1–3 eggs in May or June.

Habitat
Arid and semiarid regions, from Pacific Coast to about 5000′ (1500 m). Desert grassland to open mountain woodland, frequently in hilly areas and near streams.

Range
West-central Colorado through S. Utah and Nevada to central and W. California, south into Baja, Mexico.

Subspecies
Four; 3 in our range.
California (*T. p. eiseni*), light collar prominent; W. California south along coast to Baja.
Desert (*T. p. transmontana*), light collar faint; Riverside and San Diego counties, California.
Utah (*T. p. utahensis*), light collar absent; west-central Colorado through S. Utah and Nevada to SE. California.

Comments
May be seen wandering on surface at night. Eats worms, burrowing insect larvae, and centipedes.

Ground Snake
Sonora semiannulata
228, 231, 239

8–19″ (20.3–48.3 cm). Tiny, glossy snake; grayish, brownish, or reddish with great variation in back pattern. Some essentially patternless; others with a wide red, orange, or beige back stripe; others with crossbanding ranging from a single neck band to evenly spaced, saddle-shaped blotches to bands with red interspaces encircling body. Small dark blotch on back scales. Scales smooth and shiny. Scale in front of anus divided.

Breeding
Mates spring and fall. Up to 6 eggs deposited early June–late August. Young 4–5″ (10–13 cm) long hatch in 7–10 weeks.

Habitat
Dry open areas with loose sandy soil; rocky wooded or prairie hillsides, mesquite thickets along river beds, sand hummocks, vacant lots, brushy desert; sea level to 6000′ (1800 m).

Range
SW. Idaho, SE. Oregon south through Nevada, SE. California, and Arizona into Baja California and northern Mexico, east to E. Texas, and north through Oklahoma, SE. Colorado, S. Kansas, and SW. Missouri.

Comments
Until recently this secretive burrower was considered to be 2 species: *Sonora episcopa* with 2 subspecies and *S. semiannulata* with 5 subspecies. Plain-colored, striped, and crossbanded individuals may be found in the same area.

Racer
Coluber constrictor
232

33–77″ (86.4–195.5 cm). Large, slender, agile, and fast-moving. Adults uniformly black, blue, brown, or greenish above; white, yellow, or dark gray below. Young typically gray and conspicuously marked with dark spots on sides and dark gray, brown, or reddish-brown blotches down midline of back. Scales smooth. Scale in front of anus divided.

Breeding
Mates April–late May in most of range, 1–2 months earlier in Deep South. Female lays 5–28 soft leathery eggs with a rough granular texture in rotting tree stump, sawdust pile, under rocks, or in small mammal tunnel, mid-June to August. Occasionally a number of females deposit their eggs in a communal nest. Young hatch in 6–9 weeks, July–September.

Habitat
Abandoned fields, grassland, sparse brushy areas along prairie land, open woodland, mountain meadows, rocky wooded hillsides, grassy-bordered streams, and pine flatwoods; sea level to about 7000′ (2150 m).

Range
S. British Columbia and extreme S. Ontario; every state in continental United States, except Alaska; scattered populations through eastern Mexico to northern Guatemala.

Subspecies
11, poorly defined; 1 in the deserts of our range. Western Yellowbelly (*C. c. mormon*), green, olive-green, yellowish brown, or reddish brown above, belly yellow; S. British Columbia to Baja California east to SW. Montana, W. Wyoming, and W. Colorado. Some recent authors consider this form to represent a separate species.

Comments
Diurnal. The Racer may be encountered in most any terrestrial

situation except atop high mountains and in hottest deserts. Often observed streaking across roads. Although agile and a good climber, it spends most of its time on the ground. When hunting, it holds its head high and moves swiftly through cover. Often hibernates in rocky hillsides in large numbers.

Common Kingsnake
Lampropeltis getulus
234, 246

36–82" (91.4–208.3 cm). A large chocolate-brown to black kingsnake with a highly variable back and belly pattern. Light-centered scales may form distinct crossbands, "chain links," lengthwise stripes, blotches, or speckles on the back. Belly ranges from plain white to heavily blotched with dark pigment to plain black. Scales smooth. Scale in front of anus undivided.

Breeding
Mates mid-March (Florida) to June. 3–24 creamy white to yellowish elongated eggs are laid mid-May (Florida) to August. Incubation lasts 8½–11½ weeks, depending on temperature. Hatchlings are 9–12" (23–30 cm) long.

Habitat
Diverse: New Jersey Pine Barrens to Florida Everglades; dry rocky wooded hillsides to river swamps and coastal marshes; prairie, desert, and chaparral; sea level to 6900' (2100 m).

Range
S. New Jersey to S. Florida, west to SW. Oregon and S. California, south to S. Baja California and Zacatecas, Mexico.

Subspecies
California (*L. g. californiae*), chocolate-brown to black with bold light crossbands or a black stripe; SW. Oregon south to extreme S. Baja California, east to S. Utah and W. Arizona. Desert (*L. g. splendida*), back dark brown or black with narrow light crossbands, scales on sides have central light spot; central Texas west to SE. Arizona south to central Mexico.

Comments
Active during the day, especially early in the morning or near dusk, but becomes nocturnal in the warm summer months. It is primarily terrestrial, occasionally climbing into shrubs. A strong constrictor, it eats snakes—including rattlesnakes, copperheads, and coral snakes—as well as lizards, mice, birds and eggs.

Western Shovelnose Snake
Chionactis occipitalis
235, 237

10–17" (25.4–43.2 cm). Whitish or yellow, with saddle-shaped dark brown or black crossbands, sometimes with intervening reddish-orange crossbands. Snout flattened and juts well beyond lower jaw. Scales smooth.

Breeding
2–4 eggs are deposited in summer.

Habitat
Arid desert land; sandy washes, dunes, and rocky hillsides;

prefers areas with scattered mesquite-creosote bush; below sea level to 4700' (1450 m).

Range
South-central Nevada south into Baja California and Sonora, Mexico.

Subspecies
Mojave (*C. o. occipitalis*), dark crossbands, most not crossing belly, red crossbands absent; SE. California, southern tip of Nevada, west-central Arizona.
Colorado Desert (*C. o. annulata*), dark crossbands on body; most cross belly; narrow red crossbands present; SE. California and SW. Arizona, south into Mexico.
Nevada (*C. o. talpina*), brown-marked light spaces between brown crossbands appear as secondary crossbands; south-central Nevada southwestward into California.
Tucson (*C. o. klauberi*), distinct narrow secondary crossbands between black primary crossbands; south-central Arizona.

Comments
The small, shovel-shaped head, valved nostrils, flattened belly, and smooth scales allow this burrower to move quickly through sand. Occasionally seen during the day, but essentially nocturnal and most apt to be encountered crossing a road.

Banded Sand Snake
Chilomeniscus cinctus
236

7–10" (17.8–25.4 cm). Tiny, with a flattened and protruding shovel-shaped snout. Head and neck same width. Pale yellow to reddish orange above patterned with dark brown or black crossbands that encircle tail. Belly white. Scales smooth and shiny. Scale in front of anus divided.

Breeding
Habits poorly known; lays small clutches of eggs.

Habitat
Fine sandy areas in open desert dominated by creosote bush; coarse sandy areas in rocky upland washes and arroyos with paloverde and saguaro.

Range
Central and SW. Arizona south to S. Baja California and S. Sonora, Mexico.

Comments
Often emerges and moves on the surface at night. Highly specialized for desert existence; its spadelike snout, streamlined head with nasal valves, glossy skin, and angular-ended belly scales enable it to literally swim through fine sand.

Longnose Snake
Rhinocheilus lecontei
238, 247

22–41" (55.9–104.1 cm). A tricolored snake with a tapered, pointed snout protruding beyond lower jaw. Most scales under tail in a single row. Light-bordered, cream-flecked black saddle-shaped blotches extend down sides to edge of belly scales. Spaces between blotches pink or reddish with black spotting on sides. Scales smooth. Scale in front of anus undivided.

Breeding
Mates in spring. June–August, female lays 4–9 eggs in underground nest. Young, 8–10″ (20–25 cm) long, hatch in 2–3 months.

Habitat
Dry open prairie, desert brushland, coastal chaparral to tropical habitat in Mexico; sea level to 5400′ (1600 m).

Range
SW. Kansas, SE. Colorado, and New Mexico, south into Mexico, and northwest to Arizona, W. Utah, Nevada, and central California.

Subspecies
Western (*R. l. lecontei*), tip of snout not distinctly tilted upward; central California, Nevada, and W. Utah south into Baja and W. and S. Arizona. Isolated populations in Utah and SW. Idaho.
Texas (*R. l. tessellatus*), snout sharp with distinct upward tilt at tip; SW. Kansas and SE. Colorad. south through New Mexico and Texas into Mexico.

Comments
A good burrower. Active at night; hides amid rocks or in underground burrows during day. When first captured the Longnose Snake exhibits an unusual defense reaction: it tries to hide its head, then coils its body, vibrates its tail, and discharges a bloody fluid and anal gland secretions.

Sonoran Shovelnose Snake
Chionactis palarostris
240

10–15½″ (25.4–39.4 cm). A tiny yellow snake with alternating black and red saddle-shaped crossbands. Black crossbands usually extend across underside. Snout yellow, overhangs lower jaw, is slightly convex in profile. Scales smooth. Scale in front of anus divided.

Breeding
Habits unknown; presumably lays about 4 eggs in summer.

Habitat
Saguaro–paloverde-dominated upland desert in Arizona; arid mesquite–creosote-bush–bur sage terrain to the south.

Range
Organ Pipe Cactus National Park, SW. Arizona south to west-central Sonora, Mexico.

Subspecies
Two; 1 in our range, Organ Pipe (*C. p. organica*).

Comments
Nocturnal. A strong burrower with habits similar to those of the Western Shovelnose, but appears to prefer rockier terrain.

Arizona Coral Snake ⊗
Micruroides euryxanthus
241

13–21″ (33–53.3 cm). Blunt-snouted and glossy, with alternating wide red, wide black, and narrow yellow or white rings encircling the body. Head uniformly black to angle of jaw. Scales smooth. Scale in front of anus divided.

Breeding
Habits poorly known; presumably lays clutch of 2–3 eggs in late summer.

Habitat
Rocky areas, plains to lower mountain slopes; rocky upland desert especially in arroyos and river bottoms; sea level to 5900′ (1800 m).

Range
Central Arizona to SW. New Mexico south to Sinaloa, Mexico.

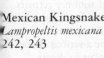

Subspecies
Three; 1 in our range, *M. e. euryxanthus*.

Comments
Do not handle! Venom is highly dangerous. This snake emerges from a subterranean retreat at night, usually during or following a warm shower. When disturbed by a predator, it buries its head in its coils, raises and exposes the underside of its tail, and may evert its cloacal lining with a popping sound. Eats blind snakes, and other small snakes.

Mexican Kingsnake
Lampropeltis mexicana
242, 243

24–47½″ (61–120.7 cm). Highly variable pattern of white-bordered gray crossbands alternating with black-bordered reddish-orange crossbands or blotches. Head distinct from neck; eyes large. Scales smooth. Scale in front of anus undivided.

Breeding
Mates in spring. 4–9 eggs are laid late May–late July, hatch in 9–11 weeks. Young are 9–11″ (23–28 cm) long.

Habitat
Arid mesquite–creosote-bush desert flats, barren rocky hillsides, canyons, limestone ledges, ranging into semimoist mountainous situations; 1200–7500′ (350–2300 m).

Range
Trans-Pecos region east to Balcones Escarpment of Edwards Plateau of Texas, south into Mexico.

Subspecies
Three, poorly defined; 1 enters our range, Gray-banded (*L. m. alterna*).

Comments
Once considered rare, this handsome snake became a favorite of collectors. A secretive, nocturnal species, it proved to be considerably more common than believed. Lizards are its staple diet, but it also eats frogs, small snakes, and rodents.

Copperhead ⊗
Agkistrodon contortrix
244

22–53" (55.9–134.6 cm). Stout-bodied; copper, orange, or pink-tinged, with bold chestnut or reddish-brown crossbands constricted on midline of back. Top of head unmarked. Heat-sensitive facial pit for locating prey between eye and nostril. Scales weakly keeled. Scale in front of anus undivided.

Breeding
Live-bearing. Mates spring to fall, peak April–May. 1–14 young, 7–10" (18–25 cm) long, are born August–early October; mature in 2–3 years.

Habitat
Wooded hillsides with rock outcrops above streams or ponds; edges of swamps and periodically flooded areas in coastal plain; near canyon springs and dense cane stands along Rio Grande; sea level to 5000' (1500 m).

Range
SW. Massachusetts west to extreme SE. Nebraska south to Florida panhandle and south-central and W. Texas.

Subspecies
Several; 1 in deserts of our range.
Trans-Pecos (*A. c. pictigaster*), dark crossbands with pale area at base of each band; Davis Mountains and Big Bend region, Texas.

Comments
Copperheads bask during the day in spring and fall, becoming nocturnal as the days grow warmer. Favored summer retreats are stone walls, piles of debris near abandoned farms, sawdust heaps, rotting logs, and large flat stones near streams. Copperhead bites are painful, but rarely pose a serious threat to life. The Trans-Pecos Copperhead may occur in desert shrublands, but is more often found near permanent water such as springs or streams lined with cottonwood.

Saddled Leafnose Snake
Phyllorhynchus browni
245

12–20" (30.5–50.8 cm). Small pink or cream snake with fewer than 17 large brown dark-edged, saddle-shaped blotches on body. Belly plain white. A large free-edged, triangular-shaped patchlike scale curves back over tip of snout and separates scales between nostrils. Pupils vertical. Scales smooth or faintly keeled. Scale in front of anus undivided.

Breeding
Poorly known habits. 2–5 eggs presumably laid in summer.

Habitat
Upland rocky or sandy desert dominated by mesquite, creosote bush, saltbush, paloverde, and saguaro; about 1000–3000' (300–900 m) in Arizona.

Range
South-central Arizona to NW. Mexico.

Subspecies
Four; 2 in our range.

Pima (*P. b. browni*), dark saddles much wider than light inner spaces; Pinal County, Arizona, south into Mexico.
Maricopa (*P. b. lucidus*), dark saddles and light inner spaces approximately equal in size; Maricopa County, Arizona, southwest into Mexico.

Comments
Usually seen crossing highways before midnight on warm humid summer nights. Feeds chiefly on lizards. Harmless, but hisses while striking.

Blacktail Rattlesnake ⊗
Crotalus molossus
48

28–49½" (71.1–125.7 cm). Greenish, yellowish, or grayish, with irregular light-edged, light-centered crossbands and sharply contrasting black tail. Individual scales are of a single color. Scales keeled.

Breeding
About 3–6 young, 9–12" long, are born in summer.

Habitat
Most common in rocky mountainous areas; among rimrock and limestone outcrops, wooded stony canyons, chaparral, rocky streambeds; near sea level to about 9000' (2750 m).

Range
Arizona east to central Texas, south through central Mexico.

Subspecies
Three; 1 in our range, Northern (*C. m. molossus*).

Comments
Generally considered an unaggressive rattlesnake; little is known of its natural history. It is seen at night and basking during cooler periods of the day. Presumably feeds mainly on small rodents. Record longevity is 15½ years.

Tiger Rattlesnake ⊗
Crotalus tigris
49

20–36" (50.8–91.4 cm). Numerous gray or brownish crossbands mark pale gray, buff, lavender, or pinkish-gray upper surface. Crossbands composed of tiny dots, often poorly defined. Head proportionally small, rattle large. Scales keeled.

Breeding
Live-bearing. Young reportedly about 9" (23 cm) at birth.

Habitat
Arid rocky foothills and canyons, primarily in ocotillo–mesquite–creosote bush and saguaro-paloverde associations; sea level to 4800' (1450 m).

Range
Central Arizona south to S. Sonora, Mexico.

Comments
Natural history poorly known. Reportedly active day and night and occasionally encountered crossing roads after warm showers. Occasionally confused with larger Speckled Rattlesnake, which enters its range.

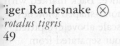

Rock Rattlesnake ⊗
Crotalus lepidus
250, 257

16–32⅝" (40.6–82.9 cm). Small-headed and slender; greenish gray, bluish gray, or pinkish tan, with widely spaced, irregularly bordered narrow black or brown crossbands. Dusky spotting between bands may be sparse or so heavy as to form secondary crossbands or appear speckled.

Breeding
2–8 young, 6¾–8¾" (17–22 cm) long, are born July–August.

Habitat
Chiefly rocky mountainous areas; talus slopes, gorges, rimrock, limestone outcrops, rocky streambeds; 1500–9600' (460–2900 m). Occasionally into rocky areas containing creosote bush.

Range
SE Arizona, west-central and SE. New Mexico southeast to Jalisco, and through the Trans-Pecos region to south-central Texas.

Subspecies
Four; 2 in our area.
Mottled (*C. l. lepidus*), spaces between crossbands heavily spotted, dark stripe from eye to angle of mouth; SE. New Mexico through Trans-Pecos region to south-central Texas, south to San Luis Potosí.
Banded (*C. l. klauberi*), crossbands distinct, no dark stripe from eye to angle of mouth; SE. Arizona to extreme W. Texas, south to Jalisco, Mexico.

Comments
May be observed during the day sunning itself among rocks. Feeds on lizards, small snakes, and small newborn rodents.

Speckled Rattlesnake ⊗
Crotalus mitchelli
251, 255

23–52" (58.4–132.1 cm). Pattern and color vary greatly; generally has a sandy, speckled appearance. Back marked with muted crossbands or hexagonal to diamond-shaped blotches formed by small cluster of dots. Large scale above eye pitted, creased, or rough-edged; or scale on snout separated from scales in front of nostrils by row of tiny scales. Scales keeled.

Breeding
July–August, female gives birth to 2–11 young, 8–12" (20–30 cm) long.

Habitat
Prefers rugged rocky terrain, rock outcrops, deep canyons, talus, chaparral amid rock piles and boulders, rocky foothills; sea level to 8000' (2450 m).

Range
Extreme SW. Utah, S. Nevada and S. California south into NW. Sonora and throughout Baja California.

Subspecies
Southwestern (*C. m. pyrrhus*), scale on snout separated from

scales in front of nostrils by small scales; SW. Utah, W.
Arizona, extreme southern tip of Nevada, S. California.
Panamint (*C. m. stephensi*), large scale above eye pitted,
creased, or roughly edged; S. Nevada and adjacent California.

Comments
Active during the day in spring and fall, at night in summer.
Eats ground squirrels, kangaroo rats, white-footed mice,
birds, and lizards. Record longevity exceeds 16 years.

Sidewinder  Ⓧ
Crotalus cerastes
252, 253

17–32⅜" (43.1–82.4 cm). A rough-scaled rattler with a
prominent triangular projection over each eye. Scales keeled.

Breeding
Mates April–May, sometimes in fall. Female gives birth to 5–
18 young, about 6½–8" (17–20 cm) long, late summer to
early fall.

Habitat
Arid desert flatland with sandy washes or mesquite-crowned
sand hammocks; below sea level to 5000' (1500 m).

Range
S. Nevada and adjacent California, and extreme SW. Utah,
south into Mexico.

Subspecies
Mojave Desert (*C. c. cerastes*), bottom segment of rattle brown;
extreme SE. Utah, S. Nevada, and Mojave Desert region of
California.
Sonoran (*C. c. cercobombus*), bottom segment of rattle black;
south-central Arizona to west-central Sonora.
Colorado Desert (*C. c. laterorepens*), bottom segment of rattle
black; SW. Arizona and SE. California and adjacent Mexico.

Comments
Travels quickly over shifting surfaces by "sidewinding," a
locomotion process in which the snake makes use of static
friction to keep from slipping when crossing soft sandy areas.

**Red Diamond
Rattlesnake** Ⓧ
Crotalus ruber
254

29–64" (73.7–162.5 cm). Stoutly built; tan to brick-red,
with diamond-shaped blotches down midline of back. Blotches
usually light-edged but may be indistinct. Black and white
rings encircle tail. Scales keeled.

Breeding
Mates February–April. Females gives birth to 3–20 young,
11¾–13½" (30–34 cm) long, in August.

Habitat
Cool coastal zone into the foothills and over the mountains
into the desert; prefers dense chaparral in foothills, brush-
covered boulders, cactus patches; sea level to 5000' (1500 m).

Range
SW. California south through Baja.

Subspecies
Five; 1 in our range, *C. r. ruber.*

Comments
Most often encountered in the spring, coiled in a shelter in partial sun or crossing the road at night. Eats rabbits, ground squirrels, and birds. Record longevity is 14½ years.

Western Diamondback
Rattlesnake ⊗
Crotalus atrox
256

34–83⅞" (86.4–213 cm). Largest western rattlesnake. Heavy-bodied with large head sharply distinct from neck. Back patterned with light-bordered dark diamonds or hexagonal blotches; blotches often obscured by randomly distributed small dark spots, which give back a mottled or dusky look. 2 light diagonal lines on side of face; stripe behind eye meets upper lip well in front of angle of jaw. Tail encircled by broad black and white rings. Scales keeled.

Breeding
Mates late March–May and in fall; 4–25 young, 8½–13" (21.5–33 cm) long, are born in late summer. Females mature in 3 years.

Habitat
Arid and semiarid areas from plains to mountains; brushy desert, rocky canyons, bluffs along rivers, sparsely vegetated rocky foothills; sea level to 7000' (2100 m).

Range
SE. California eastward to central Arkansas south into northern Mexico.

Comments
The "coon-tail rattler" is capable of delivering a fatal bite. When disturbed it usually stands its ground, lifts its head well above its coils, and sounds a buzzing warning. Take heed! Active late in the day and at night during hot summer months. Eats rodents and birds. Record longevity is nearly 26 years.

Western Rattlesnake ⊗
Crotalus viridis
258, 260

16–64" (40.6–162.6 cm). Size and color vary greatly. Brownish blotches down midline of back, generally edged with dark brown or black and often surrounded by light border; begin as oval, squarish, diamondlike, or hexagonal markings and tend to narrow into inconspicuous crossbands near tail. Scales keeled.

Breeding
Mates March–May and in fall; 4–21 young, 6–12" (15–30 cm) long, are born August–October.

Habitat
Great Plains grassland to brush-covered sand dunes on Pacific Coast, and to timberline in the Rockies and the coniferous forests of the Northwest; rocky outcrops, talus slopes, stony canyons, prairie-dog towns; sea level to 11,000' (3350 m).

Range
Extreme W. Iowa, south into Mexico and west to S. Alberta, SW. Saskatchewan, south-central British Columbia, Washington, Oregon, and coastal California, and south.

Subspecies
Nine; 2 in deserts of our range.
Prairie (*C. v. viridis*), greenish or brownish above, well-defined brown blotches; extreme W. Iowa to the Rockies, S. Alberta to northern Mexico.
Great Basin (*C. v. lutosus*), light brown or gray above; blotches narrow (roughly equal to interspaces); SE. Oregon, S. Idaho, NE. California, Nevada, W. Utah, extreme NW. Arizona.

Comments
Excitable and aggressive. In northerly areas or at high elevations, large numbers may overwinter together at a common den site. In southerly areas or those lacking rocky retreats, individuals may seek shelter in mammal burrows.

Mojave Rattlesnake ⊗
Crotalus scutulatus
359

24–51″ (61–129.5 cm). Uniformly white scales surround brown diamonds marking midline of back. Greenish gray, olive green, greenish brown, or occasionally yellow above. Black and white rings encircle tail; white rings significantly larger. Light stripe behind eye extends backward above angle of mouth. Scales keeled.

Breeding
Female gives birth to 2–11 young, about 9–11″ (23–28 cm) long, July–August.

Habitat
Upland desert flatland supporting mesquite, creosote bush, and cacti; also arid lowland with sparse vegetation, grassy plains, Joshua-tree forests, and rocky hills; sea level to 8300′ (2500 m).

Range
S. Nevada, adjacent California and extreme SW. Utah southeastward through central Mexico.

Subspecies
Two; 1 in our range, *C. s. scutulatus*.

Comments
Usually encountered on mild nights, crossing a road, or before the heat of the day, partially exposed under the bank of a dry wash or along a mesquite-bordered streambed. Its venom is extremely toxic and causes more respiratory distress than that of any other North American pit viper.

Western Hognose Snake
Heterodon nasicus
361

16–35¼″ (40.6–89.5 cm). Sharply upturned and pointed snout. Stout body with broad neck. Tan, brown, gray, or yellowish gray above with distinct or somewhat faded series of dark blotches down back and 2 or 3 rows of side spots. Belly and underside of tail distinctly patterned with large black blotches. Scales keeled. Scale in front of anus divided.

Breeding
Mates March–May. Lays 4–23 elongate, thin-shelled eggs in soft loamy or sandy soil, early June–late August depending on locality. Young, 6–7½" (15–19 cm) long, hatch in 7–9 weeks and reach maturity in 2 years.

Habitat
Sand and gravelly soiled prairie, scrubland, river floodplains. Sea level to 8000' (2450 m).

Range
SE. Alberta and NW. Manitoba, south to SE. Arizona, Texas, and into northern Mexico. Isolated populations in Minnesota, Iowa, Illinois, Missouri, and Arkansas.

Subspecies
Plains (*H. n. nasicus*), more than 35 midline body blotches in males, more than 40 in females; SE. Alberta and SW. Manitoba south to W. Oklahoma, Texas panhandle, and S. New Mexico.
Mexican (*H. n. kennerlyi*); Mexico into extreme S. Texas through the Trans-Pecos region into SW. New Mexico and SE. Arizona.

Comments
Primarily active during morning and late afternoon hours; burrows into loose soil to escape hot or cold conditions. Sense of smell enables it to find buried toads, lizards, snakes, and reptile eggs; also eats birds and small rodents.

Lyre Snake
Trimorphodon biscutatus
262, 270

24–47¾" (61–121.2 cm). A slimly built, "cat-eyed" snake; broad head bears a chevron- or lyre-shaped mark. Light brown to gray with darker brown or gray saddle-shaped blotches with light centers on back; smaller dark blotches on sides and belly scales. Scales smooth.

Breeding
Little known. A Californian female laid 12 eggs in September which hatched in 79 days. Young about 8–9" (20–23 cm) long.

Habitat
Rocky hillsides, slides and canyons, boulder-strewn mountain slopes; arid rocky coastal areas; desert to evergreen forest; sea level to 7400' (2250 m).

Range
S. California east to Big Bend region of Texas, south to Costa Rica.

Subspecies
Six; 3 in our range.
Sonoran (*T. b. lambda*), distinct chevron-shaped head mark, more than 22 body blotches, scale in front of anus divided; S. Nevada and extreme SW. Utah south through SE. California,

Arizona and SW. New Mexico to Sonora.
California (*T. b. vandenburghi*), distinct head marking, about
36 body blotches. Scale in front of anus usually undivided. S.
California into Baja California.
Texas (*T. b. vilkinsoni*), head pattern obscure, usually less than
23 body blotches, scale in front of anus divided; Big Bend
region of Texas, northwest to SW. New Mexico, and west into
Chihuahua, Mexico.

Comments
Emerges at night from its rocky retreat to explore. Enlarged
teeth toward back of jaw introduce a mild venom into prey.

Gopher Snake
Pituophis melanoleucus
63

48–100" (122–254 cm). Large and powerfully built; small
head. Light-colored with black, brown, or reddish-brown
blotches on back and sides. Snout somewhat pointed, with
enlarged scale extending upward between nostrils. Scales
keeled. Scale in front of anus undivided.

Breeding
Mates in spring. Clutches of 3–24 cream to white eggs are
laid in burrows in sandy soil or below large rocks or logs, June–
August; hatch in 64–79 days. Young are 12–18" (30–46 cm)
long.

Habitat
Dry, sandy pine-oak woodlands and pine flatwoods, cultivated
fields, prairies, open brushland, rocky desert, chaparral; sea
level to 9000' (2750 m).

Range
S. New Jersey, western Virginia, S. Kentucky, Wisconsin,
SW. Saskatchewan, S. Alberta, and south-central British
Columbia south to S. Florida, east-central and west-central
Mexico and tip of Baja.

Subspecies
Fifteen; 2 in deserts of our range.
Sonoran Gopher (*P. m. affinis*), blotches brown or reddish
brown on forepart of body, distinctly darker on rear; extreme
south-central Colorado, W. New Mexico, extreme W. Texas,
central and S. Arizona, and SE. California south into Mexico.
Great Basin Gopher (*P. m. deserticola*), wide blotches on
forepart of body usually black, connected with side blotches,
and creating isolated light blotches on back; south-central
British Columbia south through E. Washington, Nevada, SE.
California and eastward through Idaho, Utah, N. Arizona, to
Wyoming, W. Colorado, and NW. New Mexico.

Comments
Generally diurnal, but may be active at night during hot
weather. This snake takes refuge in mammal or tortoise
burrows or under large rocks or logs. Noted for its
consumption of rodents. When confronted, Gopher Snakes
hiss loudly, sometimes flattening their heads and vibrating
their tails, then lunging at the intruder.

Massasauga ⊗
Sistrurus catenatus
264

18–39½″ (45.8–100.3 cm). Unlike other rattlers, has 9 enlarged scales on top of head. Tail stocky with moderately developed rattle. Rounded dark blotches on back and sides; interspaces narrow. Light-bordered dark bar extends from eye to rear of jaw. Dark bars (often lyre-shaped) on top of head extend onto neck. Scales keeled. Scale in front of anus undivided.

Breeding
Mates April–May. Litter of 2–19 young, 6½–9½″ (16.5–24 cm) long, are born July–early September. Females mature in years.

Habitat
Rocky hillsides, sagebrush prairie, into desert grassland in the West; sphagnum bogs, swamps, marshland, and floodplains to dry woodland in the East.

Range

S. Ontario and NW. Pennsylvania south to northeastern Mexico and extreme SE. Arizona. Isolated populations in central New York.

Subspecies
Desert (*S. c. edwardsi*), smaller, faded; belly whitish and often unmarked; SE. Colorado and SW. Kansas to W. and S. Texas, S. New Mexico and extreme SE. Arizona.

Comments
Massasauga means "great river mouth" in the Chippewa language and probably alludes to the snake's habitat in Chippewa country—swampland surrounding mouths of rivers. It may be encountered sunning on mild days; becomes crepuscular or nocturnal during hot summer months. Eats lizards, small rodents, and frogs. The Desert Massasauga ordinarily inhabits shortgrass prairie, but is sometimes found in grassland-desert transition areas where creosote bush is common; for instance, along the Arizona-New Mexico border.

Spotted Leafnose Snake
Phyllorhynchus decurtatus
265, 269

12¾–20″ (32.4–50.8 cm). Stout-bodied like Saddled Leafnose Snake; bears similar triangular-shaped patchlike scale curved back over tip of snout. Pink, gray, or tan with more than 17 dark blotches from neck to tail along midline of back. Belly white. Vertical pupils. Scales smooth or keeled. Scale in front of anus undivided.

Breeding
Poorly known. Clutches of 2–4 large eggs are laid primarily June–July. Hatchlings about 7–8″ (18–20 cm).

Habitat

Open, sandy, or gravelly creosote bush desert; sea level to 3000′ (900 m).

Range
S. Nevada south through SE. California and Arizona to tip of Baja California and Sinaloa, Mexico.

Subspecies
Six; 2 in our range.
Clouded (*P. d. nubilis*), 42–60 blotches on midline of back, equal or wider than inner spaces; Pima County, Arizona, south into Sonora, Mexico.
Western (*P. d. perkinsi*), 24–48 blotches, narrower than inner spaces; S. Nevada south into Baja California and NW. Sonora, Mexico.

Comments
Nocturnal. A secretive, adept burrower, this snake is most commonly encountered in the evening on roads after rains.

Western Hooknose Snake
Gyalopion canum
466

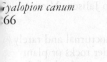

8–14¼" (20.3–36.2 cm). Pale brown and patterned with dark-edged brown crossbands; 2 prominent crossbands on head. Snout upturned and sharp-edged. Scales smooth. Scale in front of anus divided.

Breeding
One female is known to have laid a single egg early in July.

Habitat
Arid regions dominated by creosote bush, mesquite, and shadescale, and juniper-grassland or pinyon-juniper associations.

Range
W. Texas west to SE. Arizona, and south to Zacatecas, Mexico.

Comments
Although usually thought of as a desert species, the Western Hooknose Snake inhabits mountainous parts of New Mexico and Texas. It is most often seen at night after a light rain, from April to September. When first touched, it gyrates wildly and makes popping noises by everting and retracting the lining of its cloaca—the chamber into which the digestive, urinary, and reproductive systems empty.

Night Snake
Hypsiglena torquata
467

12–26" (30.5–66 cm). Slender and cylindrical-bodied; beige, yellowish, or gray, patterned with numerous dark brown or gray blotches on back and side. Large blotch on each side of neck; a third spot may be present on nape or lateral blotches may be fused at midline. Eyes with vertical pupils. Dark bar behind eye; upper lip scales white. Belly cream or white, unpatterned. Scales smooth. Scale in front of anus divided.

Breeding
Habits poorly known. Clutches of 4–6 eggs have been deposited late April–early July. Incubation takes 7–8 weeks.

Habitat
Semiarid and arid sandy or rocky situations from plains and desert flats, to heavy brush chaparral and blue oak-digger pine woodland; sea level to 7000' (2100 m).

Range
North-central California, south-central Washington, S. Idaho, Utah, and SW. Kansas south through Baja California to Costa Rica.

Subspecies
About 12; 6 in our range.

Desert (*H. t. deserticola*), 3 blotches on neck, central one greatly enlarged toward rear; south-central Washington, E. Oregon, S. Idaho, Nevada, W. Utah, and Mojave Desert region, SE. California.

San Diego (*H. t. klauberi*), 3 blotches on neck, central one not enlarged toward rear; coastal S. California, vicinity San Luis Obispo Bay south into Baja California.

Sported (*H. t. ochrorhyncha*), 2 blotches or single narrow bar across neck region, top of head flat; Arizona, W. New Mexico SW. Trans-Pecos region of Texas south to Jalisco, Mexico.

Comments
This successful, wide-ranging species is nocturnal and rarely encountered. Most of the day it hides under rocks or plant litter. Enlarged grooved teeth, located near the back of the upper jaw, hold lizard and frog prey while snake's mildly toxic saliva incapacitates them.

Glossy Snake
Arizona elegans
268

26–70" (66–178 cm). Resembles Gopher Snake but has smooth glossy scales rather than keeled scales. Snout somewhat pointed; lower jaw inset. Variable number of black-edged tan, brown, or gray blotches mark cream, pinkish, or light brown upper surfaces. Dark line runs from angle of jaw to eye. Belly unmarked. Scale in front of anus undivided.

Breeding
Mates in spring. Clutch of 3–23 eggs is laid during summer, hatches in 10–12 weeks.

Habitat
Dry, open sandy areas, coastal chaparral, creosote-mesquite desert, sagebrush flats, and oak-hickory woodland; below sea level to 5500' (1700 m).

Range
SE. Texas and extreme SW. Nebraska west to central California, south into Mexico.

Subspecies
9, poorly differentiated; 7 in our range.

Kansas (*A. e. elegans*), 39–69 large dark body blotches; extreme SW. Nebraska south through W. Texas into Mexico.

Texas (*A. e. arenicola*), 41–58 body blotches; SE. Texas.

Mojave (*A. e. candida*), 53–73 narrow body blotches; Death Valley area, S. Nevada south through western Mojave Desert in California.

Desert (*A. e. eburnata*), pale-colored with 53–83 small narrow body blotches; extreme SW. Utah, S. Nevada south through center of Mojave Desert to Gulf of California.

Arizona (*A. e. noctivaga*), body blotches slightly wider than interspaces; S. and W. Arizona south to central Sinaloa, Mexico.
California (*A. e. occidentalis*), dark with 51–75 dark brown blotches; San Joaquin Valley south into Baja California.
Painted Desert (*A. e. philipi*), 53–80 body blotches; SE. Utah, NE. and SE. Arizona, W. New Mexico.

Comments
Occasionally called the faded snake because of its bleached appearance. It is a capable burrower and is usually seen on the surface in the early evening hours during the warmer months. This species feeds chiefly on lizards, but sometimes preys on small mammals as well.

California Treefrog
Hyla cadaverina
271

1–2″ (2.5–5.1 cm). Skin rough, gray, with dark blotches. Dark stripe through eye usually absent. Expanded toe pads; webbing extends to tip of fifth toe of hind foot. Male has gray throat.

Voice
An abrupt low-pitched quack, given during the day as well as at night. Males usually call while sitting in the water, often at the base of a rock.

Breeding
March–May.

Habitat
Near slow streams and rocky washes with permanent pools. Deserts to mountains, sea level to over 5000′ (1500 m).

Range
From SW. California into N. Baja California.

Comments
Primarily nocturnal. The California Treefrog seeks shade during the day among the rock crevices near water. Protective coloration helps it avoid daytime predators. When disturbed, it leaps into the water but returns immediately to shore.

Canyon Treefrog
Hyla arenicolor
272

1¼–2¼″ (3.2–5.7 cm). Plump and warty, with a toadlike appearance. Olive to brownish gray, with darker blotches present in most populations. Dark-edged light spot beneath eye. Undersurfaces of thigh yellow to orange. Large toe pads. Male has gray to black throat.

Voice
An explosive, rather hollow and nasal series of notes, all of one tone and lasting 1–3 seconds.

Breeding
Usually March–July; may be delayed until adequate rain falls.

Habitat
Arid areas close to rocky washes, streams, permanent pools.

Range
From S. Utah to central Colorado, south into Mexico. Isolated populations in NE. New Mexico and the Big Bend region of Texas.

Comments
Primarily nocturnal; often seen along watercourses. During the day it can be found hiding among rocks or in stony crevices near streams, camouflaged by its color.

Lowland Burrowing Treefrog
Pternohyla fodiens
273

1–2″ (2.5–5.1 cm). Light yellow to brown, with large black-edged brown spots or longitudinal stripes. Skin is fused to bony skull; skin fold at back of head. Toe pads´small. Large spadelike tubercle on hind feet. Male has gray throat.

Voice
A series of loud deep squawks.

Breeding
July–August, with summer rains.

Habitat
Arid grassy areas or open mesquite woodlands. Sea level to about 5000′ (1500 m).

Range
Extreme south-central Arizona south along the Pacific coast of Mexico.

Comments
Nocturnal. This Mexican treefrog is adapted to living in burrows where humidity is high. It is easily caught when breeding or chorusing but at other times is extremely wary.

Couch's Spadefoot
Scaphiopus couchi
274

2¼–3½″ (5.7–8.9 cm). A plump toad with elongated, sickle-shaped spade on each hind foot and no hump between eyes. External eardrum apparent. Skin smooth, with many minute light-colored tubercles. Bright greenish yellow to brown with variable dark marbling. Belly mostly white.

Voice
Like the bleat of a lamb; lasts about 1 second. Very noisy chorus can be heard for a long way.

Breeding
Mates after heavy rainfall, April–September. Eggs are laid on plant stems in temporary pools and, if the spot is warm, may hatch in 36 hours. Tadpoles transform in 2–6 weeks, before pools dry up.

Habitat
Tolerant of dry terrain; likes shortgrass prairie as well as mesquite savannah and creosote-bush desert.

Range
Extreme SE. California, S. Arizona and New Mexico, and SW. Oklahoma south into Mexico.

Comments
Nocturnal. During dry periods this toad stays underground in the burrow of a small mammal or buried in loose soil.

ains Spadefoot
aphiopus bombifrons
5

1½–2½" (3.8–6.3 cm). A stout-bodied toad with round- to wedge-shaped spade on hind feet and prominent bony hump between eyes. External eardrum apparent. Skin relatively smooth with scattered small tubercles; gray to brown, often with overtones of green; tubercles orange. Usually light stripes on back are vaguely discernible. Belly white. Male throat bluish gray on sides.

Voice
A dissonant grating note given at 1-second intervals; sometimes a hoarse trill lasting 1 second.

Breeding
May–August, stimulated by rain. Eggs in masses of 10–200 are attached to submerged vegetation in shallow ponds, hatching within 48 hours. Tadpoles are omnivorous; transform within 2 months.

Habitat
Shortgrass prairie where soil is loose and dry, rainfall low. Likes sandy and gravelly soils. Occurs in several desert–grassland transitional areas.

Range

The Great Plains from S. Alberta and Saskatchewan southeast through Montana to Missouri and central Oklahoma, south through W. Texas and E. Arizona and into Mexico. Separate population in extreme S. Texas.

Comments
Nocturnal. A single sharp-edged spade on the inside of each hind foot pushes aside soil as the Spadefoot backs into the ground. Burrows may be a few inches to several feet long. They remain open but are difficult to locate in sandy soil. Occasionally, sticky matter is seen at the entrance, probably to cement soil in place and prevent burrow collapse.

estern Spadefoot
aphiopus hammondi
6

1½–2½" (3.8–6.4 cm). Stout-bodied toad with wedge-shaped spade on each hind foot and no hump between eyes. External eardrum apparent. Dusky-olive to brown or gray, with irregular light stripes and random darker blotches. Skin relatively smooth with scattered small tubercles, red- or orange-tipped in some specimens. Belly white.

Voice
A rolling trill like the purr of a cat. Males call while floating on surface of water.

Breeding
January–August, depending on rainfall. Eggs are laid in cylindrical masses attached to vegetation. Hatching occurs

within 2 days, transformation in 4–6 weeks. Tadpoles are carnivorous and feed on mosquito larvae.

Habitat
Tolerates wide range of conditions from semiarid to arid. Prefers shortgrass plains and sandy, gravelly areas such as alkali flats, washes, and river floodplains.

Range
Arizona, New Mexico, parts of S. Colorado, and W. Oklahoma south into Mexico. Separate population in California south of San Francisco through the central valley and foothills into N. Baja California.

Subspecies
New Mexico (*S. h. multiplicata*), with trill lasting longer than 1 second; S. Colorado through Arizona and New Mexico into Mexico.

Comments
Nocturnal. These toads are often numerous where soil conditions are favorable for burrowing. Deep burrows provide a microhabitat with moderate temperatures and humidity. When handled, the Western Spadefoot produces a secretion that smells like peanuts and can inflame the skin or cause hay-fever symptoms of runny nose and watery eyes.

Great Basin Spadefoot
Scaphiopus intermontanus
277

1½–2″ (3.8–5.1 cm). Stout toad with wedge-shaped spade on each hind foot and glandular hump between eyes. External eardrum apparent. Skin relatively smooth, but many minute tubercles present. Olive to gray-green, with light stripes along flanks. Belly white.

Voice
A series of low-pitched throaty notes given rapidly.

Breeding
April–July, usually following heavy rains. Utilizes springs and slow-moving water as well as temporary pools.

Habitat
Sagebrush flats and forested areas. Digs burrow in loose soil or uses burrows of other animals.

Range
From S. British Columbia south to E. California, east to Colorado and NW. New Mexico.

Comments
Primarily nocturnal. It is occasionally found abroad in daylight foraging for insects and can sometimes be brought to the surface by loud stamping near its burrow.

Red-spotted Toad
Bufo punctatus
278

1½–3″ (3.8–7.6 cm). Small flat toad with round parotoids. Olive to grayish brown, usually with reddish warts. Bony ridges on head weak or absent.

Voice
A high-pitched musical trill. Males call while sitting near water's edge.

Breeding
April–September, initiated by rainfall. The only North American toad that lays eggs one at a time, not in long strings, on bottoms of pools.

Habitat
Desert and rocky regions and prairie grasslands, usually near source of permanent water or dampness, natural or man-made, from sea level to 6000' (1800 m).

Range
From central Texas west into SE. California and south into Mexico.

Comments
Active at twilight. Red-spotted Toads are most often collected at breeding choruses, but animals have been encountered over a mile from water and even in prairie dog burrows.

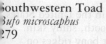

Southwestern Toad
Bufo microscaphus
279

2–3" (5.1–7.7 cm). Medium-size plump toad, olive to brown to pink, with or without dark spots. Usually has light stripe or patch on head and back. Parotoid glands oval, widely separated; forward ends light-colored. No bony ridges on head. Male throat not dark.

Voice
A pleasing musical trill; ends abruptly after 10 seconds.

Breeding
March–July; not dependent on rainfall. Egg strings are laid on bottom of pools.

Habitat
Loose gravelly areas of streams and arroyos in drier portion of range; often on the sandy banks of quiet water in other areas.

Range
Coastal S. California and N. Baja California. Scattered localities in Utah, Nevada, Arizona, and New Mexico.

Subspecies
Arizona (*B. m. microscaphus*), with dark spots on back; scattered populations along the headwaters and tributaries of the Colorado River from SW. Utah, S. Nevada, central Arizona, and SW. New Mexico, into Mexico.

Comments
Primarily nocturnal, but also found foraging by day. It hops instead of walking.

Texas Toad
Bufo speciosus
280

2–3⅛" (5.1–9.2 cm). Medium-size plump toad with indistinct bony ridges on head and widely separated oval parotoids. Olive to grayish brown, with greenish warts in darker spots. 2 sharp-edged tubercles on each hind foot; inner tubercle is sickle-shaped. Flap of skin covers deflated vocal sac.

Voice
An abrupt high-pitched trill.

Breeding
April–September, after heavy rains. Uses temporary pools or man-made waterholes and ditches.

Habitat
Prairie grasslands and open woodlands; adapted for dry conditions. Usually on floodplains in deserts, but occurs into shrublands. Prefers sandy areas.

Range
Extreme south-central Kansas through Oklahoma, Texas, and S. New Mexico into northern Mexico.

Comments
Nocturnal. An effective burrower, the Texas Toad disappears rapidly in loose soil. When threatened, it often flattens itself on the ground.

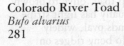

Colorado River Toad
Bufo alvarius
281

3–7" (7.7–17.9 cm). Largest native toad in the United States. Olive to dark brown, with a relatively smooth, shiny skin. Elongate parotoid glands touch prominent bony ridges on head. 1 or 2 white warts at corner of mouth. Other large warty glands on hind legs. Belly is cream-colored.

Voice
A weak low-pitched toot, lasting less than a second.

Breeding
May–July.

Habitat
Desert. Prefers damp areas near permanent springs or man-made watering holes but may be found in arid grasslands and woodlands. From sea level to 5300' (1600 m).

Range
Extreme SE. California to extreme SW. New Mexico, south into Mexico.

Comments
Nocturnal. The Colorado River Toad sometimes appears before seasonal rains fill breeding pools. When the rains finally arrive, breeding commences. It eats insects, spiders, and lizards.

**Great Plains
Narrowmouth Toad**
Gastrophryne olivacea
282

⅞–1⅝" (2.2–4.1 cm). Small, plump, smooth-skinned, with egg-shaped body, pointed snout, and fold of skin across back of head. Gray to olive, with scattered black flecks. Single spade on each hind foot. Male has dark throat.

Voice
High-pitched buzzing bleat.

Breeding
March–September, when heavy rains create favorable water
levels. Eggs are laid as a surface film.

Habitat
Desert, montane woodlands, and grasslands, from sea level to
4000' (1200 m). Moist or damp areas from marshes to leaf
litter and rodent burrows.

Range
In a band from E. Nebraska and W. Missouri through
Oklahoma and Texas into Mexico, west through northern
Mexico into south-central Arizona.

Comments
Nocturnal. This toad often shares the burrow of a tarantula
(where the 2 apparently live in harmony), a lizard, or a mole.
It feeds primarily on ants.

Great Plains Toad
Bufo cognatus
283

2–4½" (5.1–11.4 cm). Large, with prominent bony ridges on
head that converge to form bony hump on snout. Behind eyes,
bony ridges on head meet elongate parotoid glands. Gray to
olive to brown, with large, symmetrical, light-bordered dark
blotches. Sharp-edged tubercle on each hind foot. Flap of skin
conceals the deflated male vocal sac.

Voice
A high-pitched, almost metallic trill.

Breeding
April–September, usually during or after heavy rainfall. Egg
strings are attached to debris on bottom of pool.

Habitat
Grasslands of the prairie and drier bushy areas.

Range
From SE. Alberta to W. Wisconsin in the north, south
through the Great Plains to NW. Texas and into Mexico, west
to S. New Mexico, Arizona, and SE. California, and north to
parts of SE. Nevada and central Utah.

Comments
Primarily nocturnal, but sometimes found foraging on cloudy,
rainy days. This frog prefers loose soil where burrowing is
easy. When in danger, it inflates, closes its eyes, and lowers
its head to the ground. It is a voracious predator of cutworms,
which cause extensive crop damage.

Sonoran Green Toad
Bufo retiformis
284

1½–2¼" (3.8–5.7 cm). Small flat toad with green to
greenish-yellow spots surrounded by striking broad patterns of
black. Large, elongate parotoid glands extend onto sides. Bony
ridges on head weak or absent. Male has dusky throat.

Voice
A buzz. Males call from edge of grass-bordered pools.

Breeding
July, with advent of rains.

Habitat
Semiarid grassland and creosote-bush desert.

Range
A narrow band from south-central Arizona to west-central Sonora in Mexico.

Comments
Nocturnal. It is a shy toad, rarely seen in numbers except at breeding ponds. As a consequence, most specimens collected are males. Occasionally single individuals are found abroad at night among the mesquite.

Rio Grande Leopard Frog
Rana berlandieri
285

2¼–4½" (6–11.4 cm). Pale green, with large dark spots between russet ridges at juncture of back and sides; ridges broken near hind legs. Light jaw stripe poorly defined.

Voice
A short rapid trill, low in pitch.

Breeding
Year-round. Egg masses are attached to submerged vegetation.

Habitat
Any water or area with moist conditions, either natural or artificial.

Range
SW. Arizona and S. New Mexico to central Texas, south into Mexico.

Comments
Primarily nocturnal. The Rio Grande Leopard Frog can tolerate dry conditions by burrowing under rocks and shingle.

Northern Leopard Frog
Rana pipiens
286

2–5" (5.1–12.8 cm). Slender brown or green frog with large, light-edged dark spots between light-colored ridges at juncture of back and sides; ridges continuous to groin. Light stripe on upper jaw. Eardrum without light center.

Voice
A low guttural snore lasting about 3 seconds, followed by several clucking notes.

Breeding
March–June. Egg masses are attached to submerged vegetation or laid on bottom.

Habitat
From desert to mountain meadow; from freshwater sites with profuse vegetation to brackish marshes and moist fields.

Range
Throughout northern North America, except West Coast.

Comments
Primarily nocturnal. When pursued on land, it flees in zigzag leaps to the security of water. In the desert this species is confined to areas of permanent or nearly permanent water.

Green Toad
Bufo debilis
87

1¼–2⅛″ (3.2–5.4 cm). Small, flat, bright green toad with many small warts and black spots. Large parotoids extend onto sides; no bony ridges on head. Male has dark throat.

Voice
A piercing cricketlike trill. Males call while floating head-up in the water.

Breeding
March–September, but only when rains are adequate to fill pools. If conditions are not favorable, breeding season may be skipped. Egg strings are attached to vegetation.

Habitat
The shelter of rocks in semiarid regions. Also found in prairies.

Range
From SW. Kansas south through Texas to the Gulf Coast and into Mexico, north to SE. areas of Arizona, New Mexico, and Colorado.

Subspecies
Western (*B. d. insidior*), black spots usually interconnected; SE. Colorado and W. Kansas through W. Texas and E. New Mexico and Arizona to Mexico.

Comments
Active at twilight, but often will forage during the day following heavy rains. When threatened, it frequently flattens itself against the ground. Often found in roadside ditches following rains.

Bullfrog
Rana catesbeiana
88

3½–8″ (9–20.3 cm). The largest frog in North America. Green to yellow above with random mottling of darker gray. Large external eardrum; hind feet fully webbed except for last joint of longest toe. No ridges at juncture of back or sides. Belly cream to white, may be mottled with gray.

Voice
Deep-pitched, loud *jug o'rum* call.

Breeding
Northern areas, May–July; southern, February–October. Egg masses are attached to submerged vegetation. Tadpoles are large, 4–6¾″ (10.2–17.1 cm), olive-green, and may take almost 2 years to transform.

Habitat
Aquatic. Prefers ponds, lakes, and slow-moving streams large enough to avoid crowding and with some vegetation.

Tiger Salamander
Ambystoma tigrinum
289, 290, 291

Range
Eastern and central United States; also New Brunswick and parts of Nova Scotia. Extensively introduced in the West.

Comments
Nocturnal. Usually found on the bank at water's edge.

6–13⅜″ (15.2–40 cm). World's largest land-dwelling salamander. Stoutly built, with broad head and small eyes. Color and pattern extremely variable—large light spots, bars, or blotches on dark background or network of spots on lighter background. Tubercles on soles of feet. 11–14 (usually 12–13) grooves on sides.

Breeding
Prompted by rain; in North and higher elevations, eggs laid March–June; in South, December–February; in Southwest, July–August. Mates in temporary pools, fishless ponds, stream backwaters, and lakes soon after ice is out. Egg masses adhere to submerged debris. Hatching larvae are ⁹⁄₁₆″ (14 mm long; transform June–August at about 4″ (90–123 mm).

Habitat
Varied: arid sagebrush plains, pine barrens, mountain forests, and damp meadows where ground is easily burrowed; also in mammal and invertebrate burrows; sea level to 11,000′ (3353 m).

Range
Widespread from central Alberta and Saskatchewan, south to Florida and Mexico, but absent from New England, Appalachian Mountains, Far West.

Subspecies
Several; 3 in deserts of our range.
Barred (*A. t. mavortium*), dark with yellow crossbars or blotches; NE. Nebraska to extreme SE. Wyoming, south to south-central Texas and New Mexico, and Mexico.
Arizona (*A. t. nebulosum*), gray with small dark marks; W. Colorado and Utah to south-central New Mexico and central Arizona.
Blotched (*A. t. melanostictum*), dark with yellow to olive blotches or netlike lines; extreme S. British Columbia, E. Washington, and central Alberta southeast to S. Wyoming and NW. Nebraska.

Comments
Often seen at night after heavy rains, especially during breeding season, Tiger Salamanders live beneath debris near water or in crayfish or mammal burrows. In desert areas these animals are often found breeding in cattle tanks. They consume earthworms, insects, mice, and amphibians.

FISHES

Watercourses in the American deserts provide a habitat for a variety of fishes, from common shiners, which are widespread in freshwater, to the Desert Pupfish, which is found only in desert areas. Some of these species live a marginal existence, threatened by natural and manmade changes in their aquatic homes. This section covers some of the fishes that survive in the waters of the deserts.

White River Springfish
Crenichthys baileyi
292

To 3" (7.5 cm). Deep, stout, slightly compressed; back dark olive to dusky; sides silvery with 2 rows of dark spots, belly yellowish to whitish. Head large, flattened above; snout blunt, mouth wide, small. Fins small, edges black; pectoral fins inserted low on body, rounded; no pelvic fins; caudal fin edge straight. Lateral line absent.

Habitat
Warm desert spring pools and runs.

Range
White River drainage of SE. Nevada.

Comments
The White River Springfish feeds on microscopic and filamentous algae and aquatic invertebrates. Like many other fishes in desert springs, it is threatened by the alteration of its limited habitat and the introduction of exotic fishes.

Desert Pupfish
Cyprinodon macularius
293

To 2½" (6.5 cm). Stout, deep, females deeper-bodied than males; back silvery to olive; sides silvery with 6–9 dusky bars often forming irregular band along side; breeding males iridescent blue. Head short, scaled; mouth at tip of head upturned. Dorsal and anal fins rounded, dorsal fin often with dusky blotch; caudal fin edge toward rear slightly convex.

Habitat
Marshy backwaters of desert streams and springs.

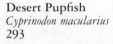

Range
S. Arizona, S. California, and NW. Mexico.

Comments
The Desert Pupfish grows very rapidly, sometimes reaching lengths of 2" (5 cm) in a year. Most of the 13 species of *Cyprinodon* in the United States are restricted to springs or streams in the deserts of Texas, New Mexico, Arizona, Nevada, and California. Several species are endangered by desert development and the introduction of exotic fishes. The best known is the Devils Hole Pupfish (*C. diabolis*), once the focal point of a U.S. Supreme Court water rights case.

Mosquitofish
Gambusia affinis
294

To 2½" (6.5 cm). Rather robust, particularly females; compressed. Tan to olive above, pale yellowish below; scales have small, dusky spots near edges; dark bar below eye; many spots present on dorsal and caudal fins; females have conspicuous black spot on belly during reproductive period. Head flattened from top to bottom; mouth small, oblique; lower jaw projects beyond upper. Anal fin of male modified to form reproductive organ.

Habitat
Near surface of fresh or brackish water in ponds, lakes, ditches, backwaters, and sluggish streams; introduced to many desert springs and ponds.

Range
From New Jersey to central Mexico along coast and in associated freshwater streams; Mississippi River basin south from Illinois.

Comments
Because it eats aquatic mosquito larvae, the Mosquitofish has been introduced into many areas to control mosquitoes. It competes with natural desert fish.

Gila Topminnow
Poeciliopsis occidentalis
95

To 2″ (5 cm). Moderately elongate, greatest depth in front of dorsal fin; back dark olive, sides olive to tan with dark stripe along side from upper margin of gill cover to tail-fin base, scales on back and sides and fin rays outlined with dark pigment. Head small; mouth small, upturned. Pelvic fins small; dorsal fin behind anal fin origin; anal fin modified in male to form reproductive organ; caudal fin rounded to almost square. Scales large.

Habitat
Springs, pools, edges, and backwaters of streams, usually with debris and aquatic vegetation.

Range
Gila River drainage from S. Arizona, SW. New Mexico to Sonora, Mexico.

Comments
Once one of the commonest fishes in the southern Colorado River drainage, the Gila Topminnow was added to the list of endangered species in 1967. Efforts are underway to remove competitors from isolated springs.

Longfin Dace
Agosia chrysogaster
296

To 3½″ (9 cm). Robust; head blunt; dark olive-gray above, with dark stripe along side ending in darker spot; whitish below. Mouth at tip of head reaches front of eye; small barbel at corner of jaw. Fins rounded except caudal fin forked; front half of anal fin elongate in females. Scales small.

Habitat
Warm desert streams to cooler mountain brooks.

Range
Bill Williams and Gila rivers of central and SE. Arizona and SW. New Mexico; Sonora, Mexico.

Comments
Longfin Dace are less common in large rivers and at high elevations. They are omnivorous, feeding on detritus, aquatic invertebrates, and algae.

Speckled Dace
Rhinichthys osculus
297

To 4″ (10 cm). Elongate, rounded, belly flattened; back dusky to dark olive; sides gray-green with dark lateral stripe, often obscured by dark speckles or blotches. Snout moderately pointed; mouth small, on underside; lips reddish in breeding males; barbels present; eye small. Fins plain, bases reddish in breeding males; caudal fin moderately forked.

Habitat
Cool to warm creeks, rivers, and lakes over gravel or rock; desert springs and their outflow.

Range
West of Continental Divide from S. British Columbia south to S. Arizona.

Comments
The Speckled Dace is one of the most widespread minnows in western waters. There are several subspecies of this highly variable species. It is an important forage fish in some trout streams and is used for bait.

Tui Chub
Gila bicolor
298

To 16″ (41 cm.) Plump, robust; back dark olive to brassy, sides lighter; lower body and fins pinkish in adults; young with dark stripe along side. Head short, somewhat pointed; mouth small, oblique; eye large. Anal fin small; caudal peduncle deep, thick.

Habitat
Quiet, shallow waters of large, slow streams, lakes, and ponds.

Range
From S. Washington south through Oregon, SW. Idaho, Nevada, E. and S. California.

Comments
Tui Chubs are omnivorous, but feed primarily on invertebrates. They are a good forage fish, but have overpopulated some reservoirs, adversely affecting some game fishes. Several subspecies are endangered, and most are restricted to streams and springs in isolated desert basins.

Golden Shiner
Notemigonus crysoleucas
299

To 12″ (30 cm). Deep, compressed; back golden to olive, sides light olive with silvery reflections, belly silvery yellow; some fish entirely silvery. Mouth upturned; snout blunt. Belly has pronounced keel between pelvic and anal fins. Dorsal fin slightly crescent-shaped; breeding males have orange on pelvic and anal fins. Lateral line curved downward.

Habitat
Clear, quiet streams, lakes, ponds, and swamps over mud, sand, or rocks, usually near aquatic vegetation.

Range
Native to eastern North America, southern Canada, and south to Texas; widely introduced elsewhere.

Comments
Golden Shiners are the most common bait fish sold in the United States and are important forage fish for several species

of game fishes. They are schooling fishes that stay mainly near shore but may venture into open water. This species has been introduced into many desert aquatic habitats to the detriment of native species.

Spikedace
Meda fulgida
00

To 3″ (7.5 cm). Elongate, slender, slightly compressed; back olive-brown with dark mottles; sides silvery with scattered black specks. Snout short; mouth extends to below eye; eye large. Base of fins, except caudal, reddish; dorsal fin with 2 spines. Scales embedded or absent.

Habitat
Over sand or gravel in pools of larger streams with moderate to swift current.

Range
Gila River system in central and SE. Arizona and SW. New Mexico.

Comments
The Spikedace was once widespread in the Gila River drainage, but has been displaced in many areas by the newly introduced Red Shiner.

TREES, SHRUBS, CACTI, AND GRASSES

Most of our desert landscape is dominated by low-growing vegetation—shrubs, cacti, and grasses—though some plants do grow to the size of small trees. All of these plants are remarkable in the many and varied ways in which they have adapted to a desert existence. Some are leafless most of the year; others have silvery or velvety foliage that helps to retain moisture under the hot desert sun. Many are armed with spikes or thorns, perhaps to discourage animals from grazing on their slow-growing branches. Often these plants are surprisingly long-lived. Some cacti are well over 100 years old, and clumps of Creosote Bush are believed to have persisted for several millennia. This section describes some of the most frequently seen trees, shrubs, cacti, and grasses that occur in our deserts.

Blue Palo Verde
Cercidium floridum
301, 316

Spiny, small tree, leafless most of the year, with a short blue-green trunk and widely spreading, very open crown.
Height: 30′ (9 m). Diameter: 1½′ (0.5 m).
Leaves: alternate; few and scattered; bipinnately compound; 1″ (2.5 cm) long, with short axis forking into 2 side axes. 2 or 3 pairs of leaflets on each side axis. ¼–⅜″ (6 mm) long; oblong; pale blue-green; appearing in spring but soon shedding.
Bark: trunk and branches blue-green and smooth; base of large trunks becoming brown and scaly.
Twigs: blue-green, smooth, slightly zigzag, hairless, with straight, slender spine less than ¼″ (6 mm) long at each node.
Flowers: ¾″ (19 mm) wide; with 5 bright yellow petals, the largest with a few red spots; 4–5 flowers in a cluster less than 2″ (5 cm) long; covering the tree in spring, sometimes again in late summer.
Fruit: 1½–3¼″ (4–8 cm) long; narrowly oblong, flat, thin pods; short-pointed at ends, yellowish brown; maturing and falling in summer; 2–8 beanlike seeds.

Habitat
Along washes and valleys and sometimes on lower slopes of deserts and desert grasslands.

Range
Central and S. Arizona, SE. California, and northwestern Mexico; 4000′ (1219 m).

Comments
Although leaves are absent most of the year, photosynthesis, the manufacture of food, is performed by the blue-green branches and twigs. Twigs and pods serve as browse for wildlife and emergency food for livestock; the seeds are eaten by rodents and birds; and the flowers are a source of honey.

Screwbean Mesquite
Prosopis pubescens
302, 311, 320

Spiny shrub or small tree with long, slender branches and odd, screwlike pods.
Height: 20′ (6 m). Diameter: 8″ (20 cm).
Leaves: alternate; clustered; bipinnately compound; 2–3″ (5–7.5 cm) long, with stalk of ½″ (12 mm) and 1 pair (sometimes 2) of side axes. 5–8 pairs of leaflets ¼–⅜″ (6–10 mm) long, ⅛″ (3 mm) wide; oblong, short-pointed, finely covered with gray hairs, dull green, stalkless.
Bark: light brown, smooth, thick, separating in long, fibrous strips and becoming shaggy.
Twigs: slender; covered with gray hairs when young; with slender, whitish, paired spines about ⅜″ (10 mm) long united with base of leafstalk at nodes.
Flowers: 3/16″ (5 mm) long; light yellow; many crowded in narrow clusters about 2″ (5 cm) long; in spring and summer.
Fruit: 1–2″ (2.5–5 cm) long; a pod tightly coiled into a narrow spiral like a large screw, pale yellow or light brown, hard, with sweetish pulp and many tiny, beanlike seeds; several to many crowded on a stalk, often abundant; maturing in summer, not splitting open, and shedding in autumn.

Habitat
Along streams and valleys in deserts; often forming thickets.

Range
Trans-Pecos Texas west to extreme SW. Utah and SE. California; also adjacent northern Mexico; to 5500′ (1676 m).

Comments
Screwbean Mesquite is easily recognized by the unusual pods, which are the basis of the common English name. The sweetish, nutritious pods can be eaten and are browsed by livestock and wildlife.

Catclaw
Acacia greggii
303, 317

Spiny, many-branched, thicket-forming shrub; occasionally a small tree with a broad crown.
Height: 20′ (6 m). Diameter: 6″ (15 cm).
Leaves: alternate; clustered; bipinnately compound; 1–3″ (2.5–7.5 cm) long; the slender axis usually with 2–3 pairs of side axes. 3–7 pairs of leaflets ⅛–⅜″ (3–6 mm) long; oblong, rounded at ends; thick; hairy; almost stalkless; dull green.
Bark: gray, thin, becoming deeply furrowed.
Twigs: brown, slender, angled, covered with fine hairs; with many scattered, stout spines ¼″ (6 mm) long, hooked or curved backward.
Flowers: ¼″ (6 mm) long; light yellow, fragrant; stalkless; including many tiny stamens in long, narrow clusters 1–2″ (2.5–5 cm) long; in early spring and irregularly in summer.
Fruit: 2½–5″ (6–13 cm) long, ½–¾″ (12–19 mm) wide; thin, flat, ribbonlike, oblong pod; brown, curved, much twisted, often narrowed between seeds; maturing in summer and shedding in winter, remaining closed; several beanlike, nearly round, flat brown seeds.

Habitat
Along streams, in canyons, and on dry, rocky slopes of plains and foothills.

Range
Central, southern, and Trans-Pecos Texas and northeastern Mexico; to 2000′ (610 m), sometimes higher.

Comments
This is one of the most despised southwestern shrubs. As indicated by the common names (including the nicknames Devilsclaw and Catclaw Acacia, as well as the Spanish, *uña de gato*), the sharp, stout, hooked spines, like a cat's claws, tear clothing and flesh.

Tamarisk
Tamarix chinensis
304, 324

Naturalized shrub or small tree with slender, upright or spreading branches and narrow or rounded crown; resembling a juniper, though not evergreen.
Height: 16′ (5 m). Diameter: 4″ (10 cm).
Leaves: alternate; about ¹⁄₁₆″ (1.5 mm) long; scalelike, crowded, narrow and pointed; dull blue-green.

Bark: reddish brown, smooth, becoming furrowed and ridged.
Twigs: green, becoming purplish; long, slender, hairless;
usually shedding with leaves.
Flowers: less than ⅛″ (3 mm) long and wide; with 5 pink
petals; numerous, crowded together in narrow clusters ¾–2″
(2–5 cm) long at ends of twigs; in spring and summer.
Fruit: ⅛″ (3 mm) long; narrow, pointed, reddish-brown
capsules; splitting into 3–5 parts; many tiny, hairy seeds;
maturing in summer.

Habitat
Wet, open areas along streams, irrigation ditches, and
reservoirs, including sand banks and alkali and salty soils.

Range
Native of Asia and southeastern Europe. Extensively
naturalized from SW. Nebraska west to Nevada and south to
S. California and S. Texas; local beyond; also in northern
Mexico; to 5000′ (1524 m).

Comments
Introduced at the beginning of this century as an ornamental
and for erosion control, Tamarisk has become an undesirable
weed in many places. It is considered a phreatophyte (literally,
a "well-plant," having deep roots and high water use).
Eradication has been difficult, since the plants spread by seeds
and cuttings and grow rapidly. However, the large thickets
provide cover for doves and other wildlife. Also known as
Saltcedar. *Tamarix,* the classical Latin name, may allude to
Tamaris, a river in Spain.

moke Tree
Dalea spinosa
05, 313, 334

Spiny, many-branched shrub or small tree with short, crooked
trunk, compact or irregular crown of smoky-gray branches,
and small leaves; leafless most of the year.
Height: 20′ (6 m). Diameter: 1′ (0.3 m).
Leaves: alternate; ⅜–⅝″ (1–1.5 cm) long, ⅛–½″ (3–12 mm)
wide. Reverse lance-shaped, rounded at tip, long-pointed at
base, edges wavy; stalkless or nearly so; gray, densely hairy
and gland-dotted. Few in early spring, shedding after a few
weeks and before flowering.
Bark: dark gray-brown, furrowed and scaly.
Twigs: smoky-gray, with dense, pressed hairs and brown
gland-dots; zigzag, slender, ending in slender, sharp spines.
Flowers: ½″ (12 mm) long; 1 broad upper petal and 2 lateral
petals nearly enclosing 2 lower petals that are joined and
shaped like the prow of a boat; dark purple or violet, fragrant,
gland-dotted; few, in clusters to 1¼″ (3 cm) long, along
twigs; in late spring or early summer when leafless.
Fruit: ⅜″ (10 mm) long; a small, egg-shaped pod ending in
curved point, hairy and gland-dotted, with 1 brown, beanlike
seed; maturing in late summer and not opening.

Habitat
Sandy and gravelly washes in desert, mainly with Creosote
Bush; in subtropical regions.

Range
W. Arizona, extreme S. Nevada, SE. California, and
northwestern Mexico; from below sea level to 1500' (457 m).

Comments
The common name describes the hazy appearance of the
leafless plants when seen from a distance. The smoky-gray
twigs produce most of the food, by photosynthesis, since the
plants have leaves for only a few weeks each year.

Desert Willow
Chilopsis linearis
306

Large shrub or small tree, often with leaning trunk; open,
spreading crown; narrow, willowlike leaves; large, showy
flowers; and very long, narrow, beanlike fruit.
Height: 25' (7.6 m). Diameter: 6" (15 cm).
Leaves: opposite and alternate; 3–6" (7.5–15 cm) long, ¼–
⅜" (6–10 mm) wide. Linear, straight or slightly curved, very
long-pointed at ends; not toothed, drooping, short-stalked;
light green, sometimes hairy or sticky.
Bark: dark brown, furrowed into scaly ridges.
Twigs: brown, very slender, sometimes hairy or sticky.
Flowers: 1¼" (3 cm) long and wide; bell-shaped corolla with
unequal lobes, whitish tinged with pale purple or pink and
with yellow in throat; fragrant; in clusters to 4" (10 cm) long
at ends of twigs; from late spring to early summer.
Fruit: 4–8" (10–20 cm) long, ¼" (6 mm) in diameter; a dark
brown, cigarlike capsule; maturing in autumn, splitting into
2 parts, and remaining attached in winter; many flat, light
brown seeds with 2 papery, hairy wings.

Habitat
Moist soils of stream banks and drainages in plains and
foothills, desert and desert grassland zones, often in thickets.

Range
SW. Texas and New Mexico west to extreme SW. Utah
and S. California; also in northern Mexico; at 1000–5000'
(305–1524 m).

Comments
Desert Willow is important in erosion control and is planted
also as an ornamental. Propagated from cuttings or seeds, it
grows rapidly and sprouts after being cut.

Mexican Palo Verde
Parkinsonia aculeata
307, 322

Spiny tree with very open, spreading crown of drooping twigs
and narrow evergreen "streamers"; usually leafless.
Height: 40' (12 m). Diameter: 1' (0.3 m).
Leaves: alternate; bipinnately compound but appearing
pinnately compound, with short, spine-tipped axis and 1–3
pairs of wiry, flattened, narrow, evergreen, drooping axes or
"streamers" 8–20" (20–51 cm) long. 25–30 pairs of leaflets
¼–⅜" (6 mm) long; narrowly oblong, light green; remaining
on tree only a short time before falling.
Bark: trunk and branches yellow-green, smooth; base of large
trunks becoming scaly.

Twigs: yellow-green, smooth, slightly zigzag, slender; finely hairy when young; with paired, short spines at nodes bordering a third, larger brownish spine of leaf axis.
Flowers: ¾" (19 mm) wide; with 5 rounded golden-yellow petals, the largest red-spotted and turning red in withering; in loose, upright clusters to 8" (20 cm) long, showy; in spring and summer or practically continuously in tropical climates.
Fruit: 2–4" (5–10 cm) long; a narrowly cylindrical, dark brown pod, long-pointed at ends, narrowed between seeds, hanging down; 1–8 beanlike seeds; maturing in summer and autumn and remaining closed.

Habitat
Moist valley soils; rare in foothills and mountain canyons of desert and desert grassland.

Range
S. to Trans-Pecos Texas and local in S. Arizona; to 4500' (1372 m). Planted and becoming naturalized across southern border of United States, sometimes as a weed. Widely distributed in tropical America.

Comments
Mexican Palo Verde, or Jerusalem-thorn, is a popular, fast-growing tree widely used as an ornamental and hedge plant in warm regions. The foliage and pods have been used as emergency forage for livestock, and are consumed by wildlife as well. Bees produce fragrant honey from the flowers.

Honey Mesquite
Prosopis glandulosa
308, 321

Spiny, large thicket-forming shrub or small tree with short trunk, open, spreading crown of crooked branches, and narrow, beanlike pods.
Height: 20' (6 m). Diameter: 1' (0.3 m).
Leaves: alternate; bipinnately compound; 3–8" (7.5–20 cm) long; the short axis bearing 1 pair of side axes or forks, each fork with 7–17 pairs of stalkless leaflets, ⅜–1¼" (1–3 cm) long, ⅛" (3 mm) wide; narrowly oblong, hairless or nearly so, yellow-green.
Bark: dark brown, rough, thick, becoming shreddy.
Twigs: slightly zigzag, with stout, yellowish, mostly paired spines ¼–1" (0.6–2.5 cm) long at enlarged nodes, which afterwards bear short spurs.
Flowers: ¼" (6 mm) long; nearly stalkless, light yellow, fragrant; crowded in narrow clusters 2–3" (5–7.5 cm) long; in spring and summer.
Fruit: 3½–8" (9–20 cm) long, less than ⅜" (10 mm) wide; narrow pod ending in long narrow point, slightly flattened, wavy-margined between seeds; sweetish pulp; maturing in summer, remaining closed; several beanlike seeds within 4-sided case.

Habitat
Sandy plains and sandhills and along valleys and washes; in short grass, desert grasslands, and deserts.

Range

E. Texas and SW. Oklahoma west to extreme SW. Utah and S. California; also northern Mexico; naturalized north to Kansas and SE. Colorado; to 4500' (1372 m).

Comments

The seeds are disseminated by livestock that graze on the sweet pods, and the shrubs have invaded grasslands. Cattlemen regard mesquites as range weeds and eradicate them. In sandy soils, dunes often form around shrubby mesquites, burying them except for a rounded mass of branching tips. The similar Velvet Mesquite (*P. velutina*) replaces Honey Mesquite in the southern half of Arizona and adjacent Mexico. The scientific names and status of mesquites are topics of dispute among biologists. At least one author recognizes all United States mesquites as varieties of a single, widely distributed species, *P. juliflora*.

Foothill "Yellow" Palo Verde
Cercidium microphyllum
309, 318

Small, spiny tree that is leafless most of the year, with yellow-green trunk and wide, many-branched, open crown.
Height: 25' (7.6 m). Diameter: 1' (0.3 m).
Leaves: alternate; few; bipinnately compound but appear as if a pinnately compound pair; ¾–1" (2–2.5 cm) long; consisting of very short axis with 2 forks, each with 3–7 pairs of minute leaflets: elliptical, slightly hairy; yellow-green; appearing in spring but soon shedding.
Bark: yellow-green, smooth.
Twigs: short, stiff, ending in long, straight spines about 2" (5 cm) long.
Flowers: about ½" (12 mm) wide; with 5 pale yellow petals, largest petals white or cream; in clusters to 1" (2.5 cm) long; covering the tree in spring.
Fruit: 2–3" (5–7.5 cm) long; cylindrical pods; constricted between seeds; remaining attached.

Habitat

Associated with Saguaro on desert plains and rocky slopes of foothills and mountains.

Range

Arizona, SE. California, and northwestern Mexico; at 500–4000' (152–1219 m).

Comments

During most of the year, in the absence of leaves, the branches and twigs manufacture food. This adaptation to a desert habitat exposes less surface to the sun, aiding moisture retention.

Velvet Mesquite
Prosopis velutina
310

Spiny tree with short, forking trunk, open, spreading crown or crooked branches, and hairy or velvety foliage, twigs, and pods.
Height: 20–40' (6–12 m). Diameter: 1–2' (0.3–0.6 m).
Leaves: generally clustered; bipinnately compound; 5–6" (13–15 cm) long; finely hairy, the slender axis with 1 or 2

pairs of side axes. Leaflets crowded, 15–20 pairs, ¼–½″ (6–12 mm) long; narrowly oblong, dull green, stalkless.
Bark: dark brown, rough and thick, separating into long, narrow strips.
Twigs: light brown, slightly zigzag, covered with fine velvety hairs; with stout, yellowish, generally paired spines ¼–1″ (0.6–2.5 cm) long at enlarged nodes.
Flowers: ¼″ (6 mm) long; light yellow, nearly stalkless, fragrant; crowded in hairy, long, narrow clusters 2–3″ (5–7.5 cm) long of many flowers; in spring and summer.
Fruit: 4–8″ (10–20 cm) long, less than ⅜″ (10 mm) wide; a narrow pod; short-pointed, slightly flattened, wavy-margined between seeds; finely hairy; sweetish pulp; maturing in summer, not splitting open; several beanlike seeds within 4-sided case.

Habitat
Along washes and valleys and on slopes and mesas in desert, desert grassland, and occasionally with oaks.

Range
Extreme SW. New Mexico west to central Arizona and northwestern Mexico; at 500–5500′ (152–1676 m).

Comments
The medium-size tree mesquite of central and southern Arizona, Velvet Mesquite reaches larger size than related species. The wood is used for fenceposts and novelties and is one of the best in the desert for fuel; even the large, deep taproots are grubbed up for that use. Southwestern Indians prepared meal and cakes from the sweet pods and livestock browse them, disseminating the seeds. Bees produce a fragrant honey from mesquites. This species and the Honey Mesquite (*P. glandulosa*) are often considered varieties of *P. juliflora*.

Elephant Tree
Bursera microphylla
312, 315

Aromatic shrub or tree with short, very thick, sharply tapered trunk with stout, crooked, tapering branches and a widely spreading but sparse, open crown.
Height: 16′ (5 m). Diameter: 1′ (0.3 m).
Leaves: alternate; pinnately compound; 1–1¼″ (2.5–3 cm) long; with winged axis; aromatic. 15–30 leaflets ⅕–⅖″ (6 mm) long; narrowly oblong, short-pointed at base, stalkless, not toothed, dull light green on both surfaces.
Bark: papery, peeling in thin flakes, white on outside; next thin layers green, inner layers red and corky.
Twigs: reddish brown.
Flowers: less than ¼″ (6 mm) wide; with 5 whitish petals, short-stalked; 1–3 at leaf base; male and female on same tree; in early summer.
Fruit: ¼″ (6 mm) long; elliptical, red, aromatic, 3-angled, splitting into 3 parts; drooping on slender, curved stalk; with 1 nutlet; maturing in autumn.

Habitat
Dry, rocky slopes of desert mountains.

Range
SW. Arizona and extreme S. California; also northwestern Mexico; to 2500′ (762 m).

Comments
As the common name suggests, the stout trunk and branches recall the legs and trunk of an elephant. The northernmost representative of a small tropical family, it is very susceptible to frost; young plants are killed back by cold weather.

Crucifixion Thorn
Canotia holacantha
314

Spiny, spreading shrub or small tree with short trunk, many upright, flexible, yellow-green branches, and twigs in broomlike masses; leafless most of year.
Height: 18′ (5.5 m). Diameter: 8″ (20 cm).
Leaves: very small, scalelike, greenish, very short-lived.
Bark: yellow-green, smooth; becoming gray, rough, slightly fissured and shreddy at base.
Twigs: ⅛″ (3 mm) in diameter; inconspicuously grooved, with small black rings at forks, often ending in spines or dead tips.
Flowers: ⁵⁄₁₆″ (8 mm) wide; with 5 rounded, greenish petals; in clusters near ends of twigs; in spring and early summer.
Fruit: ¾″ (19 mm) or more in length; egg-shaped, long-pointed capsules, upright, reddish brown, hard; 5-celled and splitting open along 10 lines; maturing in autumn, remaining attached until spring.

Habitat
Dry, rocky slopes and hillsides in desert and chaparral.

Range
Arizona and extreme S. Utah; local in northern Mexico; at 2000–5000′ (610–1524 m).

Comments
Crucifixion Thorn, or Canotia, is distinguishable from palo verdes, which it replaces to the north, by the more crowded, upright branches and twigs in broomlike masses. It is the most common of the spiny, many-branched shrubs called crucifixion thorns and the only one that commonly reaches tree size. The green branches and twigs, like those of palo verdes, manufacture food, requiring less water than leaves would.

Desert Ironwood
Olneya tesota
319

Spiny evergreen tree with short trunk and widely spreading, rounded, dense crown often broader than high and with numerous purplish flowers in late spring.
Height: 30′ (9 m). Diameter: 2′ (0.6 m).
Leaves: evergreen or nearly so; alternate; densely clustered; pinnately compound; 1–2¼″ (2.5–6 cm) long. 2–10 pairs of leaflets ¼–¾″ (6–19 mm) long; oblong, generally rounded at tip and short-pointed at base, without teeth, thick, short-stalked; blue-green, with fine pressed hairs.
Bark: gray, smooth, thin, becoming much fissured and scaly.
Twigs: greenish, slender; covered with gray hairs when young; with short, slender, straight spines paired at nodes.

Flowers: ½" (12 mm) long; 1 broad upper petal and 2 lateral petals nearly enclosing 2 bottom petals that are joined and shaped like prow of a boat; purple; in short clusters along twigs; fragrant and showy; in late spring with new leaves.
Fruit: 2–2½" (5–6 cm) long; a cylindrical pod; short-pointed, slightly narrowed between seeds, light brown; covered with sticky hairs, thick-walled; with 1–5 beanlike, shiny brown seeds; maturing in late summer, splitting in 2 parts.

Habitat
Sandy and gravelly washes in rocky foothills in deserts.

Range
S. and SW. Arizona, SE. California, and northwestern Mexico; to 2500' (762 m).

Comments
Desert Ironwood is one of the heaviest native woods; only Leadwood (*Krugiodendron ferrum*), a small tropical tree of southern Florida, is heavier. The beanlike seeds can be roasted and eaten. Desert animals also consume the seeds, and livestock browse the foliage. A parasitic mistletoe on the branches with reddish, juicy berries attracts birds, which in turn spread the sticky seeds of the parasite to other trees.

Bitter Condalia
Condalia globosa
23

Spiny, much-branched shrub or small tree with short trunk and irregular, thin crown of tangled, spreading branches.
Height: 20' (6 m). **Diameter:** 8" (20 cm).
Leaves: alternate or usually in clusters of 2–7 on short twigs; ⅛–½" (3–12 mm) long and half as wide. Spoon-shaped, without teeth, thin but stiff, almost stalkless, finely covered with rough hairs or hairless. Pale yellow-green, with raised veins beneath.
Bark: brownish gray, thin, much fissured and shreddy.
Twigs: light gray or brown, forking nearly at right angles, very slender, stiff; some short and ending in slender spine.
Flowers: less than ⅛" (3 mm) wide; cup-shaped, with 5 yellow-green, pointed sepals and no petals, short-stalked, fragrant; few clustered together on short twig; in early spring or autumn, following irregular rains.
Fruit: ³⁄₁₆" (5 mm) in diameter; black or dark blue, with thin, juicy pulp, often very bitter; 1-seeded; ripening in spring.

Habitat
Dry, sandy plains, rocky slopes, and along washes in Creosote Bush desert.

Range
SW. Arizona and SE. California; also in northwestern Mexico; at 500–2500' (152–762 m).

Comments
Bitter Condalia is plentiful at Organ Pipe Cactus National Monument in southwestern Arizona. It was originally described in 1924 as a shrub from Baja California and was later found in Arizona as a tree new to the United States.

Jumping Cholla
Opuntia fulgida
325

A very spiny cactus, commonly a shrub, occasionally a small
tree with short trunk. The stout, jointed, spreading to slightly
drooping branches are leafless except when young.
Height: 15' (4.6 m). Diameter: 6" (15 cm).
Leaves: single at tubercles; ½–1" (1.2–2.5 cm) long; narrowly
cylindrical, long-pointed, light, green, fleshy, soon falling.
Bark: on both trunk and larger branches blackish, rough,
scaly, spineless. Segments or joints 3–8" (7.5–20 cm) long,
1¼–2" (3–5 cm) in diameter; pale green, fleshy, bearing
many egg-shaped tubercles, each with 2–12 large, brown
spines ¾–1¼" (2–3 cm) long and covered with shiny, straw-
colored sheaths.
Flowers: 1" (2.5 cm) long and broad; with 5–8 pink or white
petals streaked with lavender, stalkless; scattered near ends of
joints and on fruit; in late spring and summer.
Fruit: 1–1⅜" (2.5–3.5 cm) long and ¾" (19 mm) in
diameter; pear-shaped berries; green, tubercled, spineless,
fleshy, with many seeds. Some remain attached several years
and bear new flowers and fruit annually, often without seeds.
These fruit clusters hang in long, branched chains.

Habitat
Dry, sandy soils of valleys, plains, and slopes, forming dense
"cactus forests" in deserts.

Range
Central and S. Arizona and NW. Mexico; to 4000' (1219 m).

Comments
The common name cholla is applied to various shrubby cacti
with jointed branches, of which this species is the largest. Its
segments or joints, easily detached by touching, adhere to
clothing and skin. They are fancifully said to jump out and
attack passersby, especially when one's back is turned, as the
common name implies. Their sharp, barbed spines can cause
painful wounds and are not easily removed.

Joshua-tree
Yucca brevifolia
326

A picturesque or grotesque, narrow-leaf evergreen tree with
short, stout trunk; open, broad crown of many, stout, widely
forking, spreading branches; and spiny, daggerlike leaves.
Height: 15–30' (4.6–9 m). Diameter: 1–3' (0.3–0.9 m),
sometimes larger.
Leaves: evergreen; numerous, clustered and spreading at ends
of branches; 8–14" (20–36 cm) long, ¼–½" (6–12 mm)
wide. Daggerlike, stalkless, stiff, flattish but keeled on outer
surface, smooth or slightly rough; ending in short, sharp
spine. Blue-green, the yellowish edges with many tiny teeth.
Trunk: small trunks and branches covered with dead, stiff
leaves pressed downward; larger trunks brown or gray, rough,
corky, deeply furrowed and cracked into plates.
Flowers: 1¼–1½" (3–4 cm) long; bell-shaped, with 6
greenish-yellow, leathery sepals; crowded in upright, much-
branched clusters 1–1½' (0.3–0.5 m) long; with unpleasant
odor; mostly in early spring, at irregular intervals.

Fruit: 2½–4″ (6–10 cm) long, 2″ (5 cm) in diameter; elliptical, green to brown, 6-celled, slightly fleshy becoming dry; falling soon after maturity in late spring, but not splitting open; many flat seeds.

Habitat
Dry soils on plains, slopes, and mesas; often in groves.

Range
Mojave Desert of extreme SW. Utah, Nevada, California, and Arizona; at 2000–6000′ (610–1829 m).

Comments
Joshua-tree, the largest of the yuccas, is the characteristic tree of the Mojave Desert and has come to symbolize the area. The Mormon pioneers named this species Joshua because its shape mimics a person praying with uplifted arms or gesturing wildly, referring to the Biblical leader pointing the way to a Promised Land. It is abundant at Joshua Tree National Monument in southern California and Joshua Forest Parkway in western Arizona.

California Washingtonia
Washingtonia filifera
327

Tall palm with massive, unbranched trunk and very large, fan-shaped leaves.
Height: 20–60′ (6–18 m). Diameter: 2–3′ (0.6–0.9 m).
Leaves: evergreen; alternate; numerous, spreading around top; if not burned or cut, old dead leaves hang down against trunk in thick thatch. Leafstalks 3–5′ (0.9–1.5 m) long; stout, with hooked spines along edges. Leaf blades 3–5′ (0.9–1.5 m) in diameter; gray-green, split into many narrow, folded, leathery segments, with edges frayed into many threadlike fibers.
Trunk: gray, with horizontal lines and vertical fissures.
Flowers: ⅜″ (10 mm) long; with funnel-shaped, deeply 3-lobed white corolla: short-stalked, slightly fragrant; many together in much-branched clusters 6–12′ (1.8–3.7 m) long; drooping from leaf bases.
Fruit: ⅜″ (10 mm) in diameter; elliptical black berry, with thin, sweetish, edible pulp, 1 elliptical brown seed.

Habitat
Moist soils along alkaline streams and in canyons of mountains in Colorado and Mojave deserts.

Range
SE. California (San Bernardino County to San Diego County), SW. Arizona (Kofa Mountains, Yuma County; also S. Yavapai County where perhaps introduced) and N. Baja California; at 500–3000′ (152–914 m).

Comments
The largest native palm of the continental United States as well as the only western species, it is also known as the Fanpalm or Desert-palm. Another name is Petticoat-palm from the shaggy mass of dead leaves hanging against the trunk. Groves are in Palm Canyon near Palm Springs and in Joshua Tree National Monument.

Soaptree Yucca
Yucca elata
328

Evergreen, palmlike shrub or small tree with single trunk or several clustered trunks; unbranched or with few upright branches; and very long, narrow leaves.
Height: 10–17' (3–5 m), rarely to 25' (7.6 m). Diameter: 6–10" (15–25 cm).
Leaves: evergreen; numerous, spreading, grasslike; 1–2½' (0.3–0.8 m) long, ⅛–⅜" (3–10 mm) wide. Linear, flat, leathery, and flexible; ending in sharp spine. Yellow-green, with fine whitish threads along edges.
Trunk: gray and slightly furrowed in lower part, covered by dead leaves above.
Flowers: 1½–2" (4–5 cm) long; bell-shaped, with 6 white, broad, pointed sepals; crowded on upright branches, in clusters 3–10' (0.9–3 m) or more in height including long stalk; in spring.
Fruit: 1½–3" (4–7.5 cm) long; a cylindrical capsule, light brown, dry, 3-celled; maturing in early summer, splitting open in 3 parts and remaining attached; many small, flat, thin, rough, dull black seeds.

Habitat
Dry, sandy plains, mesas, and washes; in desert grassland and desert, often in pure stands with grasses.

Range
Trans-Pecos Texas west to central New Mexico and central Arizona and local in SW. Utah; also northern Mexico; at 1500–6000' (457–1829 m).

Comments
Soapy material in the roots and trunks of this abundant specie has been used as a soap substitute. The leaves are a source of coarse fiber and were used by Indians in making baskets. Cattle relish the young flower stalks, and chopped trunks and leaves serve as emergency food during droughts.

Mojave Yucca
Yucca schidigera
329

Evergreen shrub or small tree, usually with clustered trunks, often with few upright branches, and with bayonetlike leaves.
Height: 16' (5 m). Diameter: 6–12" (15–30 cm).
Leaves: evergreen; numerous, crowded and spreading at top; usually 18–24" (0.5–0.6 m) long, sometimes to 4' (1.2 m), and 1–1½" (2.5–4 cm) wide. Bayonetlike or lance-shaped, thick and stiff, grooved, broadest at middle; ending in sharp spine. Yellow-green, with coarse fibers or threads on edges.
Trunk: gray-brown and furrowed at base.
Flowers: 1¼–2" (3–5 cm) long; bell-shaped, with 6 white and purplish-tinged sepals: on drooping stalks, crowded in upright, branched clusters usually 1½–3' (0.5–0.9 m) long; bearing flowers almost to the base; in early spring.
Fruit: 2–4" (5–10 cm) long, 1–1¼" (2.5–3 cm) wide; a cylindrical berry, often curved, blunt-pointed, dull dark brown or blackish, with thick, sweetish, edible flesh; maturing in late summer, falling before winter. Many small, flat, rough, dull black seeds.

Habitat
Creosote Bush desert and chaparral on dry, gravelly mountain and valley slopes.

Range
Mojave Desert in NW. Arizona, S. Nevada, S. California, and N. Baja California; at 1000–6000′ (305–1829 m).

Comments
Flowers in the yucca genus depend upon the small, white pronuba moth (*Tegeticula*) for pollination. The female moth gathers pollen and works it into a tiny ball before pushing it against the stigma of another flower, where she deposits her eggs in the ovary. The larvae feed on the developing fruit capsule but leave some seeds to mature. Also known as Spanish Dagger.

Torrey Yucca
Yucca torreyi
30

Evergreen shrub or small tree with irregular shape, 1 or 2 and sometimes several unbranched trunks, with long leaves.
Height: 13′ (4 m). Diameter: 4–12″ (10–30 cm).
Leaves: evergreen; usually 2–3½′ (0.6–1.1 m) long and 1¼–2″ (3–5 cm) wide. Bayonetlike or lance-shaped, tapering from enlarged base to sharp spine at end; slightly grooved, thick and stiff, rough. Yellow-green, with many coarse, whitish fibers or threads along edges.
Trunk: brown and scaly at base, covered by dead leaves above.
Flowers: 1½–3″ (4–7.5 cm) long; bell-shaped, with short tube and 6 narrow, white or purplish-tinged calyx lobes: long-stalked and showy; crowded in upright clusters (partly within foliage) usually 16–24″ (0.4–0.6 m) long; in spring.
Fruit: 3–4″ (7.5–10 cm) long, 1–1¼″ (2.5–3 cm) wide; a cylindrical or egg-shaped berry, brown to black, fleshy; falling before winter; many small, flat, rough, dull black seeds.

Habitat
Dry soils of plains, mesas, and foothill slopes; in desert grassland and shrub thickets.

Range
SW. Texas including Trans-Pecos Texas, S. New Mexico, and northeastern Mexico; at 2000–5000′ (610–1524 m).

Comments
Indians ate the pulpy fruits of this and related shrubby species either raw or roasted; they also dried and ground them into meal for winter use. The coarse fibers of the long leaves were made into ropes, mats, sandals, baskets, and cloth.

Saguaro
Cereus giganteus
31

Tall, thick, columnar spiny stems generally with several large erect or twisted branches; flowers white.
Flowers: 2½–3″ (6.3–7.5 cm) wide, funnel-shaped, in crownlike clusters near ends of branches, with many petals; May–June.
Stems: 8–24″ (20–60 cm) wide; 12–24 ribs.

Spines: stout, to 2″ (5 cm) long, in clusters on ribs, 10–25 in each cluster.
Fruit: fleshy, egg-shaped, 2½–3½″ (6.3–8.8 cm) long, green on outside, red inside.
Height: up to 50′ (15 m).

Habitat
Desert slopes and flats.

Range
Extreme SE. California to S. Arizona and northern Sonoran Desert.

Comments
The Saguaro (pronounced *sah-wah'-ro*) is the state flower of Arizona, where, like all cacti and many other plants, it is protected by law. It grows very slowly; the oldest plants are estimated to be 150–200 years old. Many are killed or injured by lightning during desert storms. Its slow growth and capacity to store great quantities of water allow it to flower each year regardless of drought. The fruits were an important source of food for Indians and are still used to some extent, the pulp eaten raw or preserved, the juice fermented to make an intoxicating drink, and the seeds ground into a butter. The woody ribs of the stems are used in building shelters. Its flowers open at night and are visited by nectar-feeding bats, moths, and a variety of insects. May also be classified as *Carnegeia gigantea*.

Teddybear Cholla
Opuntia bigelovii
332

A miniature tree, the upper half with short, stubby branches densely covered with pale golden spines. Flowers green or yellow, the petals often streaked with lavender.
Flowers: 1–1½″ (2.5–3.8 cm) wide, near ends of joints; March–April.
Stems: joints cylindrical, 3–10″ (7.5–25 cm) long.
Spines: ½–1″ (1.3–2.5 cm) long.
Fruit: about ¾″ (2 cm) long, yellow, egg-shaped, knobby.
Height: 3–9′ (90–270 cm).

Habitat
Hot, dry, rocky slopes in deserts.

Range
SE. California to W. Arizona; south to northwestern Mexico.

Comments
Though the branches resemble the arms and legs of a fuzzy teddy bear, this plant is far from cuddly: its spines stick instantly and hold tightly by means of minute, backwardly directed barbs. It is one of the most formidable and respected cacti of the Southwest. When a joint (which seems to "jump" when detached by a light touch or bump) is severely stuck, the victim's best solution is to cut the spines with scissors or nippers and pull them from the flesh with pliers. Sometimes a comb can be used to slide between the cactus and the skin to pull the cactus loose, but the process is painful.

ree Cholla
puntia imbricata
33

A small, spiny, leafless tree or bush with cylindrical, jointed branches, the deep reddish-lavender flowers blooming near ends.
Flowers: 2–3″ (5–7.5 cm) wide; many petals; May–July.
Stems: joints 5–16″ (12.5–40 cm) long, ¾–1¼″ (2–3.1 cm) wide, with sharply raised, spine-bearing knobs.
Spines: ½–1″ (1.3–2.5 cm) long, 10–30 per cluster.
Fruit: 1–2″ (2.5–5 cm) long, yellow, egg-shaped, fleshy.
Height: 3–7′ (90–210 cm).

Habitat
Plains, deserts, and among pinyon and juniper.

Range
S. Colorado and Kansas to Arizona, New Mexico, Texas, and northern Mexico.

Comments
This is the first bushlike or treelike cholla (pronounced *choy'-yah*) encountered when traveling from the East to the Southwest. Near the Rio Grande other species appear, and in Arizona there are many, making identification more difficult. Once the flesh has weathered away, their woody stems are hollow, with many holes, and are popular souvenirs.

)cotillo
ouquieria splendens
35

A funnel-shaped plant with several woody, almost unbranched, spiny, commonly straight stems leafless most of the year, and a tight cluster of red flowers at tip of branch.
Flowers: corolla tubular, ⅝–1″ (1.5–2.5 cm) long, the 5 short lobes curled back; in clusters to 10″ (25 cm) long; March–June, sometimes later.
Leaves: to 2″ (5 cm) long, narrowly ovate, broader above middle, almost without stalks, in bunches above spines.
Height: to 30′ (9 m).

Habitat
Open stony slopes in deserts.

Range
W. Texas to SE. California; northern Mexico.

Comments
The family consists of about 11 species, mostly Mexican, with Ocotillo (pronounced *o-ko-tee'-yo*) the most northern, and perhaps the Boojum Tree, *F. (Idria) columnaris,* of Baja California the most unusual. Leaves appear only after rain and wither when the soil dries, a cycle commonly repeated several times during the warm season.

Banana Yucca
Yucca baccata
36

Rigid, spine-tipped leaves in 1 or several rosettes, and a long cluster of large whitish flowers on a stalk about as tall as the leaves.
Flowers: 6 petal-like segments, each 2–4″ (5–10 cm) long, white or cream and often also purplish tinged, waxy; April–July.

Leaves: to about 3′ (90 cm) long, edges with a few whitish fibers.
Fruit: pod 2½–10″ (6.3–25 cm) long, fleshy, cylindrical, round at ends.
Height: to 5′ (1.5 m), the trunks up to 20″ (50 cm).

Habitat
Rocky soil in deserts, grasslands, and open woods.

Range
SE. California across S. Nevada and Utah to SW. Colorado; south through much of Arizona, all of New Mexico, and W. Texas to northern Mexico.

Comments
The baked fruit of Banana Yucca tastes somewhat like sweet potato. Yucca flowers are still eaten by Mexican Indians to such an extent that some species now rarely show mature pods. Identification of the many yucca species is often difficult. Those with broad leaves are sometimes called Spanish Daggers, a name generally applied to the treelike species of western Texas. Plains Yucca (*Y. angustifolia*), common from the eastern edge of the Rocky Mountains eastward almost throughout the plains and prairies of the central United States, is a small species with narrow, gray-green leaves.

Lechuguilla
Agave lecheguilla
337

A tall, narrow cluster of flowers grows from a basal rosette of erect, rigid, sharply pointed leaves.
Flowers: ¾–1½″ (2–3.8 cm) long, grouped in small clusters along the main stalk; 6 narrow, spreading, yellow to red or purplish petal-like segments; May–July.
Leaves: 12–20″ (30–50 cm) long, about 1″ (2.5 cm) wide, straight or slightly curved.
Height: 7–10′ (2.1–3 m).

Habitat
Rocky limestone slopes.

Range
S. New Mexico and W. Texas to Mexico.

Comments
This formidable plant was a dangerous obstacle in early Southwestern exploration. The sharp leaves pierced horses' legs and a rider who fell might lie impaled. Today, leaves of small plants puncture tires of off-road vehicles. Indians obtained fiber from the leaves.

Sotol
Dasylirion wheeleri
338

Thousands of tiny, greenish-white flowers in a long, narrow cluster that grows from a dense bunch of many slender, spiny leaves.
Flowers: cluster 5–8′ (1.5–2.4 m) long; 6 petal-like segments; May–July.
Leaves: to 3′ (90 cm) long, ½–1″ (1.3–2.5 cm) wide, with teeth on edges that curve forward.

Height: flower stalk 6–17′ (1.8–5.1 m), atop a trunk to 3′ (90 cm).

Habitat
Rocky desert slopes.

Range
W. Texas to S. Arizona.

Comments
Plants may be treated in the same manner as agaves to produce food and liquor (sotol). The tough leaves are woven into mats and baskets and used for thatching. The broad, spoonlike base is often used in dried floral arrangements. The smaller Smoothleaved Sotol (*D. leiophyllum*), which grows on limestone in southern New Mexico, western Texas, and northern Mexico, has teeth that curve toward the leaf base.

Parry's Century Plant
Agave parryi
39

A stout, tall flower stalk, like a huge candelabrum, grows from the center of a compact rosette of thick, rigid, broadly lanceolate grayish-green leaves.
Flowers: buds reddish, but open flowers yellow facing upward in clusters near the ends of branches, each flower with 6 petal-like parts about ¾″ (2 cm) long and 6 stamens attached near upper edge of flower tube; June–August.
Leaves: 12–18″ (30–45 cm) long, concave on upper side, each bearing a dangerously sharp terminal spine and a few smaller spines along the edges.
Height: 10–14′ (3–4.2 m).

Habitat
Dry rocky slopes.

Range
From central Arizona to W. Texas; also northern Mexico.

Comments
Century Plants require many years to flower, but not a century. They provided southwestern Indians with food, beverages, fiber, soap, medicine, and lances. Mescal, pulque, and tequila are made from Mexican species.

Rabbit Brush
Chrysothamnus nauseosus
40

A shrub with erect, slender, flexible branches covered with dense, feltlike, matted hairs (often overlooked until one scrapes the surface lightly), very narrow leaves, and small yellow flower heads in dense clusters at ends of stems.
Flowers: heads ¼–½″ (6–13 mm) high, slender, without rays, bracts oriented in 5 vertical rows, outer bracts short; August–October.
Leaves: ¾–3″ (2–7.5 cm) long.
Fruit: seedlike, with fine hairs at tip.
Height: up to 7′ (210 cm).

Habitat
Dry open places with sagebrush, or grassland or open woods.

Range
W. Canada to California, Texas, and northern Mexico.

Comments
Rabbit Brush is a common and variable species in a genus found only in western North America. Some races are light green, others have silvery hairs. Navajo Indians obtained a yellow dye from the flower heads.

Snakeweed
Xanthocephalum sarothrae
341

Many slender green branches form a round shrublet with hundreds of tiny yellow flower heads in loose clusters.
Flowers: heads narrow, ⅛–¼" (3–6 mm) long, with 3–7 ray flowers, each about ⅛" (3 mm) long, and 2–6 tiny disk flowers; August–September.
Leaves: ¼–2½" (6–63 mm) long and very narrow, less than ⅛" (3 mm) wide, resinous.
Fruit: seedlike, hairy, plump, with low scales at top.
Height: 6–36" (15–90 cm).

Habitat
In deserts, on plains, and among pinyon and juniper.

Range
E. Oregon and S. Idaho to S. California; east to Texas and the western Plains as far north as central Canada; also Mexico.

Comments
Little-head Snakeweed (*X. microcephala*), a very similar species that may grow in the same area, has 1–3 ray flowers and 1–3 disk flowers. As with many aromatic plants, Snakeweed was used medicinally, occasionally as a treatment for snakebite; hence its common name. Bundled, dried stems made primitive brooms, hence the alternate name Broomweed; the alternate names Matchweed and Matchbush refer to this species' matchlike heads. This plant poses serious problems as range weed. More frequent as a result of improper range management, it now covers thousands of square miles of once good grassland. Because it is poisonous, Snakeweed occasionally kills grazing livestock but more commonly aborts fetuses. Some authorities use the name *Gutierrizia* for this genus.

Creosote Bush
Larrea tridentata
342

Medium to large, evergreen shrub, numerous flexible stems usually arising from the base at an angle.
Flowers: yellow, 1" (2.5 cm) wide, sepals 5, twisted like blades of a fan; February–August, but some individuals have few flowers in all months.
Leaves: opposite, leaflets 2, united at base; pointed, yellowish green, resinous, pungent especially when wet; ¼–½" (6–13 mm) long.
Fruit: globose, densely woolly, white to reddish; exhibits a persistent style.
Height: usually less than 4' (120 cm) but can reach 12' (360 cm) in well-watered situations.

Habitat
On well-drained plains and slopes, especially those with a caliche layer; to 4000′ (1220 m). Often the most abundant shrub, frequently forming pure stands.

Range
S. Nevada, extreme SW. Utah, SE. California, southern third of Arizona, S. New Mexico north along major river valleys to Albuquerque, W. Texas, south into Mexico.

Comments
Creosote Bush is the most characteristic species of the hot deserts of North America. Its pungence fills the air following rains. Decoctions from its leaves are used as antiseptics and emetics. Many "bunches" of plants are actually clones. The foliage hides species of grasshoppers, praying mantids, and crickets that occur only on this plant. Leafy galls caused by a fly, the Creosote Gall Midge (*Asphondylia* spp.), are often numerous.

ittleleaf Horsebrush
etradymia glabrata
43

Small to medium-size, many-branched, stiff shrub, the young leaves and branches often covered with woolly hairs that are quickly lost.
Flowers: yellow, rayless, on ends of branches in clusters of about 4; May–July.
Leaves: alternate, linear, not modified to spines, but with sharp tips; ¼–½″ (6–13 mm) long, secondary leaves in axils.
Height: less than 42″ (105 cm); usually 10–20″ (25–50 cm).

Habitat
Open, rocky hillsides and saline flats from 2000–6000′ (610–1830 m) in pinyon-juniper woodland, but most common in sagebrush desert, and with Shadscale and Greasewood.

Range
Oregon and Idaho to Montana, south to California, Nevada, and Utah.

Comments
Horsebrushes are common species in the Great Basin, sometimes forming nearly pure stands. While the spininess of many species usually prevents them from being eaten, the young, succulent branches produced in the spring are often taken by sheep with quite toxic effects. Spiny Horsebrush (*T. spinosa*), with numerous recurved spines and solitary flower heads, and Spineless Horsebrush (*T. canescens*), a spineless, woolly species, are also common in the Great Basin.

rrow Weed
luchea sericea
44

Tall, willowlike shrub, with slender erect branches.
Flowers: purplish, clustered at ends of branches, ray flowers absent, disk flowers numerous and small; March–July.
Leaves: dense, alternate, lancelike, covered with fine white hairs giving a silvery appearance; pleasant-smelling when green, foul when dried.

Height: tall; usually more than 40" (100 cm) and often reaching 10' (300 cm).

Habitat
Along watercourses, ditches, and in some low, flat areas, including those that are quite saline.

Range
S. Nevada, southern third of California, extreme southwest corner and Colorado Plateau portion of Utah, south through W. Texas.

Comments
Indians used this plant to make shafts for arrows because of its long, straight stems. Arrow Weed forms dense stands along some rivers, including the Colorado River in Arizona. Most of its close relatives are strong-smelling herbs.

Greasewood
Sarcobatus vermiculatus
345

Perennial shrub, numerous yellowish-white to grayish, rigid branches that are very spiny.
Flowers: inconspicuous, with males and females separate. Male flowers rose-colored, on ends of branches forming dense spikes to 1½" (3.8 cm) long; female flowers small, solitary or 2 together in axils of leaves; May–August.
Leaves: linear, yellow-green, succulent, ½–1½" (1.3–3.8 cm) long; alternate, no petioles present.
Fruit: small, globular, surrounded in middle by winglike membranous disk.
Height: to 8' (240 cm).

Habitat
Flat, barren, often very alkaline areas with water close enough to soil surface for roots to get free water. Elevations of 1000–7000' (305–2134 m) in desert as well as nondesert areas.

Range
Continuous distribution from southern Canada to S. Nevada, NE. Arizona, and NW. New Mexico. Southward, scattered in California, S. Arizona, and W. Texas into Mexico. Occurs as far east as North Dakota.

Comments
Greasewood often occurs in pure stands on alkaline flats around playas. Its leaves accumulate sodium salts, giving them a salty taste. The young shoots and leaves provide forage for cattle and sheep, but when overeaten this plant may be toxic. The Hopi Indians use it for fuel. A second species, *S. baileyi*, from Nevada, is recognized by some authors.

Shadscale
Atriplex confertifolia
346

Compact, rounded perennial shrub with rigid, straw-colored stems and branches that become spiny on the tips.
Flowers: inconspicuous; sexes occur on separate plants. Male flowers in clusters in axils on short, nearly leafless branches; female flowers usually solitary in axils near branch tips; April–July.

Leaves: vary from nearly round to elliptical or oval, ¼–¾″ (6–20 mm) long and ⅛–½″ (3–13 mm) wide, covered with small scales on both sides, gray, with very short petioles, ⅛″ (3 mm) or less.
Height: usually less than 2′ (60 cm); rarely, to 5′ (150 cm).

Habitat
Widely distributed over plains and mesas below about 6000′ (1830 m), including those that are quite alkaline. In the Great Basin occurs with Big Sagebrush, grasses, and as nearly pure stands in more alkaline areas. Commonly associated with Creosote Bush in warm deserts.

Range
Generally distributed from Oregon, Idaho, and Montana east to the Dakotas; south to N. Arizona and NW. New Mexico; scattered, often abundant populations into W. and central Texas, S. California, and S. Arizona.

Comments
Shadscale is, along with Big Sagebrush, the most commonly seen plant in the Great Basin. Southward it is still very common, though more restricted in its ecological relationships. The young branches of this plant are an important food for animals, including sheep. Shadscale seems to resist overgrazing, and persists or even increases when other plants are disappearing.

Jojoba
Simmondsia chinensis
347

Bluish-green, medium-size shrub with low, broad appearance and leathery leaves. Very widely spreading.
Flowers: sexes on separate plants, flowers without petals. Males in clusters ¼–1″ (6–25 mm) long, hanging downward from stem originating in leaf axils; females similarly placed, but with single flower per axil and with prominent sepals, appearing as thick green petals; March–May.
Leaves: leathery, oval to spatulate, opposite, ¾–2″ (2–5 cm) long and up to 1″ (2.5 cm) wide, attractive, bluish green.
Fruit: acornlike, ⅓–1″ (8–25 mm) long.
Height: most individuals 2–3′ (60–90 cm); many reach 6′ (180 cm).

Habitat
Arid, rocky or gravelly slopes below 5000′ (1524 m).

Range
Sonoran Desert regions of S. California and Arizona into Mexico.

Comments
Jojoba is emerging as a potentially important desert crop species. Its fruit is about 50 percent oil, of a quality similar to that of sperm whale oil. Unlike many other oils, it does not degrade by bacterial activity. It can be used in cosmetics, lubricants, in cooking, and as a wax for cars, while the pulp remaining after oil extraction can be fed to animals. The United States alone produced 165 tons of jojoba oil in 1983.

Blackbrush
Coleogyne ramosissima
348

Small to large, densely branched, spiny shrub with dark gray bark that darkens to black with age and when wet. Branches are opposite.
Flowers: solitary, yellow, ¼–½" (6–13 mm) wide; no petals, occur on ends of short branches; March–July.
Leaves: gray, linear, about ½" (13 mm) long, apparently fascicled, covered with hairs.
Fruit: glabrous, one-seeded, dry.
Height: 1½–6' (45–180 cm).

Habitat
Gravelly slopes and mesas, 3000–6500' (914–1980 m), often in nearly pure stands.

Range
SE. California, S. Nevada, in a band along Arizona-Utah border, into E. Utah on the Colorado Plateau.

Comments
Blackbrush is a transitional form, straddling the boundary between the Mojave and Great Basin deserts and extending onto the Colorado Plateau. Despite its spininess, cattle feed on the young branches, and goats, sheep, deer, and bighorns make significant use of its branches and leaves.

Desert Sage
Salvia dorrii
349

A broad bush with many rigid, spine-tipped branches, silvery leaves, and bright blue to blue-violet bilaterally symmetrical flowers.
Flowers: about ½" (1.3 cm) long; lower lip with a very broad, spreading middle lobe bent downward and 2 small outer lobes at side of opening to tube; upper lip with 2 short, earlike lobes; 2 stamens and 1 style arch out in front of flower; bracts among flowers purple; May–July.
Leaves: ½–1½" (1.3–3.8 cm) long, broadly lanceolate, broadest near tip, tapered to a stalklike base, opposite, often clustered along the stem.
Height: 8–32" (20–80 cm).

Habitat
Dry flats and slopes, often associated with sagebrush.

Range
East of the Cascade Mountains and Sierra Nevada from Washington to S. California; east to central Arizona, Utah, and SW. Idaho.

Comments
It is this Sage, not sagebrush, that is referred to in Zane Grey's classic western *Riders of the Purple Sage*. It is a handsome plant, pretty in leaf as well as in flower.

Tarbush
Flourensia cernua
350

Medium to large resinous, aromatic shrub with dense, many-leaved branches.
Flowers: yellow, nodding, solitary, in axils of upper leaves. Ray flowers absent; September–December.

Leaves: alternate, deep green above, lighter beneath, elliptical, strongly aromatic like tar, sticky.
Height: usually less than 3', but may reach 6'.

Habitat
Dry, often calcareous soils of valleys, mesas, plains, and some slopes, below 5000' (1524 m).

Range
Extreme SE. Arizona, southern quarter of New Mexico, W. Texas into Mexico.

Comments
Tarbush characterizes the Chihuahuan Desert. It often shares dominance with Creosote Bush over large areas. In Mexico a decoction of its leaves and flowers is used to ease indigestion.

Anderson Lycium
Lycium andersonii
351

Many-branched, somewhat rounded, spiny, grayish shrub.
Flowers: tubular, ⅓–⅔" (8.5–17 mm) long, off-white to lavender with 4 or, usually, 5 lobes; March–May.
Leaves: rather flattened, but thickened and somewhat succulent, mostly without hairs, ⅛–⅔" (3–17 mm) long.
Fruit: ⅛–⅜" (3–9 mm) long, ovoid, juicy, many-seeded, bright red.
Height: 3–9' (90–270 m).

Habitat
Sandy washes, mesas, and slopes, generally below 2000' (610 m) but ranges to 6000' (1830 m) in many places. Can withstand some soil alkalinity.

Range
S. Nevada, SE. California, southern half of Arizona and into N. Arizona along the Colorado River, northward into Utah on the Colorado Plateau.

Comments
About 10 species of wolfberries, squawberries, or desert thorns, as they are often called, occur in our southwestern deserts. Their red, usually astringent fruits are eaten by man as well as by a variety of birds and mammals. *L. cooperi*, predominantly a Mojave Desert species, has woolly young twigs and fruit that has a constriction. *L. pallidum* is a widespread species in most of Arizona, S. Utah, most of New Mexico, and W. Texas. It occurs at higher elevations than most other species and is recognized by the combination of its hairless young twigs and a flower tube that is ½–⅞" (1.3–2.2 cm) long and greenish with purple veins. *L. berlandieri* has hairless young branches, and a very short flower tube, usually less than ⁵⁄₁₆" (8 mm) long. This species thrives in the southern third of Arizona and New Mexico and into Texas.

Four-wing Saltbush
Atriplex canescens
352

Roundish, quite woody but not spiny, shrub with an irregular outline and branches that become scaly with age.
Flowers: inconspicuous, male and female generally on separate

plants. Male flowers yellow, forming globular spikes about
$\frac{1}{16}$" (1–2 mm) wide near ends of flowering branches; female
flowers forming panicles 2–15" (5–38 cm) long; May–
August.
Leaves: evergreen, alternate, numerous, oblong or linear,
$\frac{1}{2}$–2" (13–50 mm) long and $\frac{1}{16}$–$\frac{3}{8}$" (1.5–9 mm) wide.
Fruit: very distinctive: 4 winglike membranous structures,
$\frac{1}{4}$–$\frac{3}{4}$" (6–20 mm) long, surrounding a small seed.
Height: usually over 3' (90 cm), often reaching 6' (180 cm)
and occasionally much larger.

Habitat
Varied, from sea level to 7000' (2134 m); usually somewhat
sandy, often alkaline soils of both flats and slopes. Occurs with
a wide variety of other shrubs in all 4 North American deserts.

Range
Western half of North America east of Sierra Nevada–Cascade
axis and excluding higher elevations of the Rocky Mountains.

Comments
Four-wing is a nutritious and important browse species. This
plant is the most widely distributed member of the genus
Atriplex in North America, where it has great economic
significance. Because it occurs in so many different habitats,
local populations of this species exhibit a wide variety of
genetic adaptations that suit it for use in the reclamation of
disturbed lands in arid or alkaline sites. Its pollen, which is
copiously produced, is known to be the cause of hay fever in
some individuals.

Big Sagebrush
Artemisia tridentata
353, 357

Many-branched, erect shrub with a definite trunk, strong
exfoliating bark, and very grayish-green and strongly aromatic
leaves.
Flowers: yellowish to greenish gray, small, occurring in dense
leafy panicles; August–October.
Leaves: $\frac{1}{2}$–1$\frac{3}{4}$" (1.3–4.4 cm) long, variable; generally
expanding from base to tip; usually 3, but sometimes as many
as 9, blunt teeth at tip.
Height: usually to 6' (180 cm) but can reach 15' (450 cm).
Largest plants occur on fertile, deep soils.

Habitat
Throughout Great Basin into northern Mojave on good,
nonsaline soils of well-drained valleys, and slopes to 10,000'
(3048 m).

Range
South Dakota to British Columbia, southward to N. Arizona
and New Mexico; south through California to Baja California.

Comments
This is the most common Great Basin Desert shrub, often
washing the landscape with the colors of its grayish-green
foliage. Big Sagebrush is eaten by a variety of animals. Its
wood makes a quick, hot fire.

Winter Fat
Ceratoides lanata
354

A small shrub, with many slender, flexible branches, becoming woody near the base; leaves and stems characteristically covered with long, conspicuous, light-colored hairs.
Flowers: inconspicuous, but white, often hairy-looking inflorescence stands out in axils or along branch tips; April–August.
Leaves: linear, ½–1¾″ (1.3–4.3 cm) long, covered with yellowish-white hairs.
Fruit: small, covered with long white hair, giving a cottony appearance to ends of branches.
Height: 1–3′ (30–90 cm).

Habitat
Not too alkaline soils on flats and mesas, 2000–8000′ (610–2438 m).

Range
Dakotas to the Nevada-California border, north to Canada, south to Arizona, New Mexico, and W. Texas.

Comments
Winter Fat is an exceptionally good food plant for sheep, deer, and rabbits, especially in winter. Recognizable from some distance, it may form nearly pure stands over large areas.

White Bur Sage
Ambrosia dumosa
355

Low, light-colored, woody shrub with many rigid, brittle branches.
Flowers: inconspicuous. Sexes are separate, but flowers of both are intermingled in terminal and lateral spikes; March–May.
Leaves: ⅜–¾″ (9–20 mm) long, with about 6 narrow, rounded lobes, silvery both above and below.
Fruit: somewhat like a small cocklebur.
Height: 1–2′ (30–60 cm).

Habitat
Alluvial slopes and plains, often a co-dominant with Creosote Bush over large areas, 500–2500′ (150–760 m).

Range
S. Nevada, extreme SW. Utah, S. California and Sonoran Desert parts of Arizona.

Comments
White Bur Sage is widespread and common in the Sonoran and Mojave deserts, where it is often called burro bush.

Mariola
Parthenium incanum
356

Grayish, low, bushy shrub.
Flowers: small, white, crowded into flat-topped terminal clusters; June–October.
Leaves: alternate, somewhat oval in outline, ⅜–¾″ (9–20 mm) long, divided into 3–7 lobes; hairy, particularly on lower surface.
Fruit: inconspicuous; old petals sometimes adhere to it.
Height: usually less than 3′ (90 cm).

Habitat
Gravelly plains and slopes, especially those high in calcium, often with a caliche layer; 2500–6000' (760–1830 m).

Range
Mainly S. New Mexico and W. Texas in the Chihuahuan Desert; eastward into Texas and scattered across Arizona, barely reaching SW. Utah.

Comments
The better-known member of this genus is *P. argentatum,* or Guayule, a species of interest for its rubber content. It enters the United States only in the Big Bend region of Texas.

Desert Holly
Atriplex hymenelytra
358

Compactly branched, silvery white, rounded shrub, covered with numerous hollylike leaves.
Flowers: inconspicuous male and female flowers on separate plants, in clusters ¼" (6 mm) wide and ¾–1¼" (2–3.1 cm) long; February–April.
Leaves: alternate, roundish or oval in outline, margins toothed; hollylike, silvery white, powdery, ½–1¼" (1.3–3.1 cm) long.
Fruit: covered with round, kidney-shaped, flattened bracts ¼–½" (6–12 mm) long; attached to fruit, forming wings above.
Height: 1–3' (30–90 cm).

Habitat
Sandy or stony plains and washes, below 3000' (914 m).

Range
S. Nevada, barely into SW. Utah, SE. California, barely into Arizona along the Colorado River.

Comments
The hollylike leaves of this extremely attractive shrub are ofte used in household decorations.

Desert Buckwheat
Eriogonum fasciculatum
359

Semi-erect shrub, often to 4' (120 cm) broad, with many flexible branches covered with thin bark, exfoliating in strips.
Flowers: white to pinkish flowers, ⅛" (3 mm) wide, formed into dense terminal heads, either solitary or on rays of an umbel; May–October.
Leaves: alternate, evergreen, in fascicles, narrowly oblong to linear, ¼–⅞" (6–22 mm) long, green or slightly white above, white below.
Height: to 3' (90 cm).

Habitat
On hillsides and flats where soils consist of fine particles, and along washes to 6500' (1980 m); usually to less than 4000' (1219 m).

Range
From the California coast to New Mexico-Arizona border, north to S. Nevada and extreme SW. Utah.

Comments
This species occupies a wide variety of habitats, including disturbed roadsides and sea cliffs. It is often abundant and conspicuous in the Mojave and Sonoran deserts.

Bur Sage
Ambrosia deltoidea
360

Low, rigid shrub with dark brown branches and sticky leaves. Flowers: inconspicuous. Male and female flowers separate, males forming terminal spikes; females are below these on lateral spikes; January–April.
Leaves: triangular to ovate, with teeth along the edges. Lower surfaces woolly.
Fruit: covered with about 20 flattened, sometimes hooked spines; remotely like a cocklebur.
Height: usually less than 2′ (60 cm).

Habitat
Alluvial plains; gravelly and rocky portions of bajadas, especially upper portions where subtrees are common.

Range
Southwestern quarter of Arizona into Mexico.

Comments
Bur Sage and White Bur Sage (*A. dumosa*) usually do not occur together, with Bur Sage more often on gravelly soils. Several other species of *Ambrosia* are common in parts of our deserts. One of the most obvious is Canyon Ragweed (*A. ambrosioides*), which occurs in washes in the southern portions of Arizona. It is recognized by its long (2–5″), lance-shaped leaves, which are green on both surfaces. Most *Ambrosia* species can cause hay fever.

Fluffgrass
Erioneuron pulchellum
361

A low, densely tufted perennial bunchgrass, sometimes forming open mats.
Flowers: short capitate achene or panicle; spikelets 4–18, covered with conspicuous silvery hairs; May–September.
Leaves: thin, crowded at base of stems, wiry; 1–2″ (2.5–5 cm) long, usually folded along midvein.
Height: 3–6″ (7.5–15 cm).

Habitat
Sites of low productivity, often rocky soils, among desert shrubs on very open sites from foothills to flats, below 5000′ (1524 m).

Range
S. Nevada, Utah, Colorado to Arizona, New Mexico, and Texas.

Comments
Although generally considered to be a poor forage grass, this plant is quite attractive, its fluffiness contrasting with the stark, open background of its relatively barren habitat.

Indian Ricegrass
Oryzopsis hymenoides
362

A densely tufted, leafy, erect bunchgrass.
Leaves: dark green, strongly bent along midrib.
Fruit: borne on open, lacy-looking panicle, each seed head with several divided branches; seeds on ends of wavy branches; May–early August.
Height: 7–18″ (17.5–45 cm).

Habitat
Many desert habitats, usually on sandy soil including dunes, seldom on gravelly or rocky soil; 3500–6500′ (1065–1980 m), lower in some places.

Range
Canada south to California and Arizona, east to Texas.

Comments
This beautiful grass often dominates sand dunes. It is a highly palatable species for many animals including livestock.

Bluebunch Wheatgrass
Agropyron spicatum
363

Tall, tufted, green to bluish-green bunchgrass.
Flowers: flower stalks slender, erect, usually 4–12 per plant; flower heads occupy up to 8″ (20 cm) of the tips. Spikelets flattened, 1″ (2.5 cm) long, with 3–6 flowers; each about ¾″ (2 cm) apart; June–October.
Leaves: flat or slightly inrolled, pointed, narrow, ⅛″ (3 mm) wide; to about 8″ (20 cm) long.
Height: 20–40″ (50–100 cm).

Habitat
Plains, dry slopes, and open woods and mixed with sagebrush in northern Great Basin.

Range
Canada, south to Arizona and New Mexico, east to the Dakotas.

Comments
This is a dominant grass of the steppe country of Washington, Oregon, and Canada, and an obvious component of the northern Great Basin. It is a prized forage species for domestic animals as well as for elk and bison in winter.

Mormon Tea
Ephedra spp.
364

Medium-size shrub with numerous jointed green, apparently leafless, branches; nodes are conspicuous.
Flowers: small male and female cones; mainly February–April.
Leaves: scalelike, 2 or 3 leaves.
Fruit: seeds surrounded with large scales in threes.
Height: to more than 4′ (120 cm).

Habitat
Mesas, plains, on gravelly or sandy soil including sand dunes; to 6000′ (1830 m) in at least one species, *E. viridis*.

Range
Arid regions of North and South America, Asia, and the Mediterranean.

Comments

Mormon teas have been used for a wide variety of medicinal purposes by various peoples in the deserts of North America. They are occasionally browsed by native and domestic animals. Several species of *Ephedra* occur in our area. Those with 3 scalelike leaves include *E. trifurca* of S. Arizona, S. New Mexico, and W. Texas and *E. torreyana* of S. Nevada, S. Utah, the Colorado Plateau, N. Arizona, most of New Mexico, and W. Texas. *E. viridis,* occurring in the Great Basin Desert and on the Colorado Plateau, and *E. nevadensis,* found from Oregon south to W. Texas, have 2 scalelike leaves.

Burrobush
Hymenoclea salsola
365

Medium-size shrub with diffuse, slender branches and a filmy appearance; copiously covered with white.
Flowers: inconspicuous; March–May.
Leaves: nearly threadlike, alternate, to 3″ (7.5 cm) long with margins rolled downward and inward.
Fruit: small, 1/16″ (1.5 mm) long, widely surrounded by 7–12 conspicuous, silvery-white wings.
Height: 3–6′ (90–180 m).

Habitat
Sandy washes, sometimes onto slopes below 1800′ (550 m).

Range
S. Nevada, SE. California, extreme SW. Utah; southern Sonoran Desert portions of Arizona.

Comments
This common wash species is a frequent cause of hay fever. A second species, *H. monogyra,* has a complementary range: from SE. Arizona across S. New Mexico, into W. Texas.

Turpentine Broom
Thamnosma montana
366

Often leafless, densely branched, yellowish-green shrub; branches are pungent and dotted with glands.
Flowers: 1/4–1/2″ (6–13 mm) long, 4 purple petals, erect, not spreading; March–May.
Leaves: simple, alternate, 1/4–1/2″ (6–13 mm) long, deciduous after flowering.
Fruit: capsule, 2–lobed, often yellowish green, each half about 1/4–3/8″ (6–9 mm) wide and dotted with glands.
Height: 1–2′ (30–60 cm).

Habitat
Slopes and mesas, usually rocky or gravelly, and below 4500′ (1370 m).

Range
S. Nevada, extreme SW. Utah, SE. California, scattered parts of western half of Arizona.

Comments
Turpentine Broom belongs to the family Rutaceae, which includes lemons, oranges, and grapefruits. The fruit is a miniature of those fruits and smells overpowering at times.

INSECTS AND SPIDERS

Among the most numerous animals on earth, insects and spiders are also among the most fascinating. Some have carved out an existence for themselves as tiny predators in an immense landscape; others have developed complex social systems of communal life. A few behave like the larger animals of the deserts, retreating to a shady burrow or a cool crevice by day, emerging in the evening to search for food. Included in this section are descriptions of some of the most common and typical desert insects and spiders and their relatives.

**Green Valley
Grasshopper**
chistocerca shoshone
67

1½–2¾" (38–70 mm). Green with yellow midline stripe on head and upper part of thorax. Hind tibiae red-pink.

Habitat
Tall grasses and open, sandy woods, a variety of shrubs and trees in desert areas.

Range
Colorado to Texas and Mexico, northwest to California.

Life Cycle
Egg masses are thrust into soft soil, hatching in a week or less except when soil is very dry. Often nymphs do not hatch until rains soften soil.

Comments
One of the largest grasshoppers, the Green Valley Grasshopper sometimes appears in devastating hordes and severely damages range grasses.

**Creosote Bush
Grasshopper**
Bootettix argentatus
568

¾–1" (20–26 mm). Green, somewhat marked with silvery-white; some brown and black. Female's antennae rather short. Male's fore wings have many transparent cells near margin.

Habitat
Arid lands with creosote bush.

Range
New Mexico, Arizona, and S. California.

Sound
Scratchy, gritty noises at night.

Life Cycle
Eggs are concealed a few inches below surface of soil, hatching after spring rain, when nymphs find soft, expanding foliage to eat. Rate of growth varies greatly. Adults are found throughout the year.

Comments
This well-camouflaged species stays in shade when possible, flying only if approached closely, and is found virtually only on creosote bush (*Larrea tridentata*).

**Pallid-winged
Grasshopper**
Trimerotropis pallidipennis
569

1¼–1⅝" (31–41 mm). Grayish to brownish or reddish. Fore wings with 1 or 2 black crossbands. Hind wings whitish to yellow except for dark edge. Hind tibiae yellow or yellowish brown.

Habitat
Many different habitats, sea level to 9150' (2789 m), including areas of alkaline soil.

Range
Manitoba to Oklahoma, Mexico to British Columbia.

Life Cycle
Up to 12 egg masses, with 100 eggs each, are deposited in

soft soil. Eggs overwinter, hatch in late spring. Nymphs become adults by June in the South or October in the North. 1 generation a year.

Comments
This is probably the most common and most often observed insect species in all of our deserts.

Lubber Grasshopper
Brachystola magna
370

1½–3⅛" (38–79 mm). Brown to gray-green with brown, green, or blue and black markings. Hind tibiae have both inner and outer spines at tip. Upper part of thorax has 3 smooth longitudinal ridges. Fore wings short, pink with black spots. Small hind wings concealed by fore wings.

Habitat
Rocky and gravelly soil and sparse vegetation; generally a grassland species but occurs in desert scrub.

Range
Minnesota to Arizona and Mexico, north to Montana.

Life Cycle
Eggs are concealed in soil, hatching after a soaking rain. Adults are active August–October. 1 generation a year.

Comments
The Lubber Grasshopper eats and sometimes destroys the scanty vegetation of its habitat. This insect retains so much internal moisture that after death it may rot.

Horse Lubber Grasshopper
Taeniopoda eques
371

1½–2½" (38–64 mm). Stout. Shiny black with orange or yellow. Veins on fore wings yellow on black background. Hind wings red with black borders, large enough in male to permit flight.

Habitat
Grasslands and woods with live oak.

Range
Texas and Arizona to Mexico; also into desert areas, especially those with mesquites (*Prosopis*).

Life Cycle
Eggs overwinter in soil and survive mild drought, hatching after spring rains. In good years adults appear August–November. In very dry years eggs do not hatch.

Comments
These grasshoppers flutter about and leap into bushes when disturbed. Males snap their fore wings together noisily.

Dragon Lubber Grasshopper
Dracotettix monstrosus
372

¾–1¾" (18–44 mm). Ash-gray. Head bulging. Crest cap has 3 deep notches on upper part of thorax. Wings short.

Habitat
Arid soil and sparse vegetation.

Range
S. California into Mexico.

Life Cycle
Eggs are laid in soil but do not hatch until rain, which allows nymphs to find newly sprouted vegetation to eat.

Comments
These grasshoppers hop on roads, feeding on dead insects, including their own kind. They are often killed by passing vehicles, especially the females, which cannot leap far.

Aztec Pygmy Grasshopper
Paratettix aztecus
473

¼–½" (5–12 mm). Dull gray, brown, or reddish, sometimes edged with yellow along sides of upper part of thorax (pronotum), which extends backward beyond tip of abdomen. Femora of middle legs extremely long. Side ridges of upper part of thorax weak toward front. Front projection of head no wider than 1 compound eye.

Habitat
Desert soil, especially gravelly edges of intermittent streams.

Range
Mexico into California, Nevada, and Arizona.

Life Cycle
Eggs are concealed in soil, usually in spring. Female overwinters. Life span 2 or more years.

Comments
Pygmy grasshoppers are found throughout North America. They are usually seen in spring and summer. All *Paratettix* species have a narrow ridge on the femur and 12–15 segments in antennae. Some species include both long-winged and short-winged members. A few species are mostly females and produce asexually by parthenogenesis. This species was previously included in the genus *Telmatettix*. *Paratettix mexicanus* occurs in all deserts, including the Great Basin, but always near water.

Mormon Cricket
Anabrus simplex
474

1–2⅜" (25–60 mm). Dark brown to bluish black, sometimes with pale markings. Large upper part of thorax extends backward, concealing female's vestigial wings and almost covering male's reduced wings. Female's egg-laying organ upcurved, swordlike, as long as body. Antennae as long as body.

Habitat
Open fields.

Range
Missouri River to N. Arizona, west to SE. California, north to Alberta.

Sound
A hoarse chirp, repeated at intervals.

Life Cycle

Dark brown eggs are deposited below soil surface in midsummer. They turn gray, overwinter, and hatch in spring Up to 100 nymphs emerge, maturing in about 60 days.

Comments

This cricket got its common name after thousands attacked th Mormon pioneers' first crops in Utah in 1848. Periodic outbreaks of the insect occurred before the 1950s.

Jerusalem Cricket
Stenopelmatus fuscus
375

1⅛–2″ (30–50 mm). Humpbacked. Very long antennae. Shiny amber-brown with darker brown crossbands on abdomen. Wingless. Head large with wide space between small compound eyes and jaws. Legs short; hind tibiae have 2 rows of spines with inside row shorter and flattened on inner surfaces.

Habitat

Hillsides and valley slopes, under rocks, on sand dunes, and even in the nests of pack rats.

Range

Nebraska to New Mexico and Mexico, north along the Pacific Coast to Washington, east to Montana.

Sound

A scratchy noise.

Life Cycle

Female prepares depression in soil for masses of oval white eggs. Nymphs and adults are extremely slow-moving. Adults are particularly slow during spring mating season. Female often devours mate. 1 generation a year.

Comments

Active both day and night, these crickets often leave distinctive smooth tracks on dusty roads by dragging their bulky abdomens.

Bee Assassins
Apiomerus spp.
376

½–⅝″ (12–15 mm). Variably colored: red with blackish-brown markings or brown with yellowish markings. Dense short hair on head, thorax, and legs. Distance between simple eyes greater than the distance between compound eyes. Second antennal segment rather comblike. Nymph is dark and reddish.

Habitat

Meadows, fields, and gardens on flowers of a variety of familie in many habitats.

Range

North America; most common in the West.

Life Cycle

Eggs are attached to foliage. Nymphs, like adults, are voracious predators. 1 generation or more a year in the North.

Comments
This insect pounces on Honey Bees and other pollinating insects. It holds the captive in its powerful legs, thrusts its cutting beak into the victim's back, injects an immobilizing digestive agent, then sucks out the body juices.

Obscure Ground Mantid
Litaneutria obscura
377

⅝–1⅛″ (15–30 mm). Gray. Male has sooty gray wings with a brown spot near base of fore pair. Female has only small wing pads, leaving all but the first abdominal segment exposed. Middle and hind legs long, slender.

Habitat
Arid lands, among dry grasses.

Range
Colorado to Mexico, northwest to California, occasionally to Texas.

Life Cycle
Eggs are laid in masses on low shrubs in fall. They overwinter and hatch in spring. Mantids sometimes go through a dormant stage during extended droughts, common in southern parts of the range.

Comments
This mantid is most active during wet periods, when prey is plentiful and conspicuous. In the same range the Agile Ground Mantid (*L. minor*), 1–1⅛″ (25–30 mm), has a brown spot only in males, and females have a rough pronotum. Unlike other mantids, this genus runs on the ground, seldom using vegetation as an avenue of escape.

Tiger Beetles
Cicindela spp.
378

⅜–⅞″ (9–20 mm). Usually shiny, metallic bronze, blue, green, or purple; sometimes shades of gray, brown, and white. Elytra are widest behind middle. Antennae arise from just above bases of jaws.

Habitat
Open, sunlit areas; in deserts on ground between shrubs; on sand dunes and open alkaline flats.

Range
Throughout North America.

Life Cycle
The S-shaped larvae construct vertical burrows, often in hard, dry soil. Larvae seize passing prey with their jaws while anchoring themselves into sides of burrow with hooks on one of their abdominal segments.

Comments
Tiger beetles are conspicuous because of their rapid running, quick flight, and striking metallic colors. Their agility makes them hard to catch without a net. Four genera and about 120 species of tiger beetles occur in North America. Over three-quarters of these occur in the West; all 4 of our deserts contain

several. Any one locality may support 4–6 species, each of which has slightly different habitat requirements. Many species are quite variable in their coloration and thus may be difficult to identify; *C. pusilla*, for example, varies from gray to blue, blue-green, or almost purple. This species is an especially good flier and can be seen catching insects on the wing in desert areas of Arizona, New Mexico, and Utah.

Ironclad Beetle
Zopherus haldemani
379

¾–1″ (20–26 mm). Extremely hard-bodied. Head, body, and elytra are dull ivory-yellow marked with black on top of head, on sides of upper part of thorax, and over elytra. Yellow marks along femora, tibiae, and on outermost leg segments.

Habitat
Deserts.

Range
Southwest.

Comments
This nocturnal beetle hides in dark crevices by day and often feigns death when picked up or disturbed. It is highly resistant to water loss.

Agave Billbug
Scyphophorus acupunctatus
380

⅜–¾″ (10–19 mm). Elongate oval, hard. Black. Beak is thickest at base, downturned. Elytra are deeply grooved, shorter than abdomen.

Habitat
Deserts.

Range
Mexico north into Texas, New Mexico, and Arizona.

Life Cycle
Eggs are laid in pits cut at the base of flower stalk. Larvae tunnel inward and pupate inside the plant or in soil.

Comments
This beetle's elytra are extremely hard, protecting it from the drying sun of its habitat. The related Yucca Billbug (*S. yuccae*), ⅝″ (15–17 mm), feeds on yucca plants in California.

Broad-necked Darkling Beetle
Coelocnemis californicus
381

⅞–1″ (22–25 mm). Front portion of thorax wider than long, almost flat above. Elytra convex, rounded. Uniformly dull black with minute to large pits in surface. Dull tan stripes on inner surface of tibiae and outermost leg segments.

Habitat
Deserts and semidesert regions.

Range
S. California into S. Oregon.

Comments
This beetle moves with its head down, abdominal end raised,

and hind legs extended. It stands stiffly if disturbed and during the heat of day burrows into cooler soil or hides beneath opaque objects.

Arizona Blister Beetle
Lytta magister
382

⅝–1⅛" (15–28 mm). Blue-black with dull orange head and upper part of thorax. Legs are brownish red, outermost leg segments blackish.

Habitat
Deserts.

Range
Arizona.

Comments
Nuttall's Blister Beetle (*L. nuttalli*), ⅝–1" (15–25 mm), is metallic purple or green with pale purplish elytra. It is widespread in east Manitoba and in the Rocky Mountains from New Mexico to Alberta.

Tarantula Hawks
Hemipepsis spp.
383

½–¾" (12–20 mm). Short "waist" between thorax and abdomen. Velvety black. Wings reddish to orange, darker and less transparent at tip and base.

Habitat
Dry hillsides and rolling arid plains.

Range
California and Mexico.

Life Cycle
Female stings spider between legs, immobilizing it. The female quickly digs a burial chamber, drags the spider inside, lays an egg, and closes burrow. Wasp larva feeds on spider.

Comments
Tarantula hawks are primarily tropical, but several large species are found in the Southwest.

Arid Lands Honey Ants
Myrmecocystus spp.
384

Worker ⅜" (8–10 mm), dark brownish red; replete worker ⅜–½" (10–12 mm), paler; reproductives ¼–⅝" (5–16 mm), male black, female brownish black. Reproductive (winged) males and females have well-developed thorax, smaller and flattened head, short jaws. Workers and repletes have much larger head and stronger jaws, smaller thorax constricted between middle and hind legs, and a more obvious slender 1-segmented "waist" between thorax and abdomen.

Habitat
Arid plains and deserts.

Range
New Mexico to northern Mexico, north to Utah.

Life Cycle
Nests are built in arid soil, where eggs are laid and larvae

develop and pupate. In some species, workers gather food and pass it to repletes—workers that store food for months or years in their swollen abdomens. They hang head-up by their claws from the ceiling of the nest and regurgitate food droplets to the colony. There are rarely more than a few hundred ants in a colony.

Comments
Some species are active by day, others at night. Certain species are strictly predatory and carnivorous, while others have a replete caste that takes in only sweet liquids of plant origin.

Spine-waisted Ants
Aphaenogaster spp.
385

⅜" (8–10 mm), depending on caste. Reddish black with 2 sharp diverging spines on rear of thorax. 1-segmented "waist" between thorax and abdomen. Antennae and legs long.

Habitat
Arid plateaus at elevations of 2690–5380' (820–1640 m), sometimes reaching lower into the upper portions of deserts.

Range
Texas to California, south to Mexico.

Life Cycle
Queen excavates brood chamber in soil and lays a few eggs. Queen regurgitates food to larvae until they can spin cocoons and transform to adults. Then workers hunt for food, expand galleries, feed queen, and tend eggs and young.

Comments
The sharp spines on these ants may be nature's way of protecting their narrow "waist," or pedicel, from attackers.

Little Black Ant
Monomorium minimum
386

Worker 1/16" (1.5–2 mm). Slender, smooth, with sparse body hair. Shiny black to dark brown. 1-segmented "waist" between thorax and abdomen. Antennae 12-segmented, first long, last 3 form club.

Habitat
Forest edges and houses; in deserts under stones in blackbrush, sagebrush, and other desert types.

Range
Throughout North America, except Pacific Northwest.

Life Cycle
Nests are constructed below ground, raising small craters around opening at the surface, or in rotting wood. Queen feeds first brood, then workers take over, tending young and feeding queen.

Comments
One of the most common ants in homes, this insect is active day and night and is often seen carrying particles of food many feet back to its nest. Because there are usually no winged females, these ants do not have nuptial flights.

Rough Harvester Ant
Pogonomyrmex rugosus
387

¼–½" (6–13 mm), depending on caste. Reddish brown. 2-segmented "waist" between thorax and abdomen. Winged female and wingless queen larger and darker than workers; winged male smaller.

Habitat
Lowlands, especially cultivated fields and relatively bare areas, and sandy areas near roads.

Range
Southwestern states.

Life Cycle
Mated female, with help from mate, digs small chamber to conceal clusters of milk-white capsule-shaped eggs and, later, larvae and pupae. First workers to emerge enlarge nest; nest opening may be level with ground or protected by conical crater of small pebbles. Separate chambers are dug to shelter eggs, developing larvae, and pupae. Ants swarm April–October.

Comments
Workers, active only by day, can bite and sting painfully. They can severely damage crops by cutting down plants and creating large barren areas.

Texas Carpenter Ant
Camponotus festinatus
388

¾–1" (18–24 mm), depending on caste. Brownish yellow, sometimes banded. 1-segmented "waist" between thorax and abdomen. Antennae 12-segmented, elbowed.

Habitat
Deadwood of upright or fallen trees, timber, utility poles, and on soil surface or under stones and cow dung.

Range
Colorado and Texas west to California, south to Mexico.

Life Cycle
Queen (mated female) begins nest in dead wood and tends first brood. As females mature, they extend galleries, tending eggs and young and hunting for food, which they regurgitate to feed queen. Large colony of thousands includes soldiers and workers of various sizes.

Comments
Battalions of ants searching for food sometimes invade houses at dusk or dark. Flying adults may come to artificial lights and pass barriers to reach dry wood suitable for constructing galleries.

Red Velvet-ant
Dasymutilla magnifica
389

Male ¾" (18 mm), female ⅞" (21 mm). Antlike, with only slight "waist" between thorax and abdomen. Head, thorax, legs, and "waist" dark wine-red to black with black hair. Male's abdomen dark wine-red with red hair on segments 3–8 and black hair on rest. Female's abdomen burnt-orange to yellow-orange. Male winged, female wingless.

Habitat
Arid and semiarid open lands.

Range
Texas to California and Nevada, south to Mexico.

Comments
These hairy wasps scurry across the ground much like true ants.

Thistledown Velvet-ant
Dasymutilla gloriosa
390

½–⅝″ (13–16 mm). Antlike, with only slight "waist" between thorax and abdomen. Antennae beadlike. Black, with covering of long white hair. Male winged, female wingless.

Habitat
Arid and semiarid open lands, on the ground, and in low vegetation. Males sometimes are found on flowers.

Range
Utah, Nevada, California, and Texas into Mexico.

Life Cycle
Female actively searches for burrows dug by sand wasps, which are stocked with flies as food for developing wasp larvae. Eggs are dropped in wasp nest. Velvet-ant larvae feed on wasp larvae and food brought by female wasp. Usually they kill wasp larvae, then pupate in host's larval chambers.

Comments
Female velvet-ants defend themselves from wasps, ants, and people by inflicting a painful sting.

Cochineal Bug
Dactylopius confusus
391

Female ¹⁄₁₆–⅛″ (2–3 mm); male one-half length. Red with deep red to pink waxy scales under body. Often concealed by dense tangled strands of white cottony wax. Legs reduced. Male has 2 diverging filaments trailing from rear and long white wings.

Habitat
Deserts and arid areas.

Range
New Mexico to Mexico, northwest to California; also in Montana, Colorado, and Florida.

Life Cycle
Nymphs escape from beneath body of dead female and begin feeding. Females mature in place without moving after the first molt. They feed in all stages. Males do not feed in last nymphal stage, nor perhaps as adults.

Comments
Conspicuous clusters of Cochineal Bugs often feed side by side, covering large areas of cacti like a white furry rug.

Termites
Order Isoptera
92

¼–⅝" (6–15 mm). Small, soft-bodied, pale-colored, social insects with biting mouthparts. Body forms various, depending on individual's role in colony. Reproductives heavily pigmented; all 4 wings finely veined and of the same size. Sterile soldier caste has enlarged jaws and defends colony.

Habitat
In wood and in the ground, some species forming "soil" tubes over vegetation or wood.

Range
Throughout our deserts, though not common in Great Basin.

Life Cycle
All castes include both sexes. Male and female reproductives leave colonies in swarms. After short mating flight, queen and mate, or king, shed their wings and found a new colony that may last for many years. Their offspring include sterile workers that collect and distribute food and maintain nest. A few species have a nasute caste, which spray a repellent fluid at intruders. Some species have no worker caste; others may lack soldiers.

Comments
Three families of termites are common in our deserts. The Kalotermitidae include 3 common desert genera: *Incisitermes,* *Paraneotermes,* and *Marginitermes. M. hubbardi* is a very common species in dry wood of the hottest parts of our deserts. The family Termitidae have opaque wings and are essentially confined to the Southwest in the United States. Members of 4 genera occur in the deserts; the earthworks of one of the several species, *Gnathitermes tubiformans,* are especially conspicuous. The family Rhinotermitidae has 2 desert genera. *Heterotermes,* and particularly the species *H. aureus,* causes serious destruction to desert dwellings.

Desert Millipede
Orthoporus ornatus
393

To 7" (18 cm). Large millipede, usually brown or yellowish, often with distinct bands; each segment has 2 pairs of legs.

Habitat
A variety of vegetation types in Sonoran and Chihuahuan deserts.

Range
Arizona, New Mexico, and western half of Texas.

Comments
This herbivorous species spends three-fourths of the year as deep as 30" below ground, often in the burrows or nests of other animals including harvester ants. When the rains come in late spring and summer, up to 600 animals per acre may be seen crawling about on the ground or up into shrubs during the cooler parts of the day or at night. These millipedes may live for several years.

Centruroides Scorpions
Centruroides spp.
394

2–2¾" (50–70 mm). Dark brown to tan, often striped with greenish yellow along midline above. Some species have greenish-yellow parallel stripe on each side of cephalothorax. Abdomen slender, constricted at each segment, pale or dark according to species. Toothlike structure beneath venom bulb on the tail.

Habitat
Dark crevices under bark, stones, and litter on the ground, and on dry abandoned dirt roads.

Range
Florida and Gulf states, west to Arizona and Mexico.

Life Cycle
Female keeps eggs in sac, then carries hatchlings on back until they can fend for themselves. Male uses pincers to pull female toward him and over a spermatophore that he lays.

Comments
These scorpions seize prey in pincer-tipped pedipalps and kill them with their stingers. Included in this genus is the dreaded Sculptured Centruroides (*C. sculpturatus*), ¼" (6–7 mm), whose sting is extremely poisonous for people and sometimes fatal. It is found in Arizona.

Giant Desert Hairy Scorpion
Hadrurus arizonensis
395

5½" (140 mm). Cephalothorax black, each segment rimmed in pale yellow. Abdomen, pincerlike pedipalps, and legs pale yellow. Undersurface pale. Abundant erect dark brown hair on legs, pedipalps, and abdomen.

Habitat
Deserts.

Range
Southwestern United States.

Life Cycle
Female bears live young, and carries brood on back for 10–15 days. Young do not feed during this period. After shedding their first skin, they scatter to live independently. Young grow slowly and shed their skin several more times before reaching maturity.

Comments
Scorpions are nocturnal and are preyed upon by owls and bats. Venom in the scorpion's stinger is used to subdue struggling prey and for self-defense. *H. arizonensis* is the largest of 9 species of *Hadrurus* inhabiting the United States. They range north as far as Idaho and east as far as Colorado.

Pale Windscorpion
Eremobates pallipes
396

Male ⅜–1" (15–26 mm), female ⅞–1¼" (22–32 mm). Yellowish brown. Fangs large, pincerlike, held forward close together. Pedipalps heavy, leglike, held like coarse antennae. First pair of walking legs as long as other pairs but much more slender.

Habitat
Arid and semiarid lands.

Range
Arizona to North Dakota and adjacent areas of Canada.

Life Cycle
Female digs out area in soil, then hides eggs there. Female stands guard until they hatch. Young are primarily nocturnal, venturing about in daylight only when they approach adult size. Males remain smaller than females and their legs are longer in proportion to body length.

Comments
These solitary windscorpions are independent hunters. Only a specialist can distinguish the 100 species in this genus.

hernetids
amily Chernetidae
97

1/16–1/8" (2–4 mm). Tan to dark brown, with 5 segmented legs. Some species have 2 eyes; others have none. Pincerlike pedipalps contain well-developed venom glands and ducts in movable part of pincer, but are poorly developed or absent in fixed part.

Habitat
Many different habitats, ranging from woods under leaf litter or bark to deserts or homes; wherever organic matter is accumulated.

Range
Throughout the United States; locally in all 4 North American deserts.

Life Cycle
Females in this family carry brood pouch until young hatch. Some females construct a brood nest.

Comments
Most members of this family of extremely common, small pseudoscorpions are predators. Some Chernetid species are found under the elytra of long-horned beetles, where they prey on mites on the beetles' bodies.

iant Vinegarone
astigoproctus giganteus
08

3–3⅛" (75–80 mm). Brown to black. Tail filament normally held curled forward over the back. Pincers turned forward; first pair of legs held forward, like feelers. 8 eyes.

Habitat
Outdoors among debris on soil, under logs and rotting wood; indoors in humid dark corners; barely reaching deserts near human habitations.

Range
Southern and southwestern United States.

Life Cycle
Female watches over eggs. Young ride on female's back until the first molt, when they disperse. Young are colorless.

Comments

This formidable-looking whipscorpion is seldom encountered, because it hides by day and hunts in darkness.

Desert Tarantula
Aphonopelma chalcodes
399

Male 2–2½" (50–65 mm), female 2–2¾" (50–70 mm); female legspan to 4" (100 mm). Body heavy, hairy. Cephalothorax gray to dark brown. Abdomen brownish black. Iridescent hair forms pad below tip of each leg.

Habitat
Desert soil.

Range
Arizona, New Mexico, and S. California.

Life Cycle
Male tries to maintain contact with female. If female moves away, male aggressively pursues desired mate. Eggs are concealed in some natural cavity. All spiderlings resemble females at first. After last molt, male emerges with distinctive pedipalps and more slender and relatively larger legs. Female continues to molt after reaching maturity and may live to 20 years.

Comments
The male spider wanders in the dim light after sunset or near dawn searching for a mate, then hides by day in abandoned holes or under stones. These spiders are reluctant to attack people. Usually the venom is no more poisonous than that of bees.

Inconspicuous Crab Spiders
Philodromus spp.
400

Female ⅛–⅜" (3–8 mm), male slightly smaller. Camouflage coloring: brownish to reddish, yellow, or grayish, with spots, bands, or mottling. Abdominal tip usually pale.

Habitat
Woods on tree bark and adjacent foliage, or on ground among litter.

Range
Throughout the United States and southern Canada.

Life Cycle
Flattened egg sac is attached to a leaf, twig, or rock, or left under bark. It is guarded by the female until spiderlings emerge.

Comments
These spiders are inconspicuous when they rest on bark. Occasionally they stray into a house.

Carolina Wolf Spider
Lycosa carolinensis
401

Male ¾" (18–20 mm), female ⅞–1⅜" (22–35 mm). Cephalothorax gray-brown. Abdomen may have darker stripe along midline. Female has sparse covering of gray hair; somewhat paler in male.

Habitat
Open fields on the ground.

Range
Throughout the United States and southern Canada.

Life Cycle
Female digs a burrow, often with a high rim around the entrance. Female often produces more than 1 egg sac, which gradually darkens from satiny white to earth color before spiderlings emerge. Female guards egg sacs in burrow but does not interfere with spiderlings as they emerge and disperse.

Comments
The Carolina Wolf Spider is the largest wolf spider in North America. It hunts almost exclusively at night.

Apache Jumping Spider
Phidippus apacheanus
402

⅜–½″ (9–12 mm). Legs and underside black. Top of body bright orange. Jaws metallic green.

Habitat
Deserts and dry woodlands.

Range
Florida west through southern states to California, north to Utah.

Life Cycle
Spectacular courtship displays involve waving and signaling with the palps and front legs.

Comments
Jumping spiders are alert and often beautifully colored animals that hunt by "cruising" the foliage of shrubs. They use their agility to pounce on prey. The genus *Phidippus* contains about 50 species in the United States, but only a small portion of these occur in deserts. Other genera of jumping spiders occur on desert shrubs and flowers and can usually be recognized by their very large, shiny middle eyes. While not harmful, some jumping spiders can give a painful bite.

BUTTERFLIES AND MOTHS

The sparse vegetation of many of North America's desert areas provides ample shelter, moisture, and nectar for a large variety of butterflies. These delicate creatures are often abundant after a rainfall, and in wet years some species may be quite numerous. Some desert butterflies occur almost nowhere else, having found perfectly suitable environments among the cacti or in the vegetation that grows on the walls of rocky canyons. A few species are migratory, turning up in the deserts at various times during the year. This section provides descriptions of some of the most conspicuous desert butterflies.

Becker's White
Pontia beckerii
403

1⅜–1⅞" (35–48 mm). White above with open, squarish black spot in fore-wing cell and bold black spotting around fore-wing tip and margin. Female may also have black spots on hind wing above. Below, gray-green or moss-green scaling broadly outlines veins of hind wing, broken by clear white band across wing; fore-wing tips below have some green scaling and black spot in fore-wing cell. Brightness of green scaling variable.

Habitat and Flight
Arid lands such as sage flats, dry coulees, foothill canyons, and lower mountains. 2 broods; May–June, August–September.

Range
Drier, intermontane western North America from interior British Columbia through Montana to Black Hills of South Dakota, SE. Colorado, and across Great Basin to Baja California.

Comments
A hardy butterfly of harsh environments, Becker's White is at home on a hot wind in a dusty canyon. Its association with sagebrush arises from a common adaptation to the desert. Look for this butterfly on rabbit brush, where it takes nectar.

Desert Orangetip
Anthocharis cethura
404

1⅛–1½" (28–38 mm). Upper side white or sometimes pale yellow with pale yellow-orange patch near fore-wing tip contained within black and white barred tip and margin. (Female sometimes lacks orange tip.) Below, hind wing yellow-washed, with heavy yellow-green marbling fusing into fairly separate swirls or bands.

Habitat and Flight
Desert chaparral, juniper hills, canyons, ridgeline meadows, and open deserts. 1 brood; late February into May.

Range
S. California, N. Nevada and W. Arizona into Baja California, especially in Mojave and Colorado deserts; also Santa Catalina Island.

Comments
Good spring rainfall brings the Desert Orangetip out on the arid desert stretches. One race limited to Santa Catalina Island off Los Angeles was feared extinct, but recent field work has proven otherwise.

Gray Marble
Anthocharis lanceolata
405

1⅝–1¾" (41–44 mm). White; fore wing above has gray, slightly hooked tip and black cell spot. Below, fore-wing tip and entire hind wing smoked and marbled with gray or brownish gray.

Habitat and Flight
South slopes of wooded, walled canyons, desert washes and edges, and ravines. Flies February–May, according to locale.

Range
Siskiyou and southern Cascade mountains of Oregon south through California mountains and Carson Mountains of Nevada into Baja California.

Comments
This uncommon, drab, and frail inhabitant of hotter mountains is not known to many people. Its liking for rock walls, where cresses cling, makes it difficult to observe closely

Pearly Marblewing
Euchloe hyantis
406

1¼–1⅜″ (32–35 mm). Small. Pure white with pearly sheen, especially between marbling below. Above, fore wing has charcoal- to black-checked tips and broad, nearly square black bar at end of fore-wing cell. Below, hind-wing marbling is green in solid, separate bars; fore-wing tips below also green.

Habitat and Flight
Sagelands, pinyon-juniper forests, rocky ravines, dry watercourses, serpentine outcrops, granite moraines, and canyon walls. 1 brood; April–May, rarely March–June.

Range
Basin and foothill country between eastern Coast Ranges and western Rockies from S. British Columbia and W. Montana south to Baja California, SE. Arizona, and N. New Mexico.

Comments
The Creamy Marblewing can be found flying over sage flats when, despite the chilly April wind, the big desert violets are in bloom.

Phoebus Parnassian
Parnassius phoebus
407

2⅛–3″ (54–76 mm). Male cream- to snow-white with black and gray markings and red spots on both fore wing and hind wing above and below, varying in size and in hue from pale salmon to brilliant scarlet; black spots on outer edge of fore wing. Female dusky or largely transparent, with more black and gray markings and spots; has waxy dark pouch at tip of abdomen. Antennae of both sexes banded in black and white.

Habitat and Flight
Meadows, clearings, sage flats, and tundra. 1 brood; June–early September, emerging later at higher altitudes.

Range
Subarctic Alaska south to central Sierra Nevada of California and down Rockies to Utah and New Mexico.

Comments
A number of features probably reflect the Phoebus Parnassian's adaptation to life in the arctic-alpine zone. The amount of dark gray scaling seems to increase in colder regions, enabling the butterflies to absorb the sun's warmth. Phoebus flies at colder temperatures than many butterflies, sometimes in snow

arge White Skipper
eliopetes ericetorum
08

1⅛–1⅝″ (28–41 mm). Milk-white above with black and white chevrons in rows along borders; blue-gray at base. (Female may have considerable bluish gray above.) Faint pinkish-brown areas cloud fore-wing tip and hind wing below, otherwise whitish. Fringes checkered.

Habitat and Flight
Vegetated spots in arid lands, especially where mallows (*Sphaeralcea*) abound. Rocky watersides in Columbia Basin. 5 broods in S. California; most of year. Fewer in north; May–September.

Range
Washington south to Baja California, across Great Basin to Colorado, New Mexico, Arizona, and northern Mexico.

Comments
The Large White Skippers colonize bush mallow in burned or disturbed portions of the southern California chaparral.

ale Blue
uphilotes pallescens
09

¾–⅞″ (19–22 mm). Male above violet-blue; narrow dark margin, sometimes broken into rows of dots on hind wing. Female above dark brown or gray-brown, sometimes with flush of grayish blue on fore-wing base; orange band just inside margin sometimes has small marginal dark spots. Both sexes below light gray to white, with small black dots; thin or wide orange band just inside margin of hind wing.

Habitat and Flight
Sandy desert washes, arid slopes, and juniper woodlands. 1 brood; late July–October, chiefly August and September.

Range
California along western border of Mojave Desert, across Nevada to W. Utah.

Comments
Female butterflies from the Stansbury Mountains of Utah have gray on the base of the fore wings. This feature is less or not at all apparent in individuals from other areas.

mall Blue
ilotiella speciosa
0

½–⅝″ (13–16 mm). Very small. Above, male uniform light blue with dark margins; female uniform brown. Both sexes white to gray below; bold black dots on fore wing; hind wing has bold black dots mostly in an irregular row or only a few tiny black dots. Wings rather long and narrow.

Habitat and Flight
Deserts, especially in the spring; also sandy washes and some areas bordering chaparral or arid woodlands. 1 brood; in deserts mostly April–early May, in Sierra Nevada early May.

Range
Chiefly western Mojave and Colorado deserts of S. California; also California from San Joaquin Valley south along western edge of Sierras and east to White Mountains into Nevada.

Comments

At the height of the brief desert wildflower season, the Small Blue may be found flying almost invisibly close to the desert floor. Small Blues from the Sierra Nevada foothills, found near Mariposa and at Briceburg on the Merced River, are among the rarest North American butterflies.

Antillean Blue
Hemiargus ceraunus
411, 412

¾–1" (19–25 mm). Above, male lavender-blue with narrow black border, female dusky brown-black, washed steel-blue at wing bases. Drab gray-brown below with 2 rows of whitish arrowheads inside margins; thin, broken, white-outlined black bars cross fore-wing and hind-wing centers. Southwestern population usually has only 1 eyespot beneath.

Habitat and Flight

Fields, roadsides, and sunny spots; principally lower deserts with mesquite and foothills westward, sporadically into mountains. Multiple broods; March–November in Southwest, year-round in Texas and Florida.

Range

S. California east through Nevada, S. Utah, and New Mexico; Texas; Alabama, Georgia, and Florida south into Mexico and Antilles. Absent from central Gulf states.

Comments

Three separate races of this species reach into the United States from the Antilles, eastern Mexico, and Baja California; two of these occur in deserts. Because the Antillean Blue's caterpillars feed on a wide array of legumes, the species is capable of inhabiting many kinds of warm places.

Western Pygmy Blue
Brephidium exilis
413

⅜–¾" (10–19 mm). Tiny. Bicolored above: white-fringed chocolate-brown with ultramarine blue inward, female larger than male and less blue. Below, gray-brown blending to bluish gray at base; tiny iridescent blue-green centered black spots on hind-wing margin; white striations across wings.

Habitat and Flight

Lowland, often disturbed places and coastlines: washes, marshes, alkali flats, railroad tracks, and vacant lots. Continuous broods in S. Texas and California, peaking in late summer and autumn.

Range

E. Oregon, California, and Great Basin south to Texas and South America, east to Nebraska and other plains states.

Comments

This smallest western butterfly is often abundant, but nevertheless usually passes unnoticed because of its diminutive size and slow flight. Despite its minuteness and seeming fragility, the Western Pygmy Blue emigrates northward each year from its year-round southern homeland.

Blue Copper
Chalceria heteronea
414, 415

1⅛–1¼" (28–32 mm). Male above bright sky-blue; female gray-blue or slate-gray with dark spots and soft brown shading. Both sexes below nearly white with black spots on fore wing; hind wing variable, with or without blurred darker spots.

Habitat and Flight
Low- to middle-elevation mountain canyons, sagelands, and flowery river flats and plateaus. 1 brood; July–August.

Range
Mainly east of Sierra-Cascade axis, across Great Basin and through Rockies to E. Wyoming; southwestern Canada to N. Arizona and New Mexico. Also west of Sierra Nevada in N. California to coast; locally in Tehachapi and Tejon ranges.

Comments
Despite its bright sky-blue color, the Blue Copper's venation and structure ally it with the coppers rather than with the blues. Common over most of their range, both male and female Blue Coppers frequent flowers, especially the blossoms of wild buckwheat.

Behr's Hairstreak
Satyrium behrii
416

⅞–1⅛" (22–28 mm). Tailless. Above, bright golden brown with dark margins broadest along leading edge of wings; male has bold patch of scent scales. Below, gray to brown with fine, white-edged black speckles, mostly on hind wing; speckles scattered over inner two-thirds of hind wing and in even row on outer third; red and black spot near outer hind-wing angle.

Habitat and Flight
Dry slopes of mountains and plateaus, foothill creeks and canyons, grass-shrub steppe; associated with sagebrush, pinyon-juniper woodland, and Joshua-tree savannah. 1 brood; mainly June–July, sometimes August.

Range
S. British Columbia south along east slope of Cascades and Sierra Nevada, locally along northern Transverse Ranges of S. California; east through Oregon and S. Idaho to SE. Wyoming, Arizona, and New Mexico to eastern Rockies.

Comments
The smallest and palest-marked individuals of this species come from California, the largest and darkest-marked from British Columbia. Unlike most hairstreaks, Behr's is passive and can be approached at close range. Adults are fond of buckwheat flowers.

Sleepy Orange
Eurema nicippe
417

1⅜–1⅞" (35–48 mm). Male bright golden orange above with broad, uneven black border and a black fore-wing cell spot; yellow beneath with small brown blotches. Female orange or yellow; black border breaks down halfway along hind wing; below, hind wing cocoa-brown with darker blotches; fore wing orange. In autumn individuals, hind wing below is darker.

Habitat and Flight
Old fields, wood edges, desert scrub, open pine woods, mountain canyons, watersides, and wet meadows. Flies March–November in South with 2–3 broods; shorter flight period northerly; all months in Deep South.

Range
Throughout South and Southwest, northward east of Rockies, rarely well into Northeast.

Comments
This sulphur cannot withstand cold winters yet annually penetrates the northerly latitudes—a characteristic pattern of many North American butterflies. The common name, Sleepy Orange, may have come from the butterfly's habit of hibernating through the cooler days of the southern winter. In summer it seems anything but sleepy with its rapid flight.

Queen
Danaus gilippus
418

3–3⅜" (76–86 mm). Large. Deep fox-brown above and below with black margins and finely lined black veins. Fine white dots speckle margins, larger ones occur on fore-wing tip and along margin. West of Mississippi, populations have white scaling along hind-wing veins above and are somewhat paler.

Habitat and Flight
Deserts, prairies, watercourses; also coasts and other open places with milkweeds. Successive broods; April–November, briefer in North, perhaps all year in Texas.

Range
Nevada and S. California east to Kansas and Texas, around Gulf to Florida and S. Georgia, south to South America.

Comments
The Queen cannot withstand cold winters. Records for northwestern Utah, Nebraska, and Kansas represent temporary immigrations. Male Queens have brushes within the tips of their abdomens. As courtship begins, these brushes are extended, releasing a compound that subdues the female.

Monarch
Danaus plexippus
419

3½–4" (89–102 mm). Very large, with fore wing long and drawn out. Above, bright, burnt-orange with black veins and black margins sprinkled with white dots; fore-wing tip broadly black interrupted by larger white and orange spots. Below, paler, duskier orange. 1 black spot appears between hind-wing cell and margin on male above and below. Female darker with black veins smudged.

Habitat and Flight
On migration, anywhere from alpine summits to cities; when breeding, habitats with milkweeds, especially meadows, weedy fields and watercourses. Encountered in all deserts during migration. Overwinters in coastal Monterey pine, Monterey cypress, eucalyptus groves in California, and fir forests in Mexican mountains. Successive broods; April–June

migrating northward, July–August resident in North, September–October migrating south, rest of year in overwintering locales. Year-round in S. California and Hawaii.

Range
Nearly all of North America from south of Hudson Bay through South America; absent from Alaska and Pacific Northwest Coast. Established in the Hawaiian Islands.

Comments
The Monarch is the only butterfly that annually migrates north and south as birds do. But no one individual makes the entire round-trip journey. In the fall, Monarchs in the North begin to congregate and to move southward. Midwestern and eastern Monarchs continue south all the way to the Sierra Madre of middle Mexico. Far western and Sierra Nevada Monarchs fly to the central and southern coast of California. Winter butterflies are sluggish and do not reproduce; they venture out to take nectar on warm days. In spring they head north, breed along the way, and their offspring return to the starting point.

Painted Lady
Vanessa cardui
420

2–2¼″ (51–57 mm). Fore-wing tip extended slightly, rounded. Above, salmon-orange with black blotches, black-patterned margins, and broadly black fore-wing tips with clear white spots; outer hind wing crossed by small black-rimmed blue spots. Below, fore wing dominantly rose-pink with olive, black, and white pattern; hind wing has small blue spots on olive background with white webwork. Fore wing above and below has white bar running from leading edge across black patch near tip.

Habitat and Flight
Anywhere, especially flowery meadows, parks, and mountaintops. 2 or more broods; all year in southern deserts, April–June until hard frosts in North.

Range
All of North America well into sub-Arctic.

Comments
This species deserves its alternate name, "Cosmopolite"; it is perhaps the most widespread butterfly in the world, found in Africa, Europe, and Asia, as well as in North America. Most of North America is devoid of Painted Ladies between the first heavy frosts and the onset of spring, although they occur year-round in the Sonoran deserts and perhaps other warm regions. In February and March, Painted Ladies begin infiltrating the North and East from the Southwest, and by late spring, they have recolonized the continent.

Desert Checkerspot
Charidryas neumoegeni
421

1¼–1¾" (32–44 mm). Above, nearly solid orange with few narrow black lines and spots. Below, orange with pearly tip on fore wing; hind wing has orange bands and pearl-white bands of spots. Arizona and New Mexico populations blacker above.

Habitat and Flight
Rocky desert washes and hills, pinyon-juniper and oak woodlands, and arid mountain canyons. 1 brood; late March–early May. Occasional second brood in fall if rainfall is heavy.

Range
Desert Southwest: SE. California, S. Nevada, and SW. Utah and Arizona, extending south into Baja California and Sonora, Mexico.

Comments
After wet winters these checkerspots may be common, and in April, many can be observed in the desert. For moisture and sugar, they visit desert asters and other brief Sonoran blooms.

Chara Checkerspot
Dymasia chara
422

¾–1⅛" (19–28 mm). Small. Above, predominantly orange with several rows of distinct black bars across wings, and whitish bar on leading edge of fore wing leading into paler band. Sexes similar. Below, fore wing orange with black lines and whitish and orange marginal bands; hind wing has alternating orange and white spot bands, the outermost band white. Arizona populations have slightly darker borders on fore wing above; white spots below more cream-colored than those of California populations.

Habitat and Flight
Deserts with mesquite and saguaro cactus, and open deserts and mountain canyons. 2 or more broods; usually early March and late October following rains; varies locally.

Range
SE. California east to SW. New Mexico; south into Mexico.

Comments
Chara Checkerspots fly slowly and often visit flowers after rains; males patrol gulches and hillsides, seeking females.

Sagebrush Checkerspot
Charidryas acastus
423

1¼–1¾" (32–44 mm). Male pale orange above with fine to heavy black lines; female is deeper orange but some females are yellowish or blackish. Below, pale mottled orange on fore wing with marginal white crescents; hind wing has narrow orange bands just inside margin and broad cream-white bands of black-rimmed spots.

Habitat and Flight
Arid grassland gulches, pinyon-juniper woodlands, sagebrush hills, and canyons. 1 brood in Oregon; May–June. Several broods from Utah to New Mexico; May–September.

Range
Great Basin and intermountain areas from SE. Washington

and Alberta to North Dakota, SE. California, and New
Mexico.

Comments
The Sagebrush Checkerspot generally inhabits pinyon-juniper
habitats that are rich in both sagebrush and rabbit brush, but
a few colonies have been discovered in open sageland.

Elada Checkerspot
Texola elada
424

⅞–1⅛" (21–28 mm). Small. Above, orange with black
borders and 3 bands of black dashes; some black dashes on
wing bases, seldom any white on leading edge of fore wing.
Below, fore wing orange with fainter black dashes, orange
margin, white band just inside, and black-edged orange band
further inside. Hind wing beneath has alternating orange and
white spot bands, the outermost band orange-red.

Habitat and Flight
Desert thorn scrub or shrub savannah with mesquite, saguaro,
and lecheguilla. Successive broods; April–October.

Range
Mexico to S. Arizona and central and S. Texas.

Comments
Elada Checkerspots fly together with the smaller Dymas
Checkerspots (*Dymasia dymas*). Like other externally similar
butterflies, these look-alikes give off sexual attractants, called
pheromones, that may help each species to recognize its own
kind.

Texan Crescentspot
Anthanassa texana
425

1–1½" (25–38 mm). Fore wing indented below tip. Above,
mostly black with white dots and bars on margin and center
disk, white band across middle of hind wing, red-orange areas
near wing bases. Below, fore wing orange at base, black-
brown on outer half, with white marks; hind wing buff-
colored with fine black lines and dots, white midband.

Habitat and Flight
Open areas: scrublands, deserts, and grasslands. Several
broods; March–November, sometimes year-round in S. Texas.

Range
S. California and S. Nevada east to South Carolina and
Florida, and south through Mexico; rarely north to Colorado,
North Dakota, Minnesota, and Illinois.

Comments
Male Texan Crescentspots often rest on bushes in gullies,
flying out to chase other butterflies. A related tropical species,
the Ptolyca Crescentspot (*A. ptolyca*), has been found in the
Santa Ana Wildlife Refuge in Texas.

Phaon Crescentspot
Phyciodes phaon
426

⅞–1¼″ (22–32 mm). Small. Above, fore wing brown with orange-tinged base, followed by black band just beyond base, whitish middle-band, orange band just inside margin, and dark margin; brown hind wing has orange bands. Beneath, fore wing similar to above; hind wing chalk-colored to yellowish cream, with dark veins and crescents (more noticeable in female); white crescents along hind-wing margin outside black dot row in brown area.

Habitat and Flight
Fairly moist open areas: desert springs, weedy fields, and marshes. 2 or more broods; April–September.

Range
SE. California and S. Nevada east to North Carolina and Florida, rarely emigrating north to Nebraska and Missouri.

Comments
Females often lay clusters of 50–100 eggs. But as with all butterflies, the mortality rate is high; only about 5% survive to the adult stage. The majority are killed by parasitic flies, wasps, and other predators.

Gray Metalmark
Apodemia palmerii
427

¾–⅞″ (19–22 mm). Above, dusky brown-gray, flushed with orange and slightly dappled with white; some species have orange margins and white fringes. Below, pale peach with extensive white overlay and scalloping; wavy, light brown line cuts across middle of fore wing and hind wing.

Habitat and Flight
Semiarid deserts near honey mesquite. 2 or 3 broods; April, June–August, October–November, time and length probably determined by summer rainfall.

Range
Desert mountains of SE. California, east through Arizona and New Mexico to W. Texas; south to Baja California, Mexico.

Comments
Gray Metalmark caterpillars spend much of their time in silken hideaways between sewn mesquite leaflets. They may occasionally emerge during winter for brief feedings, but do not mature until spring. Three small relatives of the Gray Metalmark dwell in south Texas. Hepburn's Metalmark (*A. hepburni*) has fewer reddish markings, and lacks the former's marginal row of white dots. The 2 species occupy much of the same range in southern Arizona, west Texas, and Mexico. Walker's Metalmark (*A. walkeri*) is chiefly Mexican, but has been found in southernmost Texas.

Mormon Metalmark
Apodemia mormo
428

¾–1¼″ (19–32 mm). Above, brightly patterned, varying geographically; fore-wing outer half and base of fore wing coal-black to ash-gray; inner half nut-brown to russet-orange; 4 black-bordered, pearl-white squares boldly mark inner fore-wing area, with others forming 2 indistinct bands of tooth-shaped spots outwardly; fringe strongly checkered. Hind-wing ground color and spotting similar, russet area usually confined to broad swath above outer wing margin. Below, fore wing pale brown; large white squares dot margin and interior; hind wing ash-gray, white, or russet with large, puffed, white squares and polygons. Metallic markings obscured by white.

Habitat and Flight
From beach dunes to mountains, typically in dry, often rocky, washes and slopes. 2 broods in lower areas, 1 brood northward and at higher elevations; principally March–June, August–October. In arid situations, timing of second brood depends upon summer rainfall.

Range
SE. Washington, E. Oregon through Idaho and central Rockies to W. Texas; across Great Basin to Pacific Coast south to Baja California and northwestern Mexico.

Comments
The unmistakable, common, and swift-flying Mormon Metalmarks perch vertically, either head up or head down, in blazing sunshine. Their flashing colors match mottled desert rocks and sand, making flying adults difficult to track.

Bordered Patch
Chlosyne lacinia
29, 430

1⅝–1⅞" (35–48 mm). Fore wing black above with white or orange marginal dots, followed by row of white dots, row of narrow to wide white or orange patches in middle, and occasionally whitish or orange spots at base. Hind wing above similar but middle row usually forms a broad yellow and orange band or patch. Below, fore wing similar to upper side; hind wing black with yellowish bands at base, middle, and margin; red band or spot near corner beyond middle band.

Habitat and Flight
Subtropical thorn forests, desert hills, weedy edges of fields, bottomlands, pinyon pine and oak woodlands, parks and gardens. Several broods; usually March–November.

Range
SE. California east to Texas and south to Argentina, rarely emigrating north to Utah and Nebraska.

Comments
The Bordered Patch has been called our most variable butterfly, as well as the most widespread and abundant checkerspot in the Americas.

Great Basin Wood Nymph
Cercyonis sthenele
31

1⅜–2" (35–51 mm). Above, light to dark brown. Below, striated pale brown to silvery gray-brown, with outer half of hind wing paler than inner and often bearing 2 small but prominent eyespots; hind wing also has band composed of darker scaling between 2 gently wavy or mildly zigzagged dark lines. 2 large eyespots usually appear on outer fore wing; sometimes yellow near eyespots but never in strong patches.

Habitat and Flight
Basin sagelands, dry shrub steppes, oak-lined arid canyons, and pinyon-juniper woodlands. 1 brood; June–July.

Range
E. British Columbia and Washington south and west through Great Basin to Four Corners area of Utah, Colorado, Arizona, and New Mexico; also central and S. California and Baja.

Comments
One widespread population of the Great Basin Wood Nymph has a dappled and frosty-whitish underside, but populations from outside or along the edges of the Great Basin retain the chocolate-brown hue characteristic of wood nymphs.

Desert Checkered Skipper
Pyrgus philetas
432

⅞–1⅛" (22–28 mm). Wings above blackish or grayish brown, checkered with uniform pattern of many white spots with some bluish-gray basal hair. Marginal spots on hind wing conspicuous above, with clear white or mildly checkered fringes. Below, dull gray or quite silvery, with vague bands of slightly dark hind wing.

Habitat and Flight
Arroyos, valley bottomlands, and desert waterholes. Several successive broods; February–December in Texas.

Range
S. New Mexico and Arizona, central Texas to Baja California and Mexico.

Comments
This silvery skipper whirrs up and down small gullies in the desert Southwest.

Sandhill Skipper
Polites sabuleti
433

¾–1⅛" (19–28 mm). Highly variable; generally pale orange above, with deeply toothed outer hind-wing margins. Female only slightly darker than male, with yellow to whitish spots inside of fore-wing margin above. Below, fore wing orange at leading edge, black at base, olive-yellow toward margin and tip. Hind wing blackish olive with coalesced yellow spot band on lower hind wing that runs out along veins to margin. Desert populations may be almost unmarked below.

Habitat and Flight
Coastal dunes, desert alkaline seeps and flats, urban lawns, and watercourses. 2 broods in North; May–June and August–September; longer in South, June–September in mountains.

Range
S. British Columbia and Washington south to Baja California and southeast through Idaho and Colorado.

Comments
Although this skipper's name reflects its affinity for dunes, it is hardly restricted to sandhills. In British Columbia, it uses European knotweed as a late-summer nectar source.

haska Skipper
speria pahask
4

1⅛–1½" (28–38 mm). Rich tawny-orange above, with narrow brown border except broad toward fore-wing tip. Male has conspicuous patch of scent scales, black with yellow center, female may have some blurred brown markings on fore-wing disk. Below, fore wing paler than above; hind wing brownish to greenish olive, with well-developed crescents of silver-white spots just inside margin and at base, the outer band broken toward leading edge, inner one fragmented.

Habitat and Flight
Ridges in plains and basins; valleys in mountains; desert seeps and mesas. 1 brood in northern range; June–July. 2 broods southward; May–September.

Range
S. Saskatchewan, western Dakotas, and Montana south to New Mexico and west to S. Nevada and S. California.

Comments
Specialists distinguish the very similar and variable western silver-spotted skippers by examining the structure of the genitalia and the color of a feltlike material in the stigma.

oyote Skipper
halarus toxeus
5

1⅝–2" (41–51 mm). Large, with narrow and very pointed wings. Chocolate-brown on both surfaces, slightly lighter on fore wing below. Fore wing above and below crossed by very vague brown bands of a different shade. Hind wing below crossed by 2 more dark brown bands. Hind-wing fringe white.

Habitat and Flight
Chaparral, desert and mountain scrub forests, and savannahs. Probably several broods; most of year.

Range
Arizona and Texas south to Panama.

Comments
In the Santa Ana National Wildlife Refuge of southern Texas, the Coyote Skipper flies about Texas ebony trees. Males visit the flowers while females deposit eggs deep in the foliage.

esert Gray Skipper
retta carus
6

⅞–1¼" (22–32 mm). Soft grayish yellow above with 2 rows of buff-yellow spots on fore wing, 1 row on hind wing; male has strong, slender bar of scent scales. Below, yellow-gray with 2 bands of white spots, more suffused on fore wing; female has white scales along hind wing veins, male black between fore-wing and hind-wing veins. Fringes gray.

Habitat and Flight
Moist areas in desert. April–September, year-round in Texas.

Range
S. California, Arizona, New Mexico, and Mexico to Panama.

Comments
The drab coloring of the mothlike gray skippers may have

evolved to help conceal them from predators in the desert. This skipper is found near waterholes and sandbars.

Great Basin Sootywing
Pholisora libya
437

1–1⅛" (25–35 mm). Brassy black to dark brown above, with crescents of white spots on fore wing, smaller on male, larger on female. Below, brown to brownish gold, with spots only at tip; hind wing sooty gray-brown to black with large white spots in rows—1 median row and 1 row just inside margin in Southwest, or 1 median row and basal spot in Great Basin.

Habitat and Flight
Alkaline sage flats and deserts. 1 brood in Great Basin; June–July. 2 broods in S. California; March–May and September–October.

Range
SE. Oregon, E. Montana, and W. North Dakota south to W. Colorado, Arizona, S. California, Baja California, and Mexico.

Comments
Chiefly a denizen of the Great Basin, this skipper also inhabits saltbush stands in the Mojave and Sonoran deserts; one population reaches across the Red Desert of Wyoming.

Bronze Roadside Skipper
Amblyscirtes aenus
438

⅞–1⅛" (22–28 mm). Brown above with brassy luster. Fore wing has reddish cell below; hind wing gray below, disk has transverse row of powdery, pale spots. Fringes checkered.

Habitat and Flight
Small, stony canyons, gullies on plains, rocky slopes of dry foothills and mountain ranges. 1 brood; May–June, Colorado April–July, Texas; June–September, Arizona.

Range
Colorado and Utah, south through SE. Arizona, New Mexico and W. Texas.

Comments
In west Texas, New Mexico, and southern Arizona, this species may be confused with the Texas Roadside Skipper (*A. texanae*), but the latter is paler overall, and has more extensive spots above than the Bronze Roadside Skipper. The similar Slaty Roadside Skipper (*A. nereus*), an uncommon and local species, is much grayer overall than both the Bronze and Texas Roadside skippers, and its hind wing is greenish below.

Yucca Giant Skipper
Megathymus yuccae
439

2–2⅞" (51–73 mm). Black above with yellow rays outward from bases and cloudy-yellow hind-wing borders; fore wing has bright yellow cell spot, narrow or pointed in western populations and rounded in others, and band of squarish yellow spots just inside margin above; sometimes hind wing has yellow spotting above. Below, dark hind wing frosty-violet with some black dusting and white spotting. Big, rounded body, generally black to dark brown or gray.

Habitat and Flight
Forest edges, granite outcroppings, old fields, and bottomlands with yucca. Late January–June, only about 4 weeks in any one locale except central Florida.

Range
Utah and Great Basin east through Arkansas and Carolinas, south to Florida and Gulf, west to Nevada, S. California, Baja California, and Mexico.

Comments
By far the most widely distributed giant skipper. Regional races may be quite distinctive. The western subspecies are often grouped in a separate species under the name Colorado Giant Skipper (*M. coloradensis*). The somewhat rare Ursine Giant Skipper (*M. ursus*) is the largest giant skipper in North America, with a wingspan to 3⅛" (79 mm). This distinctive black skipper has a broad, yellow-orange spot patch across the fore-wing tip above and below, and white antennae. It flies in summer and early fall in southeastern Arizona, southern New Mexico, Texas, and Mexico.

da Hairstreak
nistrymon leda
0

¾–⅞" (19–22 mm). Small. Above, blue at base, gray-black outwardly; male blue paler, may cover most of hind wing. Below, gray crossed by jagged black line just behind middle of wing with or without red outline; black-centered red spot and blue patch may or may not be present near 2 tails; faint spots at wing base.

Habitat and Flight
Thorn scrub with mesquite, often in sandy washes and flats, foothill canyons, and drier mountain forests. At least 2 broods; May–July or August, September–October or even November.

Range
Eastern Mojave Desert in New York Mountains of California, to deserts of S. California, Baja California, and S. Arizona.

Comments
The Leda Hairstreak has 2 distinct forms, with and without red markings. This kind of dimorphism may be due to different seasonal conditions, such as moisture variation, or it may be a balanced, genetically fixed set of frequencies within the population. Both forms definitely belong to the same species because eggs of one have produced the other.

esert Green Hairstreak
llophrys comstocki
1

¾–1" (19–25 mm). Tailless. Light gray above. Below, gray-green to green (summer brood more yellowish); white band of broken bars just behind middle of wing, bent at middle, and edged inwardly with black; fore-wing disk green below.

Habitat and Flight
Desert mountain ranges, rocky slopes, canyons, and washes. 2 broods, and in some years, depending on rains, 3 broods; March–April, June–July, August–September.

Range
Largely northern and eastern Mojave Desert in S. California,
W. and S. Nevada, NW. Arizona, SE. Utah, and SW.
Colorado.

Comments
In years of ample rainfall, the Desert Green Hairstreak can be
quite common. Males perch on rocks or low shrubs and behave
very territorially. Females, found less often, seem to stay
higher up the canyon walls close to the host plants.

Boisduval's Yellow
Eurema boisduvaliana
442

1⅛–1⅝" (28–41 mm). Short, sharp-tailed. Yellow with
highly angular black borders on male, restricted to black fore-
wing tip on female. Underside yellow with rust-pink
mottling, especially at tips.

Habitat and Flight
Sonoran scrub and openings. May fly any month.

Range
Mostly Mexico, possible resident in S. Texas, straying to S.
Arizona and Florida.

Comments
This species is named for Jean Baptiste Boisduval, a 19th-
century French entomologist who dispatched collectors and
named material from much of the New World.

Common Sulphur
Colias philodice
443

1⅜–2" (35–51 mm). Above, male light yellow with sharp
black borders; female yellow or white with yellow-spotted
black border. Below, both sexes greenish yellow in spring and
fall broods, clear yellow in midsummer; double red-rimmed
silvery spot near end of cell and row of brown spots near edges
of both wings. Albino female has pink fringes.

Habitat and Flight
Almost any open country; especially numerous in clover
meadows, parks, and pastures; absent from extreme deserts,
but may be found in desert areas with nearby agriculture.
Several broods; March–December, weather permitting.

Range
Throughout United States except for most of Florida.

Comments
Because it feeds on clover, alfalfa, and other pervasive
legumes, the Common Sulphur has spread dramatically.
It was probably originally a northern and eastern species.

Western Tiger
Swallowtail
Pterourus rutulus
444

2¾–3⅞" (70–98 mm). Above and below, lemon-yellow with
black tiger-stripes across wings and black yellow-spotted
margins. 1 or 2 orange spots and several blue spots near black
tail on hind wing; blue continuous all around outer margin of
hind wing below. Yellow spots along outer black margin of

fore wing below run together into band; uppermost spot on border of hind wing above and below is yellow.

Habitat and Flight
Widespread, but normally near moisture—canyons, watersides, trails, roadsides, parks, and gardens; sagelands and mesas with creeks. February in S. California, May in Washington, normally June–July in mountain areas. Up to 3 broods in low altitudes and latitudes, 1 in cooler places with shorter seasons. Present most of summer.

Range
British Columbia south to Baja California, east through Rockies to Black Hills, and High Plains of Colorado and New Mexico. Rare east of Rockies.

Comments
The Western Tiger may be the most conspicuous butterfly in the West. In canyons, males of several species of swallowtails gather in spectacular numbers around puddles or beside streams, with the Western Tiger predominating.

Desert Swallowtail
Papilio rudkini
545

2⅛–2¾″ (67–70 mm). 3 forms: black with yellow spots; black with yellow bands of larger spots; typical form mostly yellow, since broad yellow bands of spots cover up most of black. Tailed; with blue patches and orange spot with pupil in from tail on hind-wing margin. Outer edge of yellow spots tends to be scalloped outward toward margin.

Habitat and Flight
Dry washes and mountain canyons in desert. Flies year-round; most common early spring and fall in 2 broods after rains.

Range
S. Nevada, SE. Utah, S. California, and W. Arizona.

Comments
Since it occurs in several different forms, the Desert Swallowtail could be extremely hard to identify if not for its clear-cut habitat preference.

Anise Swallowtail
Papilio zelicaon
546

2⅛–3″ (67–76 mm). Yellow-banded; more yellow than black. Lemon-yellow spots in midwing band above are straight-edged and fill spaces between veins of wing; hind wing flushed with blue between broad, yellow band and medium-long tail; hind-wing eyespot orange with large, round, centered pupil. Similar below. Black abdomen has yellow side stripes.

Habitat and Flight
Sea level to 14,000′ (4270 m); vacant city lots, sage deserts, canyons, and parks. Absent from dense forests except clearings or roadsides; also avoids warm desert areas. Flight varies greatly: year-round in S. California; spring and fall broods on Northwest Coast, 1 brood midsummer high in Rockies.

Range
Pacific Coast from British Columbia to Baja California, east to Black Hills and eastern edge of Rockies; scarce or absent in most of SE. California deserts.

Comments
The Anise Swallowtail is one of the most adaptable native butterflies. Males are especially ardent hilltop fliers, and seek out any eminence on the horizon as a courtship rendezvous.

Short-tailed Black Swallowtail
Papilio indra
447

2⅛–3⅜" (54–86 mm). Small with negligible to medium-size tails. Brownish black with pale cream-colored spots and bands; hind wing has diffuse blue patches, orange eyespot with centered, round, black pupil. Great variation among subspecies; some have inner two-thirds of wing all black, no midwing band, and very extensive blue; others have narrow midwing band; still others have broad midwing band of pale cream cut off sharply by black on inner edge, so that basal third or half of wing is all black. 2 narrow gold lines on thorax; abdomen chiefly black.

Habitat and Flight
Various arid lands, including canyons, pinyon-juniper slopes, desert ranges, cliffs, boulder-strewn foothills, and serpentine barrens; also moister high mountain slopes. Most of range, 1 brood in spring and early summer; also second, late summer broods on Colorado Plateau and California deserts.

Range
Deserts, mountains, and canyonlands of all western states.

Comments
Exceptionally powerful in flight, Short-tails can be difficult to approach; but males often congregate at damp earth to drink, and the retiring females sometimes come down from the canyon rims to take nectar from streamside mint flowers.

White-lined Sphinx
Hyles lineata
448

2½–3½" (65–90 mm). Fore wings brown with a buff-colored band from near base to tip; veins outlined in white. Hind wing mostly pink, dark brown to black near body and along outer margin. Head prominent, brown between eyes above. Thorax brown with 6 white stripes. Abdomen brown with paired dark spots on each segment, separated by 3 pale lines on back broken lengthwise.

Habitat and Flight
Meadows and gardens, especially where portulaca grows; found on plants after rains in deserts. Flies in midsummer.

Range
Throughout North America.

Comments
These moths whirr like hummingbirds as they visit garden flowers at dusk or in darkness. Often they fly in numbers to

artificial lights. Sometimes they seek nectar in daylight. There are 2 or more generations a year, one overwintering as pupae underground. The Galium Sphinx (*H. gallii*), wingspan not more than 3" (75 mm), is similar except it lacks the white stripes on thorax and its veins are not outlined in white.

California Cankerworm Moth
Paleacrita longiciliata
449

1–1⅜" (25–35 mm). Male's fore wings grayish brown or gray with brownish or blackish scales, small grayish-black spot in discal cell. Hind wings above light grayish brown, somewhat translucent. Female's wings vestigial, less than ¹⁄₁₆" (1 mm) long; body grayish brown with some gray scales.

Habitat and Flight
Open scrub areas and deserts. Flies November–May.

Range
California.

Comments
Females of this species are wingless. The caterpillars, called cankerworms, occasionally cause severe defoliation of forest and shade trees.

Large California Spanworm Moth
Procherodes truxaliata
450

1⅜–1¾" (35–45 mm). Fore wings yellowish brown, slightly incurved from tip to middle of outer margin producing 2 projecting points. Hind wings paler with 1 projecting point midway along outer margin. Wings are variably speckled with gray-brown; fore wings crossed by 2 transverse bands, which vary from strongly contrasting dark gray to an almost completely indistinguishable yellow-brown.

Habitat and Flight
Sandy, arid regions to mountain forests; not specialized. Flies May–August.

Range
Colorado and New Mexico to California Sierras, south to Baja California.

Comments
This species is occasionally abundant enough in southern California to become a minor pest of trees and shrubs.

MAMMALS

Animal life is diverse and abundant in deserts, yet some of the most interesting mammals venture out only at sunset or during the night, when it is cooler and the chance of being seen by a predator is less great. Small mammals, such as shrews and mice, are especially numerous; many species construct complex systems of burrows for nesting and food storage. Bats are also plentiful, emerging at night, sometimes by the thousands, to scour the air for flying insects. Among the larger mammals that the patient visitor may see are foxes, the Coyote, and the Desert Bighorn. This section covers these and other common mammals of the desert.

Ghost-faced Bat
Mormoops megalophylla
451

2⅜–2⅝″ (5.9–6.6 cm) long. Reddish brown to dark brown. Short tail projects from upper side of membrane connecting hind legs. Unique folds of skin across chin from ear to ear.

Habitat
Desert or scrub, usually in caves or mines that are often very hot and humid; seldom in buildings.

Range
Only in S. Texas and S. Arizona.

Comments
Strong, swift flyers, these bats emerge late in the evening to hunt just above the ground. They roost in loose colonies.

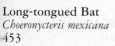

California Leaf-nosed Bat
Macrotus californicus
452

3⅜–3⅝″ (8.4–9.3 cm) long. Grayish to dark brownish above, with fur nearly white at base; paler below. Large ears. Erect triangular flap on nose.

Habitat
Desert scrub. By day, abandoned mine tunnels.

Range
S. California, extreme S. Nevada, and W. and S. Arizona.

Comments
The only bat in our area with large ears and a leaf nose. It roosts by day, usually fairly close to the entrance of a mine tunnel, in small groups of up to 100 bats, which do not touch.

Long-tongued Bat
Choeronycteris mexicana
453

2¼–3⅛″ (5.5–7.8 cm) long. Gray or brownish above, paler below. Large eyes. Long, slender nose has an erect arrowhead-shape flap of skin. Tiny tail extends less than halfway to end of interfemoral membrane.

Habitat
Canyons in mountain ranges rising from the desert. By day, usually caves and mines, sometimes in buildings, where they tend to hang near the entrance.

Range
Extreme SW. California, SE. Arizona, and extreme SW. New Mexico.

Comments
The long tongue, tipped by a brush of tiny nipple-like projections, and the lack of lower incisors make it easy for this bat to lap up flower nectar and fruit juices.

Mexican Long-nosed Bat
Leptonycteris nivalis
454

3–3½″ (7.6–8.8 cm) long. Grayish brown above; paler on shoulders and underparts. Long nose has a leaflike projection. No tail. Medium-size ears.

Habitat
Colonies in caves, particularly in pine-oak habitat.

Range
In the United States only, in Big Bend National Park, Texas.

Comments
This bat emerges late from its daytime roosting cave, apparently moving to lower elevations to feed on nectar and pollen.

Sanborn's Long-nosed Bat
Leptonycteris sanborni
455

2¾–3⅜" (6.9–8.4 cm) long. Reddish brown on back; brownish on belly. No visible tail. Long nose has erect leaf-shaped projection on tip. Large eyes.

Habitat
Caves and mines where mountains rise from the desert.

Range
S. Arizona and extreme SW. New Mexico.

Comments
This bat emerges late to feed on nectar and pollen as well as insects. It either alights on vegetation while feeding or hovers somewhat like a hummingbird.

Yuma Myotis
Myotis yumanensis
456

3⅜–3⅞" (8.4–9.9 cm) long. Short, dull fur. Variable shades of brown above; lighter below, with throat sometimes whitish.

Habitat
Always near ponds, streams, or lakes. By day, under sidings or shingles. Night roosts are often in buildings; nursery colonies in caves, mines, buildings, or under bridges.

Range
California to British Columbia, east to W. Montana, Idaho, W. Nevada, Utah, Colorado, New Mexico.

Comments
Closely associated with water, the Yuma Myotis feeds by flying very low over the surface.

Cave Myotis
Myotis velifer
457

3½–4½" (9–11.5 cm) long. Large. Light brown in eastern part of range to black in western part. Calcar not keeled. Ears reach tip of nose when extended forward.

Habitat
Arid Southwest; in summer, caves, mines, sometimes buildings; in winter, caves.

Range
W. Texas north to S. central Kansas, west through S. New Mexico, S. Arizona, extreme SE. California.

Comments
These bats sometimes form very large colonies, estimated at 15,000–20,000 in Kansas nurseries. All but those in Kansas migrate between summer and winter quarters.

California Myotis
Myotis californicus
458

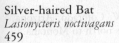

2⅞–3⅜" (7.4–8.5 cm) long. Dull fur, light to dark brown with yellowish or orangish cast above; paler below. Ears, wings, and interfemoral membrane dark. Tiny foot.

Habitat
Desert to semidesert areas; in Southwest, especially rocky canyons. By day, in buildings, under bridges, under bark, in hollow trees; by night, buildings.

Range
Western North America north to SW. British Columbia, east to Idaho, Colorado, and New Mexico.

Comments
In winter, some of these bats hibernate in mines, while others remain active. An ability to veer suddenly sideways, up, or down makes their flight conspicuously erratic.

Silver-haired Bat
Lasionycteris noctivagans
459

3⅝–4¼" (9.2–10.8 cm) long. Medium-size. Nearly black; silvery-tipped hairs on back, look frosted. Interfemoral membrane lightly furred above. Short, rounded, naked ears.

Habitat
In summer, north woods in protected spots (under bark; in dead trees, woodpecker holes, bird nests). In winter, hibernates in trees, crevices, buildings, and other places.

Range
Most of United States and southern Canada.

Comments
This beautiful, solitary bat emerges in early evening, flying very slowly to feed on a variety of insects but especially favoring moths and flies. Generally migrating south for the winter, it possesses a well-developed homing instinct; one bat traveled 107 miles to its home roost.

Southwestern Myotis
Myotis auriculus
460

3⅛–3½" (7.8–8.8 cm) long. Dull brownish fur. Large brown ears and a long, thin tragus. Calcar not keeled.

Habitat
Deserts, mesquite or chaparral to forests, especially in areas of rocky outcroppings.

Range
SE. Arizona and SW. New Mexico.

Comments
Little is known of this species except that it roosts at night in buildings and caves; its day roosts have not been found.

Western Pipistrelle
Pipistrellus hesperus
461

2⅜–3⅜" (6–8.6 cm) long. Smallest bat in United States. Light yellow or grayish to reddish brown above; belly whitish. Wings, membrane connecting ears, nose, and feet blackish. Calcar keeled. 1 tiny premolar behind canine.

Habitat
Caves, deserts, rocky areas, scrub, buildings.

Range
North-central and Big Bend areas of Texas, W. New Mexico, Utah north to E. Oregon, SE. Washington.

Comments
Usually the first bat to appear in the evening, it often flies before dark and is even seen in broad daylight. Its flight is erratic and slow, less than 6 mph.

Spotted Bat
Euderma maculatum
462

4¼–4½″ (10.7–11.5 cm) long. Black above with 3 large white spots on back; white below. Huge ears.

Habitat
Primarily in crevices in rocky cliffs and canyons.

Range
S. California and S. Nevada through SW. Colorado, Arizona, W. New Mexico, with scattered records north to Montana.

Comments
One of the rarest North American bats, this species emerges late, carrying its huge ears forward during flight and giving a loud, high-pitched call. Also called the Death's Head Bat.

Townsend's Big-eared Bat
Plecotus townsendii
463

3½–4⅜″ (8.9–11 cm) long. Pale gray or brown above; buff underparts. Wings and membrane connecting hind legs naked. Enormous ears extending to middle of body when laid back; 2 large glandular lumps on nose.

Habitat
Usually in caves; sometimes in buildings, especially on West Coast. Also scrub deserts, pine and pinyon-juniper forests.

Range
Western United States north to S. British Columbia, east through Idaho, Wyoming, Colorado, New Mexico, Oklahoma, Texas; scattered populations farther east.

Comments
This bat emerges late to feed almost entirely on moths. In summer, females form nursery colonies of up to about 200.

Pallid Bat
Antrozous pallidus
464

4¼–5⅛″ (10.7–13 cm) long. Large. Creamy to beige above; nearly white below. Big ears separated at base. Wings and membrane connecting hind legs essentially naked.

Habitat
Deserts; daytime roosts are in buildings and crevices, less often caves, mines, hollow trees, and other shelters.

Range
Deserts from north-central British Columbia and E. Washington to S. California, S. Kansas, W. Texas.

Comments
Emerging late at night and beating its wings more slowly than many bats (only 10–11 beats per second), this stately bat is unique in feeding primarily on the ground. It gives several distinctive calls.

Brazilian Free-tailed Bat
Tadarida brasiliensis
465

3½–4⅜" (9–11 cm) long. Smallest free-tailed bat. Dark brown or dark gray above, with hairs whitish at base. Ears separated at base. Calcar pointed backward, extending the interfemoral membrane more than half the length of tail.

Habitat
Buildings on West Coast; caves from Texas to Arizona.

Range
Throughout southern United States. In the West, north to S. Oregon and S. Nebraska. Also farther east.

Comments
The Brazilian Free-tailed Bat is by far the most common bat in the Southwest; a United States population of at least 100 million also makes it one of the most numerous mammals in the country. Most individuals from this region migrate to Mexico for the winter, usually toward the end of October, and return in March to mate. The Carlsbad Caverns in New Mexico were discovered as a result of the bats' emergence. At sunset, bats begin flitting about inside the cave. After circling for several minutes they begin to emerge in a spiral, ascending 150–180' from the depths of the cave into the night air. When flight is at its heaviest, 5000–10,000 bats emerge each minute. The return to the cave is even more spectacular than the emergence: most bats appear just at sunrise and from heights of 600–1000' plummet straight down at speeds of more than 25 mph.

Pocketed Free-tailed Bat
Tadarida femorosacca
466

3⅞–4⅝" (9.8–11.8 cm) long. Dark gray or brown above and below; lower half of hairs nearly white. Wings long and narrow. Tail free about half its length. Ears joined at base.

Habitat
Rock outcrops in desert.

Range
S. California, S. Arizona, small area in SE. New Mexico, Big Bend area of Texas.

Comments
By day, this bat roosts in rock crevices or other shelters in rocky areas, in small colonies usually composed of less than 100 members. As it drops from its perch into the air at night it gives a loud, high-pitched call.

Big Free-tailed Bat
Tadarida macrotis
467

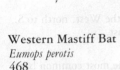

5⅛–5¾" (12.9–14.4 cm) long. Large. Reddish brown, dark brown, or black, with hairs white at base. Tail free for an inch or more. Ears joined at base and extending beyond tip of nose when laid forward.

Habitat
Rocky areas; day roosts in rocky cliffs.

Range
Widespread but usually uncommon; sometimes locally abundant in parts of California and Nevada east to Kansas and Texas. Scattered fall records in British Columbia and Iowa.

Comments
This colonial bat emerges late to feed on moths as well as crickets, ants, and other insects. It sometimes chatters loudly.

Western Mastiff Bat
Eumops perotis
468

5½–7½" (14–18.5 cm) long. Largest bat in United States. Body sparsely furred, with dark brown hairs white at base. Enormous ears joined at base and protruding over forehead.

Habitat
Rocky cliffs and canyons; also buildings.

Range
S. California, extreme S. Nevada, S. Arizona, extreme SW. New Mexico, Big Bend area of Texas.

Comments
By day these bats form small colonies, usually with fewer than 100 members. Because of their large size and long wings, they require considerable space to launch into flight, so roosting sites are placed to permit a free fall for at least 10′

Botta's Pocket Gopher
Thomomys bottae
469

6⅝–10¾" (16.7–27.3 cm) long. Usually dark brown to grayish above, with purplish cast on sides; slightly lighter below. Tail tan to gray, essentially hairless. Variable coloration includes white individuals in the Imperial Desert of southern California, almost black ones in some coastal areas. Individuals in Arizona have white spotting under chin. Rounded ear with a similar-sized dark patch behind it.

Habitat
Various: deserts to mountain meadows, in soils ranging from sand to clay, with loam preferred.

Range
Extreme SW. Oregon through California, S. and E. Nevada, Utah, SW. Colorado, Arizona and New Mexico, W. Texas.

Comments
This pocket gopher spends most of its time in underground burrows. Tunnels are extensive; one in Texas was 150′ long. Botta's Pocket Gopher is solitary, living one to the burrow, and often fights if it meets another.

Desert Shrew
Notiosorex crawfordi
470

3–3¾" (7.7–9.3 cm) long. Grayish, washed with brown above; pale gray below. Long grayish tail, lighter below. The only North American shrew with 3 teeth on each side of the jaw with only one cusp (point) on each. Ears more noticeable than in most shrews.

Habitat
Arid regions, especially in semidesert scrub. Sometimes found in woodrat nests or in large masses of vegetation at the base of agave, cactus, or other plants in desert areas.

Range
S. California east through Arizona, New Mexico, S. Colorado to W. Arkansas, W. Texas.

Comments
Like many desert animals, the Desert Shrew obtains water from its food, usually the soft inner parts of larger insects.

Silky Pocket Mouse
Perognathus flavus
471

3⅞–4¾" (10–12.2 cm) long. Soft-furred. Pale yellowish above, often with many black hairs; belly white. Yellow patch behind ear, white spot below ear. Small feet. Juveniles gray.

Habitat
Prairies; sandy, gravelly, or rocky areas with sparse vegetation.

Range
SE. Wyoming and W. Nebraska south to W. Texas, New Mexico, Arizona, extreme SE. Utah.

Comments
This mouse makes small burrows, usually not more than 4" deep, often with 3–4 openings. Blind passages near the surface enable the Silky Pocket Mouse to escape underground predators.

Arizona Pocket Mouse
Perognathus amplus
472

4⅕–6⅔" (12.3–17.0 cm) long. Tawny with hints of pinkish or salmon above with many interspersed black hairs. Belly white or slightly off-white. Hind foot less than ⁸⁄₁₀". Tail about 70 percent or more the length of body. Best told from Little Pocket Mouse by the size of the lower premolar tooth.

Habitat
Desert areas with scattered shrubs and fine-textured soils.

Range
Scattered in central and S. Arizona into Sonora, Mexico.

Comments
The diet consists of about 80 percent of seeds. When food is unavailable these mice can go into a lowered metabolic state of torpor, thus conserving their energy.

Little Pocket Mouse
Perognathus longimembris
473

4¼–5⅞" (11–15.1 cm) long. Soft-furred. Grayish yellow or buff above interspersed with black hairs, varying from lighter to darker with color of soil; underparts buff, brownish, or white. Tail light brown. 2 small white patches at base of ears.

Habitat
Gravelly soils in desert areas.

Range
SE. Oregon, Nevada, W. and S. Utah, S. California, and isolated small areas in N., S. central and SW. Arizona.

Comments
This seasonally active pocket mouse may hibernate for long periods under adverse conditions; in California it is inactive from October to January. It can survive in the wild 3–5 years. In Nevada, the Kit Fox is an important predator.

Great Basin Pocket Mouse
Perognathus parvus
474

5¾–7¾" (14.8–19.8 cm) long. Medium-sized. Soft-furred. Pinkish buff or yellowish above, interspersed with blackish hairs, white or buff below; indistinct olive-greenish line on sides. Long tail dark above, whitish below; crested near tip.

Habitat
Arid, sparsely vegetated plains and brushy areas.

Range
South-central British Columbia south through E. Washington. E. Oregon, S. Idaho, to NE. and central California, Nevada, Utah, extreme NW. Arizona and SW. Wyoming.

Comments
This species is active from April through September, eating many kinds of insects and collecting seeds to be stored in its burrow. Water is metabolized from food. Summer nesting and storage burrows are shallow, but a deep tunnel is dug to a hibernation nest of dry vegetation in a chamber 3–6' deep, where it spends the winter.

Long-tailed Pocket Mouse
Perognathus formosus
475

6¾–8¼" (17.2–21.1 cm) long. Soft-furred. Gray or brown above; belly white, tipped with yellowish. Long tail, grayish above, whitish below, distinctly crested and tufted on terminal third. Large hind foot. Ears lack white hairs.

Habitat
Usually rocky or gravelly ground, sometimes along riverbeds and sandy wastes in hard-packed sand; open mesquite.

Range
Nevada, W. Utah, NW. Arizona, S. California.

Comments
In extreme heat or cold, the Long-tailed becomes torpid and stays in its burrow. Its life span is 4–5 years. In Nevada, the Kit Fox is an important predator.

ailey's Pocket Mouse
erognathus baileyi
76

7⅞–9⅛" (20.1–23 cm) long. Rough-haired. Grayish with
yellow hairs interspersed; rump with black hairs but usually
not spines; underparts clear white. Long tail tufted at tip.
Small white spot at base of ear.

Habitat
Rocky slopes in desert areas.

Range
Extreme S. California, S. Arizona, and Hidalgo County, New
Mexico.

Comments
It feeds on the seeds of various green plants and also carries
some seeds in its cheek pouches back to its burrow as reserves
for winter. It does not hibernate.

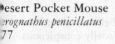

esert Pocket Mouse
erognathus penicillatus
77

6⅜–8½" (16.2–21.6 cm) long. Rough-haired. Yellowish
brown to yellowish gray above, interspersed with black hairs;
belly and underside of tail white. Long tail crested and tufted
No spines on rump. Soles of hind feet naked.

Habitat
Sandy deserts, among cactus or mesquite, especially along
stream beds or washes.

Range
S. California, extreme S. Nevada, S. and W. Arizona, S. Ne
Mexico, W. Texas.

Comments
During the heat of the day, the Desert Pocket Mouse closes i
burrow and retires within; like other pocket mice, it is active
at night. It feeds on weed and grass seeds, which it carries in
cheek pouches to be stored in side passages of its burrow.

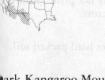
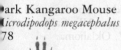

ark Kangaroo Mouse
icrodipodops megacephalus
78

5¾–7" (14.8–17.7 cm) long. Blackish or dark grayish abov
with hairs gray at base; white below. Tail thickest in middle
tapering at both ends, with black tip, no tuft. Incisors not
grooved. Soles of hind feet haired.

Tracks
Prints are almost round, slightly longer than wide, about ½'
long; forefeet usually print almost side by side, followed by
hind feet, also side by side. Trails may meander about colon'
area.

Habitat
Shadscale and sagebrush scrub.

Range
SE. Oregon, extreme NE. California, Nevada, NW. Utah.

Comments
This species apparently stores no food in its burrow. Report
to feed heavily on the black seeds of Desert Star (*Mentzelia*)
when available, it eats many other kinds of seeds as well.

Pale Kangaroo Mouse
Microdipodops pallidus
479

5⅞–6¾" (15–16.9 cm) long. Small. Light pinkish cinnamor above; hairs white to base on belly and underside of tail. Tail thickest in middle and lacking tuft, distinct markings, and black tip. Incisors not grooved. Soles of hind feet haired.

Habitat
Fine sand around scattered brush in deserts.

Range
W. Nevada and adjacent Mono and Inyo counties, California.

Comments
Burrows are 4–6' long, 1' deep; no food is stored in them, at least in summer. Various seeds and other vegetation form this species' diet. The "kangaroo" tail stores fat, which serves as a reserve energy source, and also helps maintain balance during jumps.

Ord's Kangaroo Rat
Dipodomys ordii
480

8⅛–11⅛" (20.8–28.2 cm) long. Buff above; white below. Long tail, usually not white-tipped. Usually conspicuous white spots at base of ears and above eyes. 5-toed. White tail stripes narrower than dark ones. Lower incisors round in fron

Tracks
When moving slowly, all 4 feet touch ground and heel of hir foot leaves a complete print about 1½" long, somewhat triangular, much wider at front than rear; foreprints much smaller, round, and between hindprints; when resting on ground, tail leaves a long drag mark; when hopping, heel of hind foot is off ground, so hindprints are shorter, little or no tail mark shows, and forefeet may or may not print. Width o straddle over 2". Trails radiate and crisscross.

Habitat
Sandy waste areas; sand dunes; sometimes hard packed soil.

Range
SE. Alberta, SW. Saskatchewan, S. Idaho, south-central Washington, E. Oregon south to extreme NE. California, Arizona, New Mexico, W. Texas, W. Oklahoma.

Comments
This species spends its days in deep burrows in the sand, which it plugs to maintain stable temperature and humidity. Extra holes serve as escape hatches.

Chisel-toothed Kangaroo Rat
Dipodomys microps
481

9⅝–11¾" (24.4–29.7 cm) long. Buff to dusky above; whitish below. Long tail with white side stripe narrower thar dark stripes. 5-toed. Lower incisors flat in front.

Habitat
Sagebrush and shadscale scrub, pinyon-juniper woodlands.

Range
SE. Oregon, SW. Idaho near Murphy, E. California, most of Nevada, W. Utah, extreme NW. Arizona.

Comments
A male drums on sand with its hind feet, evidently to attract a female and arouse her. Males fight over females, rolling in the sand, growling, and sometimes leaping high off the ground.

anamint Kangaroo Rat
ipodomys panamintinus
2

11¼–13⅛" (28.5–33.4 cm) long. Brownish gray above, cinnamon on sides; white below. Dark stripe on bottom of tail tapering to point near tip. Light cheek patches and white spot behind ear. 5-toed. Lower incisors rounded in front.

Habitat
Creosote bush scrub and pinyon-juniper woodlands.

Range
Extreme W. Nevada, south through scattered areas in S. California, and in S. Nevada near Searchlight.

Comments
Like other kangaroo rats, the Panamint has a prominent oil-secreting gland on its back; it regularly bathes in dust, which prevents its fur from becoming matted with excess oil.

anner-tailed Kangaroo
at
ipodomys spectabilis
3

12¼–14⅜" (31–36.5 cm) long. Dark buff above; white below. Long tail with narrow, white side stripes extending only two thirds its length and with a prominent white tip preceded by black band. 4-toed.

Habitat
Scrub or brush-covered slopes, often with creosote bush or acacias on hard or gravelly soil.

Range
SE. Arizona, most of New Mexico, W. Texas.

Comments
This kangaroo rat with its spectacularly white-tipped tail usually lives alone in its impressively mounded burrow system, which may have as many as a dozen openings.

esert Kangaroo Rat
ipodomys deserti
4

12–14¾" (30.5–37.7 cm) long. Yellowish buff above; white below. Tail crested, with tip white, sometimes with a short, dark red stripe on top only. No dark facial markings. 4-toed.

Habitat
Areas of soft sand, such as dunes; creosote bush or shadscale scrub.

Range
S. Nevada, S. California, SW. Arizona.

Comments
When excited, this species kicks sand and drums the ground with its large hind feet. It is abroad at night but keeps to its burrow when the moon is bright and predators could see it.

Merriam's Kangaroo Rat
Dipodomys merriami
485

8¾–10¼" (22–26 cm) long. Smallest kangaroo rat in United States. Light yellowish buff above; white below. Long tail with white side stripe wider than dark stripes and dusky tufted tip. Facial markings paler than in most species; dark line on either side of nose but not connected across it. 4-toed

Habitat
Sagebrush, shadscale, creosote bush desert scrubs, on a great variety of soil types.

Range
W. Nevada, S. California, SW. Utah, NW. and S. Arizona, S. New Mexico, W. Texas.

Comments
Merriam's Kangaroo Rats feed mostly on seeds, especially of mesquite, creosote bush, purslane, grama grass, and ocotillo.

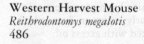

Western Harvest Mouse
Reithrodontomys megalotis
486

4½–6¾" (11.4–17 cm) long. Brownish above; buff along sides; white below. Grooved incisors.

Habitat
Early-stage dry weedy or grassy areas.

Range
Much of western United States and extreme southwestern Canada east to SW. Wisconsin, NW. Indiana, NE. Arkansas and W. Texas.

Comments
Although primarily a seed-eater, in spring this species also eats new growth and in summer consumes many insects, especially grasshoppers.

Fulvous Harvest Mouse
Reithrodontomys fulvescens
487

5¼–7⅞" (13.4–20 cm) long. Reddish brown interspersed with black above, shading to yellowish on sides; white below. Tail more than half total length. Feet reddish above.

Habitat
Grassy or weedy areas; arid inland valleys.

Range
SE. Arizona, SW. and E. Texas, E. Oklahoma, SE. Kansas, SW. Missouri, W. Arkansas, Louisiana and W. Mississippi.

Comments
In arid areas, these mice live in burrows; elsewhere they inhabit nests constructed up to 4' above ground. This species eats mostly seeds and the soft parts of green plants.

Southern Grasshopper Mouse
Onychomys torridus
488

4¾–6½" (11.9–16.3 cm) long. Stocky. Grayish or pinkish cinnamon above; white below. Tail white-tipped, thick, short, between one third and one half total length. Juveniles gray.

Habitat
Low deserts with creosote bush, mesquite, and yucca.

Range
S. California, S. Nevada, extreme SW. Utah, W. and S. Arizona, S. New Mexico, and W. Texas.

Comments
The Southern Grasshopper Mouse digs its own burrows or appropriates those of other small mammals. Its home range, up to 8 acres for males, is unusually large for a small rodent. Grasshopper Mice have developed efficient strategies for dispatching prey: small mammals are killed by a bite through the back of the neck; before killing scorpions, the mouse immobilizes that arachnid's deadly tail.

Deer Mouse
Peromyscus maniculatus
489

4¾–8¾" (11.9–22.2 cm) long. Grayish to reddish brown above; white below; tail distinctly bicolored and short-haired. Woodland forms usually larger, with tail longer and feet larger than prairie form.

Tracks
In dust, hindprint ⅝" long, with 5 toes printing; foreprint ¼" long and wide, with 4 toes printing; straddle 1⅜", with foreprints printing behind and between hindprints. In mud, foreprints and hindprints each approximately ⁵⁄₁₆" wide; straddle 1½".

Habitat
Prairies, brushy areas including scrub deserts; woodlands.

Range
Mexico to S. Yukon and Northwest Territories; in the East, Hudson Bay to Pennsylvania, the southern Appalachians, central Arkansas, and central Texas.

Comments
Deer Mice occur in a great variety of habitats in deserts, and are often among the most abundant mouse species. They have broad tastes in food, eating both plant and animal matter, and are very adaptable to local conditions.

Brush Mouse
Peromyscus boylii
490

7⅛–9⅜" (18–23.8 cm) long. Brownish or grayish above to buff or tawny on sides; white below. Tail distinctly bicolored, hairy, equal to or longer than head and body. Ankles dusky. Large ears.

Habitat
Arid to semiarid brushlands, especially rocky areas.

Range
California, S. and extreme W. Nevada, Utah, SW. Colorado, Arizona, New Mexico, W. Texas, Oklahoma, NW. Arkansas, and SW. Missouri.

Comments
A skilled climber, this mouse often runs up trees to avoid predators. Foods include conifer seeds, acorns, and insects. It also eats cactus fruits extensively when in season.

Northern Grasshopper Mouse
Onychomys leucogaster
491

5⅛–7½″ (13–19 cm) long. Heavy-bodied. 2 color phases above: grayish or cinnamon-buff; white below. Short, thick, bicolored tail with white tip, usually less than one third total length. Juveniles dark gray.

Tracks
In mud or dust, foreprints and hindprints overlap partially or completely, each about ⅝″ long, ½″ wide, with hindprints sometimes slightly longer; straddle 1¼″.

Habitat
Low valleys; deserts; prairies.

Range
SE. Washington, S. Alberta and SW. Manitoba south to NE. California, E. Arizona, and W. Texas.

Comments
As their name suggests, they feed heavily on grasshoppers, but they also eat other insects, scorpions, mice, and a small amount of plant material. Grasshopper Mice either dig burrows or take over those abandoned by other animals. They maintain a complex system of burrows throughout their rather large territories, and give several calls.

Cactus Mouse
Peromyscus eremicus
492

6¾–8⅝″ (16.9–21.8 cm) long. Pale gray above; white below. Tail sparsely haired, indistinctly bicolored, longer than head and body. Ears nearly hairless.

Habitat
Rocky outcroppings with cactus or yucca stands.

Range
S. California, extreme S. Nevada, extreme SW. Utah, Arizona, S. New Mexico, and SW. Texas.

Comments
Well adapted to desert living, the Cactus Mouse tolerates higher temperatures and needs less water than most other North American *Peromyscus* species. It may nest in clumps of cactus, among rocks, or in the abandoned burrows of other animals.

Desert Woodrat
Neotoma lepida
493

8¾–15⅛″ (22.5–38.3 cm) long. Buff-gray above; grayish below, often washed with buff. Tail similarly bicolored. Hind feet white. All hairs gray at base.

Habitat
Deserts; pinyon-juniper areas.

Range
SE. Oregon, SW. Idaho, Nevada, Utah and S. and extreme NE. California.

Comments
The Desert Woodrat often appropriates an old burrow of a ground squirrel or kangaroo rat, fortifying the entrance with a

house of sticks and cactus spines. This species is adept at moving about among spiny cacti without injuring itself. It eats spiny cacti, yucca pods, bark, berries, pinyon nuts, seeds, and any available green vegetation, metabolizing its water from the succulent vegetation.

White-throated Woodrat
Neotoma albigula
494

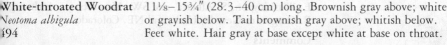

11⅛–15¾" (28.3–40 cm) long. Brownish gray above; white or grayish below. Tail brownish gray above; whitish below. Feet white. Hair gray at base except white at base on throat.

Tracks
In mud, hindprint ¾" long, with 5 toes printing; foreprint ½" long with 4 toes printing. Hindprints ahead of foreprints; distance between individual walking prints, approximately 1¼–3".

Habitat
Brushlands of southwestern dry plains and deserts.

Range
Extreme SE. California east to W. Texas, but extending north into SE. Utah and S. Colorado.

Comments
The White-throated Woodrat generally chooses the base of a prickly pear or cholla cactus as the site for its house; however, if vegetation is scarce, it will build in rocky crevices and sometimes add an underground chamber. It is skilled at climbing spiny cacti and uses the needles to help cover the entrance to its houses.

House Mouse
Mus musculus
495

5⅛–7¾" (13–19.8 cm) long. Grayish brown above; nearly as dark below. Long tail dusky above and below, nearly naked. Ungrooved incisors.

Habitat
Buildings; areas with good ground cover, including cultivated fields. Uncommon in undisturbed or natural habitats.

Range
Throughout United States and southwestern Canada north to central British Columbia, and along Pacific to Alaska.

Comments
When they occur in great numbers, mice, though generally timid, have been known to bite people and even to run over them. In cultivated fields, they feed heavily on weed seeds, but they are entirely destructive indoors, eating and contaminating grain and other valuable foodstuffs. They chew or shred furniture and wires, sometimes starting fires; gnaw holes in walls, floors, and baseboards; and, like other rodents, spread disease.

Sagebrush Vole
Lagurus curtatus
496

4¼–5⅝" (10.8–14.2 cm) long. Pale gray above; whitish to silvery or buff below and on feet. Bicolored, well-furred tail usually less than 1" (2.5 cm) long. Ears and nose buff.

Habitat
Sagebrush and grass-sage communities.

Range
E. Washington, S. Alberta, and SW. Manitoba south through E. Oregon to Nevada, Utah, and NE. Colorado.

Comments
These voles are usually found in colonies, which vary greatly in size and density from year to year. They feed on grass heads and other green plants in summer, bark and twigs of sage and various roots in winter. It does not store food.

Least Chipmunk
Eutamias minimus
497

6⅝–8⅞" (16.7–22.5 cm) long. Small. Color varies: in drier regions, muted yellowish gray above with tan dark stripes; in moister areas, brownish gray with black side stripes. Stripes continue to base of tail. Sides orange-brown; belly grayish white. Long tail light brown above, yellowish below, with hairs black-tipped. Ears tawny in front.

Habitat
Sagebrush deserts; pastures; piney woods; rocky cliffs; often abundant in open coniferous forests.

Range
Most of southern Canada from Ontario to S. Yukon; W. North Dakota to New Mexico, NW. California, and SE. Washington.

Comments
Lightest in color of all the western chipmunks, it often lives in the most desertlike habitats and generally enters hibernation rather late. Seeds, fruits, berries, and grasses are its main foods but it also eats fungi, invertebrates, and (rarely) small vertebrates.

Harris' Antelope Squirrel
Ammospermophilus harrisii
498

8¾–9¾" (22–25 cm) long. Upperparts pinkish buff in summer, gray in winter; underparts white. A single white stripe on sides. Tail mixed black and white below. Ears small.

Habitat
Low deserts with little vegetation.

Range
S. and W. Arizona, extreme SW. New Mexico.

Comments
Like the White-tailed Antelope Squirrel, the Harris' has pale coloration, helping it blend with its arid environment. Like many desert mammals, it metabolizes its water from food.

White-tailed Antelope Squirrel
Ammospermophilus leucurus
499

7⅝–9⅜″ (19.4–23.9 cm) long. Upperparts buff in summer, gray in winter; underparts white. 1 narrow white stripe on each side. Underside of tail clear white with black-tipped hairs forming narrow black border. Ears small.

Habitat
Deserts, foothills; hard gravelly surfaces.

Range
SW. Idaho, SE. Oregon, Nevada, Utah, W. Colorado, S. California, N. Arizona, NW. New Mexico.

Comments
Like the other antelope squirrels, the White-tailed runs fast with its tail held over the back, exposing white underparts. It usually lives in burrows but also in rock crevices and sometimes in abandoned burrows of other animals. Usually foraging on the ground, but sometimes in yucca or cactus, it eats seeds and fruit. It hibernates in northern parts of its range.

Texas Antelope Squirrel
Ammospermophilus interpres
500

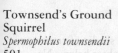

8⅔–9¼″ (22.0–23.5 cm) long. Chipmunklike. White stripes on either side of back from shoulder to base of tail. Underside of tail white. Ears short. Hairs on tail have 2 black bands.

Habitat
Rocky foothills from desert to low-elevation woodlands.

Range
South-central New Mexico, Big Bend of Texas into Mexico.

Comments
This squirrel is most common at middle elevations. It generally has dens at bases of large rocks or boulders. Active throughout the year, it feeds on seeds or fruits.

Townsend's Ground Squirrel
Spermophilus townsendii
501

6⅝–10¾″ (16.7–27.1 cm) long. Plain gray above, tinged pinkish; belly whitish or buff. Short tail reddish or tawny below, with white edge. Face and hind legs reddish.

Habitat
Open sagebrush.

Range
South-central Washington, E. Oregon, extreme NE. and SW. California, most of Nevada, W. Utah, S. Idaho.

Comments
These ground squirrels sometimes form large colonies, yet they are not very social. Each adult digs two burrows—a small one in the feeding area, evidently used as an escape hatch, and a much bigger home burrow, 50′ long or more and up to 6′ deep. It is inactive from June or July through winter. Seeds of green plants and green plant parts are favored foods.

Mexican Ground Squirrel
Spermophilus mexicanus
502

11–15″ (28–38 cm) long. Brown, with about 9 rows of squarish white spots on back; belly whitish or buff. Long, bushy tail. Small rounded ears. Males larger than females.

Habitat
Brushy or grassy areas, or mesquite or cactus deserts, usually on sand or gravel.

Range
SE. New Mexico, SW. Texas.

Comments
This somewhat colonial ground squirrel hibernates in winter in the cooler parts of its range. Each squirrel has several burrows: a home burrow, usually with 2 entrances, in which the young are born in the deepest part of a side tunnel, and 2 or more secondary refuges. It feeds primarily on green vegetation in spring, later on insects and often on dead animals.

Spotted Ground Squirrel
Spermophilus spilosoma
503

7¼–10″ (18.5–25.3 cm) long. Grayish or brownish above, with small, squarish indistinct light spots scattered on back; whitish below. Rather scantily haired tail similar to back, with black tip; buff below. Ears small.

Habitat
Dry sandy areas especially; also grassy areas and pine woods.

Range
SW. South Dakota south to W. Texas, New Mexico, Arizona.

Comments
Active in the morning and late afternoon, in the heat of the day it often retires to its burrow. In southern parts of its range it is active all year but may hibernate farther north. Green vegetation and seeds are primary foods.

Round-tailed Ground Squirrel
Spermophilus tereticaudus
504

8–10½″ (20.4–26.6 cm) long. Various shades of cinnamon with drab grayish cast above; slightly lighter below. No stripes or mottling. Round tail long, slender, not bushy; cinnamon or drab below.

Habitat
Flat sandy desert areas, creosote scrub.

Range
SE. California, S. Nevada, SW. Arizona.

Comments
To avoid the most intense heat, it is most active mornings and evenings. Seeds, other plant parts, and insects are chief foods. It hibernates from late September or early October to early January; in some areas it is active all year.

Rock Squirrel
Spermophilus variegatus
505, 506

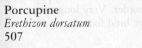

16⅞–20¾″ (43–52.5 cm) long. Largest ground squirrel in its range. Mottled above, grayish brown in front, brownish behind: buff-white or pinkish buff below. Long bushy tail variegated buff and brown with white edges.

Habitat
Open rocky areas; oak-juniper growth in canyons.

Range
S. Nevada, Utah, Colorado, panhandle of Oklahoma, W. Texas, Arizona, New Mexico.

Comments
Active in early morning and late afternoon. In the north it hibernates, but only for short periods, and is often abroad during winter warm spells; in the southern parts of its range it is active all year.

Porcupine
Erethizon dorsatum
507

25½–36½″ (64.8–93 cm) long. Large, chunky body with high-arching back, short legs. Long guard hairs in front half of body; yellowish in the West. Quills on rump and tail. Feet have unique soles with small, pebbly textured fleshy knobs and long curved claws; 4 toes on forefeet, 5 toes on hind feet.

Tracks
Distinctive; toe in; pebbled knobs on soles leave stippled impression, long claws mark far ahead of oval main prints; foreprint, including claw marks, about 2½″ long, hindprint well over 3″ long, usually but not always printing ahead of foreprint. Stride is short and waddling, with prints 5–6″ apart; straddle up to 9″ wide. In snow, feet may drag or shuffle, connecting prints. Trail occasionally blurred, as if swept by a small broom when belly brushes ground and stiff heavy tail swishes from side to side in waddling walk.

Habitat
Woods.

Range
Most of Canada and western United States; in the East, south to New England, New York, and most of Pennsylvania, northern half of Michigan, and Wisconsin.

Comments
The solitary Porcupine is active year-round, though in bitter cold it may den up in a hole in a rocky bluff, sometimes with other Porcupines in the area. A strict vegetarian, in spring the Porcupine feeds on leaves, twigs, and green plants. In winter, it chews through the rough outer bark of various trees, including pines, fir, and hemlock to get at the inner bark on which it then mainly subsists. Although the Porcupine is usually found in forests, individuals wander widely, and have been observed in the Great Basin desert as well as in the Sonoran and Chihuahuan, often roaming among creosote bushes. Primarily nocturnal, it may also rest by day in a hollow tree or log, underground burrow, or treetop.

Desert Cottontail
Sylvilagus audubonii
508

13¾–16½″ (35–42 cm) long. Buff brown above; white below. Nape bright rust. Moderately long ears.

Habitat
Grassland to creosote brush and deserts.

Range
California to Texas, E. Montana and SW. North Dakota.

Comments
Unlike most cottontails, the Desert Cottontail seldom rests in shallow depressions but will readily climb sloping trees. In areas of sparse vegetation it occasionally rests in the burrows of other animals. Its chief foods are grasses, mesquite, and cactus.

Black-tailed Jack Rabbit
Lepus californicus
509

18–25″ (46–64 cm) long. Buffy gray or sandy above, peppered with black; white below. Tail has black stripe above, extending onto rump, with white border. Very long ears brownish with black tips. Very large hind foot.

Habitat
Barren areas and prairies, meadows, cultivated fields, also areas where vegetation exceeds height of 2′.

Range
Texas and California north to south-central Washington.

Comments
This most abundant and widespread jack is not really a rabbit but a hare, as its young are born well furred and with eyes open. By day, it generally rests in dense vegetation or in a shallow depression, or form, becoming active in late afternoon. In summer, it eats many kinds of plants, favoring alfalfa; in winter, it depends on woody and dried vegetation.

Antelope Jack Rabbit
Lepus alleni
510

21⅝–26⅛″ (55.3–67 cm) long. Grayish brown above; lower sides largely white. Face, throat, and ears brownish. Tail black above. Very long ears with no black on tips.

Habitat
Deserts.

Range
South-central Arizona and SW. New Mexico.

Comments
This jack rabbit's long ears play an important role in regulating body temperature: in hot weather, they stand erect, and their dilated blood vessels give off heat, thus cooling the jack; in cold weather, ears lay back close to the body, and blood vessels constrict to maintain body warmth. It feeds on various coarse grasses, prickly pear, mesquite, and cat's-claw.

Ringtail
Bassariscus astutus
511

24½–31⅞" (61.6–81.1 cm) long. Yellowish gray above; whitish buff below. Body catlike; face somewhat foxlike. Very long, bushy tail with 14–16 bands, alternately black and white, ending with black at tip; black bands do not meet on underside. Relatively large ears and eyes. White or pale eye ring. 5 toes on each foot; claws partially retractile.

Tracks
Unlike its relatives, the Ringtail leaves no long heel prints. Prints 1–2¾" long, 2" wide, catlike, with no noticeable differences between foreprints and hindprints. 5 toes on each foot, with no claws showing. Because habitat is usually dry and often rocky, tracks are not easily found.

Habitat
Various; most common in rocky situations, such as jumbles of boulders, canyons, talus slopes, rock piles; less common in wooded areas with hollow trees; sometimes about buildings.

Range
SW. Oregon, California, S. Nevada, southern two thirds of Utah, W. Colorado, and S. Kansas south through Arizona, New Mexico, Oklahoma, and Texas.

Comments
In a narrow den often padded with moss, grass, or leaves, the Ringtail, or Cacomistle, sleeps by day. By night it ambushes prey, then pounces, forcing the prey down with its paws and delivering a fatal bite to the neck. Its diet includes grasshoppers, crickets; small mammals, small birds; fruit, spiders, and frogs.

Raccoon
Procyon lotor
512

23¾–37⅜" (60.3–95 cm) long. Reddish brown above, with much black; grayish below. Distinguished by a bushy tail with 4–6 alternating black and brown or brownish-gray rings and a black mask outlined in white. Ears relatively small.

Tracks
Hindprint 3¼–4¼" long, much longer than wide; resembles a miniature human footprint with abnormally long toes. Foreprint much shorter, 3", almost as wide as long; claws show on all 5 toes. Tracks are large for animal's size because Raccoon is flat-footed, like bears and men. Stride 6–20", averaging 14". When walking, left hindfoot is almost beside right forefoot. When running, makes many short, lumbering bounds, bringing hindfeet down ahead of forefeet in a pattern like oversize squirrel tracks.

Habitat
Various, but most common along wooded streams; in deserts, occurs along water courses and in tree-lined areas; occasionally in dry areas with artificial water sources (such as cattle tanks).

Range
Southern Canada; most of United States except for portions of the Rocky Mountain states, central Nevada, and Utah.

Comments
Native only to the Americas, the Raccoon is nocturnal and solitary except when breeding or caring for its young. During particularly cold spells, the Raccoon may sleep for several days at a time but does not hibernate. It will eat almost anything.

Coati
Nasua nasua
513

33⅜–52¼" (85–134 cm) long. Grayish brown. Long, thin, somewhat indistinctly banded tail (6–7 bands). Long, pointed snout; white toward tip and around eye, sometimes with black or dark brown patches on upper part. Ears small; dark feet. Male twice as large as female.

Tracks
3" long, 2" wide, hind- and foreprints; all with 5 toes; claws show on foreprints only. Because not as plantigrade as the Raccoon, less of hind heel pad registers, and prints are shorter.

Habitat
Mountain forests, usually near water; rocky, wooded canyons.

Range
Southeastern quarter of Arizona, SW. New Mexico, Big Bend and Brownsville areas of S. Texas. Abundant in Huachuca, Patagonia, and Tumacacori mountains of SE. Arizona.

Comments
Active by day and gregarious, Coatis are conspicuous as they travel about in troupes of 4–25, usually females and their young. They hold their long tails high and nearly erect. The Coati spends its days foraging for food, which includes invertebrates and lizards; very fond of fruit, including that of the manzanita, a troupe may ignore customary foods and visit a fruit-bearing tree daily until it is stripped.

Badger
Taxidea taxus
514

20½–34¼" (52.1–87 cm) long. Flattish body, wider than high, with short, bowed legs. Shaggy coat grizzled gray to brown. White stripe from shoulder to pointed, slightly upturned snout. Short, bushy, yellowish tail; cheeks white with black patch; ears small; dark feet with large foreclaws. Males larger than females.

Tracks
Turn in sharply. Foreprint 2" wide (as long as wide even though little heel pad shows), longer when claw tips show; hindprint narrower than foreprint, 2" long. Gait variable, with hind foot printing before or behind forefoot. Stride 6–12"; straddle 5–7", wider in snow.

Habitat
Open plains, farmland, and sometimes edge of woods.

Range
Western United States east to E. Texas, Oklahoma, N. Missouri, N. Illinois, N. Indiana, N. Ohio, north to SE. British Columbia, Alberta, Manitoba, and S. Saskatchewan.

Comments
This powerful burrower has become nocturnal in areas where it encounters man, but otherwise it is often active by day. It feeds mainly on small mammals—especially ground squirrels, pocket gophers, rats, and mice—which it usually captures by digging out their burrows. Few animals will attack the Badger, because it is a formidable adversary: its thick fur, loose, tough hide, and heavy neck muscles protect it as it bites, claws, and exudes (not sprays) a skunklike musk.

triped Skunk
Mephitis mephitis
15

20½–31½" (52.2–80 cm) long. Black with 2 broad white stripes on back meeting in cap on head and shoulders; thin white stripe down center of face. Bushy black tail, often with white tip or fringe. Coloration varies from mostly black to mostly white. Males larger than females.

Tracks
Show 5 toes when clear, sometimes claws. Hindprints 1¼–2" long, less wide, broadest at front, more flat-footed; foreprints 1–1¾" long, slightly wider; stride 4–6" (because skunk shuffles and waddles, tracks are closer than in other mustelids, and fore- and hindprints usually do not overlap); when running, stride longer and hind feet print ahead of forefeet. Trail undulates slightly because of waddling walk.

Habitat
Deserts, woodlands, grassy plains, and suburbs.

Range
Most of United States; southern tier of Canadian provinces.

Comments
This skunk's anal glands hold about a tablespoon of a fetid, oily, musk, enough for 5 or 6 jets of spray—though 1 is usually enough. Striped skunks usually den in a burrow abandoned by another animal. They feed on a wide variety of vegetable matter: insects and grubs, small mammals, eggs of ground-nesting birds, and amphibians.

Hog-nosed Skunk
Conepatus mesoleucus
516

20¼–35¾" (51.3–90 cm) long. Top of head, back, and tail white; lower portions black. Long snout, naked on top, with broad nose pad. Foreclaws large. Males larger than females.

Tracks
Similar to Striped Skunk's but forefeet toeprints are longer, often longer than heel pad.

Habitat
Foothills, brushy areas.

Range
S. Arizona, SE. Colorado, much of New Mexico, and S. Texas.

Comments
Although primarily nocturnal like other skunks, in winter the Hog-nosed Skunk may forage by day. Its broad nose pad is an

adaptation for rooting up insects; vegetation, arachnids, reptiles, mollusks, and small mammals are also eaten. It dens in rocky crevices.

Bobcat
Felis rufus
517, 520

28–49⅜" (71–125 cm) long. Tawny (grayer in winter), with indistinct black spotting. Short, stubby tail with 2 or 3 black bars and black tip above; pale or white below. Upper legs have dark bars. Face has thin, black lines radiating onto broad cheek ruff. Ears slightly tufted. Males larger than females.

Tracks
Fore- and hindprints about same size, 2" long, slightly longer than wide, with 4 toes, no claw marks. If clearly outlined, heel pad distinguishes from canine print: dog's or Coyote's is lobed only at rear; Bobcat's is lobed at rear and concave at front, giving print scalloped front and rear edges. Trail very narrow, sometimes as if made by a 2-legged animal, because hindfeet are set on, close to, or overlapping foreprints; 9–13" between prints. This manner of walking may be an adaptation to stalking: hunting as it travels, cat can see where to place its forefeet noiselessly, then brings down hind feet on the same spots.

Habitat
Primarily scrubby country, broken forests, but adapts to swamps, farmlands, and arid lands if rocky or brushy.

Range
Spottily distributed from coast to coast from southern Canada into Mexico. Probably most plentiful in Far West, from Idaho, Utah, and Nevada to Pacific and from Washington to Baja California.

Comments
Found only in North America, where it is the most common wildcat, the Bobcat gets its name from its stubby, "bobbed," tail. It lies up by day in a rock cleft, thicket, or other hiding place. It preys mostly on the Snowshoe Hare and cottontails but also eats mice, squirrels, Porcupines, and cave bats. Its scream is piercing and when threatened, it utters a short, sudden, and resonant "cough-bark." It yowls loudest and most often during breeding season.

Mountain Lion
Felis concolor
518, 519

59⅛–108" (150–274 cm) long. Yellowish to tawny above; white overlaid with buff below. Unspotted. Long tail with black tip. Backs of ears and 2 whisker patches on upper lip dark. Head fairly small; ears small and rounded; feet large. Young buff with black spots.

Tracks
Prints quite round, usually with all 4 lower toes showing but no claw marks, as claws are retracted. Foreprint 3¼–4" long; hindprint slightly smaller. Lobed heel pad has single scalloped edge at front, double scalloped edge at rear. Tracks usually in

a fairly straight line, staggered in pairs, with hindfoot track
close to or overlapping forefoot track but seldom registering
precisely within it. Straddle 8–10″; length of stride 12–28″.
Longer gaps indicate bounding, when all feet come down close
together. In snow, prints slightly larger, sometimes blurred
by thicker winter fur, and elongated by foot drag marks; in
deep snow, tail may drag and leave trace between prints.

Habitat
Originally varied, now generally mountainous areas.

Range
British Columbia and S. Alberta south through W. Wyoming
to California and W. Texas. Also farther east.

Comments
The most widely distributed cat in the Americas, the
Mountain Lion is a solitary, strongly territorial hunting
species that requires isolated or undistured game-rich
wilderness; it has therefore declined or become extinct in
much of the habitat where it once thrived. Unlike most cats,
it may be active by day in undisturbed areas. It feeds
primarily on large mammals, preferring deer, but also eats
Coyotes, mice, Raccoons, birds, and even grasshoppers.
Sometimes it waits for passing game but more often travels
widely after prey; a male may cover up to 25 miles in 1 night.
It can outrun a deer, but only for short distances. The
bloodcurdling mating call has been likened to a scream. Also
called Puma and Cougar.

it Fox
ulpes macrotis
21

15–20″ (38–51 cm) long. Buffy gray above with buff along
sides and underside of tail. Tail tip is black. Ears large.

Tracks
Small, less than 1½″ long; prints may not show pads or claws
because of heavy hair on the feet.

Habitat
Deserts, grasslands, and montane areas with trees.

Range
SE. Oregon; SW. Idaho and Utah, south into Mexico. East to
central and SE. New Mexico, W. Texas.

Comments
This mostly nocturnal fox excavates its own den or enlarges
burrows of ground squirrels and kangaroo rats. Food includes
rodents, birds, and even scorpions. These alert and elusive
foxes can be quite irascible when trapped or cornered.

ay Fox
ocyon cinereoargenteus
2

31½–44¼″ (80–113 cm) long. Grizzled gray above, reddish
below and on back of head; throat white. Tail with black
"mane" on top and black tip; feet rusty. Prominent ears.

Tracks
When in straight line, similar to those of a very large

domestic cat, except that nonretractile claws may show. Foreprint about 1¼–1⅞" long, 1⅜–1½" wide; hindprint as long, slightly narrower; 4 toes with claws. Pad marks set apart from one another. On fairly hard ground, hind heel pad leaves only a round dot if side portions fail to print. A fox digs in when running, leaving claw marks even in hard ground where pads do not print.

Habitat
Varied, but associated often with wooded and brushy habitats.

Range
E. North and South Dakota, Nebraska, Kansas, Oklahoma, most of Texas, New Mexico, Arizona and California, north through Colorado, S. Utah, S. Nevada, and W. Oregon; eastern United States.

Comments
Although primarily nocturnal, the Gray Fox is sometimes seen foraging by day in brush, thick foliage, or timber. The only American canid with true climbing ability, it occasionally forages in trees and frequently takes refuge in them, especially in leaning or thickly branched ones. Favored den sites include woodlands and among boulders on the slopes of rocky ridges.

Coyote
Canis latrans
523, 524

41⅜–52" (105–132 cm) long. Grizzled gray or reddish gray with buff underparts; long, rusty or yellowish legs with dark vertical line on lower foreleg; bushy tail with black tip. Nose pad to 1" (25 mm) wide. Ears prominent.

Tracks
Similar to dog's, but in a nearly straight line; 4 toes, all with claws; foreprint about 2½" long, slightly narrower; hindprint slightly smaller; stride 13" when walking, 24" when trotting, 30" or more when running, often with much wider gaps signifying leaps. Tracks and scat most often seen where runways intersect or on a hillock or open spot, vantage points where Coyotes linger to watch for prey.

Habitat
In the West, open plains.

Range
E. Alaska, northern and western Canada, all of western United States east to at least New England, N. New York, New Jersey, Ohio, Tennessee, and Louisiana.

Comments
The best runner among the canids, the Coyote can leap 14' and cruises normally at 25–30 mph and up to 40 mph for short distances. Tagged Coyotes have been known to travel great distances, up to 400 miles. The Coyote runs with its tail down, unlike wolves, which run with tail horizontal. Vocalizations are varied, but the most distinctive are given at dusk, dawn, or during the night and consist of a series of barks and yelps followed by a prolonged howl.

ollared Peccary
icotyles tajacu
25

34¼–40″ (87–102 cm) long. Piglike. Grizzled grayish or blackish above and below, with yellowish tinge on cheeks and whitish to yellowish irregular collar from shoulder to shoulder. Heavy, bristly hair from head to back can be erected into a mane. Inconspicuous tail; piglike snout; tusks (canines) nearly straight. 4 toes on forefeet, 3 on hind feet; all feet with 2 hooves. Young brownish with a black stripe down back.

Tracks
Similar to pig's but smaller. Cloven hooves are rounded oblongs, generally about 1–1½″ long, with hindprint slightly smaller than foreprint. Stride, short, usually 6–10″ between pairs of overlapping fore- and hindprints.

Habitat
Brushy deserts, rocky canyons, wastelands.

Range
SE. Arizona, extreme SE. and SW. New Mexico, central and S. Texas.

Comments
Active mainly in the early morning and late afternoon, the Peccary often beds down in a hole rooted in the earth or takes shelter in a cave during the midday heat. Peccaries travel in herds of 6–30, grunting softly while feeding. A Peccary's alarm call is a barking cough; it can squeal but does so only if terrified or injured. Peccaries prefer cactus, particularly prickly pear, which provides water as well as food; they devour even the spines. Mesquite fruit, sotol, and lechuguilla are some succulents they favor. They sometimes eat animal matter.

ighorn Sheep
vis canadensis
26

Rams: 5¼–6′ (160–185 cm) long. Ewes: 4¼–5¼′ (128–158 cm) long. Muscular body with thick neck. Color varying from dark brown above in northern mountains to pale tan in deserts; belly, rump patch, back of legs, muzzle, and eye patch white. Short, dark brown tail. Coat shed in patches June–July. Rams have massive brown horns that curve up and back over ears, then down, around, and up past cheeks in a C shape called a "curl." A 7- or 8-year-old may have a full curl, with tips level with horn bases; a few old rams exceed a full curl, but often horns are "broomed"—broken off near tips or deliberately rubbed off on rocks when they begin to block ram's peripheral vision. Ewes' horns are short, slender, never forming more than a half curl. Horn spread to 33″ (83 cm). Ewes much smaller than rams.

Tracks
Double-lobed prints, 3–3½″ long, with hindprints slightly smaller than foreprints; similar to deer's but with straighter edges—less pointed and often more splayed at front, less heart-shaped. When walking downhill on soft ground, dewclaws may print 2 dots behind hoofprint. Walking gait about 18″; bounding gait on level ground, 15′, down steep incline, 30′.

Habitat
Foothills near rocky cliffs near permanent water.

Range
S. British Columbia, SW. Alberta, Idaho, and Montana south
to SE. California, Arizona, and New Mexico.

Comments
Bighorns inhabit areas rarely disturbed by man. In the desert
of North America, 4 subspecies are grouped under the
common name of Desert Bighorn. These forms inhabit dry,
relatively barren desert mountain ranges. Bighorns are active
by day, feeding in early morning, midday, and evening, lying
down and chewing their cud at other times, and retiring to
bedding spots for the night. These may be used for years.

Pronghorn
Antilocapra americana
527

49¼–57⅛″ (125–145 cm) long. Medium-size; long-legged;
deerlike. Upper body and outside of legs pale tan or reddish
tan; sides, chest, belly, inner legs, and rump patch white. 2
broad white blazes across tan throat. Cheeks and lower jaw
usually white. Buck has broad, black band from eyes down
snout to black nose and black neck patch. Horns black: bucks
12–20″ (30–50 cm) long when full grown, lyre-shaped,
curving back and slightly inward near conical tips, each with
1 broad, short prong jutting forward and slightly upward
usually about halfway from base; does' seldom more than 3–4
(7.5–10 cm) long, usually without prongs. Short erectile
mane, about 2¾–4″ (7–10 cm) long.

Tracks
Shaped like split hearts about 3″ long; hindprints slightly
shorter than foreprints. Tracking usually relatively
unimportant for field observer since Pronghorn inhabits open
terrain and can often be seen at a great distance.

Habitat
Grasslands; grassland-brushlands; bunch grass-sagebrush areas

Range
S. Saskatchewan south to California, Arizona, New Mexico,
and W. Texas.

Comments
The fastest animal in the Western Hemisphere and among the
fastest in the world, the Pronghorn, making 20′ bounds, has
been clocked at 70 mph for 3–4 minutes at a time. Speeds of
45 mph are not unusual, and 30 mph is an easy cruising
speed. Active night and day, it alternates snatches of sleep
with watchful feeding. Because it inhabits open terrain, it
relies for safety on sight and speed; protruding eyes can detect
movement 4 miles away. In summer, it grazes on a number of
plants, including grasses, various forbs, and cacti; in winter,
it browses, favoring sagebrush.

Iule Deer
docoileus hemionus
28

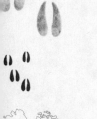

3¾–6½' (116–199 cm) long. Stocky body with sturdy legs. In summer, reddish brown or yellowish brown above; in winter, grayish above. Throat patch, rump patch, inside of ears, inside of legs white; lower parts cream to tan. Large ears, 4¾–6" (12–15 cm). Bucks' antlers branch equally, each a separate beam forking into 2 tines. Antler spread to 4' (120 cm). 2 major subspecies: Mule Deer with tail white above, tipped with black; Black-tailed Deer, with tail blackish or brown above. Males larger than females.

Tracks
Fore- and hindprints 3¼" long (males), 2⅜" long (females); walking stride 22–24". Distinctive bounding gait ("stotting"), with all 4 feet coming down together, forefeet printing ahead of hind feet.

Habitat
Mixed habitats, forest edges, mountains, and foothills.

Range
S. Yukon and Mackenzie south through western United States to Wisconsin and W. Texas.

Comments
These deer have large ears that move independently and almost constantly and account for the common name. Primarily active in mornings, evenings, and on moonlit nights, deer may also be active at midday in winter. Summer forage is chiefly herbaceous plants but also blackberry, salal, and thimbleberry; winter browse includes twigs of Douglas-fir, cedar, yew, aspen, willow, and dogwood. Deer in mountainous areas migrate up and down seasonally to avoid heavy snows. They seldom form large herds.

BIRDS

Numerous birds—large and small, silent and noisy—find a suitable home in the American deserts. Birds of prey are adapted to hunt in the open country, while other species search for insects in the rocky canyons or lead a secretive existence among the thorny desert shrubs. Tiny, brightly colored hummingbirds seek out red flowers to take nectar, while the inconspicuous nightjars perch lengthwise on the ground, camouflaged against the rocky landscape. This section describes many typical desert birds.

Black Vulture
Coragyps atratus
29

23–27″ (58–69 cm). Wingspan 54–60″ (1.4–1.5 m). Smaller than the Turkey Vulture. Black, with broad wings in flight showing a whitish "window" near the tip. Black face is naked but is enveloped in a feathered "hood." In flight its short, square tail usually does not seem as long as its legs.

Voice
Generally silent. Croaking or hissing notes when annoyed.

Habitat
Similar to that of the Turkey Vulture's open, broken country.

Range
Southeastern and, sporadically, southwestern United States and south to South America. Can be locally common in areas such as Organ Pipe Cactus National Monument.

Comments
These vultures soar, often in numbers high in the skies, until one of them discovers carrion, whereupon all converge on it. It soars in short spurts that alternate with short glides.

Turkey Vulture
Cathartes aura
30

26–32″ (66–81 cm). Wingspan 72″ (1.8 m). One of America's largest birds of prey. Brown-black overall; with unfeathered red head (dark in young); yellow feet. In flight, conspicuously short-necked; broad wings appear two-toned with dark gray flight feathers looking lighter than black wing linings. Wings in flight are held at a slight V angle, or dihedral, often with primaries separated.

Voice
Rarely gives a soft hiss or groan, but generally silent.

Habitat
Dry open country or along roadsides, where it forages for carrion.

Range
Common from southern Canada throughout North America. Also widespread through Central and South America. In the West, winters in California (locally), and S. Arizona.

Comments
Vultures are often called buzzards, a Western misnomer originally applied to Buteo hawks in the Old World.

Northern Harrier
Circus cyaneus
31

17½–24″ (45–61 cm). Slim, with long wings, tail, and legs. Male is light gray above, white underparts with reddish spotting; in flight, black wing tips and barred tail. Female is brown above with some brown streaks below. Both sexes have white rump. Immature is brown above, cinnamon below. Slow, hesitant flight and intermittent, tilting glide on wings held in a shallow "V" are characteristic.

Voice
Generally silent. It may utter a short chatter around the nest.

Habitat
Marshes, meadows, and fields; in deserts, often seen hunting over sagebrush stands.

Range
Throughout North America, excluding the southeastern seaboard and the South. Winters mainly in western, central, and southern United States.

Comments
"Harriers," the old English name of these hawks, are specialized mousers in tall vegetation; their owl-like disk-shaped face mask directs the squeaks of field mice to their sensitive ears. They surprise small waterfowl or the young of other birds among the reeds.

Cooper's Hawk
Accipiter cooperii
532

14–20″ (36–51 cm). Medium-sized hawk. Rounded (not square) tail and slower wingbeat. Male slate blue above, barred rusty below, female larger and brownish blue above. Immatures brown above, streaked with brown below.

Voice
A rapid series: *kek kek kek kek kek.*

Habitat
Woodlands, forest edges, river groves, and even wooded city areas. May nest along desert watercourses.

Range
Widespread from southern Canada to northern Mexico; winters as far south as Costa Rica.

Comments
This still is a relatively common bird of prey in most parts of the West. A fast and powerful flier, this hawk hunts by flying low over trees, traveling short distances at a time, and using the terrain to hide. It feeds on small birds and mammals.

Harris' Hawk
Parabuteo unicinctus
533

17½–29″ (44–74 cm). Wingspan 42–45″ (1–1.1 m). Slim, medium-sized hawk. Dark, with chestnut shoulder, wing linings, and thighs (hence sometimes called "Bay-winged Hawk"). Long tail is black with white terminal band and flashy white tail coverts, and in flight appears white with broad black band. Juveniles paler and streaked below.

Voice
Call is a harsh squeal.

Habitat
Mesquite shrub and desert areas; requires trees for nesting and prefers those in woods in river bottoms.

Range
A tropical or semitropical hawk, widespread from the border areas of the United States (the lower Colorado River Valley of California east to S. Texas) south to Chile and Argentina.

Comments
During incubation and brooding, the male, which is smaller than the female, supplies the whole family with food.

Swainson's Hawk
Buteo swainsoni
534, 535

19–22″ (48–56 cm). Wingspan 48–56″ (1.2–1.4 m). Medium-sized buteo. Dark brown above, white throat and body accentuated by a dark biblike band across breast. Darker gray flight feathers highlight whitish wing linings. Tail gray above, light below with dark border; terminal band has white trailing edge. In the dark phase, body and wings dark.

Voice
Like many other large raptors, usually silent. Around the nest it may give a downslurred whistle.

Habitat
Plains, prairies, dry meadows with few trees, and tundra.

Range
Commonest hawk of Canadian prairies. Breeds from Alaska south to the Mexican Plateau. Winters mainly in Argentina.

Comments
This hawk has a slightly dihedral or V-angled gliding pattern when soaring on thermal air currents. It perches near the ground and feeds mainly on rodents when available; otherwise it takes grasshoppers and locusts. In migration it forms huge flocks of several thousand individuals en route to South America.

Red-tailed Hawk
Buteo jamaicensis
536, 537

19–25″ (48–64 cm). Wingspan 48–51″ (1.2–1.4 m). Large hawk. Dark brown above, most typically light below with a dark belly band. Rufous tail has a narrow dark band and light tip. Finely streaked grayish tail of immature is often light at base. Plumage variation includes several color phases.

Voice
A loud, harsh downslurred scream, often quite prolonged *kee-ahrrr*.

Habitat
A variety of habitats from tundra to semidesert, wherever there are open hunting areas with nearby woodlands.

Range
North and Central America.

Comments
Commonly sighted at roadsides, perching atop telephone poles, haystacks, or fence posts, this hawk may sit for hours, then suddenly glide off to surprise a ground squirrel, lizard, or other ground-dwelling prey. At mating time it soars high in the air with conspicuous flight displays and cries.

Ferruginous Hawk
Buteo regalis
538

22½–25″ (57–64 cm). Wingspan 56″ (1.4 m). Largest buteo. Light phase: rufous above, whitish below, with rufous wrist patch and leg feathers. Black primary tips. Dark phase (rare): deep rufous above and below. Whitish tail. Legs feathered down to talons. Immatures resemble light-phase adults but lack rufous markings.

Voice
A loud, descending *kre-ah;* gull-like *krag* notes.

Habitat
Prairies, brushy open country, badlands.

Range
Nests from the Canadian prairie provinces south to Oregon, Nevada, Arizona, and Oklahoma. Winters in southern half of breeding range and southwestern states.

Comments
These hawks lay more eggs when prey abounds, fewer in years when rodent populations decrease. They feed mainly on prairie dogs and ground squirrels, less regularly on locusts, Jerusalem crickets, and birds.

Rough-legged Hawk
Buteo lagopus
539

19–24″ (48–61 cm). Wingspan 48–54″ (1.2–1.4 m). Large hawk. Legs feathered to talons. In light phase, has buffy head, chest, and leg feathers with dark streaking; broad black belly band, wrist patch, and broad terminal tail band edged with white. Primary tips and trailing edge of wing are black. In dark phase (rare), head, body, and underwing coverts dark; white flight feathers with dark edge; dark tail band.

Voice
Silent on wintering grounds. At the nest it may give a squeal.

Habitat
Nests in upland tundra; in winter, open plains or marshes with elevated lookout posts.

Range
Circumpolar. Winters in southern Canadian provinces south to S. California (uncommon), Arizona, and Texas and to central states in the East. Migrant and winter visitor to Great Basin.

Comments
Hovers above its prey like a Kestrel. Lemmings and ptarmigans are its main sources of food on its breeding grounds; on its wintering grounds, it takes larger rodents and upland birds. In snowy areas it is usually the only large buteo, with the exception of a few Red-tailed Hawks.

Golden Eagle
Aquila chrysaetos
540

30–41″ (76–104 cm). Wingspan 76–92″ (2–2.4 m). Shaped like a hawk but when soaring its wingspan is much greater; bill also larger, and the "eagle look" of the eye seems more pronounced because of the deep socket. Adult dark brown overall with golden to tan nape (visible only at close range).

Legs feathered to talons. Immatures in flight show large white
wing patch at base of primaries and white tail with dark
terminal band.

Voice
Rarely heard: soft mewing or yelping notes, a high squeal.

Habitat
Remote rangeland, alpine tundra, mountainous badlands, and
canyons.

Range
Mountains and rangeland of the West, from Alaska to Mexico;
rare in Northeast. Northern populations migratory.

Comments
These majestic birds are common in many places in the West.
They feed mainly on rabbits and large rodents, and sometimes
scavenge dead lambs. The damage attributed to eagles by
sheep herders, however, has been exaggerated.

Crested Caracara
Polyborus plancus
541

20–25″ (51–64 cm). Wingspan 48″ (122 cm). A long-legged
hawk often seen on ground. Dark above and below, with black
cap, white face, neck, and brown-barred breast. Facial skin
red. In flight, appears long-necked and long-tailed, with
conspicuous white head, wing patches, and base of tail.
Immatures browner.

Voice
Generally silent except for a cackling cry, from which its name
is derived.

Habitat
Open or semi-open country, brushland, seashore, plantations
with scattered tall trees, desert scrub; perches on tall cactus.

Range
Tropical; reaches Arizona, Texas, and Florida.

Comments
An omnivorous raptor, the Caracara feeds on small vertebrates
as well as carrion. This bird, magnificent in flight, is the
"Mexican eagle" of the flag of Mexico.

American Kestrel
Falco sparverius
542

9–12″ (23–30 cm). Wingspan 22¼–23½″ (57–60 cm).
Smallest North American falcon. Male has rufous crown, back,
and tail; blue-gray wings and head; buff breast and nape;
white underparts with side spotting. Black markings behind
ear; black mustache and terminal tail band. The lateral ear
markings are said to resemble eyes as seen from above by large
hawks. Female's head resembles that of male but back and
wings are darker rufous overall with heavier streaking below.

Voice
A loud, rapid *killy-killy-killy-killy.* Among the most vocal of
birds of prey.

Habitat
Partly open country, farmland, forest edges, and cities.

Range
Throughout the Americas. From Alaska to Tierra del Fuego.
Winters throughout range; northern birds are migratory.

Comments
This small falcon is commonly seen at roadsides, where it
perches atop telephone poles and trees. It often hovers in the
air before swooping on its prey. It feeds mainly on grasshoppers
and small rodents. Formerly known as the "Sparrow Hawk."

Aplomado Falcon
Falco femoralis
543

15–18″ (38–46 cm). Medium-sized falcon. Adult bluish gray
above, with striking striped head. Black mustache and black
stripe behind each eye. Pale stripe over eye stretching to rusty
nape; white throat, buff breast, and black band on lower
breast. Russet thighs and belly not always visible. Tail black
with many white crossbars. Juvenile brown above, streaked on
breast, plain brown on flanks.

Voice
A rapid *gacking* cry quickly repeated, quite similar to the call
of other falcons of the same size. Also a shrill *eek, eek.*

Habitat
Open arid country, grassland, desert, and savanna.

Range
Formerly ranged from SE. Arizona to S. Texas south to
Patagonia. Extremely rare and sporadic in the border country,
although fairly common farther south. A few are found in
New Mexico.

Comments
This beautiful falcon strikes its small bird prey in the air,
where it also catches large flying insects. In behavior and
appearance it resembles a Kestrel more than a big falcon.

Chukar
Alectoris chukar
544

13–15½″ (33–39 cm). Round, stocky. Light brown back and
wings with gray-tinged cap, breast, and rump. White cheek
and throat framed by broad black band. Bold chestnut-and-
black diagonal striping on flanks, creamy white belly, and
bright rufous outer tail feathers. Bill and legs orange-red.
Sexes look alike.

Voice
A low, harsh, cackling *chuk-karr,* often repeated at length.

Habitat
Arid mountainous areas, canyons, and grassy slopes with rock
outcroppings.

Range
Mainly the Great Basin, from S. British Columbia south to
Baja California and east to Colorado.

Comments
The Chukar partridge was successfully introduced to the West from the "Mediterranean" dry belt of Eurasia. This hardy bird can outrun a hunter, first running uphill, then flying down. Its loud calls enliven desolate country.

age Grouse
entrocercus urophasianus
45

Male, 26–30" (66–76 cm); female, 22–23" (56–58 cm). Both sexes streaked gray above with a black belly. Male has a long pointed tail; black throat, white collar, and white breast flanked by elongated neck plumes. Female's head, back, and breast uniformly barred. In courtship display male's tail is fanned and tilted forward; white neck and breast are inflated by pair of naked yellowish-green air sacs.

Voice
When flushed, it may give a chickenlike *cluck cluck cluck*.

Habitat
Open country, plains, foothills, sagebrush semideserts.

Range
From S. British Columbia, Alberta, and Saskatchewan south to W. Colorado, Utah, Nevada, and E. California.

Comments
As its name suggests, this grouse feeds on sagebrush buds and leaves, where it also nests and hides. The males gather each spring on a traditional display ground, or lek, for the courtship ritual. After strutting with neck feathers raised and wings and tail spread, the male stops with breast inflated, making popping and burbling noises by inflating and deflating his air sacs. Females crisscross the male's territories, squatting before the mate of their choice.

caled Quail
allipepla squamata
46

10–12" (25–30 cm). White, cottony topknot; pale unstreaked gray head; bluish-gray feathers of breast and mantle have black semicircular edge, creating scaled effect; belly also has brown "scales"; white lines on flanks. Sexes look alike.

Voice
The call is often interpreted as a nasal *pay-cos, pay-cos*.

Habitat
Semideserts such as yucca flats, juniper hillocks, canyon bottoms.

Range
Chihuahuan Desert of Mexico; north to SE. Arizona, New Mexico, Utah, S. Colorado, and parts of Texas.

Comments
Though birds of arid habitat, Scaled Quails must visit water holes regularly. They nest in the rainy season, when moisture produces some vegetation, and do not breed during extremely dry summers.

Gambel's Quail
Callipepla gambelii
547

10–11½″ (25–29 cm). Principal American desert quail. Buffy white, unscaled belly with central black patch on male (black lacking in female) and chestnut on crown and flanks. Teardrop-shaped head plume in both sexes.

Voice
Loud, cackling calls, usually of 3 syllables, with second syllable accented and highest pitched.

Habitat
Desert thickets; arid country often near springs.

Range
Southwestern United States to northwestern Mexico; introduced on a small scale elsewhere.

Comments
An ingenious watering device has been invented to fill the main environmental need of these quail: a slanting metal roof open to the cool night air of the desert accumulates dew, which drips down into a trough, providing water by day.

California Quail
Callipepla californicus
548, 549

9–11″ (23–28 cm). Colorfully and intricately patterned. Small and plump with black forward-curving plume arising from chestnut crown. Creamy forehead and black throat. Crown and throat edged in white. Grayish-blue breast and softly mottled nape; unstreaked brown back and creamy belly scaled with brown markings. Creamy diagonal flank streaking. Female less boldly marked than male.

Voice
A loud, distinctive *ka ka kow,* the second note highest. Sometimes expressed as *chi-ca-go* or *who are you?* Often with 2-noted "warmup" phrases. Calls include loud *pit!* notes.

Habitat
Brush with open areas such as coastal or foothill chaparral and live-oak canyons; also adjacent desert and suburbs.

Range
Originally, both California and Baja California. Introduced to S. Vancouver Island, British Columbia; also found in S. Oregon and N. Nevada.

Comments
Perched on tree or fence post, the male claims his territory by cackling and posturing; the entire family takes to trees for roosting as well as for safety. After the breeding season, these birds become gregarious and gather in large coveys, often visiting city parks, gardens, and yards.

White-winged Dove
Zenaida asiatica
550

11–12½″ (28–32 cm). Length of Mourning Dove but tail is much shorter and body is larger. Drab brown body with a purplish sheen on crown, neck, and shoulder. Primaries charcoal gray; white upper wing coverts conspicuous in flight. Tail is rounded with white-tipped outer tail feathers.

Voice
A harsh cooing reminiscent of a crowing rooster; sometimes
represented as *who cooks for you-all?*

Habitat
Desert scrub and fields, cottonwoods along watercourses and
willow thickets, suburbs.

Range
S. California, Arizona, New Mexico, Texas to South America.

Comments
Many northern species of pigeons and doves are seed-eaters,
but tropical species feed primarily on fruit. The White-
winged Dove enjoys both: in the desert its main seasonal fruit
is that of cactus; elsewhere it also consumes berries.

Mourning Dove
Zenaida macroura
551

11–13″ (28–33 cm). Light brownish gray above, pale buffy
below; wings darker, with black spots along inside edge; light
blue eye-ring, large black spot at lower base of ear patch;
iridescent light violet neck shield. Very long central tail
feathers (shorter in female), with sharply tapered white-tipped
outer tail feathers.

Voice
Its name comes from the male's melancholy cooing, the last 3
notes lower than the first: *coo-ooh, coo, coo-coo.* It is uttered from
a prominent perch and followed by a courtship flight, which
begins with an upward arc and audible wing clapping and
ends in a glide with flamboyant tail display.

Habitat
Dry uplands, grain fields, suburban areas; deserts.

Range
Throughout temperate North America including Mexico but
not in montane and boreal forests. Migratory in the North.

Comments
The breeding season starts early—in March in California—
and continues to mid-September. Bird may nest 2 to 4 times
each year. Thus the Mourning Dove is easily able to maintain
its numbers even though it is hunted extensively.

Inca Dove
Columbina inca
552

7½–8″ (19–20 cm). Small pale dove somewhat larger than
Ground-Dove. Rufous primaries, long, narrow tail with white
sides; upperparts look scaled. At a distance it seems paler,
with less rust color showing than on Ground-Dove.

Voice
A monotonous *coo-hoo*, repeated; first note higher.

Habitat
Suburban gardens, city parks, ranches, fields.

Range
SE. California, S. Arizona, New Mexico, and Texas and south.

Comments
This tropical bird has become a city dweller, its spread made possible by watered "oases"—cities and suburbs.

Common Ground-Dove
Columbina passerina
553

6–6¾" (15–17 cm). A tiny dove. Short black tail and rufous primaries, most noticeable in flight. Light brown; adult male has blue crown; purplish on neck-shield area and shoulders, and is slightly scaled. Folded wings show big black spots.

Voice
Rapidly repeated *woo-oo,* the 2 syllables often blending.

Habitat
Mesquite, brushy areas, roadsides, edges of woods.

Range
Widespread in tropical America, extending into the border areas of the United States from S. California through S. Arizona and New Mexico east to the Gulf Coast, Florida, and South Carolina.

Comments
The Ground-Dove flies incredibly fast, with its short wings beating rapidly, almost like those of a quail. When it walks, it nods like a pigeon. It searches for seeds on the ground, but requires low brush for nesting and roosting.

Greater Roadrunner
Geococcyx californianus
554

20–24" (51–61 cm). A large, elongated terrestrial bird. Brown with green sheen, streaked with black and white above; buff below with brown streaks on breast; oversized heavy bill and crest; long graduated tail, which it occasionally flicks up; white-tipped outer tail feathers. Runs rapidly on strong feet; seldom flies.

Voice
"Song" is a mournful series of low cooing notes, dropping in pitch: *cooo cooo cooo cooo-ah coo-ah.*

Habitat
Chaparral, desert scrub, and other arid brush.

Range
Central Valley of California throughout the Southwest into the southern part of the prairie states, and south to Mexico.

Comments
Famous for its rather unusual behavior, the Roadrunner is a reticent bird that when surprised on a road runs rapidly away, vanishing into cover. It feeds on a wide variety of desert life including insects, scorpions, lizards, and snakes.

Common Barn-Owl
Tyto alba
555

14–20" (36–51 cm). Medium-sized owl. White, heart-shaped face ringed with tan; back light tan with fine pearl gray streaks; white below suffused with tan. Sits upright on long feathered legs.

Voice
A loud rasping hiss, quite unlike the typical hooting of owls. Also a clicking note and, when alarmed, a snapping of bill.

Habitat
Hunts in rodent-rich savanna, woodlands, farmlands, or suburbs; needs trees for perching.

Range
Cosmopolitan, it lives in tropical and temperate regions on all continents; absent from coniferous forests in the mountains.

Comments
In the glare of auto headlights, a flying Barn-Owl looks snow-white, often giving the impression that it is a Snowy Owl. Barn-Owls are effective mousers and take many rats.

reat Horned Owl
ubo virginianus
56

18–25″ (46–64 cm). Large owl. Ear tufts set wide apart, yellow eyes. Mottled gray-brown above with fine dark gray horizontal barring below.

Voice
A deeply resonant hooting, *hoo, hoo-hoo-hoo, hoo;* also 3 hoots.

Habitat
In all habitats, including deserts, as long as shelter such as woods or cliffs is close.

Range
Common in North America up to the northern tree limit.

Comments
This owl hunts rabbits, rodents, and birds, including crows, ducks, and other owls. On occasion, it even captures skunks. It is the largest and best known of the common owls.

erruginous Pygmy-Owl
laucidium brasilianum
57

6½–7″ (17–18 cm). A small, rust-colored owl. Especially characteristic is red, faintly cross-barred tail. Crown streaked with white, underside streaked with red-brown, and white-bordered black patch on sides of nape. Undulating flight.

Voice
Monotonous, repeated, harsh whistle, *poip,* and other whistles.

Habitat
Saguaro desert; mesquite or other streamside growth.

Range
Rare and local from S. Arizona and the lower Rio Grande of Texas to South America.

Comments
The male calls incessantly in spring at a rate of 90–150 times a minute (1 individual is reported to have called for 3 solid hours). This tiny tropical owl is rare and local in the United States, and the small population around Tucson, Arizona, is a great attraction to bird-watchers.

Elf Owl
Micrathene whitneyi
558

5–6" (13–15 cm). Smallest American owl, sparrow-sized. N
ear tufts; white eyebrows, yellow eyes; underparts faintly
streaked with buff. Short tail extending only to wing tips; ro
of white spots above shoulder.

Voice
The calls, high-pitched for an owl, consist of various whistles
and whinnies, most typically a downslurred *kew kew kew.*

Habitat
Southwestern saguaro deserts, arid scrub, and wooded canyon

Range
Breeds from SE. California to Texas, south to central Mexico

Comments
At night in the desert, this tiny nocturnal owl is most often
located by its tremulous call. It feeds on large insects.

Burrowing Owl
Athene cunicularia
559

9–11" (23–28 cm). Small owl of open country; no ear tufts;
generally earth-brown with white spots, whitish eyebrows an
throat interrupted by a dark collar. Long legs and short,
stubby tail. It stands upright whether perching or on ground

Voice
The alarm note is a cackle. Also a mellow rolling *coo-c-o-o.*

Habitat
Open country such as prairies, sagebrush flats, pinyon-junipe
slopes, and deserts with numerous rodent burrows.

Range
Throughout the West; also in Florida and the dry region of
South and Central America. Leaves colder areas in winter.

Comments
In urban areas the Burrowing Owl occurs at airports and
vacant lots where open spaces resemble those of its natural
habitat. When agitated, it frequently bobs and bows.

Lesser Nighthawk
Chordeiles acutipennis
560

8–9" (20–23 cm). Similar to but smaller than Common
Nighthawk. Mottled above and below with buff, brown, gray
and white; both sexes have buffy cast to underparts. Long,
pointed wings; tail long, notched, rectangular. White wing
patch (buff in female) two-thirds of the way between bend of
wing and wing tip (visible in flight). Male's throat white;
female's buffy. Whereas Common Nighthawk hunts and calls
from high up, Lesser Nighthawk flies low and utters no calls.

Voice
Call is a soft, sustained, tremolo whirring.

Habitat
Dry, open scrub; desert valleys; prairies and pastures.

Range
Southwestern United States (mainly S. California, Arizona,

parts of Nevada, Utah, New Mexico, and Texas) south to Brazil. Winters mainly south of the United States.

Comments
The Lesser is more nocturnal than the Common Nighthawk and it hunts its insect prey flying low above the canopy of trees or the brush and grass of open plains.

Common Nighthawk
Chordeiles minor
1

8½–10″ (22–25 cm). Robin-sized. Long notched tail and long pointed wings with broad white wing bar halfway between bend and tip. Mottled brownish black above and below, perfectly matching its surroundings. Male has white throat patch and white subterminal tail bar. Female has buffy throat patch and no tail bar.

Voice
A nasal call, *peent* or *spee-ik,* heard primarily at dusk. Courtship display involves aerial dives ending in a loud, vibrant buzz.

Habitat
Open woodlands, clearings, fields, towns with roosting trees or fence posts. While breeding elsewhere, they often hunt desert areas by night.

Range
Widespread in North America except for tundra and low deserts of the Southwest. Winters in subtropics.

Comments
This bird is found in a wide variety of habitats, including forests, meadows, sagebrush, and even cities.

Common Poorwill
Phalaenoptilus nuttallii
2

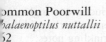

7–8½″ (18–22 cm). Smallest nightjar. Its mottled, gray-brown body serves as camouflage; no white mark on wings but whitish collar separates black throat from mottled underparts. Dark outer tail feathers are tipped with white, more conspicuously in male; tail is rounded.

Voice
On warm nights in the breeding season this bird reveals its presence by uttering a melancholy call, the first note lower than the second; this sounds like its name, *poor-will.* In flight it utters a low *wurt, wurt.*

Habitat
Desert, chaparral, sagebrush, and other arid uplands.

Range
Breeds from SE. British Columbia and Alberta south throughout the western United States. Winters in southern United States and Mexico.

Comments
The Poorwill has been discovered hibernating in the desert in California, surviving a long cold spell in torpid condition

without food and with its body temperature lowered almost
that of the environment.

Black-chinned Hummingbird
Archilochus alexandri
563

3¼–3¾" (8–10 cm). Small hummingbird. Male green abov
with black chin, underlined by violet-purple throat band.
Female green above with white throat and breast, buff sides,
and white-tipped outer tail feathers.

Voice
Calls are a low *tup* and a buzz. Male makes a dry buzz with
wings in flight.

Habitat
Mountain and alpine meadows, woodlands, canyons with
thickets, chaparral, mesquite thickets, and orchards.

Range
British Columbia south to Mexico and W. Texas; absent fror
humid northern Pacific Coast. Winters in Mexico.

Comments
The male Black-chinned, like all hummingbirds, maintains a
mating and feeding territory in spring. He courts his female
with a dazzling aerial display involving a pendulumlike fligh
pattern. When mating interest wanes, the male often takes u
residence elsewhere, near a good food supply.

Costa's Hummingbird
Calypte costae
564

3–3½" (8–9 cm). Tiny hummingbird. Male has violet-purpl
crown and gorget, which is flanked with very long,
conspicuous side feathers. Costa's habit of soaring between
flower clusters is helpful in distinguishing it.

Voice
In display, male's outer tail feathers produce a very high-
pitched whine, highest in pitch and intensity in the middle.
Call notes include a light *chip* and high tinkling notes.

Habitat
Low desert and, in California and Baja California, chaparral.

Range
Southwestern desert states extending south from central
California and S. Nevada to northwestern Mexico.

Comments
Hummingbirds feed on both insects and nectar, but they hav
a decided preference for red flowers. In southern and central
California, Costa's feeds extensively on the red beardtongue.
This bird is probably the plant's chief pollinator.

Gila Woodpecker
Melanerpes uropygialis
565

8–10" (20–25 cm). Medium-sized woodpecker; above, has
pattern of black and white checks, including upper tail
coverts. Head and underparts gray-brown. Male has small re
cap. Female and juvenile similar but lack red cap. White wir
patches are prominent in flight.

Voice
Has a vibrato call, a rolling *churrr,* as well as one like a barnyard hen.

Habitat
Low desert scrub with saguaro and mesquite trees for nesting; also farther south in tropical deciduous thorny bush and forest, often interspersed with organ-pipe cactus.

Range
From SE. California through the Sonoran Desert to central Mexico.

Comments
This bird is characteristic of the Sonoran Desert and nests in holes in giant saguaro cacti.

Golden-fronted Woodpecker
Melanerpes aurifrons
566

8½–10½″ (22–27 cm). Medium-sized. Back and wings have "zebra-backed" barring. Tail black. White rump and wing patch show in flight. Head and underparts pale buff; some yellow on belly. Yellow tuft of feathers above bill in both sexes; nape patch is bright orange in male and yellow-orange in female; male has bright red cap edged with gray. Juveniles lack head patches.

Voice
A rolling *churrrr,* similar to that of the other "zebra-backed" woodpeckers.

Habitat
A great variety, including stream woodlands, mesquite, flood-bed growth, thorn forest.

Range
Texas and Oklahoma south through Central America, where it is the most common woodpecker.

Comments
The range of this species lies between those of 2 very similar "zebra-backed" species, the Red-bellied and Gila woodpeckers. It hybridizes with the eastern Red-bellied in Texas. The Gila Woodpecker of the Sonoran Desert is isolated and adapted to the driest conditions.

Ladder-backed Woodpecker
Picoides scalaris
567

6–7½″ (15–19 cm). Zebra-backed woodpecker with small black ear patch and face stripe, usually separated from black of nape and back by white band. Male's with red cap. Best identified by voice and habitat.

Voice
A sharp *pik* call. During encounters with rivals it utters a harsh *jeee jeee jeee.*

Habitat
Deserts and their borders; also mesquite, pinyon-juniper woodland, and scrub oaks.

Range
S. California, Utah, and Colorado south to Baja California, northern Mexico; locally to Nicaragua.

Comments
This "agave woodpecker" lives in an unusual microcosm. After pollinating the century plant, the agave beetle lays eggs in the flower stalk, where its larvae consume some of the growing seed. The woodpecker eats the larvae, thus controlling their number. After the century plant seeds mature and the plant dies, the stalk serves as a nest site for the Ladder-backed Woodpecker.

Northern Flicker
Colaptes auratus
568

12½–14" (32–36 cm). A large woodpecker. Barred cinnamon-brown back and white rump. Brown head, gray face and neck, red mustache of male separated from boldly black-on-white spotted underparts by black crescent on breast. Salmon-pink wing and tail linings of western flickers are conspicuous in flight.

Voice
A piercing *keee-ar.* Also *flicka-flicka-flicka,* and a loud prolonged series: *wick wick wick wick wick.*

Habitat
Deciduous or mixed woods, semi-open country, edge or replacement growth in northern conifer belt, saguaros and woods along desert washes.

Range
Woodlands from Alaska to Mexico and coast to coast, including deserts of the Southwest.

Comments
Northern Flickers occur in three color variants, the "Red-shafted" of the West; the "Gilded," living in the desert; and the "Yellow-shafted," found east of the Rocky Mountains. The "Yellow-shafted Flicker" has a brilliant golden-yellow underside of wings and tail, a red crescent on the nape, and a black mustache in the male. The "Gilded" has wings and tail like the "Yellow-shafted," red mustache like the "Red-shafted." The "Red-shafted" and "Yellow-shafted" hybridize in the Great Plains.

Gray Flycatcher
Empidonax wrightii
569

5½" (14 cm). Gray above, white below. Lower bill flesh-colored.

Voice
Song is in 2 parts, rising in tone: *chiwip* (or *chi-bit*) *cheep.* Call is a soft *wit.*

Habitat
Sagebrush and pinyon-juniper woodland.

Range
Great Basin states.

Comments
Four other *Empidonax* species that occur in the West—the Willow, Dusky, Hammond's, and Western flycatchers—are very similar to this species. However, the Gray Flycatcher lacks the olive and yellow tinges to the back and underparts that mark other flycatcher species.

Black Phoebe
ayornis nigricans
70

6–7″ (15–18 cm). Slate-black except for white belly and undertail coverts and outer tail feathers. Its tail-wagging, erect posture, and insectivorous feeding habits are helpful in field identification.

Voice
Song is a repetition of the phrase *fee-bee,* the second syllable alternately lower and higher in pitch. Call is a sharp, downslurred *chip.*

Habitat
Shady watered areas, streams, pond and lake banks; in winter, city parks, open chaparral. Occasionally seen in moister areas of deserts, particularly in winter.

Range
Southwestern United States and western Mexico south to Argentina.

Comments
Black Phoebes are territorial and solitary nesters, often remaining year round in an established territory. The wanderers found in atypical winter habitats (chaparral or grassland) are thought to be first-year, nonbreeding birds.

Say's Phoebe
ayornis saya
71

7–8″ (18–20 cm). Dusky head, breast and back with darker wings and black tail. Light rust-colored belly and undertail coverts.

Voice
A mellow, whistled *pee-ur* with a plaintive quality.

Habitat
Plains, sparsely vegetated country, dry sunny locations, often near ranch houses, barns, and other buildings.

Range
Widespread in the West from central Alaska, the Yukon, and N. Mackenzie south to central Mexico; not present west of the Cascades and Sierras except locally in south-central California and W. Oregon. Winters from Southwest to Mexico.

Comments
Although primarily insect-eaters (as are all flycatchers), Say's Phoebes will eat other foods, such as berries, during long spells of cold, inclement weather when insects are unavailable.

Vermilion Flycatcher
Pyrocephalus rubinus
572

5½–6½″ (14–17 cm). Male has bright vermilion head and underparts. Brownish-black narrow mask, back, wings, and tail. Female and immatures are lighter brown above, lightly streaked on white breast; yellow-tan or pink wash on belly and undertail coverts.

Voice
Generally silent except for springtime aerial displays of the male. In flight, the male utters a stuttering outburst: *pit-pit-pit-pitty-zeee!*

Habitat
Deserts; thickets adjacent to watercourses, subtropical scrub.

Range
The Southwest to South America.

Comments
Despite its brilliant color, the Vermilion Flycatcher is hard to detect in cottonwoods, willows, or mesquite, since it hunts from the highest canopy and generally remains well concealed. In sparsely vegetated areas, however, it may descend to the ground after insect prey.

Ash-throated Flycatcher
Myiarchus cinerascens
573

7½–8½″ (19–22 cm). Medium-sized. Slender bill and gray-white throat. Olive-brown above, light yellow underparts. Cinnamon-rust primaries and tail feathers. Two white wing bars.

Voice
Common call is a rolling *quee-eer* suggestive of a low-pitched playground whistle. Also various *pip* or *pwit* notes and various croaking sounds.

Habitat
Open woodland, pinyon-juniper, chaparral, oak canyons, deserts, and riverside groves.

Range
S. Washington and Idaho south into California and Mexico, east to Colorado and Texas. Winters from extreme S. California and Arizona southward.

Comments
These birds launch their pursuit of insects from the dead upper branches of mature trees at the edge of woodlands. Trunk rot in these trees creates cavities useful as nesting sites.

Brown-crested Flycatcher
Myiarchus tyrannulus
574

8½–9½″ (22–24 cm). Large. Olive-brown above, darkest on crest; 2 whitish wing bars. Pale gray throat and breast; yellow belly. Bill black. Nearly identical to Ash-throated Flycatcher, but can be distinguished by larger darker bill, paler gray throat and breast, and brighter sulphur-yellow belly. In flight conspicuous reddish tail and primaries.

Voice
Very loud, rolling *prrrreeep!* notes. Call is a sharp *weep*.

Habitat
Desert where saguaro cactus is available for nest sites; also
river groves and woodlands and in sycamore canyons.

Range
S. Arizona east to S. Texas.

Comments
Biologists have found that when closely related similar species
such as the Brown-crested, Ash-throated, and Dusky-capped
flycatchers occur together, ecological specializations such as
differences in size, feeding habits, and vocalizations allow the
species to coexist without competing.

Western Kingbird
Tyrannus verticalis
575

8–9″ (20–23 cm). Olive-brown above, yellow below; gray
head, lighter grayish throat and upper breast. Dusky wings
and blackish tail with white margins. Red crown feathers not
normally visible.

Voice
A *whit* call, in various combinations, also chattering notes and
longer flight song.

Habitat
Arid savanna—natural or man-made (e.g., alfalfa fields with
fences, orchards alternating with pasture), open chaparral,
pinyon-juniper brushland, roadsides.

Range
Throughout the West, from southern Canada south to Mexico,
east to Great Plains. Winters in Central America.

Comments
The Western Kingbird is found on almost every ranch in the
West, where alfalfa and livestock pastures provide many of the
flying insects that make up the bulk of its diet. After the
young fledge it is not uncommon to see half a dozen or more
kingbirds sally from the dry upper branches of shade trees.

Horned Lark
Eremophila alpestris
576

7–8″ (18–20 cm). Pale brown, with black bib, yellow wash
on throat and face; black whisker marks, black "horns"
(difficult to see in the field). Black tail feathers with white
margins. Young lack the black face pattern and have silver-
speckled back.

Voice
The male often sings his tinkling song from a mound of earth
or as he circles high above his territory. Each phrase builds to
an emphatic close. Thin *tsee-eep* and a *buzz*.

Habitat
Open patches of bare land alternating with low vegetation,
such as on the tundra, alpine meadow, and sagebrush plains.

Range
Widespread in Arctic and mountain tundras of the Northern

Hemisphere; in North America, all suitable habitats and fields except southeastern seaboard.

Comments
The Horned Lark walks or runs instead of hopping; when feeding, it moves in an erratic pattern. On its breeding territory and when it flocks during winter, it feeds on seeds and ground insects. This bird is philopatric, or faithful to its birthplace, where it returns after every migration.

Purple Martin
Progne subis
577, 578

7¼–8½" (18–22 cm). Largest swallow in North America. Adult male glossy blue-black; wings and forked tail duller black. Female and yearling birds dusky black above, light below with smoky gray throat and breast.

Voice
A rich, low *chew* note. Song is a series of rich gurgling notes.

Habitat
Open woodlands, burns with snags, edges, hollow trees, and city buildings. Common in some desert sites, where it nests in woodpecker holes in saguaros.

Range
Southern Canada to northern Mexico; scarce in the West. Absent from the Central Plateau and its mountain-chain rims. Winters in South America.

Comments
In much of the West the Purple Martin is becoming scarcer, probably because of competition with Starlings for nest sites. Western representatives do not occupy "martin houses," preferring the open countryside or downtown areas.

Violet-green Swallow
Tachycineta thalassina
579

5–5½" (13–14 cm). Dark metallic bronze-green upperparts, iridescent violet rump and tail, the latter slightly forked; white underparts. White cheek extending above eye and white on the sides above rump.

Voice
A high *dee-chip* given in flight. Also varying *tweet* notes.

Habitat
Breeds in forests, wooded foothills, mountains, suburban areas. Commonly feeds over bodies of water in desert sites, especially in the Great Basin.

Range
From Alaska east to South Dakota, south to Baja California, Texas, and central Mexico. Winters south to Central America.

Comments
This species lives in colonies, basically because of its feeding needs; where one individual finds food there is usually enough for all, and when feeding communally these birds can more readily detect and defend themselves from hawks.

Black-billed Magpie
Pica pica
580

17½–22″ (44–56 cm). Large black and white bird with long tail and dark bill. Bill, head, breast, and underparts black, with green iridescence on wings and tail. White belly, shoulders, and primaries that are conspicuous as white wing patches in flight.

Voice
A rapid, nasal *mag? mag? mag?* or *yak yak yak.*

Habitat
Open savanna, brush-covered country, streamside growth.

Range
Northern part of the Northern Hemisphere. In North America from Alaska south to E. California, and east to Oklahoma.

Comments
Magpies generally nest individually but can sometimes be found in loose colonies; they are social when feeding or after the breeding season.

Chihuahuan Raven
Corvus cryptoleucus
581

19–21″ (48–53 cm). Crow-sized, but with heavy bill, wedge-shaped tail, and long, pointed throat feathers. All black; its heavy black ruff conceals white upper neck feathers, except in display. It flies with the raven's typical flat-wing glide.

Voice
Call is a harsh, prolonged *caaaa,* higher than that of a raven.

Habitat
Yucca desert, mesquite groves, and arid grasslands. Trees or powerline poles are required for nesting.

Range
More common from the Oklahoma Panhandle south through Texas, New Mexico, and Arizona across the open areas of Mexico. Scarce from Nebraska south through prairie region.

Comments
A scarcity of trees may have originally led to this bird's habit of reusing the same nest year after year. Gregarious birds, they feed in groups on insects as well as carrion. They roost communally, and soar high in the air in group displays.

Common Raven
Corvus corax
582

21½–27″ (55–69 cm). Large, black bird. Thick bill, shaggy ruff at throat, and wedge-shaped tail. Alternately flaps and soars like a hawk, flapping less and soaring more than American Crow.

Voice
Utters a hoarse, croaking *kraaak* and a variety of other notes, including a hollow, knocking sound and a melodious *klook-kluk,* usually in flight.

Habitat
A great variety, including deserts, mountains, canyons, boreal forests, Pacific Coast beaches.

Range

Alaska and Canada to Greenland. South, in the West, to Central America and east to the foothills of the Rockies.

Comments

A very "intelligent" bird, the Common Raven seems to apply reasoning in situations entirely new to it. Its "insight" behavior at least matches that of a dog. It is a general predator and opportunistic feeder, like other members of the crow family, and often feeds at garbage dumps.

Verdin
Auriparus flaviceps
583

4–4½″ (10–11 cm). Smaller than a chickadee. Gray with yellow head and throat; chestnut patch at bend of wing; white underparts. Juveniles lack both yellow and chestnut coloration of adults and are distinguishable from Bushtit by shorter tail.

Voice

The call most often heard is a single sharp *seep!* Its infrequent song is a 3-note *kleep-er-zee!*, the final note being highest.

Habitat

Low desert, containing brush and taller shrubs.

Range

SE. California east to S. Texas and south to northern Mexico.

Comments

Verdins behave like the more familiar chickadees and bushtits, feeding on insects, seeds, and berries. The small clutch size may be an adaptation to assure sufficient food in an area of climatic extremes.

Cactus Wren
Campylorhynchus brunneicapillus
584

7–8¾″ (18–22 cm). The largest North American wren. Long white eye-stripe, brown head, upperparts striped with white; cross-barred wings and tail, white spotting on outer tail feathers. Dark spotting of underparts is concentrated on upper breast. Pale rust color on lower belly.

Voice

Calls are low, harsh, and repetitious, and frequently unbirdlike. For example, a harsh *chug chug chug chug . . .* or *ka ka ka ka . . .*

Habitat

Deserts and arid hillsides with clumps of yucca or mesquite.

Range

Southwestern United States to central Mexico.

Comments

Cactus Wrens forage for food very methodically, searching under leaves and other ground litter. Like other wrens, they build roosting nests and even use them for shelter in rainy weather. They are late sleepers and an early bird-watcher may surprise them still dozing in the snug nest.

Rock Wren
Salpinctes obsoletus
585

5–6" (13–15 cm). Finely mottled gray above with rust-colored rump. Light eye-stripe and fine streaking on pale breast; buffy tips of outer tail feathers.

Voice
Song is a series of 3–5 trilling notes on one pitch, usually cricketlike in quality. Call is a loud *ki-deeeee*.

Habitat
Cliffs, rocks, talus slopes, from desert to coastal islands.

Range
British Columbia east to Saskatchewan and south throughout the West to Central America. Winters from California south.

Comments
The Rock Wren frequently constructs a "path" of rock chips leading to its nest. The purpose of this behavior is unclear.

Canyon Wren
Catherpes mexicanus
586

5½–5¾" (14–15 cm). Finely mottled brown above with rust-colored rump and tail; pure white throat and breast with finely streaked dark chestnut-brown belly.

Voice
The pleasing song is a descending series of clear, whistled notes, decelerating in tempo: *tee-tee-tee-tee-tee-tee-teer teer teer*. Call is a harsh *zzeep*.

Habitat
Canyons and rocky barrens.

Range
Resident from S. British Columbia to Montana, and south to southern Mexico.

Comments
This wren is found in remote canyons and on rocky mountainsides but has also adapted to man-made structures such as stone buildings and rock walls.

Bewick's Wren
Thryomanes bewickii
587

5–5½" (13–14 cm). Plain, unpatterned warm brown above, white or grayish white below, with distinct long white eyebrow-stripe. When tail is fanned, white outer tips of tail feathers are conspicuous, as is its slow flicking of tail sideways.

Voice
The loud, cheerful song usually begins with a soft buzz, as if the bird is inhaling, followed by a trill and a series of slurred notes. As in many birds, its singing perches are often higher than its foraging areas. Scold notes include a harsh *vit vit vit* and a harsh, drawn-out buzzing note.

Habitat
On or near the ground in a brush-covered, partly open area, including the edge of deciduous forest, coniferous woods with underbrush, chaparral, and pinyon-juniper woodland and down to desert edges, but not on open plains.

Range
Locally from British Columbia east to the Appalachians and south to southern Mexico

Comments
Bewick's Wren uses its long, narrow, slightly downcurved bill for scavenging on the ground and picking in crevices for insects and spiders.

Black-tailed Gnatcatcher
Polioptila melanura
588

4½–5″ (11–13 cm). Tiny bird. Gray above, whitish below. Male has black crown during summer, which extends to eyes. Long black tail with white corners. Winter male, female, and juveniles duller.

Voice
The common call is a harsh 2- or 3-note scold: *chee chee chee.*

Habitat
Deserts and arid country; dry washes in the low desert.

Range
S. California, Nevada, Arizona, New Mexico, Texas, southward into Mexico.

Comments
Identification of gnatcatchers is difficult, particularly in the Southwest, where the ranges of 2 species, the Black-tailed and the Blue-gray, overlap. The tail of the Black-tailed Gnatcatcher is black underneath with only 1 outer white-tipped feather on each side, whereas that of the more widespread Blue-gray is mostly white as seen from beneath, and when fanned, the 3 feathers on each side have diminishing amounts of white.

Western Bluebird
Sialia mexicana
589

6–7″ (15–18 cm). Long-winged, rather short-tailed. Male has deep blue hood and upperparts; rusty red breast and crescent mark across upper back; white belly. Female sooty gray above, with dull blue wings and tail. Juveniles like female but grayer, with speckled underparts.

Voice
Soft calls sound like *phew* and *chuck*. Song is a short, subdued *cheer, cheer-lee, churr.*

Habitat
Open woodland and pasturelands where old trees provide nest sites; occasionally occurs in sagebrush-dominated areas.

Range
From southern half of British Columbia and W. Alberta south to Baja California, central Mexico; west along the Rocky Mountains to W. Texas.

Comments
Females are attracted by the vivid blue of the male and by the availability of nesting holes, which are often in short supply.

Once the male secures a nesting hole he entices the female
with a colorful display that serves to repel rivals.

Northern Mockingbird
Mimus polyglottos
590

9–11″ (23–28 cm). Robin-sized. Gray above, white below;
white wing bars, and nervous motion of tail. In flight, tail is
black with striking white borders, and wing flashes white.
Characteristic sudden opening and closing of wings when on a
lawn perhaps scares hidden insects into movement. Also a
sideways flicking motion of the tail.

Voice
A persistent bubbling, sometimes gurgling or fluty song,
consisting of stanzas of repeated phrases. This bird is famous
for imitating many other birds as well as the noises of cars,
sirens, and other objects. Call notes include a harsh *chock*.

Habitat
Originally found in scrubby woodland, canyons, and the like,
it is now also a common garden bird and occurs even in arid
desert shrublands.

Range
From southernmost Oregon through N. Utah to
Newfoundland and south to southern Mexico.

Comments
At mating time, the male becomes increasingly exuberant,
flashing his wings as he flies up in aerial display, or singing
while flying from one song post to another. Mockingbirds
require open grassy areas for their feeding; thick, thorny, or
coniferous shrubs for hiding the nest, and high perches where
the male can sing and defend his territory.

Sage Thrasher
Oreoscoptes montanus
591

8–9″ (20–23 cm). Robin-sized; smaller than other thrashers.
Grayish brown above, light underparts with heavy brown
streaking. White wing bars and yellow eyes. White-tipped
outer tail feathers.

Voice
Song is a rich pattern of various musical phrases. Call is a low
blackbirdlike *chuck*.

Habitat
Sagebrush, and rabbit-brush cover in cold winter deserts.

Range
South-central British Columbia to S. Nevada, Utah, through
Texas and Oklahoma, and in the San Joaquin Valley of
California. Winters from central California to Mexico.

Comments
A good songster from a conspicuous perch or in flight,
the Sage Thrasher is a less repetitious mimic than the
Mockingbird. It feasts on fruits and vegetables in gardens of
desert towns, but also eats many damaging insects in alfalfa
fields near its sagebrush nesting area.

Bendire's Thrasher
Toxostoma bendirei
592

9–11″ (23–28 cm). Robin-sized. Shorter, less curved bill than other desert thrashers. Body light grayish brown with faint streaking on sides of neck and on breast. Yellow eyes.

Voice
The beautiful song is a clear, melodious warble with some repetition and continuing at length. Call is a low *chuck*.

Habitat
Desert scrub of the Southwest.

Range
Sonoran Desert, extending from Baja California to S. Utah, SE. New Mexico, and NW. Oklahoma, south into mainland Mexico. In winter it moves slightly to the south.

Comments
This thrasher flies from bush to bush, whereas other desert thrashers almost never fly. However, most of its feeding is done on the ground.

Curve-billed Thrasher
Toxostoma curvirostre
593

9½–11½″ (24–29 cm). Robin-sized, with long curved bill, pale red-orange eyes, and faint streaking on breast. Grayish brown above with darker long tail; narrow light wing bars occasionally present.

Voice
Song is a long but halting carol with little if any repetition. Distinctive call is a loud *whit-wheet?*

Habitat
Permanent resident in the cactus desert of the Southwest.

Range
S. Arizona to W. and S. Texas and south to Mexico.

Comments
This bird forages on the ground in search of insects.

Le Conte's Thrasher
Toxostoma lecontei
594

10–11″ (25–28 cm). Palest of the thrashers. Light sand color with lighter, unstreaked underparts and darker tail. Dark bill, dark eyes, and dark eye-line. During breeding season adults have deep buff undertail coverts.

Voice
Song is a loud, rich melody that is less harsh and with less frequent repetition than songs of other thrashers. Calls are a rising *whit* and *tu-weep*.

Habitat
Deserts with scant vegetation (mostly cholla and creosote bush), where the bird blends with the light-colored soil.

Range
Sonoran Desert and neighboring hot areas, the lower San Joaquin Valley of California, S. Nevada and Utah, Arizona, Sonora, and Baja California.

Comments
This thrasher is a permanent resident in the Southwest. Like most other desert thrashers, it prefers to escape by scurrying away through the sparse vegetation, but will fly if pressed.

hainopepla
hainopepla nitens
95

7–7¾″ (18–20 cm). Larger than a sparrow. Slender, elegant bird with conspicuous crest; longish tail and upright posture. Male shiny black with white wing patch that shows only in flight. Females and juveniles plain gray with pale wing patch.

Voice
Common calls include an upslurred whistled *hoooeet* and a low *quirk*. The short warbled song is rarely heard.

Habitat
Known as a desert scrub bird, yet it does not have strong preference for desert; it favors hot country with single, tall trees, preferably with mistletoe or other berries available when flying insects are scarce.

Range

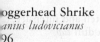

Central California, Arizona (extending into extreme S. Nevada and Utah), east to W. Texas; south through arid areas of Mexico. In the northerly parts of its range, it is migratory.

Comments
The Phainopepla is the northernmost of a group of tropical birds that feed on mistletoe. In the Southwest the berries are seasonal, so this species supplements them with insects, which it takes from the air in long sallies, like a flycatcher.

oggerhead Shrike
anius ludovicianus
96

8–10″ (20–25 cm). Large. Gray above, white below with wide black face mask, which meets over the strong hooked bill. Small white patch on rump and on back adjacent to wing; black wings with small white window at base of primaries. Juveniles are brownish, with barring below.

Voice
A harsh, scolding *bzee, bzeee*. Song is a series of coupled phrases, such as *queedle-queedle*.

Habitat
Roadside vegetation, thickets, savanna, desert, or any open country with high perches as lookouts.

Range

North America south of the coniferous forest region into Mexico. Winters in southern United States.

Comments
The shrike feeds mainly on large insects, such as locusts. In cold weather when insects are hard to find, it will hunt small birds or mice. When hunting is good, it stores excess food by impaling it on thorns, barbed wire, or the like.

European Starling
Sturnus vulgaris
597

7½–8½" (19–22 cm). Chunky; with short tail. In spring black with iridescent green-purple gloss and yellow bill. In winter duller, heavily speckled with light spots; dark bill. Fledged young, which roam together in flocks, look like a different bird: grayish brown above, lighter below.

Voice
A simple, low-pitched, chirpy chatter without musical quality, interspersed with whistles, clicks, and mimicked songs and calls. Call note is a loud grating *veer*.

Habitat
A wide variety of habitats, including cities, fields, orchards, and woodlands; in deserts, often nests in cavities of saguaro and other cactus species.

Range
Alaska and southern half of Canada south to the Gulf Coast and northern Mexico.

Comments
Hordes of these birds damage vegetable or fruit crops and do considerable damage around orchards and feedlots, consuming and fouling the feed of domestic cattle. They join blackbirds and feed on locusts, ground beetles, and the like.

Black-throated Gray Warbler
Dendroica nigrescens
598

4½–5" (11–13 cm). Head striped black and white, black bib on throat, white below with black stripes on sides, blue-gray back with black striping; yellow spot between bill and eyes. white wing bars and white outer tail feathers. Winter male, female, and juveniles lack black bib.

Voice
The song is a series of buzzes, rising in pitch and intensity, then falling: *zee zee zee zee bzz bzz*. Call is a dull *tup*.

Habitat
Shrubby openings in coniferous forest or mixed woods, dry scrub oak, pinyon and juniper, chaparral, and other low brushy areas; also in forests. Often seen foraging during migration in desert areas.

Range
Coastal forests from S. British Columbia (except Vancouver Island) to N. Baja California. Also found in the Great Basin states. Winters in the Southwest and Mexico.

Comments
This bird resembles Townsend's Warbler in every respect except that it lacks the green and yellow colors of the latter. Whereas the bright plumage of Townsend's blends well with the bright green of the spruces and pines of the coast forest, the drab appearance of the Black-throated Gray is a good adaptation to the bluish gray-green of western junipers.

Western Tanager
Piranga ludoviciana
599

6–7½" (15–19 cm). Adult male has brilliant red head, bright yellow body, with black back, wings, and tail. 2 wing bars; smaller uppermost bar yellow, lower white. Female is yellow-green above, yellow below; wing bars similar to male's.

Voice
Song is strong and carries far; Robin-like in its short fluty stanzas rendered with a pause in between. The quality is much hoarser, however. Call is a dry *pit-r-ick*.

Habitat
Open coniferous forests.

Range
Widespread in the West, from Alaskan Panhandle and S. Mackenzie south to N. Baja California, skirting the deserts; in the mountains of the Southwest. Often seen in summer in Great Basin; a conspicuous migrant and winter visitor to Sonoran desert. Winters in Mexico and Central America.

Comments
In late spring and early summer it feeds on insects, often like a flycatcher from the high canopy; later it feeds on berries and other small fruits.

Northern Cardinal
Cardinalis cardinalis
600, 601

7½–9" (19–23 cm). Male brilliant red, crested, with black face and throat framing conical red bill; female olive-buff with some red on crest, wings, and tail. Immatures drab buff.

Voice
Whistles a loud, melodious *cheer, cheer, cheer,* followed by a rapid *woight-woight-woight-woight.* Calls are soft *tsip* and *pink* notes.

Habitat
Gardens, streamside thickets, mesquite patches, mixed woodland margins.

Range
From the Colorado River Valley of California through S. Arizona to Baja California and Mexico. Introduced in Hawaii and around Los Angeles. Widespread in the East.

Comments
Feeding mainly on the ground in the open and nesting in thickets, it is well suited to a garden area. Nonmigratory, it stays around bird feeders even in the snowy winters of southern Canada and the northeastern states, but it does best where winters are milder.

Pyrrhuloxia
Cardinalis sinuatus
602, 603

7½–8" (19–20 cm). Shaped like Cardinal, but with parrot-like bill. Male gray with crimson crest, rose stripe down middle of breast and belly, with darker red flashes in wings and tail. Female more buffy than gray and lacks red markings except in front of eyes, on crest, wings, and tail. Bill yellow in summer, horn-colored in winter; never pink.

Voice
Song like that of a Cardinal, but thinner and usually downslurred: a clear *tseeu tseeu tseeu tseeu*. Call is *quit*.

Habitat
Mesquite scrub, less vegetated than the Cardinal's habitat.

Range
A Mexican bird, entering the United States in S. Arizona, New Mexico, and Texas.

Comments
Pyrrhuloxias feed on seeds and insects, and benefit cotton fields by destroying great numbers of cotton worms and weevils. When an observer approaches, a pair will fly up to a high watch post, erect their crests, and sound a loud, piercing alarm.

Blue Grosbeak
Guiraca caerulea
604

6–7½" (15–19 cm). Smaller than other American grosbeaks but with same large conical bill. Male dark blue with 2 rusty wing bars; female and juveniles tan with lighter buff underparts and faintly blue-tinged primaries and rump and rust-colored wing bars.

Voice
The male's song is a simple warble, rising and falling in pitch and lasting from 2 to 5 seconds. Call is a sharp *pink*.

Habitat
Streamside woodlands with much open area; riparian areas of deserts; marshy meadows with tall vegetation and hedgerows; overgrown fields.

Range
Breeds from California, S. Colorado, and South Dakota, east to New Jersey, and south to Costa Rica. Winters from northern Mexico to Panama.

Comments
After breeding, small flocks feed together or mix with other seed-eating finches and sparrows. They also search out insects, especially grasshoppers, that live in open fields.

Green-tailed Towhee
Pipilo chlorurus
605

6¼–7" (16–18 cm). Ground finch, smaller than other towhees. Sexes similar; rufous cap, olive-green above, with white throat and belly, gray breast. White between eye and base of bill, with dark mustache stripe. Yellow wing linings.

Voice
Song loud and lively, consisting of slurred notes and short, buzzy trills, usually delivered from atop a shrub or young conifer. Call is a short, nasal *mew*.

Habitat
Sagebrush, mountain chaparral, pinyon-juniper stands, and thickets bordering alpine meadows.

Range
Central Oregon south through mountains to S. California and the Great Basin to SE. New Mexico. Winters at lower elevations and south to S. Arizona, south-central Texas and into Mexico.

Comments
This shy bird hops and scratches for food under low cover, flicking its tail and erecting its rufous cap into a crest. It prefers low scrub and occurs in brushy openings in boreal forests on western mountains, as well as in sagebrush habitats.

Abert's Towhee
Pipilo aberti
606

8–9″ (20–23 cm). Grayish brown above, slightly paler underparts with buffy belly and tawny undertail. Black facial patch surrounding pale bill.

Voice
Call is a single bell-like note.

Habitat
Along arroyos in desert thickets; associated with cottonwood, willow, and mesquite, although it is also found around farms, orchards, and urban areas.

Range
Arizona, parts of neighboring Utah, New Mexico, and California southward into Baja California and Mexico.

Comments
This bird, while related to and closely resembling the Brown Towhee, is paler, more secretive, and has a different song. They do not interbreed, even though their ranges overlap.

Brown Towhee
Pipilo fuscus
607

8–10″ (20–25 cm). Earth-brown above with buffy, faintly streaked throat, light brown underparts, and rust-colored undertail coverts. Birds of the Southwest are paler and grayer and have a rufous cap.

Voice
Song is a series of squeaky *chips* on the same pitch, accelerating into a rapid trill. The pattern varies according to the area. The call is a sharp *chink* and thin *tseeee*.

Habitat
Shady underbrush, open woods, pinyon-juniper woodlands, and suburban gardens.

Range
Coastal and foothill chaparral from Oregon to S. Baja California; brush country of the southwestern states of Arizona, Colorado, Oklahoma, and Texas to southern Mexico.

Comments
The Brown Towhee is rarely noted because it often forages quietly among chaparral bushes or garden cover. Although its range in the chaparral overlaps during winter with that of the

Rufous-sided Towhee, it lives in low scrub, whereas the Rufous-sided keeps to scrub oaks and taller "forest edge" areas.

Brewer's Sparrow
Spizella breweri
608

5″ (13 cm). Light brown upperparts with black streaks; unmarked pale underparts. Solid, finely streaked crown. Well-defined darker ear patch bordered by fine black eye-line and 2 parallel whisker marks. Unstreaked breast; darker, finely streaked back with buff wing bars.

Voice
Alternating trills, musical or buzzy, often quite prolonged. Call note is a soft *seep,* most often given in flight.

Habitat
Sagebrush and alpine meadows.

Range
From British Columbia east to Saskatchewan south to New Mexico, Arizona, and S. California. Absent from the cool Pacific coastal belt.

Comments
This sparrow is unusual in having 2 distinct nesting populations, one in the alpine meadows of the Rocky Mountains of the Yukon; the other found in sagebrush deserts.

Vesper Sparrow
Pooecetes gramineus
609

5–6½″ (13–17 cm). Streaked brown above, with streaked head, throat, and breast. Light, narrow eye-ring, chestnut bend of wing, and white outer tail feathers.

Voice
A finchlike song, with variations similar to Song Sparrow's: 2 introductory notes followed by 2 or 3 short higher trills, ending in a rapid melody.

Habitat
Open grassy areas with some elevated song posts; hayfields and grainfields, meadows, roadsides.

Range
Coast to coast from Canada to south-central United States. Winters to southern Mexico.

Comments
The name Vesper Sparrow (the Latin word vesper means evening) is a misnomer, as this species does not sing more often in the evenings than other sparrows.

Black-throated Sparrow
Amphispiza bilineata
610

4¾–5½″ (12–14 cm). Gray above, darkest on head, dusky on wings; sooty black tail has white margins and corners. Eyebrow, mustache, and a spot below eye are white; large black bib; white below. Sexes similar; juveniles lack black bib and have finely streaked breast.

Voice
A quick little song starting with 2 or 3 melodious phrases, ending in a fast, tinkling trill. Calls are various tinkling notes.

Habitat
Driest and hottest cactus and sagebrush desert.

Range
From NW. Nevada and S. Wyoming through the deserts of the Southwest and northern Mexico.

Comments
The Black-throated Sparrow is well adapted to the extremes of its habitat. During the hot months of late summer and early fall, it maintains itself on dry seeds and drinks regularly at water holes. After the rains, these sparrows scatter into small flocks and feed on vegetation and insects, from which they derive all the moisture they need. They raise their young in the dry upland desert. This bird is thus known as the "Desert Sparrow" in the Southwest.

Sage Sparrow
Amphispiza belli
11

5–6″ (13–15 cm). Gray above; white belly with small black midbreast spot. Back and sides striped, wings lighter with buffy feather edges that also form 2 wing bars. Pronounced white eye-ring. Gray cheek, white eyebrow stripe, black mustache stripe. Immatures browner and have white throat and fine dark streaking on buff breast and belly.

Voice
Song is a short pattern of jumbling notes, rising, then falling. Call is a soft tinkling.

Habitat
Sagebrush, chaparral, dry foothills.

Range
From Washington south to Baja California, and throughout the Great Basin. Winters in small flocks in the low desert of S. California, Arizona, New Mexico, and Mexico.

Comments
The Sage Sparrow is secretive, moving under cover rapidly when approached, except during the spring breeding season, when males sing from a sagebrush perch to announce their territory. It has a habit of flicking its tail while hopping around on the ground.

Dark-eyed "Oregon" Junco
Junco hyemalis
12

5–6¼″ (13–16 cm). This species shows much geographic variation in color. Typically, males of western populations ("Oregon Junco") have black hood, buff sides. Pink bill and dark gray tail with white outer tail feathers. Western females have gray hood; females of all forms less colorful.

Voice
Ringing metallic trill on the same pitch. Members of a flock

may spread out widely, keeping in contact by constantly
calling *tsick* or *tchet*. Also a soft buzzy *trill* in flight.

Habitat
Openings and edges of conifers and mixed woods; in winter,
roadsides, parks, suburban gardens, and sagebrush plains and
foothills of the Great Basin.

Range
In wooded regions of North America from Alaska to
Newfoundland, and south across the northern United States.
In the West, south through the coastal rain forest and the
mountain forests of the northwestern states to Baja California.
Western birds winter mostly in Pacific coastal areas,
occasionally wandering to the East Coast. A few eastern birds
occur on the West Coast in winter.

Comments
This lively territorial bird is a ground dweller and feeds on
seeds and small fruits in the open. It also moves through the
lower branches of trees and seeks shelter in tangles of shrubs.

Brown-headed Cowbird
Molothrus ater
613

6–8″ (15–20 cm). Smallest North American blackbird. Short,
wide bill nearly conical. Male is metallic green-black with
coffee-brown head; female lighter gray-brown overall.
Juveniles like female, with lightly streaked breast, and
"scaled" upperparts, caused by gray margins of feathers.

Voice
The courting male delivers a variety of high, squeaking
whistles and gurgling notes accompanied by head-throw
postures and spread tail; females, a rattling call and soft *tsip*.

Habitat
During breeding season, woodlands, light stands of trees along
rivers, suburban gardens, city parks, and ranches; may also
breed in some desert areas. At other times, in mixed flocks
with other blackbirds in fields; winter visitor to desert areas.

Range
Widespread from southern Canada to the Mexican Plateau,
but a newcomer to the Northwest, expanding as the virgin
forest was opened up in the last few decades. Winters in
milder areas of United States.

Comments
Cowbirds are promiscuous; no pair bond exists. In late spring
the female cowbird and several suitors move into the woods.
The males sit upright on treetops, uttering sharp whistles,
while the female searches for nests in which to lay her eggs.
Upon choosing a nest, she removes one egg of the host's
clutch, and deposits one of her own in its place. The young
cowbird is so much larger than the young of the host that it
crowds and starves them out.

Hooded Oriole
Icterus cucullatus
614, 615

7–7¾" (18–20 cm). Breeding male is orange below with orange cap, black back, wings, and tail; large black bib from face to upper chest. Female olive green above, olive-yellowish below. Both sexes have 2 white wing bars. Immature male is like the female, but has a small black bib.

Voice
Call is a whistled *wheet?* Also a series of deliberate chattering notes. The song is a series of jumbled phrases including whistles, guttural trills, and rattling notes.

Habitat
Originally streamside growth, but it quickly adapted to tree plantations, palm rows, city parks, and suburbs with palm or eucalyptus trees and shrubbery. In the desert, occurs along water courses; also seen clinging to flowering plants.

Range
Central California, central Arizona, New Mexico, southernmost Texas, and south to Central America.

Comments
This oriole is easy to observe as it moves slowly through the taller trees in search of insects. Its nest is often parasitized by cowbirds, the aggressive young cowbird usually receiving the most food and starving the oriole nestlings.

Scott's Oriole
Icterus parisorum
616

7½–8¼" (19–21 cm). Male has black head, mantle, throat, and central breast area, bright lemon-yellow underparts, rump, and outer tail feathers. Wings, central tail feathers, and wide terminal band are also black. Male has one slender white wing bar. Female lime-yellow with dusky streaks on back; 2 wing bars. First-year male resembles female, but with small faint black throat and bib.

Voice
The song, a series of rising and falling flutelike notes, delivered from atop a yucca, juniper, or other tree. Call is a harsh *chuck.*

Habitat
Breeds in the pinyon-juniper woodland of montane semidesert areas; yucca trees or palms in deserts; sycamores or cottonwoods in canyons.

Range
Desert region from SE. California, S. Nevada, Utah, and Arizona's Chihuahuan Desert through S. New Mexico and W. Texas. South of the border, found in the deserts of northwestern Mexico and Baja California.

Comments
Besides gleaning insects, this fine songster feeds on available fruits, including those of cacti, and has been observed taking nectar—a habit practiced by many tropical orioles.

House Finch
Carpodacus mexicanus
617, 618

5–5¾" (13–15 cm). Sparrow-sized. Most adult males shiny red on crown, breast, and rump. Female has plain, unstriped head and heavy streaking on light underside. Immature males less highly colored, often yellowish on head and breast.

Voice
A *chirp* call like that of a young House Sparrow. The song is an extensive series of warbling notes ending in a *zeee*. Canarylike but without the musical trills and rolls. Sings from a high tree, antenna, or similar post for prolonged periods.

Habitat
Chaparral, deserts, and orchards, as well as coastal valleys that were formerly forested with redwood, cedar, or Douglas-fir but have now become suburbs.

Range
Throughout the West, from southern Canada to southern Mexico, and east to Nebraska. Introduced and now widespread in eastern United States.

Comments
These social birds are omnivorous, gleaning insect pests and, in winter, grass and weed seed. Garden-bred birds join large field flocks during the fall, often feeding in farmers' fields.

PART IV APPENDICES

GLOSSARY

Abdomen In insects, the hindmost of the three subdivisions of the body; in spiders, the hindmost of the two subdivisions of the body.

Achene A small, dry, hard fruit that does not open and contains one seed.

Alternate Arising singly along the stem, not in pairs or whorls.

Annual Having a life cycle completed in one year or season.

Anther The saclike part of a stamen, containing pollen.

Axil The angle formed by the upper side of a leaf and the stem from which it grows.

Bipinnate With leaflets arranged on side branches off a main axis; twice-pinnate; bipinnately compound.

Bract A modified and often scalelike leaf, usually located at the base of a flower, a fruit, or a cluster of flowers or fruits.

Brood A generation of butterflies hatched from the eggs laid by females of a single generation.

Calcar In bats, a small bone or cartilage that projects from the inner side of the hind foot into the interfemoral membrane.

Calyx Collective term for the sepals of a flower, usually green.

Caste In social insects, a specialized form of adult.

Catkin A compact and often drooping cluster of reduced, stalkless, and usually unisexual flowers.

Cell The area of a butterfly's wing that is entirely enclosed by veins; also called discal cell.

Cephalothorax The first subdivision of a spider's body, combining the head and the thorax.

Cloaca In certain vertebrates, the chamber into which the digestive, urinary, and reproductive systems empty.

Compound eye One of the paired visual organs consisting of several or many light-sensitive units, or ommatidia, usually clustered in a radiating array.

Corolla Collective term for the petals of a flower.

Coverts In birds, small feathers that overlie or cover the bases of the large flight feathers of the wings and tail, or that cover an area or structure (e.g., ear coverts).

Diurnal Active during the daytime hours.

Drupe A stone fruit; a fleshy fruit with the single seed enveloped by a hard covering (stone).

Elytron The thickened forewing of beetles, serving as protective covers for the hind wings (*pl.* elytra).

Femur The third segment of an insect's leg.

Flight feathers In birds, the long, well-developed feathers of the wings and tail, used during flight.

Follicle A dry, one-celled fruit, splitting at maturity along a single grooved line.

Head A crowded cluster of flowers on very short stalks, or without stalks as in the sunflower family.

Host plant The food plant of a caterpillar.

Inflorescence A flower cluster on a plant; especially the arrangement of flowers on a plant.

Introduced Intentionally or accidentally established in an area by man, and not native; exotic or foreign.

Involucre A whorl or circle of bracts beneath a flower or flower cluster.

Key A dry, one-seeded fruit with a wing; a samara.

Lanceolate Shaped like a lance, several times longer than wide, pointed at the tip and broadest near the base.

Larva A post-hatching immature stage that differs in appearance from the adult and must metamorphose before assuming adult characteristics (e.g., a tadpole).

Leaflet One of the leaflike parts of a compound leaf.

Lichen Any of a large number of small plants made up of an alga and a fungus growing symbiotically on various solid surfaces, such as rocks.

Lobed Indented on the margins, with the indentations not reaching to the center or base.

Lore In birds, the space between the eye and the base of the bill, sometimes distinctively colored.

Margin The edge of the wing.

Molt The periodic loss and replacement of feathers; most species have regular patterns and schedules of molt.

Node The place on the stem where leaves or branches are attached.

Oblanceolate Reverse lanceolate; shaped like a lance, several times longer than wide, broadest near the tip and pointed at the base.

Obovate Reverse ovate; oval, with the broader end at the tip.

Opposite leaves Leaves occurring in pairs at a node, with one leaf on either side of the stem.

Ovary The swollen base of a pistil, within which seeds develop.

Ovate leaf Egg-shaped, pointed at the top, technically broader near the base.

Palmate Having three or more divisions or lobes.

Palp A sensory structure associated with an insect's mouthparts.

Parotoid gland A large glandular structure on each side of the neck or behind the eyes of toads and some salamanders.

Pedicel The stalk of an individual flower.

Pedipalp One of the second pair of appendages of the cephalothorax of a spider, usually leglike in a female but enlarged at the tip in a male as a special organ for transferring sperm; used by both sexes for guiding prey to the mouth.

Peduncle The main flowerstalk or stem holding an inflorescence.

Perennial Living more than two years; also, any plant that uses the same root system to produce new growth.

Petiole The stalklike part of a leaf, attaching it to the stem.

Pinnate leaf A compound leaf with leaflets along the sides of a common central stalk, much like a feather.

Pistil The female organ of a flower, consisting of an ovary, style, and stigma.

Pod A dry, one-celled fruit, splitting along natural grooved lines, with thicker walls than a capsule.

Pollen Spores formed in the anthers of a flower that produce the male cells.

Pome A fruit with fleshy outer tissue and a papery-walled, inner chamber containing the seeds.

Primaries The outermost and longest flight feathers on a bird's wing.

Proboscis A prolonged set of mouthparts adapted for reaching into or piercing a food source.

Pupation In insects, the transformation from caterpillar to chrysalis or from larva to adult.

Raceme A long flower cluster on which individual flowers each bloom on a small stalk all along a common, larger, central stalk.

Ray flower The bilaterally symmetrical flowers around the edge of the head in many members of the sunflower family; each ray flower resembles a single petal.

Regular flower A flower with petals and/or sepals arranged around the center; always radially symmetrical.

Rhizome A horizontal underground stem, distinguished from roots by the presence of nodes, often enlarged by food storage.

Rosette A crowded cluster of leaves; usually basal, circular, and appearing to grow directly out of the ground.

Secondaries In birds, the large flight feathers located in a series along the rear edge of the wing.

Sepal A basic unit of the calyx, usually green, but sometimes colored and resembling a petal.

Sheath A more or less tubular structure surrounding a part, as the lower portion of a leaf surrounding the stem.

Simple eye A light-sensitive organ consisting of a convex lens bulging from the surface of the head, concentrating and guiding light rays to a cup-shaped cluster of photoreceptor cells. Also called an ocellus.

Simple leaf A leaf with a single blade.

Spadix A dense spike of tiny flowers, usually enclosed in a spathe, as in members of the arum family.

Spathe A bract or pair of bracts, often large, enclosing the flowers.

Spike An elongated flower cluster, each flower of which is without a stalk.

Spur A stout, spinelike projection, usually movable, such as is present commonly toward the end of the tibia.

Stamen One of the male structures of a flower, consisting of a threadlike filament and a pollen-bearing anther.

Stigma The tip of a pistil, usually enlarged, that receives the pollen.

Stipules Small appendages, often leaflike, on either side of some petioles at the base.

Stolon A stem growing along or under the ground; a runner.

Style The narrow part of the pistil, connecting ovary and stigma.

Tarsus In butterflies, the foot section of the leg; it has hooks at the end for clinging; in birds, the lower part of the leg.

Thorax The subdivision of the body between head and abdomen, consisting of three segments (the prothorax, mesothorax, and metathorax) and bearing whatever legs and wings are present.

Tragus In bats, the lobe that projects upward from the base of the ear.

Tubercle A raised, wartlike knob.

Umbel A flower cluster in which the individual flower stalks grow from the same point, like the ribs of an umbrella.

Vent Anus; opening of the cloaca to the outside of the body.

Whorl A circle of three or more leaves, branches, or pedicels at a node.

Wing bar A conspicuous, crosswise wing mark.

Wing stripe A conspicuous mark running along the opened wing.

BIBLIOGRAPHY

General References
Sierra Club Guide to the National Parks of the Desert Southwest.
New York: Random House, 1984.

Bender, G. L., ed.
Reference Handbook on the Deserts of North America.
Westport, Connecticut and London: Greenwood Press, 1982.

Brown, G. W., Jr.
Desert Biology, Vols. I and II.
New York and London: Academic Press, 1968 and 1974.

Chronic, H.
Roadside Geology of Arizona.
Missoula, Montana: Mountain Press Publishing Co., 1983.

Crawford, C. S.
Biology of Desert Invertebrates.
Berlin, Heidelberg, New York: Springer Verlag, 1981.

Hunt, C. B.
Death Valley. Geology, Ecology, Archaeology.
Berkeley, Los Angeles, London: University of California Press, 1975.

Louw, G. N. and M. K. Seely.
Ecology of Desert Organisms.
London and New York: Longman, 1982.

McGinnies, W.G.
Discovering the Desert.
Tucson: University of Arizona Press, 1981.

Naiman, R. J. and D. L. Soltz.
Fishes in North American Deserts.
New York: John Wiley & Sons, 1981.

Nations, D. and E. Stump.
Geology of Arizona.
Dubuque, Iowa: Kendall/Hunt Publishing Co., 1981.

Sheldon, R. A.
Roadside Geology of Texas.
Missoula, Montana: Mountain Press Publishing Co., 1979.

Wallwork, J. A.
Desert Soil Fauna.
New York: Praeger Publishers, 1982.

Desert Plants. A magazine published 4 times per year. May be obtained from Desert Plants, Boyce Thompson SW Arboretum, P. O. Box AB, Superior, Arizona, 85273.

Plant Identification
Benson, L. and R. A. Darrow.
Trees and Shrubs of the Southwestern Deserts, 3rd edition.
Tucson: University of Arizona Press, 1981.

Benson, L.
The Cacti of the United States and Canada.
California: Stanford University Press, 1981.

Correll, D. S. and M. C. Johnston.
Manual of the Vascular Plants of Texas.
Renner, Texas: Texas Research Foundation, 1970.

Cronquist, A., A. H. Holmgren, N. H. Holmgren, and J. L. Reveal.
Intermountain Flora. Vascular Plants of the Intermountain West, U.S.A., Volume 1, Volume 6, Volume 4.
New York and London: New York Botanical Gardens, Hafner Publishing Company, 1972, 1977, and 1984.

Kearney, T. H. and R. H. Peebles.
Arizona Flora, 2nd edition.
Berkeley and Los Angeles: University of California Press, 1964.

Martin, W. C. and C. R. Hutchins.
A Flora of New Mexico, Volume 1, Volume 2.
Vaduz, Germany: J. Cramer, 1980 and 1981.

Munz, P. A.
A Flora of Southern California.
Berkeley, Los Angeles and London: University of California Press, 1974.

Niehaus, T. F. and C. L. Ripper.
A Field Guide to Pacific States Wildflowers.
Boston: Houghton Mifflin Company, 1976.

Niehaus, T. F., C. L. Ripper, and V. Savage.
A Field Guide to Southwestern and Texas Wildflowers.
Boston: Houghton Mifflin Company, 1984.

Shreve, F. and I. L. Wiggins.
Vegetation and Flora of the Sonoran Desert, Volumes 1 and 2.
California: Stanford University Press, 1964.

Warnock, B. H.
Wildflowers of the Big Bend Country Texas.
Alpine, Texas: Sul Ross State University, 1974.

Wauer, R. H.
Naturalists Big Bend.
College Station and London: Texas A & M University Press, 1980.

Animal Identification
Kaston, B. J.
How to Know the Spiders, 3rd edition.
Dubuque, Iowa: Wm. C. Brown Co. Publishers, 1978.

Soltz, D. L. and R. J. Naiman.
The Natural History of Native Fishes in the Death Valley System.
Los Angeles: Natural History Museum of Los Angeles County, Science Series, 30, 1978.

White, R. E.
A Field Guide to the Beetles of North America.
Boston: Houghton Mifflin Company, 1983.

CREDITS

Photo Credits

The numbers in parentheses are plate numbers. Some photographers have pictures under agency names as well as their own.

David Ahrenholz (424 left and right, 429 right)
Ronn Altig (479, 481, 501)

Amwest
Dennis Anderson (67, 114, 150) Joseph J. Branney (519)
Charles G. Summers, Jr. (524)

Animals Animals
Tom Brakefield (283, 285) Breck P. Kent (399) Zig Leszczynski (171, 184, 185, 188, 228, 238, 254, 256, 257, 259, 284, 290) Raymond Mendez (173) John C. Stevenson (513) Stouffer Productions Ltd. (520)

Charles Arneson (347 left, 359 left)
Ray E. Ashton, Jr. (175, 202, 289)
Ron Austing (532, 557, 604)
Stephen F. Bailey (569, 594)
Gregory Ballmer (403–405, 408, 410, 421 left, 422 left, 423 left, 437 right)
Frank S. Balthis (4)
Roger Barbour (451 left and right, 454, 455 left and right, 456, 457 left and right, 458 left and right, 460, 462, 466, 467 left and right, 468, 470, 472, 476, 477, 483, 487, 488, 491, 494)
Erwin Bauer (518)
Greg Beaumont (535)
W. Frank Blair (180, 280)
Regan Bradshaw/The Photo Circle (506)
Tom Brakefield (485)
Linda Broome (496)
Ben M. Burns (417)
Stewart Cassidy (507)
David Cavagnaro (27, 301, 302, 305, 306, 313 left and right, 315 left and right, 316 left and right, 317 left, 319 left and right, 320 left, 321 left, 322 left and right, 326, 327, 329 left and right)
Scooter Cheatham (320 right, 321 right)
Roger Clapp (597)
Herbert Clarke (31, 342 right, 359 right, 551, 567, 574, 583, 589, 608, 612, 615, 616)
C. J. Cole (206–210, 241)

Bruce Coleman, Inc.
Jen and Des Bartlett (2nd frontispiece, 154, 331 left) Bob and Clara Calhoun (263, 521, 587) Clara Calhoun (163) Lois and George Cox (51, 473) Kenneth Fink (122) Kit Flannery (65) M.P.L. Fogden (123, 338, 499) G. Meszaros (269) Wardene Weisser (248) Gary Zahm (148)

Ed Cooper (41 right, 159, 335 left)
Steve Crouch (308, 312)
Douglas Danforth (432, 436, 438)

Thase Daniel (93, 152, 153, 503)
Harry Darrow (425, 426 right, 442, 529, 531, 541)
Thomas W. Davies (367, 372, 429 left, 431, 448)
Edward R. Degginger (73, 172, 178, 221, 223, 235, 294, 328 left, 394, 515, 536)
David M. Dennis (196, 272, 273, 277)
Larry Ditto (582)
Georges Dremeaux (579)

DRK Photo
Stephen Krasemann (4th frontispiece, 28, 511, 565) Wayne Lankinen (613)

John F. Eisenberg/Smithsonian Institution Photographic Services (482)

Harry Engels (130)

Entheos
Steven C. Wilson (1st frontispiece)

Chuck Farber (434)
P. R. Ferguson (58, 79, 109, 136 right, 156)
William E. Ferguson (351, 382, 389, 390, 449, 450)
Ken Ferrell (41 left)
Kenneth Fink (502, 538, 550)
Richard Fischer (350)
Jeff Foott (545, 607)
R. S. Funk (190)
John Gerlach (559)
Jeff Gnass (8, 29)
François Gohier (17)
Gilbert Grant (452 left and right, 465)
James M. Greaves (572)
Joseph A. Grzybowski (609)
David Hafner (500)
William Hammer (447)
Frank Hedges (427 left, 435)
Douglass Henderson (9, 23, 30, 38 left, 132, 342 left, 344, 354, 361–363, 366)
Elizabeth Henze (62, 103)
Noel Holmgren (44 left and right, 68)
Charles Johnson (55, 63, 64, 72, 78, 80, 81, 83, 92, 95, 107, 111, 115, 140, 146, 157)
J. Eric Juterbock (182, 197, 200, 201, 247, 270, 278, 287)
R. Y. Kaufman (618)
G. C. Kelley (528, 546, 547, 554, 566, 571)
E. F. Knights (573, 591)
Peter Kresan (12)
Frank A. Lang (116)
Wayne Lankinen (514, 537, 580)
Frans Lanting (539)
Calvin Larsen (530)
Herbert W. Levi (401)
Jack Levy (406, 414, 421 right, 437 left, 440, 441, 444, 445)

Betty Randall and Robert Potts (310)
William Ratcliffe (52, 108)
John Ratti (544)
C. Gable Ray (577, 578)
Tim Reeves (332 right)
Alan Resetar (195)
John N. Rinne/U.S. Forestry Service, Rocky Mountain Station (292, 295–297, 300)
Edward S. Ross (155, 160, 371, 373, 375–377, 380, 381, 383, 386, 391, 407 left, 415, 422 right, 427 right, 428, 430)
James P. Rowan (392)
Leonard Lee Rue III (497, 508)
Clark Schaack (307, 309, 314 left and right, 323 left and right, 325 right, 328 right, 330 right)
Perry Shankle, Jr. (516)
John Shaw (400, 412 left, 413 left and right, 418 right, 419 right, 420 left and right)
Ervio Sian (586, 611)
Robert S. Simmons (214, 219, 232, 243, 249–253, 260, 262, 271, 274, 286)
Arnold Small (14, 15, 357, 360, 364, 365, 533, 552, 558, 575, 596, 598–600, 602, 603, 606, 614)
Arlo I. Smith (325 left)
Robert Burr Smith (463 right)
Paul Spade (446)
Richard Spellenberg (45, 49, 56, 77, 94, 102, 104, 105, 110, 117–119, 131, 133, 134, 138 left, 139, 142–144, 149, 162, 165, 304, 311, 317 right, 318 left and right, 324 left and right, 343 left and right, 345 left, 346, 348, 355, 356)
Joy Spurr (38 right, 46, 99, 121, 167, 340 right)

Tom Stack and Associates (7)
Rod Allin (32) Harry Ellis (443) Celta Luce (5th frontispiece)
Rick McIntyre (474) Bob McKeever (203) Brian Parks (26)

Alvin E. Staffan (279, 495, 522)
Gayle Strickland (439)
K. H. Switak (20, 187, 189, 194, 220, 226, 230, 240, 242, 244)
Scott B. Terrill (561)
T. K. Todsen (47, 54, 61, 66, 71, 74, 84, 87, 89, 120, 129, 141, 151, 334, 337 left and right, 341)
Merlin D. Tuttle (453 left and right, 459 left and right, 461, 463 left, 464)
University of California at Berkeley/Jepson Herbarium (106, 164 left and right)
University of Colorado Museum (50, 76, 91, 101, 124, 126)
William Vandivert (489)
R. Van Nostrand (590, 617)
Charles S. Webber (113)
Wardene Weisser (48, 86, 97, 98, 147, 335 right, 469, 504, 570, 588, 610)
C. Wershler (407 right)

Larry West (330 left, 397, 416 left)
Richard R. Whitney (298)
Jack Wilburn (3, 5, 345 right, 352, 353, 526)
John Wilkie (411, 426 left)
Michael A. Williamson (258, 264)
Eleanor Yarrow (166)
Gary R. Zahm (576)
Dale and Marian Zimmerman (22, 40, 59, 82, 100, 336, 471, 480, 525, 540, 605)
Jack Zucker (145)
Richard G. Zweifel (179, 186, 205, 211, 213, 216, 217, 234, 267, 275, 276)

Illustrations

The drawings of plants and the tree silhouettes were executed principally by Margaret Kurzius and Mary Jane Spring. The following artists also contributed to this guide: Bobbi Angell, Dolores R. Santoliquido, and Stephen Whitney. Dot Barlowe contributed the drawings of mammal tracks.

INDEX

Numbers in boldface type refer to plate numbers. Numbers in italic refer to page numbers.

A

Abronia villosa, 53, 362
Acacia, Whitethorn, 68
Acacia
constricta, 68
greggii, 303, 317, 482
neovernicosa, 87
Acamptopappus schockleyi, 51
Accipiter cooperii, 532, 578
Achalarus toxeus, 435, 539
Acleisanthes longiflora, 104, 387
Agave
Desert, 65
False, 85
Harvard, 86
Agave
deserti, 65
harvardiana, 86
lecheguilla, 337, 496
parryi, 339, 497
shawii, 69
Agkistrodon contortrix, 244, 454
Agosia chrysogaster, 296, 477
Agropyron spicatum, 363, 508
Alectoris chukar, 544, 582
Allenrolfea occidentalis, 39, 108
Allionia incarnata, 59, 365
Amblyscirtes aenus, 438, 540
Ambrosia
ambrosioides, 68
deltoidea, 360, 507
dumosa, 355, 505
eriocentra, 50
Ambystoma tigrinum, 289, 290, 291, 474
Ammospermophilus
harrisii, 498, 562
interpres, 500, 563
leucurus, 499, 563
Amphispiza
belli, 611, 609
bilineata, 610, 608
Anabrus simplex, 374, 513
Anemone, Desert, 91, 381
Anemone tuberosa, 91, 381
Ant
Arid Lands Honey, 384, 517
California Harvester, 54

Little Black, 386, 518
Red Velvet-, 389, 519
Rough Harvester, 387, 519
Spine-waisted, 385, 518
Texas Carpenter, 388, 519
Thistledown Velvet-, 390, 520
Anthanassa texana, 425, 535
Anthocharis
cethura, 404, 527
lanceolata, 405, 527
Antilocapra americana, 527, 574
Antirrhinum filipes, 116, 393
Antrozous pallidus, 464, 550
Anulocaulis leiosolenus, 105, 387
Apache Plume, 96, 383
Aphaenogaster spp., 385, 518
Aphonopelma chalcodes, 399, 524
Apiomerus spp., 376, 514
Apodanthera undulata, 141, 404
Apodemia
mormo, 428, 536
palmerii, 427, 536
Aquila chrysaetos, 540, 580
Archilochus alexandri, 563, 590
Arctomecon merriami, 95, 382
Aristida longiseta, 46
Arizona elegans, 268, 464
Aroga websteri, 40
Arphia
conspersa, 40
pseudonietana, 40
Arrow Weed, 344, 499
Artemia salina, 35
Artemisia
arbuscula, 37
filifolia, 37
tridentata, 353, 357, 504
Asclepias
albicans, 82, 376
subverticillata, 80, 375
Aster, Mojave, 61, 366
Astragalus
amphioxys, 50, 361
lentigenosus, 163, 414
Athene cunicularia, 559, 588
Atrichoseris platyphylla, 85, 378

Atriplex
  canescens, 352, 503
  confertifolia, 346, 500
  hymenelytra, 358, 506
  lentiformis, 102
  parryi, 49
  polycarpa, 50
  spinosa, 51
Auriparus flaviceps, 583, 598

B
Baccharis
  glutinosa, 52, 103
  sarothroides, 68
Badger, 514, 568
Baileya multidradiata, 128, 398
Balloon Flower, 44, 358
Balsam Root, Arrowleaf, 130, 399
Balsamorhiza sagittata, 130, 399
Bassariscus astutus, 511, 567
Bat
  Big Free-tailed, 467, 552
  Brazilian Free-tailed, 465, 551
  California Leaf-nosed, 452, 547
  Ghost-faced, 451, 547
  Long-tongued, 453, 547
  Mexican Long-nosed, 454, 547
  Pallid, 464, 550
  Pocketed Free-tailed, 466, 551
  Sanborn's Long-nosed, 455, 548
  Silver-haired, 459, 549
  Spotted, 462, 550
  Townsend's Big-eared, 463, 550
  Western Mastiff, 468, 552
Battarrea phalloides, 167, 416
Bear Grass, 86
Beaver, 99
Bebbia juncea, 65
Bee Assassins, 376, 514
Bee Plant, Yellow, 111, 390
Beetle
  Arizona Blister, 382, 517
  Blister, 90

Broad-necked Darkling, 381, 516
  Ironclad, 379, 516
  Tiger, 378, 515
Beloperone californica, 160, 413
Billbug, Agave, 380, 516
Blackbrush, 348, 502
Bladderpod, Fendler's, 146, 407
Blue
  Antillean, 411, 412, 530
  Pale, 409, 529
  Small, 410, 529
  Western Pygmy, 413, 530
Bluebird, Western, 589, 600
Blue-eyes, Arizona, 69, 370
Boa, Rosy, 219, 224, 443
Bobcat, 517, 520, 570
Boojum Tree, 69
Bootettix argentatus, 368, 511
Bouteloua breviseta, 88
Brachylagus idahoensis, 42
Brachystola magna, 370, 512
Brephidium exilis, 413, 530
Brittlebush, 136, 402
Brome, Cheatgrass, 38
Bromus tectorum, 38
Broom, Turpentine, 366, 509
Broomrape, Spike, 76, 373
Bubo virginianus, 556, 587
Buckwheat
  Desert, 359, 506
  Sand Dune, 105
Bufo
  alvarius, 281, 470
  cognatus, 283, 471
  debilis, 287, 473
  microscaphus, 279, 469
  punctatus, 278, 468
  retiformis, 284, 471
  speciosus, 280, 469
  woodhousei, 92
Bullfrog, 288, 473
Bunting, Varied, 96
Burrobush, 365, 509
Burrograss, 88
Bursera microphylla, 312, 315, 487

Buteo
albonotatus, 95
jamaicensis, 536, 537, 579
lagopus, 539, 580
regalis, 558, 580
swainsoni, 534, 535, 579
Buttercup, Bur, 38

C
Cactus
Barrel, 122, 395
Beavertail, 41, 357
Claret Cup, 42, 357
Cushion, 40, 356
Desert Christmas, 162, 414
Fishhook, 39, 355
Fishhook Barrel, 66
Hedgehog, 65
Organ Pipe, 66
Prickly Pear, 66, 86
Rainbow, 123, 396
Simpson's Hedgehog, 38,
355
Calico, Desert, 51, 361
Calliandra eriophylla, 48,
360
Callipepla
californicus, 548, 549, 584
squamata, 546, 583
Callisaurus draconoides, 203,
434
Callophrys comstocki, 441,
541
Calochortus
kennedyi, 152, 154, 409
nuttallii, 99, 384
Calypte costae, 564, 590
Camponotus festinatus, 388,
519
Campylorhynchus
brunneicapillus, 584, 598
Candelilla, 86
Canis latrans, 523, 524,
572
Canotia holacantha, 314,
488
Caracara, Crested, 541,
581
Cardinal, Northern, 600,
601, 605
Cardinalis
cardinalis, 600, 601, 605
sinuatus, 602, 603, 605
Cardon, 69

Carpodacus mexicanus, 617,
618, 612
Cassia
armata, 51
bauhinioides, 144, 406
Castilleja chromosa, 159,
412, 412
Castor canadensis, 99
Catclaw, 303, 317, 482
Cathartes aura, 530, 577
Catherpes mexicanus, 586,
599
Cattle Spinach, 50
Caulanthus inflatus, 164,
415
Celtis pallida, 68
Centipede, 89
Centrocercus urophasianus,
545, 583
Centruroides spp., 394, 522
Century Plant, Parry's,
339, 497
Ceratocephalus testiculatus, 38
Ceratoides lanata, 354, 505
Cercidium
floridum, 301, 316, 481
microphyllum, 309, 318, 486
Cercyonis sthenele, 431, 537
Cereus, Night-blooming,
87, 379
Cereus
gigantea, 331, 493
greggii, 87, 379
pringelei, 69
schotti, 66
thurberi, 66
Chaenactis stevioides, 84, 377
Chalceria heteronea, 414,
415, 531
Chamaesaracha, Dingy,
119, 394
Chamaesaracha sordida, 119,
394
Charidryas
acastus, 423, 534
neumoegeni, 421, 534
Checkerspot
Chara, 422, 534
Desert, 421, 534
Elada, 424, 535
Sagebrush, 423, 534
Chernetidae, 397, 523
Chernetids, 397, 523
Chia, 64, 367

Chicory, Desert, 86, 378
Chilomeniscus cinctus, 236,
451
Chilopsis linearis, 306,
484
Chinchweed, 133, 400
Chionactis
occipitalis, 235, 237, 450
palarostris, 240, 452
Chipmunk, Least, 497,
562
Chlosyne lacinia, 429, 430,
537
Choeronycteris mexicana, 453,
547
Cholla
Buckthorn, 66
Cane, 66
Golden, 65
Jumping, 325, 490
Pencil, 64
Teddybear, 332, 494
Tree, 333, 495
Chordeiles
acutipennis, 560, 588
minor, 561, 589
Chrysothamnus nauseosus,
340, 497
Chub, Tui, 298, 478
Chuckwalla, 189, 427
Chukar, 544, 582
Chuparosa, 160, 413
Cibolacris parviceps, 54
Cincindela spp., 378, 515
Circus cyaneus, 531, 577
Clammyweed, 81, 376
Clavellina, 87
Cleome lutea, 111, 390
Clover, Jackass, 110, 390
Cnemidophorus
exsanguis, 210, 438
inornatus, 208, 437
neomexicanus, 211, 439
tesselatus, 207, 437
tigris, 206, 436
uniparens, 209, 438
velox, 46
Coachwhip, 223, 229,
230, 233, 445
Coati, 513, 568
Cochineal Bug, 391, 520
Coelocnemis californicus, 381,
516
Colaptes auratus, 568, 592

Coleogyne ramossissima, 348, 502
Coleonyx
brevis, 177, 178, *422*
reticulatus, 92
variegatus, 176, 179, *422*
Colias philodice, 443, *542*
Coluber constrictor, 232, *447*
Columbina inca, 552, *585*
Columbina passerina, 553, *586*
Condalia, Bitter, 323, *489*
Condalia globosa, 323, *489*
Conepatus mesoleucus, 516, *569*
Cophosaurus texanus, 204, *435*
Copper, Blue, 414, 415, *531*
Copperhead, 244, *454*
Coragyps atratus, 529, *577*
Corvus
corax, 582, *597*
cryptoleucus, 581, *597*
Coryphantha vivipara, 40, *356*
Cottontail
Desert, 508, *566*
Mountain, *42*
Cottonwood, Fremont, *52, 106*
Cowbird, Brown-headed, 613, *610*
Coyote, 523, 524, *572*
Crenichthys baileyi, 292, *476*
Creosote Bush, 342, *498*
Crescentspot
Phaon, 426, *536*
Texan, 425, *535*
Cricket
Jerusalem, 375, *514*
Mormon, 374, *513*
Crotalus
atrox, 256, *458*
cerastes, 252, 253, *457*
lepidus, 250, 257, *456*
mitchelli, 251, 255, *456*
molossus, 248, *455*
ruber, 254, *457*
scutulatus, 259, *459*
tigris, 249, *455*
viridis, 258, 260, *458*
Crotaphytus
collaris, 200, 201, *433*

insularis, 186, *425*
Croton, *105*
Croton wigginsii, 105
Crucifixion-thorn, 314, *488*
Cucurbita foetidissima, 140, *404*
Cutthroat, Lahontan, *33*
Cynomys gunnisoni, 46
Cyprinodon
macularius, 293, *476*
milleri, 54
pecosensis, 91
tularosa, 91

D
Dace
Longfin, 296, *477*
Speckled, 297, *477*
Dactylopius confusus, 391, *520*
Daisy
Blackfoot, 92, *381*
Tahoka, 62, *367*
Woolly, 127, *398*
Yellow Spiny, 131, *400*
Dalea
Feather, 49, *360*
Fremont, *51*
Dalea
formosa, 49, *360*
fremontii, 51
spinosa, 305, 313, 334, *483*
Danaus
gilippus, 418, *532*
plexippus, 419, *532*
Dandelion, Desert, 125, *397*
Dasylirion wheeleri, 338, *496*
Dasymutilla
gloriosa, 390, *520*
magnifica, 389, *519*
Datura wrightii, 100, *385*
Deer, Mule, 528, *575*
Delphinium nuttallianum, 63, *367*
Dendroica
coronata, 77
nigrescens, 598, *604*
petechia, 77
Descurainia pinnata, 38
Desert Bell, 70, *370*
Desert Broom, 68, *103*

Desert Candle, 164, *415*
Desert Gold, 145, *406*
Desert Holly, 85
Desert Ironwood, 319, *88*
Desert Peach, *40*
Desert Star, Mojave, 90, *80*
Desert Trumpet, 108, *89*
Desert Velvet, 118, *393*
Devil's Claw, 117, 165, *93*
Diapheromera covilleae, 90
Dicotyles tajacu, 525, *573*
Dipodomys
deserti, 484, *557*
merriami, 485, *558*
microps, 481, *556*
ordii, 480, *556*
panamintinus, 482, *557*
spectabilis, 483, *557*
Dipsosaurus dorsalis, 188, *426*
Distichlis spicata, 108
Dithyrea wislizenii, 79, *375*
Dock, 68
Winged, 46, *359*
Dove
Common Ground-, 553, *586*
Inca, 552, 585
Mourning, 551, *585*
White-winged, 550, *584*
Dracotettix monstrosus, 372, *512*
Dugesiella echina, 89
Dymasia chara, 422, *534*
Dyssodia pentachaeta, 134, *401*

E
Eagle, Golden, 540, *580*
Echinocactus
horizonthalonius, 87
texensis, 87
Echinocereus
engelmannii, 65
pectinatus, 123, *396*
triglochidiatus, 42, *357*
Elaphe subocularis, 214, *440*
Elephant Tree, 312, 315, *487*
Elymus cinereus, 38

Emmenanthe penduliflora, 115, *392*
Empidonax wrightii, 569, *592*
Encelia farinosa, 136, *402*
Enceliopsis nudicaulis, 132, *400*
Ephedra spp., *364*, *508*
Eremobates pallipes, 396, *522*
Eremophila alpestris, 576, *595*
Erethizon dorsatum, 507, *565*
Erigeron divergens, 89, *380*
Eriogonum
deserticola, 105
fasciculatum, 359, *506*
inflatum, 108, *389*
umbellatum, 112, *391*
Erioneuron pulchellum, 361, *507*
Eriophyllum wallacei, 127, *398*
Erodium cicutarium, 57, *364*
Eschscholtzia mexicana, 148, *408*
Euchloe hyantis, 406, *528*
Eucnide urens, 150, *408*
Euderma maculatum, 462, *550*
Eumeces obsoletus, 213, *440*
Eumops perotis, 468, *552*
Euphilotes pallescens, 409, *529*
Euphorbia
albomarginata, 102, *386*
antisyphilitica, 86
Eurema
boisduvaliana, 442, *542*
nicippe, 417, *531*
Eutamias minimus, 497, *562*
Evolvulus arizonicus, 69, *370*

F
Fagonia, 55, *363*
Fagonia californica, 55, *363*
Fairy Duster, 48, *360*
Falco
femoralis, 543, *582*
sparverius, 542, *581*
Falcon, Aplomado, 543, *582*
Fallugia paradoxa, 96, *383*
Felis
concolor, 518, 519, *570*

rufus, 517, 520, *570*
Ferocactus
acanthodes, 122, *395*
wislizenii, 66
Filaree Storksbill, 57, *364*
Finch, House, 617, 618, *612*
Five Spot, Desert, 43, *358*
Flax, Chihuahua, 149, *408*
Fleabane, Spreading, 89, *380*
Flicker, Northern, 568, *592*
Flourensia cernua, 350, *502*
Fluffgrass, 361, *507*
Flycatcher
Ash-throated, 573, *594*
Brown-crested, 574, *594*
Gray, 569, *592*
Vermilion, 572, *594*
Fouquieria
columnaris, 69
macdougalii, 70
splendens, 335, *495*
Four O'Clock
Desert, 52, *362*
Trailing, 59, *365*
Fox
Gray, 522, *571*
Kit, 521, *571*
Frog
Bull-, 288, *473*
Northern Leopard, 286, *472*
Rio Grande Leopard, 285, *472*

G
Gaillardia pulchella, 60, *366*
Galleta, 38, 46
Big, 51, 64
Gambelia
silus, 187, *426*
wislizenii, 191, *428*
Gambusia, Big Bend, 91
Gambusia
affinis, 294, *476*
gaigei, 91
Gastrophryne olivacea, 282, *470*

Gecko
Big Bend, 92
Leaf-toed, 175, *421*
Texas Banded, 177, 178, *422*
Western Banded, 176, 179, *422*
Geococcyx californianus, 554, 586
Geomys arenarius, 99
Gerea canescens, 135, *401*
Ghost Flower, 147, *407*
Gila bicolor, 298, *478*
Gila Monster, 180, *423*
Glaucidium brasilianum, 557, 587
Globemallow
Coulter's, 157, *411*
Desert, 158, *412*
Gnatcatcher, Black-tailed, 588, *600*
Goldeneye, 85
Goldenhead, *51*
Gopher
Botta's Pocket, 469, *552*
Desert Pocket, 99
Yellow-faced Pocket, 99
Gopherus agassizii, 169, *418*
Gourd, Buffalo, 140, *404*
Grama, Gypsum, 88
Grasshopper
Aztec Pygmy, 373, *513*
Cream, 54
Creosote Bush, 368, *511*
Desert Clicker, 54
Dragon Lubber, 372, *512*
Green Valley, 367, *511*
Horse Lubber, 371, *512*
Lubber, 370, *512*
Pallid-winged, 369, *511*
Red-winged, 40
Speckled Rangeland, 40
Graythorn, 64, 88
Greasewood, 345, *500*
Little, 39
Grosbeak, Blue, 604, 606
Groundcherry, Purple, 67, *369*
Groundsel, Threadleaf, 129, *399*
Grouse, Sage, 545, *583*
Guiraca caerulea, 604, 606
Gyalopion canum, 266, *463*

H
Hackberry, Desert, 68
Hadrurus arizonensis, 395, 522
Hairstreak
Behr's, 416, *531*
Desert Green, 441, *541*
Leda, 440, *541*
Halogeton, 38
Halogeton glomeratus, 38
Haplopappus spinulosus, 131, *400*
Harrier, Northern, 531, 577
Hawk
Common Night-, 561, 589
Cooper's, 532, 578
Ferruginous, 558, 580
Harris', 533, 578
Lesser Night-, 560, 588
Red-tailed, 536, 537, 579
Rough-legged, 539, 580
Swainson's, 534, 535, 579
Zone-tailed, 95
Hechtia texensis, 85
Heliopetes ericetorum, 408, 528
Heliotrope, Sweet-scented, 101, *385*
Heliotropium convolvulaceum, 101, *385*
Heloderma suspectum, 180, *423*
Hemiargus ceraunus, 411, 412, *530*
Hemipepsis spp., 383, *517*
Hesperia pahaska, 434, *539*
Hesperocallis undulata, 98, *384*
Heterodon nasicus, 261, *459*
Hibiscus
coulteri, 151, *409*
denudatus, 45, *358*
Hilaria
jamesii, 38, 46
mutica, 88
rigida, 51, 64
Holbrookia maculata, 192, *429*
Holly, Desert, 358, *506*
Hopsage, *51*
Horse Crippler, 87
Horsebrush, Littleleaf, 343, *499*

Horsenettle, White, 73, 372

Hummingbird
Black-chinned, 563, 590
Costa's, 564, 490

Hyla
arenicolor, 272, 465
adaverina, 271, 465
Hyles lineata, 448, 544
Hymenoclea salsola, 365, 509
Hypsiglena torquata, 267, 463
Hyptis emoryi, 65

I

Ice Plant, Common, 88, 379
Icterus
cucullatus, 614, 615, 611
parisorum, 616, 611
Iguana, Desert, 188, 426
Indian Blanket, 60, 366
Indigo Bush, 64
Inky Cap, Desert, 166, 415
Iodinebush, 39
Ipomopsis
aggregata, 161, 413
longiflora, 66, 368
Isoptera, 392, 521

J

Jack Rabbit
Antelope, 510, 566
Black-tailed, 509, 566
Jatropha
cardiophylla, 68
dioca, 85
Jewel Flower, Arizona, 107, 388
Jojoba, 347, 501
Joshua-tree, 326, 490
Jumping Bean, Mexican, 68
Junco, Dark-eyed "Oregon," 612, 609
Junco hyemalis, 612, 609
Juncus balticus, 39

K

Kallstroemia grandiflora, 155, 410
Kestrel, American, 542, 581

Kingbird, Western, 575, 595
Kingsnake
Common, 234, 246, 448
Mexican, 242, 243, 453
Kinosternon
flavescens, 170, 418
sonoriense, 171, 419
Krameria parvifolia, 56, 364

L

Lagurus curtatus, 496, 562
Lampropeltis
getulus, 234, 246, 448
mexicana, 242, 243, 453
Langloisia, Spotted, 97, 383
Langloisia
matthewsii, 51, 361
punctata, 97, 383
Lanius ludovicianus, 596, 603
Lark, Horned, 576, 595
Larkspur, Nuttall's, 63, 367
Larrea tridentata, 342, 498
Lasionycteris noctivagans, 459, 549
Latrodectus hesperus, 40
Lavender, Desert, 65
Lechuguilla, 337, 496
Lepidium
flavum, 113, 391
montanum, 78, 374
perfoliatum, 38
Leptonycteris
nivalis, 454, 547
sanborni, 455, 548
Leptotyphlops
dulcis, 225, 449
humilis, 226, 449
Lepus
alleni, 510, 566
californicus, 509, 566
Lesquerella fendleri, 146, 407
Leucophyllum frutescens, 47, 359
Lichanura trivirgata, 219, 224, 443
Ligurotettix coquilletti, 54
Lily
Desert, 98, 384
Desert Mariposa, 152, 154, 409

Rain, 153, 410
Sego, 99, 384
Limber Bush, 68
Linanthus aureus, 145, 406
Linum vernale, 149, 408
Lion, Mountain, 518, 519, 570
Litaneutria obscura, 377, 515
Lizard
Black-collared, 186, 425
Bluntnose Leopard, 187, 426
Brush, 190, 427
Collared, 200, 201, 433
Crevice Spiny, 198, 431
Desert Horned, 55, 74
Desert Night, 183, 184, 424
Desert Spiny, 199, 432
Eastern Fence, 93
Flat-tail Horned, 194, 430
Fringe-toed, 182, 424
Granite Night, 185, 425
Greater Earless, 204, 435
Lesser Earless, 192, 429
Longnose Leopard, 191, 428
Mojave Fringe-toed, 181, 423
Regal Horned, 195, 430
Roundtail Horned, 193, 429
Sagebrush, 212, 439
Short-horned, 197, 431
Side-blotched, 202, 433
Texas Horned, 196, 430
Tree, 205, 435
Zebratail, 203, 434
Loco, Melon, 141, 404
Lophophora williamsii, 37, 355
Lophortyx gambelii, 547, 584
Lubber, Furnace Heat, 54
Lupine, Coulter's, 72, 371
Lupinus sparsiflorus, 72, 371
Lycium, Anderson, 351, 503
Lycium andersonii, 351, 503
Lycosa carolinensis, 401, 524
Lytta magister, 382, 517

M

Machaeranthera
tanacetifolia, 62, 367

tortifolia, 61, *366*
Macrotus californicus, 452, *547*
Magpie, Black-billed, 580, *597*
Maguey, *69*
Malacothrix
coulteri, 126, *397*
glabrata, 125, *397*
Malvastrum rotundifolium, 43, *358*
Mammilaria microcarpa, 39, *355*
Mantid, Obscure Ground, 377, *515*
Marble, Gray, 405, *527*
Marblewing, Pearly, 406, *528*
Marigold
Desert, 128, *398*
Five-needle Fetid, 134, *401*
Mariola, 356, *505*
Martin, Purple, 577, 578, *596*
Massasauga, 264, *462*
Masticophis
bilineatus, 222, *445*
flagellum, 223, 229, 230, 233, *445*
taeniatus, 221, *444*
Mastigoproctus giganteus, 398, *523*
Maurandya
antirrhiniflora, 74, *372*
wislizenii, 71, *371*
Meda fulgida, 300, *479*
Megathymus yuccae, 439, *540*
Megetra cancellata, *90*
Melampodium leucanthum, 92, *381*
Melanerpes
aurifrons, 556, *591*
uropygialis, 565, *590*
Melon Loco, 141, *404*
Menodora
Rough, 142, *405*
Spiny, *51*
Menodora
scabra, 142, *405*
spinescens, *51*
Mentzelia involucrata, 120, *394*
Mephitis
macroura, *98*

mephitis, 515, *569*
Mesembryanthemum crystallinum, 88, *379*
Mesquite
Honey, 308, 321, *485*
Screwbean, 302, 311, 320, *481*
Velvet, 310, *486*
Metalmark
Gray, 427, *536*
Mormon, 428, *536*
Micrathene whitneyi, 558, *588*
Microdipodops
megacephalus, 478, *555*
pallidus, 479, *556*
Micruroides euryxanthus, 241, *453*
Milkvetch
Crescent, 50, *361*
Freckled, 163, *414*
Milkweed
Climbing, 83, *377*
Poison, 80, *375*
White, 82, *376*
Millipede, Desert, 393, *521*
Mimus polyglottos, 590, *601*
Ministrymon leda, 440, *541*
Mirabilis multiflora, 52, *362*
Mockingbird, Northern, 590, *601*
Mohavea confertiflora, 147, *407*
Molothrus ater, 613, *610*
Monarch, 419, *532*
Monomorium minimum, 386, *518*
Monoptilon bellioides, 90, *380*
Mormon Tea, 364, *508*
Mormoops megalophylla, 451, *547*
Mortonia scabrella, *87*
Mosquitofish, 294, *476*
Moss, Ball, *69*
Moth
California Cankerworm, 449, *545*
Large California Spanworm, 450, *545*
Sagebrush Defoliator, *40*
Mouse
Arizona Pocket, 472, *553*

Bailey's Pocket, 476, 555
Brush, 490, 559
Cactus, 492, 560
Canyon, 58
Dark Kangaroo, 478, 555
Deer, 489, 559
Desert Pocket, 447, 555
Fulvous Harvest, 487, 558
Great Basin Pocket, 474,
554
House, 495, 561
Little Pocket, 473, 554
Long-tailed Pocket, 475,
554
Nelson's Pocket, 98
Northern Grasshopper,
491, 560
Pale Kangaroo, 479, 556
Plains Harvest, 98
Rock Pocket, 79, 98
Silky Pocket, 471, 553
Southern Grasshopper, 488,
588
Western Harvest, 486, 558
White-ankled, 99
Muhlenbergia porteri, 51
Muhly, Bush, 51
Mus musculus, 495, 561
Myiarchus
cinerascens, 573, 594
tyrannulus, 574, 594
Myotis
California, 458, 549
Cave, 457, 548
Southwestern, 460, 549
Yuma, 456, 548
Myotis
auriculus, 460, 549
californicus, 458, 549
velifer, 457, 548
yumanensis, 456, 548
Myrmecocystus spp., 384, 517

N
Nama demissum, 54, 363
Nasua nasua, 513, 568
Neotoma
albigula, 494, 561
lepida, 493, 560
micropus, 99
Nerisyrenia, Velvety, 94,
382
Nerisyrenia camporum, 94,
382

Nettle, Desert Rock, 150,
408
Nicotiana
glauca, 114, 392
trigonophylla, 103, 386
Nighthawk, Common,
561, 589
Nolina
microcarpa, 86
texana, 86
Notemigonus crysoleucas, 299,
478
Notiosorex crawfordi, 470,
553

O
Octillo, 335, 495
Tree, 70
Odocoileus hemionus, 528,
575
Oenothera
brevipes, 156, 411
deltoides, 93, 381
tanacetifolia, 139, 403
Olneya tesota, 319, 488
Onychomys
leucogaster, 491, 560
torridus, 488, 588
Opuntia
acanthocarpa, 66
basilaris, 41, 357
bigelovii, 332, 494
echinocarpa, 65
fulgida, 325, 490
imbricata, 333, 495
leptocaulis, 162, 414
lindheimeri, 86
phaeacantha, 66, 86
polyacantha, 121, 395
ramosissima, 64
schotti, 87
spinosior, 66
Orange, Sleepy, 417, 531
Orangetip, Desert, 404,
527
Oreoscoptes montanus, 591,
601
Oriole
Hooded, 614, 615, 611
Scott's, 616, 611
Orobanche multiflora, 76, 373
Orthoporus ornatus, 393, 521
Oryzopsis hymenoides, 362,
508

Ovis canadensis, 526, 573
Owl
Burrowing, 559, 588
Common Barn-, 555, 586
Elf, 558, 588
Ferruginous Pygmy-, 557,
587
Great Horned, 556, 587

P
Paintbrush, Desert, 159,
412
Painted Lady, 420, 533
Pale Face, 45, 358
Paleacrita longiciliata,
449, 545
Palo Verde
Blue, 301, 316, 481
Foothill "Yellow," 309,
318, 486
Mexican, 307, 322, 484
Paperflower, 137, 403
Papilio
indra, 447, 544
rudkini, 445, 543
zelicaon, 446, 543
Pappogeomys castanops, 99
Parabuteo unicinctus, 533,
578
Paratettix aztecus, 373, 513
Parkinsonia aculeata, 307,
322, 484
Parnassian, Phoebus,
407, 528
Parnassius phoebus, 407, 528
Parthenium incanum, 356,
505
Passerina versicolor, 96
Patch, Bordered, 429,
430, 537
Peccary, Collared, 525,
573
Pectis papposa, 133, 400
Pediocactus simpsonii, 38,
355
Penstemon, Jones, 68,
369
Penstemon
dolius, 68, 369
palmeri, 44, 358
Peppergrass
Western, 78, 374
Yellow, 113, 391
Pepperweed, Clasping, 38

Perezia nana, 85
Perognathus
  amplus, 472, 553
  baileyi, 476, 555
  flavus, 471, 553
  formosus, 475, 554
  intermedius, 79, 98
  longimembris, 473, 554
  nelsoni, 98
  parvus, 474, 554
  penicillatus, 477, 555
Peromyscus
  boylii, 490, 559
  crinitus, 58
  eremicus, 492, 560
  maniculatus, 489, 559
  pectoralis, 99
Peyote, 37, 355
Phacelia, Scalloped, 65, 368
Phacelia
  campanularia, 70, 370
  integrifolia, 65, 368
Phainopepla, 595, 603
Phainopepla nitens, 595, 603
Phalaenoptilus nuttallii, 562, 589
Phidippus apacheanus, 402, 525
Philodromus spp., 400, 524
Philotiella speciosa, 410, 529
Phlox, Long-leaved, 58, 365
Phlox longifolia, 58, 365
Phoebe
  Black, 570, 593
  Say's, 571, 593
Pholisora libya, 437, 540
Phrynosoma
  cornutum, 196, 430
  douglassi, 197, 431
  m'calli, 194, 430
  modestum, 193, 429
  platyrhinos, 55, 74
  solare, 195, 430
Phyciodes phaon, 426, 536
Phyllodactylus xanti, 175, 421
Phyllorhynchus
  browni, 245, 454
  decurtatus, 265, 269, 462
Physalis lobata, 67, 369
Pica pica, 580, 597
Pickleweed, *108*

Picoides scalaris, 567, 591
Pincushion, Esteve's, 84, 377
Pipilo
  aberti, 606, *607*
  chlorurus, 605, 606
  fuscus, 607, *607*
Pipistrelle, Western, 461, 549
Pipistrellus hesperus, 461, 549
Piranga ludoviciana, 599, 605
Pituophis melanoleucus, 263, 461
Plecotus townsendii, 463, 550
Pluchea sericea, 344, 499
Plume, Golden Prince's, 109, 389
Podaxis pistillaris, 166, 415
Poeciliopsis occidentalis, 295, 477
Pogonomyrmex
  californicus, 54
  rugosus, 387, 519
Polanisia dodecandra, 81, 376
Polioptila melanura, 588, 600
Polites sabuleti, 433, 538
Polyborus plancus, 541, 581
Pondweed
  Fennelleaf, *109*
  Horned, *109*
Pontia beckerii, 403, 527
Pooecetes gramineus, 609, *608*
Poorwill, Common, 562, 589
Poppy
  Desert, 155, *410*
  Great Desert, 95, *382*
  Mexican Gold, 148, *408*
Populus fremontii, 52, *106*
Porcupine, 507, 565
Potamogeton pectinatus, 109
Prairie Dog, White-tailed, 46
Prickly Pear
  Plains, 121, 395
  Texas, 86
Primrose
  Birdcage Evening, 93, *381*
  Desert, 156, *411*
  Tansy-leaved Evening, 139, *403*

Proboscidea altheaefolia, 117, 165, 393
Procherodes truxaliata, 450, 545
Procyon lotor, 512, 567
Progne subis, 577, 578, 596
Pronghorn, 527, 574
Prosopis
glandulosa, 308, 321, 485
pubescens, 302, 311, 320, 481
velutina, 310, 486
Prunus fasciculatus, 40
Psathyrotes ramosissima, 118, 393
Pseudemys scripta, 172, 419
Pseudosermyle straminea, 90
Psilostrophe cooperi, 137, 403
Psorothamnus schottii, 64
Pternohyla fodiens, 273, 466
Pterourus rutulus, 444, 542
Puffball
Buried-stalk, 168, 416
Desert Stalked, 167, 415
Puncture Vine, 143, 405
Pupfish
Cottonball Marsh, 54
Desert, 293, 476
Pecos River, 91
White Sands, 91
Purple Mat, 54, 363
Purslane, Sea, 108
Pyrgus philetas, 432, 538
Pyrocephalus rubinus, 572, 594
Pyrrhuloxia, 602, 603, 605

Q
Quail
California, 548, 549, 584
Gambel's, 547, 584
Scaled, 546, 583
Quail Bush, 102
Queen, 418, 532

R
Rabbit
Antelope Jack, 510, 566
Black-tailed Jack, 509, 566
Pygmy, 42
Rabbit Brush, 340, 497
Raccoon, 512, 567
Racer, 232, 447

Rafinesquia neomexicana, 86, 378
Ragweed, Canyon, 68
Rana
berlandieri, 285, 472
catesbeiana, 288, 473
pipiens, 286, 472
Rat
Banner-tailed Kangaroo, 483, 557
Chisel-toothed Kangaroo, 481, 556
Desert Kangaroo, 484, 557
Hispid Cotton, 98
Merriam's Kangaroo, 485, 558
Ord's Kangaroo, 480, 556
Panamint Kangaroo, 482, 557
Ratany, 56, 364
Rattlesnake
Blacktail, 248, 455
Mojave, 259, 459
Red Diamond, 254, 457
Rock, 250, 257, 456
Speckled, 251, 255, 456
Tiger, 249, 455
Western, 258, 260, 458
Western Diamondback, 256, 458
Rattlesnake Weed, 102, 386
Raven
Chihuahuan, 581, 597
Common, 582, 597
Reithrodontomys
fulvescens, 487, 558
megalotis, 486, 558
montanus, 98
Resurrection Plant, 112
Rhabdotus schiedeanus, 89
Rhinichthys osculus, 297, 477
Rhinocheilus lecontei, 238, 247, 451
Rhus
aromatica, 106
microphyllum, 87
Ricegrass, Indian, 362, 508
Ringstem, Southwestern, 105, 387
Ringtail, 511, 567
Roadrunner, Greater, 554, 586

Rosemallow, Desert, 151, 409
Rubber Plant, 85
Rumex
hymenosepalus, 68
venosus, 46, 359
Ruppia maritima, 109
Rushes, 39

S
Sacahuista, 86
Sacaton, Alkali, 39
Sage
Bladder, 75, 373
Bur, 360, 507
Death Valley, 77, 374
Desert, 349, 502
Mojave, 49
White Bur, 355, 505
Wooly Bur, 51
Sagebrush
Big, 353, 357, 504
Black, 37
Sand, 37
Saguaro, 331, 493
Salamander, Tiger, 289, 290, 291, 474
Salazaria mexicana, 75, 373
Salicornia rubra, 108
Salmo clarki henshawi, 33
Salpinctes obsoletus, 585, 599
Salsola Kili, 38, 84
Saltbrush
Four-wing, 352, 503
Parry, 49
Saltgrass, 108
Salvadora
deserticola, 217, 442
hexalepis, 218, 442
Salvia
columbariae, 64, 367
dorrii, 349, 502
funerea, 77, 374
mohavensis, 49
Sandpaper Bush, 87
Sapium biloculare, 68
Sarcobatus
vermiculatus, 345, 500
baileyi, 39
Sarcostemma cynanchoides, 83, 377
Satyrium behrii, 416, 531
Sauromalus obesus, 189, 427

Sayornis
 nigricans, 570, 593
 saya, 571, 593
Scaphiopus
 bombifrons, 275, 467
 couchi, 274, 466
 hammondi, 276, 467
 intermontanus, 277, 468
Sceloporus
 graciosus, 212, 439
 magister, 199, 432
 poinsetti, 198, 431
 undulatus, 93
Schistocerca shoshone, 367, 511
Scleropogon brevifolius, 88
Scolopendra heros, 89
Scorpion
 Centruroides, 394, 522
 Giant Desert Hairy, 395, 522
Scyphophorus acupunctatus, 380, 516
Seepweed, 108
Selaginella lepidophylla, 112
Senecio douglasii, 129, 399
Senita, 66
Senna, Spiny, 51
Sesurium verrucosum, 108
Shadscale, 346, 500
Sheep, Bighorn, 526, 573
Shiner, Golden, 299, 478
Shrew, Desert, 470, 553
Shrike, Loggerhead, 596, 603
Shrimp, Brine, 35
Sialia mexicana, 589, 600
Sidewinder, 252, 253, 457
Sigmodon hispidus, 98
Silverleaf, Texas, 47, 359
Simmondsia chinensis, 347, 501
Sistrurus catenatus, 264, 462
Sitanion hystrix, 38
Skink, Great Plains, 213, 440
Skipper
 Bronze Roadside, 438, 540
 Coyote, 435, 539
 Desert Checkered, 432, 538
 Desert Gray, 436, 539
 Large White, 408, 528
 Pahaska, 434, 539

 Sandhill, 433, 538
 Yucca Giant, 439, 540
Skunk
 Hog-nosed, 516, 569
 Hooded, 98
 Striped, 515, 569
 Western Spotted, 98
Skyrocket, 161, 413
Sleepy Orange, 417, 531
Slider, 172, 419
Smoke Tree, 305, 313, 334, 483
Snail, Creamy White, 89
Snake
 Arizona Coral, 241, 453
 Banded Sand, 236, 451
 Big Bend Patchnosed, 217, 442
 Blacknecked Garter, 220, 444
 Checkered Garter, 216, 441
 Common King-, 234, 246, 448
 Glossy, 268, 464
 Gopher, 263, 461
 Ground, 228, 231, 239, 447
 Longnosed, 238, 247, 451
 Lyre, 262, 270, 460
 Mexican King-, 242, 243, 453
 Night, 267, 463
 Saddled Leafnosed, 245, 454
 Sonoran Shovelnosed, 240, 452
 Sonoran Whip-, 222, 445
 Spotted Leafnosed, 265, 269, 462
 Striped Whip-, 221, 444
 Texas Blind, 225, 449
 Trans-Pecos Rat, 214, 440
 Western Blackhead, 227, 450
 Western Blind, 226, 449
 Western Hognose, 261, 459
 Western Hooknose, 266, 463
 Western Patchnosed, 218, 442
 Western Shovelnosed, 235, 237, 450
 Western Terrestrial Garter, 215, 441
Snakehead, 126, 397

Snakeweed, 341, *498*
Snapdragon, Yellow
Twining, 116, *393*
Snapdragon Vine
Little, 74, *372*
Net-cup, 71, *371*
Softshell, Spiny, 174, *420*
Solanum elaeagnifolium, 73, *372*
Sonora semiannulata, 228, 231, 239, *447*
Sootywing, Great Basin, 437, *540*
Sotol, 338, *496*
Spadefoot
Couch's, 274, *466*
Great Basin, 277, *468*
Plains, 275, *467*
Western, 276, *467*
Sparrow
Black-throated, 610, *608*
Brewer's, 608, *608*
Sage, 611, *609*
Vesper, 609, *608*
Spectacle Pod, 79, *375*
Spermophilus
mexicanus, 502, *564*
spilosoma, 503, *564*
tereticaudus, 504, *564*
townsendii, 501, *563*
variegatus, 505, 506, *565*
Sphaeralcea
ambigua, 158, *412*
coulteri, 157, *411*
Sphinx, White-lined, 448, *544*
Spider
Apache Jumping, 402, *525*
Carolina Wolf, 401, *524*
Inconspicuous Crab, 400, *524*
Spikedace, 300, *479*
Spilogale gracilis, 98
Spizella breweri, 608, *608*
Sporobolus airoides, 39
Springfish, White River, 292, *476*
Squawberry, *106*
Squirrel
Harris' Antelope, 498, *562*
Mexican Ground, 502, *564*
Rock, 505, 506, *565*
Round-tailed Ground, 504, *564*

Spotted Ground, **503**, *564*
Texas Antelope, **500**, *563*
Townsend's Ground, **501**, *563*
White-tailed Antelope, **499**, *563*
Squirreltail, Bottlebush, 38
Stanleya pinnata, 109, *389*
Starling, European, 597, *604*
Stenopelmatus fuscus, 375, *514*
Stick-leaf, White-bracted, 120, *394*
Storksbill, Filaree, 57, *364*
Streptanthus arizonicus, 107, *388*
Sturnus vulgaris, 597, *604*
Suaeda depressa, 108
Sulphur, Common, 443, *542*
Sulphur Flower, 112, *391*
Sumac, Little Leaf Desert, 87
Sunflower, Desert, 135, *401*
Sunray, 132, *400*
Swallow, Violet-green, 579, *596*
Swallowtail
Anise, 446, *543*
Desert, 445, *543*
Short-tailed Black, 447, *544*
Western Tiger, 444, *542*
Sweetbush, 65
Sylvilagus
audubonii, 508, *566*
nuttalli, 42

T
Tachycineta thalassina, **579**, *596*
Tadarida
brasiliensis, **465**, *551*
femorosacca, **466**, *551*
macrotis, **467**, *552*
Taeniopoda eques, 371, *512*
Tamarisk, 304, 324, *482*
Tamarix chinensis, 304, 324, *482*
Tanager, Western, 599, *605*
Tansy Mustard, 38

Tantilla planiceps, 227, *450*
Taproot, Woody, 88
Tarantula, Desert, 399, *524*
Tarantula Hawk, 383, *517*
Tarbrush, 350, *502*
Taxidea taxus, 514, *568*
Tequilia hispidissima, 88
Termites, 392, *521*
Terrapene ornata, 173, *420*
Tetradymia glabrata, 343, *499*
Texola elada, 424, *535*
Thamnophis
cyrtopsis, 220, *444*
elegans, 215, *441*
marcianus, 216, *441*
Thamnosa montana, 366, *509*
Thomomys bottae, 469, *552*
Thorn Apple, Southwestern, 100, *385*
Thrasher
Bendire's, 592, *602*
Crissal, 76, *95*
Curve-billed, 593, *602*
Le Conte's, 594, *602*
Sage, 591, *601*
Threeawn, 46
Thryomanes bewickii, **587**, *599*
Tillandsia recurrata, 69
Toad
Colorado River, 281, *470*
Great Plains, 283, *471*
Great Plains Narrowmouth, 282, *470*
Green, 287, *473*
Red-spotted, 278, *468*
Sonoran Green, 284, *471*
Southwestern, 279, *469*
Texas, 280, *469*
Woodhouse's, 92
Tobacco
Desert, 103, *386*
Tree, 114, *392*
Tobacco Weed, 85, *378*
Tobosa, 87
Topminnow, Gila, 295, *477*
Tortoise, Desert, 169, *418*
Towhee
Abert's, 606, *607*

Brown, 607, *607*
Green-tailed, 605, *606*
Toxostoma
bendirei, 592, *602*
curvirostre, 593, *602*
dorsale, 76, 95
lecontei, 594, *602*
Treefrog
California, 271, *465*
Canyon, 272, *465*
Lowland Burrowing, 273, *466*
Tribulus terrestris, 143, *405*
Trichoptilium incisum, 124, *396*
Trimerotropis pallidipennis, 369, *511*
Trimorphodon biscutatus, 262, 270, *460*
Trionyx spiniferus, 174, *420*
Trixis, 106, *388*
Trixis californica, 106, *388*
Trumpets
Angel, 104, *387*
Pale, 66, *368*
Tulostoma simulans, 168, *416*
Tumble Weed, 38, *84*
Turk's Head, *87*
Turtle
Sonoran Mud, 171, *419*
Western Box, 173, *420*
Yellow Mud, 170, *418*
Twinleaf, 144, *406*
Tyrannus verticalis, 575, *595*
Tyto alba, 555, *586*
Tytthoytle maculata, 54

U
Uma
notata, 182, *424*
scoparia, 181, *423*
Urocyon cinereoargenteus, 522, *571*
Urosaurus
graciosus, 190, *427*
ornatus, 205, *435*
Uta stansburiana, 202, *433*

V
Vanessa cardui, 420, *533*
Verbena, Desert Sand, 53, *362*
Verdin, 583, *598*

Vermivora luciae, 77
Viguiera stenoloba, 85
Vinegarone, Giant, 398, *523*
Vole, Sagebrush, 496, *562*
Vulpes macrotis, 521, *571*
Vulture
Black, 529, *577*
Turkey, 530, *577*

W
Walkingstick, *90*
Gray, *90*
Warbler
Black-throated
Gray, 598, *604*
Lucy's, *77*
Yellow, *77*
Yellow-rumped, *77*
Washingtonia, California, 327, *491*
Washingtonia filifera, 327, *491*
Wheatgrass, Bluebunch, 363, *508*
Whipsnake
Sonoran, 222, *445*
Striped, 221, *444*
Whiptail
Chihuahuan Spotted, 210, *438*
Colorado Checkered, 207, *437*
Desert Grassland, 209, *438*
Little Striped, 208, *437*
New Mexico, 211, *439*
Plateau, *46*
Western, 206, *436*
Whispering Bells, 115, *392*
White, Becker's, 403, *527*
Whitehorn, *87*
Widgeongrass, *109*
Widow, Western, *40*
Wildrye, *38*
Willow
Desert, 306, *484*
Seep, 52, *103*
Windscorpion, Pale, 396, *522*
Winter Fat, 354, *505*
Wislizenia refracta, 110, *390*
Wood Nymph, Great

Basin, 431, *537*
Woodpecker
Gila, 565, *590*
Golden-fronted, 566, *591*
Ladder-backed, 567, *591*
Woodrat
Desert, 493, *560*
Southern Plains, *99*
White-throated, 494, *561*
Wren
Bewick's, 587, *599*
Cactus, 584, *598*
Canyon, 586, *599*
Rock, 585, *599*

X
Xanthocephalum sarothrae, 341, *498*
Xantusia
henshawi, 185, *425*
vigilis, 183, 184, *424*

Y
Yellow, Boisduval's, 442, *542*
Yellow Head, 124, *396*
Yucca
Banana, 336, *495*
Mohave, 329, *492*
Soaptree, 328, *492*
Torrey, 330, *493*
Yucca
baccata, 336, *495*
brevifolia, 326, *490*
elata, 328, *492*
schidigera, 329, *492*
torreyi, 330, *493*
Yvretta carus, 436, *539*

Z
Zanichellia palustris, 109
Zenaida
asiatica, 550, *584*
macroura, 551, *585*
Zephyranthes longifolia, 153, *410*
Zinnia
Desert, *84*
Little Golden, 138, *403*
Zinnia
acerosa, *84*
grandiflora, 138, *403*
Ziziphus obtusifolia, 64, *87*
Zopherus haldemani, 379, *516*

ACKNOWLEDGMENTS

It is impossible to thank all of the people who influence a book like this. After all, the book represents experiences covering the major portion of my life, and I should include everyone who has been part of those experiences. Instead, I have chosen to single out three people from my formative years, to whom I dedicate this work.

E. J. Koestner, then director of the Dayton Museum of Natural History, once told an obnoxious high school freshman to stop tapping on the snake cages in his museum. That episode started a series of events that changed a curious, adolescent naturalist into a practicing scientist. My first knowledge of biology as a formal discipline occurred at the museum under the guidance of "D.C."

From my junior year at Michigan State University's field station through graduate school—and even now—my scientific life has been influenced by Dr. Robert McIntosh of the University of Notre Dame, an ecologist par excellence. "Mac" is always there to critique my work and to listen to new ideas. He taught me (somewhat) to harness my youthful exuberance and channel it into formal science. His imprint is ever on me.

Dr. James McCleary of Northern Illinois University was a friend, colleague, and teacher when I was becoming seriously interested in desert biology. "James the Greater's" knowledge of the desert and his generous sharing of that knowledge allowed me to shortcut beyond many of the problems of understanding and identifying desert plants. We always talked about writing a book on deserts together. I hope he knows he is very much a part of this one.

This particular project has involved a lot of time and patience on the part of the staff at Chanticleer Press. I want to thank all for their contributions, especially Ann Whitman, Susan Costello, Marian Appellof, David Allen, Constance Mersel, and—last but not least—Mary Beth Brewer.

My own crew at Utah State University labored long and hard on this whole project. Important characters include Rand Hooper, Mark Mesch, Ellen Parker, and Teri Waldron. Of special importance—because she does everything in my lab, and does it well—is Linda Finchum. Her tasks included the preparation of virtually the entire manuscript from my hand-written, big yellow sheets, which she hated.

Fred Wagner read the entire manuscript, to its benefit. Eric Zurcher, my academic son, also read every word of the manuscript, the species accounts, and at times even read my thoughts. His contribution to the project is inestimable—but obvious to all who know Eric and me.

Tache, my Bernese Mountain Dog, listened to me read every word of the manuscript out loud. She generally liked it, which is strange for a cold-adapted dog only recently introduced to the desert.

Finally, much of my research over the years has been funded by the National Science Foundation and, to a lesser extent, by the Ecology Center of Utah State University.

James A. MacMahon

Prepared and produced by Chanticleer Press, Inc.

Founding Publisher: Paul Steiner
Publisher: Andrew Stewart

Staff for this book:

Editor-in-chief: Gudrun Buettner
Executive Editor: Susan Costello
Managing Editor: Jane Opper
Series Editor: Mary Beth Brewer
Text Editor: Ann Whitman
Associate Editor: Marian Appellof
Assistant Editors: David Allen, Constance Mersel
Production Manager: Helga Lose
Production: Amy Roche, Frank Grazioli
Art Director: Carol Nehring
Art Associate: Ayn Svoboda
Picture Library: Edward Douglas, Dana Pomfret
Maps and Symbols: Paul Singer
Natural History Consultant: John Farrand, Jr.
Original series design by Massimo Vignelli

All editorial inquiries should be addressed to:
Chanticleer Press
665 Broadway, Suite 1001
New York, NY 10012

To purchase this book, or other National Audubon Society
illustrated nature books, please contact:
Alfred A. Knopf, Inc.
201 East 50th Street
New York, NY 10022
(800) 733-3000